Culture and Identity

Culture and Identity

The History, Theory, and Practice of Psychological Anthropology

Charles Lindholm
Boston University

Boston   Burr Ridge, IL   Dubuque, IA   Madison, WI   New York
San Francisco   St. Louis   Bangkok   Bogotá   Caracas   Kuala Lumpur
Lisbon   London   Madrid   Mexico City   Milan   Montreal   New Delhi
Santiago   Seoul   Singapore   Sydney   Taipei   Toronto

McGraw-Hill Higher Education

A Division of The **McGraw-Hill** Companies

CULTURE AND IDENTITY
THE HISTORY, THEORY, AND PRACTICE
OF PSYCHOLOGICAL ANTHROPOLOGY
Published by McGraw-Hill, an imprint of The McGraw-Hill Companies, Inc.
1221 Avenue of the Americas, New York, NY, 10020. Copyright © 2001, by The
McGraw-Hill Companies, Inc. All rights reserved. No part of this publication
may be reproduced or distributed in any form or by any means, or stored in a
database or retrieval system, without the prior written consent of The McGraw-
Hill Companies, Inc., including, but not limited to, in any network or other electronic storage or transmission, or broadcast for distance learning.
Some ancillaries, including electronic and print components, may not be available to customers outside the United States.

This book is printed on acid-free paper.

1 2 3 4 5 6 7 8 9 0 FGR/FGR 0 9 8 7 6 5 4 3 2 1 0

ISBN 0-07-037995-5

Publisher: *Phillip A. Butcher*
Sponsoring editor: *Carolyn Henderson*
Editorial assistant: *Sue Driscoll*
Marketing manager: *Leslie Kraham*
Project editor: *Christina Thornton-Villagomez*
Production supervisor: *Michael McCormick*
Cover Designer: *Pam Verros*
Supplement coordinator: *Matthew Perry*
Cover Images: *© Stock Market Inc./© Corbis Images/Cherry Lindholm*
Compositor: *Carlisle Communications, Ltd.*
Typeface: *10/12 Palatino*
Printer: *Quebecor Printing Book Group/Fairfield*

Library of Congress Cataloging-in-Publication Data
Lindholm, Charles, 1946-
    Culture and identity: the history, theory, and practice of psychologi-
cal anthropology /
    Charles Lindholm.
       p. cm.
    Includes index.
    ISBN 0-07-037995-5 (alk. paper)
    1. Ethnopsychology. 2. Personality and culture. I. Title.
GN502 .L56 2001
155.8—dc21
          00-033921

*To two of my mentors in psychological
anthropology—Robert Murphy and Richard Christie*

About the Author

CHARLES LINDHOLM is a university professor and professor of anthropology at Boston University. He received his bachelor's degree from Columbia University in 1968 and then went to Pakistan, Afghanistan, Iran and South Asia as a Henry Evans travelling Fellow. He returned to Columbia for graduate studies in anthropology and did his ethnographic research among the Swat Pukhtun of Northern Pakistan, which led to the publication of his first book, *Generosity and Jealousy*. After receiving his doctorate in 1979, he taught at Columbia and Harvard before going to Boston University in 1990.

Professor Lindholm has published a number of articles on the Pukhtun, some of which are included in the book *Frontier Perspectives*; he has also written a general text entitled *The Islamic Middle East: An Historical Anthropology*. His other major research has been on the psychological anthropology of idealization, and he has written essays on romance and a book entitled *Charisma*. His most recent project was an analysis of American culture called *Is America Breaking Apart?* coauthored with John A. Hall. Professor Lindholm is currently doing research on the cultural meaning of pleasure and on issues of identity and authenticity in a comparative perspective.

Preface

OVERVIEW

In one sense, psychological anthropology is a discipline with a long intellectual tradition. Western thinkers have been theorizing about the influence culture has on character since the time of the Greeks, and the question of the relative power of nature versus nurture has continued to vex philosophers and scientists ever since.[1] Yet in another sense, psychological anthropology is one of the most contemporary of academic studies; the scholarly study of the relationship between the individual and culture arguably began in the late nineteenth century, when W. H. R. Rivers and his colleagues undertook an expedition to Melanesia to test the perceptions of the local people. The heyday of the discipline was reached in the 1930s and 1940s with the investigations of Margaret Mead, Ruth Benedict, and others. Although their work exerted tremendous influence on the intellectual life of America during that period, research on the topic fell into disfavor in the 1950s. But in the past few years the anthropological study of the dialectic between personal and collective identity has reemerged as one of the most intellectually exciting fields in academia.

Considered historically, a renewed interest in psychological anthropology makes good sense, since the discipline addresses fundamental questions about the nature of humanity that have become especially pressing in the present era of multiculturalism and globalization, as taken-for-granted, everyday realities have been challenged within a fluid and dynamic world. Today, perhaps more than ever, people want to know to what degree their perceptions, emotions, beliefs, values, and even their experiences of themselves may be shaped and changed by shifts in culture and context. What about us is consistent? What is malleable? What does it mean to be an individual and also a member of a community?

To begin to answer these difficult questions, this book draws material from three great and sometimes contradictory paradigms for the human condition: the anthropological, which analyzes and interprets ethnography gathered from a multiplicity of cultures; the sociological, which compares collective social

vii

organizations and the institutional structures of power; and the psychological, which investigates the mental states of individuals. My overall goal in this book is to describe and contribute to the ongoing effort by present-day practitioners to overcome disciplinary boundaries and establish a unified theory of the human experience.

To accomplish this goal, I provide the reader with an historical and critical outline of the fundamental debates in Western thought about the relationship between personal and collective identity; I then show how cross-cultural research has contributed to these debates, and ask how findings from this research relate to modern questions concerning the nature of self-awareness, perception, cognition, emotion, and the experience of love and community. In proceeding on this exploration, I give my own critical perspectives and explanations whenever I can. Doing so is not meant to supply the final answer, but rather, to inspire argument and debate. A discipline is dead when all the fights have been won and there is nothing left to discuss. As the reader will discover, psychological anthropology today is very far indeed from that moribund state.

ORGANIZATION

The book is divided into five parts. Part One introduces the reader to the central question of the text: Who am I? This question is located within the modern American context, and its ramifications are considered: How is it possible not to know who one is? What conditions lead to doubting self-identity? The introductory chapter provides an outline of the disciplinary methods of anthropology and psychology as well as a general construction of the argument as a whole, along with an account of the author's own perspective.

Part Two of the book consists of two chapters giving a rapid historical sketch of some of the major Western theories about the nature of the self, beginning with St. Augustine's depiction of the individual soul seeking redemption and ending with Sigmund Freud's portrait of human beings dominated by unconscious desires. Along the way, I connect changes in theories of the nature of the self to larger transformations in social organization and the economy. For example, the utilitarian belief that the individual is primarily a rational maximizer of benefits is shown to correspond with the rise of capitalism. In response to this narrowed vision, romantic theorists argued in favor of the priority of the emotions and developed an aesthetic theory of human nature. The various permutations of these paradigms are outlined, as are later efforts by Marx, Weber, and Durkheim, to provide a synthesis.

This sketch of Western theories of the relationship between the individual and the collective provides the basis for understanding contemporary theoretical discussions, which always take their terms from previous arguments—although their authors do not necessarily acknowledge their debts. The review also makes the reader conscious of how much his or her own assumptions about the relationship between personal being and the larger social world are culturally and historically constituted.

Part Three builds on this foundation. Its four chapters are a synopsis of the development of the academic discipline of psychological anthropology, moving from an account of Rivers's expedition and concluding with a critical assessment of the most recent phenomenological theories of embodiment. Debates over primitive rationality are outlined, and the origin, contribution, and downfall of the culture and personality school are described at length, as is the influence of Freud, both positive and negative, on various practitioners of the discipline. The work of Abram Kardiner, Erik Erikson, and the Frankfurt school is presented and compared with alternative theories, such as A. I. Hallowell's evolutionary approach and Erving Goffman's dramaturgic model. This section also examines efforts by anthropologists such as Melford Spiro and Robert LeVine to establish a more scientifically adequate means of analyzing the influence of culture on the individual. Part Three ends with a critical summary of contemporary debates about the nature of interpretation, the role of the fieldworker, and the applicability of Freudian, neo-Marxist, phenomenological, and dialectical approaches within the discipline. Included is an extensive analysis of contemporary theorists, such as Obeyesekere, Shweder, Taussig, and Scheper-Hughes.

Having explored the history and theory of the discipline, the next step is to show how it is actually practiced. In Part Four of the book, the research of modern psychological and cognitive anthropologists is utilized to investigate complex problems such as the nature of the self, the structure of the mind, the content of the emotions, the basis of mental illness, and the appeal of charismatic leaders. In these four chapters various approaches to these crucial questions are outlined and evaluated in cross-cultural context: For example, the egocentric Western self is compared with the sociocentric self of Japan, and it is argued that the differences between the two are actually less than they might appear to be.

Part Five, the concluding section of the book, comprises two chapters in which theory is applied to practice in a way that personally touches the reader. These are chapters on the nature of romantic love and on the experience of being an American. My hope is that these chapters in particular will stir debate and awaken in the reader the realization that the theories in question are not abstract formulas pertaining only to distant others, but instead are relevant concepts for understanding our own lives here and now.

LEARNING AIDS

Cohesive Theme

This book ties together fundamental themes in psychological anthropology by following a single narrative thread: the inquiry into the nature of personal identity. This approach means that the text is not just a compendium of facts, but has a dramatic structure and movement, as well as a personal voice. The text also engages the reader in a debate that is connected to issues of relevance in daily life. As mentioned, this aspect is especially evident in the concluding section of the book, which deals with romantic love and American culture. But throughout I continually link theoretical debates to topics that are of significance to the reader, such as the nature of emotion or the social construction of deviance. This makes the complex arguments both relevant and compelling.

Up-to-Date Coverage

The book also engages the reader by dealing with up-to-date material, covering the most important developments in psychological anthropology in the past decade. To give only a few examples: Chapter 8 considers contemporary theories of hybridity, hegemony, and the decentered self; Chapter 9 outlines recent debates that have been inspired by computer programming and investigations into artificial intelligence; Chapter 10 presents arguments about the distinction between thinking and feeling, and the possible existence of emotions that cannot be named.

Chapter-Opening Vignettes, Outlines, and End-of-Chapter Summaries

In every chapter, I have tried to engage the reader's attention by beginning with an opening vignette that personalizes the material. To increase understanding, I have also included substantial chapter-opening outlines of the arguments to follow. Each subsection within the chapter is also preceded by an outline of its content, and every chapter ends with a summary of the main points covered. These aids provide the reader with a quick synopsis of the material and the arguments, and reinforce his or her grasp of the theories presented.

In-Text Examples and Summaries

Within each chapter are numerous concrete examples relating theory to practice. Whenever possible, I have also included bulleted lists that condense important arguments. For instance, in Chapter 4, Margaret Mead's famous analysis of three Melanesian peoples is summarized as follows:

- *Arapesh.* Both men and women are peaceful, caring, and feminine according to Western standards.
- *Mundagumor.* Both sexes are violent, aggressive, and masculine.
- *Tchambuli.* The women are masculine traders and activists; the men are feminine aesthetes.

Illustrations and Photographs

The book includes plentiful illustrations and photographs to enliven the text and heighten reader involvement. For example, Freud's model of the mind is illustrated by his own drawing; a discussion of initiation ceremonies is accompanied by a photo of such a ceremony; a segment on trance is illustrated by a photo of a shaman. Tables are also inserted when appropriate: Erik Erikson's "eight ages" paradigm is encapsulated by his own tabular presentation. Other aids include a timeline of important events and the birth and death dates of historical figures, as well as publication dates of significant books. These offer the reader a quick sense of the time frames involved and the historical relationships between various authors and events.

Bibliographical Material

The book also has a wide-ranging and up-to-date bibliography of over 700 entrees, many explicitly included in order to provide the most complete available commentaries on the complex material that is outlined in the text. Extensive endnotes point readers toward the relevant literature and give them the basis for undertaking more in-depth library research.

Boxed Features

I have added a number of substantial boxed features to each chapter. For example, in Chapter 5, which discusses the role psychoanalytic thought has played in psychological anthropology, I included four such features:

- A discussion and critique of the immensely popular theories of myth and archetype associated with Carl Jung and Joseph Campbell.
- A description of projective tests and an analysis of their use and abuse in psychological anthropology.
- To show the difficulty of distinguishing between primary and secondary aspects of culture, I present contrasting anthropological arguments about food prohibitions, such as the Hindu prohibition on eating beef. Are these prohibitions reflections of material conditions, or are they symbolic expressions of worldviews?
- In a section on alternative psychoanalytic theories, I add an account of the life and work of Wilhelm Reich, the brilliant German analyst of sexuality, who lost credibility through his manufacture of "orgone boxes" meant to capture cosmic energy.

Boxes in other chapters deal with such topics as the debate over the quality of Margaret Mead's fieldwork, the way the Oedipal myth has been interpreted by anthropologists, the relationship between German philosophy and Eastern religion, the notion of history in several non-Western cultures, the models of human nature proposed by Melanie Klein and other object relations theorists, the relationship between prototypes and racial categories, Durkheim's concept of secular religion, and anthropological explanations of spirit possession and witchcraft. All these boxed features are integrated into the text and serve to explicate aspects of the narrative that are not covered in the main argument; they also add variety and widen the appeal of the discussion.

IN A NUTSHELL

In sum, *Culture and Identity* is a unified and up-to-date text that uses much material not considered in other texts. It provides a philosophical groundwork for dealing with the issues central to psychological anthropology, gives a solid base in classic and contemporary theory, and then deals with questions that are of importance to the readership, such as the nature of love, the sources of racism and sexism, the quest for transcendence, the structure of the mind, and the character of Americans. The material is regularly summarized and outlined to make it more understandable, and numerous learning aids are provided throughout. In all, the intent is to present a coherent perspective that can provoke debate and discussion among the readers.

SUPPLEMENTS

As a full-service publisher of quality educational products, McGraw-Hill does much more than just sell textbooks. It creates and publishes print, video, and digital supplements for students and instructors as well. This particular text is accompanied by the following instructor supplement:

- Instructor's Manual—chapter outlines, lecture notes, key terms, discussion questions, assignments, exam questions, and more.

The Instructor's Manual is provided free of charge to instructors. Orders of new textbooks help McGraw-Hill defray the substantial cost of developing supplements like this. Please contact your local McGraw-Hill representative for more information on the supplements available with any of our texts.

ACKNOWLEDGEMENTS

In this book I have chosen not to attempt an encyclopedic record, but to concentrate on specific writers whose work is representative of an important school or approach. This has meant that I have left out many worthwhile contributions. I regret these omissions, especially since preparing the book led me to be increasingly impressed by the intellectual quality of earlier writing, and by the incredible liveliness and exciting variety of the work being done at present.

I would like to give special credit to the authors of some of the classic textbooks and collections of readings in the field: Victor Barnouw,[2] Philip Bock,[3] Erika Bourguignon,[4] Yehudi Cohen,[5] John Honigmann,[6] Francis Hsu,[7] Gustav Jahoda,[8] Robert LeVine,[9] George Spinder,[10] and Anthony F. C. Wallace,[11] to name just a few. Now that I have written a text myself, I appreciate more than ever the excellence of their work and the work of other contributors to the field.

Many people have helped me with this project in various ways, and I can thank only a few of them here. At McGraw-Hill, Phil Butcher originally recruited me to write a book on psychological anthropology and remained enthusiastic despite my long delays. A number of other editors participated in the process as well. Miriam Beyer and Jill Gordon have moved on to other pastures, but I am much indebted to them for their help in the early phases. I am also grateful to Christina Thornton-Villagomez, Inge King, Sue Driscoll, Leslie Kraham, and the rest of the McGraw-Hill team for their hard work and their expertise in the construction of the text. I am especially thankful to Carolyn Henderson, whose oversight, encouragement, good advice, and editing skills made a huge difference in the final product. It was a great pleasure to work with such a competent group of professionals.

In the academic world, I would like to thank Judy Pugh, J. Patrick Gray, and Douglas Hollan, who anonymously reviewed an earlier draft manuscript and who were insightful, thorough, encouraging, and very useful in their criticisms—most of which I tried to address; their input strengthened the book greatly. I am also much obliged to Steve Parish, who had many valuable comments to make during the early stages of writing and who reviewed the entire manuscript in its final version. And I am once again indebted to Dr. Rebecca Norris for her helpful editorial assistance. I also want to thank Michael McKernan for his excellent fact checking, while noting that the errors that remain are purely my responsibility. And, as ever, I am deeply grateful to Cherry Lindholm for her encouragement, tolerance, and unfailing critical judgment. I wish as well to express my appreciation to the many students who have studied psychological anthropology with me throughout the years at Columbia, at Harvard, and now at Boston University. Working with them has always been tremendously rewarding.

Finally, I want to do justice to my own teachers and colleagues. Abe Rosman and Paula Rubel, my graduate advisors at Columbia, encouraged me to explore psychological anthropology when it was decidedly unfashionable, and I am very appreciative of both their tolerance and their critical insights. I was also fortunate to have taught at Harvard when John and Beatrice Whiting, Robert LeVine, Arthur Kleinman, Byron Good, and their students were doing much to revive interest in the field. I benefited greatly from the innovative atmosphere they created. A similarly creative environment exists as well at Boston University, where the interdisciplinary University Professors Program supported my research assistants and allowed me to explore my interests freely. The Anthropology Department has also always been extraordinarily encouraging and stimulating. In conclusion, I want to acknowledge my great intellectual debt to two of my mentors at Columbia, Richard Christie and Robert Murphy, both sadly now deceased. In their very different ways, they inspired me to think creatively about psychological issues in anthropology. This book is dedicated to their memories.

Charles Lindholm
Boston University

Endnotes

1. For more on the Greeks and their relationship to psychological anthropology, see Rodney Needham, 1985, "Skepticism and Forms of Life," in Rodney Needham (ed.), *Exemplars*, Berkeley: University of California Press.
2. Victor Barnouw, 1985, *Culture and Personality* (4th ed.), Chicago: Dorsey Press.

3. Philip Bock, 1988, *Rethinking Psychological Anthropology*, New York: Freeman.

4. Erika Bourguignon, 1979, *Psychological Anthropology: An Introduction to Human Nature and Cultural Difference*, New York: Holt.

5. Yehudi Cohen (ed.), 1961, *Social Structure and Personality*. New York: Holt, Rinehart and Winston.

6. John Honigmann, 1967, *Personality in Culture*, New York: Harper and Row.

7. Francis Hsu (ed.), 1961, *Psychological Anthropology: Approaches to Culture and Personality*, Chicago, IL: Dorsey.

8. Gustav Jahoda, 1982, *Psychology and Anthropology: A Psychological Perspective*, London: Academic Press.

9. Robert LeVine, 1973, *Culture, Behavior and Personality: An Introduction to the Comparative Study of Psychosocial Adaption*, Chicago: Aldine.

10. George Spindler (ed.), 1978, *The Making of Psychological Anthropology*, Berkeley: University of California Press. See also Marcelo Suarez-Orozco, George Spindler, and Louise Spindler (eds.), 1994, *The Making of Psychological Anthropology II*, Fort Worth, TX: Harcourt Brace.

11. Anthony F. C. Wallace, 1961, *Culture and Personality*, New York: Random House.

Brief Contents

Part 1
INTRODUCTION

Part 2
CULTURE AND THE INDIVIDUAL IN WESTERN PHILOSOPHY

Part 3
THE ANTHROPOLOGY OF PERSONAL BEING

Part 4
PROBLEMS AND SOME SOLUTIONS

Part 5
APPLICATIONS

Contents

Part 1
INTRODUCTION

Part 2
CULTURE AND THE INDIVIDUAL IN WESTERN PHILOSOPHY

Part 5
APPLICATIONS

List of Illustrations

List of Boxes

5. THE PSYCHOANALYSIS OF CULTURE

6. QUANDARIES AND ALTERNATIVES

7. CREATIVITY AND ALTERITY

8. DIALECTICS OF SELF AND OTHER

9. THE THINKING ANIMAL

10. FEELING AND BEING

11. Outsiders and Charismatics

12. Love and Culture

13. Being an American

Time Line

1690	Publication of John Locke's *Essay concerning Human Understanding*
1711–1776	David Hume
1712–1778	Jean Jacques Rousseau
1724–1804	Immanuel Kant
1739	Publication of David Hume's *A Treatise of Human Nature*
1744–1803	Johann Gotfried Herder
1748–1832	Jeremy Bentham
1749–1832	Johann Wolfgang Goethe
1755	Publication of Jean Jacques Rousseau's *Discourse on the Origins of Human Inequality*
1757–1827	William Blake
1759–1805	Johann von Schiller
1762–1814	Johann Fichte
1770–1831	Georg Wilhelm Friedrich Hegel
1770–1850	William Wordsworth
1774	Publication of Goethe's *The Sorrows of Werther*
1775	Invention of the steam engine
1775	American Revolution begins
1775–1854	Friedrich von Schelling
1781	Publication of Immanuel Kant's *Critique of Judgment*
1783–1842	Stendahl (Marie Henri Beyle)
1788–1860	Arthur Schopenhauer
1789	French Revolution begins; Declaration of the Rights of Man
1793	Louis XVI executed
1799	Formation of Société des Observateurs de l'Homme, Paris
1805–1859	Alexis de Tocqueville
1808	Publication of G. W. F. Hegel's *The Phenomenology of Mind*
1809–1882	Charles Darwin
1813–1855	Søren Kierkegaard
1813–1883	Richard Wagner
1818–1881	Lewis Henry Morgan
1818–1883	Karl Marx
1820–1903	Herbert Spencer
1821–1881	Fyodor Dostoyevsky

1832–1917	Edward B. Tylor
1835	Publication of Alexis de Tocqueville's *Democracy in America*
1839–1914	Charles Peirce
1842–1910	William James
1844–1900	Friedrich Nietzsche
1844–1942	Bronislaw Malinowski
1854–1941	James G. Frazer
1856–1939	Sigmund Freud
1857–1913	Ferdinand de Saussure
1857–1939	Lucien Levy-Bruhl
1858–1917	Émile Durkheim
1858–1942	Franz Boas
1859–1952	John Dewey
1863	Emancipation of slaves in the United States
1863–1931	George Herbert Mead
1864–1920	Max Weber
1864–1922	W. H. R. Rivers
1865	Publication of E. B. Tylor's *Researches into the Early History of Mankind*
1872–1950	Marcel Mauss
1872	Publication of Charles Darwin's *The Expression of Emotions in Man and Animals*
1873–1957	Arnold Van Gennep
1874–1948	Charles Beard
1874–1936	G. K. Chesterton
1875–1961	Carl Jung
1876–1960	Alfred Kroeber
1877	Publication of Lewis Henry Morgan's *Ancient Society*
1881–1915	Robert Hertz
1883–1957	Robert Lowie
1883–1962	Louis Massignon
1884–1939	Edward Sapir
1884	Publication of Friedrich Engels's *The Origin of the Family, Private Property, and the State*
1887–1948	Ruth Benedict

1887	Publication of Friedrich Nietzsche's *On the Genealogy of Morals*
1888	Boas's first classes at Clark University
1889–1969	Martin Heidegger
1890	Publication of James G. Frazer's *The Golden Bough*
1891–1937	Antonio Gramsci
1891–1981	Abram Kardiner
1891–1953	Geza Roheim
1892–1974	A. Irving Hallowell
1893–1953	Ralph Linton
1895–1970	Vladimir Propp
1895–1973	Max Horkheimer
1895–1975	Mikhail Bakhtin
1896–1982	Roman Jakobson
1897–1990	Norbert Elias
1897–1957	Wilhelm Reich
1897–1941	Benjamin Lee Whorf
1898	Torres Straits expedition
1898–1979	Herbert Marcuse
1900	Publication of Sigmund Freud's *The Interpretation of Dreams*
1900–1980	Erich Fromm
1901–1978	Margaret Mead
1902–1972	Julian Steward
1902–1973	E. E. Evans-Pritchard
1902–1977	A. R. Luria
1903–1969	Theodor Adorno
1904–1980	Gregory Bateson
1905	Theory of Relativity
1908–1999	John Whiting
b. 1908	Claude Lévi-Strauss
1908–1961	Maurice Merleau-Ponty
1909	Publication of Arnold van Gennep's *The Rites of Passage*
b. 1909	David Riesman
1911–1975	Max Gluckman
1912	Publication of Émile Durkheim's *Elementary Forms of the Religious Life*

1913	Publication of Sigmund Freud's *Totem and Taboo*
1914–1918	World War I
1916	Publication of Ferdinand de Saussure's *Course in General Linguistics*
1917	Russian Revolution
1920–1983	Victor Turner
1920	Publication of Max Weber's *The Protestant Ethic and the Spirit of Capitalism*
1922	Publication of Bronislaw Malinowski's *Argonauts of the Western Pacific*
1922–1983	Erving Goffman
b. 1926	Clifford Geertz
1926–1984	Michel Foucault
1928	Publication of Margaret Mead's *Coming of Age in Samoa*
1928	Publication of Vladimir Propp's *The Morphology of the Folk Tale*
1929–1939	Great Depression
1930	First seminar on culture and personality, Yale University
1931–1932	A. R. Luria's expedition to Uzbekistan and Kirgizia
1932–1994	Christopher Lasch
1934	Publication of Ruth Benedict's *Patterns of Culture*
1934	Publication of G. H. Mead's *Mind, Self and Society*
1936	Publication of Gregory Bateson's *Naven*
1939–1945	World War II
1939	Publication of Abram Kardiner's *The Individual and His Society*
1939	Publication of Norbert Elias's *The Civilizing Process*
1941	Publication of Erich Fromm's *Escape from Freedom*
1944	Publication of Cora Du Bois's *The People of Alor*
1949	Publication of Claude Lévi-Strauss's *The Elementary Structures of Kinship*
1950	Publication of Erik Erikson's *Childhood and Society*
1950	Publication of Theodor Adorno et al.'s *The Authoritarian Personality*
1950	Publication of David Riesman et al.'s *The Lonely Crowd*
1950	Publication of Geoffrey Gorer and John Rickman's *The People of Great Russia: A Psychological Study*
1952	Publication of Frantz Fanon's *Black Skin, White Masks*
1954	Publication of W. R. Fairbairn's *The Object-Relations Theory of the Personality*

1957	First space satellite
1957	Publication of Noam Chomsky's *Syntactic Structures*
1961	Publication of Anthony F. C. Wallace's *Culture and Personality*
1963	Publication of Erving Goffman's *Stigma: Notes on the Management of a Spoiled Identity*
1965–1973	Vietnam War
1969	Publication of Brent Berlin and Paul Kay's *Basic Color Terms*
1973	Publication of Robert LeVine's *Culture, Behavior and Personality*
1975	Publication of Beatrice and John Whiting's *Children of Six Cultures*
1975	Publication of Mikhail Bakhtin's *The Dialogic Imagination*
1977	Publication of Pierre Bourdieu's *Outline of a Theory of Practice*
1977	Publication of Victor Turner's *The Ritual Process: Structure and Anti-Structure*
1978	Publication of Christopher Lasch's *The Culture of Narcissism: American Life in an Age of Diminishing Expectations*
1980	Publication of Vincent Crapanzano's *Tuhami: Portrait of a Moroccan*
1980	Publication of Michelle Rosaldo's *Knowledge and Passion: Ilongot Notions of Self and Social Life*
1981	Publication of Gananath Obeyesekere's *Medusa's Hair: An Essay on Personal Symbols and Religious Experience*
1987	Publication of George Lakoff's *Women, Fire and Dangerous Things: What Categories Reveal about the Mind*
1988	Publication of Arthur Kleinman's *Rethinking Psychiatry: From Cultural Category to Personal Experience*
1988	Publication of Catherine Lutz's *Unnatural Emotions: Everyday Sentiments on a Micronesian Atoll and Their Challenge to Western Theory*
1990	Publication of Unni Wikan's *Managing Turbulent Hearts: A Balinese Formula for Living*
1991	Publication of Richard Shweder's *Thinking Through Cultures*
1992	Publication of Nancy Scheper-Hughes's *Death without Weeping: The Violence of Everyday Life in Brazil*
1993	Publication of Michael Taussig's *Mimesis and Alterity*
1996	Publication of Bradd Shore's *Culture in Mind: Cognition, Culture, and the Problem of Meaning*
1996	Publication of Steven Parish's *Hierarchy and Its Discontents: Culture and the Politics of Consciousness in Caste Society*

PART ONE

Introduction

CHAPTER 1

Who Am I?

The Search for the Self

A Sufi teaching story tells of the holy fool Mulla Nasrudin who ventured to a strange city. Before he left on his journey, his wife put a sign around his neck with his name on it so that he would not forget his identity. When he arrived, he spent the first night at a caravanserai; while he slept, a joker took the sign and put it around his own neck. When the Mulla awoke, he was appalled to find his name tag on the joker's chest. "It seems," he cried, "that you are me. But if you are me, then who am I?"[1]

The Mulla's dilemma is a ridiculous one, but it nonetheless touches on central problematics of human existence: the relationship between self and other, and the construction of identity. This introductory chapter lays the groundwork for the discussion of these issues throughout this book.

Chapter Outline

I Identity in America
  A The Self among Others: Diversity and Identity
  B Socialization for Self-Expression
  C Authenticity in Psychoanalysis
II Questioning Self-Certainty
  A Self-Knowledge
  B Self-Doubts
  C Problems of Authenticity
III On the Borderline of Psychology and Anthropology
  A What Is Psychological Anthropology?
  B Psychology and Anthropology: Complementary Perspectives?
  C Boundaries and Possibilities
IV Outline of the Argument
  A History, Theory, Practice
  B The Author's Point of View

I. IDENTITY IN AMERICA

A The Self among Others: Diversity and Identity
   Immigration, difference, and the problem of self-knowledge in the United States.

B Socialization for Self-Expression
   American training in expressivity, autonomy, and choice leads to a quest for the "authentic" self.

C Authenticity in Psychoanalysis
   Modernity and identity in psychoanalysis.

A. The Self among Others: Diversity and Identity

The question asked by Mulla Nasrudin—Who am I?—is a question that is asked, in one form or another, by many in today's America, where vast cultural diversity seems to undermine any unified or shared sense of personal being. Unlike other societies whose members affirm—rightly or wrongly—a historically evolved ethnic and national character, citizens of the United States find themselves in a world that has been manufactured by people from many different cultural backgrounds. With the exception of Native Americans, we live in a community of immigrants who proudly proclaim their distinctiveness from one another and their autonomy from the past.

Yet the affirmation of personal uniqueness leaves us with certain problems of self-conception, since we must then define ourselves without reference to our cultural commonalities or shared history. We therefore are sometimes confused about who we really are and about our relationship with our cultural heritage and social circumstances. That this is so is revealed in our everyday language. Most of us immediately understand the term "identity crisis" and talk easily about the virtues of "finding ourselves," of "getting in touch with our feelings," and of "self-expression." We say casually that we are "not ourselves today," and we make efforts to "get ourselves together." Becoming ourselves is, it seems, a matter of personal effort and is opposed to social demands. We dislike people who play roles; those who do are insulted as phonies, while those we like are praised as real and authentic.

B. Socialization for Self-Expression

The characteristic American concerns for self-expression and distaste for social authority that are revealed in ordinary discourse are not just matters of cliché—they inform and motivate our worldviews and actions at every stage of life. Although self-expression is concretely realized in different ways by different social groups, American children generally are socialized by their parents and teachers to explore options for themselves, to have their own points of view, to be independent of the group, and to choose what they personally like and dislike as a way of revealing their distinctive tastes and character. This attitude is

Diversity in the United States: A crowd watching a show at a shopping mall in Miami.

inculcated in infancy. American parents expect their babies to express individual preferences before they can even speak. This process of self-discovery and self-assertion is thought to lead to individual autonomy and empowerment, and therefore, to personal success and a more rewarding life in a highly competitive world.

American children, especially those of the middle class, who are trained to be autonomous and to choose for themselves, tend to grow into teenagers stereotypically preoccupied with finding out who they are—a preoccupation often leading them to rebel against the very parents who encouraged them to "be themselves." College students continue the struggle to find and nurture their authentic identities, though by this time they realize that they are obliged to play roles in public—acting attentive in class, for example, or wearing a suit and a serious expression to work in an office setting. The "real self" of spontaneous emotion, open affection, and self-revelation can be shown only to close friends and lovers.[2] College is also a time to try out unusual philosophies and alternative lifestyles, as students attempt to develop new identities outside the realms of parental or institutional control.

Nor does the quest for authenticity stop with graduation; many American adults feel alienated from their existences and search for ways to find, cultivate, and expand what they believe to be their genuine being. This search leads not only to a high divorce rate, as people seek new relationships where they can grow and find themselves, but also to the proliferation of therapy groups, 12-step programs, and New Age religions. All these are voluntary collectives that have as their ostensible aim the release of hidden potentials of the self. Even the military lures new soldiers with the slogan "Be all that you can be . . . in the Army." The journey of self-discovery thus has a profound effect on the life courses of many contemporary Americans, whether children, adolescents, or adults.

C. Authenticity in Psychoanalysis

The pervasive rhetoric of authenticity in our culture indicates that Mulla Nasrudin's question is one of our overriding concerns, one that dominates much of our personal and public lives. Yet, although our preoccupation with self-discovery and authenticity may seem to be an inescapable fact of life, the quest to be ourselves is actually a fairly recent development. Consider, for example, the short history of psychoanalysis. During the late nineteenth century, when the discipline was young, the arbitrary sexual prohibitions and double standards characteristic of the Viennese patriarchal bourgeois family drove some young women to exhibit hysterical neurotic symptoms in which their frustrations were symbolically acted out. These patients were not searching for their true selves; instead, they were desperately unhappy with the restricted and repressed lives they were obliged to live. There was no suspicion that identity itself might be a problem. In contrast, hysteria is nowadays almost a completely forgotten diagnosis. Instead, therapy treats primarily newly diagnosed problems, such as borderline personality disorders, anorexia nervosa, post-traumatic stress syndrome, and multiple personality disorders, all of which involve the fragmentation or disintegration of the self.[3]

This shift in therapeutic practice from a concern with repression and neurosis toward a concern with identity and its construction reflects larger changes in social circumstances: Society has become ever more fluid, complex, and hybrid, as the old family system and the patriarchal values it instituted have come increasingly under fire; and the boundaries of reality have been challenged by technology and global change. In this shifting context, old verities have been shaken, and the very nature of what it means to be human has been questioned. This book aims to place our modern problems and preoccupations with identity within a larger philosophical and anthropological context.

II. QUESTIONING SELF-CERTAINTY

A Self-Knowledge
  Identity is confirmed by feelings, emotions, hopes, memories, plans, the acknowledgment of others, and spiritual experience.

B Self-Doubts
  Identity is disconfirmed by philosophical skepticism, delusions, spirit possession, psychological disorders, and introspection.

C Problems of Authenticity
  What would it mean to be truly ourselves? Are we more than machines?

A. Self-Knowledge

On the face of it, asking the modern question Who am I? and seriously seeking one's authentic identity seems an absurd thing to do. Isn't it obvious to everyone but a fool like Mulla Nasrudin that all human beings are always and forever themselves and no one else? Don't we all know ourselves absolutely, indisputably, intuitively, and immediately as living bodies, compelled by physical sensations of hunger, thirst, pain, and sexual desire, and carried away by emotions of grief, anger, shame, longing, and fear? All these inner forces, and a myriad more, must inevitably require all persons, no matter how metaphysically inclined, to recognize themselves as embodied beings interacting with concrete objects and active others. In short, if a person says she does not know who she is, an hour in the dentist's chair will quickly remove her doubts.[4]

Nor is the physical body with its pains and pleasures the only proof of our selfhood. Obviously, all human beings have hopes and dreams that they hold as their own; they certainly have memories of a unique past that confirm their identities to themselves; they have as well a mind full of personal thoughts, beliefs, and ideas. These belong to the self and orient its existence in the world and its trajectory over time. Furthermore, all people have their personal self-certainty confirmed by others, who acknowledge them, remember them, and call them by name. These others provide a world where the individual has a place in an ongoing network of human relationships. Finally, according to the Abrahamic tradition, all human beings have unique souls that will be saved or damned when the body is dead and gone; this eternal part of the individual yearns toward good and is repelled by evil. From the theological point of view, pangs of conscience and moments of religious communion reveal our true spiritual essence in a manner that cannot be denied. All these aspects—corporeality, memories, thoughts, plans, social placement, and the sense of spirituality—give the self an immediate reality that would seem hard to dispute.

B. Self-Doubts

Nonetheless, despite the indubitable tangibility of the self, questions still arise when one thinks seriously about what that self actually *is*. What is most truly one's self in this mixture of body, mind, soul, instinct, logic, and imagination that is called by one's name? Are impulses and desires, which are certainly felt, the aspects that are most essential, or is an individual's truest being to be found in an inner sense of spirituality, which is much less definite? Is the self located in the ego that remembers and plans, or is authenticity to be found in the capacity for reverie and imagination, or in lust and fear? Do we discover our most essential selves when alone, or can we find out who we are only in the reflecting mirror of those who surround us? Do individuals have essentially the same identities they had as children, or do people change from day to day? What if all one's memories were somehow erased, or if one's face were changed so that it would no longer be recognizable? What if someone else's memories and face were magically substituted for our own? What if a person were completely paralyzed and could no longer communicate, or if, in science fiction fashion, a person's mind were put in the body of a fly? What about zombies, robbed of soul and will? More realistically, what happens to the self when the brain is dead, but the body is still alive?

In all these hypothetical cases, the "me" becomes problematic. And what about the selves of others? How do they vary from my own? In what way do the identities of those of another race or ethnicity or gender, or of those raised in a different culture or a different time, diverge from mine? Can machines, animals, trees, spirits have selves? In the same vein, what might it mean to say we are "not ourselves"—for instance, when we are so tired or intoxicated that we "don't know who we are," or when we are "beside ourselves" with anger? In these instances, if we are not ourselves, who are we? Can we be held accountable for our acts if "we didn't know what we were doing"? And if "we" are not responsible, who then *is* responsible? What about those who seem to us to be delusional, imagining themselves to be Jesus or Napoleon? How different are they from us, and are their realities as real—or unreal—as our own? How responsible are they for their actions, feelings, and thoughts? What about people who claim to have multiple personalities, or who believe they can remember past lives, or who say they are possessed by demons or have been abducted by aliens, or who go into trances and channel supernatural entities through themselves? What about those who believe they are imprisoned in a sexual body that is not their own—men who say they are really women, women who say they are really men? How can we accommodate these extraordinary concepts and experiences into our notions of personal identity?

Furthermore, if, as the questions above seem to imply, the self as experienced comprises a number of aspects, some of which at least are liable to alter with circumstances, and if there is perhaps a hierarchy of these different parts of the self, then it must be possible for the individual to be in conflict with the self, to lie to the self, to sin against the self, even to lose the self and become somebody else, as Mulla Nasrudin feared. Our ordinary language often makes just these claims: "I was just kidding myself"; "I'm only hurting myself"; "I don't feel like myself"; "I can't stop myself." And since among modern Americans the highest value is to be authentic, it follows that we must then struggle against such conflicts, ambivalences, and transformations to cleave to what are really our truest and deepest selves.

C. Problems of Authenticity

Yet the urge to purify also has its predicaments. How can we know for certain which of our feelings, thoughts, desires, and memories are really our own? Perhaps we have been programmed to accept as our own the ambitions and plans of our parents and teachers and bosses, plans that are actually corrosive of our true identities. Perhaps the recognition of others, the expectations they have of us, forces us to act against ourselves, imposing an inauthentic being upon us. Society itself may be ultimately destructive, obliging us to obey rules and codes of conduct that alienate us from ourselves. If we tear the socially imposed mask away, we will discover who we really are. This is, in fact, the fundamental message promoted in the shelves of self-help literature found in bookstores in America today.

But even if we could eliminate what is false and imposed, what would our cleansed authentic beings actually consist of when they have been purified of the past and of the demands of others? Would we then achieve, as some contemporary gurus argue, a kind of mystical communion with God, or, in a more secular mode, would we discover the authentic ground of our being that would allow us to be more productive, happy, and aware? Or would we experience something rather less appealing—a sense of anxiety and even of terror as all our history and training are undermined and we are left floating without moorings in a void?

Whether the disintegrating of social identity structures will lead to ecstasy or panic (or both), the fact is that the markers that give secure boundaries to our selves have become ever more blurred in our present era. Contemporary challenges to our self-certainty are epitomized in the difficulties we now have in distinguishing between ourselves and the machines we build, which have reached a level of sophistication undreamt of until very recently. It is now plausible for workers in the field of artificial intelligence seriously to consider constructing a machine that is in many respects the equivalent of a human being. If this can be done convincingly, it would then seem by analogy that a person is no more than a machine—albeit born of flesh and not built of metal—but still containing the biological counterparts of the machine's implanted memories, logic chips, and programmable emotion circuits. Undo the circuitry and nothing is left but a pile of scrap in the one case and dead meat in the other, and machines and humans can merge into one another—a scenario popularized in the modern genre of cyberpunk.[5] If this is so, then it is hard to deny that the self is indeed an illusion. If that is the case, who then is writing this manuscript? And who is reading it?

These metaphysical questions and doubts, with many others, occur when one begins to think about identity and about the dizzying problems involved in making claims to being an individual in the contemporary world. They will continue to be asked in the following pages, since these questions, and others concerning the nature of being, are central to our modern condition. Exploring such core concerns can stimulate us to more critical and more creative understanding of our own condition and of ourselves—whether those selves are illusory or not! Identity issues also offer a pathway to discuss, in a coherent narrative, some of the central questions about the conjunction between individual psychology and cultural context.

III. ON THE BORDERLINE OF PSYCHOLOGY AND ANTHROPOLOGY

A What Is Psychological Anthropology?
We know ourselves only by knowing our culture.

B Psychology and Anthropology: Complementary Perspectives?
Psychology analyzes individual differences through controlled experiments; anthropology interprets cultures using the method of fieldwork.

C   Boundaries and Possibilities
   Problems and potentials of bridging the gap between psychology and anthropology.

A. What Is Psychological Anthropology?

For my discussion in the pages to follow I will rely for the most part on the data and theory provided by my own discipline of anthropology, which takes as its mandate the discovery and explication of the limits and potentials of the human condition through the study of the beliefs and experiences of individuals in cultures other than one's own. More specifically, I will focus on the subdiscipline of psychological anthropology—once known as culture and personality, and now sometimes known also as cultural psychology. This is the part of anthropology that undertakes the cross-cultural study of the social, political, and cultural-historical constitution of the self; it also analyzes the manner in which human identity is variously disintegrated and reintegrated, conceptualized and realized, in diverse cultural and temporal settings. Because of its comparative thrust and its effort to reach universal truths while still giving credit to cultural specificities and the agency of individuals, psychological anthropology offers us the material and the means to think more clearly and objectively about the central issues of selfhood and identity I outlined above. The fundamental claim is that the individual exists only within a social and cultural context. Therefore, we can really know ourselves only if we know others, and we can really know others only if we know the cultures in which they exist.

B. Psychology and Anthropology: Complementary Perspectives?

As expected, such an ambitious field of study is itself internally conflicted and ambiguous, and has a checkered history and reputation. This is in large part because psychological anthropology, as its title indicates, attempts to bridge the gap between two very disparate disciplines. Unfortunately, academic communities, like most other self-defined collectives, cultivate their distinctiveness zealously, and they fear nothing more than losing their autonomy to the claims of rivals. As a result, any attempt to marry academic disciplines is a dangerous enterprise, one that is likely to be perceived as a threat to the integrity of each partner, and one that is likely to produce bastard offspring, not acceptable to either parent. Such has generally been the case with anthropology and its closely associated discipline of psychology, which have maintained their separateness by specializing in studies that consider only certain aspects of the human experience. The majority of academic psychologists have seen their research as a process of identifying, clarifying, and quantifying a set of interrelated variables. From this exercise, hypotheses then could be generated and tested within the confines of the university, using the captive local population of college students or, just as often, the ubiquitous white rat; there was usually no need for investigators to venture out of the laboratory or to doff their lab coats. Results of such

Psychology versus anthropology: A psychologist shapes the behavior of a white rat in a laboratory; an anthropologist talks with his informants in Highland, New Guinea.

research could be rigorously evaluated and compared according to scientific standards of replicability and predictability, and new hypotheses could be generated and tested by ever more elegant and precise means.

In contrast, most anthropologists have spent their careers in distant and exotic environments, confronted by people whose language, customs, institutions, and rituals were unfamiliar and hard to decipher. Laboratory studies and the isolation of relevant variables were rarely possible in such complex and opaque settings, nor were most anthropologists able to follow the scientific model for investigation, where researchers are tidily detached from their experimental subjects. Instead, they lived among the people they studied, following the method of participant observation, which requires immersion of the ethnographer within the disorderly clamor of daily life. Whereas the psychologist could remain remote, the anthropologist was obliged to be intimate; whereas the psychologist could control the laboratory setting and retain a sense of superiority, the anthropologist was at the mercy of those he or she worked among. And whereas the psychologist sought context-free, experimentally verifiable results, the anthropologist produced an ethnographic account that could not easily be reduced to weighted factors or otherwise quantified. Instead, the anthropologist was usually satisfied with what Clifford Geertz called thick description: a rich narrative that made sense of seemingly inexplicable cultural beliefs and practices by placing them within a coherent and consistent meaning system. In other words, anthropology has generally made use of an interpretive rather than an experimental method, and has validated its claims in ways very different from those of academic psychology.

Furthermore, anthropologists generally studied culture as *sui generis*—self-generated, with its own rules and goals that stand quite outside the realm of psychology. If individuals were looked at, it was mostly to show how external culture constructed their inner realities. As a result, anthropologists were able to ignore personality differences almost entirely, setting such investigations aside as irrelevant for their inquiries. In return, psychologists working within their own society and in the sanitized environment of the laboratory kept the confusing variables of the cultural setting completely in the background. For psychologists, the object of their science was the discovery of parsimonious models of inputs and outputs in mental and emotional functioning among their subjects. That these discoveries might be culturally relative was rarely considered—and for good reason—since such a consideration would challenge the foundations of their research.

The major differences between psychology and anthropology can be summarized as follows:

- *Psychology.* Focus on individual; located in the laboratory; practice scientific method; concern with replicability and validity of narrow experiments.
- *Anthropology.* Focus on culture; located in the field; practice interpretive ethnography; concern with accurate description of multiple realities.

C. Boundaries and Possibilities

Given the wide gap in theory and practice between anthropology and psychology, there has not been a great deal of communication between the two disciplines, and what there has been has often enough been acrimonious. Psychological anthropology, as I intend to explicate it, seeks to close that gap. Since I am an anthropologist, however, the weight will naturally enough be placed on the interpretive anthropological side of the equation.[6] Nonetheless, as we shall see in later chapters, considerable work in psychological anthropology, especially in the area of cognitive anthropology, has aspired to develop experimental models capable of being tested and quantified in cross-cultural contexts. However, because controls are so difficult to achieve in cross-cultural conditions, absolutely verifiable conclusions have been few and far between, though interesting claims have been made for the existence of psychic, emotional, and cognitive universals.

Although the results of anthropological investigations may rarely be readily verifiable, the material marshaled to answer our queries about the nature of human experience and the relationship between culture and the individual has become ever more evocative and challenging; the questions being asked have also become more sophisticated and perhaps more disturbing as well. This is as it ought to be. Places where boundaries are crossed are indeed dangerous spots, but they are also places of great promise for creativity, where new ideas and even new ways of being can sometimes appear. This risky territory is the region we shall explore in the chapters to follow.

IV. OUTLINE OF THE ARGUMENT

A History, Theory, Practice
  A synthetic and dialectical approach.

B The Author's Point of View
  The intersection of psychoanalysis, history, sociology, and culture. The role of resistance and adaption.

A. History, Theory, Practice

The book you are about to read has a simple outline. In the next two chapters, I will provide a very brief intellectual history of some of the basic Western philosophical debates about the vexing questions of the relationship between culture and the individual psyche. I do so because I believe that anthropologists, who pay great attention to the fundamental premises of other worldviews, often neglect the assumptions that underlie their own. If we are to understand ourselves as cultural creatures, then we ought to be aware of the intellectual history that predicates our inquiry.

In subsequent chapters, I will show how standard Western notions of the relationship between self and society have been challenged and expanded by cross-cultural research. These research projects include inquiries into the perceptions and intelligence of "primitive" peoples on the one hand, and on the other hand, efforts to apply psychoanalytic theory to cultures very different from our own. I will discuss as well the difficulties of reconciling a strong Western faith in individual creativity with an equally strong anthropological belief in the overwhelming authority of culture, and describe some of the methodological problems of applying Western measurement devices and conceptual frameworks to other worldviews. I will also outline some new theoretical approaches, relate them to their philosophical heritages, and consider to what degree they offer viable solutions to the fundamental question of the relationship between personal being and cultural context.

The next section of the book will apply theory to practice, demonstrating how the insights of psychological anthropology can help us understand some specific problems of Western selfhood. What, for example, is the self? Are Westerners uniquely egotistical, and are other cultures more communal in their self-experience? To what degree is identity malleable, and to what degree do humans everywhere share the existential sense of personal being? These questions lead into a discussion of advances in cognitive anthropology, which attempts to discover the extent to which thought itself may be culturally conditioned and whether a universal mind operates beneath the variety of constraints. Another route of inquiry leads to the investigation of emotions across cultures. Do others feel as we do? Can we begin to develop a theory of the passions that is not culturally biased? And what of the psychic realities of those afflicted with mental diseases, or immersed in dissociative states of trance, or excluded as deviants by the mainstream, or caught up in radical social movements? Finally, the book concludes with two chapters that connect what has gone before with the everyday reality of the modern American reader, showing how the powerful inner experience of romantic love is culturally constructed and conditioned, and discussing the relationship between American worldviews and personal being.

B. The Author's Point of View

Throughout this book, I have tried my best to do justice to the different theoretical perspectives that have been taken by various thinkers, while also showing the implications (sometimes unintended) of their thoughts. But my ambition to be evenhanded and objective does not mean that I do not have a theoretical point of view of my own. In truth, no writer can write without taking a theoretical position—even the claim not to be taking a position is a position in itself. All writers must look through their own theoretical lenses to see and organize the vast range of material on hand. When the author's point of view is made explicit, it can help give a unifying narrative voice to a text; it also makes it easier for readers to offer critique and to compensate for the author's biases.

To alert the reader to my orientation, I will state my premises in the simplest form: I believe an adequate psychological anthropology must take account of the dialectical interpenetration of at least three levels of human experience. The first is that of the psyche, with its compulsions and inhibitions. This is the level best understood through a modified version of psychoanalysis. The second is that of social organization, consisting of institutional structures and authority systems. This level is susceptible to historical and sociological inquiry. The third is that of meaning construction, which connects the personal and the social through the elaboration of symbolic systems and ritual performances. This level is best understood through anthropological analysis.

I believe as well in the evolutionary principle of adaption. Our thoughts, feelings, acts, and, indeed, our selves are limited and shaped by our circumstances. Yet, at the same time, adaption is never perfect; we continually struggle to escape from constraints, seeking to become something other and greater than our mundane selves. I think the best method for psychological anthropology is ethnography that focuses on the contradiction between "is" and "ought," tracing the varied life trajectories taken by individuals within and against the framework of a particular culture. By concentrating on the complex relationship between constraint and desire, adaption and resistance, we can render the human condition, if not more comfortable, at least more comprehensible.[7]

Summary

This chapter introduces the human problem of identity and self-knowledge. These issues are especially salient in the United States, where historical and sociological factors render personal identity fluid and problematic. At the same time, Americans are socialized to value authenticity and to view life as a journey of self-discovery. This preoccupation is a modern one, as the history of psychoanalysis shows. Interest has shifted there from a concern with repression to a focus on identity. This shift reflects larger global changes, as the erosion of traditional support systems has led to self-questioning.

Of course, in some senses, questioning of identity is absurd. Obviously, each individual exists as a self-conscious corporeal body in time and space. Nonetheless, reasonable doubts can be raised about identity, especially in extreme cases where mind and body are disconnected, or when people are deluded or intoxicated. And even in ordinary life, it seems that individuals can feel self-alienated. How then do we know our true selves? Some argue that the real self can be discovered only beneath social and cultural programming, but perhaps deprogramming leads to panic, not enlightenment. In any case, it is clear that questions about identity offer a pathway for the investigation of the relationship between culture and the individual.

These questions have been investigated by psychological anthropology, which seeks to bridge the gap between psychology and anthropology. This task is difficult, because each discipline has its own research agenda and methodology: Psychologists work mostly within laboratories, focus on individuals, and attempt to develop narrow but verifiable hypotheses; anthropologists work in exotic locations and produce ethnographic interpretations of whole cultures. However, despite the differences, there is potential for a creative rapprochement.

The chapters that follow attempt to build such a link, beginning with an account of the Western philosophical and historical underpinnings of the concept of identity, following with a discussion of the foundation and progress of psychological anthropology, a description of its contribution to solving some essential problems about the nature of the self, and ending with a cultural interpretation of romantic love and American identity. The book conveys a wide range of theoretical material, but is based on the author's own version of psychological anthropology, which is dialectical and aims to interconnect psychic, social, and cultural levels of the human experience.

Endnotes

1. A slightly different version of this story is to be found in Idries Shah, 1972, *The Exploits of the Incomparable Mulla Nasrudin*, New York: E. P. Dutton, p. 152.
2. See Michael Moffatt, 1989, *Coming of Age in New Jersey: College and American Culture*, New Brunswick, NJ: Rutgers University Press.
3. Some of these contemporary disorders are discussed in Chapter 11.
4. Embodiment is discussed at greater length in Chapter 7.
5. For more on computers and their relation to humanity, see Chapter 9.
6. For a recent effort from the other direction, see Michael Cole, 1996, *Cultural Psychology: A Once and Future Discipline*, Cambridge, MA: Harvard University Press.
7. For a more complete account of my own version of psychological anthropology, see the conclusion to Chapter 7.

PART TWO

Culture and the Individual in Western Philosophy

CHAPTER 2

The Discovery of the Individual

Perhaps the first time the question Who am I? was asked was in 386 A.D. The questioner was an intensely ambitious and successful 32-year-old man who had already risen from a modest background to reach the high position of public orator of Milan. A great career was his for the taking. Yet he was suddenly overcome with anguished uncertainty about his identity. As he wrote in his autobiography, "I had placed myself behind my own back, refusing to see myself."[1] He felt that his "inner self was a house divided against myself . . . Beside myself with madness . . . I tore my hair and hammered my forehead with my fists." Falling into the depths of despair, he was rescued only when he heard what he took to be God's voice exhorting him to take up the Bible and read.[2] At that moment, he felt himself reborn as a Christian, and as a wholly new person. This tortured convert was later to become St. Augustine (354–430 A.D.), the bishop of Hippo in North Africa, and the most famous cleric and intellectual of his age.

Augustine's anguished experience of inner disintegration and his subsequent conversion marked his radical departure from the pagan universe into which he had been born. In his dramatic narrative, Augustine provides us with the first description of a self-conscious individual at odds with his time and culture, and, even more extraordinary, at odds with himself. He thus began the Western preoccupation with identity and self-discovery. Augustine reached a sense of his true being through conversion to the Catholic Church; others in later centuries would find different answers, some more satisfying, some less, but none of them conclusive. This chapter and the next will outline some of the most important moments in this long Western quest for authentic identity.

Chapter Outline

I The Discovery of the Unified Self
   A Augustine's Quest
   B The Self in Antiquity
   C Plato's Model

The vision of St. Augustine.

II A Human-Centered Universe: The Renaissance
    A From Sacred Hierarchy to the Sacred Self
    B Heroic Individualism
    C Machiavellian Realism

III Protestantism, Capitalism, and Individualism
    A Protestantism and the Anxieties of Freedom
    B The Rise of the Entrepreneur

IV New Paradigms: Montaigne, Hobbes, Descartes, Hume, and Kant
    A Transitory Meditations: Montaigne
    B Solitary, Poor, Nasty, Brutish, and Short: Hobbesian Man
    C The Mind Floating Alone: Descartes
    D The Self Disintegrates: Hume
    E Kant and the Enlightenment

I. THE DISCOVERY OF THE UNIFIED SELF

A Augustine's Quest
    St. Augustine's discovery of a unified, developmental, questioning
    self. His notions of spiritual equivalence and progress.

B   The Self in Antiquity
The classical model of selves as multiple, ranked, porous, communal, and changeless.

C   Plato's Model
True identity is achieved through subduing the passions and embracing reason.

A. Augustine's Quest

Augustine's autobiography (aptly entitled *Confessions*), in which his conversion was recorded, was written during an era when Christianity took decisive hold in the Roman Empire. Augustine's life story reflects the transformation from paganism to Christianity. He was educated in the classical tradition at great expense and with sacrifice from his parents. As noted above, prior to becoming a Christian, he had achieved considerable success, but without ever finding himself at ease in the pagan world. His conversion, which stands as the turning point of his autobiography, was emblematic of a definitive shift in the fortunes of the new religion, as it evolved from a persecuted sect into the dominant faith of the Western world.

Written as an act of public contrition for his past sins and as an attempt to understand the meaning of his life, Augustine's book was something entirely novel. Previously, the rare self-descriptions written in the ancient worlds of the Greek and Roman empires were laudatory histories of great deeds done, obstacles overcome, and public honors achieved. Self-portraits and biographies were static set pieces, not dynamic narratives of personal development, and they were constructed according to stereotypical models that offered little leeway for giving any of what we now call insight.[3]

Augustine was the first to step out of this conventional form. Written with a new awareness of sin and personal responsibility, his autobiography attempts to present to the reader, and to God, an accurate picture of the author's journey toward salvation, including all his errors along the way. He vividly recalls his infantile rage and frustration and his resistance to the discipline of schooling; he describes his youthful sexual adventures, which his pagan father approved, though they were condemned by his Christian mother; he recounts impressing his friends by stealing pears from a neighbor's tree, an act that he later regretted greatly.

In Augustine's narrative of these episodes, we find no adherence to a standardized classical model, but instead "self-searching, self-questioning, self-discovery, self-description, and self-assessment."[4] It is perhaps the first account of the individual as flawed and unheroic, and is the first instance of ambivalence toward the constraints of society on the individual—an ambivalence that remains as a critical potential in our thought today. Augustine's narrative of a personal drama of existential doubt, inner fragmentation, and eventual spiritual reconstitution is also the archetype for the stories of conversion and self-construction that many people still tell nowadays, not only as religious parables, but also as secular tales of addiction and cure, stories of redemption by love, and so on.

History: Linear, Changeless, or Cyclical?

The Judeo-Christian image of history as a drama moving toward a millennial end point is in contrast with the world-views of most other societies. The aboriginal peoples of Australia pictured themselves existing within an eternal dream time in which myths were continually relived. In contrast, Hindu cosmology depicts vast cycles of diminution and expansion, with no end point possible. Our modern era, in the Hindu worldview, is much inferior to the past, when giants roamed the earth and when people were of a far higher quality than they are now. But this too is bound to pass, as the cycle renews itself.

Augustine's conversion provided him with a grounding from which he could construct a single unified narrative for his whole life. From his newfound position as a redeemed Christian, the moral quandaries and vagaries of his previous existence could be interpreted as serving the divine purpose of teaching him his absolute dependence on God. In other words, as he gained a new spiritual identity, Augustine's past was made sensible; instead of being simply a sequence of random events, his history became a coherent narrative with its own intrinsic structure and goal. The image of life as an evolutionary development toward an end point has remained central to our present-day self-concepts and to our larger notion of progress.

Other revolutionary and influential aspects of Augustine's work also deserve mention. For instance, in the moral universe that he inhabited, every individual gained a new and cosmic importance, since every soul was equally worthy of God's love. This new egalitarian morality would later find expression in notions of natural rights and personal liberty. The idea of all human beings as humble pilgrims on a quest for salvation also carried with it greater responsibilities: An introspective, interrogating, and confessional attitude came to prevail, as each individual had continually to test, hone, refine, and purify his or her soul in preparation for redemption. Only a unitary and historical self-consciousness could cultivate itself in this manner and organize its own personal pilgrimage.

By searching for God within, Augustine inaugurated a new way of imagining the self, in which the individual became critically aware of himself or herself as experiencer and actor. The "I" comes into the foreground, and the external world fades into the background. Augustine taught Western humanity that the truest knowledge derived only from the discovery of the truth within—a truth that we now, in a secularized world, take not to be God, but instead, our most authentic selves.[5]

B. The Self in Antiquity

After reading Augustine's text, the reader has a vivid picture of a concrete and unified personality unafraid of displaying his own doubts and weaknesses, his longings and hopes. It is a wholly new image of a human being, one that contrasts starkly with the notion of the individual characteristic of the pagan Greco-Roman culture—a contrast worth exploring to indicate the originality of Augustine's position.[6]

For both the Greeks and the Romans, human beings were not regarded as regent actors, as Augustine regarded them. Instead, they were enmeshed in family and clan relationships that tied them inextricably to their ancestors and to their contemporaries. Personal being was deeply linked to ancestry: The Homeric warrior proudly recited his genealogy whenever asked his identity, since he felt that only through the blood of his forefathers could he assert his proper place among men. The power of the patrilineage over the individual remained so strong in imperial Rome that the cult of ancestor worship flourished as a household religion until the final victory of Christianity, and a father had the right to kill his sons without punishment by the state. In both Greece and Rome, participation in the community was a value held much higher than private life. Honorable men existed primarily as citizens taking part in the politics of the city; slaves, foreigners, women, and those who wished to seek personal economic advantage or withdraw into the family were by definition hardly human.

Inside these aristocratic societies, the Christian notion of the equality of souls was quite foreign: Only men of the patrician clans deemed themselves full human beings. To them, slaves and plebeians were nameless entities, regarded with the same disdain as children or women.[7] Ordinary people were thought to lack the character automatically transmitted by a noble genealogy, and of course, they also lacked the accumulated wealth and power of a family estate. Without the intertwined attributes of blood and property, the plebs, like women, children, and slaves, had neither the capability nor the privilege of acting as men ought, that is, as contestants in battles for glory and respect, straining to stand out from others and earn glory for themselves and their lineages. Only the patricians who engaged in noble contestation could claim virtue and full human status; only they could rise above the undifferentiated masses.

The same competitive ambition is at the core of the Greco-Roman epic literary tradition, with its heroes whose names are still known today: Achilles, Odysseus, Aeneas. But these heroes did not seek to discover themselves in the way that Augustine did. Indeed, there was no way for the Greeks even to refer to the self, nor did they imagine any organizing principle at the core of the human agent.[8] The Greek term *psyche,* often translated into English as "mind" or "soul," was actually not the central locus of thoughts and feelings that such a translation would indicate; rather, it was a shadowy life force that left the body at death.[9] Other aspects of the human being were also seen differently by the Greeks: Bile from the liver, for example, was the source of anger; intelligence and sensibility were located in the lungs, which were the seat of speech, and in the heart, from whence blood vapor could rise and infuse the breath. For the Greeks, and for their Roman imitators, the self had no core.[10]

As Ruth Padel, a scholar of ancient Greece, has remarked, from within this worldview, "persons, mind and body, were porous to divine entry"[11]—human beings could be mysteriously energized by the whims of a god or crippled by attacking malevolent spirits. Thus Agamemnon lamented his disastrous quarrel with Achilles but did not blame himself or Achilles for it—the fight was caused by madness sent by Zeus. Dido and Aeneas fell in love, not because they were naturally attracted to each other, but because they were overcome by the poisons administered by Eros.

Everywhere in the Greco-Roman epics, heroes are driven by their mysterious fates and by the whims of deities who used men as surrogates in their own never-ending battles for glory and revenge.[12] According to Padel, "they 'split' *reality* instead of themselves. One god made you commit a crime, another punished you for it."[13] The moral codes of this universe were automatic mechanisms, like the taboos of tribal societies, rendering personal responsibility and motive irrelevant. Oedipus, who killed his father and married his mother, did so unconsciously, inexorably propelled by his evil fate, and his punishment unfolded in an equally mechanical manner.[14]

This model of character provided a framework for the daily lives of ordinary men and women in classical antiquity, a framework in which questions about identity, distinctiveness, and personality development were mostly irrelevant. What was really important for the Roman and Greek patricians was living up to the standard expectations of exemplary action, gaining public recognition, and adding to the luster of their lineages. Underlying the continual striving for success was its opposite: a pervasive fear of public failure, of shaming oneself and tarnishing one's heritage. In the culture of honor and shame, people lived very much in the eyes of their kin and rivals, not inside their private souls.[15]

For the would-be hero, it was no consolation to have tried and failed, or to have had virtuous intentions. The only thing that could satisfy the public eye and validate the honor of the actor and his lineage was triumph in contests with co-equals. Yet in such contests one could never be certain of the outcome, since the world was, after all, uncontrollable and since one's opponents might be favored by the gods, or the fates, or the stars. In an uncertain universe of continual contest, the Greek and Roman obsession with omens and portents and with propitiating the deities made perfect psychological sense: One looked outside, not inside, for both help and meaning. The world of antiquity was not a social

---

Taboo

While the word "taboo" derives from anthropological studies of Polynesian society, the fear of breaking taboos exists everywhere. Taboo forbids certain acts or contact with certain objects or persons; breaching the injunction automatically leads to supernatural punishment. The tabooed act or entity can be either sacred or polluted. Common proscriptions are against touching or coming close to kings (or outcasts), engaging in sexual relations with close relatives, having contact with menstrual blood, and eating certain foods (for example, pork is taboo for Jews and Muslims).

setting that favored, or even could imagine, modern concepts of introspection, self-reflection, and guilt.

In short, the biographies and epics of Greece and Rome give us a portrait of societies where human beings conceived of themselves as existing only within larger communal units. Locked into the overarching community, each person's life mission was to avoid shame and to seek public approval. For men, esteem came from triumphing over their rivals. This was a dangerous and uncertain task, and those engaged in it felt themselves the playthings of forces beyond themselves and the loci of supernatural entities and overwhelming passions that could harm or elevate them. They were not autonomous and solitary individuals but, rather, were permeable, multiple, and fragmented.

C. Plato's Model

Prior to the advent of Christianity and of Augustine, the main challenge to this worldview was developed by the philosopher and teacher Plato (427–347 B.C.) and his followers, who argued that human beings could gain self-mastery and reach spiritual enlightenment through marshaling the higher, rational part of the soul to subdue the lower, passionate parts. By giving first place to reason, Plato challenged the pagan image of humankind ruled by a chaotic mix of irresistible passions, inscrutable fate, and the whims of the gods. In its place he offered a hierarchical distinction between reason and emotion, a distinction that would later be spiritualized in Christianity and that remains a key element in Western notions of the self to this day.

Plato's model also assumed a central agent capable of rationally grasping reality and acting according to that understanding. His theory of agency moved him away from classical ideas of porous and multiple identity and toward the notion of the unitary and reflective core self that we now take for granted. From his premises, it followed as well that Plato would stress the capacity of enlightened human beings to make free choices as they struggled to reach the ultimate good—another notion that had a great influence on Augustine. But it was Augustine who transformed Plato's ideas, adding to them the emphasis on introspection and the concerns for human fallibility, guilt, and self-doubt, which we now accept as central to personal identity.[16]

II. A HUMAN-CENTERED UNIVERSE: THE RENAISSANCE

A From Sacred Hierarchy to the Sacred Self
   The rise of the individual in the context of the breakdown of feudal hierarchy.

B Heroic Individualism
   The Renaissance and worship of creative genius. Cellini as exemplary.

C Machiavellian Realism
   Machiavelli's portrait of humanity "as it really is": craven, power-hungry, untrustworthy.

A. From Sacred Hierarchy to the Sacred Self

In the centuries after Augustine the bureaucratic and encompassing Catholic Church gradually triumphed throughout medieval Europe, changing Augustine's individualistic doctrine of striving into a far more static doctrine of acceptance. Medieval church creed sanctified a rigid feudal system that granted everyone a place in an immutable hierarchical corporate order. The pope was the spiritual chief of an obedient army of bishops, cardinals, and priests. The king was the pope's secular counterpart, commanding the fealty of princes, knights, and serfs. Similarly, all of creation was envisaged as organized in an eternal and orderly chain of being, leading from heaven down through the various links of angels, humans, animals, plants, and minerals. People were expected to remain within their positions in this stratified and "natural" order; there was little space for exploration of individuality.

This stable universe was not to last. The feudal status system and its attendant worldview was gradually dismantled during the Renaissance—an era that extended from the fourteenth to the early seventeenth century. Of course, despite changes, older modes of being and doing continued to inform the lives of many ordinary people, who maintained their beliefs in magical powers and fluid selves through the medieval period, into the Renaissance, and even until today.[17] But it was during the Renaissance that an elite class of thinkers and artists began to take an increasingly activist stance toward their world—one that at first put human beings at the center of the cosmic picture, as the living images of God, then slowly began to nudge God from the scene altogether, venerating the creative individual capable of making the world over to suit himself [18] (the predominance of men in the public sphere during this period makes the use of the masculine pronoun appropriate).

This shift began in the city-states of northern Italy and was in large measure an unintended by-product of political chaos. Faced with a corrupt and dissolute church and prey to the machinations of rapacious princes and the predatory commanders of armies for hire, Italians of the era were increasingly thrown upon their own resources. Under the circumstances, many could no longer afford to, and others no longer wished to, adhere to feudal codes and religious constraints that had proved inadequate. Also aiding in the transformation was the importation from the Middle East of the ideal of romantic love and of the practice of independent scholarship, which arrived in Europe as a result of the Crusades of the eleventh, twelfth, and thirteenth centuries. These new concepts greatly influenced the rise of humanistic learning in Europe, heightened the importance of the individual, and further subverted the already collapsing hierarchical values of the feudal order.[19]

As a consequence of these and other factors, an opening was made in northern Italy for the construction of new sorts of identities. One such alternative, the one that gave the Renaissance its name, was a self-conscious return to antiquity, as people repudiated the values of the unreliable present and sought some moral grounding by imitating the magnificence of the Hellenic and Roman past. But of course, the recapture of the past was only superficial: Renaissance men and women, steeped in Christian values, could in no way truly emulate the multiple and permeable classical character, nor could they negate the deeply ingrained Augustinian notion of a unified and introspective self whose life was a journey—though often enough, the journey was now understood to be a pursuit of creative self-expression, not a quest for God's love.

B. Heroic Individualism

The new notion that self-development was to be sought not solely as a pathway to something higher but rather as an absolute value in itself was the most fundamental contribution of the Renaissance to Western thought. Many believed that men (again, with some important exceptions, women had little part in this new belief system) could achieve their own kind of immortality by dint of their conscious actions. A burgeoning interest in scientific experiment reflected this human-centered vision; by breaking the natural world into its separate components, which could be categorized, manipulated, and transformed, ambitious thinkers sought to control their fates in ways never imagined by the ancients. Associated with the new activist stance toward nature was a more positive attitude toward work, as labor became a way in which the creative Renaissance man could transform the material world in his own image. The emphasis on self-definition through labor would later find its way into our own active stance toward ourselves and our world.

The most characteristic first-person description of this change is found in the *Autobiography* of the flamboyant Italian adventurer and sculptor Benvenuto Cellini (1500–1571), who has been described as "a wholly recognizable prototype of modern man."[20] Unlike Augustine, who was tormented by his own sins and weakness, Cellini proudly proclaimed himself a genius capable of rivaling God in the beauty of his creations. Despite his modest background, he felt no awe for any king or prince and affirmed "that I was quite able to conduct my quarrels to an end by myself, and that I had no need of stouter fighters than I was."[21] For the competitive and headstrong Cellini, talent alone was enough to set him above others, regardless of their inherited rank or wealth. He spent much of his autobiography arrogantly recounting his vast capacity for hard labor and bragging about his technical innovations, his aesthetic genius, his vigor in love and war, his successful duels, and, above all, his resolute unwillingness to accept the authority of anyone besides himself.

C. Machiavellian Realism

While heroic artists like Cellini portrayed themselves as demigods, another more jaundiced view of human nature was put forward by Niccolò Machiavelli (1469–1527), a Florentine historian whose response to the political unrest of his time was not to glorify himself but rather to delve into the study of history, searching through the past for a way to achieve stable rule. His research into the violent and checkered record of his beloved city made him painfully aware that the Florentine people rarely acted according to idealized standards, nor did they live in a world of ethical certainties. Yet this truth had been ignored by moralistic chroniclers who piously painted over the ambiguities and weaknesses of the men and women of the past. This, Machiavelli said, was a grave mistake, one that kept rulers from understanding the real necessities of governing and therefore promoted political chaos.

To discover and remedy the sources of social discord, it was necessary, Machiavelli thought, to reject idealized images of human beings and describe them not as they ought to be, not as they wished they were, but as they really are. This meant putting aside a quest for otherworldly salvation and observing the actual events of history to discover the underlying psychology of all-too-human actors. Such an exercise in dispassionate observation, Machiavelli declared, showed quite clearly that the Florentine people were desirous above all of fame and glory; though sometimes heroic, they were mostly fearful, cowardly, jealous, and vengeful. These unpleasant human characteristics had to be taken into account by a ruler if any political stability was to be obtained. Machiavelli's greatest work—*The Prince*—was an instruction manual for achieving political authority, which denied, or rather bracketed, precisely that moral aspect of humanity Augustine had underscored. His unflattering portrait of human beings as they really are made Machiavelli's name a byword for manipulative cynicism, but it also originated modern realism and gave rise to the science of psychology.

III. PROTESTANTISM, CAPITALISM, AND INDIVIDUALISM

A Protestantism and the Anxieties of Freedom
Self-consciousness and autonomy among Protestants. Community and the sacred covenant of worshipers.

B The Rise of the Entrepreneur
Capitalist entrepreneurship and individualism. Community and the unseen hand of market competition.

Realist Visions of Human Nature

The unflattering portrait Machiavelli drew of human vanity, deceit, violence, and greed is not unique. In medieval China, for example, Han Fei Tzu and the legalist school contended that human nature is naturally evil and counseled the king to be cruel and rigorous for the state to survive. Similarly, in medieval Baghdad, Nizam al-Mulk, the great prime minister of the Seljuk dynasty, presented a jaundiced view of human motivation to his sultan, warning him that a network of secret police was a necessity for safeguarding the empire. Similar examples of realist political philosophy can be found in other premodern states, where the cruel necessities of centralized rule often undermined idealism.

Martin Luther nails his protest against the sale of indulgences to the door of the church at Wittenburg.

A. Protestantism and the Anxieties of Freedom

The next step in the development of the modern notion of the individual came with the Reformation, which began when German theologian Martin Luther (1483–1546) protested against papal infallibility and the sale of indulgences in 1517. The movement against the authority of the Catholic Church spread rapidly throughout Northern Europe, as Protestants called for an end to priestly hierarchy and affirmed the equality of all worshipers. By 1536, the English parliament declared the authority of the pope void in England. The undermining of papal authority helped inspire massive wars, including the devastating Thirty Years' War (1618–1648) and the English civil war, which ended only with the execution of King Charles I (1648). This disorder led to increased political centralization, greater bureaucratization, and more emphasis on personal responsibility—particularly in England and France.

But there were other, more theological factors that had a part in the Protestant reconfiguration of earlier concepts of individuality. Denied the Catholic possibility of absolution, and without any mediators between themselves and God, Protestants experienced anxiety about salvation, which often led to a highly introspective turn of mind, as believers compulsively sought to discover the workings of faith—and the devil—in themselves. In the mode of Augustine, but with far greater anxiety, apprehensive Protestant self-scrutiny led to a huge increase in the numbers of autobiographies and spiritual diaries among the English Puritans and German Pietists of the seventeenth century.

These pious Protestants deeply suspected emotion and the body, and embraced method and calculation as a way to control the wayward soul, thus indirectly helping set the stage for the scientific revolution. They were gripped as well by a pervasive fear of self-deception and damnation, terrified that the devil could delude them. Continually self-questioning, they struggled to root out all doubt and duplicity. In their relentless self-explorations, these men and women contributed both to the notion that the self can and should be worked on and to a debilitating uncertainty about what is truly one's own. Haunted above all by a deep inner anxiety about their own integrity and salvation, they presaged the modern obsession with authenticity and the gnawing sense that the self is not what it ought to be.

B. The Rise of the Entrepreneur

Simultaneous with the rise of Protestantism was the nascence of capitalism—a hugely complex historical-social process that gradually evolved in Europe, especially in England, after the breakup of the old feudal system. The exact reasons why capitalism began and flourished in Europe rather than elsewhere pose a problem that has exercised many social thinkers.[22] Here I will note only that the advent of capitalism was aided by the relative freedom of European cities, particularly those in the north, from direct princely domination. This freedom permitted the evolution of the independent merchant class who were the backbone of capitalism. Furthermore, as Max Weber argued,[23] the Protestant ethic, with its values of innovation, efficiency, and asceticism, had a central part in developing a new sort of person who would be better suited to capitalist enterprise. We need also to take into account the gradual collapse of feudal authority, which liberated workers from their traditional ties, allowing for the development of a more fluid social system where labor could be freely bought and sold.[24]

Whatever the causes of the gradual advent of the new capitalist economic system, it is certain that its arrival was a painful and disruptive process; it destroyed old bonds, tore people away from home and family, and eroded traditional forms of security. But by devaluing preexistent social relationships as the primary sources of identity, it opened the way for a new vision of human beings as self-directed free agents. What arose as a result was an entrepreneurial society where independent producers and free workers negotiated with one another for advantage under the umbrella of contractual agreements that ensured the unimpeded flow of goods and services. The dangerous pursuit of glory that had animated both the Renaissance and antiquity was now replaced with the socially less destructive and more calculating calm passion of bourgeois greed.[25]

Because capitalism liberated individuals to sell themselves and their skills on the open market, it fit well with the Protestant belief that the covenanted community was to be freely chosen by believers, not given by tradition. Within this ideological framework, the primacy of the collective, taken for granted by the thinkers of antiquity, decisively gave way to a preference for the individual. In a similar way, capitalism and Protestantism also overturned traditional notions of hierarchy. For Protestants, every person was a priest, equal in the eyes of God; each had complete responsibility for his or her own spiritual life. Likewise, in capitalism, all individuals had control over their own labor and could advance themselves according to their own skills and abilities.

It is evident that the increased dominance of these two linked modes of being led to new ways of understanding the self and its relationships to the world: Henceforth, the self-actualizing and striving individual would be regent, while notions of an encompassing community, or of inherent hierarchy, would be in decline. The image of society as a conglomerate of free, equal, independent actors who choose to live together continues today—especially in America, where an aristocracy has never ruled and which has been deeply capitalistic (and Protestant) from its beginnings.

IV. NEW PARADIGMS: MONTAIGNE, HOBBES, DESCARTES, HUME, AND KANT

A Transitory Meditations: Montaigne
   The human psyche is in continual flux.

B Solitary, Poor, Nasty, Brutish, and Short: Hobbesian Man
   Humans are driven by fear and the pursuit of power.

C The Mind Floating Alone: Descartes
   Truth is to be found in detachment from all preconceptions and sensations.

D The Self Disintegrates: Hume
   The self has no rational core. People are governed not by reason but by emotion.

E Kant and the Enlightenment
   Humanity cannot exist without reason, which has a transcendent source.

A. Transitory Meditations: Montaigne

The great upheavals occasioned by the twinned rise of Protestantism and capitalism inspired many different intellectual responses, but here I wish to discuss a few that have been most influential or typical in terms of our modern understanding of human nature. The first is that of the French nobleman Michel de Montaigne (1533–1592), who chose to withdraw from the dislocations and debates of his time. Like Augustine, he turned inward, seeking knowledge within himself, but without the passion and agony of Augustine, and without Augustine's faith. Rather, Montaigne immersed himself in introspection primarily as a kind of experiment in self-analysis, assuming—in narcissistic Renaissance fashion—that his own moods and musings would be well worth recording.

In his many years of writing his *Meditations*, Montaigne chronicled no conversion experience, no transcendent narrative of salvation. He simply took pleasure in discovering and describing a self that was full of ambiguities, idiosyncrasies, and outright contradictions. As he says: "My footing is so unsteady and so insecure. I find it so vacillating and ready to slip, and my sight is so unreliable that on an empty stomach I feel myself another man than after a meal."[26] Montaigne turned inward Machiavelli's injunction to study man as he really is, away from politics and the pragmatic pursuit of power; he inaugurated the playful fascination with self-exploration and self-revelation that would be later elaborated by the romantics, become central to psychoanalysis, and find its final expression in our present-day concern with individual uniqueness.

B. Solitary, Poor, Nasty, Brutish, and Short: Hobbesian Man

The second response, initiated by Thomas Hobbes (1588–1679), was quite different in character. As an advisor to both English royalty and rebellious reformers, Hobbes managed to survive to ripe old age through judicious shifts in loyalty. Marked by his terrifying experience of the English civil war, Hobbes expanded Machiavelli's realist political perspective on human nature in his great book *The Leviathan* and thereby gave self-interest a new philosophical base. Hugely influenced by Protestant egalitarianism, he vigorously argued that medieval notions of noble blood, papal infallibility, and the divine right of kings were false: Human beings are created by nature as equals, all with more or less the same abilities, intelligence, and strengths. Elite pretensions of innate superiority, he said, were purely a product of the brute fact of political domination: "Honorable is whatever possession, action, or quality is an argument and sign of power."[27] Morality too, Hobbes said, is a matter of convention, enforced solely by the might of the dominant classes. In defense of his position, Hobbes

Original frontispiece to Hobbes's *Leviathan*.

noted wryly that piracy is commended among pirates, while the gods of Greece were revered for committing rape and pillage.

Hobbes believed that honest insight into one's own nature would reveal, beneath all the masks of honor and morality, a fundamental human psychological truth, which has nothing to do with the quest for either God or glory. Rather, it is the "perpetual and restless desire of power after power, that ceases only in death."[28] An unrelenting struggle for power is a necessity, Hobbes said, because human beings naturally attempt to protect themselves against being injured or enslaved, and the only sure way to do this is try to acquire authority over and enslave others. This means, in turn, a war "of every man against every man" where "the notions of right and wrong, justice and injustice have there no place."[29] According to Hobbes, this fearsome situation could be remedied only by a ruler's stern assertion of might over a subordinate population.

Hobbes's Calvinist beliefs were also reflected in his famous theory of the origin of the state. He argued that government arose when primitive men and women, tired of the war of each against all and of lives that were "solitary, poor, nasty, brutish and short,"[30] rationally undertook a voluntary social contract among themselves in which they ceded authority to a ruler who could restrain the perpetual violence of co-equals. As long as the ruler fulfilled the duty of protecting the people, the citizenry were obliged to obey. But if the ruler failed, the contract was abrogated, and obedience was no longer required. Therefore, Hobbes advised a soldier captured in war to immediately change sides, since the state had failed in its duty of protection!

Hobbes's radical individualism was in stark contrast to the classical notion of the citizen whose essential identity was located in the polis and the clan, and for whom self-sacrifice and deference to the demands of the group were the ultimate virtue. Instead, Hobbes presented an image of the collective as a group of equal free agents, united solely for mutual benefit. His individualistic view of the nature of human community obviously corresponded to the marketplace mentality of nascent capitalism.[31]

C. The Mind Floating Alone: Descartes

Quite different in content, but even more influential in effect, was the writing of French philosopher and scientist René Descartes (1596–1650), who constructed a revolutionary portrait of humanity, one that combined the Reformation virtues of rationality, introspection, and self-control in a remarkable manner. Like Plato, he put reason at the pinnacle of human existence. His belief is summed up in his famous statement, *cogito ergo sum*—"I think, therefore I am."[32] For Descartes, the pursuit of reason meant a methodical and rigorous process of detaching the mind from the body, the influence of emotions, and the pull of tradition, and then deducing unchallengeable premises through the use of pure logic. As he wrote:

> I shall now close my eyes, stop my ears, withdraw all my sense. I shall even efface from my thinking all images of corporeal things; or since that can hardly be done, I shall at least view them as empty and false.[33]

When the world was made to vanish, the thinker assumed priority; truth was no longer simply there to be found, but was to be *built* by an act of arduous discipline that permitted a mental grasping of the world as if one were—like God—outside it. His method of detached observation led Descartes to his pioneering studies of the mechanisms of perception (see Figure 2.1). Imitating Plato, Descartes hoped by this exercise of intellectual rigor to achieve communion with a rational deity.

Far removed from the musings of Montaigne or the anxieties of Hobbes, the disembodied intellectual methodology of Descartes inaugurated a new capacity for control over the self and the external world, and paved the way for the rationalism of the Enlightenment and the scientific discoveries of the Industrial Revolution.[34] But by affirming the centrality of his own reasoning ego, Descartes undermined all particularity, since he assumed that the path of reason would always lead to the same end: Rational people will necessarily agree. At the end of his affirmation of the power of the self to think correctly, there are no individuals, only abstract truths.

Despite its weaknesses, Descartes's method appealed greatly to many thinkers in the era of the Enlightenment (seventeenth and eighteenth centuries) that followed the Reformation. The Enlightenment was a period in which educated and thoughtful people were struggling to find their moorings in a moral universe where the verities of religion and society had been deeply compromised by more than a century of upheaval and revolution. In response to pervasive uncertainty, theorists and scientists throughout Europe attempted to discover more stable and eternal principles to replace the outdated dogmas of the Catholic Church and the divine king. Descartes's rigorous procedures seemed to offer just such universal truths.

For Descartes, the pursuit of ultimate reality through reason meant that only absolutely verifiable conclusions were admissible. When experimentally applied to the analysis of the nature of our material world, the Cartesian mode of disinterested deduction from verifiable truths—which we now call the scientific method—provided humanity with a new and more adequate picture of reality. The revolution in method also led to new technological inventions and revitalized scholarship, and made the Cartesian scientific model overwhelmingly powerful. This approach remains today—as it should—the primary paradigm for explaining and controlling our material world.

D. The Self Disintegrates: Hume

The scientific revolution inspired by Descartes and his fellows proved much less satisfactory when applied to grasping the nature of human beings themselves. Such was the case with the research of David Hume, the English empiricist philosopher (1711–1776), who applied Descartes's methods to appraise the workings of his own mind.[35] To his surprise, Hume found it quite impossible to make a valid proof for the existence of any core of personal identity within himself. Instead, he came to the startling conclusion that what we usually call human consciousness is "nothing but a bundle or collection

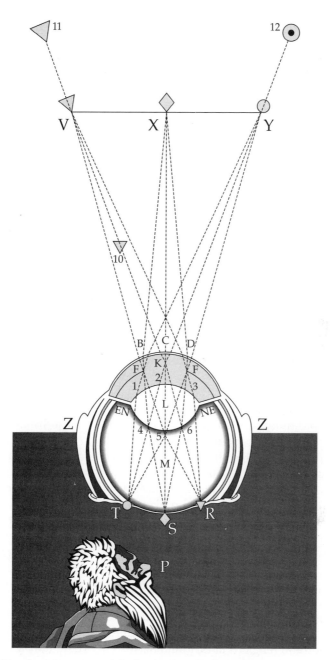

FIGURE 2.1. Sketch of the optics of the human eye by René Descartes. Note the homunculus looking through the eye—an indication of the mind/body dichotomy in Descartes's theory.

Source: Charles Adam and Paul Tannery (eds.), 1897–1910, Oeuvres de Descartes, Vol. 6, "La Dioptrique". Paris: Leopold Cerf publishers, (original publication 1637), p. 119

of different perceptions, which succeed each other with an inconceivable rapidity, and are in a perpetual flux and movement."[36]

Confronted with his inability to observe and record any agent behind his own perceptions, Hume was then obliged to argue that the common belief in a coherent, individual, and bounded self is a result of the illusion that there is a predictable causal relationship between past and present sequences of perception; this illusion leads in turn to the mistaken presumption that there is a consistent and coherent actor who is doing the perceiving. But the existence of a coherent self behind perception, Hume argued, cannot be proved, because there is no way to demonstrate irrefutably that cause and effect actually exist outside the delusions of memory and habit. There is, therefore, no sure way to establish without doubt the endurance or even the existence of the self. And since neither cause and effect nor a stable perceiving self can be experimentally proved to exist, they must, according to Descartes's strict rules of evidence, be rejected as false.

Having called the foundations of his own selfhood into doubt, Hume then asked: What leads human beings to undertake action? He argued that although people claim they act according to reason, in fact, their actions are far from reasonable, since the very premises upon which they base their reasoning are illogical and unprovable. Rather, Hume asserted that human beings are in truth motivated primarily by their fears, desires, and passions. As he wrote in 1737: "Reason alone can never be a motive to any action of the will . . . it can never oppose passion in the direction of the will . . . Reason is, and ought to be the slave of the passions, and can never pretend to any other office than to serve and obey them."[37] It is ironic that the most rigorous follower of Cartesian ideals of dispassionate objectivity was led by those very ideals to the affirmation of human irrationality and psychic fragmentation.

Hume further declared that the ruling passions of a particular individual are intrinsically neither good nor evil. They simply exist as products of habit, disposition, and interest. As a result of differing experiences, histories, and cultural experiences, all persons are also likely to have a multiplicity of different emotions with differing motivational strengths. One person's meat, Hume suggested, is likely to be another's poison. But whatever the various motivations of individuals, Hume claimed that for all of them, rationality is a mask, applied post hoc to justify deeds that are actually motivated by desire; the task of the analyst is to get beneath that mask in order to reveal the cut and thrust of the arousing passions.

Although Hume had come to the same conclusions as had Montaigne 200 years previously, his reaction was very different. Montaigne, secure in his social position and religious faith, found his insight to be simply an amusing datum. Hume, a product of a far more fluid and secular society, was plunged into deep despair by his failure to discover any stable core within himself. To forget his disturbing conclusions, he headed to the local tavern, where "I dine, I play a game of backgammon, I converse, and am merry with my friends."[38] Relieved of his worries by amiable companionship and beer, he set aside philosophical inquiry and devoted his later career to the study of history.

Hume's Theory of Religion

Although he did not again attempt philosophical analysis, the iconoclastic Hume remained an astute student of human psychology throughout his life. He was especially fascinated with religion, which seemed to him to exemplify human irrationality and the power of hope and fear. He argued in a scandalous posthumous essay that monotheism results from the flattery of frightened worshipers who wish to calm the violent natural forces that might harm them. To do so, they imagine those forces to be persons who can be moved by obsequious flattery. This flattery is exaggerated by ambitious priests wishing to make great claims for the power of their particular god, and eventually transforms multiple local deities into a single omnipotent divinity. But the difficulty of making a personal appeal to such a distant deity then leads in the opposite direction, to the invention of intervening saints, who can be influenced to carry the petitioner's message to the supreme being. The anthropologist Ernest Gellner has made brilliant use of Hume's psychological model of religious evolution to explain the presence of living saints in Islamic society.[39]

E. Kant and the Enlightenment

After Hume, it would no longer be possible for Western philosophy to take for granted the Platonic principle that the highest and most vital organizing force of human life is pure intelligence. Instead, his contemporaries and successors had to cope with Hume's discomfiting portrait of a humanity ruled by sensation, habit, and desire. In Germany, the preeminent philosopher of the Enlightenment, the Pietist Protestant theologian Immanuel Kant (1724–1804), attempted to defeat Hume and resuscitate the transcendental power of thought by making a claim for the existence of absolute and universal logical prerequisites for all human understanding and action—abstraction, generalizability, consistency, and noncontradictoriness. Kant contended that we cannot think at all without the use of these prerequisites; therefore, whatever we understand to be real must (in the largest sense) also be rational. Kant's effort to comprehend the essentials of human reason has continued to have a great influence on the development of cognitive anthropology, which, as we shall see in Chapter 9, has sought to discover by comparative methods whether Kantian universal categories actually exist.[40]

As a theologian, Kant was not satisfied simply to posit the universal prerequisites for thought; he argued as well that since these conditions exist before reason itself, they cannot be created by humankind, but must have a transcendental source. In other words, like Descartes before him, Kant believed that God created the parameters of logic, which humans then must attempt to follow. Kant went on to assert that our God-given rational capacity, if used properly, will necessarily lead us to discover and enact our highest moral obligation, that is, to treat ourselves and others as ends, not as means. What this Kantian rendering of the

Golden Rule signifies is that one ought to influence others by offering rational reasons for acting, giving credit to the rationality and freedom of the other, and one should refrain from influencing others in nonrational ways (such as by force or through appeals to emotion), because this would deny the other's rationality and agency. This moral way of relating, Kant thought, must be accepted by anyone who has truly developed his or her God-given capacity for self-reflection; it is the goal sought by both intellectual discipline and Christian spirituality. The good person is also—and must be—the reasonable person.

In asserting the moral imperative behind the use of reason, Kant hoped to replace Hume's vision of human beings enslaved by their emotions with a more uplifting picture of autonomous free agents working toward the evolution of higher moral consciousness through a continuous effort to perceive both the world and themselves accurately. His motto (which became the motto of the Enlightenment) is both heroic and individualistic: *sapere aude*—"think for yourself!" Like Descartes, and in the rebellious spirit of Protestantism, he opposed the forces of tradition and dogma in favor of a strenuous personal search for a truth that could be found only by looking within the mind—which contained, he believed, the highest expression of the soul.

Perhaps because of his experience as a Protestant divine, Kant was not as hopeful as Descartes had been about the absolute power of reason. Real human beings are made, as he put it, of crooked wood, and are inevitably plagued by deep contradictions between desires and principles, passions and duties. This conflict, Kant said, is a painful truth: We are both attracted to and repelled by the world around us and enmeshed in our own complex inner reactions to it— a formulation that would later have a great influence on Freud. It is this nuanced awareness of human ambiguity, and not his theory of reason, that makes Kant a true precursor of modernity.[41]

Summary

This chapter traces in broad strokes the gradual transformation in the Western notion of the individual from antiquity to the eighteenth century. We have seen how the old Greco-Roman vision of persons as multiple, porous, and collective was transformed by the Christian message of St. Augustine, who presented an image of the individual as a spiritual seeker, striving to discover God within. His human-centered vision was eclipsed in the hierarchical order of feudalism, but reappeared in the heroic self-representation of the Renaissance man and then, in inverted form, in Machiavelli's injunction to know human beings as they really are.

Later, the dual and intertwined rise of Protestantism and capitalism led to an even greater emphasis on the regent and self-sufficient individual, capable of exploring and controlling the world through the use of reason. This new vision was expressed, in contrasting forms, by the aesthetic meditations of Montaigne, the pragmatic psychology of Hobbes, and the scientific detachment of Descartes. The latter was the most successful in offering a means for understanding and regulation of the external world.

However, the effort to apply Cartesian logic to the exploration of the self foundered unexpectedly; Hume found no core of being, but only a welter of desire and perception. Kant's effort to refute Hume's corrosive argument stressed the God-given obligation for all persons to reason logically and act responsibly, while positing as well a compassionate awareness of human frailty. As we shall see in the next chapter, in the market-ruled environment of the nineteenth century, Kant's sophisticated discourse fell on deaf ears and was displaced by far more radical visions of humanity.

Endnotes

1. St. Aurelius Augustinus, 1961, *Confessions,* Baltimore: Penguin Books, Sect. 8.7 (written 397–401, p. 169).
2. Ibid., Sect. 8.8, pp. 170–171.
3. For a discussion of classical biography, see Karl Joachim Weintraub, 1978, *The Value of the Individual: Self and Circumstance in Autobiography,* Chicago: University of Chicago Press.
4. Ibid., p. 26.
5. For this discussion, see Charles Taylor, 1989, *Sources of the Self: The Making of the Modern Identity,* Cambridge, MA: Harvard University Press, p. 130.
6. Of course, ancient Greece and Rome were very different in many essential respects, and each society underwent centuries of internal development and expansion as well. In this section, however, I intend to focus on their fundamental commonalities.
7. For a psychoanalytic study of the fraught relationships between men and women in ancient Greece and in other patrilineal societies, see Philip Slater, 1971, *The Glory of Hera,* Boston: Beacon Press.
8. Taylor, *Sources of the Self,* p. 113. The linguistic notion of the self will be discussed at greater length in Chapter 8.
9. For more on the problems of translation and the historical development of the notion of psyche, see Ruth Padel, 1992, *In and Out of the Mind: Greek Images of the Tragic Self,* Princeton, NJ: Princeton University Press.
10. For discussion and references, see Andrew Strathern, 1996, *Body Thoughts,* Ann Arbor: University of Michigan Press, pp. 41–62.
11. Ruth Padel, 1981, "Madness in Fifth-century (BC) Athenian Tragedy," in Paul Heelas and Andrew Lock (eds.), *Indigenous Psychologies: The Anthropology of the Self,* London: Academic Press, p. 126.
12. Simone Weil, 1986, "The Poem of Force," in Sian Miles (ed.), *Simone Weil: An Anthology,* New York: Weidenfeld and Nicholson.
13. Padel, "Madness in Fifth-century (BC) Athenian Tragedy," p. 111.
14. For some accounts of notions of the individual in antiquity, see Amélie Rorty, 1988, *Mind in Action: Essays in the Philosophy of Mind,* Boston: Beacon Press; Marcel Mauss, 1979, "A Category of the Human Mind: The Notion of Person, the Notion of 'Self' " (original publication 1938), in Marcel Mauss, *Sociology and Psychology: Essays,* London: Routledge and Kegan Paul; Strathern, *Body Thoughts.* See Chapter 8 for more on culture and the concept of the self.
15. For a contemporary example of a society governed by very similar ideals, see Pierre Bourdieu, 1977, *Outline of a Theory of Practice,* Cambridge, England: Cambridge University Press.
16. For more on the differences between Plato and Augustine, see Taylor, *Sources of the Self.*
17. For example, see Carlo Ginzburg's influential research on ordinary life in medieval Europe: 1980, *The Cheese and the Worms: The Cosmos of a Sixteenth Century Miller,* Baltimore: Johns Hopkins University Press; 1983, *The Night Battles: Witchcraft and Agrarian Cults in the Sixteenth and Seventeenth Centuries,* Baltimore: Johns Hopkins University

Press. See also Tanya Luhrmann's work on contemporary witchcraft: 1989, *Persuasions of the Witch's Craft: Ritual Magic and Witchcraft in Present-day England,* Cambridge, MA: Harvard University Press.

18. Of course, creative artists and thinkers existed in the medieval period, as they exist in every era and culture, but during the Renaissance, such figures were idolized and creativity was made a central value.

19. For the standard account of the rise of the Renaissance in northern Italy, see Jacob Burkhardt, 1960, *Civilization of the Renaissance in Italy,* New York: Mentor Books. For the influence of Islamic society, see George Makdisi, 1981, *The Rise of Colleges: Institutions of Learning in Islam and the West,* Edinburgh, Scotland: Edinburgh University Press. For more on romantic love in the West, see Chapter 12.

20. Burkhardt, cited in Weintraub, *The Value of the Individual,* p. 115.

21. Benvenuto Cellini, 1927, *Autobiography,* Garden City, NY: Garden City Publishing, p. 131 (original publication 1728).

22. For the standard view, see Max Weber, 1930, *The Protestant Ethic and the Spirit of Capitalism,* New York: Scribner (original publication 1920). For an alternative, see Jack Goody, 1996, *The East in the West,* Cambridge, England: Cambridge University Press.

23. For example, see Weber, *The Protestant Ethic;* Charles MacPherson, 1962, *The Political Theory of Possessive Individualism: Hobbes to Locke,* Oxford, England: Oxford University Press.

24. Alan MacFarlane (1987, *The Culture of Capitalism,* Oxford, England: Basil Blackwell) has argued that Northern Europe already had just such an independent workforce prior to capitalism, which is partly why capitalism found such fertile soil there.

25. Albert O. Hirschman, 1977, *The Passions and the Interests: Political Arguments for Capitalism before Its Triumph,* Princeton, NJ: Princeton University Press.

26. Michel de Montaigne, 1958, Apology for Raymond Sebond" (original publication 1580), in Michel de Montaigne, 1958, *The Complete Essays of Montaigne,* Stanford: University of California Press, p. 425.

27. Thomas Hobbes, 1980, *Leviathan,* Book 1, Chap. 10, Indianapolis, IN: Bobbs-Merrill, p. 81 (original publication 1651).

28. Ibid., Chap. 11, p. 86.

29. Ibid., Chap. 13, p. 108.

30. Ibid., p. 107.

31. For more on Hobbes and capitalism, see MacPherson, *The Political Theory of Possessive Individualism.*

32. In a sense, his was simply a reiteration of the old Platonic apotheosis of reason. But, unlike the Greek philosophers, for Descartes there was no preexistent eternal ideal to be discovered by contemplation of the ever-changing particular worldly forms.

33. René Descartes, 1972, *Discourse on Method and Meditations on First Philosophy,* Harmondsworth, England: Penguin, p. 193 (original publication of *Meditations* 1641).

34. Descartes is often taken as the prototype of the modern scientist, unswayed by sentiment in the quest for truth. In fact, this is not quite accurate, since he had no great interest in experimentation and falsification, relying instead on his own inner capacities to discover his principles (in this sense, he was the first phenomenologist and was also a true exponent of the egoism of the Renaissance).

35. Aside from that of Hume, the most important philosophical research on consciousness was undertaken by Locke, whose strictly sensationalist psychology deserves far more attention than space permits here.

36. David Hume, 1978, *A Treatise of Human Nature,* London: Oxford University Press, p. 252 (original publication 1739), Note that the question of who the "I" is in Hume's questioning discourse is left aside.

37. Hume, *A Treatise of Human Nature,* pp. 413, 415.
38. Hume, quoted in John A. Hall, 1987, *Liberalism,* Chapel Hill: University of North Carolina Press, p. 12.
39. Hume, *The Natural History of Religion;* Ernest Gellner, 1981, "Flux and Reflux in the Faith of Men," in E. Gellner (ed.), *Muslim Society,* Oxford, England: Blackwell.
40. Franz Boas, the father of American anthropology, took Kant's *Critique of Pure Reason* with him during his first fieldwork with the Eskimos. According to the anthropological historian George Stocking, Boas was directly influenced by Kant in his work on Eskimo verbal categories and in his larger interest in the relation between objective and subjective reality (see George Stocking, 1974, *The Shaping of American Anthropology, 1883–1911: A Franz Boas Reader,* New York: Basic Books).
41. For a more nuanced appreciation of Kant than I can undertake here, see Charles W. Nuckolls, 1996, *The Cultural Dialectics of Knowledge and Desire,* Madison: University of Wisconsin Press.

CHAPTER 3

Authenticity and Its Vicissitudes

The modern notion of the self changed irrevocably in 1749, when an unknown, self-educated, ambitious, and deeply unhappy journeyman writer, with a checkered past as a private secretary and gentleman's valet, sat down to ponder a question that had recently been asked by the Academy of Dijon. The question was this: Has the restoration of the sciences and arts tended to purify morals? With sudden inspiration, the author realized that the answer was an unequivocal no. He understood "that man is naturally good and that it is through these institutions alone that men became bad."[1] His own maladjustment, alienation, and misery were therefore not his responsibility; the fault lay with the world itself! Thus Jean Jacques Rousseau (1712–1778), at the age of 37, began writing his great book *Discourse on the Origin of Inequality,* which made him famous and inaugurated a career that would shake the world.

Jean Jacques Rousseau

According to Rousseau, playing social roles destroyed human integrity; reason estranged people from feeling; civilization itself was catastrophic. True being could be found only deep within the innocent childlike heart, still beating warmly beneath the distorting distinctions and vanities of society. Instead of the austere Augustinian quest for God within, Rousseau's ultimate aspiration was to tear away all social masks in order to reveal his genuine emotional essence. By disavowing his entire culture in favor of a search for inner authenticity, Rousseau set the stage for a debate about the nature of human existence that would influence Western thought until today.

Chapter Outline

I. ROUSSEAU AND ROMANTICISM

A The Solitary Walker
    Rousseau's character, his quest for authenticity, and the role of public confession.

B The Road to Self-Estrangement
    Human evolution leads away from innocence to a civilized condition of envy and vanity.

A. The Solitary Walker

Jean Jacques Rousseau was born in the Calvinist city of Geneva to a working-class family; he left home at an early age and wandered aimlessly through Europe, settling at last in France. During his meanderings, he survived by working at a number of menial and degrading jobs, which aroused in him a deep hatred of inequality that would motivate his later philosophy. Naturally introspective, Rousseau spent much of his time ruminating on his state of being and on his place in the cosmos. His soul-searching left him alienated from and repelled by the world as it existed. In his last book, poignantly entitled *Reveries of the Solitary Walker,* Rousseau describes himself as follows:

> Wrenched somehow from the natural order, I have been plunged into an incomprehensible chaos where I can make nothing out . . . I live here as in some strange planet on to which I have fallen from the one I knew . . . Let me give myself over entirely to the pleasure of conversing with my soul, since this is the only pleasure that men cannot take away from me.[2]

The estrangement Rousseau felt for his society had its spiritual roots in the Christian rejection of the material world. But in his more secular era, Rousseau could not find salvation by retreating to a monastery. Nor was he psychologically inclined to suppose, as did his Enlightenment compatriots, that reason could lead him to deliverance from his alienation. Instead, Rousseau (and the romantic poets and thinkers who followed him) sought redemption in the enhancement of feeling and in the quest for an authentic and natural self.[3] Social rules and regulations, as well as Cartesian theorems and methods, were perceived as obstacles to the pursuit and revelation of inner truth.

Like Montaigne, then, Rousseau looked for ultimate reality within himself, but unlike the cosmopolitan, detached, amused, and amusing meditations of his predecessor, Rousseau's *Confessions*[4] were perverse and disturbing. In this unvarnished autobiography, he bared his most intimate and humiliating thoughts and experiences, revealing himself as self-serving, cowardly, obsequious, masochistic, sexually deviant, paranoid, and achingly proud. In his litany of failings, Rousseau consciously paralleled himself with St. Augustine, but where Augustine presented his sins (very minor ones) as a prelude to his conversion and salvation, Rousseau did something very different. In his often embarrassing autobiography, Rousseau proudly revealed his vices and weaknesses with unprecedented honesty and candor for everyone to see and judge. Could his readers be as honest with themselves?

Making a claim to moral superiority through the very act of displaying his worst moral defects was a characteristic Rousseauean gambit, and heralded a new vision of the self in which the important thing is the free and full expression of one's essential nature, whatever it is, regardless of the moral standards of society. For Rousseau, as long as one remains true to the prompting of one's inner being, the judgments of others count for nothing. As he characteristically writes: "Under pressure from all sides, I remain upright because I cling to nothing and lean only on myself."[5] Only such resolute solipsism, Rousseau felt, could lead to authenticity.

B. The Road to Self-Estrangement

Rousseau also believed that being true to the essential self had become almost impossible to achieve under the conditions of civilized society. As he famously remarked in the first pages of *The Social Contract,* "Man was born free, and everywhere he is in chains. Many a one believes himself the master of others, and yet he is a greater slave than they."[6] Not only are we enchained, but we have even grown to love our chains and to embrace the social world that has destroyed our freedom. How is it, he asked, that we have lost our way so badly?

To answer this question, Rousseau wrote one of the first, and one of the most influential, explorations in speculative anthropology, *The Origins of Inequality.* In it, he argued that human beings originally lived in a pure state of "noble savagery." Unlike the Hobbesian portrait of early humans engaged in perpetual war, Rousseau's view claimed that our ancestors were unmoved by desire or jealousy; motivated only by *amour de soi* (self-love), they lived in harmony with nature. Only with the gradual development of the division of labor, and the differences in wealth and property that resulted, did humans learn to covet their neighbor's possessions. Motivated by *amour propre* (vanity), they sought prestige and status at the expense of others. This led in turn to the imposition of the state and to the present degraded condition. Born and raised in iniquitous circumstances created by a long history of oppression and inequality, humans were trained in envy and deceit, and became so vain that they forgot their original autonomy. According to Rousseau, humans today are capable of experiencing their being only when they are reflected in the eyes of others. If others admire us, we are proud; if others hold us in contempt, we despise ourselves.[7]

Civilization, Rousseau said, has robbed us of our independence and made us slaves of power and imitators of fashion; the true character of humanity can be seen only in simple folk cultures, which are naturally closer to the original state of nature. As we shall see in the following pages, Rousseau's nostalgia for the primitive would have much influence on later French and German romantics, and would contribute mightily to the foundation of anthropology as a discipline devoted to the study of such cultures.

Equally influential was Rousseau's belief that children were repositories of humanity's original innocence. Some of Rousseau's most important works were therefore concerned with developing what we would now call a child-centered

---

Rousseau's Evolutionary Model

- The noble savage: No passions, no desires; motivated by *amour de soi* to fulfill basic needs; individual is self-sufficient.
- Division of labor develops distinctions between humans.

- Civilized humanity: Passionate, with expanding desires; motivated by *amour propre* to envy and greed; individual exists only in the opinions of others.

education, one that would train the child to resist cultural brutalization and remain an "amiable foreigner" in his or her own society.[8] Rousseau was thus the first Western social thinker to take the Christian emphasis on childhood purity seriously and to focus on the crucial effects of socialization—an orientation that was later to have a great influence on Freud and on the development of psychological anthropology.

In sum, Rousseau presented the Enlightenment with a challenge as radical as Hume's, and one with far more influence on the larger public. Like Hume, he argued for the essential irrationality, multiplicity, and emotionality of human nature, but unlike Hume, he did not question the existence of an inner self through the exercise of philosophical self-analysis. Rather, relying on poetic intuition instead of Cartesian logic, he made the startling claim (redolent with Biblical imagery of the Fall) that an authentic self did indeed exist and could be discovered among primitives and innocent children; but sadly, true being had been distorted by the influences of an alienating civilization. His dissenting message—reflecting the ideals of his Calvinist childhood training—was resolutely against the world as it actually exists, and passionately in favor of the rediscovery of an indefinable yet deeply felt authentic self. His radical faith inspired the French Revolution and has continued to appeal to rebels and poets from his time until today.[9]

II. HUMAN BEINGS AS MAXIMIZERS: UTILITARIANISM

A Industrialism and Philosophy
      The social context of utilitarian thought.

B Quantifying Pleasure and Pain
      Human beings as rational calculators.

C Ambiguities in the Calculations
      Contradictions of utilitarian reason.

A. Industrialism and Philosophy

Rousseau's fears about the destructive potential of reason seemed to many to have been borne out by the ruthless rise of the Industrial Revolution, which began in England in the late eighteenth century. The invention of the steam engine by James Watt in 1775 and the installation of steam power in a cotton-spinning factory in 1785 were benchmarks in the marriage of entrepreneurship and technology, a marriage that would soon lead to vast increases in production and completely transform the earth. By the end of the eighteenth century, factories and mills dotted the English landscape, and sooty London was the center for commerce not only in Europe but in the entire world.

In this pragmatic environment, Kantian transcendental categories and Rousseauean ideals were equally irrelevant to the task of discovering new and better ways to manufacture commodities, organize labor, speed exchange, and

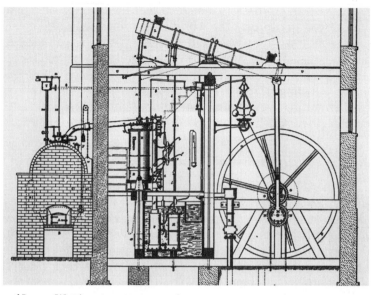

Diagram of James Watt's rotary steam engine.

create and sell products. Efficiency, innovation, hard work, self-control, rational calculation, and hard-headed investment were the dominant values of the rising class of entrepreneurs and inventors. To be sure, these attitudes were derived from the same Protestant ethic that had so inspired Kant's own individualistic philosophy, but they had been transformed by economic success into a capitalistic code of behavior that was far removed from its original religious foundations.[10]

The successes of the Industrial Revolution were undeniable. But so were the costs. Some romantics argued that the pursuit of Enlightenment virtues of individualism and rationality had led to more innovation and efficiency but had not brought humankind a more humane social environment. Rather, the reverse seemed to be the case: Reason and egoism had run amuck, forging a highly productive technological and capitalistic world where hearts and souls were destroyed in service to the inhuman needs of industry.

Nor had the Enlightenment call for the overthrow of tradition and the increase of human freedom fared any better. The French Revolution, which had begun in 1789 by proposing to replace religious bigotry and aristocratic tyranny with the principled rule of reason and democracy, had disintegrated within 5 years into anarchy and arbitrary mass executions. After this cataclysm, it seemed clear to many formerly sympathetic thinkers that the rational principles espoused by the Enlightenment had dismally failed to produce the expected benevolent effects.

Early nineteenth-century disenchantment with the Enlightenment faith in the transcendental power of reason promoted a backlash of poetic romanticism. The visionary English engraver and mystical poet William Blake (1757–1827) fulminated against the "man-forged manacles" blighting the human soul,[11] and

William Wordsworth (1770–1850) lamented that the triumph of capitalism inevitably destroyed the spirit: "The world is too much with us; late and soon. Getting and spending, we lay waste our powers."[12] And, as we shall see, in Germany, revulsion against the brutalities of the age led to the philosophical romanticism of Johann von Schiller (1759–1805), Johann Fichte (1762–1814), and Friedrich von Schelling (1775–1854). But the Industrial Revolution also gave rise to a very different intellectual response—utilitarianism, best articulated by Jeremy Bentham, the English philosopher and reformer (1748–1832).

B. Quantifying Pleasure and Pain

Bentham accepted Hume's argument in favor of the primacy of sensation and went on to reduce Hume's multiplicity of desires to a mere two: the desire to avoid pain and the desire to gain pleasure. The next step for the pragmatic Bentham was to attempt to calculate which acts and policies would give the most people the maximum amount of pleasure and the least amount of pain. Keeping this simple goal in mind, Bentham spent his long career trying to discover psychological techniques that could measure the duration, intensity, and amount of sensations in order to build a social system in which pleasure and production would be maximized and pain and waste minimized. Bentham practiced what he preached. Shocked at the uselessness of burial of the dead, he had his own body stuffed and preserved as an ornament. He continues, in this useful capacity, to preside to this day over the meetings of the syndics of the London School of Economics.

Those who followed Bentham's lead emphasized the calculating aspect of his theory, and as good capitalists, they focused on what they assumed to be the essential human passion: greed. No longer the complex and often self-contradictory creatures described by Kant and Hume, or romantic seekers thirsting for authenticity and feeling, human beings were envisaged as buyers and sellers negotiating in the marketplace of life to fulfill personal needs, wants, and desires. Each autonomous individual was assumed to be fully conscious of what he or she valued and capable of calculating trade-offs for exchange with other fully conscious calculating agents.[13] One advantage of this severe reduction of the passions was that theorists could now envision human life as economic exchange, subject to the same kinds of rulelike mathematical formulas of supply and demand as the rest of the marketplace. The study of human behavior could then once again make claims to Cartesian scientific rigor, without the worries about the irrational nature of humanity that had so troubled Hume or romantic qualms about civilization's corruption of spontaneous, natural human beings.

C. Ambiguities in the Calculations

This apparently simple philosophy rests on an insecure base. Although the utilitarian portrait of human beings as machines designed for pursuing pleasure and avoiding pain seems concrete and scientific enough, the commonsense premise of utility actually disguises the undeniable fact that Hume had noted long ago: The desires of individuals are often polymorphous, complex, contra-

---

The Origins of Functionalism

The social theory that developed from utilitarian principles had many paradoxes, not least of which was the assertion that the continual competition of each against all in an open market actually contributed to social order behind the back, as it were, of the actors. According to utilitarian theory, social order appeared because entrepreneurs, producers, and consumers had to count upon one another to conduct relations of exchange and worked together (albeit unconsciously) to maintain peace, stability, and growth. This theory of social order arising through competition in the marketplace is one of the origins of the hugely important concept of functionalism, that is, that a society is built and maintained by independent actors fulfilling different but interrelated social roles, much as a body maintains itself through the operations of its integrated and interdependent organs. This model of society has had great influence on anthropological thought, as we shall see in the next chapter.

---

dictory, and rarely reducible to easy calculation. Furthermore, wants are culturally conditioned and vary historically, a problem utilitarians simply ignored. Nor could utilitarian theory make sense of the apparently irrational excesses of the French Revolution[14] or other later outbreaks of collective violence, and it could not account for instances of self-sacrifice and devotion that flew in the face of its central premise of calculated interest.[15]

Despite these limitations, utilitarianism expanded outside the realm of economic philosophy and has become, to a very large degree, the standard Western folk model for understanding human action, explaining and unmasking all behavior as an attempt to get something for the maximizing individual actor. This triumph reflects the correlation between utilitarianism and our dominant capitalist economic ethic, and also coincides with the predominant Western—and especially American—ideology of the autonomous and self-actualizing individual. Nonetheless, it must be stressed that the premises of utilitarianism, however realistic they seem, are historical and cultural products, reflecting and validating the social structure. They are no more (or no less) eternal and universal than other value systems.

III. THE GERMAN REACTION: HEGEL, SCHOPENHAUER, MARX, AND NIETZSCHE

A Hegel's Spiral
   The Hegelian model of thesis, antithesis, and synthesis, leading toward unity with the spirit.

B The Dialectical Study of History
   Hegel's method. History can be grasped through comparative studies of characteristic individuals. Identity is culturally constituted.

C The Triumph of the Will: Schopenhauer
   Schopenhauer's proto-Darwinism. Humanity is propelled by the deep, universal Will to procreate and expand.

D Marx's Materialist Dialectics
   Marx's materialist revision of Hegel. The inevitable rule of the proletariat.

E Nietzsche and the Death of God
   Nietzsche's debunking of transcendental assumptions. His method of comparative interpretation.

F The Psychology of Power and the Quest for Authenticity
   Nietzsche's psychology of resentment. His apotheosis of the *übermensch*—the superman.

A. Hegel's Spiral

The development of an anti-utilitarian theoretical framework that incorporated the insights of romanticism within an analytical system was left to German philosophers, who produced new, more dynamic models of the social world and the physical universe. For these thinkers, the systems of civilization were thought to resemble living things driven by inner contradictions to strive toward an ultimate completion—much like the organic growth and flowering of plants. This notion stood at the heart of the philosophies of Schelling, Fichte, and Schiller, among others, but the greatest exponent was G. W. F. Hegel (1770–1831), who (much influenced by his intensive reading of European mystical Hermetic philosophy and of Buddhist and Hindu texts) portrayed human history as a continually upwardly moving spiral of heightened awareness. Each historical thesis about the nature of life and community generated a contrary antithesis, and then a synthetic combination of the two, which provided the basis for a new thesis, and so on.

Thesis → antithesis → synthesis

In Hegel's system, the evolving tensions and oppositions within society could then be analyzed to account for social change.[16]

Hegel's emphasis on the dynamics of contradiction and dialectical movement radically challenged the prevailing individualism and linear thinking of the utilitarians; he also denied the existence of Kantian transcendental categories and disparaged the romantic quest for an essential inner being. Against these ahistorical and acultural theories, Hegel declared that persons exist only when they are engaged with others and are immersed in a particular time, place, and community. Knowledge likewise is socially constructed and cannot be seen as either eternal or external to human action. The same is true of the self: The quest for authenticity is wholly a product of a particular worldview. For Hegel, reality and significance are to be found only within the multiplicity and continual transformation of human relationships; his is a completely social theory of the human condition. In a sense, then, he returned to the classical notion that hu-

man beings exist only in community, but balanced this with a modern emphasis on individual uniqueness and historical change.

Hegel's portrait of history had great poetic as well as intellectual power, for
it resonated with the Christian narrative of redemption. History had meaning
and humankind could indeed reach the promised land through struggle and
discipline, though it would be a promised land not of milk and honey but of
philosophical self-consciousness, where God (or *Geist,* the "world spirit") was
revealed as immanent in society itself.

B. The Dialectical Study of History

However, the question remained as to how this stage of philosophical insight
can be reached if our ideas and feelings are inevitably entangled in and even
constructed by our own particular time and place and the relationships we have.
Hegel's answer was that we are at an advanced stage of development where we
can look back through history and across cultures to see—with the help of
Hegel's own writings—that all humans have faced parallel quandaries of being,
but from different historical and cultural positions. We can therefore grasp the
reality of others (not as individuals, but as general types) by comparing how,
within the objective constraints of their time and place and culture, they struggled with the fundamental dilemmas of existence—a perspective that I will argue in favor of throughout this book.

Hegel thus reimagined personal identity as neither a disembodied essence
nor an expression of feeling, but something far more complex and ambiguous:
For him, the particular individual is a fleeting moment in the ongoing flow of
opposition and synthesis. Human beings necessarily struggle for uniqueness,
yet with equal necessity are merged in community and can realize themselves
only through active relations with others.[17] What Rousseau found so repellent—
that individuals discover their being through participation in their culture—
was in Hegel's terms the very essence of reality, a revelation that could be
achieved through assiduous reading of Hegel's own writings. In a secular age,
the philosopher donned the robe of the prophet.

C. The Triumph of the Will: Schopenhauer

Hegel's oracular writings inspired and enraged many later thinkers. One of the
most irate was another German philosopher, Arthur Schopenhauer (1788–1860),
who, like Hegel, was very much influenced by Eastern philosophy, but who
heartily detested Hegel's idealism. Prefiguring Darwinian evolutionary theory,
Schopenhauer stated that human civilization has no transcendental goal; it is
merely the consequence of the blind workings of the Will, a universal life force
that seeks nothing more than to reproduce and expand itself. All forms of human experience are adaptive responses to the demands of the impersonal and
omnipotent Will: There is no dialectics—only the inexorable pressure of the Will
to overcome resistance. Awareness of this mechanical reality does not lead to
philosophical contentment, but only increases unhappiness. To escape from the

Eastern Religion and German Philosophy

Eighteenth-century German philosophy often was influenced by early translations from Eastern religious traditions. Hegel was familiar with Western mystical thought, but his portrait of the world as a whirling multiplicity divided from and yet continually returning to an original unity bears a striking resemblance to Hindu cosmology. Chinese yin-yang theory, in which there is an eternal dialectical struggle between opposing elements, also has much in common with Hegel's model. (See Figure 3.1.) Hegel, however, as a Christian, believed that history moves toward a redemptive end point—a faith in progress that neither Indian nor Chinese thought share.

Schopenhauer's debt to Asian philosophy, especially Buddhism, is even more obvious, especially since he often quoted from Buddhist and Hindu texts to make his case. The material world, Schopenhauer argued, is governed by the relentless movement of blind forces. There is no end to this process, which

FIGURE 3.1. The yin-yang symbol of Chinese cosmology, depicting the masculine, active (light) and the feminine, passive (dark) principles of nature, which are combined in different ways in all of nature and society.

continually draws us, as material beings, into participation and suffering. In line with Buddhist teachings, Schopenhauer counseled detachment from desire and a stoic withdrawal into pure contemplation as the only solution to humanity's existential misery.

relentless drive of the Will, Schopenhauer counseled an ascetic withdrawal from the world. Instead of a prophet, the philosopher becomes a monk.

D. Marx's Materialist Dialectics

Another German philosopher, Karl Marx (1818–1883), was equally critical of Hegel, but from a very different direction. Unlike the pessimistic Schopenhauer, Marx retained Hegel's faith in human progress, and he accepted as well the dialectical model Hegel had posited for the explanation of history. But whereas Hegel had focused on the clash of ideas, Marx argued for a materialist approach. He was preoccupied not by historical shifts in notions of self and other, but by changes in the mode of production and in the relations of production, picturing history proceeding through more and more complex and encompassing economic forms, culminating in capitalism, in which one class (the capitalists) had appropriated control over the means of producing a living. But that too would pass, Marx claimed, as internal contradictions would inevitably lead to the overthrow of the capitalists and to the dictatorship of the proletariat—the universal class. Then, Marx said, history would cease, and humanity would reach its full potential—though it was not

Friedrich Nietzche

quite clear what the content of that potential would be, but it seemed to involve fishing in the morning and philosophizing in the afternoon.

While Schopenhauer favored retreat from the world, Marx took the opposite tack. He was the philosopher as revolutionary: a brilliant polemicist, an impassioned journalist, and an active propagandist. He implored workers to unite and throw off their chains, following his belief that the role of philosophy was not simply to interpret the world but to change it. However, his model of the world was, in fact, oddly impersonal. The psyches of individuals were mere reflections of their period and class positions; ethics and values were ideology serving the interests of the dominant class; history would proceed mechanically to its end. Regardless of the desires and ambitions of the various actors, the proletariat would triumph and humanity would be saved from itself.

E. Nietzsche and the Death of God

It was left to another German scholar, Friedrich Nietzsche (1844–1900), to follow Schopenhauer's path and completely deny the possibility of any dreams of ultimate redemption, whether Marxist or Hegelian, and supply an unprecedentedly dark portrait of humanity. Beginning his career as a brilliant linguistic scholar, Nietzsche, like Rousseau, was deeply alienated from the world around him. He especially despised his fellow academics, whom he characterized as "coquettish bedbugs with their insatiable ambition to smell out the infinite, until at last the infinite smells of bedbugs."[18] Disgust with the sterility of standard scholarship, combined with his increasingly bad health (he was infected with syphilis, a disease that eventually drove him insane), led Nietzsche to withdraw from the university and devote himself entirely to writing. His first works showed the striking language and originality of thought that would henceforth be his trademark, as he used Hegelian dialectics to argue for the transcendent power of dramatic opera.

But Nietzsche was soon disappointed in the healing potential of art and in the transcendent claims of Hegelianism. He dismissed both as delusions, masking the true wounded and alienated condition of humanity. Nor could Nietzsche accept the Cartesian or Kantian apotheosis of reason, while utilitarianism, in its narrowness and psychological simplicity, seemed to him hardly worth refuting. Instead, Nietzsche argued that to cure humanity of its diseased reliance on illusion, philosophy must undertake research that did not take anything for granted, including the very notion of God and of absolute truth. Only in this way could humankind hope to escape from bondage to fantasies.

Like Hegel, Nietzsche believed our modern age of comparisons allows us to unveil the contingent nature of our culturally and historically manufactured truths.[19] However, problematizing all claims to verity as social and historical constructions left Nietzsche—again, like Hegel—with a severe methodological difficulty. How could he carry on research about the nature of humanity if truth itself is multiple and malleable, and if there is no ultimate goal to history? Well aware of this quandary, he argued that the only appropriate method was to incorporate as many different interpretations as possible, making him a precursor of the comparative method that undergirds anthropology.

The Birth of Tragedy

In his first great book, *The Birth of Tragedy*, Nietzsche claimed the operatic works of his hero, Richard Wagner (1813–1883), were the modern incarnation of ancient Greek tragedy; for him, Wagner's operas embodied a dialectical conflict between the fundamental forces of Dionysius (Will) and Apollo (Thought), uniting them in an overwhelming aesthetic synthesis—a work of art that could raise society to a higher spiritual level. Later, after he had a falling-out with Wagner, Nietzsche revised his opinion of Wagnerian opera downward. Incidentally, it is from Nietzsche that the anthropologist Ruth Benedict drew inspiration for her characterization of American Indian cultures as Apollonian or Dionysian, as will be discussed in Chapter 4.

F. The Psychology of Power and the Quest for Authenticity

Although stressing the importance of multiple perspectives for gaining understanding, Nietzsche also believed certain fundamental psychological premises could be drawn from the study of history and culture. Indeed, Nietzsche saw himself primarily as a psychologist and took as his teachers and equals not philosophers or academics but the novelists Stendahl (1783–1842) and Dostoyevsky (1821–1881).[20] Nietzsche believed desire lay at the heart of being, but for him the fundamental desire was what he, following Schopenhauer, called the will to power—the naked and innate animal impulse to expand and control. Nietzsche's picture of the workings of this essential drive was complex and troubling. He denied Bentham's utilitarian calculation that suffering and pleasure vary inversely. Instead, he believed that "without cruelty there is no festival"; and that in the overflowing of the life force, "even pain acts as a stimulus."[21]

Most famously, Nietzsche argued that self-sacrifice, restraint, piety, and other forms of conventional ethical behavior are actually distorted expressions of the aggressive will to power, turned against the self by weaklings incapable of action in the world. The lacerations and restrictions that ensue are the expressions of a slave morality dedicated to judging and destroying the natural vitality of the strong. According to Nietzsche, it is the hypocritical self-wounding morality of the weak and pious that has made humanity into the sick animal, burdened with bad conscience, motivated solely by resentment against the strong, and therefore incapable of acting with vitality or immediacy.

If virtue is delusion, and an unhealthy delusion at that, what then remains? From early in his career Nietzsche had the answer—one that Rousseau would have recognized:

> The man who does not want to belong to the mass has only to stop being lazy with himself. Let him follow his conscience, which cries out to him: "Be yourself! You are none of those things you now do, think, desire" . . . In this world there is one unique path which no one but you may walk. Where does it lead? Do not ask; take it.[22]

Individualism, understood as the revelation of uniqueness and the overflowing of psychic energy breaking out of the constraints of ordinary morality, was for Nietzsche the pure expression of the life force, a force that must be cultivated for humankind to escape its crippled state.[23]

Thus, Nietzsche arrived at a conclusion that Rousseau would have found compatible: The true human quest must be for the recovery and expansion of the inner self that had been degraded and distorted in a corrupt civilization based on envy and resentment. There is a deep division, however, between Rousseauean and Nietzschean visions of what constitutes genuine being, since for Nietzsche, the authentic noble savage is not the peaceful dreamer envisaged by Rousseau. Rather, like Schopenhauer and Hobbes, Nietzsche saw the quest for power as the ultimate motivation—leading him to a wholly amoral vision of humanity.

Following from his apotheosis of power, Nietzsche claimed in his later work that the superior human (the *übermensch*) is one whose will to power and passions are strong and violent; it is precisely the savage vitality that makes that human being the *übermensch*, a "blond beast" exercising an innate capacity to dominate. For Nietzsche, then, the affirmation of the self became the pure expression of vital energy, while human passions were reduced to desire for power and the fear of subjugation. In finally arguing that the force of the passions is all that really matters, Nietzsche carried the premises of the primacy of preference and emotion that underlie utilitarian thought to their logical and extreme conclusion. It is this aspect of Nietzsche that made him a favorite of the Nazis, who believed that they embodied the *übermensch* and were establishing the rule of force.[24]

IV. RECONSTRUCTING SOCIAL BEING: WEBER, DURKHEIM, AND FREUD

A   Weber's Cultural Comparative Method
   Weber's value-free analysis of alternative worldviews from the actor's point of view (*verstehen*).

B   Meaning, Suffering, and the Irrational
   Weber's psychology: meaning as an escape from suffering. The role of charisma and emotion.

C   Society Is God: Durkheim's Collective Morality
   The sacred collective versus the profane individual. The central importance of action and ritual.

D   Dissecting the Soul: Sigmund Freud and Psychoanalysis
   Background, methods, and critiques of Freudian psychoanalytic practice.

E   Psychoanalysis and the Evolution of Society
   The Oedipal conflict. Freud's model of the mind. Male and female. The discontents of civilization.

F   Freud's Metapsychology
   Eros versus Thanatos. The potential of Freud's theory for cultural analysis.

A. Weber's Cultural Comparative Method

Nietzsche's vigorous deconstruction of what remained of old verities left a tremendous rift in social theory and philosophy. How was it possible to construct a new vision of humanity that did not fall back on discredited religious and Enlightenment values, and yet did not succumb to Nietzsche's corrosive message? Max Weber (1864–1920), the great German sociologist, met this challenge by moving beyond the value system of the West, bringing cultural differences into social theory, and by making the quest for meaning, rather than the will to power or the structure of the economy, the center of his model.

Weber began his career as an economic historian and was intrigued throughout his career by the question of why capitalism should have originated and grown only in the West. His investigations into this topic led him to the study of the economies of non-Western societies, where capitalism had not occurred, and from there to the realization that the economy could be understood only in relation to the wider values of the society at large. Each culture, Weber argued, developed its own particular worldview, and this worldview provided the tracks along which social life flowed. In other words, the Marxist claim for the priority of the economy was incomplete, nor was Nietzsche correct in assuming people were invariably driven by a will to power. Rather, grasping human motives for action required that particular cultural ideas and world images, with their implications for determining ultimate ends and permissible means, always had to be taken into account.

Weber's great contribution was the method of *verstehen*—understanding through an imaginative identification with the position of the other—which has had such great influence in anthropology. Following this interpretive method allowed Weber to explain much of what seemed irrational in history and in other societies. For example, a European nobleman might bankrupt himself through extravagant entertaining, gambling, and ostentatious display. The practice of conspicuous consumption was irrational in a capitalist economy, since it led to impoverishment, but it was nevertheless rational within the moral world of the courtiers, who looked down on anyone putting profit over generosity.[25]

Although notions of rationality could vary infinitely across cultures, particular worldviews had, Weber said, an elective affinity for certain social strata. Warriors, for example, tended to embrace superstitious belief systems emphasizing the arbitrary power of fate; such a faith fit well with the risky and competitive aspects of warrior life. In modern times, professional athletes and actors have a similar affinity for superstitious beliefs, since they too are dependent on fate for success. Weber also argued that the spread of a belief system depended, to a large degree, on the cultural authority of the social strata who were its natural bearers. For instance, the success of Buddhism in Asia was largely due to the cultural dominance of scholars, who were naturally attracted to its mystical and intellectual ethic.

Although Weber believed that for technical reasons, capitalism was bound to triumph over all other economic systems, he nonetheless affirmed the validity of alternative cultural ways of apprehending the world and setting goals for the self. None of these modes of apprehension and the goals they entail, he said, are of intrinsically greater value or of any greater truth than any other—though some are undoubtedly more economically efficient. He even claimed no privilege for his own thought.

B. Meaning, Suffering, and the Irrational

Although Weber affirmed cultural relativism in terms of values, he nonetheless did assume that human nature entails certain crucial psychological elements: a universal fear of suffering, a desire for self-justification and explanation, and a concomitant tendency to evolve ever more complex intellectual systems.

In emphasizing the deep impulse of humans to manufacture meaning systems, Weber opposed Nietzsche's claim that humans are motivated primarily by fear and resentment. Rather, Weber said that human beings are essentially free agents, rationally seeking to maximize benefits and reduce pain for themselves by acting within the moral constraints of a worldview they believe to be valid. At the same time, by their actions men and women continually reconstitute and revitalize the cultural universe they live within. His is, in fact, a revamped utilitarianism, one that recognizes the powerful role of culture and meaning in constituting human life.

While Weber, as a rationalist, believed that the only possible subject of social science had to be the analysis of the consciously held values and ideas that motivate action, as a realist, he also gave credit to the romantic view that a great deal of human experience is not conscious, and that men and women are often driven by powerful desires they cannot even name. In particular, he posited that the equivalent of the Nietzschean superman—whom Weber called the charismatic—is at the center of social change. According to Weber, when a culture has lost its capacity to supply meaning to its members and when traditional leaders no longer have legitimacy, revolutionary figures are likely to appear, figures who are obeyed simply because of their irrational capacity to emanate an aura of supernatural power. Followers are emotionally bound to these leaders and submit to them with passionate fervor. As a result, the leader can become the prophet of a new order that seeks to transform the world. Paradoxically, great historical change originates not in the quest for meaning but in irrational attraction and ecstatic devotion.[26]

C. Society Is God: Durkheim's Collective Morality

While Weber brought the irrational superman back into his individualistic, meaning-centered, and culturally sensitive social science through the back door, the French sociologist Émile Durkheim (1858–1917) had a very different response to the Nietzschean challenge. The inheritor and torchbearer of the French tradition of ameliorative social science and faith in the revolutionary power of the masses, and the descendant of generations of orthodox rabbis, he placed much greater emphasis on collective solidarity and irrationality than did Weber. For him, society is an entity *sui generis* (self-generated). It exists according to its own rules and pursues its own goals, which do not correspond with the desires of the individuals who constitute it. Society is able to follow its goals and enforce its rules because it is endowed with the transcendent power to compel loyalty and awe its members. In fact, Durkheim's famous premise is that humanity does not and cannot live in a Nietzschean universe where God is dead. God does indeed exist and does provide human beings with ultimate meaning. God, however, does not live in the sky, nor does the deity exist apart from humanity. Rather, God is a symbolic representation of society itself, which actually unites human beings in participation in something real that exists above and beyond themselves.

To argue his extraordinary premises, Durkheim first agreed with Weber that individuals are naturally instrumentally oriented, searching for personal aggrandizement and salvation. But the conclusions he drew from this utilitarian understanding of human nature were quite different from Weber's. According to Durkheim, the premises of utilitarianism operate only within the competitive realm of economics, where human beings are like Hobbesian beasts of prey, battling each other in a meaningless struggle of each against all for survival and domination. The winners in this struggle are the violent blond beasts Nietzsche worships.

But the competitive and aggressive actor is decidedly not the end point of Durkheim's analysis. For him, to be a human being is precisely *not* to be an autonomous individual, but requires instead an escape from individuality into the collectivity. From Durkheim's perspective, collective awareness is not only separate and different from that of the individual, but also unquestionably superior to and more powerful than individual consciousness. The collective exists over and above the people who make it up; it is timeless, encompassing, vital, and emotionally compelling, and it provides a higher moral order for its members.

According to Durkheim, involvement in this higher order is inculcated into individuals through their spontaneous participation in transformative group rituals, which Durkheim envisioned as ecstatic performances where individual differences are blurred and the communicants lose themselves in the trancelike states Durkheim called collective effervescence. Such unifying rituals, Durkheim thought, are the emotional fountainhead of religion, and continue to be enacted, albeit in attenuated form, not only in churches, but in the modern-day worship of the nation, as well as in other secular aspects of group life, such as sports and entertainment.

These ritual performances also provide the various symbolic collective representations that penetrate deeply into the consciousness of the individual. For example, the flag (the symbol of our society) has the power to inspire nationalist fervor akin to religious faith. Durkheim even believed that the spatial concepts of a society express the symbolic divisions arising in ritual performance. Thus our thought, our language, our perception of time and space—all those logical prerequisites to being that Kant attributed to the intervention of God—are derived from the common emotional experience of ritual and of collective symbolic representations.

Although Durkheim affirmed, as no other modern writer has, the power of collective consciousness, he did not deny men and women their embodied personal identities. Rather, the tension between group and individual is fundamental to human existence. The body is instrumentally oriented and therefore beastlike, incapable of the self-sacrifice needed to form social bonds; the human part of humankind, in contrast, participates in the collective and is deeply attached to the ideals the collective supports. Durkheim proposes a social psychology of ebb and flow between singularity and community, one in which reason is often merely a rationale for action that is in actuality socially motivated. There is no place for the Nietzschean superman here, but there is plenty of space for tragedy, since human beings are portrayed as deeply torn between irreconcilable opposites: personal desire versus the larger moral demands of society.[27]

Weber versus Durkheim

- *Weber.* Humans are rational maximizers of cultural values. They are motivated by a desire to escape from suffering and make life meaningful. Tragedy is the inability of any prophetic system to solve existential problems.

- *Durkheim.* Humans are irrational. They are formed by ecstatic participation in collective ritual. Tragedy is the inevitable conflict between social demands and individual desires.

The divergent assumptions made by these two great thinkers about individual action can be seen clearly by comparing their writings. Weber's most famous book, *The Protestant Ethic and the Spirit of Capitalism*[28] (which I have used in my own analysis of the rise of capitalism in the last chapter), argues persuasively that the rise of capitalism can best be understood in the light of the values inculcated in the business class by Protestantism. According to Weber, Protestants, following the austere precepts of their creed, were psychologically prepared to save and invest. Because of the Protestant notion of the calling, they also were prepared to focus their entire energies on their jobs. Most importantly, the Calvinistic devaluation of the world and the notion that each person is responsible for his or her own fate favored a calculating and rational approach to work, one that permitted innovation. Protestantism therefore provided a worldview compatible with successful participation in capitalism. The conclusion is that social science can correlate motivating value systems with their worldly consequences.

The book of Durkheim's most comparable to *The Protestant Ethic* is his masterly study *Suicide: A Study in Sociology.*[29] In it, he tried to show that what would seem the most personal and individualistic of all decisions, the decision to end one's own life, is in fact a result of measurable social influences. Comparing suicide rates of urban and rural populations, and of different countries and religious groups, he concluded that suicide was more prevalent where social ties were eroded, boundaries were uncertain, and meanings were under threat. Thus Protestants, disconnected from one another by their belief in individual responsibility, had a much higher suicide rate than Catholics or Jews, who were far more communal in orientation. For Durkheim, then, the major conclusion was that an absence of community is deeply destructive to the individual psyche.

D. Dissecting the Soul: Sigmund Freud and Psychoanalysis

The Viennese doctor and founder of psychoanalysis, Sigmund Freud (1856–1939), is probably the best-known thinker to be discussed in this book. Almost everyone in the United States has some vague notion of Freud's essential concepts: the unconscious, repression, regression, infantile sexuality, projection, and so on. But it is rarely understood that Freud was a social thinker who, like Durkheim and Weber, wished to construct an alternative to Nietzsche's dark portrait of society. Whereas Durkheim and Weber developed theories of the collective and applied them to individual motivation, Freud took the opposite trajectory, using his concept of the psyche to make sense of the larger social world.

It is something of a paradox that Freud, the student of the irrational, was in many respects a direct inheritor of the Enlightenment rationality that Nietzsche so deplored. Trained as an experimental scientist, Freud was heavily influenced by empiricism and the pragmatism of the utilitarians.[30] He took for granted the utilitarian principle that human beings are machines fundamentally motivated to seek pleasure and avoid pain, and he believed implicitly that the psyche was animated by a vague energy (libido) that was distributed through the body and toward various objects in a manner reminiscent of a hydraulic pump. His work, he hoped, was moving toward a reliable measurement of this distribution of energy, and he described himself as a biologist of the mind seeking a mechanistic theory of the human soul.

The scientific (or perhaps scientistic) aspect of Freud's work reflected his early schooling in medicine, which was cut short by the anti-Semitic atmosphere of Vienna. Had he been allowed to follow his own inclinations, Freud would probably be known today as a minor contributor to early German neurology. But because he was unable to pursue his chosen career, Freud was obliged to turn to a new type of study, one in which results were not to be found in test tubes or through the use of microscopes, but through the slow, shared interpretation of material elicited in therapeutic sessions—a method very like the interpretive *verstehen* approach favored by Weber for the analysis of culture.[31] In Freud's case, this method became the famous talking cure of psychoanalysis, in which the patient was expected to free-associate, decode dreams, and otherwise explore unconscious motivations with the sympathetic encouragement of the therapist. It was believed this method could bring the patient to an understanding of the hidden significance of his or her symptoms. When this understanding occurred, there was an emotional upheaval (an abreaction) and the symptoms were relieved.

Freud's ambition as a healer was to alleviate neurosis, but his real ambition was as a theorist, and his claim was that the success of psychoanalytic therapy was proof of the validity of his ideas. This claim has caused no end of controversy, since we lack strong evidence demonstrating that psychoanalytic therapy is actually any more successful than many other types, including the techniques of witch doctors and other local practitioners. Furthermore, as we have seen, although Freud used the physical sciences as his reference model, the practical reality of his method was interpretive, and such an approach can never achieve the strong proofs required by Cartesian principles. As a result of these (and other) problems, Freudian theory has generally been repudiated by academic psychologists.

In this instance it is worth remembering Hume's demonstration that it is quite impossible to prove scientifically that the self or the psyche actually exists; therefore all of academic psychology—not just psychoanalysis—is based on

Sigmund Freud

unprovable assumptions. Freud's inability to meet strict scientific standards for his therapeutic practice should therefore not be assessed too harshly. Rather, his theory of human nature ought to be judged, like any other philosophical hypothesis, on the bases of its coherence, intellectual range, applicability, and capacity to answer previously unanswerable questions.

E. Psychoanalysis and the Evolution of Society

In the tradition of the great thinkers of the past, Freud first developed his theory by looking within himself. What was unique was that Freud focused not on his thoughts but on his unconscious fantasies. After the death of his father, Freud was deeply depressed and troubled by a series of frightening dreams. Interpreting their symbolic content, he gradually realized the hidden depths of his hostility toward his father, which he had unconsciously sought to expiate by punishing himself; he realized as well his equally powerful, and equally repressed, desire for his mother. This was the famous Oedipal complex: the triangle of love and jealous rivalry within the family itself. Freud believed this complex arose as the male child tries to possess the mother and destroy the father[32] but is overcome with guilt and fear because of these illicit desires. It was precisely this conflict that Freud believed to be at the nexus of the repression and resistance that he found in himself, and then discovered among his patients.

Oedipus in Anthropology

Freudian psychology claims the Oedipal conflict is universal, but some anthropologists have disagreed. The most famous was Bronislaw Malinowski (1844–1942), who had done extensive fieldwork in the Trobriand Islands of Melanesia, where the matrilineal, avunculocal nature of society meant that a son inherits from his mother's brother and leaves home to join his lineage. In this instance, Malinowski said, the father was not a stern patriarch, but rather, loving and nonjudgmental, while the mother's brother was the authority figure. Therefore, Malinowski argued, the mother's brother, not the father, is the focus of the male child's anxieties, and sexual fantasies are directed not at the mother but at the boy's sisters.

Later analysts have argued that the Trobrianders did indeed have an Oedipus complex, as revealed in their extraordinary belief that sex has nothing to do with pregnancy. This belief was taken as evidence of Oedipal repression of the fact of the parents' sexuality and of strong hostility toward the father. Myths and folklore also indicated hostility to the father and incestuous desires toward the mother. And, in fact, the relationship between a Trobriand son and his mother was traditionally very close, as a result of a long nursing period when mother and son slept together and the father was forbidden sexual access to his wife.[33]

However, Malinowski's point was not that the Oedipal complex did not exist, only that the different family structures would lead to different configurations of desire and resentment that complicate the archetypical Freudian model. This point has been made by a number of other anthropologists and fieldworkers. For example, in southern Italy, the mother is the dominant person in the family; men idealize wives and mothers as virgins, other women are whores, and the father-daughter relation is sexually tinged.[34] Among the matrilineal Navaho, the maternal grandmother is the authority and the brother-sister relationship is eroticized.[35]

According to Freud, the existence of the Oedipal conflict explained the puzzling clinical phenomenon of transference, wherein the patient experienced strong yet deeply ambivalent feelings toward the therapist, despite the therapist's principled aloofness. Freud interpreted this seemingly inexplicable occurrence as a reexperiencing of the original Oedipal bond, liberated within the safety of the therapeutic relationship. Only by working through the emotional onslaught of forbidden desire could the patient achieve the emotional catharsis necessary for a cure.

Like Rousseau, Freud made the experiences of childhood central in the development of his theory, but, scandalously, Freud did not portray the child as an innocent victim corrupted by the world.[36] On the contrary, for Freud, children were propelled by powerful erotic and aggressive instinctual libidinal impulses seeking release. These drives evolved developmentally and were connected to organ modes. Infants were primarily oral; then as muscular control evolved, the center of pleasure shifted to the anus, and then to the genitals during the Oedipal phase. Libido would be repressed during the latency phase, only to reawaken in adolescence.

In Freud's early theory, he divided the mind into three porous regions: unconscious, preconscious, and conscious. Later, he revised this division into what he called the topographic model of the mind. In this model the instinctual drives emanated from the first part of the mind, the id—the "it"—which Freud pictured as the cauldron of the unconscious, where the rules of logic do not apply, only the pressures of sheer impulse. The id is unfathomable, beneath awareness, and its content can only be grasped fleetingly through analysis of the surreal world of dreams, in slips of the tongue, in the illogic of comedy, in the symptoms of madness, or in the raging appetites of the infant.[37]

For Freud, then, a child is nothing more than a vortex of unmitigated desire, which must eventually be controlled and channeled if the individual is ever to survive a hostile world and become a member of society. It is the second part of the mind, the ego—the "I"—that has this function. The ego develops out of the id as a result of inevitable confrontations between desire and reality. It is the rational aspect of the self. But the ego is not the strong autonomous agent imagined by utilitarian thinkers. Rather, in Humean fashion, it is anxious and weak, without energy of its own, constantly serving the irrational needs of the id. In Freud's memorable imagery, the ego is akin to a rider on a wild horse, trying desperately to hold on and steer the animal in a less dangerous direction.[38]

But the ego has some important weapons in its arsenal. For one thing, it can present itself to the id as an object of desire, and thus gain a degree of energy and power.[39] This occurs in part through identification, in which the ego fantasizes that it has incorporated and transformed itself into some aspect of the object the id desires. This process is especially important during the Oedipal moment—around the age of three—when the child, unable to merge with the mother in actuality and frightened of the father's vengeance, assimilates the values and ideals of the parents. The subconscious logic is: If I cannot have what I love, I will become what I love.

Here the psychological trajectories of boys and girls, who originally have exactly the same capacities, begin to differ, since girls can actually become imitations of the mother while the boy must somehow separate himself, seeking love and denying aggression by identifying with his rival, the father, in the hope of eventually sexually possessing a woman as his father possessed his mother. Freud believed that women, because of their general capacity to achieve their deepest desires, were more emotionally grounded (more in touch with their primary narcissism) than men, who must continually struggle to reconcile themselves to their inevitable alienation. In this sense, women are closer to nature, while men are the bearers of culture, which Freud portrayed as an effort both to expiate and enact the guilt and aggression of the Oedipal triangle through the rituals and symbols of religion and politics.[40]

The agent of this cultural struggle is a new actor on the psychic stage: the third part of the mind, the superego, which, in a manner reminiscent of Durkheim's notion of the collective, imposes social values on the asocial individual. Like the conscience we refer to in ordinary language, the superego punishes bad deeds and even bad thoughts by inflicting pangs of guilt. Freud argued that the punitive superego is a product of the process of identification that resolves the Oedipal triangle, as the child (especially the male child) takes into itself as its own the morals and values of the parents (particularly those of the father) and punishes itself for any faults or errors.

Totem and Taboo

The formation of the superego and the origin of culture is the topic of Freud's most anthropological work, *Totem and Taboo: Resemblances between the Psychic Lives of Savages and Neurotics*.[41] Here Freud argued that civilization is a symbolic expression of a primitive Oedipal conflict between the all-powerful patriarch and his sons. In this scenario the band of brothers actually kill the father and incorporate his power into themselves by cannibalism; overcome with guilt, they then seek to expiate their crime by punishing themselves as the father had previously done and by imagining new father figures (gods and kings) to whom they could submit themselves—while simultaneously directing aggression toward them. Freud argued that Catholic mass is a symbolic transformation of this ancient sin: The perfect son saves his brothers by being sacrificed as expiation for the original murder of the father; the community participates in this act by eating the flesh and drinking the blood of the son.

At some points, Freud seems to believe this primal event actually occurred and is the crucial turning point in human prehistory; elsewhere, he describes this account as a myth. Certainly, the Freudian notion of the intrinsic tensions of family life and the conflict of human drives would mean that children everywhere would have fantasies of this type.

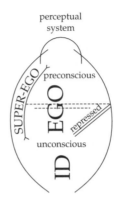

FIGURE 3.2. Sketch of the mind by Sigmund Freud, portraying the relation of the id, ego, and superego. Note how the superego merges into the id, and how the id's relationship to the outside world is mediated by the ego. In his commentary, Freud cautioned that the space occupied by the id should be much larger than shown in this diagram, and that in fact the different sections of the mind melt into one another, and are not rigidly divided.
Source: Sigmund Freud, 1965, New Introductory Lectures on Psychoanalysis, New York: Norton, p. 98.

Freud believed that without the internalized coercion of the superego, civilization could not exist. Two basic reasons underlie this belief. The obvious one is that guilt eliminates the necessity of an external force maintaining order; guilty people keep themselves in line. The less obvious reason is taken from Nietzsche: Self-laceration satisfies the human lust for violence; by masochistically injuring ourselves, we are less likely to injure others. In this sense, the superego is a reflection of the id—irrational and cruel. (See Figure 3.2.)

Unfortunately, the superego can be too violent; its unreasonable demands can lead to paralyzing anguish and depression. Freud thought that the ability of a human being to bear such suffering was limited. To escape from self-imposed guilt, and to maintain good relations within the community, people would often seek a scapegoat upon whom their unbearable rage could be vented. As Freud wrote: "It is always possible to band together a considerable number of people in love, so long as there are other people left over to receive the manifestations of their aggressiveness."[42] This was the case, Freud believed, in modern civilization, where the intensity of denial and repression led to a depth of personal neurosis and to occasional explosions of unparalleled public violence, such as World War I, which Freud witnessed, and to the rise of the Nazi movement, which eventually forced him to leave Austria for England, where he died in exile.[43]

F. Freud's Metapsychology

Faced with human irrationality, Freud, like Nietzsche, exhorted humankind not to rely on imaginary gods and powers, which both men saw as childish efforts to escape the pain of our true existential condition. Psychoanalysis, Freud said, could reveal the depth of human ambivalence, the symbolic nature of religion and culture, and the degree to which we are capable of self-delusion. Although Freud and Nietzsche are very close in these and other respects, Freud's pragmatic understanding of his mission as a philosopher and healer put him strongly in opposition to the excesses of Nietzschean romanticism: Civilization might indeed be repressive, but savagery was even more destructive, and blond beasts ought to be jailed, not worshiped. Freud hoped that psychoanalysis, instead of unleashing raw vitality, would do just the opposite. Common unhappiness, not the Nietzschean outburst of violent energy, was his ideal.

Freud also believed that the Nietzschean theory of the will to power and the resentment of the weak was far too simplistic. Rather, like Durkheim and Hegel, Freud saw human nature constructed through a dynamic and continually evolving dialectical struggle between opposing forces, though he did not follow Durkheim's opposition between the social and the individual, nor did he accept Hegel's belief in a transcendent conclusion for the dialectical process. Freud's portrait of the nature of the dialectic changed over time; he began with an antagonism between sexuality and self-preservation, and progressed to a final theory of an eternal and universal war between Eros (love) and Thanatos (death), expressed variously in the dialect of attraction and repulsion, tension and equilibrium, unity and distinctiveness, community and isolation, sexuality and aggression.[44] According to Freud, all human experience develops in response to these deep and intrinsically contradictory impulses that must find expression in any social milieu. Religion and culture symbolically express this fundamental battle, serving, like neurotic symptoms, as a means both to reveal and yet simultaneously to deny the violence and lust that are desired yet forbidden.

According to Freud, all humanity suffers from the same existential problems; however, the manner and form in which resolution is attempted will vary in each individual case, and from culture to culture, because of differences in personal character, family dynamics, and the limits and directions imposed by the social structure and environment. Freud did not, as many assume, reduce everything to sex: Not all cigars are phallic symbols (Freud himself was an avid cigar smoker). But he did argue that, in principle, individual and cultural differences could be understood within the larger framework of the psychoanalytic model, which provided a set of propositions about human nature and therefore a basis for exploring the seemingly infinite variety of human experience.

Summary

This chapter begins by tracing the romantic reaction to the Enlightenment faith in reason. Jean Jacques Rousseau, alienated from the world around him, longed for authentic emotion and a return to the halcyon world of the primitive and the child. The appeal of the romantic message increased in response to the upheavals and dehumanization of the Industrial Revolution, but even more influential was the rise of utilitarianism. This practical philosophy reflected the marketplace mentality of the era and envisaged human beings as autonomous and freely negotiating self-maximizers, eternally pursuing pleasure and avoiding pain.

Alternatives to the severe reduction of human nature by utilitarianism were soon proposed by German philosophers. G. W. F. Hegel's dialectical model was based on an organic image of growth and transformation. History, he said, is an upwardly spiraling process of thesis, antithesis, and synthesis; individuals exist only within this process, both reflecting and enacting the contradictions of the moment. Arnold Schopenhauer countered with a stark picture of humanity inexorably driven by an impersonal Will, always seeking to expand and reproduce, while Karl Marx offered a materialist reworking of Hegel's dialectics, ending history with the inevitable triumph of the proletariat. Friedrich Nietzsche echoed Schopenhauer's pessimism and produced a nihilistic psychology of human beings impelled solely by resentment and the ambition for power. His hero was the blond beast whose only virtue was overwhelming vitality.

Twentieth-century thinkers, living in an environment that was ever more secular and capitalistic, had to cope with Nietzsche's corrosive vision of a demythologized world. Max Weber did so by expanding utilitarianism across cultures, showing that many goals and values are possible, and by providing a rudimentary psychology in which human beings are seekers for a meaningful explanation of existential suffering. Émile Durkheim, in contrast, found God in the human emotional attachment to the collective, which provides a moral basis for existence because it transcends the individuals who make it up. Finally, Sigmund Freud argued that culture and religion are actually symbolic expressions of the psychic conflicts of individuals. Counseling the end of all illusion, he offered humanity a new therapeutic model of the soul.

This chapter continues to trace the Western debate on the nature of the self. The thoughts of the authors discussed here and in the previous chapter provide the foundation upon which modern thinkers will build, as they too seek to answer the question Who am I? It is to these later efforts that we now turn.

Endnotes

1. Rousseau, quoted in James Miller, 1984, *Rousseau: Dreamer of Democracy,* New Haven, CT: Yale University Press, p. 5.
2. Jean Jacques Rousseau, 1979, *Reveries of the Solitary Walker,* London: Penguin, pp. 27, 32 (original publication 1782).
3. However, it should not be thought that Rousseau was in favor of the later romantics' worship of ecstacy. He mistrusted strong emotion and desired above all a dreamy state of almost depersonalized trance.
4. Jean Jacques Rousseau, 1953, *The Confessions of Jean Jacques Rousseau,* Harmondsworth, England: Penguin (original publication 1781).
5. Rousseau, *Reveries of the Solitary Walker,* p. 126.
6. Jean Jacques Rousseau, 1967, *The Social Contract and Discourse on the Origins of Inequality,* New York: Washington Square Press, p. 7 (original publication 1762 and 1755).
7. This insight will be discussed at greater length in Chapters 6 and 11.
8. Rousseau's ideas about children are in fact far more complex than this and deeply ambiguous as well. It is worth noting that by his own admission, he placed his own children in a foundling home—an act that he attempted to justify all his life.
9. The political aspects of Rousseau's work are highly contradictory: In some instances, he favors a republic; in others, an absolute tyranny. For a discussion of Rousseau's political thought, see Judith Shklar, 1969, *Men and Citizens: A Study of Rousseau's Social Theory,* Cambridge, MA: Harvard University Press.
10. For the standard version of this argument, see Max Weber, 1930, *The Protestant Ethic and the Spirit of Capitalism,* New York: Scribner (original publication 1920).

11. William Milton Blake, "London," in Michael Mason (ed.), *William Blake: Poems, Selections*, Oxford, England: Oxford University Press, p. 124 (original publication 1793).
12. William Wordsworth, 1888, "The World Is Too Much with Us," in *The Complete Poetical Works of William Wordsworth*, New York: Crowell, p. 398 (original publication 1807).
13. For a recent incarnation of utilitarian social theory pushed to its limits, see Anthony Giddens, 1992, *The Transformation of Intimacy*, Stanford, CA: Stanford University Press.
14. Some of these irrational aspects of human behavior will be discussed in Chapters 11 and 12.
15. More insightful utilitarian thinkers soon realized the limits of their theories: As the moral theorist Henry Sidgwick lamented: "Where he had looked for Cosmos, he had in fact found only Chaos." Quoted in Alasdair MacIntyre, 1981, *After Virtue: A Study in Moral Theory*, London: Duckworth, p. 63.
16. The following passage gives the flavor of his often baffling prose: "We have to think pure flux, opposition within opposition itself, or Contradiction . . . Appearance is the process of arising into being and passing away again, a process that itself does not arise and does not pass away, but is *per se*, and constitutes reality and the life-movement of truth. The truth is thus the bacchanalian revel, where not a member is sober." Yet at the same time "the revel is just as much a state of transparent unbroken calm." G. W. F. Hegel, 1967, *The Phenomenology of Mind*, New York: Harper and Row, pp. 206, 105 (original publication 1808).
17. Ibid., p. 422.
18. Friedrich Nietzsche, 1969, *On the Genealogy of Morals and Ecce Homo*, New York: Vintage, p. 158 (original publication *On the Genealogy of Morals* 1887).
19. Friedrich Nietzsche, 1996, *Human, All Too Human: A Book for Free Spirits*, Lincoln: University of Nebraska Press, p. 29 (original publication 1878–79).
20. The only philosopher with a psychological astuteness comparable to Nietzsche's was Søren Kierkegaard (1813–1855), whose work I cannot discuss here, but who deserves more attention from anthropologists.
21. Friedrich Nietzsche, *On the Genealogy of Morals and Ecce Homo*, p. 67; 1977, *The Twilight of the Idols and the Anti-Christ*, Harmondsworth, England: Penguin, p. 110 (original publication *The Twilight of the Idols* 1889).
22. Friedrich Nietzsche, 1990 "Schopenhauer as Educator (original publication 1876) In Friedrich Nietzsche (ed.) *Unmodern Observations* New Haven CT: Yale University Press, pp. 163, 165.
23. For a good discussion of Nietzsche's complex notion of individuality, see Werner Hamacher, 1986, " 'Disgregation of the Will': Nietzsche on the Individual and Individuality," in Thomas C. Heller, Morton Sosna, and David E. Willbery (eds.), *Reconstructing Individualism: Autonomy, Individuality, and the Self in Western Thought*, Stanford, CA: Stanford University Press.
24. Nietzsche would not have approved. His superman was a lonely figure, much like himself, not a dictator. He also despised racism and hypocrisy, and had a very low opinion of Germans and of the German state. The Nazis would have seemed to him not supermen but mediocrities motivated by resentment.
25. For this analysis, see Norbert Elias, 1978, *The Civilizing Process: The Development of Manners*, New York: Urizen (original publication 1939).
26. See the essays on charisma and prophecy in Max Weber, 1978, *Economy and Society*, Berkeley: University of California Press. This aspect of Weber's theory will be discussed in more detail in Chapter 11.
27. For the most complete expression of Durkheim's thought, see his magnum opus, 1965, *The Elementary Forms of Religious Life*, New York: Free Press (original publication 1912).

28. Weber, *The Protestant Ethic.*
29. 1966, *Suicide: A Study in Sociology,* New York: Free Press (original publication 1897).
30. Freud actually translated some of the works of J. S. Mill into German.
31. At first, Freud tried to make his name in the study of drugs, working especially on cocaine, which he prescribed as a cure for morphine use. The catastrophic failure of this prescription led Freud toward his new interest in mental illness.
32. The converse occurs in the case of girls, though Freud was more concerned with what he thought was female envy of male power, as embodied in the phallus.
33. For this controversy, see Melford Spiro, 1982, *Oedipus in the Trobriands,* Chicago: University of Chicago Press; Stanley Kurtz, 1991, "Polysexualization: A New Approach to Oedipus in the Trobriands," *Ethos* 19: 68–101. In response, see Melford Spiro, 1992, "Oedipus Redux," *Ethos* 20: 358–76; John Ingham, 1996, "Oedipality in Pragmatic Discourse: The Trobriands and Hindu India," *Ethos* 24: 559–87. For more on Malinowski, see Chapter 4. For more on the Oedipal complex, see Chapter 6.
34. Anne Parsons, 1964, "Is the Oedipus Complex Universal? The Jones-Malinowski Debate Revisited and a South Italian 'Nuclear Complex,' " in W. Muensterberger and S. Axelrad (eds.), *The Psychoanalytic Study of Society,* Vol. III, New York: International Universities Press.
35. Stephen Proskauer, 1980, "Oedipal Equivalents in a Clan Culture: Reflections on Navaho Ways," *Psychiatry* 43: 43–50.
36. In his earliest work, Freud did focus on external corruption, arguing that neurosis was a consequence of sexual molestation. Later, after his self-analysis, Freud repudiated the notion of childhood trauma, preferring to focus on the internal desires of the patient. This controversial aspect of Freudian theory will be discussed more completely in Chapter 11.
37. Freud illustrated his claims in a series of books, including 1960, *Jokes and Their Relation to the Unconscious,* New York: Norton (original publication 1905).
38. Here Freud comes very close to Durkheim, who also stressed the power of unconscious motives, but with a very different moral tone and different theoretical premises. While Durkheim saw the unconscious as the moral pressure of the suprahuman collective, Freud saw it as the amoral upswelling of the biological and the prehuman.
39. This is called cathexis in the Greco-technical terminology favored by English-speaking Freudians. Freud himself did not use such neologisms. As Bruno Bettelheim (1983, *Freud and Man's Soul,* New York: Knopf) notes, Freud's German was simple and direct. Cathexis, for example, is simply *beseitzen,* or "sitting in."
40. Other differences Freud posited between men and women include male fear of castration and female penis envy. Bruno Bettelheim, in a witty reversal, has argued that it would be equally reasonable to credit men with womb envy. See Bruno Bettelheim, 1954, *Symbolic Wounds: Puberty Rites and the Envious Male,* Glencoe, IL: Free Press.
41. 1950, *Totem and Taboo,* New York: Norton (original publication 1918).
42. Sigmund Freud, 1961, *Civilization and its Discontents,* New York: Norton, p. 61 (original publication 1930). See also Freud 1959 *Group Psychology and the Analysis of the Ego,* New York: Norton (original publication 1921).
43. Freud's theory of political leadership is elaborated more fully in Chapter 11.
44. This metaphysical construct is argued most fully in Freud, 1960, *The Ego and the Id,* New York: Norton (original publication 1923).

PART THREE

The Anthropology of Personal Being

CHAPTER 4

How "Other" Is the Other?

Children in the United States are usually taught to count even before they enter preschool. In fact, the ability to count is thought to be such a fundamental cognitive skill that people who cannot count properly are likely to be considered mentally retarded. Yet when the American anthropologist Allan Holmberg went to study the seminomadic Siriono of Central America in the 1940s, he discovered that adults there could not number above 3. Any day past tomorrow was simply called "the brother of tomorrow."[1]

Holmberg's findings are not uncommon; in many simpler societies the local people have little capacity for abstract numerical reasoning. Does this mean that they have less intellectual ability than we do? Are they somehow mentally retarded? Similarly, what are we to make of the striking fact that individuals in simpler societies very often have much more rudimentary discriminations of color than we do? The Dani of New Guinea, for example, say there are only two colors: black and white.[2] Does this mean their perceptions are vastly different from, and vastly inferior to, the perceptions of people in modern society?

These are the sorts of questions that investigators have been trying to answer from the close of the eighteenth century, as expanding European colonial powers encountered other cultures very different in character and complexity from their own. The debate about human nature, which was traced in the past two chapters, now could take cross-cultural material as evidence. In particular, "primitives" could be investigated to answer questions about the range and limits of humankind. Did these others, often looking very different from us physically, often naked or nearly so, practicing strange customs, and participating in picturesque rituals, think as we do, feel as we do? Were they noble relics of an Edenic past, as the romantics thought? Or were they feral subhuman brutes, incapable of reason? What could they tell us about our history and about ourselves?

As the eighteenth century ended, these questions could be addressed with some hope of an answer. The influx of missionaries, traders, and colonial administrators into "native" societies meant that there was now a new knowledge base available for inquiry into the nature of "primitive mentality." As early as

Dani man.

1799 a research institution (Société des Observateurs de l'Homme) was founded in Paris to undertake such studies.[3] Other similar organizations were soon founded elsewhere in Europe, forming the basis for the modern science of anthropology. This early research had two goals that have remained central to the discipline ever since: to discover in what respects "we" differ from "them," and to determine whether, beneath appearances, all of "us" are somehow fundamentally alike. In other words, the question is, How much are we, as individuals, constructed by the culture we live in, and how much are we products of an underlying basic human nature? This chapter outlines some of the findings from those investigations.

Chapter Outline

I Testing Perception across Cultures
   A The Neo-Darwinian Paradigm
   B The First Expeditions
   C W. H. R. Rivers and the Study of Perception
   D Are Colors Seen as the Same Everywhere?

II Classifications, Complexity, and Intelligence
   A Classification Systems and Social Complexity
   B The Prelogical Savage
   C Primitive Rationality

III Culture, Reason, and Socialization
   A Bronislaw Malinowski and Practical Reason
   B Intelligence Tests and Socialization Practices
   C The Limits of Abstract Reason

IV Authentic Culture
   A Romantic Aestheticism
   B Franz Boas: Romantic Empiricist
   C The Internal Tensions of Boasian Anthropology

V The Foundations of Culture and Personality
   A Edward Sapir: Culture Equals Personality
   B Ruth Benedict and Margaret Mead: Culture Constructs
     Personality
   C Explaining Deviance
   D Problems and Critiques
   E Gregory Bateson and Schizmogenesis

I. TESTING PERCEPTION ACROSS CULTURES

A The Neo-Darwinian Paradigm
   Evolutionism and the theory of innate differences between primitive
   and modern humans.

B The First Expeditions
   Efforts to test evolutionist theory.

C W. H. R. Rivers and the Study of Perception
   The work of W. H. R. Rivers and his claim that differences are cultural,
   not racial.

D Are Colors Seen as the Same Everywhere?
   Color perception as a test of the evolutionary hypothesis.

A. The Neo-Darwinian Paradigm

At first, research on the mentalities and perceptions of preliterate people was conducted by armchair anthropologists who garnered their data from journals, letters, and travel books. Their theories were usually couched within the larger intellectual framework of social evolutionism: a way of understanding the world that had central importance in European intellectual life of the nineteenth century. This was a line of reasoning inspired by Charles Darwin (1809–1882), whose scientific theory of the evolution of species had been extended by Herbert Spencer (1820–1903) and others to include the study of human adaption.

The American lawyer and anthropologist Lewis Henry Morgan (1818–1881) utilized a social Darwinist perspective to argue that human evolution followed a linear trajectory: In the beginning were mobile and egalitarian "savage" tribal people who were organized on the basis of kinship, had simple technologies and lived by hunting and gathering; they developed into settled "barbarians" who had more complex tools and social organizations, lived in villages, and farmed; the culmination was the rise of "civilization," characterized by urbanized, centralized states and a complicated and hierarchical division of labor.[4] Simpler cultures were therefore at an earlier stage of development than our own, and it was assumed that cognitive differences between "them" and "us" would reflect evolutionary distinctions between simple and complex.

In a real sense, social Darwinism was an expression of the West's need to validate its newfound political authority in its nascent colonial empires. The underlying sentiment could be characterized as follows: We rule because we are the most fit; our power is justified by natural law. But social Darwinism was only the late-nineteenth-century guise of a much more deeply rooted ideology of Western supremacy. This ideology corresponded with the secular Enlightenment and Renaissance faith in the progress of humankind, which in turn was a

---

Morgan and Marx

Morgan's portrait of the evolution of society from savagery to barbarism to civilization attracted many admirers, not least of whom was Karl Marx, who took copious notes on Morgan's work. Morgan's theories also served as the basis for *The Origin of the Family, Private Property, and the State*, written by Marx's collaborator, Friedrich Engels.[5] Morgan's writing was appealing to these theorists because he argued that early society had been more communal and that changes in property rights were intimately connected to changes in family structure, political organization, and kinship. It is ironic that Morgan, a thoroughly successful capitalist who made a fortune as a lawyer representing railroads and iron-mining interests, became, through his anthropological research, a patron saint of communism.

version of an even older religious revelation. That revelation, in which the Christian nations of the West lead the rest of the world out from ignorance and animality and toward reason and salvation, was based on the earlier Greek faith that those of other nations were nothing but barbarians—subhuman speakers of gibberish. In this prophetic and racist image of history, the technological backwardness of other cultures was taken as prima facie evidence of their degraded, inhuman, and sinful state. It was the sacred duty of the Christian West to raise them from barbarity and spread the sacred word. The assumption was that the West was at the pinnacle of a historical-spiritual process—and therefore Western rule was justified by God.

B. The First Expeditions

Most early investigators of primitive cultures operated under these taken-for-granted premises. The men and women of the modern West, it was believed, must be superior in fundamental ways to members of simpler societies. But how exactly? That was the larger question to be researched. Inquiries into this matter, like the evolutionary theory that gave rise to them, were clothed in the trappings of empirical science: Psychological and physical differences between ourselves and others would be found through rational procedures of experimental testing according to the empirical Cartesian model of discovery. However, to do this, it was necessary not to rely on secondhand reports of unproven accuracy, but to investigate the natives in person. Thus began the first expeditions in which teams of scientists ventured far afield to measure (among other things) the cranial capacity of primitives. Many plaster casts of skulls gather dust today in the back rooms of museums around the world in mute testimony to this wide-ranging enterprise, which (though now discredited and forgotten) was at the origin of modern anthropology.

Much of this research, naturally enough, focused on topics easily bounded and apparently susceptible to quantification, as well as topics that would bear out (or disprove) preconceived images of the savage. For example, it was assumed that people in hunting and gathering societies would be likely to be stronger and have better eyesight than we do, as well as more acute hearing and sense of smell. This assumption rested on the idea that primitive people, because they are uncivilized, are at an evolutionary level close to animals, and therefore would have sharper natural faculties. A less pejorative version was that hunters and gatherers have been required to maintain keen hearing, eyesight, and smell to survive in the wilderness, while civilized senses have atrophied from lack of use. Such hypothesized differences in perceptual abilities could, it was thought, be easily discovered by rudimentary scientific comparisons measuring civilized and primitive reactions to the same stimuli. The earliest such study was undertaken at the end of the eighteenth century during a French expedition to Timor. Tests of strength were administered to the natives and to Europeans, the hypothesis being that the natives would be stronger. The result (though inconclusive) pointed in the reverse direction.[6]

C. W. H. R. Rivers and the Study of Perception

The most famous and influential study of the perceptions of non-Westerners had even more startling results. It was undertaken in the Melanesian islands of the Torres Straits in 1898 by W. H. R. Rivers (1864–1922) and his colleagues. Rivers was a British physician and Freudian psychologist who later became famous for his sensitive treatment of shell-shocked soldiers in World War I.[7] But his early ethnological work was of equal intellectual quality. In it, he undertook a number of experiments comparing Melanesian and English subjects in terms of reaction times, muscularity, hearing, and senses of smell and taste. The results showed that the differences that existed were due to learning, not biology, thereby overturning the presumed connection between race and culture.

In his most well-known experiment, Rivers painstakingly elicited the responses of Melanesian people to certain optical illusions, and then compared the results with the responses of Western subjects. It had been thought that the Melanesians, with more visual acuity than civilized men and women, would not be fooled by such illusions. Of course, the opposite finding would indicate that Melanesians, being less intelligent than Westerners, were more likely to be deluded. Either way, the notion of primitive mentality would be validated.

But Rivers's exemplary work—and the voluminous comparative research that followed it—soon demonstrated the complexities and ambiguities of such inquiries. Rivers did indeed discover that the Melanesians were less likely to be fooled by one type of illusion (the Müller-Lyer illusion), but slightly more likely to be fooled by another (the vertical-horizontal illusion). (See Figure 4.1.) These findings have since been validated cross-culturally by other researchers.[8] One explanation offered for the results is that Westerners are more easily fooled by the Müller-Lyer illusion because it looks like the carpentered right-angled corners of the buildings we live in. Since we are accustomed to seeing carpentered

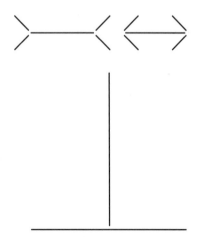

FIGURE 4.1. Müller-Lyer illusion (top) and vertical-horizontal illusion (bottom). Line segments are of equal length in each illusion.

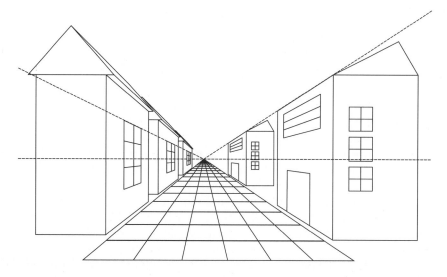

FIGURE 4.2. Drawing depicting perspectival distance.

corners, we are more prone to perceive the illusion as three-dimensional, and to be deceived by it, while Melanesians (and others living in houses with no right-angled corners) are less likely to be deceived.

Or the simple fact may be that we have been taught, through years of looking at drawings and paintings, and through training in school, to assume that the Müller-Lyer angles indicate perspectival distance. (See Figure 4.2.) It is worth remembering that this seemingly natural perception was not always the case. Perspective was known to the ancient Greeks, but forgotten for centuries, as medieval artists drew pictures in which space was distorted and condensed and the size of figures was determined by their importance, not their position in the composition. Not until the early fourteenth century was perspectival rendering rediscovered by the great Florentine painter Giotto di Bondone (1267–1337); now it seems wholly natural to us, and we are fooled by the Müller-Lyer illusion. The Melanesians, with no such painterly tradition, are not. But why Westerners are less deceived by the vertical-horizontal illusion is not so evident; perhaps it has something to do with our lack of interest in horizon lines, while such lines are of crucial importance to Melanesian ocean navigators. In any case, it is clear from this and many other related experiments undertaken by comparative perceptual psychologists over the years that preliterate people do not have better eyesight than Westerners—though they certainly pay attention to different things, as a result of variations in environment and culture.

D. Are Colors Seen as the Same Everywhere?

A similar finding was made after extensive cross-cultural research on color perception. Ever since Rivers's experiments, anthropologists have known that color vocabularies of less complex societies often combine terms Europeans keep separate. The society where I did my fieldwork has just one word for blue and green, for example. For them, the color of the sky is "shin" and so is the color of the grass. But does this mean that these people actually cannot *see* the differences, or does it simply mean that they do not have *words* to describe the differences, and are putting blue and green in the same "non-red" or "cool" category?

To answer this question, contemporary anthropologists have invented tests in which local people have been asked to sort a variety of standardized color chips. These experiments have conclusively demonstrated that even though a language may have no terms for specific colors, people can nonetheless sort the chips into groups that cluster around focal points (the best example of a color) closely resembling Western focal points, though the boundaries of the category may differ. In other words, people everywhere select approximately the same color as the "best example" of blue, even if they have no word for blue in their language, and even though they disagree as to where blue merges into green.

It appears, then, that other's perceptions of color are more or less the same as our own, though their terminologies and category boundaries may vary. The same can be said even within our own society, where the color vocabularies of women tend to be larger than those of men—probably because women, who are generally the culturally appointed arbiters of the aesthetics of the everyday, are more concerned with distinguishing hues and shades. Of course, men who are involved in fashion and design or other work that is concerned with colors are also likely to have a color vocabulary that is far more developed than average.

Cross-cultural tests of perception that were concerned with optical illusions and color were among the few that had relatively clear-cut results. As the cross-cultural psychologist Michael Cole concludes, after many years of measuring and comparing the perceptions of others, it has become evident that there are no tests that are culture-free—"only tests for which we have no good theory of how cultural variations affect performance."[9] The lone scientifically validated conclusion, reached after great efforts, is that the perceptual and physical capacities of people in simpler cultures do not differ in fundamental ways from our own. The assumption now is that any differences that do appear either are the result of an error in testing procedures or must be due to social influences, not to innate ability. All of humankind, it is now thought, have essentially the same potential to see, hear, touch, and smell—but not the same ways of talking about, focusing on, or coding the external world.

II. CLASSIFICATIONS, COMPLEXITY, AND INTELLIGENCE

    A Classification Systems and Social Complexity
           Do simple classification systems indicate low intelligence?

    B The Prelogical Savage
           Lucien Levy-Bruhl's notions of mythical thought, fusion in the collective, and primitive mentality.

    C Primitive Rationality
           E. B. Tylor and J. G. Frazer's theories of the reasonable savage, misled by mistaken premises.

A. Classification Systems and Social Complexity

Though the experiments on perception have debunked notions that people in simpler societies have physical capacities different from our own, they have raised more vexing questions about their mental abilities. For example, the research on comparative color perception demonstrated that color lexicons have an invariable pattern of expansion. A few societies divide the world into two categories, light and dark; the next step adds red. The fundamental triad of color terminology seems to be black-white-red; all other colors are predictably subsumed into these categories. The next terms added are always yellow and green; then blue is differentiated out, and, finally, brown. In other words, one never finds a society that sorts out color terminologies in a pattern of black-white-green; nor does one ever find the category blue appearing if red, yellow, and green have not already been marked out.[10] (See Figure 4.3.) It seems probable that this pattern must reflect some physical properties of human perception.

But there is an even more difficult question posed by the evolution of color terms, since the simplest lexicons are almost always associated with very simple social organizations, while the most complex are associated with complex societies. Does this mean that people in societies with primitive color lexicons and equally simple social organizations are incapable of complex thought, or, as the English philosopher John Locke (1632–1704) put it, that "general propositions are seldom mentioned in the huts of Indians"?[11] This is the answer that evolutionary theory might prefer: The natives—being childlike—just cannot conceptualize complicated differences. Or does it mean that complex lexicons for color reflect a general cultural complexity, and have nothing to do with the innate intellectual capacities of individuals? That is a more plausible answer, especially when we have already seen that people living in cultures with simple color categories can nonetheless sort colors in complex ways if given the incentive and means to do so. Yet it is also true that these societies do not offer the linguistic or conceptual tools required to perform this task. Does this mean that people in such a culture are handicapped in their capacity to reason abstractly?

This conclusion would seem to follow when we note that the classification systems of simple societies are less wide-ranging, inclusive, and complicated in general than the classification systems of complex societies. For example, although primitive peoples are sure to have complex category sets for any number of related objects that exist in their environment, they are not as likely to have an overarching category that encompasses them all—no "class of classes." For example, every society will have sets of terms that do the equivalent of

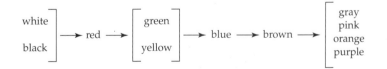

FIGURE 4.3. Color taxonomy, depicting the pattern of expansion of color terms. *Source: Brent Berlin and Paul Kay, 1969,* Basic Color Terms: Their Universality and Evolution, *Berkeley: University of California Press.*

discriminating birds from dogs, but simple societies may have no term that subsumes both, as does our category "creatures."[12] (See Figure 4.4.) Nor may people in such a society have a great capacity for counting (e.g., the Siriono). And very few societies understand what we consider basic mathematical concepts, such as zero or negative numbers (it is well to remember here that these concepts were introduced to the West only relatively recently and that many people still have only a vague grasp of their significance).

B. The Prelogical Savage

These findings, and the questions about the capacity for abstract reasoning that they raise, return us to one of the most important and long-lasting debates in the history of anthropology: that concerning the innate intellectual differences between ourselves and the so-called savages. In this debate, three positions have been taken on the causes of such differences:

- Theories of innate physical differences in brain size.
- Levy-Bruhl's notion of primitive mentality: People in non-Western cultures are immersed in a collective and think in a poetic and mythical manner.
- Tylor and Frazer's theory of primitive rationality: People in non-Western cultures think as we do, but reason from mistaken premises.

The first argument, still held by racists today, was simply that savages (who were usually people of color) had smaller brains and less capacity to reason. Evidence was taken from dubious measurements of craniums, which purported to show that white Europeans had the largest brains in the human race. There is no convincing proof, however, of innate racial differences in intelligence, and plenty of evidence to the contrary. It is well documented that children from non-Western backgrounds who are adopted at an early age into a Western environment will score as well on standard intelligence tests as their adoptive siblings. The scientific mainstream has therefore repudiated the hypothesis of innate racial differences in intelligence.[13]

A more respectable argument, associated with the French theorist Lucien Levy-Bruhl (1857–1939), was that a considerable gulf did indeed exist between the logical thought of modern individuals and the prelogical mentality of simpler societies. Using the Durkheimian notion of collective representation, Levy-Bruhl argued that native peoples had very little capacity for independent reasoning. Instead, according to Levy-Bruhl, they believed without question in a symbol system imposed upon them through their participation in the larger society. This symbol system was not logical in the sense of offering testable cause-and-effect relationships. Rather, it was made up of mystical analogies that linked the sensible universe, the spirits, and the people in a poetic unity. Everyone in a society bound together by myth and metaphor felt a profound sense of belonging—but did not do much rational thinking.

It should be stressed that Levy-Bruhl was not arguing that people in such societies are intrinsically stupid or have smaller brains. He was arguing instead that participation in a sacred and highly ritualized collective would have a deep

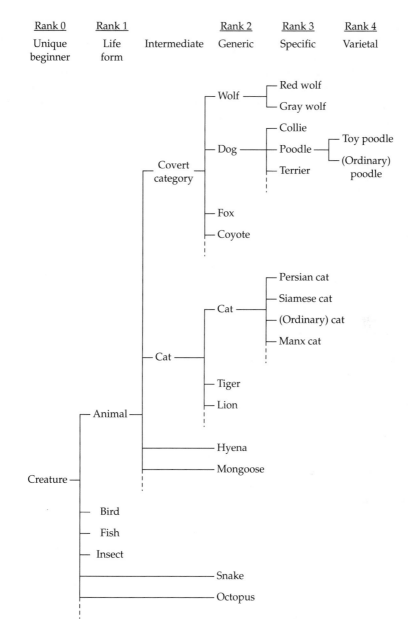

Rank 0	Rank 1		Rank 2	Rank 3	Rank 4
Unique beginner	Life form	Intermediate	Generic	Specific	Varietal

FIGURE 4.4. Partial taxonomy for "creatures" in English.
Source: Roy D'Andrade, 1995, The Development of Cognitive Anthropology. *Cambridge, England: Cambridge University Press, p. 99.*

effect on people's understanding of themselves and their world. They would not see themselves as separate actors, but as parts of something larger, which existed on the plane of imagination and mystery. Persons in such a universe would not easily recognize where the self ended and the other began, nor would they easily discriminate their own thoughts from the omnipresent and omnipotent images deriving from the shared faith of the commune. Poetic associations, symbolic analogies, emotional excitement, and synthesesia would be far more important for them than calculating rationality. In this paradigm, primitives were very much like psychotics: unable to control their impulses, lacking solid selves governed by irrational fears, prone to fantasy and to delusion. But if they became civilized, these characteristics would necessarily vanish, and they would reason as well as anyone else.[14]

C. Primitive Rationality

Levy-Bruhl's argument conformed well with Freudian theory and was later to have considerable impact on anthropologists concerned with embodiment,[15] but it was more or less discarded by the anthropologists of his era, who were far more impressed with the rationalist portrait of primitive reason offered by two English pioneers of anthropology, Edward B. Tylor (1832–1917) and his follower James G. Frazer (1854–1941). Tylor was an evolutionary theorist who believed that it would be possible to arrange all human societies in a hierarchy by comparing their different basic institutions. His definition of culture remains the one most widely cited by anthropologists everywhere:

> That complex whole which includes knowledge, belief, art, morals, law, custom, and any other capabilities and habits acquired by man as a member of society.[16]

Note that this definition does not assume any innate psychic differences between persons in different cultures. Differences that do appear are considered a result of social learning and will vary according to the stage a particular culture has reached on the evolutionary ladder culminating in Western civilization. This means that although human beings everywhere have the same capacities, those capacities are unevenly realized: According to Tylor, an uncivilized Polynesian was likely to have the mental development equivalent to that of a civilized young child.[17] Primitives might not be akin to psychotics, but they were quite certain to be very childlike and mentally unsophisticated.

Tylor's rationalist evolutionary position was elaborated by Frazer, the author of the hugely famous, but now largely unread, compendium of ethnographic information, *The Golden Bough*.[18] He envisioned himself as a "mental anthropologist" and focused his attention on the nature of what was called "magical thought," that is, apparently irrational beliefs held by natives—for example, a belief that one can harm one's enemies by burning their hair clippings or fingernails, or that impaling an effigy of a person will cause that person pain. Frazer reasoned that these beliefs—and many others—were not due to a mystical belief in participation, as Levy-Bruhl had thought, but were simply a result of mistaken premises based on false notions of the effects of association.

Frazer distinguished two types of mistaken associational reasoning: (1) contagious (objects once in contact maintain a spiritual connection—the logic behind burning hair clippings) and (2) homeopathic (like produces like, and causes resemble effects—the logic behind impaling an effigy). Once these false, but quite plausible, premises were accepted, then magical practices followed as the night follows the day. Primitive mentality then was not a result of a radically different way of thinking, in which self and other blurred together, but was simply due to lamentable, but understandable, ignorance of the actual nature of the laws of cause and effect.

Descendants of Tylor and Frazer continue to make essentially the same arguments, though with less emphasis on the superiority of Western logic. For example, is it really true that "we" have more complete categorizations of plants than "they" do? Not necessarily. One study has shown that urban American children may be able to discriminate many different vegetable products but not know the plant they came from. Spinach, some children thought, came out of a can. Children in preliterate agricultural societies, in contrast, are very well aware of the relationship between plants and their products, and are quite familiar with a wide range of plant genera. This and other differences in classification patterns obviously do not show greater intelligence on either side, but simply reflect the different interests and experiences of the two groups.[19] Likewise, American kinship terminology is among the simplest known, while the terminological structure and marriage exchange patterns of some of the world's most primitive peoples can be extremely complex. (See Figure 4.5.)

III. CULTURE, REASON, AND SOCIALIZATION

A   Bronislaw Malinowski and Practical Reason
Malinowski argues that abstract thought is unnecessary; people follow tradition and common sense instead.

B   Intelligence Tests and Socialization Practices
Cognitive differences between cultures are due to problems in testing intelligence or to socialization.

C   The Limits of Abstract Reason
Primitive forms of magical thought and false logic are pervasive in modern society.

A. Bronislaw Malinowski and Practical Reason

It is obviously the case, then, that cognition can be highly elaborate when it is applied to matters of central interest to a particular culture. But in most cases, thought may be much more uncomplicated, both for us and for them. For example, most people in the United States are probably not certain about the way electricity actually works, although they may have a vague idea about turbines churning and some probably wrong picture of atoms jumping about. Turning

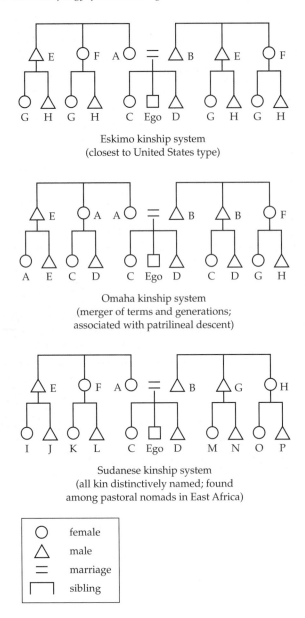

Eskimo kinship system
(closest to United States type)

Omaha kinship system
(merger of terms and generations;
associated with patrilineal descent)

Sudanese kinship system
(all kin distinctively named; found
among pastoral nomads in East Africa)

◯	female
△	male
=	marriage
⌐¬	sibling

FIGURE 4.5. Comparative kinship systems: Eskimo, Omaha, and Sudanese.

on the lights is therefore an act of faith. Nonetheless, this ignorance, though profound, is irrelevant. In order to make the lights come on, all a person has to know (most of the time) is how to turn the switch or, at worst, how to change a fuse. But we ought not feel too badly about our incapacities. It is very probable that most people in every culture are disinterested in constructing any comprehensive and systematic logical understanding of how their world works. Instead,

Trobriand girls carrying yams into their village.

they, like we, are content to know only as much as they need to know in order to get along.

This was the argument made most vigorously by Bronislaw Malinowski (1844–1942), a trained psychologist[20] who became professor of anthropology at the London School of Economics, and who was one of the most important ethnographers and theorists in the early years of the discipline. When World War I broke out, Malinowski happened to be in Australia and, as a Polish national, was interned on the Trobriand Islands of Melanesia. Turning a deficit into an advantage, he gained unparalleled knowledge of the Trobriand culture and championed a new approach to cross-cultural anthropological research in which intensive and long-term fieldwork replaced the survey methods that had previously been utilized by Rivers and others. Partly because he spent so much time studying one place, Malinowski eschewed the comparative and evolutionary approaches taken by earlier anthropologists, concentrating instead on showing how the Trobrianders manufactured a functioning society.

Anthropological Fieldwork

Ever since Malinowski's extensive fieldwork, anthropological research has typically been conducted by the method of participant observation, which implies long-term residence in a community, indepth knowledge of the local language and mores, and a high degree of integration into the society. At the same time, the investigator should maintain the role of observer and not "go native," thereby losing objectivity. Yet ethnographers are also expected to have a high degree of empathy with their subjects—one reason for the scandal that erupted with the publication of Malinowski's personal diaries, which showed that he sometimes felt antipathy toward the Trobrianders.[21]

The complex and emotionally ambiguous relationship between the fieldworker and the people being studied is central to the anthropological endeavor and has often been likened to the equally fraught relationship between therapist and patient in psychoanalysis, where transference (the intense reliving of emotions) makes objectivity hard to achieve. But whereas the therapist controls the analytic relationship and can terminate it at will, the ethnographer is a guest in a foreign society, who can be dismissed for misbehavior. Furthermore, the point of participant observation is not to cure but only to understand the other's point of view. The anthropologist is therefore much more like a pupil than a teacher and more like a patient than a doctor—at least while in the field.[22]

Doing fieldwork: The author talking to one of his friends in Pakistan.

Deeply influenced by utilitarian thought, Malinowski believed that human beings everywhere are practical individuals who rationally seek to meet their underlying basic needs with the least possible effort. These needs are material, including requirements for food, clothing, shelter, and so on. But he also posited a somewhat vaguer list of psychological needs, such as the need for reassurance, nurturance, and relief from anxiety. To meet these needs, Malinowski said, it is rarely necessary to have recourse to abstract principles. Instead, most people simply act and think according to their traditions, which have proved their efficiency over time, and solve problems as they occur without too much energy or thought. It is only when practical reason fails to meet our fundamental needs that superstition and religious belief enter in, as people call on spiritual powers to help them when ordinary means cannot. For example, Trobrianders had the technical knowledge to build a seaworthy canoe, but to cope with the actual risk of going out on the open ocean, they required ritual and magical reassurance.[23]

This distinction, as many anthropologists have pointed out since, is not quite as clear-cut as Malinowski made it seem. For example, imagine an American Indian planting corn and putting a small dead fish in with each seed; then she makes a sacred sign over the planting. It is, we think, rational to include the fish, which will rot and provide fertilizer, but irrational to make the sign, which does nothing but waste energy. The planter, however, offers the fish and the sign in the same spirit, as incentives to encourage the corn to grow. Each has its symbolic place within her larger worldview; each may be regarded as both practical and magical at once.

Despite such quibbles, Malinowski's functionalism, his practical individualism, and his theory of basic needs were all to have great influence on later anthropology. It is difficult indeed to get away from his functionalist notion that culture exists for the primary purpose of solving problems and providing the fundamental prerequisites of the people who make it up. Certainly a culture could not exist if the people within it could not feed and house themselves. However, it is harder to decide exactly what the basic psychological needs of individuals might be, and Malinowski's notion of humans motivated primarily by fear and the quest for reassurance seems rather simplistic, especially in view of the psychic conflict and ambivalence that lie at the center of Freud's theory of the psyche.[24]

Malinowski's functionalism is often derided for portraying culture as ahistorical and without conflict, but it is equally often forgotten that his emphasis on the calculating rationality of individuals has considerable affinities with modern anthropological theories that focus on agency. In a real sense, though, Malinowski's work is more sophisticated than that of his unwitting followers, since contemporary theorists of agency and process rarely lay out their underlying psychological postulates (which are usually assumptions about the innate desires of individuals for power), while Malinowski did attempt to develop a comprehensive, if rudimentary, theory of human desires in tandem with his functionalist theory of culture.

B. Intelligence Tests and Socialization Practices

Malinowski's work demonstrated that Trobriand society was enormously complicated and that the Trobrianders had constructed meaning systems of great sophistication. However, despite the complexity of indigenous knowledge, whenever Western and native intelligence were measured, the indigenous people always scored considerably lower. Certainly, part of this discrepancy was due to the simple fact that the measurements were flawed and did not operate cross-culturally.

For example, a famous test for intelligence is the Porteus maze. (See Figure 4.6.) The more quickly one negotiates the maze, the higher one's intelligence. When this test was administered to Australian aborigines, they did extremely poorly. But this had nothing to do with their native intelligence and everything to do with the fact that, as Porteus himself notes,[25] they had never been asked to hurry at anything in their lives. Such difficulties make it almost impossible to administer intelligence tests cross-culturally, or even across classes, with any degree of accuracy. What such tests mostly show is not native intelligence (however that might be defined) but the degree to which an individual shares the cultural mores and values of the people who have written the test.

Anthropologists therefore argue that differences in results of intelligence tests reflect fundamental distinctions between modern and premodern socialization practices, which can be summarized as follows:

- Premodern learning is practical, contextual, personal. Children learn by imitation.
- Modern learning is abstract, generalized, formal. Children are taught in schools.

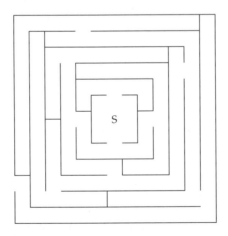

FIGURE 4.6. Item from Porteus Maze Test. Year XII.
Source: S. D. Porteus, 1965, Porteus Maze Test: Fifty Years' Application, *Palo Alto, CA: Pacific Books* p. 268.

As Levy-Bruhl knew, the meaning systems in premodern cultures tend to be bounded and contextual, not extended throughout the entire culture; they therefore differ markedly from Western knowledge structures, which are abstract and generalized. For example, the Kpelle tribe of Africa has two different systems of measurement: arm span for large distances, hand span for small distances. When the Kpelle were asked to use hand-span measurements for long distances, their estimates proved wildly wrong, though their estimates were extremely accurate when they used the proper, that is, the arm-span, method. Similarly, the Kpelle did quite poorly compared with Americans when asked to measure volumes abstractly. But when asked to estimate measurements of rice (a task they were accustomed to doing), they performed better than Americans.[26] These sorts of findings are very common in tests of the intelligence of non-Western peoples (and even among less modernized Westerners, such as the people of Sardinia).

Perhaps the most famous work on the variation between primitive and modern thought was undertaken by Soviet psychologist A. R. Luria (1902–1977) during his fieldwork in the remote regions of Uzbekistan and Kirghizia in 1931 to 1932. Luria asked a variety of local people to complete standard syllogisms, such as the following: In the far north, where there is snow, all bears are white. Zemlya is in the far north. What color are the bears there? While informants who had some rudimentary schooling quickly answered "white," his unschooled tribal informants invariably replied: "I have never been to Zemlya. How do I know what color the bears are there?"

When the same unschooled informants were shown pictures of an ax, a hammer, a saw, and a log, and asked which object did not belong, they said they all belonged together. Luria suggested that perhaps the log did not belong, but this suggestion was vehemently refuted. "You need the log," he was told, "or the ax and saw and hammer have no work!" In contrast, those who had some schooling immediately picked out the log as an object that did not belong in the abstract category of "tools." Similarly, when he presented his subjects with abstract geometrical figures and asked them to class them together, they first designated the figures with the names of everyday concrete objects. A circle, for example, was designated as a plate, a seive, a bucket, a watch, or a moon; a square was conceptualized as a mirror, a door, or a house. Objects were then grouped according to their co-occurrence in daily life. (See Figure 4.7.) Other attempts by Luria to elicit distinctions based on general categories were equally fruitless, as were his efforts to get unschooled informants to accept counterfactual statements, or to solve problems of an abstract nature, though they had no difficulties when the problems were concrete and realistic.[27]

Luria realized that the form of reasoning he found among his uneducated subjects was practical and situational. For them, items were classed together not on the basis of some assumed underlying principles, but because they functioned together or happened to co-occur in daily life. Generalizations and hypothetical conclusions were ignored in favor of personal experience. In effect, his informants refused to accept the formal and closed nature of logical arguments, and continually sought to connect problems with their daily reality.

Interviewer: Are these objects alike, or not?

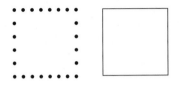

Subject 1: No, this is a watch, and this is a map. What would you have if we put them together? How can a map and a watch be put together?

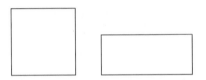

Subject 1: No, that's a window-frame and that's a ruler.

Subject 2: These are alike—this is a bird-cage, and that's a feeding-trough in a cage.

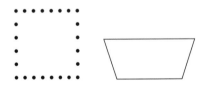

Subject 3: This is a window, and that's a frame over a doorway. But they are different.

FIGURE 4.7. Perception of abstract shapes by Uzbek subjects.
Source: A. R. Luria, 1976, Cognitive Development: Its Cultural and Social Foundations, *Cambridge, MA: Harvard University Press, pp. 36, 38 (first published in Moscow in 1974).*

Such contextualized and personalized thinking reflects not differences in innate capacity but cultural differences in learning style. Children in non-Western societies are socialized by imitating their elders ("legitimate peripheral participation," in anthropological jargon); they gradually learn proper behavior within specific cultural frameworks and become expert at doing necessary work. But formal schooling is unusual, and there is rarely any emphasis on the capacity to

As is common in non-Western societies, little girls in northern Pakistan are the major teachers and caretakers of their younger siblings.

reason abstractly and apply conclusions universally, nor is questioning encouraged. Instead, the focus tends to be on obedience and on efficiency of performance within a particular social context.[28]

In contrast, Western children are trained to learn rules, orders, and problem-solving techniques that can be extended to all aspects of life. They even spontaneously govern their games with complex regulations, which are hotly debated by the contestants and can become more important than the actual play itself. Quantification, system, and abstraction are taught from an early age, both in school and out, as is the capacity for solving the kinds of syllogisms and understanding the categorizations that Luria's informants found so baffling. While Luria's subjects believed one could not talk about what one had not seen or remove objects from their functional setting, children trained in formal operations have no difficulty applying abstract logic to any domain. In fact, assumptions that underlying rules and categories must exist make it quite difficult for Westerners to memorize random lists; we tend to spend our time trying to figure out what the hidden logic is, whereas people raised in societies where knowledge is compartmentalized and contextual usually just get on with the task.[29]

C. The Limits of Abstract Reason

If we keep in mind that Westerners are trained from infancy in the application of abstract reason and spend years in school learning formal principles, it is remarkable that we reason as badly as we do and are easily led into precisely the forms of contextualized thinking Luria found among his unschooled informants. For instance, if asked, "Father is to mother as brother is to whom?" most Westerners will answer "sister." The correct answer, technically, is "sister-in-law," since the relationship between mother and father is not one of blood, but one of marriage. But because we see mother and father as *our* blood relatives, we readily make the categorical error. Similarly, American students may have no problem accepting a syllogism such as this: If A is doing B, then C is doing D. A is not doing B; therefore C is not doing D. But they often find it difficult to accept the same reasoning when it is put in concrete terms: If Dan is drinking cola, then Bob is sitting down. Dan is not drinking cola; therefore Bob is not sitting down." Apparently we too, like the people Luria studied, refuse to keep within the rigid framework of a logical proposition that is wholly disconnected from the way ordinary reality operates.[30] Malinowski was right: Practical reason tends to trump abstract logic.

It is also apparent that both civilized and primitive people are equally easily convinced by false, but psychologically compelling, beliefs.[31] For instance, many Americans are reluctant to wear clothes that are secondhand. They apparently fear that moral dirt may cling to objects of apparel—an example of magical contagion. Fear of sitting near or interacting with people who are handicapped or scarred is equally irrational, and equally connected with magical fears of contamination. In fact, most of us, despite our schooling, are often prey to some forms of "magical" thought and "have a 'savage' mentality much of the time."[32]

It seems, then, that the anthropological premise of the psychic unity of humankind is justified. All of us have essentially the same perceptions; all of us have the same capacity to reason; all of us also tend to accept the taken-for-granted reality around us without too much criticism; and even highly educated Westerners are prone to use practical reason and to accept magical thought.

IV. AUTHENTIC CULTURE

A Romantic Aestheticism
   Herder's romantic vision of cultures as incomparable works of art.

B Franz Boas: Romantic Empiricist
   Boas's contention that cultures must be understood scientifically as well as appreciated aesthetically.

C The Internal Tensions of Boasian Anthropology
   Science and art in anthropology.

A. Romantic Aestheticism

So far, I have portrayed early anthropological research as an offshoot of Enlightenment science, seeking to make empirical tests of the differences and similarities between primitive and civilized ways of thinking and perceiving. In the quest to discover the conceptual common ground while giving credit to cultural divergence, these researchers (with the exception of Levy-Bruhl) had little interest in the romantic claims for the importance of personal authenticity and poetic expression, and they tended to assume instead that rational thought was the core of existence.

However, not all of anthropology followed the route of Frazer and Tylor; some thinkers were inspired by a more romantic vision. Like Rousseau, they believed in the existence of the noble savage and repudiated what they saw as the vulgarity of modern society; they were also wary of experimental positivist science, which seemed to denude the complexity of human experience. And, like the romantics, they sought authenticity. But while romantics generally imagined authenticity to be the spontaneous expression of an individual's personality, these theorists had a different point of view. They portrayed the authentic human being as someone integrated into a coherent and pure cultural tradition as yet unsullied by contaminating influences. The ancient Greeks were authentic until they conquered Asia Minor; the Romans before the Roman Empire were more authentic than they were afterward; uncivilized tribes were, in principle, more authentic than civilized urbanites.

Although French intellectuals like Rousseau had a penchant for romanticizing the innocence of the savage, admiration of the pure and the primitive reached its highest development in Germany, in part as a result of the pervasive influence of Johann Gottfried von Herder (1744–1803), a romantic poet, philosopher, historian, and cultural theorist, who had developed the notion that primitive societies constituted organic entities, each animated by its own distinctive genius. According to Herder, every such folk culture could be appreciated as a work of art or as a beautiful natural object. From his perspective, the study of other cultures was primarily interpretive and aesthetic, bringing the worldview and folk psychology of primitives and preliterates to the attention of the learned world. Herder was a romantic connoisseur of cultural difference, and his aesthetic approach deeply influenced early anthropology and psychology in Germany.

B. Franz Boas: Romantic Empiricist

The German interpretive approach to the anthropological investigation of other cultures later influenced Weber's notion of *verstehen* and was expressed in British anthropology by Malinowski's famous demand that the ethnographer must, above all, "grasp the native's point of view."[33] However, the romantic tradition had its greatest impact on anthropology in America, because of the huge intellectual importance of Franz Boas (1858–1942), who founded the first school of anthropology in the United States at Clark University in 1888. Boas moved to Columbia University in New York City in 1895, where he dominated the discipline until his death. Trained in Germany as an empirical scientist, Boas had a background in physics and geography, and he began his career as a psychologist. In 1883 he undertook an expedition to Baffin Island to

Franz Boas in 1895, imitating a character in the Kwakiutl winter ceremony.

explore the effects of the arctic environment on Eskimo perceptions of sea water. But while there, he was drawn more and more toward the study of Eskimo culture, and he later became a leading ethnographer of the Kwakiutl Indians of the Northwest Coast. Strongly influenced by Tylor and other evolutionists, Boas was also a diffusionist, who searched among cultures for trait complexes; at the same time, he believed in the psychic unity of humankind and maintained throughout his career that there existed "psychological laws which control the mind of man everywhere."[34]

Alongside his scientific, historical, and comparative interests, Boas was also a proponent of what Herder had called the genius of peoples. His field experiences taught him that perception was altered by cultural preconceptions about reality; the fact that his informants understood their physical world in their own culturally patterned way showed Boas the limits of an overly positivist approach and of simplistic evolutionary and diffusionist thinking. Instead, he increasingly came to admire the diversity, coherence, and complexity of American Indian cultures and the sophistication of their languages. Their world, it seemed to him, was in some ways superior to his own. This had nothing to do with the Indians' ability to reason (which Boas assumed was equal to the ability of Western peoples) and everything to do with the unconscious but pervasive symbolic system that gave the Eskimo and Kwakiutl universes their particular characters.[35] Part of the anthropologist's duty, as Boas saw it, was to protect these unique local cultures from vanishing under the unrelenting pressure of modernization and colonialism.

C. The Internal Tensions of Boasian Anthropology

As a combination of "inductive empiricist and phenomenological idealist,"[36] Boas imbued American anthropology with a dualistic character: A strong aesthetic and ethical component existed alongside the mandate to generate and test scientific hypotheses. He taught his students that the duty of researchers was to learn the language and the entire cultural repertoire of the people they were studying. Their moral mission was to preserve as much of the dwindling native world as possible—all data, including hairstyles, clothing, tool types, as well as myths, social structure, and rituals, were equally valuable as records of beautiful, intricately integrated cultures that were fast disappearing in the face of civilization.

Co-incident with the opposition between empiricism and romanticism was a parallel tension in American anthropology that also reflected Boas's experience. This was the contradiction between the ethnographer's dual role as detached researcher and participant activist. During Boas's own fieldwork, he became more than a scientific outsider with a research agenda, and the people he studied became more than his experimental subjects. They were also his friends, confidants, protectors, and teachers; he identified with them and sought to convey their understanding of their world to his audience. Ever since, anthropologists have been torn between these two positions. Those more attracted to the role of the participant have tended to focus more on the individuals who served them as interpreters and guides. These informants could be seen, not simply as the bearers of knowledge but as authentic figures—even as heroes—representing and creating their own worlds.[37] The anthropologist also could be envisioned as a heroic figure, bearing the wisdom and authentic vision of the natives back to his or her own decadent civilization, which could then be transformed for the better. As Boas wrote in his own anthropologist's credo: "How can we recognize the shackles that tradition has laid on us? For when we recognize them, we are able to break them."[38]

V. THE FOUNDATIONS OF CULTURE AND PERSONALITY

A Edward Sapir: Culture Equals Personality
   Sapir's effort to reconcile individual psychology and cultural difference.

B Ruth Benedict and Margaret Mead: Culture Constructs Personality
   Cultural configurationism: Each individual expresses the genius of his or her culture.

C Explaining Deviance
   The biological interpretation of deviance.

D Problems and Critiques
   Problems of essentialism, validity, oversimplification, one-sidedness, and ahistoricism.

E Gregory Bateson and Schizmogenesis
   The dialectic of complementary emotions.

A. Edward Sapir: Culture Equals Personality

Edward Sapir (1884–1939) is perhaps the closest anthropology has come to producing a romantic anti-establishment hero. He was recognized by Boas as his most brilliant student, even though he later rejected many of Boas's more historicist ideas. After a period of exile in Ottowa, Sapir taught at the University of Chicago and later at Yale, where he convened the first seminar on culture and personality in 1930. His major intellectual effort was the attempt (mostly fruitless) to develop an interdisciplinary study that would include psychology, psychiatry, sociology, and anthropology. A brilliant linguist and an accomplished poet, Sapir was a true Renaissance man, keenly attuned to the aesthetic aspects of language and of cultural production. He praised the "passionate temperament cutting into itself with the cold steel of intellect"[39] and appreciated the genuine integrated traditional cultures that could (he believed) foster artistic personalities—such as his own.[40] He also felt disdain for the polyglot culture of modern Western society—which he derided as spurious.

Concerned with giving due credit to the importance of the individual creative actor, Sapir argued that culture should never be seen as a superorganic entity existing over and above individuals, but could be understood only through the perceptions and responses of the various personality types who are constrained by, yet continually act upon, their world. An adequate anthropology, Sapir said, must take account of the originality of individuals (though some individuals were more original than others).

At the same time, Sapir argued that culture itself might best be understood as being analogous to a personality, which he defined as a multileveled, integrated system of symbolically interconnected patterns. From this perspective, both the individual and culture are systems of ideas imbued with meaning and intention;[41] therefore, there is not necessarily any conflict between them, only differences in levels of analysis. Like each individual, each cultural personality is unique and incommensurate with others. This argument was taken up by the linguist Benjamin Whorf and became the famous Sapir-Whorf hypothesis, which stated that differences in language coincided with differences in cognition and worldview.[42]

Although Sapir's dialectical and almost Hegelian view of the relationship between culture and individual showed great promise, it was not clear exactly how his program was to be implemented. His picture of the interacting idea systems of personality and culture was bloodless and abstract, lacking any hierarchy of levels or theory of motivation. Nor was it clear how the different systems could be interrelated, or even how a culture could integrate multiple independ-

The Sapir-Whorf Hypothesis

As an example of the Sapir-Whorf hypothesis, many languages have hierarchical markers that must be used in address. The Chinese traditionally distinguished elder and younger siblings, and also were obliged to mark all other forms of status difference linguistically. Such requisite markers, it might be conjectured, serve to inculcate a strong sense of deference to superiors in ranked society. Americans, in contrast, have no such markers and have even dispensed with the old "thee" and "thou" terms of familiarity in favor of the more egalitarian "you," which reflects the nature of our society.

Sapir's pupil, Benjamin Whorf, who did his fieldwork with the Hopi Indians of the American Southwest, took the hypothesis much further than this simple example.[43] He argued that the Hopi language, because it did not recognize linear time or concretize abstract objects, was far more suited to understanding the theory of relativity than English, with its rigid past-present-future tense structure and tendency to nominalize.

Although it is certainly true that language limits, or at least filters, thought, it is true too that new languages and new usages can be learned without great changes in cognition or behavior. Many Hindus, for example, know English and yet still participate in the caste system, with its intrinsic distinctions between groups. Most contemporary anthropologists therefore treat the extreme claims of the Sapir-Whorf hypothesis with considerable skepticism. Nonetheless, in the late 1950s the Sapir-Whorf hypothesis, in diluted form, served as the foundation of the subdiscipline of ethnoscience, where it was assumed that understanding the underlying logic of a people's linguistic categories would lead to understanding basic cognitive structures behind actions (see Chapter 9 for more on this subject).

ent character types within itself. He did concede, however, that there might be a "generalized personality . . . typical of a given society."[44] And he also suggested that certain archetypical characters might exist cross-culturally.[45]

Sapir's hope was that psychiatry and anthropology could join in a mutual inquiry, and his work was moving in that direction when he died prematurely, having written relatively little. Yet his call for an anthropology that celebrates the creative individual has continued to resonate, as we shall see in later chapters, and Sapir continues to be held up as the only genius the discipline has yet produced—perhaps in part because his early promise was never realized and because his career was tragically cut short.

B. Ruth Benedict and Margaret Mead: Culture Constructs Personality

Two other students of Boas were more successful, at least temporarily, in their attempt to bring a degree of aesthetic appreciation of other cultures into anthropology—but at the cost of erasing the individual whom Sapir had elevated. The first was Ruth Benedict (1887–1948), who took very seriously Sapir's

Margaret Mead in Samoa.

rather offhand remark that a culture might be constituted by certain typical generalized personalities. Assuming the existence of generalized personalities allowed Benedict to escape Sapir's problem of reconciling individual distinctiveness with cultural coherence. In this premise she was also inspired by German historical philosophers who, following Herder, had argued that an authentic culture was characterized by a totalizing genius that imprinted itself upon all its members.[46] Benedict called this postulate configurationism, and argued for it in pellucid prose (she, like Sapir, was an accomplished poet) in two justly famous popular books, *Patterns of Culture*[47] and *The Chrysanthemum and the Sword*.[48]

In these works Benedict presented multidimensional ethnographic portraits of several cultures (the Zuni, Plains Indian, Dobuan, and Kwakiutl in *Patterns*, the Japanese in *Chrysanthemum*) to demonstrate that each society "selects some segment of the arc of possible human behaviour" for elaboration, and thereby provides its members with a coherent model for feeling, thinking, and acting. Each culture, Benedict said, is like a language: unique, patterned, shared, selective, and changing only by a process of drift. Why exactly certain human potentials were selected by particular societies was not at all clear in Benedict's ahistorical accounts, though she indicated that each society must socialize its members so that they can survive within a specific ecological niche. Whatever the reasons for the evolution of a particular cultural form, Benedict's main point was that "most human beings take the channel that is ready made in their culture" and become the character types already provided for them.[49] Following are examples from *Patterns of Culture*:

- *Kwakiutl:* Highly competitive and status-conscious society of power-hungry Dionysian megalomaniacs. The only emotions are those of pride and shame.
- *Zuni:* Placid, orderly world of peaceful and communal Apollonian personality types. Emotions are damped down entirely.
- *Dobu:* Suspicious and hostile culture consisting of nasty and paranoid individuals who enjoy trickery and deceit.

Rather than the weak claim that culture was structured like a personality, which Sapir had made, Benedict's strong declaration was that personalities were actually reflections of culture. Each culture was envisioned, like a language, as a symbolic totality; its fundamental themes constructed every level of personal experience, including cognition and emotion. Such complex systems simply existed, Benedict said. They could not be compared, but were to be appreciated for their beauty and unity.

Benedict's theoretical orientation was shared by her younger colleague Margaret Mead (1901–1978), an indefatigable fieldworker, formidable personality, and potent cultural force, whose name remains today synonymous with anthropology for many of the general public. Much of Mead's popularity derives from the no-nonsense tone of her prolific writings—she published many books and wrote articles for everything from scientific journals to women's magazines—and from her knack for expounding on eye-catching popular issues. Like Benedict, she was an iconoclast, free thinker, and sexual experimenter, who found American society narrow-minded and repressive. Always

Mead's Fieldwork

In what is probably the most famous controversy in anthropology, Mead's work was attacked by Derek Freeman for misrepresenting the reality of Samoan culture. According to Freeman, Mead had gone into the field determined to prove that human nature was formed by culture, not by biology, and had skewed her data to make her case. In contrast, Freeman tried to show that Samoa was far from the easy going, sexually permissive society Mead had portrayed; rather, the Samoans were violent and competitive, and their sexual relations were fraught with tension and misogyny.[50] Unfortunately, Mead died before Freeman published his attack and was unable to defend herself. It is true that her youthful research in Samoa produced the least detailed and least nuanced of her ethnographic reports. But in retrospect, it seems that Freeman overstated his case as well and that Samoan culture was never so one-sided as either Mead or Freeman claimed, but rather (like every other culture) was ambiguous and contradictory in its handling of relationships between the sexes.

Nonetheless, despite posthumous attacks against her work, it remains the consensus that Mead's field research was generally of a very high quality, even if her analysis of her data was sometimes too ideologically driven and crude.[51]

Behaviorism and Configurationism

The arguments made by Benedict and Mead were very much in line with the psychological thinking of the time, which was mechanically behaviorist. Human beings, behaviorist theorists said, are almost completely conditioned by their parents, teachers, elders, and peer groups, as well as by their physical milieu.[52] According to this theory, through simple mechanisms of reward and punishment, the total learning environment teaches children to become the adults they are supposed to be; children absorb their training and respond accordingly. With its emphasis on conditioning and socialization, behaviorism had obvious similarities to traditional Boasian anthropology: Both gave dominance to the power of culture over the individual; both therefore saw learning as crucial; and both portrayed the psyche as a kind of black box, into which anything can be put if there is sufficient reinforcement. Both also accepted functionalism and evolutionism, and applauded adaption to circumstances as a requisite for promoting personal and social well-being.

confrontational, she acted directly to make her critiques and was the first to undertake problem-centered fieldwork that would attack what she believed were the shibboleths of her own society.

Her first project was typical. In *Coming of Age in Samoa: A Psychological Study of Primitive Youth for Western Civilization*[53] (written when she was just 23), Mead argued that the Samoans had little of the sexual anxiety that is typical of the West. In particular, there was no preadolescent latency period, as Freudian psychology predicted. Rather, the Samoan world, in Mead's portrait, was characterized by sexual ease, diffuseness of personal relationships, and an absence of deep feeling—a social-emotional configuration that Mead claimed favored a relatively stress-free transition to adulthood.

A similar debunking theme provided the argument for what is probably Mead's most famous book, *Sex and Temperament in Three Primitive Societies.* Here Mead characterized three Melanesian cultures in ways that were meant to challenge Western gender ideologies:

- *Arapesh:* Both men and women are peaceful, caring, and feminine, according to Western standards.
- *Mundagumor:* Both sexes are violent, aggressive, and masculine.
- *Tchambuli:* The women are masculine traders and activists; men are feminine aesthetes.

The general point Mead made throughout her work was that "human nature is almost unbelievably malleable";[54] even sexual roles are not innate, as we like to think, but are "cultural creations to which each generation, male and female, is trained to conform."[55] Socialization, Mead argued, conquers all, creating coherent and consistent cultural worlds very different from our own.

C. Explaining Deviance

It is ironic that even though the premises of configurationism forced Benedict and Mead to stress conformity, they themselves were rebels. Like Sapir, Benedict had little patience for our modern society, which she castigated as a cultural hodgepodge, incoherent, intolerant, and vulgar. She viewed America as overly individualistic, competitive, and egoistic, while at the same time she believed that Americans tended to compensate for a lack of social integration with a great pressure toward uniformity. The combination of competitive individualism and a pervasive fear of being different led, she thought, to a general atmosphere of bigotry and anxiety—of which Benedict was especially aware, since she adopted a lesbian lifestyle after suffering years of an unhappy marriage.

Part of her agenda, then, was to persuade her readers to tolerate differences; she was one of the first anthropologists to write about the mentally ill, the sexually deviant, and other social outcasts. According to Benedict, such unfortunate individuals, who challenge the boundaries of the normal, are "the exceptions who have not easily taken the traditional forms of their culture."[56] Anthropological awareness could teach such people that what is abnormal here might be quite normal elsewhere (a placid Kwakiutl would be a success among the Zuni; an aggressive Zuni would find happiness among the Kwakiutl; homosexuality is acceptable behavior among the Plains Indians). Knowledge about the relativity of normality could decrease the burden of guilt deviants feel.[57] Even more idealistic was Benedict's hope that anthropology, in its highest form, could be a kind of

---

Problems of Configurationism

- Deviance has to be accounted for biologically.
- Critique cannot be objectively validated, since it comes from within a cultural configuration favoring critique.
- The range of possible personality types is never made clear.

- Culture is seen as unitary and adaptive; contradictions, resistance, and alternatives are ignored.
- Historical change is not addressed.

---

rational social therapy, helping create a society that could analyze itself and thereby create a more just and tolerant world. Mead, too, favored greater tolerance of diversity, and she carefully documented cases of individuals who did not fit into the frameworks of their cultures (it is noteworthy that the only really detailed portraits of individuals to be found in the work of either Mead or Benedict are portraits of misfits). The underlying message is that our own norms can (and should) change and that we can become more accepting of difference.

D. Problems and Critiques

But Mead and Benedict were then left with a problem: If culture wholly constructs character, then where do aberrant individuals come from? Given their premises of the irresistible power of enculturation, they were obliged to argue that difference had to be due to innate temperament—some people just cannot fit in, despite their best efforts, because they are constitutionally incapable of adapting to their environment. Thus, even though they themselves were passionate defenders of personal liberation, their theories actually eliminated choice. People were either totally malleable or naturally deviant.

There are also other difficulties in the theoretical construct built by Mead and Benedict. For example, if culture is so encompassing and powerful, how can a commentator stand outside it to make valid and constructive criticisms? A faith in rationality and tolerance can easily be seen as wholly culture-bound and no more universally valid than any other set of beliefs—a point later taken up with great vigor by postmodern theorists. Nor is the expanse of the arc of human potential ever demarcated. We do not know what humans are capable of becoming, nor do we know what configurations are possible, or what aspects of a configuration are the most emotionally compelling.

These, however, were problems more research might solve. More worrying were the conceptual assumptions of unitary culture and seamless adaption. As a result of these premises, contrary information was often ignored, such as the fact that Arapesh men were active headhunters or that the Kwakiutl orgies were actually carefully planned. The effects of colonialism were also not addressed; for example, Samoan easy going detachment could be interpreted instead as apathy in the face of the loss of their cultural traditions under American domination.[58] Moreover, since everyone (save a tiny minority of biological deviants) was portrayed as well adjusted to the demands of society, there was no room for conflict or change either within a culture or within the individuals who make it up. By eliminating the active agent and downplaying contradiction, Mead and Benedict solved Sapir's problem of the relationship between the individual and culture by sweeping it under the rug. Clearly, a more complex and dialectical model of culture and personality was required if progress was to be made.

E. Gregory Bateson and Schizmogenesis

In fact, the beginnings of such a theory had already been provided by Gregory Bateson, Mead's second husband. Bateson, an Englishman, was a student of the natural sciences with an affinity for Hegelian philosophy. This background did not at first aid him in his anthropological studies. He had great difficulty completing his field research with the Iatmul of New Guinea; his first 3 years of work ended in failure, and it was on his second visit to the Sepik River in 1932 that he met Mead, who had just returned from her own work with the Arapesh. His meeting with Mead not only sparked a romance, but also led him to rethink his own work, which he finally published in 1936 under the ponderous title of *Naven: A Survey of the Problems Suggested by a Composite Picture of the Culture of a New Guinea Tribe Drawn from Three Points of View.*[59]

This book focused on the Naven ceremony of the Iatmul—a transvestite performance of ritualized homosexuality in which the rivalries between men and women were symbolically transformed, enacted, and parodied. In his analysis of Iatmul culture, he combined, with considerable success, a functionalist Durkheimian social structural approach with a configurationist account in the manner of Mead and Benedict. But what was really remarkable was his move beyond the static premises of configurationist and functionalist anthropology, both of which stressed social integration, and toward a more processual and dialectical vision, one based on a dynamic interaction of opposing cultural forces.[60]

Bateson's innovation was to say that culture was not a unitary totalizing force, imposing itself on individuals. Rather, Iatmul women and men were motivated by complementary, oppositional emotional attitudes, which Bateson called their ethos. Iatmul men, in Bateson's portrait, were driven to express pride and competitive individualism; women had to show contrasting moods of modesty and cooperation. Like his contemporaries, Bateson assumed these characteristic male and female attitudes were part of the great arc of human emotions, some of which each culture selects out to be amplified. But for him, these central emotions did not appear in isolation; they were defined only in relationship to one another—pride could not exist without humility.

In addition, the Iatmul emotional system was not static. Instead, it was continually in motion, each side compelling the other to express itself ever more strongly—male pride stimulating greater female humility, which arouses more pride. In acting out this cycle, individuals gained valued social identities but ran the risk of escalating conflict to the point of shattering the social order. This is the process that Bateson called schizmogenesis; it could in principle be either complementary or symmetrical—that is, the emotions accentuated could be

The Double Bind Hypothesis

Bateson's greatest success with his method was his theory of the double bind as an explanation for schizophrenia. The argument was that contradictory messages given by mothers to their infants (cuddling the child while pinching it; praising it while looking coldly away) would lead to later psychic disorganization. This hypothesis seemed sensible enough, and it was taken up by a whole school of psychologists. Nonetheless, it proved to be wrong. It is now generally agreed that schizophrenia is not caused by bad parenting, but by a combination of genetic and cultural factors.[61]

either opposite (as among Iatmul men and women) or alike (such as the competitive relations between two American businessmen).

Where Mead and Benedict had assumed equilibrium as a matter of course, Bateson wondered how culture could maintain itself in the face of the patterned oppositions that he saw at its core. Among the Iatmul, he argued, the Naven ritual served the purpose of diffusing conflict and of allowing a playful relief from tension.[62] In the ceremony, women acted like aggressive men, while men had to submit and admire their posturing wives. This gender reversal permitted both women and men to express emotions and attitudes not allowed them in ordinary life, and therefore relieved tension. Ritual performances, Bateson argued, generally function in this manner, balancing out the oppositions that characterize any social system.[63]

For Bateson, then, society is always in a state of inner tension; and, although he largely ignored individuals, he did imagine that they too are compelled by emotional impulses impossible to wholly satisfy, so they must be expressed and channeled in the symbolic arena of ritual. This formula has much in common with Freud's theory: Like Freud, Bateson focused on the constant internal conflict of dynamic systems, although for Freud, that system was the psyche while for Bateson it was the cultural ethos.[64]

Despite these parallels, Bateson apparently regarded psychoanalysis as a discipline devoted primarily to deciphering sexual symbols and never tried to utilize Freud's model of psychic conflict to enrich his own material. Instead, he spent most of his career trying to develop a scientific cybernetic model for cultural feedback systems—an effort that did not yield much fruit, though it was taken up later by a number of cognitive anthropologists. Although recognized as a brilliant thinker, Bateson, unfortunately, never had the intellectual influence on anthropology that his ideas deserved, and it was left to others to explore the possibility of a reconciliation between anthropology and psychology, as we shall see in the next chapter.

Summary

This chapter traces some of the major findings of a long history of anthropological investigations into the differences between premodern and modern mentality—in other words, the differences between "them" and "us." Although begun with neo-Darwinist notions that there would be very considerable variations in the ways that people in less complex societies perceived the world, anthropology has instead concluded that there are no essential distinctions in the perceptual capacities of people everywhere. It is now assumed that differences in perception that do exist—such as differential susceptibility to the Müller-Lyer illusion or lack of terms for various colors—are due to cultural factors that do not affect the actual content of perception.

Cognitive differences too have proved not to be innate, though measurement here has proved more difficult, due to the nearly insurmountable difficulties of applying Western intelligence tests to non-Western cultures. Nonetheless, it is evident that access to Western schooling leads fairly rapidly to higher scores on standard intelligence tests and that being raised in a Western environment offsets any differences that might be assumed to be racial.

As we have seen, there are two different intellectually respectable theories of why differences in cognition do occur across cultures. The first, associated with Levy-Bruhl, claims that immersion in a tight-knit collective, as is the case in most small-scale societies, leads to a kind of poetic, prelogical thinking, concerned mainly with participation in the larger unity. The second, associated with Tylor and Frazer, is that all thinking everywhere is more or less the same, but the premises may differ, and if wrong premises are accepted, then the results will be equally mistaken.

Malinowski, the founder of modern anthropological field methods, also assumed that human beings are reasonable and proceeded in a utilitarian fashion to portray culture as a practical problem-solving device, serving to provide for the basic material and psychological needs of its members. For Malinowski, the fundamental human prerequisites were always the same; the job of the ethnographer was to see how a particular society functioned to meet them. By undertaking in-depth fieldwork, he contributed a remarkably complex picture of life in a non-Western society, but without a comparative perspective.

In contrast, contemporary theories have concerned themselves with comparative studies of the processes of socialization in primitive societies and modern societies, showing that children in the former gain knowledge that is contextual, personal, and informal. The knowledge so learned can be highly complex and sophisticated, but it tends not to be generalized; instead, it remains situational and practical—very different from the generalized, abstract, and formal knowledge taught in the West. Nonetheless, despite these differences in learning techniques, it is remarkable how much Westerners are themselves liable to the same sorts of logical errors and contextual thinking long thought to be characteristic only of less complex cultures.

Thus there may not be as much difference between us and them as it initially might seem. At the most fundamental levels of perception and cognition, there is a psychic unity of all humanity. But differences do exist, and the appreciation of these differences was a central preoccupation of early anthropological research in the United States, which took its cue from the work of Herder and other German romantics, as carried to the United States by Franz Boas. Boas's mixture of empiricism and aestheticism greatly influenced his students, notably Edward Sapir, Ruth Benedict, and Margaret Mead.

Sapir focused on the creative individual and proposed a dialectical anthropology, with the autonomous actor and society mutually constituting one another. But he had little to say about the actual weight of the elements engaging in the dialectic, and his efforts had no practical results. Mead and Benedict, in contrast, ignored dialectical complexities and placed adaption at the center of their theories. This allowed them to paint a picture of the self constructed by a unitary culture, but at the price of eliminating all actual individuals from the picture and biologizing difference: Only innate temperament could account for resistance to the overwhelming constraints of a totally seamless society.

The one-sided and static culturology of Mead and Benedict was made more sophisticated by Gregory Bateson's pioneering work, which concerned itself with contestation between opposing forces within a society and portrayed cultures in a state of internal tension.

Endnotes

1. Allan Holmberg, 1969, *Nomads of the Long Bow: The Siriono of Eastern Bolivia,* Garden City, NY: Natural History Press (original publication 1950).
2. Eleanor Heider, 1972, "The Structure of Color Space in Naming and Memory for Two Languages," *Cognitive Psychology* 7: 532–47.
3. Joseph-Marie De Gérando, 1969, *The Observation of Savage Peoples,* Berkeley: University of California Press (original publication 1800).
4. See L. H. Morgan, 1963, *Ancient Society,* Cleveland: World Publishing (original publication 1877). Note that henceforth for stylistic reasons loaded terms such as native, primitive, savage, barbarian, uncivilized, as well as civilized, sophisticated, cosmopolitan, and so on, will not be put in quotes. The reader is asked to be aware that such terms are always provisional, inaccurate, and ironic.
5. Friedrich Engels, 1902, *The Origin of the Family, Private Property, and the State,* Chicago: Kerr (original publication 1884).
6. Reported in Gustav Jahoda, 1982, *Psychology and Anthropology: A Psychological Perspective,* London: Academic Press.
7. Rivers differed from Freud in arguing that the instinct of self-preservation, not sexuality, is the most fundamental drive. See Chapter 11 for more on Rivers's World War I research.
8. Marshall Segal, David Campbell, and Melville Herskovitz, 1966, *The Influence of Culture on Visual Perception,* Indianapolis, IN: Bobbs-Merrill. For the original reports on the Torres Straits expedition, see Alfred Haddon, 1901–35, *The Cambridge Anthropological Expedition to Torres Straits* (6 vols.), Cambridge, England: Cambridge University Press.
9. Michael Cole, 1996, *Cultural Psychology: A Once and Future Discipline,* Cambridge, MA: Harvard University Press, p. 56.
10. Brent Berlin and Paul Kay, 1969, *Basic Color Terms: Their Universality and Evolution,* Berkeley: University of California Press.
11. Quoted in Rodney Needham, 1985, *Exemplars,* Berkeley: University of California Press, p. 61.
12. See Brent Berlin, 1978, "Ethnobiological Classification," in E. Rosch and B. Lloyd (eds.), *Cognition and Categorization,* New York: Erlbaum. Chapter 9 deals with present-day cognitive anthropology in more detail. Of course, there are exceptions to the rule, as Harold Conklin documented among the Hanunoo, who have taxonomies of considerable complexity despite their relatively simple social organization. See Harold Conklin, 1954, "Hanunoo Color Categories," *Southwestern Journal of Anthropology* 11: 339–44.
13. Richard Hernstein and Charles Murray, 1994, *The Bell Curve,* New York: Free Press. For reactions, see S. Fraser (ed.), 1995, *The Bell Curve Wars,* New York: Basic Books.
14. Lucien, Levy-Bruhl, 1926, *How Natives Think,* London: Allen & Unwin (original publication 1912).
15. See Chapter 7.
16. E. B. Tylor, quoted in Michael Carrithers, 1997, "Culture," in Thomas Barfield (ed.), *The Dictionary of Anthropology,* Oxford, England: Basil Blackwell, p. 98. The definition

originally appeared in E. B. Tylor, 1871, *Primitive Culture: Researches into the Development of Mythology, Philosophy, Religion, Art and Custom* (2 vols.), London: Murray.

17. E. B. Tylor, 1865, *Researches into the Early History of Mankind*, London: Murray, p. 108.
18. J. G. Frazer, 1890, *The Golden Bough* (2 vols.), London: Macmillan.
19. J. W. Dougherty, 1978, "Salience and Relativity in Classification," *American Ethnologist* 5: 66–80.
20. He had studied with Wilhelm Wundt in Lepzig.
21. Bronislaw Malinowski, 1967, *A Diary in the Strict Sense of the Term*, New York: Harcourt, Brace and World.
22. For discussions on the relationship between fieldwork and psychotherapy, see Tanya Luhrmann, 1994, "Psychological Anthropology as the Naturalist's Art," and Waud Kracke, 1994, "Reflections on the Savage Self: Introspection, Empathy, and Anthropology," in Marcelo Suarez-Orozco, George Spindler, and Louise Spindler (eds.), *The Making of Psychological Anthropology II*, Fort Worth, TX: Harcourt Brace; Bertram Cohler, 1992, "Intent and Meaning in Psychoanalysis and Cultural Study," and Katherine Ewing, 1992, "Is Psychoanalysis Relevant for Anthropology?" in Theodore Schwartz, Geoffry White, and Catherine Lutz (eds.), *New Directions in Psychological Anthropology*, Cambridge, England: Cambridge University Press.
23. Bronislaw Malinowski, 1948, *Magic, Science and Religion*, Boston: Beacon Press.
24. Malinowski, like Freud, did have a strong awareness of the ambivalent power of human sexuality. See George Stocking, 1986, "Malinowski's Encounter with Freudian Psychoanalysis," in G. Stocking (ed.), *Malinowski, Rivers, Benedict and Others: Essays on Culture and Personality*, Madison: University of Wisconsin Press. Malinowski's famous analysis of the Oedipal complex in the Trobriands was discussed in Chapter 3.
25. S. D. Porteus, 1931, *The Psychology of a Primitive People*, London: Edward Arnold, p. 308.
26. M. Cole, J. Gay, J. Glick, and D. W. Sharp, 1971, *The Cultural Context of Learning and Thinking*, New York: Basic Books; M. Cole and S. Scribner, 1974, *Culture and Thought*, New York: Wiley; J. Gay and M. Cole, 1967, *The New Mathematics and an Old Culture*, New York: Holt, Rinehart and Winston.
27. For these and other examples, see Chapters 3 and 4 in A. R. Luria, 1976, *Cognitive Development: Its Cultural and Social Foundations*, Cambridge, MA: Harvard University Press (first published in Moscow 1974).
28. For a fine account of child raising in a traditional society, see Robert LeVine, Suzanne Dixon, Sarah LeVine, Amy Richman, P. Herbert Leiderman, Constance H. Keefer, and T. Berry Brazelton, 1994, *Child Care and Culture: Lessons from Africa*, Cambridge, England: Cambridge University Press. Of course, there are many exceptions to this generalization, the most famous being the Tiv, an African tribe with a very simple social system but a very Western-like approach to learning and thinking. See D. R. Price-Williams, 1969, "A Study Concerning Concepts of Conservation of Quantities among Primitive Children," in D. R. Price-Williams (ed.), *Cross-Cultural Studies*, Harmondsworth, England: Penguin.
29. For an excellent synopsis of research on socialization and cognition, see Chapter 5 in Robert Munroe and Ruth Munroe, 1994, *Cross Cultural Human Development* (2d ed.), Prospect Heights, IL: Waveland Press.
30. See Roy D'Andrade, 1989, "Culturally Based Reasoning," in A. Gellatly, D. Rogers, and J. Sloboda (eds.), *Cognition and Social Worlds*, Cambridge, England: Cambridge University Press.
31. For a recent example, see Paul Rozin and Carol Nemeroff, 1990, "The Laws of Sympathetic Magic: A Psychological Analysis of Similarity and Contagion," in James

Stigler, Richard Shweder, and Gilbert Herdt (eds.), *Cultural Psychology: Essays on Comparative Human Development,* Cambridge, England: Cambridge University Press. See also Richard Shweder, 1977, "Likeness and Likelihood in Everyday Thought: Magical Thinking in Judgments of Personality," *Current Anthropology* 18: 637–58; R. Nisbett and L. Ross, 1980, *Human Inference: Strategies and Shortcomings of Social Judgment,* Englewood Cliffs, NJ: Prentice-Hall.

32. Shweder, "Likeness and Likelihood in Everyday Thought," p. 638.

33. Although, as we have seen, Malinowski himself was hardly a romantic. For him, the native's point of view was primarily an understanding of his psychological needs, which were for the most part practical and adaptive.

34. Franz Boas, 1910, "Psychological Problems in Anthropology," *American Journal of Psychology* 21: 371–84, reprinted in George Stocking, 1974, *The Shaping of American Anthropology 1883–1911: A Franz Boas Reader,* New York: Basic Books p. 243.

35. Boas moved away from his early fascination with the atomistic collection of traits toward a concern for the totality of a cultural form. For a relevant essay on Boas, see George Stocking, 1992, "Polarity and Plurality: Franz Boas as Psychological Anthropologist," in Theodore Schwartz, Geoffry White, and Catherine Lutz (eds.), *New Directions in Psychological Anthropology,* Cambridge, England: Cambridge University Press.

36. The phrase is from William Manson, 1986, "Kardiner and Neo-Freudian Alternative," in George Stocking (ed.), *Malinowski, Rivers, Benedict and Others: Essays on Culture and Personality,* Madison: University of Wisconsin Press, p. 76.

37. This aspect of psychological anthropology is discussed in Chapter 7.

38. Franz Boas, 1938, "An Anthropologist's Credo," *The Nation,* August 27: 201–2.

39. Sapir, quoted in Richard Handler, 1986, "Vigorous Male and Aspiring Female: Poetry, Personality and Culture in Edward Sapir and Ruth Benedict," in George Stocking (ed.), *Malinowski, Rivers, Benedict and Others: Essays on Culture and Personality,* Madison: University of Wisconsin Press, p. 131.

40. See Edward Sapir, 1949, "Culture, Genuine and Spurious," in David Mandelbaum (ed.), *Selected Writings of Edward Sapir on Language, Culture and Personality,* Berkeley: University of California Press (original publication 1924).

41. Culture and personality thus are systems much like the grammatical and phonetic systems of language. Sapir was one of the first to make this now much-used analogy.

42. Edward Sapir, 1929, "The Status of Linguistics as a Science," *Language* 5: 207–14.

43. See Benjamin Whorf, 1956, "Science and Linguistics" (original publication 1940), in J. Carroll (ed.), *Language, Thought and Reality: Selected Writings of Benjamin Lee Whorf,* Cambridge, MA: MIT Press.

44. Quoted in Regna Darnell, 1986, "The Fate of the Sapirian Alternative," in George Stocking (ed.), *Malinowski, Rivers, Benedict and Others: Essays on Culture and Personality,* Madison: University of Wisconsin Press, p. 164.

45. See Edward E. Sapir, 1923, "The Two Kinds of Human Beings," *Freeman* 8: 211–12; 1933, "Personality," *Encyclopedia of the Social Sciences,* Vol. 12, pp. 85–87, for Sapir's usage of the categories of extravert and introvert, first made popular by the writing of Freud's erstwhile pupil and later rival, Carl Jung. Jung's influence on psychological anthropology will be discussed in Chapter 5.

46. See A. I. Hallowell, 1976, "Psychology and Anthropology" (original publication 1954), reprinted in A. I. Hallowell, *Contributions to Anthropology: Selected Papers of A. Irving Hallowell,* Chicago: University of Chicago Press. According to Hallowell, the major influences on Benedict did not include Gestalt psychology but, rather, Wilhelm Dilthey's argument that one could understand a culture by looking at the motives of its dominant philosophy and Oswald Spengler's characterization of the classical

world as Apollonian and the modern world as Faustian. Nietzsche uses the same categories in 1967, *Birth of Tragedy and the Case of Wagner,* New York: Vintage (original publication 1872).

47. 1989, *Patterns of Culture,* Boston: Houghton Mifflin (original publication 1934).
48. 1946, *The Chrysanthemum and the Sword,* Boston: Houghton Mifflin.
49. Benedict, *Patterns of Culture,* pp. 254, 113. See also Ruth Benedict, 1934, "Anthropology and the Abnormal," *Journal of General Psychology* 10: 59–80.
50. 1928, *Coming of Age in Samoa,* New York: Morrow.
51. Margaret Mead, 1963, *Sex and Temperament in Three Primitive Societies,* New York: William Morrow, p. 280 (original publication 1935).
52. See Derek Freeman, 1983, *Samoa: The Making of an Anthropological Myth,* Cambridge, MA: Harvard University Press.
53. For discussion of this controversy, see Lowell Holmes, 1987, *Quest for the Real Samoa: The Mead/Freeman Controversy and Beyond,* South Hadley, MA: Bergin and Garvey; Martin Orans, 1996, *Not Even Wrong: Margaret Mead, Derek Freeman, and the Samoans,* Novato, CA: Chandler and Sharp.
55. Mead, *Coming of Age in Samoa,* p. 191.
54. For classic texts, see John B. Watson, 1930, *Behaviorism,* New York: Norton; B. F. Skinner, 1953, *Science and Human Behavior,* New York: Macmillan.
56. Benedict, *Patterns of Culture,* p. 258.
57. These points are elaborated in Chapter 11.
58. For this point, see Victor Barnouw, 1985, *Culture and Personality* (4th ed.), Chicago: Dorsey Press.
59. 1936, *Naven,* Cambridge, England: Cambridge University Press.
60. In the ensuing analysis, I am in debt to Charles Nuckolls, 1996, *The Cultural Dialectics of Knowledge and Desire,* Madison: University of Wisconsin Press.
61. Bateson's theory has its intellectual roots in Durkheim's notion of collective effervescence, where collective ritual performances emotionally revitalize and unite society; what Bateson added is a Hegelian dialectical and processual analysis of how this renewal occurs. Why opposition should necessarily call forth self-correction was not addressed by Bateson; he assumed that what he had discovered was a cybernetic feedback loop. He later went on to explore the parallel between cultural balancing systems and naturally occurring feedback circuits.
62. For this comparison, see Nuckolls, *The Cultural Dialectics,* p. 59.
63. See Gregory Bateson, 1972, *Steps to an Ecology of Mind,* San Francisco: Chandler. See Chapter 11 for more on schizophrenia.
64. With no mention of Bateson, the notion of ritual as a kind of outlet for forbidden desires was later taken up by Max Gluckman (1954, *Rituals of Rebellion in Southeast Africa,* Manchester, England: Manchester University Press) and by Victor Turner (1957, *Schism and Continuity in an African Society: A Study of Ndembu Village Life,* Manchester, England: Manchester University Press), but it is a Freudian view as well. See Chapters 7 and 11 for more on this topic.

CHAPTER 5

The Psychoanalysis of Culture

In 1941, an event that was to prove decisive to the future of psychological anthropology occurred: The central administration of Columbia University invited Ralph Linton (1893–1953) to take over the Department of Anthropology, replacing the venerable Franz Boas. Linton, who had attended Columbia, but who had received his doctorate from Harvard, was a functionalist, interested in acculturation and the diffusion of material culture. His appointment was a direct rebuke to Boas's student Ruth Benedict, who had fully expected to inherit her mentor's position and to use her power to promote configurationism. Linton's arrival split the Columbia department into rival factions, with many students remaining loyal to Benedict and Mead.

The split in the department became even more acute when Linton embraced a brand of culture and personality research far more psychoanalytic than the configurationist approach favored by Mead and Benedict. Linton was converted to his new view through participation in seminars on the relation between psychoanalysis and anthropology held at the New York Psychoanalytic Insti-

Freud's study in London, showing his famous couch and his large collection of ethnographic objects.

tute. These seminars had been initiated by Abram Kardiner (1891–1981), a psychotherapist who had been trained by Freud and who also had studied with Boas. As soon as he was able, Linton brought Kardiner to Columbia, directly challenging Benedict and Mead, who were increasingly marginalized despite their great public fame. Thus began a trend that ended in the near complete discrediting of Benedict and Mead's brand of configurationist culture and personality theory, and the rise of a more psychoanalytic model of the relationship between individual and society. The story of this shift, and the permutations of the complex and often hostile relationship between psychoanalysis and anthropology, is the subject of the next two chapters.[1]

Chapter Outline

I. CAN THERE BE A FREUDIAN ANTHROPOLOGY?

A The Origin of Diaperology
   The use and abuse of Freud by configurationist culture and personality theorists.

B Conflicts in the Models
   Cultural diversity versus universalism. Adaption and integration versus resistance and ambivalence.

C Possibilities for a Rapprochement
   The potential for a synthesis combining interpretive psychoanalysis and anthropology.

A. The Origin of Diaperology

Could anthropology and psychoanalysis live together? Freud certainly thought so. In *Totem and Taboo: Resemblances between the Psychic Lives of Savages and*

Neurotics[2] he utilized contemporary anthropological theory, arguing, like Lewis Henry Morgan, that civilization developed through stages, becoming more and more complex over time. For Freud, however, what was important was not technical innovation or the evolution of social organization, but the way in which the psyche was transformed and the changes in worldview that resulted, as human beings progressed from infantile animism to Oedipal religion, finally evolving to civilized rationality. Freud thought that cultures could be measured as relatively mature or immature, according to the stage of development reached; they could also be psychoanalyzed much as a neurotic patient would be, with rituals conceptualized as the equivalent of dreams and symptoms. The insights gained would reveal the unconscious motivations that drive human evolution.

When anthropologists looked at Freud's ambitious efforts, they were not impressed. In a famous review of *Totem and Taboo*, Boas's student Alfred Kroeber (1876–1960), who was sympathetic to psychological explanations of cultural trends, nonetheless likened the book to a butterfly—beautiful, fragile, and easily crushed by hard facts. Freud, Kroeber said, had a poetic gift but paid no attention to the variations of culture and always found what he was looking for; his work was reductionist, inaccurate, and impossibly flawed.[3] Most other anthropologists felt the same, including those interested in the relationship between culture and individual personality, who might have been expected to be the most favorably disposed toward Freud. They distrusted psychoanalysis for two reasons: first, because it implied that humanity was universally impelled by innate dynamic drives, thus reducing the importance of culture, and second, because it appeared to be based on unprovable hypothetical premises of instincts, complexes, and mechanisms of defense.[4]

As we have seen, Bateson's dialectical model had the most significant parallels with the Freudian paradigm, yet he was drawn toward the study of cybernetics and systems theory instead. The eclectic Sapir had an intellectual interest in psychoanalysis, but he dismissed most of Freud's theory as "either ill-founded or seen in distorted perspective."[5] He was more inclined toward the Jungian notion of elemental character types interacting with culture. Benedict too had an affinity for Jungian archetypes, as is evident in her designation of entire societies as Apollonian and megalomaniac.[6] Unfortunately, this form of wholesale typologizing has proved a theoretical dead end.

Like Sapir, Benedict and Mead opposed Freud's theory of a universal pattern of psychosexual growth: Benedict asserted that the Zuni, as a matrilineal and highly ritualized society, had neither an Oedipal conflict nor a sense of guilt,[7] while Mead declared that the Samoans had no latency period and did not repress their adolescent sexuality. Both Benedict and Mead portrayed the unconscious not as a raging id, but as the passive repository of cultural symbol systems; most importantly, they saw little conflict between individual and society, or within individuals themselves. In fact, most of these early theorists simply scavenged Freud for concepts they found useful (such as repression, sublimation, projection, reaction formation, and rationalization), while discarding those

---

Jungian Anthropology

Carl Jung (1875–1961) was one of Freud's closest disciples, but he eventually split acrimoniously with Freud and developed a psychological theory of his own that became very influential with many artists and some anthropologists during the 1930s. The son of a clergyman, Jung was a prophetic figure who wished to establish an alternative to Christianity. In his new psychological metareligion, he took his inspiration from medieval alchemists, envisioning an eternal battle between reason and spontaneity that existed beneath the surface of all human life. All art, according to Jung, referred to this ageless relationship; human history was a process in which one side or the other gained power momentarily, leading inevitably to compensation; individual characters also could be placed within preexistent archetypical categories (as extroverts or introverts); the same could be said of entire cultures and religions.

More positive than Freud, Jung believed redemption could be found in the unconscious production of fantasy and myth, which he thought united intellect and passion in a creative synthesis; he spent years compiling interminable lists of myths from all over the world as illustrations of his point.[8] In terms of therapy, each individual was to look inward, to discover his or her own particular archetypical myth, and enact it in fantasy and dream.

It is evident how such a theory would appeal to artists, who found Jung's claims ratified their own faith in the power of the imagination.[9] Jung's static theory of archetypes and his method of piling up decontextualized myths as if they were proofs also greatly influenced Joseph Campbell, the hugely popular writer, who asserted in his book *The Hero with a Thousand Faces*[10] that all human myths could be read as a narrative about the eternal quest for rebirth.

Laypeople often take the writings of Campbell and Jung as fact, but, in general, anthropologists have not found any evidence of the universality or priority of the simple mythic forms they recount and dismiss them both for ransacking whole cultures to pick out narratives that are used irresponsibly to validate their own religious visions.

---

they did not like. It is striking that an anthropology bent on repudiating the old Frazerian method of collecting traits without context had no qualms about picking and choosing concepts from Freud while ignoring the larger theory that gave those concepts meaning.

One of the Freudian notions most accepted was that of the crucial importance of early childhood training in the formation of adult personality. Mead especially instructed her students to pay close attention to breast-feeding schedules and toilet training procedures, which led her opponents to satirize her approach as diaperology.

B. Conflicts in the Models

Although Mead and other culture and personality theorists did utilize Freudian theories about the importance of the oral, anal-genital socialization of children for the later development of character, in general their interest in childhood reflected the behaviorist premise that (with the exception of congenital deviants) human beings are malleable creatures who are molded to fit into the social world in which they find themselves.[11] Within this paradigm, the job of the researcher is to discover what the shaping principles of the social world are and perhaps to document the processes by which individuals are enculturated into it.

In contrast, Freud's theories about the human condition were much more conflictual. For him, human beings were innately torn by implacable and antagonistic urges toward Eros and Thanatos, communion and separation. These drives collided with each other and with the constraints of physical reality and social convention: The result was the structure of id-ego-superego (or desire-reason-conscience). This model of the mind greatly reduced the autonomy of society and the power of learning, and placed an irreducible knot of contradiction and tragedy at the core of the human experience. Civilization, Freud said, was a vast symbolic defense mechanism against dangerous impulses, offering beliefs and rituals as substitutes for forbidden objects of desire. But Freud was also certain that "it does not seem as though any influence could induce a man to change his nature into a termite's."[12] Humanity would always struggle to break the cultural chains that they—like Hobbesian men manufacturing their social contract—had forged to protect them against themselves. The tragic Promethean struggle that Freud saw as the essence of the human condition was a radical contrast to the rational and functional portrait of humanity favored by behaviorist psychology and its anthropological confederates.

Indeed, if behaviorism had an elective affinity with functionalist cultural anthropology, Freudian theory appeared to be its natural enemy. Freudian theorists such as Geza Roheim (1891–1953) insisted that culture was no more (and no less) than the comforting fantasies of a baby who is afraid of being left alone in the dark.[13] The cultural baby could make up amazing lies to comfort itself—these lies were the stuff of culture—but an enlightened psychoanalyst could see through such fictions and reveal, beneath daily practice and rationalization, the underlying truths of the repressed Oedipal conflict and deep-seated ambivalence to authority. Anthropologists rightly worried that this approach would turn their discipline into an adjunct of psychoanalysis, eliminating the variations and richness of cultural meaning systems by reducing them, as Freud himself said, to "the symptoms presented by a neurosis."[14]

The differences can be outlined as follows:

- *Configurationist anthropology.* Each culture is autonomous, unique, diverse. Humans are malleable and adaptive. The unconscious is a repository of cultural symbols. There is no fundamental conflict between individual and society, nor does Oedipal conflict exist.
- *Psychoanalytic theory.* All cultures symbolically express repressed desires. Humans are ambivalent. The unconscious is full of conflicting impulses. Individuals resist integration into society. The Oedipal conflict is universal.

C. Possibilities for a Rapprochement

Despite these seemingly irreconcilable differences, it was hard for anthropologists to deny that psychoanalytic explanations of cultural facts could be very convincing. Consider Freud's theory about the taboos that commonly surround chiefs in many societies. These taboos may prevent leaders from eating certain foods, severely limit their movements, oblige them to talk only through a mediator, forbid them from interacting freely with their subjects, and so on. Reasoning from his own clinical experiences, Freud argued that these disparate phenomena can be explained as expressions of ambivalence. The authority of the chief, like the authority of the father, awakens not only love and admiration but also profound jealousy and rage, which, through the psychic defense mechanism of the reaction formation, is sublimated in overly ostentatious demonstrations of slavish devotion and worshipful subordination. But deep negative feelings are nonetheless unconsciously expressed in the numerous restrictions imposed upon the ruler. "The ceremonial taboo of kings is *ostensibly* the highest honor and protection for them, while *actually* it is punishment for their exaltation" (italics in original).[15] In this analysis, Freud made sense of apparently inexplicable material in a new way.

In many respects, then, the cultural theory proposed by Freud provided what configurationist anthropology lacked: an encompassing and dynamic universal concept of motivation based on deep patterns of human desire. Psychoanalysis also portrayed human beings as rebellious, passionate, and conflicted creatures of flesh and blood, not as cutout, one-dimensional figures, concerned solely with maximizing their benefits or conforming to arbitrary cultural conventions. The advantages Freudian theory offered, however, were offset by the fact that psychoanalysts tended to see culture as neurosis writ large; they ignored the best of what anthropology had to offer, that is, rich descriptive portraits of specific cultural entities with their own complex symbolic realities, histories, worldviews, and economic and political systems. The sweeping generalizations made by Freud and his followers, and the tendency of some psychoanalytic theorists to regard any critics as "in denial" also convinced many anthropologists that psychoanalysis was a self-ratifying system, one that always gave the same answers to every question, yet refused to be questioned itself.

Despite these reasonable qualms, commitment to a psychoanalytic study of culture does not, in principle, have to foreclose alliance with anthropology. After all, psychoanalysis is an interpretive endeavor, mutually undertaken by patient and doctor. The patient must both intellectually participate in and emotionally connect with the analyst's interpretation. If not, the analysis is unsuccessful. Similarly, in the study of culture, psychoanalysts, like anthropologists, are interpreters who must contextualize their information and "take the native's point of view," rather than simply assume that all anger against authority is necessarily an expression of Oedipal rage or that all enclosures are metaphors for the womb. There is no need then for anthropologists to fear that psychoanalytic study of culture will automatically reduce all social facts to sexual symbols.[16]

Nor does a psychoanalytic approach necessarily block anthropological attempts to explain daily life in terms of function, economy, belief, power, or social structure; neither does it preclude historical, biological, or cognitive analysis. In principle, Freudian interpretation applies only to material that stands out as emotionally vivid, symbolically rich, and powerfully motivating. In the psychoanalysis of culture, focus ought to be fixed primarily on the intensely colored rituals, dense symbol systems, and emotionally heightened relationships that reveal the hidden anxieties and fantasies of the society. Just as analysis of a patient's dream or neurotic symptom requires knowledge of the concrete circumstances of his or her life, the analysis of cultural material requires knowledge of the ecology, politics, history, social organization, and philosophy of the society. This is where anthropological research is required. It seems, then, that despite the hegemonic tendencies of each discipline, anthropology and psychoanalysis could make an alliance, each making use of what the other has to offer. Psychoanalysis might provide a way to understand the deepest tensions of the society, while anthropology could provide the necessary contextual framework. But who would attempt such a reconciliation?

II. NEO-FREUDIAN APPROACHES: KARDINER, DU BOIS, AND ERIKSON

A Kardiner's Synthesis
   Kardiner's Marxist reading of Freud: primary institutions → basic personality structure → secondary institutions.

B Accounting for Differences
   Du Bois's theory of modal personality. Problems of understanding variation and causation.

C Erik Erikson's Weberian Perspective
   Culture and the search for meaning. Fixations and the possibility of maladaption.

D Erikson's Eight Stages and the Question of Identity
   Erikson's developmental theory. Adolescence and leadership.

A. Kardiner's Synthesis

It was clear that no synthesis between psychoanalysis and anthropology could be attained by the determinedly culturalist configurationism practiced by Benedict and Mead. Instead, it was their rival, Ralph Linton, who made the attempt to achieve a unity between the two disciplines by recruiting Abram Kardiner to offer a seminar on the psychoanalytic interpretation of cultural material. Kardiner was aided by Cora Du Bois, a postdoctoral anthropology graduate from Berkeley who had done work on psychological assessment at Harvard. She and Kardiner were strongly influenced by recent American neo-Freudian theory, which maintained that Freud had overestimated the power of the biological drives, while underestimating the adaptive capacities of the ego.[17] Minimizing the libido also meant questioning the centrality of the Oedipus complex, and Kardiner called instead for a greater emphasis on the culturally determined frustrations of a child's dependency needs; these were considered to have an especially powerful influence on personality development. For Kardiner, it was not libido, but discipline and the infant's reaction to discipline, that had to be at the center of any comparative inquiry.[18] The "I" here begins to take precedence over the "it"—a development far more congenial to the American faith in individual responsibility. At the same time, for Kardiner, as for Mead, Benedict, and Bateson, the individual still remained strangely anonymous.[19]

Because of the significance he placed on socialization and institutions, Kardiner's theory revolved around an argument about the relative weight of the various aspects of culture: Some were essential for the formation of character; others were merely secondary projections. Following Freud, but using detailed ethnographic material, Kardiner said that secondary projections consisted of religion, myth, and art; these symbolically reflect and express fundamental tensions of the collective, just as dreams symbolically reflect and express the tensions of the individual. In contrast, primary institutions are those that directly affect the developing ego in the context of the family. Mixing Freud with Marx, Kardiner affirmed that differences in the division of labor and the mode of production made for distinctive weaning methods, toilet training, and so on. The interrelation of these various influences, Kardiner said, would create typical problems for the adaption of everyone's ego in a society, resulting in a basic personality structure. The internal conflicts of this basic personality would be symbolically reflected in the secondary systems of art and religion. (See Figure 5.1.)

In developing his formula, Kardiner also introduced a mechanism for change, which had been conspicuously lacking in earlier studies. Shifts in any of the fundamental institutions would necessarily lead to alterations in personality and then in the projective systems. Thus, a new mode of production might entail a different division of labor, which could impel novel child-raising techniques, a shift in the basic personality, and changes in ritual and religion. As a present-day case, consider the new prevalence in the United States of the middle-class family with two working parents, which is a consequence of wider economic changes in capitalism. The latchkey children raised in these new households will presumably receive less maternal attention and participate more in day care centers and nursery schools than did their parents. As a result, they ought to develop basic personalities different from those of their parents, leading them to have different values, beliefs, and tastes as adults: What these might consist of must be a matter

$$C_1 \longrightarrow P_1 \longrightarrow C_2$$

FIGURE 5.1. Basic personality structure. C_1 indicates the primary institutions of culture; P_1 is the personality that develops as a result; C_2 is the projective aspect of the culture that appears as a result of personality conflicts.

of conjecture. Perhaps they will be more communally oriented, or perhaps they will have more anxieties about abandonment, or both.[20]

Kardiner's conjectures took much of what Freud had already said about family structure and personality development and mixed it with economic and cultural determinism. Freud might have agreed with a great deal of this, but he would surely have strongly objected to the emasculation of the drives and their replacement by mechanisms of ego adaption. But by reducing the importance of the id and ignoring Freud's metapsychological dialectic between Eros and Thanatos, Kardiner eliminated the tragic dimension of psychoanalysis and rendered it palatable for many skeptical American anthropologists. His revisionist paradigm shifted away from universalist arguments about the unresolvable human struggle against impulse and toward investigation of the particular combinations of economic structures, political institutions, and family structure that constructed a basic personality. This was, it seemed, a culturally nuanced psychology that anthropologists could use.

B. Accounting for Differences

The first to use Kardiner's theories was Du Bois, who was armed with them when she set off to undertake fieldwork in the small Melanesian island of Alor. There she applied her earlier training in psychological testing and employed Rorschach and other projective instruments; she also collected a number of detailed biographies that she used in her ethnography[21] in order to solve the problem of personal variability within culture, which Kardiner's formula had not really addressed. Du Bois argued that not everyone in Alor fit into one basic personality type, but that there was instead a statistically predominant modal personality. (See Figure 5.2.) In Alor, this personality was produced as a result of infant neglect, which was a consequence of the requirements of subsistence farming and the sexual division of labor, which obliged women to be away from their children most of the day.

Commenting on Du Bois's ethnography, Kardiner claimed that the tenuous relationship of Alorese children to their mothers would necessarily make for a psychically conflicted adulthood, marked by an inability to make personal connections and a pervasive sense of suspicion and resentment. These modal attitudes were reflected in myths of the trickery and deceitfulness of the gods, a folklore full of tales of maternal animosity, an apathetic affect, and an absence of

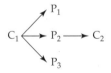

FIGURE 5.2 Modal personality structure. P_1, P_2, P_3 indicate the alternative personality structures developing from a culture's primary institutions (C_1). P_2 is the dominant or modal personality type, and gives rise to the culture's secondary institutions (C_2).

Projective Tests

Anthropologists in the 1940s and 1950s made great use of projective tests of various sorts in an effort to get at the underlying psychological states of informants in a way that was scientifically valid and verifiable. The most famous was the Rorschach, or inkblot, test. Abstract inky shapes were shown to informants who were asked to say what the figures reminded them of. Other widely used projective instruments included the TAT (thematic apperception test), in which simple drawings of enigmatic but evocative scenes were shown to informants who were asked to say what they thought the scene depicted. Another was the draw-a-man test. The idea was that these tests would serve as stimuli for fantasy. Experts would then interpret the responses and make judgments about the respondent's unconscious personality structure and underlying motivations.

But it was never clear how the experts arrived at their conclusions, nor was it possible to say that their interpretations were any more legitimate than anyone else's—particularly when cross-cultural differences in language and symbolism were taken into account. As a result, such tests lost credibility and fell into disuse. Of late, however, some anthropologists have called for a return to a more judicious and limited use of projective tests, particularly when dealing with extremely painful material. Marcelo Suarez-Orozco, for example, has discovered that children who have had horrific experiences of warfare and torture could not talk about their feelings, but could communicate them indirectly in their responses to projective tests.[22]

---

art. A psychoanalyst's examination of the Rorschach tests dutifully administered by Du Bois appeared to verify an unattractive portrait of the Alorese as "anxious, suspicious, mistrustful, lacking in confidence, with no interest in the outside world"[23]—a picture that was hard to reconcile with Du Bois's own account of the warm welcome she was accorded by the Alorese and the pleasure they were reported to take in socializing with one another.[24]

In hindsight, it is evident that despite their efforts to take into account the complexities of human motivation and their development of a statistical model of typical character, Kardiner and Du Bois had not really advanced much beyond the configurationists in their equation of personality with culture. Well aware of this problem, Du Bois had been one of the first ethnographers actually to present complex autobiographical material to flesh out her portrait of the Alorese, but this material showed that even the statistical modal personality formula she proposed was too narrow.[25] It was obvious that putting all the Alorese into a box labeled "nurturance-deprived" was an injustice to them and an oversimplification of the evidence. Nor could her material show why other societies that were equally nurturance-deprived did not display the same mangled personalities. Du Bois herself admitted that the fundamental problem of psychological anthropology still remained the discovery of "which aspects of human personality are universal, which are very frequent and which are unique to given socio-cultural groups."[26]

The Sacred Cow and Other Prohibitions

Nowhere have anthropological disputes about causation been more complex than in the discussion of food prohibitions. For instance, in India, cattle cannot be killed or harmed. Symbolic anthropologists accept the Hindu claim that cows have a special place in myth and that this is the reason they are protected. Materialist anthropologists, in contrast, have argued that the prohibition on killing cows is purely functional. Cows are not eaten because their labor is needed and because milk is a reliable source of protein. In other words, cows are more valuable alive than dead. Hindu myth is simply a way of ideologically reaffirming an ecological necessity.

A similar argument has been made about the Jewish prohibition on eating pork. Some anthropologists say this is best understood as a way to ward off the danger posed by the omniverous pig to scarce food supplies in the Middle East. Because the pig is so destructive, its meat is tabooed. An equally functional explanation is that the pig carries diseases and is forbidden for that reason. But these explanations cannot account for taboos such as the Jewish prohibition on eating lobster and shellfish, or the prohibition on mixing flesh and dairy. These can be understood only within a symbolic system in which anomalies and mixing of categories are held to be repugnant. Pigs, with their cloven hooves, and lobsters, with their shells, are not typical land or sea creatures and therefore are not to be eaten, just as milk and meat, as opposed symbolic categories, are not to be brought into contact.[27]

Kardiner and Du Bois were also stymied by the knotty problem of distinguishing between primary and secondary institutions, a dilemma that had already confounded Malinowski's efforts to divide practical reason from magical thought,[28] and that had made it impossible for Marxists to draw a hard-and-fast line between economic base and ideological superstructure. Although at first it seemed straightforward enough to say that myth is secondary and mode of production is primary, critics soon noted that beliefs can affect the mode of production in profound ways—a prohibition on female participation in hunting, for example, might very well be sanctioned by myths about female pollution; resistance to the cultivation of a new vegetable might be validated by a belief that the cultivar in question is used in witchcraft, and so on. In short, the complex constellation of personality construction that Kardiner proposed proved unwieldy and confusing, and the attractively straight causal arrow he had drawn ended up looking incongruously bent.

C. Erik Erikson's Weberian Perspective

Despite its deficiencies, the paradigm developed by Kardiner and Du Bois has continued to have great appeal to cultural theorists attempting to reconcile the psychoanalytic and the anthropological views of humanity, precisely because it offers some way of talking about the relative influence of various aspects of culture on personality. One writer who was much in debt to them was the child psychologist Erik Erikson, whose wide-ranging book *Childhood and Society* (first published in 1950)[29] continues to be read and debated. Erikson, like Kardiner, was strongly influenced by ego psychology; he too jettisoned Freud's libido theory and discarded Freud's postulate of the struggle of Eros and Thanatos. For him, as for Kardiner and later object relations theorists,[30] what was central to development was frustration of the child's fundamental desire for intimacy and dependency. Repression of that desire, Erikson believed, was the motor for human development—but only if repression was felt to be *meaningful.* Here Erikson departed from Kardiner, who had emphasized the effects of the mode of production on childhood discipline, which led in turn to typical personalities. Whereas Kardiner utilized Marx, Erikson was more influenced by Weber and stressed the importance of the coherence of beliefs and values for structuring personality and channeling the individual's energies toward a culturally sanctioned goal.

One of the most controversial aspects of Erikson's work was his claim that whole cultures are fixated at different stages of their sexual-social development as a result of the characteristic frustrations and indulgences of their child training. According to Erikson, these frustrations function to direct the individual into the pursuit of cultural goals and values. The personality of the Sioux, for instance, was said to be largely set as a result of the indulgent breast-feeding characteristic of the society, which was not curtailed even when the child began biting the mother. The free-flowing oral abundance of infancy was both validated and expressed in adulthood through the general cultural approval of generosity and selflessness, while punishment for biting created repressed anger that could then be properly released in later life as bravery in hunting and rage against tribal enemies. In other words, child-raising practices develop children who are fixated at a certain stage of their development. This fixation, however, was not neurotic. Rather, it allowed members to function well within their culture—they became adults who were psychologically impelled to do what the culture demanded they ought to do.

Like Kardiner, but in a rather more direct fashion, Erikson believed the psychic conflicts caused by the frustrations of infancy were later dealt with in the projective systems of religion and ritual. For instance, in the central performance of the Sioux faith, the sun dance, Sioux men impaled themselves and tore their chests; they were then nursed by their sisters. Erikson explained this powerful ritual as an expiation for the male child's early biting attacks on the breast and a recapitulation of the nurturing mother-son relationship. Notwithstanding his disclaimer that he was "not saying . . . if you turned a few knobs in your child-training system . . . you fabricated this or that kind of tribal or national character,"[31] it is evident that Erikson placed a very heavy emphasis on the supposed long-term effects of techniques of weaning and toilet training—a return to Mead's much disparaged diaperology.

Erikson concurred with Kardiner that shifts in production and relations of power could completely alter the personalities of people in a society. However, whereas other theorists were interested primarily in adaption, Erikson used the Sioux case to show how difficult change could be, especially under conditions of conquest, and how formerly functional behaviors could become quite the

The Sioux sun dance as portrayed by George Catlin in 1835.

opposite when one society was subordinated to another. The Sioux emphasis on generosity and their noncompetitive relationships with one another, for example, did not mesh well with the American ethos of competitive capitalism, while the bravery and anger that were easily expressed in their former culture of warfare and hunting could find no outlet in the placid agricultural life they were obliged to live. As a result, the Sioux became apathetic, depressed, and prone to bursts of alcoholic fury. In making his analysis of Sioux social dysfunction, Erikson began to bring to the fore resistance to cultural hegemony, albeit only in the form of psychic disarray. Further, he began to comment on the terrible mutilations of personal identity caused by colonialism, a factor ignored by Mead, Du Bois, and other culture and personality theorists, but one that would take on ever greater importance in modern anthropological studies.[32] Erikson also made extensive use of psychological case histories in his writing, prefiguring later anthropological interest in the lives of actual persons.[33]

D. Erikson's Eight Stages and the Question of Identity

Erikson showed originality as well in his extension of the process of character formation out of childhood into adulthood and in his stress on the moral meaning of the various stages themselves. Moving beyond the orthodox oral-anal-genital phases, Erikson said that the development of character continued throughout the life span. He outlined eight stages, each of which produced a typical set of characterological dilemmas, to be either surmounted or not. (See Figure 5.3.) In his formulation, Erikson greatly reduced the importance of drives

	1	2	3	4	5	6	7	8
VIII Maturity								Ego integrity vs. Despair
VII Adulthood							Generativity vs. Stagnation	
VI Young adulthood						Intimacy vs. Isolation		
V Puberty and adolescence					Identity vs. Role confusion			
IV Latency				Industry vs. Inferiority				
III Locomotor-genital			Initiative vs. Guilt					
II Muscular-anal		Autonomy vs. Shame, doubt						
I Oral sensory	Basic trust vs. Mistrust							

FIGURE 5.3. Erikson's eight stages of human development.
Source: Erik Erikson, 1950, Childhood and Society, New York: Norton, p. 273.

125

and addressed instead the moral issues he saw as typical of each period in a person's life. While Freud had concentrated on the libidinal pleasures felt by an infant sucking the breast and on the pain caused by weaning, Erikson portrayed the oral stage as the period of life when children learn trust by realizing that their mothers are reliable. If trust is not learned, Erikson said, then the infant will lack the ego strength to continue in development. Each stage was taken to correlate with a particular social institution; for example, trust was required for the development of religion. Thus, whereas Freud correlated religion with the Oedipal phase, in which the child internalizes the ethical demands of the punishing superego-father, Erikson portrayed religion as an expression of the encompassing love of the nurturing mother toward her baby.

Ideally, a person would successfully negotiate all the stages, dying as a respected elder after reconcilation with the limits and potentials offered by society. Erikson, as a therapist, assumed throughout his writings that certain attitudes were innately moral and healthy and that he knew quite well what the best life trajectory ought to be. He also believed that some cultures could be categorized as sick, maladapted, and neurotic, or merely primitive, while others were at a higher stage in their development.

Our own complex and technologically sophisticated culture, Erikson thought, was fixated at the adolescent stage, far removed in the developmental plane from the orality of the Sioux and other technologically simple societies where the main worries are finding enough to eat and keeping safe. Erikson believed that the problem to be solved for the adolescent is one of identity. A teenager must move away from the family of birth to establish a new and stable sense of self. This means the exploration of alternative lifestyles, participation in peer groups, emotional excesses, moralistic attitudes, hero worship, and a host of other well-known patterns of behavior. Similarly, according to Erikson, America as a culture was in the process of moving away from old European identities, but had not yet found a new stable character for itself.[34] Erikson continued drawing analogies between adolescence and nationalism throughout his career.

Of special importance in this project was his psychoanalytic reading of the characters of national leaders, such as Luther, Gandhi, and Hitler. He portrayed them as deeply divided individuals whose public enactment of their psychic dramas of personal identity mirrored the tensions of the culture as a whole. Because the masses could find both emotional release and meaning through participation in the leader's performance, these charismatic figures could gain vast authority and the power to transform society.[35] By undertaking this type of analysis, Erikson actually did what Sapir had promised: He showed the dialectical relationship between creative individuals and their larger cultural environment.

Naturally, some of Erikson's work is susceptible to the same criticisms offered to his colleagues and predecessors, particularly his overly schematic view of the relationship between child-rearing practices and adult personality. Also questionable are his evolutionary and therapeutic assumptions, which led him to accept without qualms a standardized view of mental and cultural health, a connection between stages of development and social institutions, and a moral model of personality growth that nowadays seems simplistic. But Erikson offered an advance on earlier theories in stressing the importance of development throughout the life cycle, in showing the psychic consequences of change and conquest, and in focusing on the construction of identity as a particular problem in modernity. Finally, by undertaking the analysis of culture heroes, he built a bridge between anthropology, history, and psychoanalysis.

III. FREEDOM AND REPRESSION: THE STUDY OF NATIONAL CHARACTER

A Radical Visions: The Frankfurt School
Critical theory: culture and class, repressive families, capitalism and alienation.

B The Struggle for Eros
Resistance to domination and drive for emancipation. Tensions within critical theory.

C American Interpretations
American studies of national character: Gorer, Riesman, Slater, and Lasch. Problems of interpretation.

A. Radical Visions: The Frankfurt School

Culture and personality theory, and especially research on national character, reached its apogee during World War II, when the Allies sought to utilize the insights of psychological anthropology to rally civilians, improve military esprit de corps, stimulate resistance movements, and undermine enemy morale. After Pearl Harbor, many anthropologists and psychologists were rapidly drafted into government service, where they were asked to make policy recommendations and prepare reports on the national character of America's enemies and allies.[36] Mead worked on a government committee concerned with changing the American diet, while Bateson became associated with the Secret Service, and Benedict was enlisted into the Office of Overseas Intelligence on the project that eventually led to her writing *The Chrysanthemum and the Sword.*

The study of national character was abetted by the arrival in America of members of the so-called Frankfurt school, a group of brilliant German philosophers, psychologists, and social theorists, including Erich Fromm (1900–1980) and Theodor Adorno (1903–1969), as well as Max Horkheimer (1895–1973) and Herbert Marcuse (1898–1979). These refugees willingly joined their American counterparts in the fight against Hitler, but maintained their European perspectives on the relationship between culture and personality, which had been formed by their readings of Hegel, Marx, and Freud, and which they had amalgamated into a complex philosophical approach they called critical theory. The Frankfurt school's contribution to the debate about the place of culture in the development of the individual provided an ideological counterpoint to the more conservative writings of American culture and personality theorists, and has had a great, if sometimes subterranean, influence on later writers.

Although the Frankfurt school had originally been concerned with developing a more sophisticated Marxist social theory, during the early years of the Hitler era, they had also formulated a psychological test called the F-scale, which they believed could predict authoritarian attitudes through the answers of respondents to a set of questions. To their dismay, the test showed quite decisively that the majority of German workers, who should have objectively supported the Left, were instead far more likely to follow Hitler. This is one of the few times in history that a psychological test has had practical effect, since most of the Frankfurt school, forewarned, were able to escape the Holocaust by prudently emigrating to the United States. This seminal test was eventually published in 1950 as *The Authoritarian Personality*, with Adorno as the senior author.[37]

In an effort to explain the seemingly perverse political attitudes of German workers, critical theorists sought to integrate psychoanalysis into the standard Marxist theory of class warfare and the proletariat vanguard. Faced with the reality of working-class fascism, they realized that progressive social change could not occur by merely changing the economy but required changes in family structure as well. According to this theory, authoritarian personalities arose in family constellations consisting of distant but rigid and patriarchal fathers and overwhelmingly close yet powerless mothers. So long as such family situations existed, liberation was impossible, since the children growing up under these conditions would have weak egos and would readily submit to tyranny. This postulate evidently had much in common with the notions being put forward by culture and personality theorists, in which childhood experiences were seen as central for the development of adult attitudes. The major difference was that while culture and personality theorists favored an integrative view of culture, Adorno and his colleagues argued that repression and violence in the family could lead to a wholly dysfunctional and violent society. Also, their interest was not so much in the specifics of toilet training and weaning but in patterns of authority in the household and throughout the society at large.[38]

Critical theorists also moved beyond the analysis of the authoritarian family structure to argue that the rise of the Nazis could be understood only in the wider context of modernity. In America, the most influential spokesman of this perspective was the psychotherapist Erich Fromm, who in *Escape From Freedom* (published in 1941)[39] traced the rise of individualism (much as I did in Chapters 2 and 3) in order to show that human beings, thrust out of their traditional bonds with one another by the rising forces of capitalism, gradually found themselves deprived of meaning and goals. Agreeing with Freud that "society can function socially, but cripple its members,"[40] Fromm saw the growth of the modern worldview, with its emphasis on freedom from all obligations, as the cradle for authoritarianism:

> The frightened individual seeks for somebody or something to tie his self to; he cannot bear to be his own individual self any longer, and he tries frantically to get rid of it and to feel security again by the elimination of this burden: the self.[41]

By submitting to power, the alienated individual loses unwanted autonomy, gains security, and can freely vent rage against outsiders and inferiors. This pattern, Fromm said, was characteristic of Nazi Germany, but existed as well in the United States, albeit in a culturally specific and weaker form.

Like other critical theorists, Fromm said very little about organ modes or toilet training and chided American culture and personality theorists for explaining cultural differences by differences in maternal care, while ignoring the larger political and moral dimensions of society, particularly issues of power and domination. Fromm also argued that a culture uses many other mechanisms outside the family to mold individuals into useful citizens. Foremost among these were the projective systems, such as movies and books, that Kardiner and Erikson had relegated to secondary place, but which Fromm saw as centrally determinate both of character and economy.

B. The Struggle for Eros

What was most striking about Fromm and his Frankfurt school colleagues was their principled refusal to accept the inevitability of modern conditions, and their radical assertion of the human potential to break through into a more spontaneous and authentic life of freedom, love, and happiness. What exact political and economic structures might promote the joyous, authentic life was left obscure, since critical theory opposed in principle any positivist arguments that might enchain the potential of humanity, preferring instead a relentless negative dialectic that continually revealed the inhumanity and psychic degradation inherent in modern capitalism. Only through tearing away delusory facades, the argument went, could liberation from the destructive but hidden psychological chains of contemporary culture ever be achieved. Repression would then disappear, the patriarchal family would dissolve, and humanity could move closer to achieving its potential for Eros and bliss.

Some members of the Frankfurt school were not as hopeful as Fromm. Adorno, for example, had much less faith in the possibilities of emancipation. Orthodox psychoanalysts also warned that gratification of instinct is not necessarily a purely positive good.[42] But Fromm's argument was seconded and carried even further by the radical German psychoanalyst Wilhelm Reich (1897–1957), whose analysis of German society led him to declare that "the family is the authoritarian state in miniature." Reich then proclaimed that "*sexually awakened women, affirmed and recognized as such, would mean the complete collapse of the authoritarian ideology*" (italics in original).[43] Twenty years later, similar arguments for sexual freedom as an avenue to political liberation would be made by the critical theorist Herbert Marcuse in *Eros and Civilization*,[44] and then would be taken up as well by the French philosopher Michel Foucault (1926–1984) and his school.

In their utopian aspirations, the Frankfurt school and its latter-day followers were on the side of romantic individualism and against Freud, whom they saw as actively supporting repression by concealing its social origins; at the same time, they themselves were generally rigorously intellectual and humorless, striving to use reason to dethrone reason, while still trying somehow to avoid succumbing to the rampant vitalism that had so enthralled Nietzsche and

---

Wilhelm Reich

One of the most fascinating and tragic figures in the history of psychoanalysis, Reich was a brilliant writer whose insights are still powerful. He was also a charismatic figure who used his remarkable insight into the expressive meanings of posture and movement to quickly, and usually accurately, diagnose the nature of a patient's psychic distress. He broke from orthodox Freudianism over his claim that social and psychological liberation could be achieved through sexual freedom, and soon attracted a following of artists and radical intellectuals.

Reich had a strong interest in anthropology and believed that in the Trobriands, Malinowski had discovered a free, peaceful matriarchy where sexuality is open—a template for the future. For him, self-analysis, as practiced in psychotherapy, merely accentuated psychic disorder by emphasizing the mental over the physical. All self-involved thinking, according to Reich, is a latent form of schizophrenia; only the orgasm is the source of psychic and physical health. After he migrated to the United States, Reich's beliefs became more extreme. He developed his theory that the orgasm served to channel and liberate a universal form of energy, a kind of cosmic libido that flowed through the universe and could be seen as a blue glow in the nighttime sky. He then built and sold "orgone boxes," where believers could be rejuvenated by these healthful rays. Arrested for fraud, Reich became ever more grandiose and paranoid, and spent his last years waiting for flying saucers to rescue him and his few remaining followers.[45]

---

had given spark to the Nazi explosion. There is another paradox as well within the approach taken by critical theorists. While they worshiped individualism as an ideal, they repudiated the actual individualism of their era, which they saw as based only on compulsive consumerism and mindless conformity. For the Frankfurt school, being an authentic and creative individual was much harder work than that; it required an arduous effort of continual self-monitoring and self-critique. In their moralistic and labor-intensive view of the proper duties of the human being, these theorists, though overwhelmingly Jewish, showed their great intellectual debts to Calvinism and the Protestant ethic, debts that could not be redeemed in the coin of sexual emancipation.

C. American Interpretations

While the Frankfurt school and other radical theorists were making their contribution to the study of national character, other, more American, versions were also being attempted. The first efforts were by Mead and then by her English follower, Geoffrey Gorer, who each wrote popular books on America.[46] Benedict's well-received work on Japan followed. But then Gorer and John Rickman published *The People of Great Russia*.[47] In this book, the authors argued that the common practice of tightly wrapping (swaddling) Russian infants helped produce later adult personalities marked by mood swings of depression and manic en-

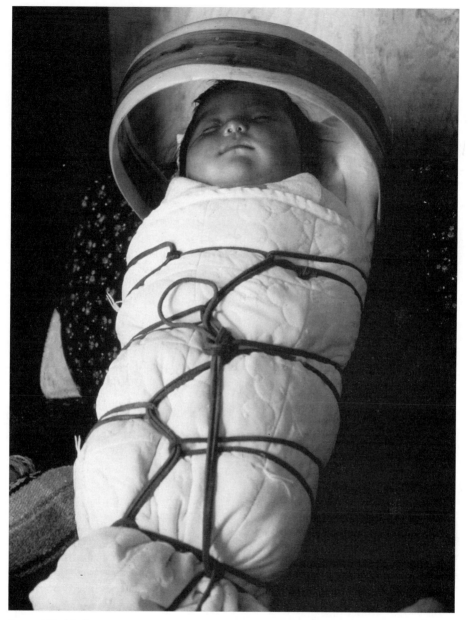

A swaddled baby.

ergy, which in turn tended to make Russians especially susceptible to tyranny. The book's claims were actually more sophisticated than this, but it was easily caricatured as diaperology at its worst—rendering all of Russian culture a reflection of infantile training. Many commentators, keen to discredit culture and personality studies, raked Gorer and Rickman over the coals for psychological reductionism and ahistorical generalization. Hostility toward their book played a large part in the general rejection of configurationist culture and personality theory that had begun with Benedict's displacement by Linton.

Although most anthropologists gave up on national character studies after the swaddling hypothesis debacle, social scientists in other disciplines were undismayed and continued to try their luck at the cultural-psychological analysis of whole nations. Foremost among these was the Harvard sociologist David Riesman (b. 1909) (and his colleagues), who wrote a hugely popular book on America, *The Lonely Crowd*,[48] which was originally published in 1950, the same year as Erikson's *Childhood and Society* and Adorno's *The Authoritarian Personality*. Giving generous credit to the intellectual influence of Fromm, as well as to Benedict, Mead, and Erikson, Riesman postulated three different social characters, which he believed existed in any society. Economic and demographic factors, Riesman said, would inevitably lead to the predominance of one type over the others. The first type, associated with premodern and relatively immobile societies, were the tradition-directed persons, who acted according to ancestral custom. The second, associated with periods of transition and population expansion, were the inner-directed individuals, who knew what they wanted and were able to act innovatively to get it. Then, if the society became more affluent and stable, this questing type would be superseded by the other-directed attitudes of the conformist, who "seeks the character he is supposed to have, and the inner experiences as well as outer appurtenances that are supposed to go with it."[49] The other-directed person is concerned, above all, with being well liked and fitting in. These values, Riesman said, allow quick adjustment to fluid circumstances. It is the other-directed character type whom Riesman saw as dominant in America today.

Riesman's typology can be summarized as follows:

- Premodern, stable society—tradition-directed individuals, accepting habitual beliefs and values.
- Transitional, expanding society—inner-directed individuals, following own beliefs and values.
- Modern, stable society—other-directed individuals, imitating companions' beliefs and values.

Riesman showed considerable sympathy for these other-directed conformists, who, he thought, were more tolerant, more self-conscious, and more compassionate than their hardy but self-centered, unfeeling ancestors. But for the other-directed, the ecstatic liberation from repression promised by Fromm and Reich was impossible. Rather, Riesman vaguely hoped for a new self-aware, autonomous character type who would arise out of precisely the restless self-doubt typical of other-directed individuals, continually trying and failing to re-manufacture themselves in accordance with the latest fads and foibles of the group.

How exactly this was to occur was left vague, as it had to be, since the picture Riesman had drawn had in fact no real oppositional elements within it. The major factors he took into account were socioeconomic development and demographic shifts, which would always lead to the same transformations in personality and culture wherever they occurred. The social characters Riesman postulated suffered no internal conflicts or social contradictions; rather like timeless Jungian archetypes, they existed in potential everywhere and at every time, rising and falling with the tide of the economy.

A more malignant, and more psychologically and anthropologically informed, version of Riesman's portrait was proposed 25 years later during the Vietnam War by Philip Slater, a social theorist who accepted the culture and personality view that "the emotional repertory of human beings is simple and straightforward . . . but every culture holds some of these human reactions to be unacceptable and tries to warp its participants into some peculiar limitation."[50] However, whereas Riesman proposed the peaceful evolution of alternative characters, Slater, as an antiwar activist, saw American society being torn apart by deep conflicts revolving around the cultural ideal of individualism, which stood, he argued, in tension with a repressed but deep inner need for community. Suppression of interdependence leads, Slater said, to a loss of feeling, sexual deadening, and an escalation of mechanized violence against outsiders, who serve as the repositories of projected hostility.

This psychic structure, Slater argued, had deep historical roots, traceable to the origins of Western civilization in ancient Greece, where a patriarchal family structure based on sexual antagonism between men and women led mothers to focus their erotic longings (and frustrated rage) onto their sons, who consequently grew up as narcissists preoccupied with self-glorification, continually proving themselves by denying all forms of dependency. They also became male chauvinists, perpetuating the system through their own hostility to women. As Slater puts it: "A society which derogates women produces envious mothers who produce narcissistic males who are prone to derogate women."[51] Slater found the source of this cycle of misery in the urbanization and increased social mobility of the Greek imperial period, which disrupted the old tightly knit kinship system.

Slater then expanded his analysis, using ethnographic material collected by anthropologists of the culture and personality school. He amassed a range of material that he believed demonstrated a correlation between sexual hostility, strong mother-son bonds, and narcissistic personality, and then claimed that an equivalent pattern existed in America, where bored housewives, excluded from meaningful work, involved themselves too deeply in their sons' lives. The resulting male narcissism was expressed in the fevered accumulation of material possessions. He concluded that "Western man is nothing but Alcibiades with a bad conscience, disguised as a plumber."[52]

A similar argument was made at about the same time by the cultural critic Christopher Lasch (1932–1994).[53] Lasch described Americans as vicious narcissists, psychically distorted by the collapse of traditional authority structures and by the incessant demands of competitive capitalism, though he did not draw the historical and cross-cultural correlations made by Slater, nor did he link his analysis so closely to a particular family configuration. Perhaps that is just as well, since Slater's argument would seem to lose all its force under contemporary conditions, when the trend is away from the housewife role he found so psychically disfiguring and toward the entrance of women into the workforce. Yet, despite quite large shifts in family structure, America is evidently just as competitive a place as it was in the 1950s and 1960s—though perhaps it is not so confident of its capacity to provide moral order everywhere.

These contrasting portraits of the United States show the variety of images that national character studies can provide of the same society. No doubt in this instance these differences in interpretation are partly historical. Riesman, writing in the stable 1950s, was much influenced by the adaptive and integrative models proposed by the culture and personality school; Slater and Lasch, writing during the Vietnam crisis of the 1970s, were swayed by critical theory and revisionist psychoanalysis. They stressed ambivalence, repression, and struggle in the relationship between the individual and culture. Controversies such as these, along with the furor over Gorer and Rickman's notorious swaddling hypothesis, contributed to a general disenchantment with national character studies, and with culture and personality studies in general, among professional anthropologists, who were more than glad to retreat to the familiar and arcane study of tribal symbol systems, political structures, and material culture.[54]

Summary

American anthropologists of the 1930s and 1940s believed they could pick and choose aspects of psychoanalysis that suited them—particularly the notion that adult character was largely structured by early childhood disciplinary practices such as weaning. Psychoanalysis itself was thought to reduce all cultural data to a symbolic expression of sex, and therefore to pose a threat to anthropology. I have argued that this image of psychoanalytic theory is far too simplistic and disregards the fact that psychoanalysis, properly understood, makes no claims to displace other, more standard, forms of anthropological inquiry. Rather, it is suitable for the study of emotionally intense and symbolically dense aspects of culture, where its use can help reveal hidden tensions within the larger system.

The rejection of psychoanalytic theory by culture and personality theorists influenced by Benedict and Mead was offset by the introduction of neo-Freudian perspectives into anthropology. Influenced by materialism, Abram Kardiner proposed a complex theory that downplayed libidinal drives and focused instead on the manner in which a culture's basic personality structure was derived from primary institutions (the mode of production and family structure). His colleague, Cora Du Bois, argued that there was no single personality in a culture, but that various personalities were clustered around a modal type.

Erik Erikson, taking a more Weberian meaning-centered approach, believed that entire cultures are fixated at various developmental points, analogous to stages in human growth. He was one of the first to recognize the psychological devastation that could be caused by cultural change and to realize that a major modern problem was the search for a stable identity. Consequently, he saw contemporary society as adolescent (since this is the phase when identity is in question) and connected the rise of charismatic nationalistic leaders to the quest for the authentic self. In hindsight, it is clear that Erikson's synthesis between psychoanalysis and anthropology was the high-water mark of classical culture and personality theory.

Meanwhile, European theorists, heavily influenced not only by psychoanalysis, but also by Hegelian dialectical theory and Marxist utopianism, arrived in the United States as refugees from just such a charismatic leader: Adolf Hitler. They added to the evolving neo-Freudian theories of culture by stressing psychic resistance to authority and the oppressive aspects of certain social and family systems, which gave rise, they said, to authoritarian personality types. Sexual freedom, some of their more radical members argued, was the sole route to emancipation. Others were not so sure. But all of them emphasized exactly what culture and personality theory ignored: the individual's struggle against the constraints of culture.

Americans also joined in the attempt to characterize whole societies psychologically, producing some controversial findings. The most controversial was the swaddling hypothesis, which connected Russian national character with the restrictions placed on infants. Attacks on this hypothesis sped the intellectual demise of configurationist culture and personality theory in anthropology, and also served to taint all other anthropological studies of the place of the individual in culture.

But in other disciplines, sophisticated variations on this type of analysis remained popular, as witnessed by David Riesman's theory of the rise of the modern other-directed individual, by Philip Slater's psychological study of sexual hostility and male narcissism in America and ancient Greece, and by Christopher Lasch's acid depiction of the correlation between capitalism and narcissism. These latter works, along with the writings of the immigrant critical theorists, relied strongly on psychodynamic interpretations of culture. Freud, it seemed, had at last entered the mainstream of American social theory. But in anthropology, there did not seem to be much room left for him.

Endnotes

1. Linton was not happy at Columbia, so he left there for Yale in 1946; he was replaced by Julian Steward (1902–1972), a materialist and evolutionist with a strong interest in cultural ecology. Someone more alien to the interests of Mead and Benedict, and to culture and personality theory, could not be imagined. Benedict died in 1948; Mead, though increasingly famous, was never granted a full professorship at Columbia and spent most of her career in relative isolation at New York's Museum of Natural History, where she was appointed curator only after 40 years of service. Kardiner too was marginalized at Columbia after World War II, and he gave up hope for realizing his project of uniting psychoanalysis and anthropology.
2. 1950, *Totem and Taboo*, New York: Norton (original publication 1913).
3. Alfred Kroeber, 1920, "Totem and Taboo: An Ethnologic Psychoanalysis," *American Anthropologist* 22: 48–55; 1939, "Totem and Taboo in Retrospect," *American Journal of Sociology* 45: 446–57.
4. See A. I. Hallowell, 1976, "Psychology and Anthropology" (original publication 1954), reprinted in A. I. Hallowell, *Contributions to Anthropology: Selected Papers of A. Irving Hallowell*, Chicago: University of Chicago Press. For other assessments of Freud's influence on anthropology, see Weston La Barre, 1958, "The Influence of Freud on Anthropology," *American Imago* 15: 275–328; Edwin Wallace, 1983, *Freud and Anthropology: A History and Reappraisal*, New York: International Universities Press.
5. Quoted in Hallowell, "Psychology and Anthropology," 210.
6. For a short history of the usage of the Jungian typological model in anthropology, see C. A. Valentine, 1963, "Men of Anger and Men of Shame: Lakalai Ethnopsychology and Its Implications for Sociopsychological Theory," *Ethnology* 2: 441–77. Anthropologists have often utilized human types for purposes of analysis, but without referring to Jung. For example, Paul Radin famously distinguished between the man of action and the thinker (1927, *Primitive Man as Philosopher*, New York: Appleton) but never mentioned Jung.

7. Following Bronislaw Malinowski, 1927, *Sex and Repression in Savage Society*, New York: Harcourt Brace. See Chapter 3 for more on Malinowski's discussion of the Oedipal conflict among the Trobrianders.
8. For example, see Carl Jung et al., 1964, *Man and His Symbols*, London: Aldus.
9. This analysis of Jung follows Philip Rieff, 1987, *The Triumph of the Therapeutic: Uses of Faith after Freud*, Chicago: University of Chicago Press.
10. 1949, *The Hero with a Thousand Faces*, New York: Pantheon.
11. Mead said that she had adopted a modified Freudian orientation in 1934; however, the effects of that shift were not particularly evident in her work. See Mead, 1962, "Retrospect and Prospect," in T. Gladwin and W. Sturtevant (eds.), *Anthropology and Human Behavior*, Washington, DC: Anthropological Society of Washington, pp. 115–49; see especially pp. 127–28.
12. Freud, 1961, *Civilization and Its Discontents*, New York: Norton, p. 43 (original publication 1930).
13. Geza Roheim, 1968, *The Origin and Function of Culture*, New York: Johnson Reprint Corporation (original publication 1943). Roheim is easy to parody, but his work is actually highly sophisticated and hard to refute if his premises are taken seriously.
14. Freud, *Totem and Taboo*, pp. 48–49.
15. Ibid., p. 51.
16. For a recent statement on the similarity between anthropological and psychoanalytic technique, see Katherine Ewing, 1992, "Is Psychoanalysis Relevant for Anthropology?" in Theodore Schwartz, Geoffry White, and Catherine Lutz (eds.), *New Directions in Psychological Anthropology*, Cambridge, England: Cambridge University Press.
17. Important in validating Kardiner's revisionism was Karen Horney's trenchant critique of Freud's biologism in her 1939 book, *New Ways in Psychoanalysis*, New York: Norton. The ego psychology of Hienz Hartmann took this typically American perspective to its limits. See, for example, Hartmann, 1958, *Ego Psychology and the Problem of Adaption*, New York: International Universities Press (original publication 1939). For an exceptionally insightful and anthropologically informed perspective on the Americanization of psychoanalysis, see Suzanne Kirschner, 1996, *The Religious and Romantic Origins of Psychoanalysis: Individuation and Integration in Post-Freudian Theory*, Cambridge, England: Cambridge University Press. For a sensitive ethnographic account of present-day conflicts faced by practitioners of psychiatry in America, see Tanya Luhrmann, 2000, *Of Two Minds: The Growing Disorder in American Psychiatry*, New York: Knopf.
18. In this, Kardiner echoes Hobbes and foreshadows Erik Erikson as well as Michel Foucault.
19. Abram Kardiner, 1939, *The Individual and His Society: The Psychodynamics of Primitive Social Organization*, New York: Columbia University Press. For a reevaluation of Kardiner's work, see William Manson, 1988, *The Psychodynamics of Culture: Abram Kardiner and Neo-Freudian Anthropology*, Westport, CT: Greenwood Press.
20. Different interpretations of changes in American family life will be discussed later in this chapter.
21. Cora Du Bois, 1960, *The People of Alor*, Vol. I, New York: Harper and Row (original publication 1944).
22. Marcelo Suarez-Orozco, 1994, "Remaking Psychological Anthropology," in Marcelo Suarez-Orozco, George Spindler, and Louise Spindler (eds.), *The Making of Psychological Anthropology II*, Fort Worth, TX: Harcourt Brace.

23. Abram Kardiner et al., 1945, *The Psychological Frontiers of Society,* New York: Columbia University Press, p. 170.
24. See Du Bois, *The People of Alor.* For a critique of Kardiner's analysis, see John Honigmann, 1967, *Personality in Culture,* New York: Harper and Row, pp. 111–12.
25. For some successful elaborations on the modal personality model, see Anthony F. C. Wallace, 1952, *The Modal Personality Structure of the Tuscarora Indians,* Bureau of American Ethnology Bulletin 150, Washington, DC: Smithsonian Institution; George Spindler, 1955, *Sociocultural and Psychological Processes in Menomini Acculturation,* Berkeley: University of California Publications in Culture and Society, Vol. 5.
26. Du Bois, *The People of Alor,* p. xxv.
27. For a materialist argument, see Marvin Harris, 1985, *Good to Eat: Riddles of Food and Culture,* New York: Simon and Schuster; for a symbolic perspective, see Mary Douglas, 1966, *Purity and Danger: An Analysis of Concepts of Pollution and Taboo,* London: Routledge.
28. See Chapter 4.
29. New York: Norton.
30. See Chapter 6 for more on these theorists.
31. Erikson, *Childhood and Society,* pp. 137–138.
32. As we shall see in Chapter 11.
33. The use of autobiography had been pioneered in anthropology by Paul Radin in his edited volumes (1920, *The Autobiography of a Winnebago Indian,* Berkeley: University of California Press; 1926, *Crashing Thunder: The Autobiography of an American Indian,* New York: Appleton).
34. American character will be explored in more detail in the conclusion.
35. For more on this subject, see Chapter 11.
36. See Virginia Yans-McLaughlin, 1986, "Mobilizing Culture and Personality for World War II," in George Stocking (ed.), *Malinowski, Rivers, Benedict and Others: Essays on Culture and Personality,* Madison: University of Wisconsin Press.
37. New York: Harper.
38. See Adorno et al., *The Authoritarian Personality;* see also Richard Christie and Marie Jahoda (eds.), 1954, *Studies in the Scope and Method of "The Authoritarian Personality,"* Glencoe, IL: Free Press.
39. New York: Holt, Rinehart and Winston.
40. Fromm, *Escape from Freedom,* p. 161.
41. Ibid., p. 173.
42. See, for example, Anna Freud, 1936, *Ego and the Mechanisms of Defense,* New York: International Universities Press, pp. 58–59.
43. Wilhelm Reich, 1970, *The Mass Psychology of Fascism,* New York: Farrar, Straus and Giroux, pp. 30, 105. See also Reich, 1972, *Sex-Pol: Essays 1929–1934,* New York: Random House.
44. 1968, *Eros and Civilization,* Boston: Beacon Press.
45. For a sympathetic essay on Reich, see Rieff, *The Triumph of the Therapeutic.*
46. Margaret Mead, 1942, *And Keep Your Powder Dry,* New York: Morrow; Geoffrey Gorer, 1948, *The American People: A Study in National Character,* New York, Norton. For more on American personality and its relationship to public life, see Chapter 13.
47. Geoffrey Gorer and John Rickman, 1950, *The People of Great Russia: A Psychological Study,* New York: Chanticleer Press.
48. Riesman, with Nathan Glazer and Reuel Denney, 1961, *The Lonely Crowd* (2d ed.), New Haven, CT: Yale University Press (original publication 1950).

49. Ibid., p. 240.
50. Philip Slater, 1976, *The Pursuit of Loneliness: American Culture at the Breaking Point*, Boston: Beacon Press, p. 3.
51. Philip Slater, 1971, *The Glory of Hera*, Boston: Beacon Press, p. 45.
52. Ibid., p. 451.
53. Christopher Lasch, 1978, *The Culture of Narcissism: American Life in an Age of Diminishing Expectations*, New York: Norton.
54. Some exceptions include Francis Hsu on China, India, and the United States (1963, *Clan, Caste and Club: A Comparison of Chinese, Hindu and American Ways of Life*, Princeton, NJ: Van Nostrand); Louis Dumont on India (1980, *Homo Hierarchicus: An Essay on the Caste System*, Chicago: University of Chicago Press); Charles Lindholm on the Middle East (1996, *The Islamic Middle East: An Historical Perspective*, Oxford, England: Basil Blackwell); Jules Henry on the United States (1963, *Culture against Man*, New York: Random House). On the United States, see also John A. Hall and Charles Lindholm, 1999, *Is America Breaking Apart?* Princeton, NJ: Princeton University Press.

CHAPTER 6

Quandaries and Alternatives

In American society, the transition from childhood to adulthood is hardly marked at all: Getting a driver's license and graduating from high school are probably the most universal rites of passage. Others, less pervasive, include entering college or joining the armed services. But this is decidedly not the case in many cultures, especially for boys. For example, among the Thonga of South Africa, every 5 years or so, boys between 10 and 16 were sent to a "circumcision school" in the bush where they learned to be adults. Their education was a brutal one, and it began immediately, when they were forced to run a gauntlet between the men of the village, who beat them with clubs; then they were stripped naked and their heads roughly shaven. Dazed, each boy was brought face to face with a frightening masked "lion man," who grabbed him and rapidly sliced off his foreskin.

That was only the beginning. The bruised and bleeding initiates spent the next 3 months secluded in the bush, hidden from women, who were forbidden to come near them on pain of death. The boys were beaten regularly, forced to sleep without blankets in the bitter winter cold, subjected to torture, tormented by thirst, and obliged to eat nauseating food. Only after surviving this long ordeal could they proudly return to the village to proclaim themselves men.[1]

The Thonga initiation process was extreme, but not unusual. Harsh transitions from boyhood to manhood are found in many premodern cultures throughout the world. How could these cruel performances be understood? What was their purpose? Why did they exist in some cultures and not in others, and why were initiation ceremonies so rare for girls? These were the questions that inspired a new attempt to bring Freud back into anthropology, and helped lead to a reformulation of culture and personality studies.

Chapter Outline

I The Whitings' Comparative Anthropology
   A Psychological Anthropology in Disarray
   B Explaining Initiation Ceremonies
   C The Six Cultures Study

New Guinea: A boy's head is shaven in preparation for the final ordeal of his 3-month-long initiation ceremony.

II Culture and Identity: Peirce, G. H. Mead, Hallowell, and Goffman
  A Two Precursors of Modern Theory
  B The Evolutionary Self
  C How World Views Make a Universe
  D The World's a Stage

III The Affirmation of Diversity: Wallace, LeVine, and Spiro
  A Culture Has No Personality
  B Maintaining Consensus in Diversity
  C Population Psychology
  D Functionalist Freudianism

I. THE WHITINGS' COMPARATIVE ANTHROPOLOGY

  A Psychological Anthropology in Disarray
    The debunking of culture and personality theory. The absence of alternative models.

  B Explaining Initiation Ceremonies
    The attempt at a scientific test of psychoanalytic theory.

  C The Six Cultures Study
    Cross-cultural comparison: its successes and limitations.

A. Psychological Anthropology in Disarray

As mentioned in the last chapter, the study of culture and personality had lost most of its credibility after the publication of Gorer and Rickman's swaddling hypothesis and other similar studies that made unsubstantiated leaps between toilet training and adult character, and implausibly linked weaning with social organization. Projective tests, which had been utilized in an effort to bolster psychological conjecture with scientific data, had proved impossible to validate. As a result, many anthropologists dismissed all the scholars studying culture and personality as diaperologists, prone to wild psychologizing and unprovable speculation. Even the commonsense notion that the socialization of children constructed the personalities of adults was challenged as unprovable, as was the idea that human beings are coherent entities.[2]

In consequence, from the 1950s into the 1970s, it was almost a taboo in most American anthropology departments for graduate students to mention the word "psychology" in their dissertations; the very term "culture and personality" became anathema, and the sophisticated cross-disciplinary research inaugurated by Kardiner, Du Bois, and Erikson was nearly forgotten.

This was unfortunate, since most of the criticisms were based on a misunderstanding of the nature of anthropological inquiry. Unlike hard scientists, who detach themselves from their subject matter, manipulate it through experiments, and reveal relationships of cause and effect according to the Cartesian

---

Socialization

Demonstrating the extent to which child-raising practices influence adult character is very difficult. Nonetheless, some studies have made a convincing case for a correlation between child training and later personality. One of the most interesting was undertaken by the psychologist Gustav Jahoda. While working with the Ashanti tribe in Africa, Jahoda was confidently informed that children born on different days of the week naturally have distinctly different characters: Children born on Wednesday will be unruly; children born on Monday are quiet and peaceful. Understandably skeptical, Jahoda researched criminal records, only to discover that indeed among the Ashanti, Wednesday children had high rates of delinquency while the rates of Monday children were much lower than normal. Unless we accept the belief that among the Ashanti the day of birth does motivate character, these findings can only be explained by socialization: Parents expect Monday children to be quiet, Wednesday children to be obstreperous, and treat them accordingly; in response, the children grow into adults with the expected characteristics.[3]

In the West, more standardized psychological studies have also demonstrated continuity of emotional disposition and self-representation. For instance, a comparison of psychological evaluations of men and women in their adolescence and evaluations done nearly 20 years later showed statistically significant stability in character type.[4] Similarly, studies of the personalities of black teenagers undertaken over a 20-year period also reveal a remarkable stability of identity.[5]

---

ideal of proof, ethnographers deal with something that cannot be dissected, that is rarely susceptible to experimental manipulation, from which the observers cannot wholly remove themselves, any more than fish can remove themselves from water. Under such circumstances, precise scientific proof is impossible. Rather, a convincing argument is one that can integrate a large number of apparently incongruous factors into a coherent picture. To defeat that postulate would require not a critique of method but a better hypothesis, one that could account more parsimoniously for a wider variety of data. This was what culture and personality theory was attempting to do, and it ought not have been castigated for failing to meet standards inappropriate to its goals. Sadly for the discipline, many anthropologists accepted the criticism as legitimate and dropped their research altogether.

Despite a generally negative atmosphere, not all anthropological work on psychological issues ceased. Mead and her students continued to defend their assertions, though their writings were cited less and less in the academic community. Other anthropologists with no respect for current intellectual fashions also contributed new research: Weston La Barre and Georges Devereux each wrote striking Freudian analyses of myth, religion, dreams, and the psychic structures of non-Western peoples;[6] George DeVos, Thomas Gladwin, George and Louise Spindler, John Honigmann, and a host of others worked to refine and expand the methods of earlier culture and personality theorists;[7] Dorothy Lee wrote a widely read book on cross-cultural concepts of human nature,[8] and so on. These writers, and others I have not the space to mention, received far less attention than they deserved.[9] Anthropology, it seemed, had left the study of the psyche to psychoanalysts.

Nor did the psychoanalysts reach out to anthropologists, even though many new psychoanalytic theories downplayed controversial Freudian premises of drive theory and the Oedipal triangle in favor of the study of the development of the ego in a manner that would seem compatible with anthropological research. For example, object-relations theorists disregarded id drives altogether and focused instead on the relationships and symbolic objects that helped children develop a healthy identity. But these theorists concerned themselves almost entirely with the inner life of infants under two years old, and so were of minor interest to anthropologists.

Another potentially promising avenue of psychoanalytic research was the self psychology proposed by Heinz Kohut, who emphasized the development of personal identity, while downplaying instinct and Oedipal rivalry. In essence, Kohut argued that children require admiration and acceptance from the outside world to develop a necessary sense of personal value and potency; he then went on to discuss the relationship between political leadership and self-conceptions in modern society.[10] In so doing, he advanced the discussion already begun by Erikson, but Kohut's work was not followed up by anthropologists, who were

---

Object-Relations Theory

Since Freud's time any number of students have focused on the pre-Oedipal bond between infant and mother. One of the most influential in the United States was Melanie Klein, who argued that innate conflicts in the infantile psyche were projected outward to "good" and "bad" objects, thereby turning attention away from internal, instinctive struggles and toward human relationships and the fantasies that surround them. Klein also posited a pattern of positions taken during growth (paranoid, schizoid, depressive).[11]

Klein's work on very young infants inspired later theorists who focused on the content of "good enough" mothering, as D. W. Winnicott termed it, and on the development of object relations (that is, relations with others) through the infant's efforts to distinguish itself from its nurturing and mirroring self-object, the mother.[12] But great controversies arose over whether the child is tortured by an inner, preexisting dynamic of love and hate, as Klein and her followers insisted, or if the child is fundamentally whole and is divided only by interaction with the mother and the environment, as the object-relations school argued. Recently, some theorists who have studied the behavior of very young children claim that the infant actually has a great deal more autonomy and active will than has generally been admitted.[13]

put off by his high evaluation of the autonomous individual. Robert LeVine, for example, writes that what Kohut lauds as healthy self-esteem would be seen elsewhere as intolerable conceit.[14]

Meanwhile, Jacques Lacan's literary French version of psychoanalysis moved in an opposite direction, portraying the individual as contingently constructed by language games in a continual process of negation. Lacan's disintegrative approach would seem to be in line with the contemporary interpretive turn in anthropology, but his work too has had little influence, perhaps because of its arcane quality.[15] In sum, the numerous theoretical shifts, controversies, and advances within psychoanalysis since the 1950s did little to revive the moribund condition of psychological anthropology.[16]

B. Explaining Initiation Ceremonies

One psychological anthropologist, however, did seek to bring the study of culture and personality back to center stage. John Whiting (1908–1999),[17] aided by his wife, Beatrice Whiting, and by a large and loyal cohort of students and colleagues, believed it was possible to conduct rigorous and scientifically verifiable comparative research that would quantify the impact of culture on character. This was to be accomplished by utilizing the Human Relations Area Files (HRAF) at Yale, which was an organized compendium of information culled from selected ethnographies, indexed and coded so that any particular cultural item or trait could be easily retrieved and correlated with similar items and traits from other cultures. In principle, the HRAF would allow researchers to test hypotheses and establish causal chains, demonstrating the validity of psychoanalytic theory.

The most impressive and influential such study aimed at discovering an explanation for the sorts of severe male initiation ceremonies described at the beginning of this chapter. Starting from the Freudian postulate of the Oedipus complex, John Whiting reasoned that a boy who had a strong Oedipal attachment to his mother would have serious psychological difficulty being separated from her and would have strong hostility toward his father. Male Oedipal dependency, Whiting thought, could be objectively measured by the presence of exclusive mother-child sleeping arrangements and a long postpartum sex taboo forbidding the husband access to his wife. Whiting and his colleagues believed that under such conditions a harsh initiation would be required to divide the boy from his mother and draw him into the world of men; furthermore, a sadistic initiation would also allow the husband to vent his rage at the son who had taken his place in his wife's bed.

As a test of this hypothesis, a sample of 56 societies was selected out of the HRAF, with every effort made to represent the widest possible diversity. Material about sleeping arrangements, postpartum sex taboos, and initiation was then coded by separate judges and tabulated. In 24 of the societies, mothers slept with their infant children, while fathers slept separately. In 27, sexual intercourse was forbidden for at least 9 months after birth. In the 20 societies where both of these variables occurred, 14 had harsh male initiation ceremonies. In the 25 societies where neither variable occurred, only 2 had such ceremonies. The

---

Juvenile Delinquency and the Family

Whiting extended his findings to make a hypothesis about juvenile delinquency in our society. If teenage male hostility to authority correlates with a strong mother-son tie and an absent father, then broken homes, female-headed households, and weak male figures would be more likely to foster delinquent behavior among boys. The solution would be some equivalent to an initiation ceremony, such as the Outward Bound program, or a change in residence, where boys were taken out of the maternal household and put under the authority of responsible adult males—such as in the Army. This model, though often debated, has had a strong influence on social welfare policy in the United States.

---

8 seeming exceptions were then explained by various means; for example, in 4 of the exceptions, teenage boys were obliged to change residence and accept the authority of a related male (usually the mother's brother), which could be considered the equivalent of initiation.[18] (See Table 6.1.) In this work, Whiting and his colleagues proved the salience of Freudian theory for understanding an otherwise opaque aspect of culture (harsh male initiation ceremonies), while also demonstrating that the strength of the Oedipal complex (attachment to the mother and rivalry with the father) varied cross-culturally according to the degree of intimacy fostered between mother and son.

Anthropological research has tended to bear out the hypothesis that boys with absent or weak fathers usually identify strongly with their mothers; societies where this occurs often do practice initiation and circumcision, expunging the feminine. But there is an alternative that occurs where the culture does not stress maleness; this is the institution of the couvade—a "male pregnancy"— wherein the husband becomes ill when his wife is pregnant. As one would expect, such a strong symbolic identification with the female role is never found where there is male initiation and circumcision. The two are complementary responses to the same problem of male identity in societies where there is intense mother-son intimacy: The first occurs where adult male roles are strongly marked; the second, where they are not.

C. The Six Cultures Study

Despite the successes of the comparative method, many anthropologists worried about the feasibility of comparing cultural items that were defined and correlated out of context, using ethnographic accounts that were of varied reliability. To offset such criticism, John and Beatrice Whiting undertook their most ambitious project, sending out six teams of carefully trained ethnographers into six different societies to discover the exact manner in which children were affected by their cultures.[19] The idea was to control for the individual interpretations of

TABLE 6.1. The Relationship between Exclusive Mother-Son Sleeping Arrangements and a Postpartum Sex Taboo* and the Occurrence of Initiation Ceremonies at Puberty

| Customs in Infancy | | Customs at Adolescent Initiation Ceremonies | |
Exclusive Mother-Son Sleeping Arrangements	Postpartum Sex Taboo	Absent	Present
Long	Long		Azande *hgs*†
			Camayura *hs*
			Chagga *hgs*
			Cheyenne *ht*
			Chiricahua *ht*
			Dahomeans *hgs*
			Fijians *gs*
			Jivaro *ht*
		Ganda	Kwoma *hgs*
		Khalapur (Rajput)	Lesu *gs*
		Nyakyusa	Nuer *hs*
		Tepoztlan	Samoans *g*
		Trobrianders	Thonga *hgs*
		Yapese	Tiv *hgs*
	Short	Ashanti	
		Malaita	Cagaba *ht*
		Siriono	
Short	Long	Araucanians	Kwakiutl *s*
		Pilaga	Ojibwa *t*
		Pondo	Ooldea *hgs*
		Tallensi	
	Short	Alorese	Hopi *hs*
		Balinese	Timbira *hst*
		Druz	
		Egyptians (Silwa)	
		Eskimos (Copper)	
		French	
		Igorot (Bontoc)	
		Japanese (Suye Mura)	
		Koryak (Maritime)	
		Lakher	
		Lamba	
		Lapps	
		Lepcha	
		Maori	
		Mixtecans	
		Navaho	
		Ontong Javanese	
		Papago	
		Serbs	
		Tanala (Menabe)	
		Trukese	
		United States (Homestead)	
		Yagua	

*Both of a year or more duration.

† The letters following the tribal designations in the right-hand column indicate the nature of the ceremony—*h* = painful hazing, *g* = genital operations, *s* = seclusion from women, and *t* = tests of manliness.

Source: J. Whiting, R. Kluckhohn, and A. Anthony, 1958, "The Function of Male Initiation Ceremonies at Puberty," in E. Maccoby, T. Newcomb, and E. Hartley (eds.), Readings in Social Psychology, New York: Holt, p. 365.

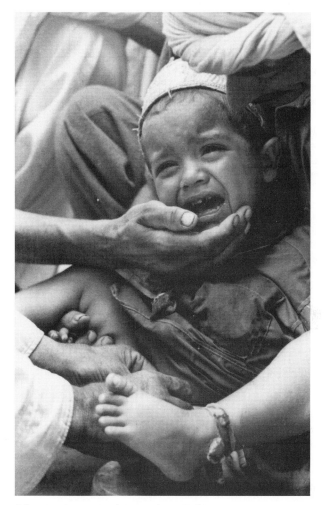

A boy is circumcised in northern Pakistan.

researchers in order to produce the very first truly scientific comparative anthropological study. Strict protocols for periodic observation of behavior were issued to the researchers (see Table 6.2), while extensive questionnaires were administered to the mothers in each community.

The organizational effort involved was massive, and every attempt was made to achieve reliability. Seventy different types of social acts were fastidiously recorded in 5-minute segments at 14 random intervals for each child in the sample. These atomistic behavior bits were coded and scored by objective readers back at Harvard and finally reduced to 12 major categories of dependent variables that were affected by the independent variables of age, sex, situation, and learning environment. The personality differences of the children were not considered. Like Mead and Benedict, the Whitings and their co-workers also placed culture first and had little interest in the character of individuals.

TABLE 6.2. Example from the Six Cultures Protocol

*Situations**

1. O assaults P.
2. O insults P.
3. O hurts self in the presence of P.
4. O encounters appreciable difficulty in an activity in the presence of P.
5. O asks help from P.
6. P hurts self.
7. P encounters appreciable difficulty in an activity in the presence of O.
8. O attempts to dominate P.
9. O reprimands P.
10. P breaks a rule.
11. O attempts to initiate friendly interaction with P.
12. P, unprovoked, initiates an interaction.

*P here refers to the particular child in whose responses we are, at the moment, interested; O refers to any other person with whom P has interaction.

Responses

1. Self-reliance
2. Obedience
3. Nurturance
4. Succorance
5. Sociability
6. Dominance
7. Achievement-oriented behavior
8. Responsible performance of duties
9. Ignoring
10. Escape
11. Aggression
12. Acceptance of reprimand
13. Refusal to accept reprimand

Source: John Whiting, Irvin Child, William Lambert, et al., 1966, Field Guide for a Study of Socialization, *New York: John Wiley, pp. 92–93.*

The results of all this labor were not what the investigators had hoped. The most well-validated results included such unremarkable findings as these: Where there are other women available to help, mothers spend less time with their children; boys are usually more aggressive than girls; children ask for help from adults and give help to infants. After much statistical manipulation, the multiple differences in children's behavior were eventually subsumed into factors of cultural complexity and domestic structure. Children in the more complex societies were more dependent and more dominant; children in the less complex societies were more nurturant and responsible. Children in nuclear households were more sociable and intimate; children in extended patrilineal households were more authoritarian and aggressive. Why these correlations occurred was not clear, though the authors offered some plausible but unprovable post hoc hypotheses, for instance, that extended family households have less intimate relationships among parents and children, and that in less complex societies, the high workload on mothers means that children have to take on more responsibility and be more protective of their siblings (which would seem to indicate that modern American latchkey children might become more kindly and nurturant in response to their mothers' absence).

In all, the heterogeneity and atomistic nature of the data and the impossibility of actually verifying the rather bland hypotheses that were generated made all the effort seem difficult to justify. Anthropologists were also disappointed that the number of variables reduced culture to just one factor among many.[20] Nor was it certain whether the correlations that had been so laboriously arrived at would hold outside the six cultures in question. Given the sparsity of results, the unresolved problems of the analysis, and the incredible difficulties of undertaking such research, no similarly ambitious project has since been attempted, and probably none ever will be.[21] What the Whitings' project seemed to prove conclusively was that it is virtually impossible to apply a rigorous comparative correlational model to actual anthropological research: Culture, like character, is simply too complex to be readily amenable to the type of atomizing investigation the Whitings and their colleagues proposed. Nonetheless, it remained quite evident, for those who wished to look, that any adequate understanding of the human experience would have to confront the methodological questions that the Whitings had tried so hard to resolve.

II. CULTURE AND IDENTITY: PEIRCE, G. H. MEAD, HALLOWELL, AND GOFFMAN

A Two Precursors of Modern Theory
   Charles Peirce: language and identity. G. H. Mead: the construction of the self through role playing.

B The Evolutionary Self
   A. I. Hallowell's theory of the evolutionary development of the ego.

C How World Views Make a Universe
   Ojibwa ontology. Hallowell's psychological assumptions.

D The World's a Stage
   Erving Goffman's dramaturgical model of social life. Parallels with Freud.

A. *Two Precursors of Modern Theory*

In the late 1950s, with the exception of the work being done by the Whitings and a few others, any connection between psychoanalysis and anthropological theory had been more or less set aside. As a result, some anthropologists and other social scientists began searching the past for theoretical models that they could apply to the study of the relationship between the individual and culture. One potentially useful theory was discovered in the writings of the obscure American linguistic philosopher Charles Peirce (1839–1914), who had argued that the personality of the individual is constituted by the social exchange of linguistic signs that circulate within an ongoing community of interpreters.[22] For him, the self appeared and existed only through communication with the external world, and was built up out of shifting feelings, acts, and thoughts that were eventually combined into bundles of habits within individuals. Even alone in their thoughts, people were engaged in a constant self-constructing dialogue, trying to convince themselves of the legitimacy of their actions.

It followed that if the individual was actually constituted by a dialogic participation in the community of language, then the community itself could be seen as "a sort of loosely compacted person, in some respects of higher rank than the person of an individual organism."[23] This theory collapsed the distinction between self and other; for Peirce, the individual became a kind of node or vortex in a constant communicative flow, and the empirical question was "discovering the bonds of feeling that hold people together or tear them apart, and what the interrelations and conditions are."[24]

Peirce's writing, while not influential during his lifetime, was to have a great effect on some cognitive and linguistically inclined anthropologists, who were impressed with his insistence on the decisive role of language and communication in constituting both the individual and society. However, Peirce's influence was limited because his major concern was developing his theory of signs; he said little specific about culture and almost nothing about how personal identity was actually constituted, save that habit—and the recognition that the world resisted one's desires—had a crucial role.[25]

More useful was the writing of another American philosopher, George Herbert Mead (1863–1931), who had provided a specifically sociological way of thinking about selves in society. Greatly influenced by Durkheim, Mead had argued strongly that we exist "only insofar as the selves of others exist and enter as such into our experience also."[26] But whereas Durkheim had been content merely to affirm the preeminence of the social over the personal, Mead wanted to understand exactly what self-consciousness entailed and how it was constructed. His argument was that self-consciousness resulted from empathetic identification with others: We become individuals when we experience in ourselves the feelings of those who surround us and respond to our actions.

Empathy, Mead said, began in children's playful ability to imitate others, especially those upon whom they depended. The act of imitation (mimesis) led to a sense of unity with those imitated (much in the way Freud pictured the origin of the superego, but without Freud's emphasis on the frustration of drives) and to the eventual incorporation within the self of socially acceptable responses and attitudes, which Mead called "the generalized other." Mead illustrated his argument by recalling the games children play in which they pretend to be other people and take turns acting out different situations, thereby learning the rules and the reciprocal balance of parts required to maintain the multiple fictions that eventually constitute social reality.

Mead thus established a rather different paradigm of the individual self than that followed by orthodox culture and personality anthropologists, who were inspired primarily by functionalism and behaviorism, and who saw the individual as a simple, stable, and direct reflection of society. Instead, for Mead, the self develops in a mimetic and dialectical relationship with the outside world. The individual in Mead's portrait, while conforming to society's demands to become what he or she ought to be, is also active, multiplex, and changeable, aware of divergence, capable of entering into the selves of others and of playing many different parts. While Mead's view gave far more credit to the autonomy of the social world than Freud's had done, it did not necessarily preclude a Freudian reading: The sorts of roles a person might adopt or shed could, in principle, be structured and motivated by preexisting psychic tensions and predilections. Individual character could therefore be constructed in response to desires and, at the same time, be reflective of the larger social universe. Mead, however, did not refer to Freud; his theory was resolutely social.

B. The Evolutionary Self

Mead's theory of the self influenced two important writers in very different ways. The first, A. Irving Hallowell (1892–1974), took Mead's ideas and placed them within an evolutionary and anthropological framework. Hallowell was a wide-ranging thinker who had worked extensively among the Ojibwa Indians of Canada. Although he published relatively little, Hallowell was well known and respected for his historical reconstructions of Indian life, for his important writing on the history of anthropology,[27] and for his advocacy of projective tests in cross-cultural research. But what is especially salient for the purposes of this book was his pioneering research on identity and culture. Like Mead and Peirce, Hallowell argued that the self is a reflexive entity: Individuals can and do think of themselves and discriminate themselves from other objects and selves; they can also see themselves as objects and have attitudes toward themselves. The self is therefore not to be confused with the ego, which Hallowell described as the cognitive, judging, adaptive aspect of the mind. In his formulation, the ego is a set of functions, whereas the self is experienced as a "phenomenal datum"— it is the subjective "I" and the objective "me."[28]

Hallowell, like Mead, spent much of his writing describing how such an extraordinary phenomenon as self-consciousness came to exist, but his inquiry turned in quite a different direction from Mead's. Heavily influenced by what was then the new field of behavioral evolution, Hallowell postulated that the capacity for self-objectification was a necessary product of the evolutionary process whereby human beings shifted from "physiological to cortical controls," that is, away from instinct and toward active learning. The cognitive ability to symbolize that permitted this transformation also allowed humans to conceptualize the self as an object—the "I" can think about "me"; this in turn aided in social organization, since people now could share internalized values and norms.[29]

Self-awareness also had another function: It made self-appraisal possible. "I" could judge "me" against the standards held by the generalized other whom "I" had incorporated as part of "my" identity. Failure to meet these self-imposed standards would lead to a painful sense of shame and guilt. This too helped maintain the social world, since an inner fear of moral failure and diminished self-respect made people try to live up to social norms. In short, Hallowell argued that for human beings, awareness of individual selfhood implies a moral responsibility to the community.

As important as he believed self-awareness to be, Hallowell did not think that it was the final source of human motivation. He assumed that unconscious impulses limit human rationality,[30] and he noted as well that the individual does not completely know his or her own psyche; human beings can therefore be deluded about motives and deceived by repression and other defense mechanisms.[31] Hallowell thereby left room in his model for a theory of the unconscious, but he did not attempt to develop such a theory himself. Like other American anthropologists of his era, he gave much more emphasis to rational adjustment and cultural integration than he did to irrational impulses and subterranean passions.

What was new in Hallowell's reworking of Mead was his impressive mixture of evolutionary theory with ego psychology. He rooted the reflexive self in human nature and made a convincing case for its adaptive necessity. All human beings, Hallowell claimed, must necessarily be self-conscious, capable of comparing themselves with others, and compelled to judge themselves against cultural norms. Hallowell deserves credit for giving an evolutionary basis and a new content to the old anthropological faith in the psychic unity of humankind, and for drawing attention to the manner in which self-consciousness is a requisite aspect of the human condition.

C. How World Views Make a Universe

Alongside these universalistic aspects, Hallowell also pointed toward a more phenomenological approach to the study of the self, asserting that the self ought to be studied and discussed from the point of view of the individual, without preexistent categories or assumptions intruding. In demanding that a Weberian *verstehen* approach ought to be taken not only to the way persons conceive of their social world, but also to how they conceive of themselves, Hallowell consciously moved away from a behaviorist concern with overt action and away from Freudian analysis that assumed an a priori knowledge of drives and defenses that constitute the individual's inner life. Rather, he argued that the self can be properly understood only from "the inside out" through grasping the social categories that the subject takes to be reality, that is, through cultural analysis. Recapitulating Durkheim, who also argued for the social construction of fundamental categories of personal being, Hallowell maintained that motives, norms, orientation toward self and other, and even awareness of space and time were provided by society. There is no objective reality, only the reality the individual experiences according to cultural precepts. Hallowell called this the world view, "the way the world looks to that people looking out."[32] Paradoxically, then, the self and its environment both turn out to be wholly culturally constituted—an odd phenomenology indeed.

Hallowell illustrated his approach most clearly in a famous article entitled "Ojibwa Ontology, Behavior and World View," in which he sought to outline the metaphysical assumptions informing notions of self and person among his Indian informants. Hallowell showed that the Ojibwa believed birds and beasts, as well as stones and rivers and other inanimate objects, had human characteristics; ghosts, spirits, demons, and other mysterious entities were also ubiquitous and constantly worked their wills on men and women. The Ojibwa be-

Lithograph of an Ojibwa woman, circa 1837.

lieved as well that these beings were capable of metamorphosis, which meant that what was not human today could become human tomorrow, and vice versa. Appearances were extremely deceiving: Hidden selves were everywhere, each with its own awareness, understanding, language, personal identity, autonomy, volition, and power; each also could be friendly if placated or dangerously hostile if offended. No Ojibwa could ever be exactly certain of the nature or agenda of any other person, animal, or thing.

Living in an ambiguous world where potential enemies lurked everywhere, the Ojibwa were beset by anxiety. They prudently believed it best to be "cautious and suspicious in interpersonal relations of all kinds."[33] An overriding fear of supernatural sanctions also lay behind the mildness and placidity that the Ojibwa invariably displayed in their relations with others. For Hallowell, the pervasive serenity of the Ojibwa was "a culturally constituted facade that often masks the hostile feelings that actually exist."[34] In fact, according to Hallowell, the whole Ojibwa personality was structured by the continuous effort to control strong emotions and to appear calm and detached, maintaining social equilibrium and avoiding the danger of giving offense. The mask of mildness was dropped only in periodic drunken rages or during acts of violent revenge.

Hallowell's *verstehen* analysis of the Ojibwa self was highly sophisticated and convincing; it showed very well the multiple influences and assumptions that constituted the indigenous notions of and expressions of Ojibwa personal being. It is for this reason that Hallowell has been widely seen as a proponent of a romantic and aesthetic phenomenological perspective on the study of the self. Yet it is ironic that the author so often congratulated for discovering the self in anthropology so rarely analyzed any real individuals. Hallowell's work, like the writings of most of his cohorts, was determinedly cultural, and the selves he discussed were socially fabricated, lacking autonomous content.

We should also note that Hallowell's interpretation of the Ojibwa world view did not proceed solely from Ojibwa concepts, but was solidly grounded in taken-for-granted Freudian notions of the punitive superego, emotional ambivalence, and the mechanisms of repression. Finally, Hallowell did not portray the Ojibwa self-concept as existing autonomously, disconnected from the larger universe. On the contrary, he carefully linked the Ojibwa self-understanding to their mode of production and social organization. As nomadic hunters and fishers in a sparse ecology, the Ojibwa were highly individualistic and lacked hierarchical leaders or external social controls. Their settlements were scattered and constantly changing, and they were continually confronted with a fluid and truly dangerous social and physical environment. Their concepts of themselves reflected this social reality, and the self-control they imposed on themselves served, Hallowell believed, to preserve their precarious way of life from disruption by human impulses of jealousy, hatred, greed, and ambition—all of which Hallowell portrayed as primordial emotions, surging upward despite strenuous Ojibwa efforts at denial. Even though he argued for an insider's interpretation of the self that started out from the Ojibwa's own vision of themselves, Hallowell's analysis also gave due credit to social factors (constituted both by culture and ecology) and to the dynamics of the psyche.

D. *The World's a Stage*

Hallowell built his theory out of Mead's premise that self-consciousness was socially constructed; and he followed Mead in envisioning self-consciousness as essential for the moral integrity of society. But while Hallowell stressed the evolutionary pathway toward the self and its particular cultural expression, Mead had concerned himself more with childhood experiences of playful mimesis. This was the aspect of Mead's theory that profoundly affected Erving Goffman (1922–1983), a brilliant sociologist who did his original field research in a hotel in Ireland. It was there, watching the shifting interactions of the customers and hotel workers, that he began to expand upon Mead's game model, developing a theory of human life as theater, with front stage and backstage areas, props, sets, audiences, and teams of performers continually trying to perfect their roles and maintain the illusion of reality. For Goffman, everyone was an actor in a constantly improvised play in which the parts are learned though emulation and identification with parents and peers.

Goffman's first book, *The Presentation of Self in Everyday Life*,[35] was a tour de force expansion of his theory, using illustrations from ordinary life to argue that human beings are indeed constructed by the roles they play for one another. Quite consciously, the book was presented as a kind of parody of Freud. Even the title is a play on Freud's early work *The Psychopathology of Everyday Life*.[36] In his book, Goffman replaced pathology with role performance; the id was equated with the intimacy and informality of backstage, while the self-control and politesse demanded in the front stage substituted for the superego. Men and women were not motivated by internal forces, but rather by the need to define the situation in a way that would gain audience approval; major anxiety was not the fear of being overwhelmed by the id, but was caused by dread that one's performance might fail. As Goffman wrote: "Behind many masks and many characters, each performer tends to wear a single look, a naked unsocialized look, a look of concentration, a look of one who is privately engaged in a difficult, treacherous task."[37] And while for Freud, the primal scene of the Oedipal conflict was expressed in neurotic symptoms, for Goffman, the primal scene was the painful discrepancy between "is" and "ought," exemplified in those with stigmatized identities, regardless of the source of the stigma. Ex-convicts, homosexuals, the handicapped, alcoholics, and the mentally ill were type cases of stigmatization.[38]

Goffman took Mead's metaphor of playacting to its ultimate. He argued that there is no real self, only roles that are socially constructed. We continually strive to act according to the parts that have been allotted to us, even when alone, and are anguished when we fail. For Goffman, there is no dynamic unconscious, only slipups and stage fright. Psychological problems are caused not by the neurotic repression of desire, but by taking the illusion of the autonomous self too seriously, judging ourselves harshly for our own failures to be the persons we believe we ought to be, castigating ourselves for discrepancies in performance while mistakenly believing in the solidity of the selves presented by others. Good mental health, Goffman seems to say, would result from the realization that we are all, in a fundamental sense, frauds; this would allow us to take ourselves less seriously and to be more accepting of the weaknesses and failures of ourselves and others.

Goffman's disintegration of the self into roles appeared to be an absolute repudiation of any theory, such as Freud's, that looks inward to find the sources of the human experience. But despite his theoretical stance, Goffman is actually much closer to Freud than is usually thought. In fact, his claim that we all share a sense of our own fraudulence and uncertainty about ourselves is structurally equivalent to Freud's postulate of shared Oedipal guilt. And Goffman's contention that we disguise our discomfort with our self-presentation by denigrating the performances of others is the counterpart to Freud's argument that people are bound together in love only so long as they can find someone to vent their hate upon. It is also worth remembering that Freud believed that character—the aspects of personality that make an individual unique—are actually defense mechanisms—efforts to stave off the existential anxiety of what Goffman calls the all-too-human. But whereas Goffman was content to relegate the all-too-human self to those eruptions and failings of the physical that might disrupt the play—farts and belches, lust, ineptitude—Freud, as we have seen, had a much more complete theory of the structure and nature of the impulses that complicate and yet compel the performance of the self. Goffman's humans, though rich in anecdote, are lacking in depth of feeling. Their main emotion (a real one, no doubt) is fear of being revealed for the fakes that they are.

There are deeper parallels with Freud as well. Although Goffman would seem, on the surface, to be in complete agreement with the premise that the private self is nothing but a reflection of the social world that molds it, in fact, he gives great credit to individual resistance to cultural authority. His most moving book is *Asylums*,[39] where he outlines in detail the operation of a mental health facility. In this "total institution" the staff exerts every effort to control the patients and adapt them to the hospital regimen. The patients, in response, attempt to provide some modicum of privacy for themselves and struggle to maintain a sense of personal integrity in the face of overwhelming odds. Here and elsewhere Goffman portrays a world where no amount of conditioning can reduce a human being to a cipher. In this, he is aligned more closely with Freud than with Margaret Mead or Ruth Benedict. But where resistance to institutional domination comes from is not discussed: It simply exists.

III. THE AFFIRMATION OF DIVERSITY:
WALLACE, LEVINE, AND SPIRO

A Culture Has No Personality
> Anthony F. C. Wallace's claim that there is no direct correlation between culture and character.

B Maintaining Consensus in Diversity
> Wallace's explanation of variability and cooperation in complex systems.

C Population Psychology
> Robert LeVine's adaptive Freudian population psychology.

D Functionalist Freudianism
> Melford Spiro's evolutionary psychoanalytic model of the generic mind.

A. Culture Has No Personality

As mentioned above, one of the major problems with much of culture and personality theory had been its obsession with demonstrating that the personalities of individuals within a culture are all essentially the same. The configurationist school of Mead and Benedict made this claim explicitly, as did Kardiner and Erikson. Even the critical theorists seemed to be saying that all Nazis had authoritarian personalities. But the concept of personality proved to be extremely slippery to define: What exactly *was* it, anyway? A set of connected traits, a certain predisposition to action, a way of organizing experience? Psychologists themselves were not sure how to answer this question. Nor were they at all sure how to test for personality cross-culturally. Furthermore, it was clear to fieldworkers that the people they studied had varied personalities, and that these personalities shifted from situation to situation. Cora Du Bois had attempted to deal with this latter problem by developing the notion of the modal personality—a statistically dominant way of being—but this only showed all the more clearly the ambiguities of the concept.

It was left to Anthony Wallace to try to shelve the notion of a common personality once and for all. Wallace himself had been a strong advocate of the modal personality approach and had written influential works demonstrating the use of highly sophisticated methods of analyzing projective tests in order to discover modal personalities.[40] But his research on the Tuscarora Indians had demonstrated that only about a third of the people in his sample could be said to share a common personality.[41] This led Wallace to wonder how useful the concept of modal personality was when two-thirds of the population had to be labeled deviant. Furthermore, Wallace realized that notions of uniform personality made internal cultural change almost impossible, except by long-term processes of drift.

In place of the assumption that culture is static, stable, and uniform, and that personality is a direct reflection of culture, Wallace proposed that in actuality, culture is fluid, multifarious, and changeable; it is characterized by "kaleidoscopic variety and . . . by diversity of both individuals and groups, many of whom are in continuous and overt competition in one subsystem and in active cooperation in another."[42] Rather than replicating uniformity, "culture may be conceived as an invention that makes possible the maximal organization of motivational and cognitive diversity."[43] In making this change in emphasis, Wallace specifically recalled Sapir's insistence that culture was made up of divergent individuals with divergent interests and could not be looked upon as a harmonious totality.

B. Maintaining Consensus in Diversity

But the problem of conceptualizing consensus remained: How can cultures endure if they do not have any core? Culture and personality theorists had proposed uniformity of character partly because they could not see how to maintain a society in which there was no equivalence of motives and values among members. Wallace denied this and returned to the old social contract model of Hobbes. Society was united, he claimed, not because its members shared a common psyche, but because they rationally accepted an implicit agreement that it was useful and profitable to work together and maintain the social peace. Culture, then, was to be understood as a kind of cognitive and moral framework within which individuals could solve problems and predict, more or less accurately, the outcomes of their behaviors. Predictability was possible because behaviors were functionally organized in reciprocally complementary ways: The feudal lord expects service from his fief, and the fief expects his lord to provide security; the elder advises and commands, and the junior listens and obeys. Individuals in different social situations will have different rights, obligations, and perceptions, but they all mesh in a cohesive cultural whole, which none of them possesses in toto, but which nonetheless contains and organizes all their divergences.

In stressing the complementarity of roles, Wallace drew attention once again to the oppositional relationships that had intrigued Bateson, but whereas Bateson had feared schism, Wallace saw congruence. So long as the framework of complementary interaction was adhered to and outcomes were positive, pleasurable, or at least tolerable, individuals had no need to know about or share in the motives or goals of others, much less to have the same personalities. In fact, Wallace claimed that incommensurate values, motives, and personalities are a positive force in complex modern societies that encompass huge numbers of people and multiple subsystems. Under these circumstances, organized diversity permits the independence and innovation necessary to maintain and expand the society. The danger to culture, Wallace asserted, is not difference and contradiction per se; these are necessarily part and parcel of any cultural system. Rather, the danger is that some persons will be left out and impoverished, or excluded from meaningful work, and driven to despair and revolt against a society that has not met its implicit contractual obligations.

No longer, Wallace concluded, should anthropologists try to deduce personality from culture or spend their time trying to outline the manner in which children are socialized to be cultural types or modal personalities. Rather, they should link the study of culture to the rest of science and search for the broader cognitive processes and evolutionary principles underlying social change. Because of his turn away from the study of personality and toward the study of culture as a problem-solving device, Wallace was especially concerned with exploring the structure of the human mind and its propensity to build schemata, or mental models, of reality, which could be utilized to structure interaction and channel behavior. Much of this presaged later cognitive anthropology.

Of special interest here was Wallace's belief that psychological material should not be understood as a reflection of culture, but rather that culture, in the broadest sense, could be understood through psychological principles, as they were worked through in various contexts. What exactly these principles were was left unclear, though Wallace did take for granted certain human universals, such as a propensity toward relationships of domination and submission, antagonistic impulses, a desire for meaning, anxiety when meaning is threatened, fear of subordination and exclusion, and, most importantly, a drive to innovate. He proposed as well a universal model for psychological transformation (he called it mazeway resynthesis, and it resembled the trajectory of psychic disintegration and reintegration among charismatic leaders that will be discussed in Chapter 11). In other words, in rejecting culture and personality theory, Wallace did not reject the use of psychology in anthropology. Far from it. Instead, he sought to reestablish psychology as an independent variable, one not reducible to cultural influence. But the content of that variable was left vague.

C. Population Psychology

While Wallace brought psychological determinism into anthropology through the back door, his scathing attack on culture and personality theory had the effect of stimulating new defenses of the old paradigms, this time from a more sophisticated evolutionary perspective, inspired by the work of Hallowell. The prime architect of this reformulation was Robert LeVine, who had been one of the fieldworkers in the Whitings' six cultures project. LeVine was well situated to try to bridge the gap between anthropology and psychology, and to resist Wallace's attempt to remove the study of personality from the anthropological agenda. In his landmark book *Culture, Behavior and Personality,*[44] he argued that Wallace's Tuscarora study did not really show that modal personality was a useless concept. If only a third of the Tuscarora showed the modal personality expected, LeVine pointed out, this was still many more than the 5 percent found in a comparative test of the Ojibwa, using the same criteria. Personalities, like biological organisms, will naturally vary a great deal, LeVine said. He agreed with Wallace that variation makes cultural innovation possible, but he also insisted that significant cross-cultural differences in personality could not be based on chance, and must indicate an adaptive fit between Tuscarora modal personality and their cultural environment.

LeVine then noted that an analysis, such as Wallace's, that remained at the level of overt behavior ignored the possibility of understanding deeper psychological roots of action and left culture without content, as merely kaleidoscopic. For example, two successful men may be objectively ranked high as achievers. But one strives for success to please his mother and increase his family's honor; the other works to gain personal recognition. These different subjective orientations will lead to different work preferences, different work styles, and so on. In any attempt to predict behavior, inner dispositions had to be taken into account in a person-centered ethnography. Furthermore, such dispositions may be culturally constructed. For example, the first man's disposition may be linked to the fact that he is Japanese, while the second man's may be linked to his being typically American. But how can the link between behavior and culture be shown, and how can valid comparisons be made between cultures?

To answer these difficult questions, LeVine called for the development of a population psychology "in which individual psychological characteristics are statistically aggregated and compared across cultures in relation to the characteristics of the sociocultural environment."[45] LeVine based his population psychology on a cost-benefit analysis of adaption. This involved a complicated research agenda that aimed at discovering the goals, rules, and sanctions of cultural institutions, as well as situational norms for responding to social pressures; the distributions of various personality dispositions, both genotypic (individual, primary, fixed) and phenotypic (cultural, secondary, malleable); and the success people had in attaining institutional goals, their satisfactions and frustrations, and the types and numbers of behavioral disorders. (See Table 6.3.) In principle, all these factors could be weighed against one another, compared cross-culturally, with costs and benefits calculated in terms of the degree of satisfaction and frustration, and the number of behavior disorders. The result

TABLE 6.3. **Categories of Data Required for Comparative Psychosocial Research**

Socialcultural environment:
A. Institutional goals
B. Institutional rules and sanctions for role performance
C. Situational norms for reacting to institutional and motivational pressures

Personality distributions:
D. Phenotypic patterns of response in social situations
E. Genotypic dispositions (normally distributed)

Hypothesized outcomes of personality-environment interaction:
F. Level of success is attaining institutional goals
G. Consciously experienced satisfaction and frustrations of population members
H. Behavior disorders (rare in frequency but stable over time)

Source: Robert LeVine, 1973, *Culture, Behavior and Personality: An Introduction to the Comparative Study of Psychosocial Adaption,* Chicago: Aldine, p. 168.

would be not only a quantification of the relative success of cultures at attaining their goals, but also a general outline of how costs could best be minimized and benefits maximized—an anthropological-psychological utilitarianism that would finally answer Bentham's problem of quantifying pleasures and pains.

LeVine himself admitted that "such grandiose goals" were a long way from being realized and required much more precise instruments for measuring the various factors he had enumerated.[46] The most intractable difficulty (among many intractable difficulties) was that of distinguishing "enduring behavioral dispositions of individuals and their reaction to transient environmental conditions."[47] But even this difficulty could be overcome, LeVine thought, by extending the methods of psychoanalysis to anthropological fieldwork. Just as psychoanalysts use their interpersonal relations with their patients as primary data, so anthropologists should be able to calibrate their personal relations with their informants to discriminate primary motivations from secondary additions. Exactly how this was to be accomplished was not clear, nor was it clear how to develop psychological tests that would be replicable and valid enough to allow anthropologists to follow LeVine's guidelines.

In fact, LeVine's project, like that of his mentor John Whiting, was swamped by its impossible methodological requirements. But on the way to reaching this impasse, LeVine articulated a strongly dialectical view of culture and the individual engaged in a mutually constitutive relationship of accommodation and adaption. No longer merely imprinted by culture, individuals had their own natures, which culture both molded and was molded by. Culture could also be internalized, and accepted, or its sanctions could be coercive, and resisted. This sophisticated and person-centered view of the human condition resisted the disintegration of culture implicit in Wallace's theory, and led LeVine to become a leading scholar of cross-cultural socialization practices. He also continued to argue throughout his career that a psychoanalytic perspective was necessary for the comparative study of human development.[48]

LeVine and Psychoanalysis

While appreciating the value of psychoanalysis LeVine questioned many of the assumptions embedded within the psychoanalytic model, observing that psychoanalysis follows Western thought in stressing the value of autonomy, although other cultures do not accent that value. In fact, the majority would see Western ideals as selfish. Nor is full autonomy ever really achieved even in the West, despite the value placed on self-actualization in contemporary therapy. As LeVine pointed out, different societies have different spheres where independence is valued and where interdependency is required. For example, the West values self-sufficiency in morality and in the experience of suffering, but interdependence in subsistence. A valid cross-cultural psychoanalysis, LeVine wrote, would have to take into account these differences.[49]

D. Functionalist Freudianism

If LeVine's last-ditch defense of a "scientific" culture and personality theory did not succeed, his spirited defense of psychoanalysis did resonate with many other theorists.[50] One of the most influential of these was Melford Spiro, a tireless fieldworker and prolific writer. Spiro had early been associated with the revisionist group gathered around Kardiner, but he soon rebuked culture and personality theory for its failure to define its terms properly and for not realizing the interpenetration of the two spheres of being. It is true, he said, that human beings require culture to develop personalities, but it is also true that personalities cannot be reduced to mere reflections of culture. Therefore, while culture socializes individuals in order to preserve and reproduce itself, it is also transmuted by those same individuals who use cultural resources for their own purposes.[51]

Spiro refused to believe that culture is simply a jumbled aggregate of behaviors, capable of taking any shape at all, or no shape in particular. Instead, he argued that human beings share universal cultural patterns, common features of social interaction, and a basic biological heritage. The interaction of these creates "a generic human mind."[52] According to Spiro, this psychological deep structure—the generic mind—was built upon panhuman psychic experiences and propensities, best explicated by Freud. By accepting the Freudian paradigm of the mind, and by connecting it to an evolutionary, functionalist anthropology, Spiro was able to provide a powerful tool for social analysis, useful for explaining aspects of human social life that appear irrational and seemingly purposeless, such as ritual exorcisms, beliefs in ghosts and witches, and monkish devotional practices.

For Spiro, as for Freud, emotionally charged cultural practices and beliefs are best understood as adaptive systems, much like neurotic symptoms in an individual, which forge a symbolic integration of the often conflicting inner fantasies of human beings with the necessities of social life, allowing the channeling and discharge of repressed desires. This means that even though these aspects of culture may seem arbitrary and illogical on the surface, they can still be explained as the culturally colored efforts at resolution of shared human conflicts. For example,

Burmese monks with their begging bowls.

Spiro understood the rigid monastic discipline of Burma as a cultural outlet for the psychic tensions of Burmese men.[53]

Spiro believed that his functional-psychodynamic model not only permitted scientific comparative research, but also could explain diversity. Human beings, Spiro insisted, must be seen first as biosocial beings, capable of existing only within cultures that provide a moral framework for behavior, organize collective outlets for desire, and supply symbolic defenses against anxiety. These cultural templates are incorporated into individuals through their socialization by family members, friends, teachers, and elders, but the incorporation is never the same for everyone: Families differ; social interactions vary; each individual's impulses, ambitions, and anxieties are never equivalently intense.[54]

As a result of endless variations in individual character and personal environment, cultural values can never simply be imposed unilaterally, but instead are differentially incorporated. Any particular individual may know some cultural doctrines only vaguely or not at all; others may be understood, but considered wrong or irrelevant; others may be accepted only as clichés; others will be internalized and used to guide decisions. Finally, some deeply held beliefs will serve as motivating forces to instigate action. These are the ideals one is willing to die defending.[55]

Spiro's levels of cultural knowledge can be summarized as follows:

- Mininal knowledge of doctrine. No motivating force.
- Doctrine known, but considered irrelevant or wrong. Minimal or negative motivating force.

- Doctrine known as cliché. Minimal motivating force.
- Doctrine internalized as correct. Motivates practical decisions.
- Doctrine internalized as a central belief. Strongly motivates action and can entail self-sacrifice.

Of course, motivating ideals are not the same for everyone; one person's absolute is another's cliché. The search for the grace of God means something quite different to an Evangelical preacher than it does to a secular sometime churchgoer. To understand motivation, the analyst would have to attend to the degree to which any norm had been internalized and made a part of the individual psyche. Spiro's early discussion of divergent degrees of engagement was later to have a great influence on cognitive anthropologists trying to understand the motivational effect of cultural models on individuals.[56]

Summary

By the 1950s, culture and personality studies had been more or less discredited, and only a few anthropologists were still working on psychological issues. Among the most important of these were John and Beatrice Whiting, who, with their colleagues, tried to test Freudian theory through the comparative method, using information culled from the HRAF to establish a correlation between harsh male initiation rites and strong Oedipal complexes. They also attempted to undertake a strictly controlled fieldwork study of six different cultures to show the relationship between socialization and character. However, the results were somewhat disappointing.

Looking for new paradigms, anthropologists turned to the past, resurrecting the writings of G. H. Mead and Charles Peirce, who had both concerned themselves with social construction of the self. Peirce focused on the role of language in forging an identity, while Mead emphasized the importance of self-awareness for the maintenance of order, and the playful, mimetic manner in which selves are tried on, discarded, and identified with. A. Irving Hallowell took up the first aspect of Mead, linking it to his own interest in evolutionary biology. Goffman took up the second, constructing a dramaturgical theory of human social life. Both authors gave credit, in their different ways, to impulse, to difference, and to resistance; they also assumed an internal human emotional structure, and a kind of unconscious—opening the possibility of assimilating psychoanalytic theory.

Meanwhile, the study of culture and personality was dealt another serious blow by one of its foremost practitioners, as A. F. C. Wallace argued that cultures are united not by shared personality structures, but by rational agreements negotiated among divergent individuals. At the same time, Wallace did not deny the existence of underlying psychological universals, such as a tendency to construct mental models of reality.

In response, two anthropologists strongly influenced by psychoanalysis proposed more complex models of the relationship between the individual and culture than had previously been attempted. Robert LeVine argued in favor of a cost-benefit population psychology that could compare and assess the inputs and outputs of a particular cultural pattern; Melford Spiro affirmed the existence of a generic human mind created by the interaction of biology, culture, and social life. In their writings, both argued that psychoanalysis offered a needed theoretical grounding to anthropology; both tried to connect a psychodynamic paradigm with Hallowell's Darwinian evolutionary model, and both emphasized the functional manner in which culture operated to release and disguise unacceptable psychic tensions that would otherwise threaten the social fabric. For both of them, as for Freud, the superego was the hero of the story, the conveyer of culture into the mind.

Even though LeVine, Spiro, and Wallace were interested in variation within culture and developed theories to account for difference, their real focus was on the typical, on processes of accommodation, and on the testing of large-scale theories about the relationship between psyche and society—not on distinction and creation, or on the experiences of individuals.[58] The writers whose work is to be considered in the next section take a very different approach.

Endnotes

1. See Henri Junod, 1927, *The Life of a South African Tribe*, London: Macmillan, pp. 74–95.
2. The most convincing examples of such criticism are to be found in Richard Shweder, 1979–80, "Rethinking Culture and Personality Theory," *Ethos* 7: 255–311; 8: 60–94. See also Katherine Ewing, 1990, "The Illusion of Wholeness: Culture, Self and the Experience of Inconsistency," *Ethos* 18: 251–73.
3. See Gustav Jahoda, 1954, "A Note on Ashanti Day Names in Relation to Personality," *British Journal of Psychology* 45: 192–95.
4. Jack Block, 1981, "Some Enduring and Consequential Structures of Personality," in A. Rabin et al., *Further Explorations in Personality*, New York: Wiley; cited in John Ingham, *Psychological Anthropology Reconsidered*, 1996, Cambridge, England: Cambridge University Press, p. 113.
5. John Rohrer and Munro Edmunson, 1960, *The Eighth Generation Grows Up*, New York: Harper and Row; Allison Davis and John Dollard, 1964, *Children of Bondage*, New York: Harper and Row (original publication 1940).
6. See, for example, Weston La Barre, 1972, *The Ghost Dance*, New York: Delta Press; Georges Devereux, 1969, *Reality and Dream: Psychotherapy of a Plains Indian*, New York: New York University Press.
7. For representative works, see George DeVos, 1973, *Socialization for Achievement: Essays on the Cultural Psychology of the Japanese*, Berkeley: University of California Press; T. Gladwin and S. Sarason, 1953, *Truk: Man in Paradise*, New York: Wenner-Gren; George Spindler and Louise Spindler, 1971, *Dreamers without Power: The Menomini Indians*, New York: Holt, Rinehart and Winston; John Honigmann, 1954, *The Kaska Indians: An Ethnographic Reconstruction*, New Haven, CT: Yale University Publications in Anthropology, 51.
8. Dorothy Lee, 1959, *Freedom and Culture*, Englewood Cliffs, NJ: Prentice-Hall.
9. For an excellent and thorough summary of the entire field during this era, see John Honigmann, 1967, *Personality in Culture*, New York: Harper and Row.
10. See Heinz Kohut, 1977, *The Restoration of the Self*, New York: International Universities Press; 1985, *Self Psychology and the Humanities*, New York: Norton.
11. Melanie Klein, 1975, *Envy and Gratitude and Other Works*, New York: Dell.
12. D. W. Winnicott, 1965, *The Maturational Process and the Facilitating Environment*, London: Hogarth; W. R. Fairbairn, 1954, *The Object-Relations Theory of the Personality*, New York: Basic Books.
13. See, for example, Virginia Demos, 1988, "Affect and the Development of the Self," in Arnold Goldberg (ed.), *Frontiers in Self Psychology*, Vol. 3, Hillsdale, NJ: Analytic Press.
14. Robert LeVine, 1979, "The Self and Its development in an African Society: A Preliminary Analysis," in Benjamin Lee (ed.), *Psychosocial Theories of the Self*, New York: Plenum Press. For other critiques, see Louis Sass, 1988, "The Self in Contemporary Psychoanalysis: Commentary on Charles Taylor," in Stanley Messer, Louis Sass, and

Robert Woolfolk (eds.), *Hermeneutics and Psychological Theory: Interpretive Perspectives on Personality, Psychotherapy, and Psychopathology,* New Brunswick, NJ: Rutgers University Press; Ewing, "The Illusion of Wholeness."

15. For an exception, see Katherine Ewing, 1997, *Arguing Sainthood: Modernity, Psychoanalysis and Islam,* Durham, NC: Duke University Press.

16. An important exception is psychoanalyst Nancy Chodorow's recent call for a new dialogue between psychological anthropology and psychoanalysis. Her claim is that psychoanalysis has not paid proper attention to social and cultural factors, while anthropologists have ignored the individual's capacity for creativity and self-transformation. For her, the cultural and psychological are dialectically united through transference, which is understood as the projection and introjection of personal fantasies onto the external world, rendering it both meaningful and emotionally compelling. See Nancy Chodorow, 1999, *The Power of Feelings: Personal Meaning in Psychoanalysis,* New Haven, CT: Yale University Press.

17. Whiting was prepared for this task by his training at Yale, where Sapir's project to study personality through anthropology still had some prestige, and where Linton had gone after his tenure at Columbia. At Yale some experimental psychologists—most notably John Dollard—had already tried to integrate Freudian insights with a more scientific methodology.

18. J. Whiting, R. Kluckhohn, and A. Anthony, 1958, "The Function of Male Initiation Ceremonies at Puberty," in E. Maccoby, T. Newcomb, and E. Hartley (eds.), *Readings in Social Psychology,* New York: Holt. For a critique, see Frank Young, 1965, *Initiation Ceremonies,* Indianapolis, IN: Bobbs Merrill.

19. The communities studied were Nyansongo (Kenya), Jaxtlahuaca (Mexico), Taira (Okinawa), Khalapur (India), Tarong (Philippines), and Orchard Town (United States). The major findings were published in Beatrice Whiting and John Whiting, 1975, *Children of Six Cultures: A Psycho-Cultural Analysis,* Cambridge, MA: Harvard University Press.

20. For a recent, balanced appreciation of the Whitings' contributions, see Sara Harkness, 1992, "Human Development in Psychological Anthropology," in Theodore Schwartz, Geoffrey White, and Catherine Lutz (eds.), *New Directions in Psychological Anthropology,* Cambridge, England: Cambridge University Press.

21. Using HRAF data, Whiting himself continued to develop ever more sophisticated and complex cross-cultural models of cause and effect, stressing the priority of climatic factors and power relationships over psychosexual fixations. For a recent statement, see John Whiting, 1990, "Adolescent Rituals and Identity Conflicts," in James Stigler, Richard Shweder, and Gilbert Herdt (eds.), *Cultural Psychology: Essays on Comparative Human Development,* Cambridge, England: Cambridge University Press.

22. Peirce's theory of semiotics was based on a tripartite concept of signs. A sign existed first in relation to a second, its object, within the context of the third, the interpretant. This latter element brought culture into the linguistic model. For a cogent exploration of Peirce's complex thought and its application to anthropology, see Milton Singer, 1984, *Man's Glassy Essence: Explorations in Semiotic Anthropology,* Bloomington: Indiana University Press.

23. See Charles Peirce, 1940, *Philosophical Writings of Peirce,* New York: Dover, p. 258.

24. Singer, *Man's Glassy Essence,* p. 72.

25. In his portrait of human beings as bundles of habits, Peirce reproduced Hume. His concern with physical habit also prefigured the notion of habitus, used later by Marcel Mauss and Pierre Bourdieu. Anthropologists recently influenced by Peirce include Vincent Crapanzano, whose work will be discussed in Chapter 7, and E. Valentine Daniel (1984, *Fluid Signs: Being a Person the Tamil Way,* Berkeley: University of

California Press), who wittily demonstrates how Tamil pilgrims reverse Peirce's movement from synthetic to analytic knowledge.

26. George Herbert Mead, 1934, *Mind, Self and Society*, Chicago: University of Chicago Press, p. 164.

27. His 1954 essay "Psychology and Anthropology" (reprinted in A. I. Hallowell, 1976, *Contributions to Anthropology: Selected Papers of A. Irving Hallowell*, Chicago, University of Chicago Press) is a classic, from which I have taken much.

28. A. I. Hallowell, 1976, "Personality, Culture and Society in Behavioral Evolution" (original publication 1963), reprinted in A. I. Hallowell, *Contributions to Anthropology: Selected Papers of A. Irving Hallowell*, Chicago: University of Chicago Press, p. 280.

29. Ibid., pp. 283, 289.

30. Hallowell, "Psychology and Anthropology," p. 229.

31. Hallowell, "Personality, Culture and Society in Behavioral Evolution," p. 280.

32. A. I. Hallowell, 1976, "Ojibwa World View and Disease" (original publication 1963), reprinted in A. I. Hallowell, *Contributions to Anthropology: Selected Papers of A. Irving Hallowell*, Chicago: University of Chicago Press, p. 399.

33. A. I. Hallowell, 1976, "Ojibwa Ontology, Behavior, and World View" (original publication 1960), reprinted in A. I. Hallowell, *Contributions to Anthropology: Selected Papers of A. Irving Hallowell*, Chicago: University of Chicago Press, p. 378.

34. Hallowell, "Ojibwa World View and Disease," p. 437.

35. 1959, New York: Doubleday.

36. Sigmund Freud, 1989, *The Psychopathology of Everyday Life*, New York: Norton (original publication 1904).

37. Goffman, *The Presentation of Self in Everyday Life*, p. 235.

38. For more on Goffman's theory of stigma, see Chapter 11.

39. Erving Goffman, 1961, *Asylums: Essays on the Social Situation of Mental Patients and Other Inmates*, Garden City, NY: Doubleday.

40. See Anthony F. C. Wallace, 1950, "A Possible Technique for Recognizing Psychological Characteristics of the Ancient Maya from an Analysis of Their Art," *American Imago* 7: 239–58.

41. Anthony F. C. Wallace, 1952, *The Modal Personality Structure of the Tuscarora Indians as Revealed by the Rorschach Test*. Bureau of American Ethnology Bulletin 150, Washington, DC: Smithsonian Institution.

42. Anthony F. C. Wallace, 1961, *Culture and Personality*, New York: Random House, p. 24.

43. Ibid., p. 36.

44. Robert LeVine, 1973, *Culture, Behavior and Personality: An Introduction to the Comparative Study of Psychosocial Adaption*, Chicago: Aldine.

45. Ibid., p. 281.

46. Ibid., p. 286.

47. Ibid., p. 203.

48. See, for example, Robert LeVine, 1981, "Psychoanalytic Theory and the Comparative Study of Human Development," in R. H. Munroe, R. L. Munroe, and B. Whiting (eds.), *Handbook of Cross-Cultural Human Development*, New York: Garland Press.

49. Robert LeVine, 1990, "Infant Environments in Psychoanalysis: A Cross-Cultural View," in James Stigler, Richard Shweder, and Gilbert Herdt (eds.), *Cultural Psychology: Essays on Comparative Human Development*, Cambridge, England: Cambridge University Press.

50. For some recent examples, see the special 1987 issue of *Ethos* 15, devoted to interpretation in psychoanalytic anthropology.

51. Melford Spiro, 1951, "Culture and Personality: The Natural History of a False Dichotomy," *Psychiatry* 14: 19–47.

52. Melford Spiro, 1984, "Some Reflections on Cultural Determinism and Relativism with Special Reference to Emotion and Reason," in Richard Shweder and Robert LeVine (eds.), *Culture Theory: Essays on Mind, Self and Emotion,* Cambridge, England: Cambridge University Press, p. 335.

53. Melford Spiro, 1965, "Religious Systems as Culturally Constituted Defense Mechanisms," in M. Spiro (ed.), *Context and Meaning in Cultural Anthropology,* New York: Free Press, p. 109.

54. See Spiro, "Culture and Personality."

55. For an early formulation of this model of differential motivation, see Melford Spiro, 1982, "Collective Representations and Mental Representation in Religious Symbol Systems," in Jacques Maquet (ed.), *On Symbols in Anthropology: Essays in Honor of Harry Hoijer 1980,* Malibu, CA: Uneda.

56. For a recent appreciation of Spiro's work, see Kevin Avruch, 1990, "Melford Spiro and the Scientific Study of Culture," in David K. Jordan and Marc J. Swartz (eds.), *Personality and the Cultural Construction of Society: Papers in Honor of Melford E. Spiro,* Tuscaloosa: University of Alabama Press.

57. LeVine's later work on the Gusii does make a point of considering alternative modes of mothering, using specific cases. His wife, Sarah, also wrote a pioneering study of individual Gusii women: Sarah LeVine, 1979, *Mothers and Wives: Gusii Women of East Africa,* Chicago: University of Chicago Press.

CHAPTER 7

Creativity and Alterity

"My adviser smiled. 'How would you like to study poetry which *pretends* to be scientific?' he asked me. 'Is such a thing possible?' I said. He shook my hand. 'Welcome to the field of social or cultural anthropology,' he said."[1]

Kurt Vonnegut's anecdote about his days as an undergraduate expresses a truth about American anthropology. As noted in Chapter 4, since its beginnings in the days of Franz Boas, the discipline has always walked the fine line between poetry and science, sometimes tilting in one direction, sometimes in the other. The culture and personality research undertaken by Benedict and her cohort leaned strongly toward poetry; in recent times, the same tendency has occurred, and with a greater magnitude, so that even the pretense of "doing science" has been dropped by many important anthropologists.

The shift to a more aesthetic and literary perspective was an inevitable reaction to research agendas of the 1950s that overreached themselves attempting to deliver valid, predictive, and universal models for understanding the relationship between culture and the psyche. The failure of projective tests was often cited as evidence of the uselessness of science for anthropological work, as were the fragmentary results of the Whitings' ambitious comparative trait analysis. Attempts to save the scientific aspect of psychological anthropology, such as LeVine's population psychology and Spiro's Freudian functionalism, did not convince opponents, who claimed that those efforts to understand the relationship between culture and the individual undermined the autonomy and distinctiveness of both, without providing any justifying valid results.

In response, a number of anthropologists tried to develop a psychological anthropology that gave more credit to personal agency, process, and invention, while still retaining some of the universalistic principles derived from Freud. Others decided to dispense entirely with any claims to comparativism or science, and to resurrect Benedict's configurationism in the construction of aesthetic thick descriptions of particular cultures. More politically motivated writers saw their task as providing the "other" with a voice to protest against injustice. Finally, a few anthropologists decided to look toward the body itself as the source of truth—aiming at the universal through the physical. This chapter outlines and critiques these recent theoretical innovations, and concludes with my own version of psychological anthropology—a dialectical model that attempts to do justice both to poetry and to science in the study of the relationship between culture and identity.

Chapter Outline

I. AGENCY AND ACTION: TURNER, OBEYESEKERE, AND CRAPANZANO

A Ritual Performance and Rites of Passage
  Victor Turner's study of ritual processes and cults of affliction. Performance theory.

B Liminality and Transformation
  Personal and social transformation through social dramas of liminality.

C The Psychoanalysis of Ritual
  Gananath Obeyesekere's linkage of personal trauma and creativity through subjectification.

D An Asian Psychodynamic
  Are Eastern cultures more in touch with the unconscious than Western cultures? Obeyesekere's critique of Freud.

E Self-Reflection in Ethnography
  Vincent Crapanzano's reflexive anthropology.

F   The Dialogic Creation of Self and Other
    Metapragmatics, doubt, and instability in ethnography.

A. Ritual Performance and Rites of Passage

An early champion of a new and more individualistic approach to the relationship between culture and identity was Victor Turner (1920–1983). Like Spiro and LeVine, he was profoundly influenced by the Freudian model, and he too attempted a synthesis; but whereas Spiro and LeVine were interested in adaption and adjustment, Turner was preoccupied with innovation and opposition; whereas they mostly set aside the study of individuals, Turner made them the focus of much of his later work, which was concerned above all with the creative potential of ritual and theatrical performance.

Turner began his career in England as a functionalist with no particular interest in psychology. He was a student of Max Gluckman (1911–1975), who had long argued that rituals permitted the symbolic expression of opposition and so could promote social stability.[2] Turner followed his mentor by describing how the Ndembu people of Africa maintained order despite deep internal contradictions within their society. They did so, he said, by the enactment of social dramas, wherein a breach of social norms leads to a crisis, which is resolved by redress, usually through performance of a ritual, and ends in social reintegration.[3]

Turner's functionalism was therefore never static, and was grounded in an analysis of ongoing ritual processes; it contained within itself the implication that failures in ritual could lead to social change (an implication Gluckman also accepted). Naturally enough, his interest soon shifted to analysis of the rituals themselves, particularly to the manner in which Ndembu cults of affliction enlisted the entire community to heal the ills of individuals. Turner gradually developed a subtle and complex method of examination in which practice, cultural knowledge, and symbolic systems were all brought into play to tease out the many levels at which curative ritual operated.[4] From his original functionalism, he was increasingly drawn toward the study of the relationship between culture and the psychology of the individual, as enacted in ritual.

As his theory evolved, Turner brought more psychoanalytic and biological material into his paradigm, arguing that ritual is a behavior found in both animals and humans, and that it serves in every instance as a symbolic means for channeling unacceptable emotions. Turner also acknowledged that humans differ from animals in their powers of imagination and their capacity to construct complex meaning systems. These too are metaphorically expressed through the symbolic enactments of ritual performance. Ritual symbols, Turner then argued, are the multivalent molecules that connect the two opposing poles of life, which he variously termed the instinctive and the cultural, the emotional and the cognitive, the natural and the collective, the id and the superego, the orectic and the ideological.

For Turner, ritual could best be understood as the communal equivalent of the ego, serving to mediate between elemental desire and cultural constraint, "putting at the service of the social order the very forces of disorder that inhere

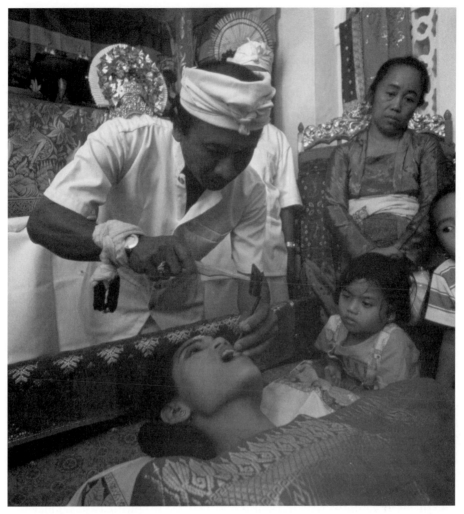

Bali: During a rite of passage into puberty, the canine teeth are filed down to eradicate the intiate's "wild" nature.

in man's mammalian constitution."[5] In a Freudian manner, he argued that in every culture, threatening sexual and aggressive impulses provoke elaborate symbolic formations "like grit in an oyster." These ritualized symbols have the power to command both mind and heart, and relate thought to feeling and action. They do so by saturating norms and ideas with passion; simultaneously, the emotions are "ennobled or 'sublimed' " through contact with social values.[6]

B. Liminality and Transformation

Turner gradually came to understand the emotional intensity and bonding of ritual performance as the necessary balance to the structure, practical reason, and authority of ordinary life, providing antistructure, fantasy, and a sense of merger in the equalizing experience of communitas. Following the classifications first formulated by Durkheim's rival, Arnold van Gennep (1873–1957),[7] and heavily influenced by Bateson's Hegelian notions of the inner dialectics of culture, Turner claimed that human society and the individuals who make it up are always moving through rites of passage.

According to van Gennep, these rites fall into two categories. The first occurs when persons move from one social status to the next; the second, when whole social worlds move through calendrical time. The first includes ceremonies commemorating personal milestones, such as birth, maturity, marriage, and death. The second includes regular communal celebrations signaling the cycle of the seasons, such as Christmas and Easter. These categories are not mutually exclusive, and more communally minded societies may have seasonally linked group ceremonies that denote, for instance, an individual's passage from one age grade to another.

Although the content of any particular rite is specific, van Gennep said they always went through three stages: (1) separation from a previous state, (2) liminality (an ambiguous phase between stages), and (3) reintegration at a different level. Typical symbols of this process include breaking, tearing, cutting, shaving, stripping away, followed by a period of isolation and magical instruction, and concluding with some form of symbolic bonding back into the community.

Where Turner contributed something new to van Gennep's model was in his connection of the notion of the liminal state to both the therapeutic process of psychoanalysis and the production of charisma. Returning to his Ndembu material and Gluckman's notion of rituals of rebellion, Turner claimed that ritual provided a healing social drama wherein the norms of the larger society could be breached and alternative worlds could be explored prior to the return to normal life. In such creative ritual performances, the unconscious impulses of individuals, ordinarily repressed, could be enacted with impunity and approved by the community of the performers and onlookers. Turner then applied his analysis to more complex social worlds, arguing that ritual performance allowed the excluded and impoverished to lose themselves momentarily in ecstatic states, feeling themselves united with the spirits and elevated to spiritual ascendancy.

In ritual, then, the psychic tensions of individuals, often exacerbated by oppression and estrangement, could be transformed into symbolic form and enacted as a form of public therapy that would heal not only the sufferer but also the other participants in the ritual. Turner also recognized that the liminal state might have a less conservative function: It could serve as the locus for opposition to the culture at large, inspiring the weak and excluded to open revolt. The radical potential of ritual derived from the indeterminacy of the performance, and the individuality of the actors, which meant that it was never certain what the outcome might be; sometimes new worldviews might be espoused by individuals energized by the force of their ecstatic communion. New anti-authoritarian symbol systems, given force by the emotional power of liminality and ecstasy, could then give alienated individuals the ideology and the strength to resist and rebel.[8]

Following this line of thought, Turner gradually moved toward a consideration of the actual persons involved in social movements and ritual performances, as he attempted to enter into their experiences to grasp the interplay of ideas, symbols, and conscious and unconscious motivations that lay behind processes of social and individual change. He thought that life histories, personal documents, and first-person accounts ought to be used to free anthropology from its reliance on purely abstract, impersonal structural paradigms, and allow anthropologists "to see in the very flaws, hesitations, personal factors, incomplete, elliptical, context-dependent, situational components of performance, clues to the very nature of human process itself."[9] Turner's ultimate hope was to show how the creative individual could transform the larger culture.

Unfortunately, Turner never actually managed to accomplish his stated goal of analyzing the interplay between individual psychic tensions, cultural processes, and social change.[10] Rather, he shifted his attention to the study of theater, increasingly focusing on the aesthetic and cultural aspects of performance in modern society, and on the priority of experience and enactment over theory. To an extent, he himself became so involved in the liminal and experiential that he was unable, or unwilling, to reconnect himself to structure, and so his contribution to theory was left incomplete.

C. The Psychoanalysis of Ritual

Another, quite different and potentially more productive, psychological anthropology of ritual performance and the manner in which the creative individual initiates cultural innovation has been offered by Gananath Obeyesekere in his book *Medusa's Hair*.[11] A native of Sri Lanka, Obeyesekere early on applied a psychodynamic approach to understanding the complex religious beliefs and practices of his homeland, focusing on the zealots who perform fantastic feats of self-laceration, such as hanging themselves on hooks, having themselves buried alive, and walking on fire, during the fêtes held annually at the syncretic shrine of Kataragama.

Obeyesekere began his attempt to bring psychoanalysis into ethnography by postulating that the characteristic long, greasy, and matted hair of the devotees he was studying was not merely an arbitrary cultural symbol marking out religiously inclined individuals. He insisted instead that their snakelike hair ought to be interpreted psychoanalytically as a sign of sexual repression, in which "the sublated penis emerges through the head."[12] This seemingly far-fetched interpretation was borne out by the believers themselves, who said that their renunciation of sexuality had been rewarded by a mystical unification with the phallic God of the shrine, who was represented in their winding, reptilian hair. It was this incorporated god who granted them the gift of overcoming pain in their ritual performances.

Obeyesekere interpreted the masochistic ceremonies of Kataragama as expiations of primary guilt caused by the infantile rage and desire stimulated by the Oedipal conflict, for which penance must somehow be made. Following Freud, Obeyesekere said that primary guilt is found among all human beings everywhere;[13] but in the life histories of the performers whom Obeyesekere analyzed, familial neglect and abuse had horribly exaggerated the Oedipal

Self-laceration is common in religous rituals, such as this one in Thailand.

Symbolic Hair

Whether Freudians are right to say that hair has universal sexual significance may be doubtful, but it is true that everywhere in the world, hairstyles are used to indicate not only ethnicity, occupation, and gender but also states of mind. In the United States during the 1960s, long hair among men was a visible, outward expression of a challenge to conventional authority—it was assumed to coincide with radical politics, drug use, and sexual experimentation. The Rastafarians of Jamaica also wear long, matted dreadlocks that express their countercultural lifestyles. While much of this symbolism has faded as long hair has become simply another style, it still retains implications of rebellion and sexual freedom. The shaven tonsure of the Catholic monk, in contrast, represents submission, restraint, and chastity—just as it does for Buddhist monks in Asia.

trauma; as a result the performers were psychologically compelled to pursue far more extreme forms of expiation than is normal. All followed the same dramatic pattern in their lives: Attacked by spirits and overwhelmed by terrifying visions, they ran away from unhappy homes and took on roles as celibate and self-torturing renunciants who experienced spiritual ecstasy in their trance states. Obeyesekere calls this transformation objectification, that is, "the expression (projection and externalization) of private emotions in a public idiom."[14] Henceforth, the punishing Oedipal demon became a loving guardian, protecting and nurturing his acolytes, who now were able to create and endure the most radical tortures without flinching.

Although the patterns of misery and redemption in the lives of Obeyesekere's informants are parallel, none of them are alike, nor are their ritual performances enacted by rote, like the standardized prayers of monks. Because each is compelled by his or her unique Oedipal experience, and because each is an individual human being, with unique psychic tensions and different family and cultural backgrounds, each shows a range of originality in his or her performances of exculpatory suffering, which may be adopted into the larger cultural framework of the Kataragama ritual and of religious ecstatics in Sri Lanka.

This creative potential is subjectification, a process in which "cultural ideas are used to produce, and thereafter justify, innovative acts, meanings, or images that help express the personal needs and fantasies of individuals."[15] If the new style of self-lacerating ritual performance resonates sufficiently with the preexistent symbolic framework of the society, it will enter the cultural repertoire and the individual will gain a position of respect and even spiritual authority. But if the individual's performance is merely idiosyncratic, there are no such rewards, and the presentation becomes nothing more than compulsive repetition, without any larger significance. Instead of being worshiped as a god, the performer is likely to be designated psychotic. For example, Obeyesekere describes a Muslim ecstatic whose performance of tongue cutting and breaking coconuts on his head was not accepted by his community, and who was in danger of becoming a pariah.

Obeyesekere argues that difference in outcome is a consequence of the mix between motive and meaning, symptom and symbol, in any given case. Symptoms, in his definition, are strongly and directly motivated by childhood trauma, with scant room for elaboration or substitution, and like the symptoms of a physical disease, such as smallpox or cholera, they vary little cross-culturally. Symbolic expressions of deep motivations, in contrast, have greater variation and show only family resemblances across cultures;[16] they are far more susceptible to the influence of culture and to personal manipulation, and more capable of expressing meaning. In summary:

- Symptoms are universal, constant, and motivated by trauma.
- Symbols are specific, variable, and transformative.

D. An Asian Psychodynamic

Individuals who are psychically capable of transforming their motivated symptoms into meaningful symbols are also capable of overcoming their mental anguish and of contributing new cultural forms to their society. This capability, which Obeyesekere calls symbolic remove, is a result of personal background, but also reflects cultural factors. According to him, Western societies permit only those public, symbolic performances that are detached from deep motivations; others societies, such as that of Sri Lanka, favor far more direct ritual expressions of powerful desires; still others favor a combination of both, in alternation.

This brings us to one of the most interesting and problematic aspects of Obeyesekere's theory. He argues that Sri Lankan and Asian societies in general easily express deep emotional material in public rituals, while in Western society such material is suppressed in public and remains on the level of personal fantasy, rising to the surface only in cases of mental illness. He believes that this is the case because of the strong Western notion of the differentiated ego and punitive superego. According to Obeyesekere, this psychic structure, with its rigid repression against id impulses, is inculcated in the Western nuclear family and correlates with a capitalist and Protestant emphasis on self-control. Under such constraints, public symbols are wholly detached from deep psychic reality. Fantasy is limited in favor of efficiency. Those who remain connected to their unconscious impulses are labeled mentally ill; there is no place for them in the society.

Among South Asians, in contrast, the society is less achievement-oriented; fantasy is permitted and even encouraged. Furthermore, the family is collectivist; the child is immersed in an extended household and experiences a strong symbiosis with its mother. Autonomy is not valued, while unity and merger are. Under these circumstances, individuals have more access to their unconscious fantasies, and there is more tolerance for transferring these fantasies into public space.

Obeyesekere concludes that the late Freudian paradigm of superego, ego, and id is mistaken. These categories are, he says, Western reifications: The cruel superego is a symbolic representation of the patriarchal Victorian father; the ego expresses the high value the West places on independent action and rationality; the id reveals a deep Judeo-Christian fear of emotion and passion. More accurate for describing South Asia, Obeyesekere claims, is the earlier Freudian model of the porous unconscious, preconscious, and conscious mind. Also, Freud's drive theory should be abandoned, since we are not at all sure which drives exist. Rather, analysts should pay attention to fantasy and its repression. Greater repression, as in the West, leads to an infantile fantasy life and a naive ignorance of the dark side of life; tolerance, as in South Asia, favors hypnomantic trance states, and a humane awareness of suffering.

To recapitulate:

- *Western thought.* Ideal of autonomy and self-control, patriarchal superego, fantasy forbidden. Correlates with capitalism, nuclear family. Individuals are repressed, infantile, and naive.
- *Eastern thought.* Ideal of merger and collective unity, maternal symbiosis, fantasy expressed. Correlates with precapitalism, extended family. Individuals are easily entranced, humane, and tolerant.

Obeyesekere contends that we must reconsider the psychoanalytic assumption that the entrance of unconscious material into the mind is inevitably catastrophic. He claims that for the ecstatics he studied, tragic circumstances have been transfigured and rendered positive precisely through the entrance of unconscious fantasies, transmuted through the dialectical process of objectification and subjectification into appropriate cultural form during trance states. These individuals have achieved, Obeyesekere thinks, a remarkable spiritual grace because Sri Lankan society contains appropriate cultural narratives for expressing psychic distress as spiritual enlightenment.

There are problems with this rosy picture. Although Obeyesekere's Sri Lankan informants have lived extraordinary and meaningful lives that are certainly worth recounting, they are not representative of the lives of ordinary Sri Lankans, who seem, from other ethnographic accounts, to be just as tormented by guilt, just as egoistical, and just as rational (or irrational) as people anywhere else. And while it may be the case, as Obeyesekere suggests, that some forms of mental disorder are transfigured in Sri Lanka by the twin processes of objectification and subjectification, he presents no evidence that mental illnesses per se are actually less prevalent there, or treated more compassionately, than in the West. Nor is it evident that Westerners repress their fantasy lives more than Asians; it seems instead that in the West, unlike in Sri Lanka, religious ritual is no longer the locus where fantasy is expressed. We have movies and television for that purpose. Furthermore, by making claims about the supposed spiritual capacities and cultural creativity of his informants, Obeyesekere is in danger of romanticization, awarding his hook-hanging supplicants a halo. Finally, it is hard to accept his denigration of impulse in favor of fantasy, and his substitution of the unconscious-preconscious-conscious triad for that of the id-ego-superego. In his paradigm, fantasy is taken as unmotivated, which seems unlikely, while the dissolution of the superego-ego-id relationship ignores precisely the problem of repression that this formula was meant to solve, that is, how and why some aspects of experience are denied entrance into awareness, so that they can be revealed only symbolically.

Nonetheless, despite these problems, Obeyesekere has offered one of the most culturally sensitive and most sophisticated versions of psychoanalytic anthropology yet written: a person-centered theory based on a constitutive dialectic between individual consciousness and cultural systems of meaning.[17]

E. Self-Reflection in Ethnography

A third author who has made innovative use of a person-centered anthropological method is Vincent Crapanzano, a philosophically inclined and psychoanalytically sophisticated American anthropologist who did his original fieldwork in Morocco, where he wrote a fine account of the psychological processes at work in an ecstatic cult, the Hamadsha. In that ethnography, he analyzed, in Turneresque fashion, the complex relationship between the overarching spiritual symbolic system of Morocco and the Hamadshas' therapeutic experience of trance.[18]

In his next book, Crapanzano moved away from symbolic analysis of ritual to write instead about his personal relationship with his Moroccan informant and friend Tuhami, a man disturbed by deep psychological problems, who sought cure through entranced identification with the female demon (Àisha) he believed had bewitched him.[19] In his communion with Àisha, Tuhami resembled the Hamadsha, who also felt themselves carried away by Àisha when they performed their ecstatic prayers; for Tuhami, however, the relationship was not a public one, and it required no prescribed ritual. Rather, Àisha entered into his soul while he was alone and transformed him permanently.

In his book, Crapanzano tried to enter as well into Tuhami's complex and highly idiosyncratic psychic world. He argued that the spirit possessing Tuhami provided him with an imaginary alter ego who could articulate and realize desires forbidden in his daily life. In identifying with the spirit, Tuhami collapsed the distinction between self and other, male and female, leading Crapanzano, like Obeyesekere, to question the universality of the autonomous ego and the punishing paternal superego. But, unlike Obeyesekere, Crapanzano did not try to develop any viable alternative theory; instead, his deep knowledge of Tuhami's unique, shifting, and extraordinary mental state made him wary of any claims to theoretical closure whatsoever.[20]

Renouncing the possibility of reaching objective conclusions out of his years of discussion with Tuhami, Crapanzano was left in a quandary. What exactly ought his ethnography accomplish? His decision was to dissect his own emotional and psychological relationship with Tuhami, much as a psychoanalyst might recount a case study. In so doing, he became more than an information collector. Transference—the intense and ambivalent emotional identification between patient and analyst first described by Freud—bound Crapanzano to his subject, and much of his ethnography consists of a public working through of this highly charged relationship. In a sense, then, the ethnography was as much about Crapanzano as it was about Tuhami—a personalization that many anthropologists found unprofessional and embarrassing.

Yet, in bringing his own reflections to the foreground, Crapanzano highlighted, more than had been done before, the problematic but also productive psychological relationship between self and other that remains at the heart of anthropological fieldwork. His reflexive ethnography was one kind of solution to the very early concerns voiced by Boas and his students about the moral aspect of investigating others. Furthermore, by discarding objective tests in favor of an account of his personal responses, Crapanzano was also reacting to the general loss of faith in psychological measurement techniques.[21]

F. The Dialogic Creation of Self and Other

Even more important for the development of his theoretical position, Crapanzano came to be obsessed with the fact that the very act of writing his account of Tuhami was an act of appropriation and transformation, reshaping and rendering coherent a relationship that was actually ambivalent and blurred. Crapanzano's realization of the power of discourse and transference in creating a published version of Tuhami's world led him away from an orthodox Freudian view of the psyche, away from the anthropological effort to locate identity within social organization, and toward a more linguistic, dialogical image of the self as "an arrested moment in a continuous dialectical movement."[22]

Heavily influenced by the writings of Peirce, Crapanzano henceforth called attention to the way selves are constructed through the reciprocal exchange of discourse located within a taken-for-granted frame of reference, which gives the limits of what can and cannot be said, thought, or felt. This metapragmatic framework provides a set of assumptions about the solidity of culture, of the self, and of the other, but these assumptions, Crapanzano declares, are illusions. Taken-for-granted notions of personality, character, culture, and so on simply provide a conventional sense of fixity that masks real instability and the unending flux of desire. Memory distortion, condensation, repression, and other mechanisms of forgetting let us ignore the discrepancies, alternatives, and openings that threaten to disrupt our delusory equilibrium.[23]

Crapanzano thus takes Turner's call for an anthropology of the particular and experiential to its limits, leaving no room for any objective or comparative research. Instead, anthropologists are called upon to "question the most fundamental epistemological assumptions of our social, cultural, and psychological understandings."[24] However, it is not evident how such questioning is to occur, especially since Crapanzano argues strongly that any exposition whatsoever falsely solidifies the flowing circularity and endless permeability of being and desire. Perhaps since we cannot begin without falsity, silence is best—as readers of some painfully self-conscious contemporary anthropological accounts might agree. But by denying the possibility of even beginning an inquiry, or of drawing plausible conclusions, Crapanzano has made a virtue of failure. Most anthropologists are not ready (at least not yet) to accept such dispiriting counsel.

II. INTERPRETATION AND CRITIQUE: GEERTZ, SHWEDER, TAUSSIG, AND SCHEPER-HUGHES

A Interpreting the Surface
   Clifford Geertz's new configurationism. Psyche reflects culture.

B Cultural Psychology
   Richard Shweder's relativist cultural psychology.

C No Anchor: Problems of Interpretivism
   Assumptions and implications of Shweder's approach.

D The Theory of Mimesis
   Michael Taussig's theory of alterity and mimesis.

E Oppression and Being
   Nancy Scheper-Hughes: the effects of persecution and suffering on the psyche.

A. Interpreting the Surface

Crapanzano's swing toward language and communication and away from traditional anthropological concerns with social organization and systems of power reflected a larger movement in anthropology. Often called the interpretivist turn, this movement is closely associated with Clifford Geertz (b. 1926), who is undoubtedly modern America's best-known, most quoted, and most intellectually influential cultural anthropologist. Strongly influenced by Weber and the *verstehen* tradition, and by Herder and other German romantic cultural theorists, Geertz opposed the functionalist paradigm that had dominated American anthropology of the 1950s. He argued vigorously that the task of anthropology was not the discovery of laws, patterns, and norms, but rather was the interpretation of what he called the culturally specific, symbolic webs of significance that people both spin and are caught up in.

Like Ruth Benedict, with whom he has often been compared, Geertz emphasized an aesthetic appreciation of the unique worldviews of other cultures, as revealed in their public interaction and discourse. These worldviews could be communicated to a Western audience only through ethnographic thick description that gave the readers an intuitive sense of the motives and values of other cultures. As might be expected, Geertz's concern with writing and interpretation led him gradually away from any notion of objective truth and toward a literary vision of anthropology. From this point of view, the anthropologist, in a real sense, makes up the world he or she is representing; criticism of that presentation is criticism of style, not of validity.

Geertz's position that culture existed only in public symbols and discourse meant that he had no interest whatsoever in any psychological theory that posited an internal dynamic outside of or resistant to culture. Even more than early culture and personality writers, Geertz saw culture exerting untrammeled hegemony over its members, who unresistingly took on identities that immediately reflected the dominant worldview of their society. For instance, he portrayed his Moroccan informants as animated by a mixture of "restlessness, practicality, contentiousness, eloquence, inclemency and moralism."[25] Their identities were not fixed, but constantly shifted, as individuals sought the best way to impress others in a marketplace based on personal relationships. Even more striking was his writing on the Balinese, whom he portrayed as Goffmanesque shadow performers in a vast and timeless cultural play. According to Geertz, the Balinese had no inner lives whatsoever, no feelings beyond stage fright and pride in a good performance.[26]

B. Cultural Psychology

With his one-sided culturalist view of the relationship between culture and the individual, Geertz would seem to have little to offer psychological anthropology. But some anthropologists believed otherwise. Foremost among them has been Richard Shweder, a widely traveled American fieldworker who made his reputation originally as an inventive cognitive anthropologist, expert in cross-

A Balinese ritual performance: orchestrated, aesthetic, and controlled.

cultural testing techniques. Shweder's extensive work with these instruments led him to be more and more skeptical of their validity, and he wrote some scathing and important articles demonstrating the limitations and faulty assumptions of cross-cultural testing. This corrosive work apparently persuaded him to doubt the value of his earlier training altogether, and he increasingly came to identify himself directly with an antipositivist Geertzian anthropology that emphasized personal interpretation and literary quality over empirical investigation and hard facts.

As a fervent convert to the romantic wing of anthropology, Shweder passionately defended the incommensurate and arbitrary nature of culture, and he wholeheartedly expounded the benefits of difference and of noncomparative relativism:

> Polytheism is alive and well. Its doctrine is the relativistic idea of multiple objective worlds, and its commandment is participation in the never-ending process of overcoming partial views.[27]

To further this participatory revelation, Shweder inaugurated a new kind of anthropological study of psychology, which he called cultural psychology and defined as follows:

> Cultural Psychology is the study of the ways subject and object, self and other, psyche and culture, person and context, figure and ground, practitioner and practice, live together, require each other, and dynamically, dialectically, and jointly make each other up.[28]

This new discipline, Shweder affirmed, is by its very nature heretical, self-contradictory, and playful, moving freely between alternative realities and accepting none of them as ultimate. It is also an anthropology of signs and communication, since people and cultures make each other up only through shared public discourse. For the romantic cultural psychologist, the purpose of writing ethnography is not to present facts but to conduct an intellectual exorcism that can wrench readers out of complacency, forcing them to challenge their own taken-for-granted senses of self.[29] In making up worlds, the cultural psychologist must also studiously avoid the essentialist and reductionist errors of earlier work, which assumed the existence of deep universal psychological laws acting beneath or outside (or even in tandem with) the influence of culture. Instead, cultural psychology eschews all abstractions, all essential distinctions, all hierarchies of motivation: Nothing is permanent or fixed; nothing has more gravity or priority than anything else; world and individual continuously interpenetrate in a Hegelian whirl of endless motion—but without direction or the possibility of any resolution.[30]

C. No Anchor: Problems of Interpretivism

All this was presented in striking and invigorating prose, yet the content was perhaps not as radical as it appeared to be. Most anthropologists probably would agree with Shweder's dialectical premises and accept the interpenetration of subject and object. However, many might not take the arbitrary nature of culture so much to heart, nor would they admit that there is no objective reality or hierarchy of motivations. Many might also look askance at a theory that gives talk so much importance. Most would say that by putting imagination and difference first, Shweder—like other interpretivist postmodern scholars—has given too little weight to the authority of biology and evolution, slighted the common processes of socialization, and ignored the shared dilemmas of human existence. Floating without moorings may be exhilarating, but it is not conducive to grounded analysis.

Shweder has often seemed to recognize this himself. Despite his assertion of limitless flux and his stated opposition to any first principles, his own research projects have been fairly conventional and even rather conservative. For example, his best-known ethnographic article attempted to show, through structured interviews and formal pencil-and-paper tests, that his South Asian informants had a much different notion of self than did Westerners.[31] (The findings of this study will be considered in more depth in the next chapter.) Methodologically, it was a straightforward piece of psychological research, one based upon fundamental scientific principles of construct validity. It has been criticized on the grounds that it made comparisons between incommensurate samples, but it certainly offered no radical methodological departure. It seems, then, that the rhetoric of Shweder's cultural psychology is more incendiary than its practice. He has not liberated himself from the paradoxical notion that making a case for the absence of rationality requires rational argumentation.

Shweder also was obliged to make certain presumptions about human nature, in spite of his claims to inhabit no fixed intellectual abode. The most important was a postulate of intentionality. According to Shweder, human beings are impelled to search for meaning within the semantic universes they themselves have imagined and communicated to one another. They are necessarily "mindful, soulful, willful, and full of goals and judgements."[32] They also pursue dignity, try to keep up appearances, and, like Goffman's actors, eternally strive to exemplify the values of their culture. Shweder also admitted, without much comment, certain fundamental emotions held by all—though how and why such emotions should exist was left unexamined.

Shweder's theory presumed as well certain moral values, most notably the virtues of tolerance and openness to other cultural worldviews, which are implicitly supposed to have their own irreducible beauty and authority.[33] Shweder argued too that his notion of culture will free "some portion of man's mind from the universal dictates of logic and science, permitting diversity while leaving man free to choose among irreconcilable presuppositions, schemes of classification, and ideas of worth."[34] Choice, tolerance, and freedom are seen here unproblematically as absolute goods, though one might plausibly ask whether these are not actually culture-bound Western enlightenment values. Finally, Shweder preached that moving in and out of differing worldviews without judging or comparing them brings with it a valuable decentering of the self and a capacity for "transcendence without ... scorn."[35] In other words, cultural psychology became, for Shweder, a religious quest. Pursuing it properly led to a higher form of experience, a closer contact with the "really real."

D. The Theory of Mimesis

A similarly messianic tone is to be found in the work of Michael Taussig, an anthropologist whose work also has special resonance for theories of cultural identity. Taussig's intellectual background, however, is very different from Shweder's; his major work has been oriented toward uncovering the physical and psychological injuries inflicted by colonialism on native peoples.[36] Like

Crapanzano's and Geertz's, his writing of late has moved in a highly literary direction, as he has attempted to portray in broken and impassioned narrative the fragmenting world of his informants, and to reproduce the historical disjuncture caused by colonial power.[37] Whereas Shweder's anthropological methods have been conservative, Taussig's have been radical. His books combine philosophical ruminations with fiery moral exhortations, and are certainly not traditional research documents.

But beneath the glitter and rhetoric, much of Taussig's writing, like Shweder's research, is founded on quite conservative anthropological ideas. In the book most relevant for our discussion,[38] he resuscitated Frazer's notion of sympathetic magic, arguing that imitation (mimesis) is an act of communion and identification that is believed to bring power to the imitator. In simple societies, Taussig claimed, mimesis thrives because the world is full of powerful spirits and animals; mimicry in dance and ritual is an effort to gain command over potent others by becoming like them. In Durkheimian fashion, collective mimesis also binds the society together in felt communion. But in our modern society, nature and the spirits who used to inhabit it are no longer alive, so we no longer have the magical capacity to imitate, lose ourselves, and thereby enter into the sacred. Instead, we rely on our individual capacity to work efficiently and physically dominate a universe devoid of vitality.

But there is payment to be made for our domination. With the spread of capitalism, people everywhere now imitate the West, attempting to gain our power by becoming like us, producing simulacra of Western objects of desire. This process of endless mirroring undermines the stability of Western identity, which needs the foreign and inferior other to define it. As the third world simulates the first, the Western self and the other who is emulating that self merge ecstatically together, leading to the destruction of all stable identity in "a crescendo of . . . 'mimetic excess' spending itself in a riot of dialectical imagery." All that will remain after this cataclysm are "gasps of unaccountable pleasure, or cartwheeling confusion."[39]

Like Shweder, Taussig is thrilled at the prospect of a future where "all land is borderland . . . where Self and Other paw at the ghostly imaginings of each other's powers . . . where words fail and flux commands"; where "selves dissolve into senses" and identity is "just chimeras of possible longings lounging in the interstices of quaint necessities."[40] The felt experience of mimetic excess, Taussig says, can teach us the redeeming truth that the self is only imaginary; through the endless reflection of compulsive copying we can regain the magical power to "become any Other and engage the image with the reality thus imagized" and "the freedom to live reality as really made up."[41]

Taussig's strong identification with the oppressed ignites here in a literary version of the psychic merger Obeyesekere found so lacking in Western society, though we may wonder whether it is actually the experience the natives had in mind when they first made dolls dressed in Western clothes. And we may also wonder whether the freedom to shift shape and live a made-up reality is really possible for any but a very privileged few who have converted to the anthropological creed.

E. Oppression and Being

Less apocalyptic, and arguably more effective in her union of political activism with psychological anthropology, Nancy Scheper-Hughes began her career not as an anthropologist but as a Peace Corps worker in the favelas (slums) of Brazil during the 1960s. She was appalled at the poverty, as well as the physical and psychological suffering, she found there. She was also impressed with the resilience and joy of the people of the community. This intense experience was to underlie her work throughout a career spent writing about the destructive effects of domination and destitution on the physical and psychological health of individuals.

After chronicling the relationship between mental illness and culture in Ireland and the United States (work to be discussed in Chapter 11), Scheper-Hughes returned to Brazil to write an ethnography of the favela where she had spent her Peace Corps years.[42] In it she paints a compelling picture of a harsh world: Brutal social, historical, and economic factors severely limit the choices of people; poverty and violence are commonplace, hunger is pervasive, life is cheap, and desperate measures are required to ensure mere survival. The typical psychological disorder of the favelas is *nervos*—"nerves"—a debilitating feeling of irritability, depression, and fatigue. Scheper-Hughes understands this disease to be a transformation of untreatable chronic hunger into treatable mental illness. Drugs can be given to calm the nerves of the poor, but their fundamental problems of poverty and starvation remain.

A favela in Recife, Brazil.

Under these conditions, Scheper-Hughes discovered that the attitude of mothers toward newborn children is not one of unconditional love and nurturance. Instead, in the favela, mothers are guided by "lifeboat ethics" of saving the salvageable. They are obliged to practice selective infanticide, allowing some children to die through neglect and starvation. The mothers hide this cruel but necessary strategy from themselves through projection and denial; the cause of a child's death is seen as a deficiency in the infant, not as an act by the mother. Women believe that some children simply want to die, or are favorites of God, or are naturally weak. Such children are allowed to starve to death. If the child happens to survive, then the mother gradually grows attached to it. But when such a baby perishes, mothers do not cry; they have remained aloof from emotional involvement, and they believe tears would impede the child's entrance into heaven.

In her controversial book, Scheper-Hughes contradicted American psychiatric assumptions about the naturalness of mother love and called instead for a pragmatics of motherhood that would take into account the reality of the historical and cultural circumstances of mothers. In the favela, she argued, it makes perfect cultural sense for mothers to behave as they do, just as it makes perfect cultural sense for mothers in the isolated nuclear households of the American suburbs to be intensely emotionally involved with their children—an involvement made "natural" by psychiatric advice.[43]

Scheper-Hughes did not paint the whole of favela life in melancholy hues. She argued that because of their continual concern with physical survival, poor Brazilians have a somatic culture that contrasts with the privileged psychological culture of the Brazilian middle classes. As a result, the poor live more directly and immediately in their bodies, and have a zest for the sensual aspects of existence that partially compensates for the hardships and the cruelty of their lives. However, she does not romanticize her informants, nor does she excuse them from all responsibility for their actions. The sufferings and violence of the others, she reminds us, are not simply creations of colonialism or capitalism or hegemonic practice. Local cultures have their own oppressive practices that need to be critiqued and changed.[44]

Scheper-Hughes herself can rightly be criticized for privileging culture over biology (mental illness is seen by her as primarily a cultural phenomenon), and for making claims that are too dramatic (the mothers in Brazil obviously do bond with their infant children; otherwise, the elaborate psychological mechanisms of projection and denial would be unnecessary). But she is to be commended for returning psychological anthropology to its earlier Boasian concern with social justice. In place of unrealistic postmodern fantasies of fusion between self and other, Scheper-Hughes has addressed issues of poverty, starvation, and oppression, and the possibilities of equity. Her job, as she sees it, is to recognize, record, and convey the struggles of voiceless people. She has done this not only by providing cultural context and political and economic history, but also by including biographies that turn her informants into concrete, living individuals. And she has made it clear that as far as she is concerned, indifference to the struggles of the disenfranchised, whether under the guise of scientific objectivity or poetic reflexivity, is a crime that anthropologists ought not commit.

III. THE CULTURAL BODY

A The Body: Personal, Social, Political
   Nancy Scheper-Hughes and Margaret Lock on the relationship between class, history, and the body.

B Precursors to an Anthropology of the Body
   Understanding of the body in social science: Montaigne, Durkheim, Mauss, and others.

C Phenomenology and Anthropology
   Thomas Csordas's attempt to build a psychological anthropology based on Pierre Bourdieu and Maurice Merleau-Ponty.

D The Usefulness of a Phenomenological Approach
   Strengths and weaknesses of a phenomenological account.

A. The Body: Personal, Social, Political

Scheper-Hughes's work with people undergoing physical suffering led her to reconsider the complex relationship between the body, personal identity, and culture. As noted above, she posited that the impoverished favela dwellers had a more somatic sense of themselves than middle-class Brazilians, and she extended this insight to argue for wider class-based differences in the relationship between mind and body. The bourgeois classes everywhere, she claimed, would have less bodily capacity to express themselves physically. For them, "the language of the body is silenced and denied."[45] This class-based incapacity infected anthropology as well, leading to a characteristic privileging of the mental and symbolic over the physical and intuitive.

Scheper-Hughes aimed to overturn this attitude in a seminal paper she wrote with Margaret Lock. In it, the authors followed critical theory to argue that the body must be seen as "simultaneously a physical and symbolic artifact, as both naturally and culturally produced, and as securely anchored in a particular historical moment."[46] The body, Scheper-Hughes and Lock said, exists in at least three different semantic realms of representation and practice: the body as it is experienced phenomenologically; the body that is used to symbolize social relations; the body as regulated by political and legal restrictions. The realms can be summarized as follows:

1. The experienced body—phenomenological.
2. The body as symbolic object—sociological.
3. The body as object of control—political.

This paper pointed to a new direction for psychological anthropology in which the theories of self and other are anchored in the concrete experience of physical being.[47]

B. Precursors to an Anthropology of the Body

Although quite new in some respects, the present concern with embodiment has as its (usually unrecognized) intellectual ancestor Montaigne, who, as we have seen, tirelessly connected the shifts in his own opinions to the momentary states of his mood, his health, and his digestion. Nietzsche, too, stressed the physical locus of thought—no proper thinker could live in Germany, he said, because of the heavy quality of the food. And Freud, of course, made the energizing impulses of the libido the center of his theory.[48]

In the social sciences, it was Durkheim who stressed the importance of the body above all. The experience of collective effervescence, which he saw as the originating force of society, was a physical experience of group trance, brought on through participation in rhythmic dance and music. Durkheim believed that individuals were intoxicated by the excitement of the collective performance, and would lose their sense of separateness and be empowered by the shared energy engendered by immersion in the ecstatic crowd. As the usually restrained Durkheim writes:

> Feeling himself dominated and carried away by some sort of external power which makes him think and act differently than in normal times, he naturally has the impression of being himself no longer. It seems to him that he has become a new being . . . Everything is just as though he really were transported into a special world, entirely different from the one where he ordinarily lives, and into an environment filled with exceptionally intense forces that take hold of him and metamorphose him.[49]

According to Durkheim, the extraordinary sensation of being physically lifted above the self in ecstatic collective trance is the source of the human experience of the sacred; it is also the source of the bonding with others necessary for maintaining society. We might call this the rave theory of social life.

Although Durkheim made physical delirium centrally important to his theory, it was left to his greatest disciple, Marcel Mauss (1872–1950), to try to bring the formal study of the body into the disciplines of sociology and anthropology. It was Mauss who coined the term "habitus"—a neologism later made famous by Pierre Bourdieu—to refer not only to the authority exercised by taken-for-granted assumptions but also to the ingrained movements and postures of the body transferred over eons of experience.[50] Recalling Durkheim's notion that society and religion began in the physical experience of a collective ecstatic dance, Mauss called for an exploration of the effect of rhythm on consciousness, and for a theory that could link body and mind by focusing on automatic physical reactions, such as the mother's response to her crying child or the worker's habituation to the use of his tools.

We have already noted how anthropologists have been concerned with understanding habitual bodily acts and with the symbolic significance of parts of the body (Obeyesekere's Freudian reading of hair is an example). Culture and

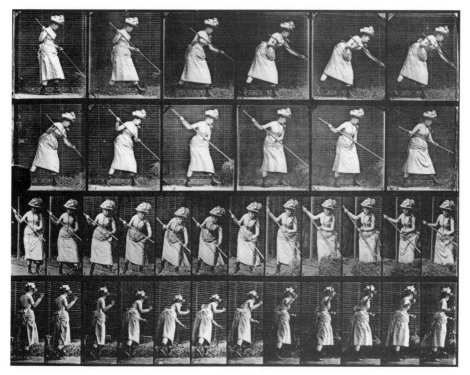

1887: A study of human locomotion by Eadweard Muybridge.

personality theorists, and all other psychoanalytic interpretations of society, have portrayed the training of the infantile body as a major source of later cultural adaptions. Trance as an embodied state has also long attracted anthropological attention, as we shall see in a later chapter.[51] And the whole field of medical anthropology has devoted itself to understanding the interplay between culture, the body, and the experience of illness.[52] In linguistics, George Lakoff and Mark Johnson have put the body at the center of their theory, arguing that experienced bodily images are well formed, easily projected into the outer world, and central to our being; as a result, such images very often serve as standardized mental models structuring all aspects of human behavior, feeling, and belief.[53] Feminist and poststructuralist anthropology has also called attention to the way bodies are manipulated and controlled by powerful institutions.[54] Moving from critique to prescription, the anthropologist Paul Stoller has insisted that a new sensuous scholarship must overturn Cartesian dualities and "eject the conceit of control in which mind and body, self and other are considered separate."[55] What Taussig saw as a millennial endpoint has here become an anthropological prescription.

C. Phenomenology and Anthropology

Leaving this last radical (and impossible) prospect aside, let us consider a less drastic alternative, voiced by Thomas Csordas, who has provided anthropology with yet another pathway for discovering the relationship between body and society—one based on a linkage between phenomenology and anthropology. Csordas's fieldwork has been in the United States with congregations of charismatic Catholics who believe fervent in the power of prayer and religious trance to cure their ills.[56] On the basis of his research with these believers, Csordas wanted to develop a theory that could explain how a symbolic system was engaged in the physical experience of trance, and this in turn required a way to bring the body into the analysis.

Csordas chose to solve this problem by turning to the French phenomenologist Maurice Merleau-Ponty (1908–1961), who—influenced by German post-Hegelian philosophy, particularly the work of Martin Heidegger (1889–1969)—had argued that any valid understanding of consciousness and identity must start not with objects (which are, after all, "other" to us), or with self-awareness (which is contingent on having a self in the first place), but with perceptions, which concretely situate the individual inside a body existing in the world and in relation to other bodies.

Merleau-Ponty had argued that this so-called preobjective state of primal perceptions provided the concrete basis for the self to reach out to grasp the external world and to discover its own identity at the same time. Csordas took this notion and paired it with Pierre Bourdieu's version of habitus, defined as "history made nature," which provides the taken-for-granted physical and psychic universe in which practice takes place and makes ordinary life seem sensible and reasonable.[57] By linking the two, Csordas put Merleau-Ponty's phenomenological posit into cultural context: The preobjective perceiving body lives within an already existent culturally constituted framework of a habitus.

Of special importance to Csordas's phenomenological theory is Merleau-Ponty's contention that the self has no essence; all that exists are fluid self-processes, movements toward and withdrawals from the perceived world. Yet the embodied self is not empty; it does have some specific characteristics. For example, it is responsive to the world and others, and it is motivated primarily by the desire not to slip into the void of the inchoate; it is this fear that leads to continuous struggles to become oriented and to see ourselves as "someone," in other words, to become objects to ourselves.[58] The intentional self-processes that manufacture this necessary self-awareness are reflexive and effortful; we perceive as constituted entities (the self-awareness discussed by Hallowell); we act within worlds we manufacture. As intentional and constituted beings within constituted worlds, we continually try to convince ourselves of our own certainty and permanence, but in truth our actual being is indeterminate and never solidified. Like Crapanzano, Csordas argues that the never-ending struggle toward the objectification of our fundamentally fluid being is at the heart of culture.

But whereas Crapanzano devoted himself to demonstrating the dangers of trying to dam the flow, and thus developed no theory beyond negation, Csordas combined a standard analysis of the American and Catholic meaning systems within which his subjects live, and a more interesting (and problematic) account of the self-processes orienting them to that world.[59] In brief, his claim is that the inevitable splitting of the primal unified self (also postulated by object-

---

Phenomenology and American Pragmatism

Phenomenology, insofar as it puts aside theory in order to study how reality is experienced from the inside, has what Weber would call an elective affinity for the American philosophical tradition, which has always concerned itself with pragmatic action, ignoring universalistic theoretical claims and concentrating instead on achieving usable results. The argument is this: Since results are what count, then what is important is knowing what good results might be, and that means finding out what people think is good or bad, what works and what doesn't. The American philosopher William James (1842–1910) was a pragmatist in his famous argument that religion exists because it has tangible and beneficial results for believers. His research methodology also was phenome-nological, in that he recorded what people actually thought and felt about their religious experiences, assuming that their words and deeds expressed their own felt truth.

Pragmatism has the difficulty of being unable to defend itself from attack except by reference to its own assumptions about what is beneficial. But what is taken for common sense is actually a culturally constructed perspective, very American in nature, that sees the world as a place to be manipulated, taken apart, and put together again for individual benefit. Similarly, phenomenology, as usually practiced, cannot defend itself except by reiterating its own assumptions about the inner nature of human experience. Each would benefit from more rigorous cross-cultural testing.

---

relations theorists) is a wound that the image of Jesus heals for believers by "a benevolent objectification of this preobjective sense of alterity."[60] In other words, Jesus is the other who cures difference. Demons, in contrast, are the malevolent aspect of existential otherness. They arise whenever "there is too much of a particular thought, behavior or emotion"; this excess is objectified into a possessing spirit.[61] The bodily differences in possession indicate the phenomenological distinction: People spontaneously rest passively when overcome by the Holy Spirit; they writhe and growl when fighting with demons.

D. The Usefulness of a Phenomenological Approach

Csordas has provided the best union yet achieved between anthropological and phenomenological theory. As such, it has many advantages. It provides a remarkably complete conceptual framework while resisting the interpretivist's tendency to turn human experience into a groundless and arbitrary symbolic system; it stays within the body and its perceptions, and does not posit the causal explanatory force of any imagined and unproven entities, such as the id or the Oedipal complex, or Jesus and the devil. Rather, it offers its own set of emergent parameters, which are taken as universal and explanatory.[62]

But while getting rid of Freudian (and Biblical) metaphysics, Csordas substitutes his own, making many assumptions about the ultimate nature of human experience, which may or may not be accurate, complete, or useful. It is not at all evident, for example, that self-processes are necessarily activated by an existential fear of the void, nor that others within the same habitus are automatically perceived as "another myself," as Merleau-Ponty claimed. Indeed, it is perfectly possible to argue that Csordas's picture of the indeterminate, yet reflexive, intentional and active self, struggling futilely toward an impossible certainty, is a heroic Western model of being: one that echoes the Protestant ethic of personal responsibility, inner interrogation, and the guilty need for redemption from the fall from grace. In contrast, we may recall the ancient Greeks, who believed in "decision without choice, responsibility divorced from intention,"[63] and note that in many societies very different interpretations indeed would be given to the heroic self-processes Csordas has postulated.[64]

Csordas's argument also journeys quite far from his informants' own understandings: His zealous Catholic informants certainly would be amazed to discover that Jesus is a "benevolent objectification of their preobjective sense of alterity." The abstraction and detachment of Csordas's theorizing also takes him away from the specificity of his subjects' actual experiences. It is never clear, for example, what the income level or job experience of his informants is, or what sort of families they come from, or what other concrete social and personal circumstances constitute their habitus and activate their self-processes. Ahistorical and abstract, his is a phenomenology that hardly ever reveals any actual phenomena at all, aside from the presumed inner lives of his respondents. In this sense, it stands very far indeed from Scheper-Hughes's sympathetic, yet pragmatic, biographical accounts of her friends in the favela.

IV. BEING IN CULTURE

A Psychic Structure
   The psyche has its own autonomy and is grounded in fundamental conflict.

B Culture and Contradiction
   The social system is an emergent collective organization that is adaptive and functional, but it is also coercive and restrictive.

C The Production of Meaning
   Humans try to construct meaningful theodicies, even though the effort can never succeed. This paradox leads to further creativity.

D Conclusion: The Dialectics of Being
   A dialectical theory of psychological anthropology must unite the different levels of human experience.

A. Psychic Structure

Let me now offer my own thoughts on what general directions seem most promising for the future study of psychological anthropology, along with some warnings about the paths I believe are less worth traveling.

To me, it is evident that the configurationists were mistaken in presenting culture as overwhelmingly hegemonic. This mistake has been repeated by some modern theorists who, understandably, have wanted to give credit to the specificity of each culture, and who have stressed the ultimate importance of linguistic structures and symbolic systems in their analyses. As a result, they have tended to see individuals as mere reflections, mirroring the authority of culture in their every thought, deed, and feeling.

While not in any way denying the crucial importance of local understanding and the heavy weight of culture, language, and history, I find such theory to be one-sided. Individuals are certainly motivated by what their fellows believe; they think and feel in the linguistic categories provided for them. But they also are certain to have emotions they cannot account for, thoughts they dare not speak aloud, dreams they cannot reveal, ideals that are never realized. As Steven Parish writes: "We all experience this gap between desire and reality where discontent brews in a cauldron of fantasy, hope and despair . . . it is the self-contradiction that signals our humanity."[65] Any valid theory needs to take into account this reality and cannot do so by simply conceding that some people are innate misfits. Explaining human resistance to cultural authority through biology is surely an act of unwarranted reductionism, and an abdication of responsibility.

Far better, I think, is to follow Freud and Durkheim and Goffman and acknowledge that all persons—not just the most obvious mavericks and rebels—are rent by fundamental psychic tensions. At the very least, we can say that human beings are riven by deep-rooted urges to love and to rage, to merge and to separate, that are impossible to realize, since those cravings are in conflict with each other, with reality, and with society. Whether we premise this dynamic to be metaphysical and innate, as Freud did, or as a consequence of the process of individuation and frustration of the desire for unity, as object-relations theorists have done, the effect is the same: The human soul is a battleground. Nor can these painful and contradictory desires be annulled; they must find release, and the way they are sublimated, projected, and distorted in their expression constitutes much of what is fundamental about our cultural and personal lives. In an existential sense, human life is a problem without a solution or, perhaps, a problem with a great many solutions, none of them wholly satisfactory.

B. Culture and Contradiction

Not only are human beings more conflicted than configurationists and interpretive anthropologists have thought, so is culture. Instead of being a seamless symbolic whole imposed in toto on its members, culture is no more without tension than are the people who live within it—as Wallace and Bateson both noted. The question is why. A strictly psychoanalytic view would be that culture is full of contradiction because it serves as a vehicle for directing, limiting, and transmuting human desires. Since culture is essentially a symbolic collective expression of our own ambivalence, it must also be full of ambivalence. This is surely so, to an extent, but turning the anthropological fallacy of cultural domination upside down and making culture a mere reflection of the psyche is equally one-sided, as is the tendency of psychoanalytic theorists to find the origin of all social life in childhood experiences.

It is more realistic to see that culture is not only a mirror of human hopes and fears, but also an objective reality, an evolving collective entity enduring over eons of time, providing its members with roles, identities, and morals that further the viability of the group as a whole. As Durkheim argued, culture exists in and for itself: Its principles and goals are carried by powerful institutions and structures, and are not necessarily beneficial or pleasant for its members. It is at base a complex system that has as its first task survival. To accomplish this task, it must cope with ecological, political, economic, structural, and technical constraints and pressures. Conflicts with external rivals must be resolved, production must be organized; a viable society must also somehow overcome failures of communication, obstacles to distribution, difficulties of organizing labor, problems in the construction of hierarchy and the maintenance of order, and so on. Any society—human or termite—faces these dilemmas. In human society, they are exacerbated by the fact we are not totally controlled by instinct, nor are we completely dominated by our infantile training. Our obedience, unlike that of the social insects, is tentative and provisional, so on top of the normal tensions implicit in any complex social order, we add the conflict between the desires of the individual and the will of the collective, and the suffering, violence, and oppression that conflict entails.

Clearly, society is not only adaptive and functional, but also necessarily full of coercion, imbalance, ambivalence, and conflict. As the psychological anthropologist Theodore Schwartz has wisely remarked, "culture creates worlds so premised that it may be as much or more the source of such conflicts and anxieties as it is the cure."[66] Even though societies strive to achieve some degree of efficiency and adjustment, this effort always entails a certain level of struggle and pain among the individuals and subgroups who make up the society. Of course, some societies can be more stable and fixed than others, often at the cost of severely limiting human freedom. In every case, however, the difficulty of organizing complexity in a constantly shifting universe and of coordinating the actions of potentially independent individuals means that a true social equilibrium is a chimera. This in turn means that anthropological theories emphasizing social integration and adaption are seeing only one-half of the matter.

C. The Production of Meaning

We can say then with confidence that every society is necessarily rent with conflict, as multiple and often competing internal requirements and external pressures must be dealt with. There is no way around this purely objective fact. Society must also channel and control the expression of the psychic tensions that drive individuals, and this too is necessarily a process fraught with considerable ambivalence.

Now let me add one other source of tension to the mix. Human societies are not only problem-solving devices and symbolic projections of sublimated desires, but also organizations for the production of meaning. As Weber and Geertz have argued, humankind is above all a meaning-making animal; our very indeterminacy, our imaginative capacity, our existential anxiety, the quandaries of our species-being, all continually press us to seek to make some sense of the world we live in. Yet these meaning systems are necessarily incomplete, inconsistent, ambivalent, and unsatisfying.

Max Weber made this very clear in his discussion of the various value standpoints from which the problem of human suffering could be rationalized. In an effort to understand and control their circumstances, human beings are pressed, he argued, to seek to widen the range, coherence, and comprehensibility of their explanatory systems.[67] Yet these efforts must founder, and lead inevitably to disenchantment, because any attempt to explain the world rationally must, at the very minimum, cope with the brute facts of physical frailty and social inequity. As Weber writes:

> The age-old problem of theodicy consists of the very question of how it is that a power which is said to be at once omnipotent and kind could have created such an irrational world of undeserved suffering, unpunished injustice and hopeless stupidity."[68]

Theological attempts to answer this basic problem have been many, and each one generates a formative value system that structures human thoughts and feelings. But they all meet with the inevitable contradiction of human misery and inequality; therefore, human beings are continually obliged to expand and reformulate their conceptual frameworks. This attempt to extend and refine a comprehensive meaning system is inevitably in tension with the disparate, contradictory, and pitiless nature of the objective world. In these respects, among others, all human meaning systems are culturally specific efforts to provide answers to quandaries of being and of community, which are, in their essence, not resolvable. But the very act of attempting a resolution is in itself transformative, as human beings develop more complex knowledge systems and continually struggle to achieve impossible cultural goals. We are creatures of paradox, and it is this paradoxical truth that makes us human.

A concrete example of the complex nature of the relationship between culture values, social organization, and the psyches of individuals can be found among the Pukhtun tribe of northern Pakistan, where I did my fieldwork. Independence and honor are valued above all in an egalitarian social organization where most of the men are engaged in continual competitive struggles for control over the all-important scarce resource of farmland. The society is structured so that any final victory is almost impossible, though defeat can and does occur. Men are therefore condemned to spend their lives zealously defending their interests against those of their nearest neighbors and relatives. Trust is in very short supply in this society, and personal relationships between men are necessarily tense and laden with anxiety. Cultural values also divide men and women, making the household no peaceful haven. Women find compensation for this antagonism in their relationships with their children, while men are expected to maintain a dignified distance from the family.

Unexpectedly, the society also has a pervasive value of hospitality, which is offered to any wayfarer, as well as an ideal of male friendship that is extolled in songs and poems. Such friendship ought to be exclusive, and it entails total trust and generosity. It is enacted with those who are outside the realm of male rivalry: strangers, Hindus, men of the nonwarrior castes, and the occasional anthropologist. The friendship ideal and the donation of hospitality stand at right angles to the overwhelmingly antagonistic atmosphere of the society as a whole.

This oddity can be understood only if we posit an underlying emotional structure acting in a dialectical relationship of tension with the social organization and cultural values of the Pukhtun. Emotions associated with communion and nurturance, forbidden to men in the harsh realm of daily life, are expressed both in rituals of hospitality and in the idealized quest for the perfect friend.[69] Among the Pukhtun, as everywhere, individual hopes and dreams are both structured by, and provide a space for resistance against, the larger social and cultural framework.

D. Conclusion: The Dialectics of Being

To reiterate, there are at least three intertwined levels at which contradictions and ambivalence exist in human life: the level of the individual psyche, the level of objective social organization, and the level of meaning construction. The latter level is the intermediate area where symbolic construction takes place. It is the realm of the objectification and subjectification processes documented by Obeyesekere; it is here that ritual performances connect the individual and the social. Theories of psychological anthropology must give credit to these dialectically intersecting levels of being, to the polarizing conflicts they contain and express, and to the limits they place on human freedom. At the same time, we must not ignore the fact that humans everywhere are not total slaves to either biology or socialization; they can and do imagine other ways of being, and they struggle to break the chains that bind them. An adequate anthropology cannot forget that along with the experience of limitation always goes the hope for liberation. This also is part of our common condition.

I would argue then that contemporary psychological anthropology should not forget Freud, who provided us with the most comprehensive model of the psyche yet presented, but should take him not at his most literal level, as a theorist of Oedipal conflict and investigator of hysteria.[70] Rather, we ought to recall the Freud who was a philosopher of the human condition, who outlined the existential dilemmas faced by adult men and women, and who gave a sympathetic account of the never-ending effort of human beings to overcome those dilemmas. This version of psychoanalysis need not stand in opposition to social theory, but rather can contribute a deeper level to Durkheimian and Weberian paradigms, which also acknowledge the dialectical and existentially conflictual nature of the human condition.

A dialectical psychoanalytic-cultural frame can also accommodate those theorists, descended from Sapir and the romantic tradition, who have called for an anthropology that offers more room for the individual and allows for human creativity. Person-centered studies like Obeyesekere's and Scheper-Hughes's, which are focused on individuals but also situated within a social context and psychologically informed, can give credit to character and to resistance, but refrain from the moralizing, the solipsism, and the relativism that romantic anthropology is prone to, while also avoiding the abstraction and impersonality of positivism. The discipline of anthropology, from its beginnings, has been divided between those who want to be poets and those who want to be scientists. In the field of psychological anthropology, one needs to be both.[71]

Summary

This chapter outlines the three major responses to the positivist trends of the 1950s and 1960s: a focus on individual creativity, a concern with cultural interpretation and critical assessment, and an effort to develop an anthropological phenomenology. Finally, a more synthetic approach is proposed.

Like Edward Sapir in his era, Victor Turner, Gananath Obeyesekere, and Vincent Crapanzano were particularly concerned with individual freedom and creativity. Turner's contribution was to portray ritual as a performance that linked meaning with emotion, and to discover within it liminal moments of antistructure in which new possibilities could be imagined and old injustices protested. Out of such moments, social and personal change could occur. Obeyesekere also focused on ritual, but he traced psychic histories of participants, showing how their personal traumas were translated into innovation. He argued that only certain social settings—such as those found in India and Sri Lanka—favored such transformations, and that Freudian theory needed revision to account for cultural differences. Crapanzano took the modern appreciation for creative individuality to its extreme, writing a psychic biography of his informant and moving toward a literary, metapragmatic perspective that deprecated all forms of stabilizing theory as delusions stifling creativity.

The interpretivist turn of anthropology championed by Clifford Geertz went in quite a different direction, emphasizing not creative agency but the authority of culture. Returning to the aesthetic romanticism of Benedict, Geertz portrayed culture as a shared, public world, completely shaping the psychic lives of individuals. His follower Richard Shweder carried this perspective forward, inaugurating a new discipline of cultural psychology: a thoroughly relativist enterprise that eschews any search for deep truths in favor of the study of how people and cultural institutions make each other up. Despite its avowed aim to respect difference, cultural psychology rests on presumptions of intentionality and assumes moral values of tolerance, choice, and freedom.

A similar quasi-evangelical tone pervaded Michael Taussig's work, which is far more political in its orientation than Shweder's or Geertz's. Taussig followed Frazer in his understanding of the sympathetic magic worked by mimesis, and he imagined a future in which the short-circuiting of the mimetic impulse would end in an ecstatic fusion of self and other. Less apocalyptic, but equally critical of capitalism and domination, Nancy Scheper-Hughes graphically portrayed the baneful effects of oppression and hunger on the human psyche, focusing especially on mothers' ambivalent attitudes toward their starving children.

Scheper-Hughes's attention to suffering led her to posit differences in somatic culture between rich and poor, and to argue that the body must be seen not only as personal but also as social and political, thus inspiring a growing anthropological interest in the physical. This perspective, which hopes to locate humanity in physical being, has roots dating at least to Montaigne, Nietzsche, Freud, and Durkheim. Marcel Mauss, Durkheim's disciple, connected the body to culture in his notion of habitus, which was then appropriated first by Pierre Bourdieu and then by Thomas Csordas, who sought to wed it to the phenomenology of Maurice Merleau-Ponty. The promise was that phenomenology could discover preobjective perceptions that are beneath culture and serve to construct the self and its relationships. This would then give anthropology an indisputable base for analysis.

The chapter closed with a statement of the dialectical theory that I favor. There are three levels of human experience: the psychic structure, which is driven by fundamental conflicting desires; social organization, which structures life but also restrains and coerces; and meaning systems, which attempt to make sense of existence. A successful account of the relationship between culture and the individual must give credit to intersection and interplay of all three levels, paying attention not only to adaption but also to conflict, resistance, and the infinite power of the imagination.

Endnotes

1. Kurt Vonnegut, 1976, *Wampeters, Foma and Granfalloons*, New York: Dell, p. 176.
2. See Max Gluckman, 1954, *Rituals of Rebellion in Southeast Africa*, Manchester, England: Manchester University Press.
3. Victor Turner, 1957, *Schism and Continuity in an African Society: A Study of Ndembu Village Life*, Manchester, England: Manchester University Press.
4. Victor Turner, 1967, *The Forest of Symbols: Aspects of Ndembu Ritual*, Ithaca, NY: Cornell University Press.
5. Victor Turner, 1977, *The Ritual Process: Structure and Anti-Structure*, Chicago: Aldine, p. 93.
6. Victor Turner, 1969, "Forms of Symbolic Action," in R. Spencer (ed.), *Forms of Symbolic Action*, Seattle: University of Washington Press, pp. 19, 21.
7. Arnold van Gennep, 1960, *The Rites of Passage*, Chicago: University of Chicago Press (original publication 1909).
8. For more on this topic, see Chapter 11.
9. Victor Turner, 1985, "The Anthropology of Performance," in Edith L. B. Turner (ed.), *On the Edge of the Bush: Anthropology as Experience*, Tucson: University of Arizona Press, p. 182.
10. Turner attempted to accomplish this in his analysis of the crisis initiated by Thomas à Beckett (Turner, *The Ritual Process*), but remained primarily on the level of historical conjecture.
11. Gananath Obeyesekere, 1981, *Medusa's Hair: An Essay on Personal Symbols and Religious Experience*, Chicago: University of Chicago Press.
12. Ibid., p. 33.
13. Obeyesekere distinguishes primary existential guilt (which is repressed and must be expressed in symbolic forms) from secondary guilt (which is culturally conditioned and has to do with breaking social norms). The energy generated by primary guilt is channeled into secondary guilt to maintain social control.
14. Obeyesekere, *Medusa's Hair*, p. 77.
15. Ibid., p. 137.
16. Gananath Obeyesekere, 1990, *The Work of Culture: Symbolic Transformation in Psychoanalysis and Anthropology*, Chicago: University of Chicago Press.
17. Obeyesekere and Turner were not the only innovators calling for the use of case studies and person-centered research focused on extraordinary individuals. For example, Robert Levy, in his monumental book *Tahitians: Mind and Experience in the Society Islands* (1973, Chicago: University of Chicago Press), brought together classical field-

work technique with extensive analytic interviewing to produce one of the most well-rounded and psychologically astute ethnographies yet written. Another book of the same calibre, but with a very different structure, was Waud Kracke's cultural-psychoanalytic study of two leaders in an Amazonian tribe (1978, *Force and Persuasion: Leadership in an Amazonian Society*, Chicago: University of Chicago Press).

18. Vincent Crapanzano, 1973, *The Hamadsha: A Study in Moroccan Ethnopsychiatry*, Berkeley: University of California Press.

19. Vincent Crapanzano, 1980, *Tuhami: Portrait of a Moroccan*, Chicago: University of Chicago Press.

20. Vincent Crapanzano, 1994, "Rethinking Psychological Anthropology: A Critical View," in Marcelo Suarez-Orozco, George Spindler, and Louise Spindler (eds.), *The Making of Psychological Anthropology II*, Fort Worth, TX: Harcourt Brace, p. 235.

21. Denigration of objective tests in favor of introspection is not new: Margaret Mead had argued early on that anthropologists ought to use as primary data their own psychic reactions to those they studied. For this reason, she recommended that anthropologists of the future should be psychoanalyzed, since psychoanalysis would hone the individual's skills of self-monitoring.

22. Vincent Crapanzano, 1990, "On Self-Characterization," in James Stigler, Richard Shweder, and Gilbert Herdt (eds.), *Cultural Psychology: Essays on Comparative Human Development*, Cambridge, England: Cambridge University Press, p. 403.

23. As he writes: "This fixity may comfort those who find intolerable a Heraclitean view of the world—one that stresses change and resists closure—the Parmenidean solace it offers is not without cost, for it precludes understanding of the pragmatic, the rhetorical, dimensions of social engagement, ultimately of the creative, the non-creative and the destructive." See Vincent Crapanzano, 1992, "Some Thoughts on Hermeneutics and Psychoanalytic Anthropology," in Theodore Schwartz, Geoffrey White, and Catherine Lutz (eds.), *New Directions in Psychological Anthropology*, Cambridge, England: Cambridge University Press, p. 304.

24. Ibid.

25. Clifford Geertz, 1979, "Suq: The Bazaar Economy in Sefrou," in C. Geertz et al. (eds.), *Meaning and Order in Moroccan Society*, Cambridge, England: Cambridge University Press, p. 235.

26. This view was much contested by other ethnographers, notably Unni Wikan (1990, *Managing Turbulent Hearts: A Balinese Formula for Living*, Chicago: University of Chicago Press), as we shall see in Chapter 10.

27. Richard Shweder, 1991, *Thinking Through Cultures: Expeditions in Cultural Psychology*, Cambridge, MA: Harvard University Press, p. 68.

28. Ibid., p. 73.

29. See Richard Shweder, 1986, "Storytelling among the Anthropologists," *New York Times Book Review*, September 21: 39.

30. For a critique of Shweder from a Hegelian perspective, see Charles Lindholm, 1997, "Logical and Moral Problems of Postmodernism," *Journal of the Royal Anthropological Institute* 3: 745–60.

31. Richard Shweder and Joan G. Miller, 1991, "The Social Construction of the Person: How Is It Possible?" in Richard Shweder, *Thinking Through Cultures: Expeditions in Cultural Psychology*, Cambridge, MA: Harvard University Press.

32. Shweder, *Thinking Through Cultures*, pp. 97, 101.

33. In this respect Shweder stands against the postmodern deconstruction of culture and against the Foucaultian tendency to see power relations behind all cultural forms.

34. Richard Shweder, 1984, "Anthropology's Romantic Rebellion, or There's More to Thinking than Reason and Evidence," in Richard Shweder and Robert Levine (eds.),

Culture Theory: Essays on Mind, Self and Emotion, Cambridge, England: Cambridge University Press, p. 48.

35. Shweder, *Thinking Through Cultures,* p. 68.
36. For example, see Michael Taussig, 1980, *The Devil and Commodity Fetishism in South America,* Chapel Hill: University of North Carolina Press.
37. Especially in Michael Taussig, 1992, *The Nervous System,* New York: Routledge.
38. Michael Taussig, 1993, *Mimesis and Alterity: A Particular History of the Senses,* New York: Routledge.
39. Ibid., p. 246.
40. Ibid., pp. 249, 253, 254.
41. Ibid., p. 255.
42. Nancy Scheper-Hughes, 1992, *Death without Weeping: The Violence of Everyday Life in Brazil,* Berkeley: University of California Press.
43. Ibid., pp. 341, 412. For an earlier statement, see Nancy Scheper-Hughes, 1990, "Mother Love and Child Death in Northeast Brazil," in James Stigler, Richard Shweder, and Gilbert Herdt (eds.), *Cultural Psychology: Essays on Comparative Human Development,* Cambridge, England: Cambridge University Press.
44. Nancy Scheper-Hughes, 1994, "The Violence of Everyday Life: In Search of a Critical and Politically Engaged Psychological Anthropology," in Marcelo Suarez-Orozco, George Spindler, and Louise Spindler (eds.), *The Making of Psychological Anthropology II,* Fort Worth, TX: Harcourt Brace.
45. Ibid., p. 185.
46. Margaret Lock and Nancy Scheper-Hughes, 1987, "The Mindful Body," *Medical Anthropology Quarterly* 1: 6–41, 7.
47. For two excellent histories, see Bryan Turner, 1991, "Recent Developments in the Theory of the Body," in Mike Featherstone, Mike Hepworth, and Bryan Turner (eds.), *The Body: Social Process and Cultural Theory,* San Francisco: Sage; and Andrew Strathern, 1996, *Body Thoughts,* Ann Arbor: University of Michigan Press.
48. Oddly, however, contemporary theorists of the body rarely refer to Freud, preferring instead to link themselves to existentialist and phenomenologist philosophers.
49. Émile Durkheim, 1965, *The Elementary Forms of the Religious Life,* New York: Free Press, pp. 249–50 (original publication 1912).
50. Marcel Mauss, 1979, "Body Techniques" (original publication 1935), in Marcel Mauss (ed.), *Sociology and Psychology: Essays,* London: Routledge and Kegan Paul, p. 27; see also Pierre Bourdieu, 1977, *Outline of a Theory of Practice,* Cambridge, England: Cambridge University Press.
51. For an overview, see Erika Bourguignon, 1968, "World Distribution and Patterns of Possession States," in Raymond Prince (ed.), *Trance and Possession States,* Montreal, Canada: Burke Memorial Society.
52. For a set of readings on this subject, see Mary Jo Good (ed.), 1992, *Pain as Human Experience: An Anthropological Perspective,* Berkeley: University of California Press.
53. See George Lakoff and Mark Johnson, 1980, *Metaphors We Live By,* Chicago: University of Chicago Press; George Lakoff, 1987, *Women, Fire and Dangerous Things: What Categories Reveal about the Mind,* Chicago: University of Chicago Press; Mark Johnson, 1987, *The Body in the Mind: The Bodily Basis of Meaning, Imagination, and Reason,* Chicago: University of Chicago Press. For more on this linguistic model, see Chapter 9.
54. For examples, see Emily Martin, 1987, *The Woman in the Body: A Cultural Analysis of Reproduction,* Boston: Beacon Press; Janice Boddy, 1989, *Wombs and Alien Spirits: Women, Men and the Zar Cult in Northern Sudan,* Madison: University of Wisconsin Press.
55. Paul Stoller, 1997, *Sensuous Scholarship,* Philadelphia: University of Pennsylvania Press, p. xvii.

56. Thomas Csordas, 1994, *The Sacred Self: A Cultural Phenomenology of Charismatic Healing,* Berkeley: University of California Press.

57. Bourdieu, *Outline of a Theory of Practice,* p. 78.

58. See James W. Fernandez, 1982, "The Dark at the Bottom of the Stairs: The Inchoate in Symbolic Inquiry and Some Strategies for Coping with It," in Jacques Maquet (ed.), *On Symbols in Anthropology: Essays in Honor of Harry Hoijer,* Malibu, CA: Uneda.

59. Csordas makes an interesting synthesis combining a Peircean semiotics and a Sartrean psychology of imagery; he also incorporates recent theories of memory as well as object-relations psychology (especially notions of the false self and of transitional objects), which I cannot elaborate here.

60. Csordas, *The Sacred Self,* p. 158.

61. Ibid., p. 226.

62. Note that Csordas is not the only anthropologist to favor a phenomenological approach, though his is the effort that is most connected to psychological anthropology. For a different reading, see the work of Michael Jackson, especially 1989, *Paths toward a Clearing: Radical Empiricism and Ethnographic Inquiry,* Bloomington: Indiana University Press.

63. Jean-Pierre Vernant and Pierre Vidal-Naquet, 1981, *Tragedy and Myth in Ancient Greece,* Sussex, England: Harvester Press, p. 33.

64. For examples, see the essays in Lawrence Rosen (ed.), 1995, *Other Intentions: Cultural Contexts and the Attribution of Inner States,* Santa Fe, NM: School of American Research Press.

65. Steven M. Parish, 1996, *Hierarchy and Its Discontents: Culture and the Politics of Consciousness in Caste Society,* Philadelphia: University of Pennsylvania Press, p. 3.

66. Theodore Schwartz, 1992, "Anthropology and Psychology: An Unrequited Relationship," in Theodore Schwartz, Geoffrey White, and Catherine Lutz (eds.), *New Directions in Psychological Anthropology,* Cambridge, England: Cambridge University Press, p. 337.

67. As he writes, "rationality, in the sense of logical or teleological 'consistency' . . . has and always has had power over man." See Max Weber, 1946, "Religious Rejections of the World and Their Directions" (original publication 1915), in Hans Gerth and C. Wright Mills (eds.), *From Max Weber: Essays in Sociology,* New York: Oxford University Press, p. 324.

68. Max Weber, 1946, "Politics as a Vocation" (original publication 1919), in Hans Gerth and C. Wright Mills (eds.), *From Max Weber: Essays in Sociology,* New York: Oxford University Press, p. 122.

69. For this argument, see Charles Lindholm, 1980, *Generosity and Jealousy: The Swat Pukhtun of Northern Pakistan,* New York: Columbia University Press. For more on Pukhtun society, see Chapter 10.

70. This is not to deny that interesting arguments may still occur in this arena, for example, in the continuing controversy over the nature of the Oedipal conflict in the matrilineal, avunculocal society of the Trobriands (see Chapter 3 for references) and in the communal environment of Hindu India. For a discussion of the Indian case, see Stanley Kurtz, 1992, *All the Mothers Are One: Hindu India and the Cultural Reshaping of Psychoanalysis,* New York: Columbia University Press.

71. Two ethnographies utilizing the dialectical approach I favor are Charles Nuckolls, 1996, *The Cultural Dialectics of Knowledge and Desire,* Madison: University of Wisconsin Press; and Parish, *Hierarchy and Its Discontents.* Examples of my own research agenda can be found in my books: Lindholm, *Generosity and Jealousy;* 1990, *Charisma,* Oxford, England: Basil Blackwell; 1996, *The Islamic Middle East: An Historical Anthropology,* Oxford, England: Basil Blackwell; John A. Hall and Charles Lindholm, 1999, *Is America Breaking Apart?* Princeton, NJ: Princeton University Press.

PART FOUR

Problems and Some Solutions

CHAPTER 8

Dialectics of Self and Other

In Japan, when children misbehave, they are sent outside and forbidden to reenter the family unit. In America, when children misbehave, they are grounded, that is, prevented from leaving the house. In Japan, when children eat sugary junk food, they are said to become lethargic, withdrawing from participation in the group. In America, when children eat the same food, they are said to become hyperactive, causing chaos by their excesses.[1] In Japan, a favorite adage is "The nail that stands out gets pounded down." In America, the comparable maxim is "The squeaky wheel gets the grease."[2]

These and many other examples have often been cited to buttress the presumption that Japanese and Americans experience antithetical family lives, attitudes, and ideals. Americans, according to cliché, are self-assertive, contentious, and individualistic. The Japanese, in contrast, are said to be far more group-oriented. Their major fear is exclusion from the community. They wish above all to occupy their proper place in a well-organized social unit, so they readily subordinate themselves to the demands of others, muffling their emotions in favor of a measured, calm demeanor to avoid any possibilities of confrontation.

Japanese exchanging bows at a wedding reception.

205

These differences have been documented by batteries of psychological tests, which have shown (among other things) that Japanese self-reported emotions are less intense than those of their American counterparts, that Japanese are more modest in their behaviors than are Americans, blame themselves more when anything goes wrong, and are more intuitive of the needs of others, more nurturant, less aggressive, more obedient, more concerned with reciprocity, and more attentive to fitting in than to demonstrating personal achievement.[3] Do these differences mean that Japanese and Americans are fundamentally different in terms of their inner experiences of self?

Chapter Outline

I Defining the Self
   A Is the Category of Self a Western Invention?
   B Defining the Self

II Sociocentric and Egocentric Selves
   A Defining Sociocentrism and Egocentricism
   B Socializing for Independence or Interdependence
   C Independent Japanese?
   D Interdependent Americans?
   E The Social Context of the Self-Concept

III Hegemony, Hybridity, and the Decentered Self
   A Control and Resistance
   B Disintegrating the Boundaries of the Self

IV Hierarchical Categories: Race, Sex, and Caste
   A Discrimination and Identity
   B Difference and Rank
   C "Natural" Differences: Sex and Race
   D *Homo Hierarchicus:* Caste in India
   E *Homo Aequalis:* Resistance to Caste

I. DEFINING THE SELF

A Is the Category of Self a Western Invention?
   Some arguments that the category of self is ethnocentric.

B Defining the Self
   A compilation of some contemporary theories of the nature of identity.

A. Is the Category of Self a Western Invention?

Before we begin an inquiry into the way the self may vary cross-culturally, some definition of terms is required. Throughout this book, I have used "self," "role," "person," "identity," and "individual" or "agent" more or less interchangeably. To a degree, this has been a matter of style, but it also has been a conscious intellectual strategy on my part that would allow me to avoid becoming entangled in confusing knots of competing definitions and to illustrate my meaning through example.

In the following pages, though, I intend to discuss recent research that has argued strongly that there are real differences between the selves constituted in Western society and the selves found elsewhere. Before considering this question, we first ought to explore its premises and ask whether the self is a useful analytic category. Many commentators have said it is not. The Norwegian anthropologist Unni Wikan has noted that "self" does not figure as a noun in her language, and that the use of the term rings to her of Anglo-Saxon ethnocentrism. Similarly, the Singhalese anthropologist Gananath Obeyesekere has stated that the entrance of the self into anthropological discourse is "too radical an appropriation of other minds into Anglo-American language games and life forms." And the linguist Anna Wierzbicka has argued that the concept of self is a "highly culture-specific creation" found as a noun perhaps only in English. According to her, a far less culture-bound term is "person," defined everywhere as a living, thinking, knowing, desiring, feeling, speaking, hearing active being.[4]

There is much to be said for these claims. We know that even in the Anglo-American world, the notion of the self as an active agent is not very ancient.[5] Until the thirteenth century, in English and other Germanic languages, the term "self" was used primarily as a reflexive pronoun, as in "I myself." The word was gradually expanded into a substantive, and finally came into use as a generalized noun in English only relatively recently. The most famous early example of modern usage was in 1690 when the philosopher John Locke defined the self as "that conscious thinking thing, . . . concerned for it self, as far as that consciousness extends."[6] As many commentators have agreed, this Lockean personal self is singular; it endures over time, space, and physical changes; and it can be empirically investigated and understood.[7]

B. Defining the Self

Ever since the time of Locke, Western thinkers have struggled with properly defining and delimiting the self. For example, in the field of psychology Roy Shafer has distinguished the person as agent, while the self is reflective;[8] object-relations theorists divided the self into true and false aspects, the first authentic and instinctive, the second a mask worn to fit into society;[9] Kenneth Gergen has even dissolved the self entirely, describing it as an illusion forced upon us by language.[10] The most thorough and convincing formulation is that of Ulrich Neisser, who has argued that there are five different selves that must necessarily be experienced by everyone: the ecological self known through bodily experience; the interpersonal self of emotional rapport and communication, as formulated by G. H. Mead; the remembered self, existing in time; the private inner self we discover through the realization that our conscious experiences are internal; and, finally, the conceptual self learned through cultural models.

Although these aspects are analytically distinct, their existence does not indicate a sense of fragmentation. As Niesser says, people everywhere feel themselves to be "unitary and coherent individuals."[11]

Neisser's five selves can be summarized as follows:

1. Ecological—bodily experience.
2. Interpersonal—communication.
3. Remembered—memory.
4. Private—internal consciousness.
5. Conceptual—cultural models.

In anthropology, matters are equally complex. In his famous essay on the notion of self, Marcel Mauss traced the way the concept of personal being changed over time. Like Durkheim and Levy-Bruhl, he argued that the individual was originally fused with the clan during the performance of ritual roles. It was in Rome, with the revolt of the plebs, that the persona become linked to the true nature of the individual, an aspect extended by Christianity, where moral responsibility was crucial. After the Enlightenment and with the rise of Protestantism, the self became the primordial category of psychological and spiritual being. As Mauss stated:

> From a mere masquerade to the mask, from a role to a person, to a name, to an individual, from the last to a being with a metaphysical and ethical value, from a moral consciousness to a sacred being, from the latter to a fundamental form of thought and action—that is the route we have now covered.[12]

The anthropologically informed philosopher Amélie Rorty has extended Mauss's categories.[13] She begins her catalogue with the hero of ancient Greece, fated to a noble destiny by the gods and known solely by deeds. A later development is the protagonist, who reveals his admirable nature only in combat. Character, a democratization of identity, is the next step; while only a few are heroes or protagonists, everyone has a character, which is fixed at birth, is public, and consists of a set of immutable traits. A figure is character writ large, providing an idealized image for emulation.

Like Mauss, Rorty portrays the person as a more internalized identity that is derived from two sources: theater and law. In Greek theater, the actor in a mask is a persona, "that through which the sound comes."[14] In law, the person is the one held legally responsible. In both senses, the person stands behind his or her acts and must look within to make a moral decision to act.

Introspection leads in two directions: One can imagine agency derived from a pure soul, unfathomable and unconditioned, judged only by God; or one can become a self, constructed by one's own powers and capacities. The latter, Rorty says, is a consequence of the capitalist transformation that freed people from their traditional feudal obligations to one another and made them reliant on their own qualities; they could now have experiences and make the most of themselves. As they did so, they became individuals—free agents who resist being typed and who claim to be unique.[15]

As we saw in Chapter 6, Hallowell was the first anthropologist to stress that people everywhere reflect upon, discuss, and judge themselves. He took this self-reflective capacity as the aspect of the self to be analyzed cross-culturally.[16] Certainly, this made considerable sense, especially because in English grammar, "the term 'self' has been a reflexive ever since its appearance."[17] But as we saw in Chapter 7, phenomenologically inclined anthropologists, like Csordas, have insisted, equally plausibly, that self-consciousness relies upon having a preobjective sense of self to reflect about. This preobjective self is immediate and experiential, perceiving the world, yet differentiated from it. Self-consciousness builds upon that existential duality of "me" and "not me," and it is the unfolding of this self that ought to be the focus of study.

Meanwhile, Grace Harris, in an influential article, added even more complications to the argument. She divided human beings into three parts.[18] The self is the existential locus of experience; it encompasses both the I and the self-reflective me. The individual consists of the species-specific aspects of being, including language. The person is the social actor playing parts in public. The latter, Harris suggested, is an achieved status, which can be lost or denied, and requires continual effort to maintain (as Goffman also argued). Because the person is preeminently social, it is the aspect of being that can most readily be investigated.

Harris's model can be summarized as follows:

1. Self—the experiential I and me.
2. Individual—species-specific aspects, including language.
3. Person—public role.

It seems, then, that the notion of the self, which appears to us to be self-evident, is actually not so easily grasped. Perhaps in the contemporary West the self is simply a cliché, exploited, packaged, and marketed to sell books on self-help and self-understanding in a complex and fluid modern society where there is ever greater anxiety about identity.[19] It may even be possible (as many postmodern theorists have claimed) that the whole notion of a coherent self is nothing but an imposition of Western values aimed at preventing the spontaneous expression of the playful, discontinuous, and polyglot identities said to be characteristic of our present age. And in fact it is (as noted in Chapter 6) quite difficult (but not impossible) to demonstrate scientifically that the personality has any continuity over the life span, or even that the self is cohesive at any particular point.

Yet even admitting that men and women put on different masks for different occasions, that they are oftentimes inconsistent about what they think and feel, and that the cultural content of the notion of personal identity shifts over time does not negate the experiential reality of the self. Our commonsense faith in the continuity of individual character is borne out in research indicating that people are very unwilling to alter the way they characterize themselves, show considerable continuity in the expression of feelings, and are recognizable as distinct personalities over time. At minimum, we can conclude that while concepts of self are vague and malleable, the actual experience of being *someone* is a real and essential aspect of our human existence. Even Buddhists who believe the self is an illusion must begin by apprehending and living within the very selves they wish to dissolve.

II. SOCIOCENTRIC AND EGOCENTRIC SELVES

A Defining Sociocentricism and Egocentricism
   Sociocentric-interdependent and egocentric-independent selves. The Japanese and Americans as prototypical.

B Socializing for Independence or Interdependence
   Learning to be a person in sociocentric and egocentric cultures.

C Independent Japanese?
   Evidence that the Japanese are actually more egocentric than is usually supposed.

D Interdependent Americans?
   Evidence that Americans are actually more sociocentric than is usually supposed.

E The Social Context of the Self-Concept
   The relationship between social organization and self-representation.

A. Defining Sociocentricism and Egocentricism

Undeterred by the fact that an absolute and precise definition of the elusive nature of personal being can probably never be attained, anthropologists have recently become concerned with the degree to which the self is altered by culture. Much of this debate was inspired by Clifford Geertz, who declared:

> The Western conception of the person as a bounded, unique, more or less integrated motivational and cognitive universe, a dynamic center of awareness, emotion, judgment and action organized into a distinctive whole and set contrastively both against other such wholes and against a social and natural background is, however incorrigible it may seem to us, a rather peculiar idea within the context of the world's cultures.[20]

In a manner reminiscent of Benedict's evocation of archetypes, Geertz then placed the bounded, unique, self-actualizing entity assumed to exist in the West in contrast to a more socially embedded, less bounded, more other-directed being said to be characteristic of non-Western societies.

A number of authors took up Geertz's formula and sought to demonstrate that the taken-for-granted aspects of Western psychology actually did not hold cross-culturally, and that a more sociocentric self could be found everywhere from America to Africa to Asia.[21] In India, for example, people were said to be not individuals, but "dividuals"; they were constituted not by self-actualization and personal enterprise, but by exchanges of substances, especially foods, that created being.[22] In this worldview, persons are permeable, absorbing the moral qualities of their families, their castes, and even their homes and villages. For instance, among the Tamils studied by E. Valentine Daniel, people who had the same ur, or home village, were thought to manifest the same essential character, since "a person absorbs the nature of the soil . . . by eating the food grown in village fields and by drinking the water that springs from the soil into village wells."[23]

The gradual assumption of identity through immersion in a social and physical world is to be found as well in South America and Melanesia. For example, among the Warí of the Amazonian basin, a child can have many fathers, since each man who has had intercourse with the mother is thought to have added semen that builds the child's flesh and bones. The Warí also believe that personhood can be attenuated, or even lost, if an individual does not continue to interact and share bodily substances with his or her social group. Marrying an outsider, for example, is said to make a woman's blood change, transforming her into the bodily image of her mate.[24]

A less processual and more structural form of sociocentric identity is found in Japan and other Asian societies, where the self is located within a dense, preexistent network of social obligations and hierarchical distinctions. As Dorinne Kondo reports in her account of her fieldwork in Japan: "I was never allowed to be an autonomous, freely operating 'individual'. . . I was 'always already' caught in webs of relationships." Invoking the Sapir-Whorf hypothesis, she argues that because Japanese pronouns vary according to whom one is speaking, "identity and context are inseparable, calling into question the very distinction between the two."[25] Japanese sociocentricism is said to be manifested at every level of society: In the workplace, instead of being focused on maximizing profit, managers concern themselves with the contextual skills of maintaining sociability among colleagues;[26] in therapy, the stress is on integration with society and maintaining relationships of dependency and protection, not, as in the West, with finding one's true self and asserting autonomy.[27]

B. Socializing for Independence or Interdependence

The differences between sociocentric and egocentric selves have often been correlated with socialization practices. For example, among groups such as the sociocentric Gusii people of Kenya, children are never left alone: A mother constantly holds her infant and soothes it, but she does not want to arouse or excite her baby, and does not interact with it or talk to it, which she thinks would be silly anyway, since babies cannot understand what is said to them. Gusii children are not praised; they are socialized to be obedient, docile, and quiet—persons who will fit into the collective.

This is in marked contrast to the practices of American mothers, who hold babies much less, but often talk to them in high-pitched baby talk, excite them by interactive play and response, and praise them effusively. Unlike Gusii children, American infants are often left alone, since Americans tend to assume that children, as autonomous individuals,[28] need privacy; parents provide children

In a sociocentric society, infants are constantly held and soothed.

with their own space, full of child-sized objects and toys that their parents cannot touch. But when the American child is with people, it is very likely to be the center of attention. This leads the child to be self-assertive, attention-seeking, and linguistically expressive.[29] Only in the United States would an adult seriously ask a three-year-old, "What do you want for dinner?"[30]

The American model of childhood training also means, as one American mother said, "letting kids evaluate their feelings, talk about their feelings, get their feelings out . . . Empowering them to take charge of their feelings."[31] In this context, middle-class American mothers "expressed respect for young children's willfulness and appreciated the 'clever' ways their youngsters attempted to get what they wanted."[32] When children do disobey, American middle-class mothers tend to explain the rationale for the rules to them and try to persuade them to comply, in the faith that autonomous individuals should cooperate not out of coercion, but out of free will—even if the individual is a three-year-old.

Again, none of these American beliefs and practices are at all characteristic worldwide. For example, studies of recent Chinese immigrants to the United States show that mothers have little or no interest in building children's self-esteem, nurturing their awareness of their emotional needs, encouraging them to make choices, or establishing a child-centered environment. Rather, children are expected to fit into the social milieu of their parents; they learn to maintain public decorum, not disgrace their families, and keep harmony within the household.[33] Discipline is also conceived of quite differently: Shaming is common, as children are strictly judged and publicly humiliated for their transgressions. These mothers certainly do not tend to be proud of the child's cleverness in breaking rules, nor do they feel it necessary to convince their children that the rules are reasonable.

Asian schooling also aims at promoting group responsibility, though there are considerable differences even among these sociocentric cultures (Chinese schools encourage authoritarian groupism, while Japanese groupism is spontaneous[34]). Class sizes in Japanese preschools are much larger than in the United States, since even very small children are expected to know how to manage their own relationships in the group, without requiring intervention from a teacher. At the same time, behavior is highly regulated among children in Japanese elementary schools, including a rule about the angle one should hold the arm when raising one's hand. Restrictions also extend outside the classroom, since children are thought of as being representatives of their schools wherever they are.[35] These distinctions in child-raising practices correspond with the attitudes toward the individual, who is expected to subordinate his or her individuality to the family and the community.

C. Independent Japanese?

These distinctions in attitude and in practice are usually thought to indicate that Japanese (or Chinese, or Indian) interdependent sociocentric selves are essentially different from autonomous, egocentric American selves. Unlike the autonomous, private, inwardly turned Western self, the selves of Japanese, Indians, Chinese, and other non-Western collectively oriented peoples are taken to be public, shaped by others, fluid, and flexibly adaptive to the requirements of the community.[36] Anthropologists who have argued in favor of such absolute internal differences have assumed that indigenous models of being "provide a basis for the organization of activities, responses, perceptions, and experiences by the conscious self."[37]

Is this so?[38] Let's consider the Japanese sociocentric self, which, as we have seen, is generally portrayed as the polar opposite of the egocentric self of Westerners.[39] The Japanese, it is often claimed, assiduously manipulate their own opinions, abilities, and characteristics to fit into the larger social world that enmeshes them. In this cultural universe, maturity is measured by the capacity of individuals to control and constrain themselves and to conform to the demands of others. In contrast, in the United States, maturity is often said to be indicated by the capacity to get in touch with one's inner emotional desires and to become self-actualized by fulfilling them. If this characterization is accurate (a large assumption), it is an indication of differing ethical value systems in East and West—one favoring adaptive self-control; the other, emotional self-expression.

But adapting to others does not necessarily mean that the interdependent self actually changes according to the contextual relationships that constitute it while the independent self of Westerners remains constant. In fact, one could argue just the opposite: Active self-regulation is required for the Japanese and other interdependent peoples to properly reflect surrounding social circumstances. In other words, self-effacement does not mean the individual has no ego; it only means that the ego must assert constant control to fit in as one is supposed to do.

To meet this goal, interdependent selves must manage their emotions carefully, since they are deeply concerned with accommodating themselves to others, and must carefully avoid giving offence or causing conflict.[40] Because of the demand for a controlled public performance, it is sometimes argued that the interdependent Japanese and other sociocentric peoples are actually able to eliminate feelings of anger or other strong emotions from their repertoire. But if this were actually the case, why then make the effort to organize conversation and interaction in such highly formal fashion?[41]

It would seem more reasonable to argue instead that the ritualized etiquette so characteristic of sociocentric societies does not necessarily indicate an absence of disruptive emotions, but rather reveals a pervasive and realistic anxiety about the dangerous consequences of displaying those emotions. Such ritualized constraint would be functional in environments consisting of relatively high-density, kinship-oriented, socially immobile communities where power is not easy to escape and insults are not forgotten. As one commentator writes, among the prototypically interdependent Chinese, "individuals do not have the choice to just change or cancel out their relationships with those individuals in their social world. Therefore, their primary concern would be how to live with each other's differences and 'get along.' "[42]

Under such restricted circumstances, a strong effort must be made to monitor and control unwanted feelings and thoughts so as not to offend others. Paradoxically, the interdependent self then can be seen to be governed by a strong, calculating, self-regulating inner overseer capable of systematically adapting behavior to conform to social demands, repressing emotions, and generally maintaining strict control in an effort to meet the cultural demand for self-effacement. It would appear from this perspective that the self-denial and restraint demanded by a sociocentric society requires a strong ego; such an ego must continually struggle to maintain the appropriate face in a difficult and challenging environment.

D. Interdependent Americans?

If the sociocentric self is not so sociocentric after all, perhaps the Western independent self is equally chimerical. And, in fact, a number of commentators have been struck by the remarkable conformity and other-directedness of Americans, existing in secret tandem with the loudly asserted values of autonomy and free-dom.[43] Conformity and a concern for the opinions of others are inculcated in Americans from childhood on, and are intensified by the requirements of a mobile and corporate economy. To survive, Americans must learn to subordinate themselves to the community, to fit in, and to participate together as co-equal citizens working for the common good.

Training toward these goals is clearest in the school system, where popular students are elected as student-body leaders whose job is to represent their fellows, where school spirit is heavily promoted, and where children are actually graded on the quality of their citizenship. Students are also expected to participate in extracurricular activities, practice teamwork, and cooperate on a voluntary basis. Sports especially are highly valued as an expression of school spirit and local pride, as individuals can show off their personal talents and also help their teammates to victory through disciplined self-sacrifice and cooperation.

As adults, Americans continue to denigrate self-display and the personal search for power, while teamwork and modesty are favored. Those who do not meet this norm are accused of acting big and thinking they are better than everyone else. For instance, the anthropologist Elvin Hatch reports that people in an American small town "avoided responsibility for decisions as much as possible. Events were normally engineered in such a way that a large number of people were involved in arriving at a course of action and responsibility was diffused throughout the community."[44] Similarly, Michael Moffatt, writing about his students at Rutgers, describes how studiously they sought to avoid any appearance of being unfriendly or snobby.[45]

Emotional control is also characteristic of Americans. Despite the idea that independent Westerners freely vent their anger, frustration, and pride, studies show that middle-class Americans typically display muffled emotions even within the family, while also downplaying differences of opinion or other potentially disrupting factors that might incite hostility, jealousy, or anger. In place of the formality characteristic of high-density and socially static interdependent communities, American relationships are emotionally muted and detached. But the result is the same: avoidance of conflict.

The American pattern correlates with the middle-class world of the suburb, where, in contrast to more sociocentric worlds, there is no need for individuals to confront one another, where it is perfectly possible for members of the same household to have separate rooms, separate schedules, and separate meals—and hardly ever meet. In the most extreme cases, when friction becomes too intrusive, middle-class Americans know that they can simply pack up and move away, an option generally unavailable to those living in the spatially fixed, kinship-based Asian societies where interdependence is a necessity.

E. The Social Context of the Self-Concept

In a very real sense, then, East Asian interdependent communities and mainstream American culture have much in common in terms of the values they pursue. In neither case does anyone wish to disrupt a smooth social surface with emotional outbursts or angry confrontations, and in each instance there is a cultural premium placed upon maintaining inner autonomy. But whereas interdependent individuals must continually interact with one another in their households and in densely packed, face-to-face, kin-based communities that cannot be escaped, Americans have the enviable capacity to retreat from interaction. This does not necessarily mean they have different selves, only that actual historical and cultural circumstances permit them a degree of physical and psychological distancing from others that is less possible for their East Asian counterparts, who must rely on formal etiquette to maintain the boundaries of potentially conflictual social worlds while protecting the psychic space of individuals.

Differences in the way people present themselves thus may correlate with differences in social structure and cultural values, particularly the values inculcated by indigenous patterns of authority and subordination. Let me make this latter point more forcefully by considering the meaning of two characteristic aphorisms that were cited in the introduction to this chapter as illustrations of the distinctions between Japanese and Americans: The American maxim is "The squeaky wheel gets the grease"; the Japanese, "The nail that stands out gets pounded down."[46]

These quotes can be taken to mean that the Japanese sociocentric self actively avoids distinction, while the American egocentric self demands attention. However, we can better understand these sayings by putting them in a more political light. The Westerners who are "squeaky wheels" make noise in the belief that they can thereby better their situations. The cultural assumption is that the political and social world will respond positively to those who make demands upon it. The Japanese proverb, in contrast, is an expression of the fear of the *punishment* that will inevitably occur if one dares to "stand out." Japanese subordinate themselves to the community not because they have essentially different selves, but because of a culturally embedded and quite realistic fear of the negative consequences of acting in a manner that is seen as egotistical.

It seems then that the Japanese and Chinese selves do not necessarily differ from those of Westerners, if by "self" is meant the fundamental manner in which reality is subjectively experienced. The differences are in the ideals of proper ways of being and in the premises about how to guide their lives.[47] These cultural ideals of self-representation serve as convenient moral yardsticks for measurement of individual behavior. When they are deeply internalized, they will profoundly affect the types of inner conflicts and guilt that beset people, and the sorts of psychological defenses they erect. The psychoanalyst Alan Roland, for example, has discussed the variations in mental illness characteristic of India, Japan, and the United States, and has related them to the degree of enmeshment in what he calls the familial self.[48]

Although self-representations may have powerful psychic effects, they are hardly the whole story. Notions of selfhood are likely to be partial, situational, and unrealistic; as the anthropologist Alan Howard writes, the ideals of the cultural superego are also likely to stand at odds with the actual experience of "the corporeal reality of the body—the fact that it urinates and defecates and experiences hunger, thirst and sexual urges."[49] As Goffman knew, conventional self-representations will never fit exactly with subjective experience; multiple sources of bodily and psychic perception, often not directly available to conceptual thought, will intervene, complicate, and contradict whatever our ideals demand. Thus, Fredrik Barth, an anthropologist who has done fieldwork probably in more societies than any other living ethnographer, notes that no matter how different the cultural construction of selfhood might be, the persons and self-concepts molded by participation in such radically alternative worlds do not come out as differently as one might have expected.[50]

In truth, human beings everywhere are inevitably and inextricably linked by the shared awareness of the unavoidable onslaught of death, the irresolvable problem of finding meaning in life, and, especially, by the demands and constraints set by equally self-aware persons whose desires and fears are as compelling for them as our own are for us. They are the capitalized Others—both generalized and specific—from whom we try to distinguish ourselves and in whose eyes we also find ourselves. It is the culturally mediated confrontation with those around us, the tension between immersion and separation, that is at the core of our recognition (albeit often muted or denied) that the other—who also is enmeshed in the same net—is not so very different from the self. Every society celebrates, in its own way and to differing degrees, both self-loss and autonomy. The subtext of sociocentric interdependence is and must be the reinstatement of an independent, bounded self—just as the subtext of independence is interdependence.[51]

III. HEGEMONY, HYBRIDITY, AND THE DECENTERED SELF

A Control and Resistance
Postcolonialism, imperialism, and Antonio Gramsci's theory of hegemony.

B Disintegrating the Boundaries of the Self
Hybridity, marginalization, and the erosion of identity. Ideals and reality.

A. Control and Resistance

The battle between autonomy and merger is fought most ferociously around relationships of domination. The study of such relationships, and their psychological effect, has recently become one of the most significant fields in anthropology, and has also assumed prominence in the new disciplinary area of cultural studies. Part of this new interest is due to the slow withdrawal of colonial forces from the third world, leaving anthropologists free to trace the scars left by the imposition of often cruel and always alien imperial power. Part is also due to the important work of Michel Foucault and feminist theorists, who have drawn the attention of social scientists and humanists to the silent infiltration of power relationships into the organization of knowledge itself. And part is a reaction against formalist and structuralist arguments that removed individual actors from social life.

Although psychological anthropology has only begun to explore this area, studies of subalterns, colonial mentality, and class consciousness have a distinguished intellectual pedigree, dating back at least to Marx and Engels, who sought to understand the false consciousness of workers who did not join the revolutionary movement. We have seen already in Chapter 5 how Marxist critical theorists were driven to psychological explanations to account for the rise of Nazism. Wrestling with a similar dilemma during Mussolini's rule, the Italian Marxist Antonio Gramsci (1891–1937) developed the notion of cultural hegemony to explain the hold Fascism had on the popular imagination of his fellow citizens. Culture, Gramsci argued, can be the most useful tool of the powerful. It is employed in many ways, both consciously and unconsciously. As an emotionally charged image of what is right and good, it penetrates into and shapes the manner reality and being are experienced. Insofar as the dominant ideology is psychologically internalized, it can completely obscure the possibilities of transformation. But in return, it must offer its believers a sense that the universe they inhabit is meaningful and gratifying, and, especially, some way to manage and rationalize suffering and injustice.

In many respects, then, Gramsci's notion of cultural hegemony is nothing more than a Marxist discovery of Weber's theory of *verstehen*. But whereas Weber stressed the manner in which individuals act to maximize their status positions within any particular ethical system, Gramsci—a more utopian thinker—emphasized the possibility of counterhegemonic acts of resistance. One could, he thought, "choose one's sphere of activity, take an active part in the history of the world, be one's own guide, refusing to accept passively and supinely from the outside the molding of one's personality."[52] This could occur, he thought, through the awakening of the reflective philosopher that exists in everyone, though exactly how the consciousness of the indigenous organic intellectual might be aroused was left unclear. In general, it was hoped that an intellectual vanguard would educate the workers and kindle their latent capacities for critique.

A number of modern sociological and anthropological works have been influenced by some version of the notion of cultural hegemony. For example, Paul Willis has shown how working-class English boys are socialized to consent to their inferior position; Jay Mcleod has explored the self-fulfilling expectations of failure prevalent among young men in a Cambridge, Massachusetts, housing project; Phillippe Bourgeois's ethnography of crack dealers in El Barrio in New York reveals how deeply the gang members have internalized the values of the very system that marginalizes and oppresses them. Kathy Newman describes how middle managers, fired from their jobs, condemn themselves, not the corporate system, for their situations.[53] This work suggests the extent to which individuals may be made complicit in their own degradation.

B. Disintegrating the Boundaries of the Self

At the same time, much attention has also been paid to protest and rebellion, now with a focus not on actual social movements (as was traditionally the case in anthropology), but on hidden, even unconscious, acts of resistance by subordinated groups. Cultural studies, in particular, has devoted considerable attention to the role of popular music and art in expressing the oppositional feelings and creative impulses of oppressed or marginalized subcultures.[54] There has also been great praise for boundary-crossing forms of cultural hybridity as a field of resistance establishing a liminal "third space" where, as the cultural theorist Homi Bhaba exults, we "may elude the politics of polarity and emerge as others of our selves"[55]—a rather daunting prospect.

As noted in the previous chapter, admiration of the marginalized, a dream of the erasure of boundaries between us and them, and a desire to escape from the constraints of personal identity all resonate with anthropology's romantic heritage. As a result, arguments taken from cultural studies have found an important place with a number of anthropological writers. One such writer, Lila Abu-Lughod, has argued that the very notion of culture should be discarded, since its use must inevitably "make these 'others' seem simultaneously more coherent, self-contained and different from ourselves than they might be . . . This in turn allows for the fixing of boundaries between self and other."[56] For theorists of this persuasion, any divisions between human beings are necessarily destructive, and even the notion of a unified self is a delusion. The anthropologist therefore becomes, as Renato Rosaldo writes, "a busy intersection through which multiple identities crisscross," whose aim is achievement of "new forms of polyglot cultural creativity."[57]

The preceding pastiche is a bit of a parody, but the message is accurate. Postmodern anthropologists do tend to believe that welcoming a decentered identity would free humanity to enter joyfully into a porous, playful, and hybrid postmodern world. But a glance at the record shows that this dream is a long way from reality.[58] The young working-class and underclass men studied by Willis, McLeod, and Bourgeois were highly unlikely to engage in creative acts of cultural hybridity; instead, they most often vented their explosive anger in violence against women and against despised others. In Bosnia, Ireland, Central Africa, Germany, Israel, Algeria, and many other places in the world, we find that threats to identity arouse not celebration, but misogyny, prejudice, and brutality.

Although morally reprehensible, these pervasive expressions of cruelty and rage are psychologically understandable as responses to anxieties about one's own self-certainty; scapegoating and demonizing others are powerful ways to relieve inner fears of chaos and psychic disintegration that can be aroused when boundaries between self and other are undermined. These ugly aspects of the human condition cannot simply be set aside in favor of a romanticized embrace of the downtrodden or in an idealistic hope for the erasure of difference. As anthropologist Jonathan Friedman writes, we cannot interpret history as "an intellectual conversation in which problems can be solved by convincing people that they have got it all wrong."[59]

IV. HIERARCHICAL CATEGORIES: RACE, SEX, AND CASTE

A Discrimination and Identity
   Frantz Fanon and the psychic effects of racism and sexism.

B Difference and Rank
   Evidence that discrimination does not necessarily follow from difference.

C "Natural" Differences: Sex and Race
   Cultural variations in sexual and racial categories.

D *Homo Hierarchicus:* Caste in India
   Caste as a cultural system based on ranking of human beings.

E *Homo Aequalis:* Resistance to Caste
   Ambivalence and opposition within caste.

A. Discrimination and Identity

A more complex and psychologically adequate picture of the effects of inequity and injustice on both oppressor and oppressed was offered in the 1960s by the psychoanalyst and philosopher Frantz Fanon (1925–1961).[60] Born in the French West Indies, Fanon was a black intellectual who was peripheralized in multiple ways: as a black man in a white culture, as a Creole speaker, and as a native of a colony. His books[61] are introspective chronicles of his personal dilemma as well as many-sided dissections of the ramifications of the human experience of prejudice. His particular topic was racism, which Fanon saw as an especially virulent form of discrimination, since it automatically places persons within publicly visible, stigmatized categories that they can neither escape nor accept. As he wrote:

> When people like me, they tell me it is in spite of my color. When they dislike me, they point out that it is not because of my color. Either way, I am locked into the infernal circle . . . For the black man there is only one destiny. And it is white.[62]

Caught within the infernal circle of racism, Fanon believed the black could only dream of being what is impossible: white. And the rage, self-doubt, and injury felt as a result of this impossible quandary leads the colonized black "to run away from his own individuality, to annihilate his own presence . . . the Negro, having been made inferior, proceeds from humiliating insecurity through strongly voiced self-accusation to despair."[63] Meanwhile, racist whites are equally distorted by the dehumanizing practice of bigotry, locked into narrow identities in which they exist only through their violent negation of nonwhite others.

As a number of feminists have argued, similar dynamics occur in traditional Western male-female relationships, as men are deemed intellectually

1957: A white onlooker taunts an African-American student attempting to attend a segregated school in Alabama.

superior and dominant in the high-status public world of work, while women are seen as emotional and irrational, destined for child-raising and nurturance. Insofar as these one-sided images are internalized, they cripple the potential of both sides to escape from rigid sexual stereotypes. Despite considerable social change, these conventions of feminine and masculine, black and white, remain compelling today, showing how deeply rooted and "natural" they have become.

Fanon's picture of the destructive psychic effects of colonialism and racial bigotry was not totally bleak. Like Gramsci, he believed in the possibility of critical consciousness. His books remain powerful tools for that purpose. As he says: "The fact of the juxtaposition of the white and black races has created a massive psychoexistential complex. I hope by analyzing it to destroy it."[64] To carry on Fanon's mission, psychological anthropology should continue its comparative analysis of the real consequences, psychological and experiential, of other forms of discrimination, the degree to which and the manner in which invidious distinctions are both internalized and resisted, and the sorts of distinction that are most destructive.

Fanon on Race

Fanon's understanding of race must be taken in the context of his own experiences in France as an immigrant from the French colonial territory of Martinque. His history of migration from the Caribbean periphery—where a creolized French is spoken—to the metropolitan center of Paris is very different from the histories of African Americans in the United States, who, while marginalized, have never been so differentiated from mainstream culture. It also must be recalled that his work was written before the civil rights struggle in the United States, when the claim to black power went along with the assertion that black is beautiful.

Fanon would have approved of this combination, since he believed that the only way for blacks to escape from self-hatred was through a confrontation with their oppressors and through identification with positive black role models; but he also would have fiercely repudiated any assertion of absolute racial distinctions. For him, the opposition of black and white could not simply be turned upside down, with blacks made superior to whites. Nor would a policy of separate but equal satisfy him. Both of these outcomes simply reiterated what he saw as a pernicious dichotomy that had to be utterly destroyed to free both blacks and whites from the chains of racism.

B. Difference and Rank

The potential for harm in the attribution of difference is most virulent when ranking is based on the belief that certain groups of human beings are innately and unchangeably biologically inferior. Racism assumes that skin color is the outer emblem of a degraded character; sexism assumes that women are intrinsically less able than men; anti-Semites believe that Jews have polluted blood. The malignant use of such negative biological categories, which can be neither escaped nor changed, is both vicious and absolute.

Yet even though it is evident that almost any physical or cultural difference can easily be elaborated, naturalized, and turned into a justification for bigotry, we have to be wary of seeing all forms of distinction as necessarily repressive, as some postmodernist theorists appear to believe. A moment's thought will show that difference does not necessarily mean relationships of subordination. Difference may be complementary, or simply aesthetic, or symbolically significant. As blue is different from yellow, so white is different from black and male is different from female. There are no necessary moral judgments implied in these categorical statements. Only when differences are ranked (white is better than black, male is naturally superior to female) do we have the ideological grounds for domination.[65]

In fact, everywhere and always, human beings have spontaneously divided themselves and others into groups based on residence, parentage, custom, gender, age, history, appearance, and so on. As Durkheim demonstrated, even in the simplest societies, people separate into symbolic moieties and mark differences of age, sex, and social category. And although cultural, ethnic, physical, and na-

---

Moieties

Many simpler societies have as their main organizational principle a division into two descent groups, called moieties by anthropologists. These moieties often perform complementary roles in rituals and are thought to have cosmic symbolic significance: the people of one moiety representing the night; the other, the day; and so on. Moieties also often serve as the basis for marriage, as marriage within the moiety is forbidden, while marriage with persons of the other moiety is prescribed.

---

tional distinctions have too often been exploited for purposes of oppression, and may sometimes decline into biological essentialism, these culturally constructed distinctions also provide the necessary incentive for attraction and exchange, and serve as the inspirations for much of human creativity.[66] The mission, then, for psychological anthropology is not to destroy difference, but to discover how difference becomes destructive, and how such destructive difference may be opposed and overcome.

C. "Natural" Differences: Sex and Race

The most obvious example of a "natural" distinction that is used to legitimize discrimination is sex. Anthropologists usually define sex as a physical distinction that is overlain and sometimes crosscut by culturally constructed gender. This follows Margaret Mead's demonstration (discussed in Chapter 4) that standardized American masculine and feminine ways of acting and feeling were not at all universal and biologically based, but varied widely across cultures: Whole societies, Mead said, could be effeminate or masculine; gender roles could even be reversed. New research has made the understanding of gender even more complex. At present, in the West there are four genders, defined primarily by sexual attraction. Male and female are thought to be naturally erotically attracted to each other and are culturally defined as normal; homosexual and lesbian are erotically aroused by the same sex, and are culturally defined as perverted.

This four-category system is by far the most prevalent cross-culturally, but certain societies have quite different understandings of gender categories. There may be intermediate gender classifications such as the xanith of Oman or the mahu of Tahiti—men who dress and act in a manner distinctively blending masculine and feminine attributes—who form a culturally specific third gender. While in the West we see these liminal categories either as the result of deeply rooted biological drives and fundamental temperamental differences or as sinful lapses, in Oman and Tahiti they have no necessary connection to one's inner nature, nor do they imply any innate sexual attraction to persons of the same sex. Rather, they are understood as social roles, to be entered or left at will. This flexibility may be connected, a number of authors have argued, to "a gender system based on contrasting social roles, as opposed to contrasting temperaments."[67]

Not only does gender presentation vary considerably across cultures, but even biological sex may be understood in culturally variable ways. In Western history, Thomas Laqueur has argued that until the late eighteenth century, medical and popular theory proclaimed that there was really only one sex—male. The female was thought to be nothing more than an incomplete man with undeveloped sexual organs.[68] Randolph Trumbach has claimed, in contrast, that seventeenth-century people assumed there were three sexes—man, woman, and hermaphrodite—and only two genders—male and female. Those who broke sexual codes of conduct were classified as hermaphrodites. Thus it was believed that lesbian women could actually change into men when "what was ordinarily hidden inwardly in a woman's body had by manipulation been brought outside of the body."[69] Effeminate males appeared as a new gender type only in the late part of the seventeenth century, and only after 1750 did some homosexual men cease to marry and have children.[70] Other cultures may also have a three-sex system, making a special category for the biologically ambiguous hermaphrodites who, in our resolutely dimorphic society, are immediately operated upon to turn them into either little boys or little girls.[71]

If even so evident a biological distinction as sex is culturally shaped, then clearly, all forms of difference that are supposedly natural have a very large cultural component. Races, for example, have no absolute or substantive content, but are intersections of many multiplex genetic and environmental influences. Genotypical analysis of clusters of genetic similarities may prove useful for tracing ancient migration patterns, but these clusters do not coincide with the culturally formed understanding of race in the United States. The genetic illogic of our categorizations can be easily discerned in the notorious one-drop rule, which classifies anyone with a black ancestor as black, regardless of appearance. According to this rule, it is perfectly possible for someone who is phenotypically white to pass for black; the reverse, however, is completely impossible. In other words, for most Americans, anyone who looks black *is* black, but someone who looks white could also be black—if he or she has "black blood."

The cultural tendency to manufacture biologically nonsensical categories is evident as well in the United States census, which refuses to acknowledge mixed-race heritages, despite the fact that "30-70 percent of African Americans by multi-generational history are multiracial; virtually all Latinos and Filipinos are multiracial, as are the majority of American Indians and Native Hawaiians."[72] We must remember that in America it was not long ago that Irish, Italians, Poles, and other Europeans were considered to constitute entirely different and inferior "races" who could not be married or admitted into the Anglo-Saxon mainstream.[73]

But since 1950, 80 percent of Italian Americans; 75 percent of those with English, Irish, and Polish backgrounds; and 50 percent of those with a Jewish background have married outside their communities; the rate of out-marriage among Asian-American immigrants is equally high. This pattern allows the descendants of these marriages to decide which ancestors they wish to accentuate: For example, a woman of Swedish-Scottish-Serbian heritage can identify herself as belonging primarily to any of her ancestral groups, according to circumstances.[74]

The above facts demonstrate that ethnicity, like nationalism, is actually founded on a shared culture, which is learned and changeable, and is a product of multiple historical influences. People can master cultural codes and acquire ethnic characteristics, just as they can become citizens of a nation. For this reason, ethnic and national identities are not as divisive as racism or other biological forms of discrimination, which undercut flexibility, since the one-drop rule is often applied. In America, biracial and multiracial individuals are increasingly resisting such rigid categorization and are making up mixed categories for themselves. Tiger Woods is not the only "cablinasian" (a term he has used to designate his Caucasian, black, Indian and Asian heritage).

In polar contrast to the effort to disintegrate restrictive racial categories is the assertion that ethnic and national identities are natural, appositional, and hierarchical. As a result, what is in principle an open category turns into a closed one. The danger of naturalizing ethnicity (and viewing the nation as an ethnic entity) can be seen in the destructive internal wars that recently tore apart Yugoslavia.[75]

D. Homo Hierarchicus: *Caste in India*

Perhaps the most pervasive hierarchical ranking of human beings occurs in Indian caste society, which orders groups of persons by their occupations, according to the degree of pollution incurred by their work. In India the top caste are the twice-born Brahman priests; beneath them are Kshatriya warriors, Vaisiya merchants, and Sudra peasants. Underneath all these are the Untouchables (Gandhi's Harijans, or "children of God," now self-designated as Dalits, or "oppressed"), who undertake the most polluting occupations, such as cleaning latrines, sweeping streets, and disposing of carcasses. These positions are justified by the notion of karma; that is, they reflect their members' spiritual attainments in an earlier life. Untouchables are paying for their past evil deeds; Brahmins are being rewarded for their austerities.

Theodicies

The caste legitimation of hierarchy and inferiority on the grounds of karma is, as Max Weber said,[76] one of the logically most perfect theodicies (explanations for suffering) ever conceived by humanity. The others are the Calvinist notion of the unknowable will of God and the Zoroastrian division of the universe into warring good and evil principles. Each of these makes a totally coherent system. However, in each case an aspect of humanity is denied: Caste obscures the desire for equality, Calvinism takes away control over one's fate, and Zoroastrianism excludes the possibility of perfection or progress.

An Untouchable woman.

Although caste rank is presented as absolutely immutable and encompass-ing, traditionally, there were alternative hierarchies within the Indian context, for instance, when religious renunciants abandoned all caste ties and claimed special spiritual powers, or when warrior rulers asserted their secular authority over their Brahman advisors. Among ordinary people, local, endogamous oc-cupational groups (jatis) sometimes contested their relative positions and at-tempted to rise in the ranks by taking up less polluting occupations and habits, hoping over the generations to have their claims to higher status accepted within the larger community.[77]

But even when mobility was possible, it occurred only in the face of the dominant worldview, which absolutely divided persons into ranked groups based on the types of contamination inherited through one's forebears and propagated through one's work and associations. Some scholars have seen this ranking system as much like American race relations, with blacks and Un-touchables alike excluded from the system as inferior and polluting.[78] Certainly, Untouchables have been discriminated against and treated as contemptible, and it has been the Untouchables who have initiated what might be called a civil rights struggle in India, successfully claiming legal compensation for their centuries of degradation. Other scholars, though, have stressed the systemic and totalizing nature of Indian caste. They note that whereas racism in America is in contradiction to the predominant cultural faith in human equality, discrimination in India is a central cultural and theological principle.[79]

Those who see caste as a total system tend to believe that "Untouchables and higher-caste actors hold virtually identical cultural constructs, that they are in nearly total conceptual and evaluative consensus with one another."[80] From this perspective, there is no space for even imagining resistance. In contrast, those who have seen parallels between caste ranking and other forms of injustice have stressed opposition.[81] But in these latter instances, what is generally missing is any sense of the multiple ambivalences and internal conflicts, both for those above and those below, that are entailed in challenging an overarching cultural value. Instead, rebellion is taken for granted, as a reasonable and rational response to felt oppression. In this instance, the Indian subaltern loses cultural specificity, and is subsumed into Western images of a self-determined individual struggling for freedom.[82]

E. Homo Aequalis: *Resistance to Caste*

Psychological anthropology can overcome this unrealistic antimony, as Steven Parish has shown in his recent work on the Hindu city of Bhaktapur in Nepal. Parish argues persuasively that "every complex culture carries within it multiple critiques of itself."[83] In particular, he insists that the notion of hierarchy is impossible without the recognition of the other as an embodied human being, essentially like oneself. Even in Bhaktapur, where hierarchy is asserted as the foundational principle of being, people make egalitarian affirmations such as "I am a person, you are a person." Expectedly, such declarations occur especially when one is complaining of ill treatment from above; yet even the elite sometimes remark that all humans are essentially alike physically and mentally, and that all carry a spark of God.

Parish explores the tensions between these alternative views by means of a person-centered ethnography in which different individuals in different caste positions are not only placed in context, but also encouraged to express their feelings and thoughts about that context. This technique brings us the voices—sometimes articulate or confused, sometimes angry or resigned, often inconsistent—of people struggling to make sense of their lives and conditions. And when the subordinates—and their superordinates—do speak,[84] they give credit to the power of caste to penetrate deeply into the minds and hearts of people at every level. Even for the Untouchable, caste provides a firm grounding for lived experience as well as a bulwark against anarchy. Like most other people, they too believe that "any order is better than chaos and violence."[85] They also recognize the pragmatic necessity of making a living and avoiding confrontation with those more powerful. As a result, there exists in

---

Egalitarian Society and Hierarchical Relations

If a hierarchical cultural model suppresses egalitarian aspects of experience, the opposite is true of egalitarian societies, which obscure or deny stratification. This partly explains the difficulty Americans have in conceptualizing the realities of class divisions within our society. It also may account for the way in which social inferiority is often equated with some form of physical taint. Black ghettos, then, can be seen as impoverished and crime-ridden as a result of the debased inner nature of their inhabitants; women do not deserve equal pay because they are emotionally and mentally lesser than men. In this way, the fact of hierarchical distinction can be made to seem biologically based, therefore unavoidable, natural, and unchangeable.[87] (For more on this topic, see Chapter 13.)

Bhaktapur (and, by implication, in every society) a silencing of alternatives, which are relegated to a repressed political unconscious. As Parish notes:

> Every time social actors "know" themselves and their society in terms of particular models of self and society, they must "not know" themselves and their world in terms of other models (of and for reality) available to them.[86]

Nonetheless, some Untouchables and even some members of higher castes do still sometimes manage to disavow the hierarchical worldview, though they are as yet unable to articulate any viable alternative. The impulse to seek equality, while disguised, thwarted, and suppressed, manages to reveal itself in multiple forms, even in this extraordinarily hierarchical society.

Parish's conclusion is that any hegemonic hierarchical order, however dominant, is always both accepted and resisted in various degrees, according to the social circumstances and psychological condition of the individual. People do internalize the worldview that subordinates them, and they repress alternatives into the political unconscious. Yet, as Freud knew, that which is repressed never vanishes; thus Parish writes that "the desire to remake the world—to make the pain go away, to realize dreams of justice, equality, liberty—is perennial."[88] If this is the case in India, in the most hierarchical system in the world, then we can say that, like Parish's informants, people everywhere will struggle to reconcile, deny, or overcome the existential quandaries and contradictions that arise whenever domination is asserted. This struggle is never completed, and it involves suffering, disjuncture, ambivalence, inconsistency—within both the society and the psyche. Yet, despite its painful consequences, it is clear that the desire for freedom—however inchoate—is as deeply human as is the impulse to domination. One major task of psychological anthropology is to delineate the psychic and cultural forces at work in the eternal dialectic between these opposing impulses.

Summary

This chapter begins with a discussion of the modern anthropological interest in the cultural constitution of the self, as elaborated in a distinction between sociocentric, interdependent selves—the prototype are the Japanese—and egocentric, independent selves—the prototype here are the residents of the United States. This distinction makes some sense, but it is too simple: The Japanese manifest many egocentric aspects, and Americans are far more sociocentric than is usually admitted. It is true that all cultures socialize children to accept and internalize the culturally appropriate relationship between individual autonomy and immersion in the community. Insofar as these resolutions vary, human beings vary, but insofar as the quandary is the same, human beings everywhere are alike.

One of the most important points where the dialectic between independence and fusion is engaged is in the relationship of power. This relationship was conceptualized in cultural terms in Antonio Gramsci's proto-Marxist theory of cultural hegemony. Gramsci stressed the power of culture to dominate consciousness, but also argued for the possibility of counterhegemonic resistance. Both aspects have been documented by anthropologists and other social scientists studying the marginalized and impoverished, but some have argued as well for a total erosion of distinctions between self and other as a necessary move in the struggle for liberation. However, actual instances of boundary blurring very often lead to rage, not to emancipation.

The best analysis of the psychic consequences of invidious discrimination was written by Frantz Fanon, who analyzed the internalization of and resistance to racist ideology among colonized blacks in France. From an anthropological perspective, even apparently natural categories of identity such as race and sex are, in large measure, culturally constituted and permeated with ambivalence. The chapter concludes with an illustration of this point through a discussion of the complex way caste hierarchy is understood and opposed among Hindus.

Endnotes

1. These examples are cited in Joseph J. Tobin, David Y. H. Wu, and Dana H. Davidson, 1989, *Preschool in Three Cultures: Japan, China, and the United States,* New Haven, CT: Yale University Press.
2. According to Hazel Markus and Shinobu Kitayama, 1991, "Culture and the Self: Implications for Cognition, Emotion and Motivation," *Psychological Review* 98: 224–53.
3. As documented in Markus and Kitayama, "Culture and the Self."
4. Unni Wikan, 1995, "The Self in a World of Urgency and Necessity," *Ethos* 23: 259–85, 265; Gananath Obeyesekere, 1990, *The Work of Culture: Symbolic Transformations in Psychoanalysis and Anthropology,* Chicago: University of Chicago Press, p. xx; Anna Wierzbicka, 1993, "A Conceptual Basis for Cross-Cultural Psychology," *Ethos* 21: 205–31; see also Frank Johnson, 1985, "The Western Concept of Self," in Anthony Marsella, George de Vos, and Francis Hsu (eds.), *Culture and the Self: Asian and Western Perspectives,* London: Tavistock. For a more complete discussion of the ambiguity of the contemporary notion of the self in anthropology, see Gerald Erchak, 1992, *The Anthropology of Self and Behavior,* New Brunswick, NJ: Rutgers University Press. For a variety of essays on the way the notion of self is utilized, see Debbora Battaglia (ed.), 1995, *Rhetorics of Self-Making,* Berkeley: University of California Press.

5. For the following paragraph, I am indebted to Charles Webel, 1983, "Self: An Overview," in B. Wolman (ed.), *International Encyclopedia of Psychiatry, Psychoanalysis, Psychology and Neurology,* New York: Asclepias.

6. John Locke, 1959, *Essay Concerning Human Understanding,* Section XXVII. New York: Dover Press, pp. 458–59 (original publication 1690).

7. See, for example, Charles Webel, 1996, "From Self-Knowledge to Self-Obsessed Self-Interest," *New Ideas in Psychology* 14: 189–95.

8. Roy Schafer, 1978, *Language and Insight,* New Haven, CT: Yale University Press.

9. D. W. Winnicott, 1965, *The Maturational Process and the Facilitating Environment,* London: Hogarth.

10. Kenneth Gergen, 1988, "If Persons Are Texts," in Stanley Messer, Louis Sass, and Robert Woolfolk (eds.), *Hermeneutics and Psychological Theory: Interpretive Perspectives on Personality, Psychotherapy, and Psychopathology,* New Brunswick, NJ: Rutgers University Press.

11. Ulrich Niesser, 1988, "Five Kinds of Self-Knowledge," *Philosophical Psychology* 1: 35–59, 22.

12. Marcel Mauss, 1979, "A Category of the Human Mind: The Notion of Person, the Notion of 'Self' " (original publication 1938), in Marcel Mauss, *Sociology and Psychology: Essays,* London: Routledge and Kegan Paul, p. 90.

13. Amélie Rorty, 1988, *Mind in Action: Essays on the Philosophy of Mind,* Boston: Beacon Press.

14. The mask is not always seen in this way. As Raymond Fogelson notes, among the Indians of Eastern North America, masks were social persons, who had to be fed and praised. The mask wearer became the spirit of the mask incarnated. See Fogelson, 1979, "Person, Self, and Identity: Some Anthropological Retrospects, Circumspects, and Prospects," in Benjamin Lee (ed.), *Psychosocial Theories of the Self,* New York: Plenum Press.

15. Rorty ends her account with two less well formed contemporary categories: the subject acknowledging arbitrariness and the presence who is an unchartered soul, drifting without will or choice.

16. A. I. Hallowell, 1976, "Personality, Culture and Society in Behavioral Evolution" (original publication 1963), in A. I. Hallowell, *Contributions to Anthropology: Selected Papers of A. Irving Hallowell,* Chicago: University of Chicago Press, p. 280.

17. Webel, "Self: An Overview," p. 398.

18. Grace Harris, 1989, "Concepts of Individual, Self and Person in Description and Analysis," *American Anthropologist* 91: 599–612.

19. As noted by Erik Erikson, 1950, *Childhood and Society,* New York: Norton.

20. Clifford Geertz, 1975, "From the Native's Point of View: On the Nature of Anthropological Understanding," *American Scientist* 63: 47–53, 48.

21. For the most thorough statement on Asia, see Markus and Kitayama, "Culture and the Self." For Africa, see Paul Riesman, 1986, "Person and the Life Cycle in African Social Thought and Life," *African Studies Review* 29: 71–138.

22. McKim Marriott and Ronald Inden, 1974, "Caste Systems," *Encyclopaedia Britannica,* Vol. 3, pp. 982–91.

23. E. Valentine Daniel, 1984, *Fluid Signs: Being a Person the Tamil Way,* Berkeley, University of California Press, p. 84.

24. Beth A. Conklin and Lynn M. Morgan, 1996, "Babies, Bodies, and the Production of Personhood in North America and a Native Amazonian Society," *Ethos* 24: 657–94.

25. Dorinne Kondo, 1990, *Crafting Selves: Power, Gender and Discourse of Identity in a Japanese Workplace,* Chicago: University of Chicago Press, pp. 26, 29.

26. Masahiko Aoki, 1988, *Information, Incentives and Bargaining in the Japanese Economy,* Cambridge, England: Cambridge University Press, p. 50.

27. See Takeo Doi, 1981, *The Anatomy of Dependence,* Tokyo: Kodansha International; Tsunetsugu Munakata, 1986, "Japanese Attitudes toward Mental Illness and Mental Health Care," in T. Lebra and W. Lebra (eds.), *Japanese Culture and Behavior,* Honolulu: University of Hawaii Press.

28. Sara Harkness, Charles M. Super, and Constance H. Keefer, 1992, "Learning to Be an American Parent: How Cultural Models Gain Directive Force," in Roy D'Andrade and Claudia Strauss (eds.), *Human Motives and Cultural Models,* Cambridge, England: Cambridge University Press, p. 169.

29. For sensitive accounts of cultural differences in child language training in the United States, see Shirley Brice Heath, 1983, *Ways with Words: Language, Life and Work in Communities and Classrooms,* Cambridge, England: Cambridge University Press; 1986, "What No Bedtime Story Means: Narrative Skills at Home and School," in B. Schieffelin and E. Ochs (eds.), *Language Socialization across Cultures,* Cambridge, England: Cambridge University Press. See also Elinor Ochs and Bambi Schieffelin, 1984, "Language Acquisition and Socialization: Three Developmental Stories and Their Implications," in Richard Shweder and Robert LeVine (eds.), *Culture Theory: Essays on Mind, Self and Emotion,* Cambridge, England: Cambridge University Press.

30. Cited in Richard Shweder and Edmund Bourne, 1984, "Does the Concept of the Person Vary Cross-Culturally?" in Richard Shweder and Robert LeVine (eds.), *Culture Theory: Essays on Mind, Self and Emotion,* Cambridge, England: Cambridge University Press, p. 194. For more on the Gusii–United States comparison, see Robert LeVine, Suzanne Dixon, Sarah LeVine, Amy Richman, P. Herbert Leiderman, Constance H. Keefer, and T. Berry Brazelton, 1994, *Child Care and Culture: Lessons from Africa,* Cambridge, England: Cambridge University Press, Chap. 8.

31. Quoted in Ruth Chao, 1995, "Chinese and European American Cultural Models of the Self Reflected in Mothers' Childrearing Beliefs," *Ethos* 23: 328–54, 338.

32. Peggy J. Miller, Heidi Fung, and Judith Mintz, 1996, "Self-Construction through Narrative Practices: A Chinese and American Comparison of Early Socialization," *Ethos* 24: 237–80, 249.

33. For a representative study, see Chao, "Chinese and European American Cultural Models."

34. See Tobin et al. *Preschool in Three Cultures.*

35. Merry White, 1993, *The Material Child: Coming of Age in Japan and America,* New York: Basic Books, pp. 222–25.

36. For the most sustained version of this argument, see Markus and Kitayama, "Culture and the Self." A parallel argument is made by Shweder and Bourne, "Does the Concept of the Person Vary Cross-Culturally?"

37. Michelle Rosaldo, 1984, "Toward an Anthropology of Self and Feeling," in Richard Shweder and Robert LeVine (eds.), *Culture Theory: Essays on Mind, Self and Emotion,* Cambridge, England: Cambridge University Press, p. 140.

38. Some of the critiques developed in the following discussion can be found in more detailed form in Melford Spiro, 1993, "Is the Western Conception of the Self 'Peculiar' within the Context of the World Cultures?" *Ethos* 21: 107–53; David Hollan, 1992, "Cross-Cultural Differences in the Self," *Journal of Anthropological Research* 48: 283–300; Unni Wikan, 1995, "The Self in a World of Urgency and Necessity," *Ethos* 23: 259–85; Fredrik Barth, 1997, "How Is the Self Conceptualized? Variations between Cultures," in Ulric Niesser (ed.), *The Conceptual Self in Context: Culture, Experience, Self-Understanding,* Cambridge, England: Cambridge University Press; some of the

following ideas were originally explored in Charles Lindholm, 1997, "Does the Sociocentric Self Exist? Reflections on Markus and Kitayama's 'Culture and the Self,' " *Journal of Anthropological Research* 53: 405–22.

39. For a relatively objective, statistical description of measurable distinctions, see Seymour M. Lipset, 1996, *American Exceptionalism: A Double-Edged Sword*, New York: Norton, Chap. 7. For more nuanced views, see Nancy Rosenberger (ed.), 1992, *The Japanese Sense of Self*, Cambridge, England: Cambridge University Press; Gordon Mathews, 1996, "The Stuff of Dreams, Fading: Ikigai and 'the Japanese Self,' " *Ethos* 24: 718–47.

40. Markus and Kitayama, "Culture and the Self," p. 235.

41. More will be said on this topic in Chapter 10.

42. Chao, "Chinese and European American Cultural Models," p. 348.

43. Alexis de Tocqueville, 1969, *Democracy in America*, Garden City, NY: Doubleday (original publication 1835). See also David Riesman, with Nathan Glazer and Reuel Denney, 1961, *The Lonely Crowd* (2d ed.), New Haven, CT: Yale University Press; Robert Jay Lifton, 1970, *Boundaries: Psychological Man in Revolution*, New York: Vintage; Erving Goffman, 1959, *The Presentation of Self in Everyday Life*, New York: Doubleday. See also Chapter 5 on national character and Chapter 13 on American values.

44. Elvin Hatch, 1979, *The Biography of a Small Town*, New York: Columbia University Press, p. 234.

45. Michael Moffatt, 1989, *Coming of Age in New Jersey: College and American Culture*, New Brunswick, NJ: Rutgers University Press.

46. Markus and Kitayama, "Culture and the Self."

47. This point is made by Spiro, "Is the Western Conception of the Self 'Peculiar'?"

48. Alan Roland, 1988, *In Search of Self in India and Japan: Toward a Cross-Cultural Psychology*, Princeton, NJ: Princeton University Press. Cultural differences in mental illness will be discussed in Chapter 11.

49. Alan Howard, 1985, "Ethnopsychology and the Prospects for a Cultural Psychology," in G. White and J. Kirkpatrick (eds.), *Person, Self and Experience*, Berkeley: University of California Press. See also J. Wellenkamp, 1988, "Notions of Grief and Catharsis among the Toraja," *American Ethnologist* 15: 486–500.

50. Barth, "How Is the Self Conceptualized?"

51. For an example, see Marina Roseman, 1990, "Head, Heart, Odor, and Shadow: The Structure of the Self, the Emotional World, and Ritual Performance among Senoi Temiar," *Ethos* 18: 227–50.

52. Antonio Gramsci, 1971, "The Study of Philosophy," in Quintin Hoare and Geoffrey N. Smith (eds.). Selections from the Prison Notebooks of Antonio Gramsci. New York: International Publishers, pp. 323–4.

53. Katherine S. Newman, 1988, *Falling from Grace: The Experience of Downward Mobility in the American Middle Class*, New York: Free Press.

54. For a classic study, see Dick Hebdige, 1979, *Subculture: The Meaning of Style*, London: Methuen. See also Paul Gilroy, 1993, *The Black Atlantic: Modernity and Double Consciousness*, Cambridge, MA: Harvard University Press.

55. Homi Bhabha, 1994, *The Location of Culture*, London: Routledge, p. 38. For a cogent criticism, see Jonathan Friedman, 1997, "Global Crises, the Struggle for Cultural Identity and Intellectual Porkbarrelling: Cosmopolitans versus Locals, Ethnics and Nationals in an Era of De-Hegemonisation," in Pnina Werbner and Tariq Modood (eds.), *Debating Cultural Hybridity: Multi-Cultural Identities and the Politics of Anti-Racism*, London: Zed Books.

56. Lila Abu-Lughod, 1993, *Writing Women's Worlds: Bedouin Stories*, Berkeley: University of California Press, p. 7.

57. Renato Rosaldo, 1989, *Culture and Truth: The Remaking of Social Analysis,* Boston: Beacon Press, pp. 194, 216.
58. For some extended critiques of postmodern anthropology, see Adam Kuper, 1994, "Culture, Identity and the Project of a Cosmopolitan Anthropology," *Man* N.S. 29: 537–54; Steve Reyna, 1994, "Literary Anthropology and the Case against Science," *Man* N.S. 29: 555–82; Charles Lindholm, 1997, "Logical and Moral Problems of Postmodernism," *Journal of the Royal Anthropological Institute* 3: 745–60. For a witty general critique, see Terry Eagleton, 1996, *The Illusions of Postmodernism,* Oxford, England: Basil Blackwell.
59. Friedman, "Global Crises," p. 88. See also Nancy Scheper-Hughes, 1994, "The Violence of Everyday Life: In Search of a Critical and Politically Engaged Psychological Anthropology," in Marcelo Suarez-Orozco, George Spindler, and Louise Spindler (eds.), *The Making of Psychological Anthropology II,* Fort Worth, TX: Harcourt Brace.
60. See also Erikson, *Childhood and Society.*
61. Frantz Fanon, 1968, *Black Skin, White Masks,* London: Macgibbon and Kee (original publication 1952); 1965, *The Wretched of the Earth,* London: Macgibbon and Kee (original publication 1961).
62. Fanon *Black Skin, White Masks,* pp. 116, 12.
63. Ibid., p. 60.
64. Ibid., p. 14.
65. For a discussion of the historical circumstances in which the hierarchical coding of race occurs, see Ann Stoller, 1995, *Race and the Education of Desire: Foucault's History of Sexuality and the Colonial Order of Things,* Durham, NC: Duke University Press.
66. Claude Lévi-Strauss, 1985, "Race and Culture," in Claude Lévi-Strauss (ed.),*The View from Afar,* Oxford, England: Basil Blackwell. See also Pnina Werbner, 1997, "Essentialising Essentialism, Essentialising Silence: Ambivalence and Multiplicity in the Constructions of Racism and Ethnicity," in Pnina Werbner and Tariq Modood (eds.), *Debating Cultural Hybridity: Multi-Cultural Identities and the Politics of Anti-Racism,* London: Zed Books. On the problematic but necessary distinction between open categories of nationhood and closed categories of race, see Benedict Anderson, 1991, *Imagined Communities: Reflections on the Origin and Spread of Nationalism* (rev. ed.) London: Verso.
67. Jeannette-Marie Mageo, 1996, "Samoa, on the Wilde Side: Male Transvestism, Oscar Wilde, and Liminality in Making Gender," *Ethos* 24 (4): 588–627, 589.
68. Thomas Laqueur, 1990, *Making Sex: Body and Gender from the Greeks to Freud,* Cambridge, MA: Harvard University Press.
69. Randolph Trumbach, 1994, "London's Sapphists: From Three Sexes to Four Genders in the Making of Modern Culture," in Gilbert Herdt (ed.), *Third Sex, Third Gender: Beyond Sexual Dimorphism in Culture and History,* New York: Zone Books, p. 118.
70. Theo Van der Meer, 1994, "Sodomy and the Pursuit of a Third Sex in the Early Modern Period," in Gilbert Herdt (ed.), *Third Sex, Third Gender: Beyond Sexual Dimorphism in Culture and History,* New York: Zone Books.
71. See Gilbert Herdt, 1994, "Mistaken Sex: Culture, Biology and the Third Sex in New Guinea," in Gilbert Herdt (ed.), *Third Sex, Third Gender: Beyond Sexual Dimorphism in Culture and History,* New York: Zone Books. For the tragic story of someone who did not stay within category, see Michel Foucault, 1980, *Herculine Barbin: Being the Recently Discovered Memoirs of a Nineteenth Century French Hemaphrodite,* New York: Pantheon.
72. Maria Root, 1992, "Within, Between, and Beyond Race," in M. Root (ed.), *Racially Mixed People in America,* Newbury Park, CA: Sage, p. 9.

73. For a discussion, see Michael Lind, 1995, *The Next American Nation: The New Nationalism and the Fourth American Revolution*, New York: Free Press.

74. For an account, see Mary Waters, 1990, *Ethnic Options: Choosing Identities in America,* Berkeley: University of California Press. Her data also show that some ethnic identities are more appealing than others. Apparently, someone who is half Scottish and half Italian is much more likely to claim Italian heritage.

75. For differing accounts of the modern origins of ethnicity and nationalism, see Ernest Gellner, 1983, *Nations and Nationalism,* Oxford, England: Basil Blackwell; Liah Greenfeld, 1992, *Nationalism: Five Roads to Modernity,* Cambridge, MA: Harvard University Press; Anderson, *Imagined Communities.*

76. For a rapid outline of possible theodicies, see Max Weber, 1946, "Religious Rejections of the World and Their Directions" (original publication 1915), in Hans Gerth and C. Wright Mills (eds.), *From Max Weber: Essays in Sociology,* New York: Oxford University Press.

77. For jati mobility, see M. N. Srinivas, 1962, *Caste in India and Other Essays,* London: Asia Publishing House; Frederick Bailey, 1957, *Caste and the Economic Frontier: A Village in Highland Orissa,* Manchester, England: Manchester University Press. For warrior claims to ascendancy, see Nicholas Dirks, 1987, *The Hollow Crown: Ethnohistory of an Indian Kingdom,* Cambridge, England: Cambridge University Press. For the spiritual power of renunciants, see Jonathan Parry, 1982, "Sacrificial Death and the Necrophagous Ascetic," in M. Bloch and J. Parry (eds.), *Death and the Regeneration of Life,* Cambridge, England: Cambridge University Press.

78. John Ogbu, 1978, *Minority Education and Caste: The American System in Cross-Cultural Perspective,* New York: Academic Press.

79. The foremost proponent is Louis Dumont, 1980, *Homo Hierarchicus: An Essay on the Caste System,* Chicago: University of Chicago Press. For a somewhat different perspective, focusing on exchange of substances in the manner outlined earlier in this chapter, see McKim Marriot (ed.), 1990, *India through Hindu Categories,* New Dehli, India: Sage.

80. Michael Moffatt, 1979, *An Untouchable Community in South India,* Princeton, NJ: Princeton University Press, p. 291.

81. See, for example, Ranajit Guha (ed.), 1982–83, *Subaltern Studies,* Vols. I and II, New Dehli, India: Oxford University Press.

82. See R. O'Hanlon, 1988, "Recovering the Subject: Subaltern Studies and Histories of Resistance in South Asia," *Modern Asian Studies* 22: 189–224.

83. Steven Parish, 1996, *Hierarchy and Its Discontents: Culture and the Politics of Consciousness in Caste Society,* Philadelphia: University of Pennsylvania Press, p. 222; 1994, *Moral Knowing in a Hindu Sacred City: An Exploration of Mind, Emotion and Self,* New York: Columbia University Press.

84. The reference is to Gayatri C. Spivak, 1993, "Can the Subaltern Speak?" in P. Williams and L. Chrisman (eds.), *Colonial Discourse and Post-Colonial Theory: A Reader,* Hemel Hempstead, England: Harvester Wheatsheaf. For a variety of reasons, Spivak denies the possibility of subaltern communication.

85. Parish, *Hierarchy and Its Discontents,* p. 143.

86. Ibid., p. 11.

87. This later example comes from Dumont, *Homo Hierarchicus.* For a book-length discussion of the way hierarchy is manifested in a strongly egalitarian society, see Charles Lindholm, 1996, *The Islamic Middle East: An Historical Anthropology,* Oxford, England: Basil Blackwell.

88. Parish, *Hierarchy and Its Discontents,* p. 3.

CHAPTER 9

The Thinking Animal

INTRODUCTION

The people of the remote Caroline Islands of the Pacific are able to navigate great distances in the open sea, paddling simple outrigger canoes without modern compasses or directional devices. How do they do it?

Like Western sailors, the Islanders know that the stars take predictable paths across the sky according to the seasons, and they have developed accurate star charts that have been handed down orally from generation to generation. Tracking the stars gives the seamen their approximate locations on the open ocean, but does not solve the problem of measuring the distances traveled in a day—a problem answered mathematically in the West by multiplying the velocity of the boat by the time traveled, keeping a close record of any changes in speed. The Caroline Islanders do not have the arithmetical skills or measuring devices to do this. Instead, they assume that their canoe is stationary on the sea, and that a "reference island" about halfway between their origin and destination is slowly passing them by as they paddle. Continually referring to the assumed position of this moving, unseen (and sometimes imaginary) island, the pilot estimates his time of arrival—usually successfully.

This indigenous model for long-distance navigation is one example of the cognitive frameworks applied by people everywhere to solving problems in their environments. The notion that an imaginary island is moving past a motionless canoe may seem very odd to us, but for the Caroline Islanders, it is a logical device that has proven its usefulness, and it occurs in congruence with a taken-for-granted worldview that makes considerable intuitive sense. After all, in the open sea it does indeed seem as if islands are moving, while the boat itself stays fixed under the equally immutable tracks of the sun and stars.[1]

As we saw in Chapter 4, psychological anthropology began with the investigation of just such variant forms of cognition and perception. These efforts eventually led investigators to the morally laudable but intellectually not very exciting conclusion that any differences in perceptual ability that existed between peoples were cultural in origin, and that fundamental physical and mental capacities of people everywhere were more or less the same—though exactly

Boys in a small outrigger canoe in the Pacific.

what those capacities were and how they could be measured was left in doubt. Later, culture and personality theorists attempted to use projective tests and similar instruments to discover the inner dispositions and underlying psychic structures of people in other societies. As noted in Chapter 6, these tests were prey to deep and apparently unresolvable methodological problems of validation and of translation, and fell out of favor. But even as culture and personality theorists abandoned their efforts to measure the mind, other branches of anthropology took up the challenge. Their investigations are the subject of this chapter.

Chapter Outline

I Thinking about Thinking
    A Interpreting Rationality
    B Analogical Thinking
    C The Structural Theory of the Mind

II The Evolution of Cognitive Anthropology
    A Componential Analysis
    B Universal Cultural Scripts
    C Ethnoscience and the Classification of Nature
    D The Body in the Mind: Experiential Linguistics
    E Ethnopsychology and the Interpretation of Culture

III Computers, Consciousness, and Cultural Models
  A Computer Science and Anthropology
  B New Models of the Mind: Parallel and Serial
  C Motivating Schemas and Cultural Models
  D Critiques and Amplifications of Schema Theory

I. THINKING ABOUT THINKING

A Interpreting Rationality
  Interpretive anthropologists assume people are motivated by culturally mediated reason.

B Analogical Thinking
  Durkheim and Mauss argue that thought is poetic and emotionally
  motivated, structured in terms of analogies and oppositions.

C The Structural Theory of the Mind
  Linguistics, Lévi-Strauss, and the theory of mental structures.

A. Interpreting Rationality

In declaring "cogito ergo sum" (I think, therefore I am), Descartes presumed that
he knew what thought was: a purely rational and universal process, closely akin
to mathematical logic. The true self is therefore the calculating self, centered in
the brain; the proper task of all humankind is to reason well and to discover the
objective truths that empirically exist out there in reality. But this assumption
takes for granted what actually needed to be proved: What indeed was thinking? How much did reason and logic actually typify the human condition? Is
thought the same everywhere, or is it culturally constructed? Is the thinking self
seeking reality, or manufacturing it?

We have seen in Chapter 3 that Descartes's easy assimilation of thinking to
being was challenged early on by a number of thinkers. Hume found through
introspection that there did not seem to be any central entity rationally processing information, and that passions, not logic, ruled human actions. Nietzsche
and Freud also argued for the priority of desire and the weakness of reason.
However, most anthropologists and social scientists followed the rationalist
philosophy of Max Weber, who assumed that all human beings act consciously
and intelligently to maximize their valued goals. The problem for analysis, then,
was not the nature of reason itself, which was assumed to be more or less alike
everywhere, but the cultural and historical differences in value systems that render the rationality of others opaque. The analysis of other value systems could
be accomplished through *verstehen:* putting oneself into the world of others, realizing the goals and values that motivate them.[2]

Weber's followers, most especially the American interpretivist school headed
by Clifford Geertz, also took for granted the rationality of human beings. They too

---

Weber and the Nonrational

Unlike his American successors, Weber himself was well aware that a great deal of human life—indeed, *most* of human life—is *not* undertaken by rational actors trying to achieve valued goals within coherent webs of meaning. As he wrote: "In the great majority of cases actual action goes on in a state of inarticulate half-consciousness or actual unconsciousness of its subjective meaning"; in other words, most of the time we thoughtlessly fit into the taken-for-granted world around us, habitually imitating others and acting according to tradition and custom.[3] In sum, Weber did not believe that human beings are primarily rational calculators; he believed only that social science could not adequately analyze anything other than the rational and calculating aspects of human life.[4]

---

presumed that any action that was not intentionally aimed toward achieving a goal, and that was not rational according to the cultural beliefs of the society, was outside the realm of meaning, therefore unintelligible, and must be excluded from analysis. As a result, many cultural anthropologists set aside any discussion of mental operations, presuming that the brain is simply a central processor, continually calculating costs and benefits in pursuit of culturally defined ends. Phenomenologists make the same assumption. For example, as noted in Chapter 7, Meleau-Ponty's perceiving eye is primarily an active agent, with goals and an agenda.

B. Analogical Thinking

However, there is another tradition of social thought that did not so quickly dismiss the study of mental processes—the French structuralist school, inspired by Émile Durkheim, whose work we have already briefly outlined in Chapter 3. There we focused on Durkheim's discussion of ritual and emotion, and the importance of collective representations in the constitution of individual consciousness. But Durkheim also had highly original notions about the nature of thought itself, which he insisted is *not* primarily constituted by causal chains of rational calculation seeking to realize some goal, but rather, by more poetic relations of analogy and metaphor.

He made his case by focusing on systems of classification, that is, on the manner in which the natural world is divided into categories such as animal and human, natural and cultural, male and female, inside and outside. All societies, he believed, manufacture complex systems of classification that serve to order their universe for them into patterned symbolic relationships of opposition and analogy, arranged in taxonomies of hierarchical inclusion (see page 83 for an example). For instance, in our society the overarching category of animal is opposed to the category of vegetable. Both together are opposed to the category of mineral. Within the animal category are vertebrates and invertebrates, and so on. In simple societies, these pervasive classification systems can reach out to embrace the whole world in intersecting metaphorical webs. Thus clan A is opposed to clan B as the cockatoo (the emblem of clan A) is believed to be opposed to the kangaroo (the emblem of clan B), which are in turn opposed as light and dark, sun and moon, right and left. So, instead of saying that human thought consists of logical chains in which A leads to B leads to C leads to D, Durkheim proposed that human thought is analogical: A is to B as C is to D.[5]

The connections and oppositions of binary classification systems provide what Durkheim called the vast symbolism that is at the core of human life and society. These pervasive categories, Durkheim argued, are not given a priori, as Kant had said, but are modeled after social organization. "It is because men were organized that they have been able to organize things . . . The unity of these first logical systems merely reproduces the unity of society."[6] In particular, logical systems derive from the very first opposition of all: the opposition experienced, as Durkheim thought, in the original ritual performance of collective ecstasy. The fleeting sensation of group rapture aroused by the ritual is contrasted to the mundane emotional life of the individual, thereby giving rise to the primal distinction between the sacred and the profane. It is this felt polarity that flowers into distinctions of time, space, nature, and culture.

But the question remained as to why some things should be classed within the same category or seen as analogous. A traditional rationalist approach would search for some underlying practical reason that could account for the reasons certain objects, creatures, or concepts were thought to go together. For instance, totemic animals might be held sacred because they are good to eat. In contrast, Durkheim and his colleague Marcel Mauss said that pragmatism has nothing to do with it. Concepts arise in emotion and are organized by sentiment, not reason. "It is this emotional value of notions which plays the preponderant part in the manner in which ideas are connected or separated."[7] It was here that Durkheim's analysis stopped, since he believed that emotions were too vague to be grasped by social science. But by then, he had already presented a striking counter to the positivist notion that human beings are essentially creatures of practical reason, pursuing goals and thinking in terms of cause and effect.

C. The Structural Theory of the Mind

Durkheim's interest in thought as a symbolic system of binary analogies was taken up and transformed two generations later by Claude Lévi-Strauss (b. 1908), a French anthropologist trained in philosophy and heavily influenced by linguistic theory. Like Durkheim, he too rejected a rationalistic vision of humanity, but whereas Durkheim saw social life arising in the collective emotional experience of the sacred ritual, Lévi-Strauss focused instead on the structure of the relationships of exchange that bound groups together. According to Lévi-Strauss, deciphering the logical implications of exchanges of "women, goods and words" could reveal "a principle of intelligibility behind an apparently chaotic jumble of arbitrary and irrational practices and beliefs."[8] Such a principle would predict patterned metamorphoses occurring when any element is changed, and coherently locate all observable social facts

---

Right and Left

One symbolic opposition found everywhere in the world is the opposition between right and left. The classic cross-cultural study of this opposition was undertaken by one of Durkheim's star pupils, Robert Hertz (1881–1915), who died in World War I.[9] Hertz followed Durkheim in arguing that the universal differentiation between right and left reflected the primordial distinction between the sacred and the profane: Right everywhere represents the sacred; left, the profane. However, Hertz went beyond Durkheim in asking whether the opposition had a biological basis.

Clearly, the universal preponderance of the right indicated that there was some underlying physical predisposition toward favoring that side. But Hertz also concluded that this slight tendency was not sufficient to explain the amazing proliferation of symbolic imagery surrounding laterality. He concluded, sensibly, that the right-left opposition can be understood only through a combination of biological and cultural analysis: a conclusion that ought to serve as a positive example for present-day researchers.

---

within the deduced systemic model. Discovering these relations of exchange was the task of structuralism—a mode of analysis pioneered by Lévi-Strauss that would have a profound influence on anthropologists of the 1960s and 1970s on both sides of the Atlantic.

Lévi-Strauss applied his structuralist method to tease out the patterns of exchange that organized kinship relations, writing a groundbreaking comparative study that he entitled *The Elementary Structures of Kinship*[10] in homage to Durkheim. He later turned his attention to spatial arrangements, economics, political hierarchy, totemism, art, ritual, and so on, in a myriad of cultures. Comparisons were undertaken to relate cross-cultural differences in exchange patterns to contrasts in social organization, mode of production, and ecology. But his most important work for our purposes was in myth analysis, which drew on the linguistic research of Roman Jakobson (1896–1982) in phonology. Jakobson, inspired by Ferdinand de Saussure's (1857–1913) claim that language is constituted by patterns of differential oppositions, had analyzed sounds as bundles of contrastive sonic elements; thus /b/ was described as a "voiced bi-labial plosive" distinct from other sonic bundles, such as /p/, which is an "unvoiced bi-labial plosive." In other words, the sole difference between /b/ and /p/ is that /b/ is plus for voice while /p/ is minus.[11]

In Jakobson's elegant theory of contrastive phonemic pluses and minuses, Lévi-Strauss thought he saw the makings of a model that could explain both the logic of culture and the inner structure of the brain. If sound could be broken into significant patterns consisting of simple binary contrasts, so could meaning, and this primordial grammar of meaning could best be found in the collective dreams of humanity: myths. In Lévi-Strauss's analysis of myth, the line of narrative and the particularity of a text were put in the background; what mat-

---

Vladimir Propp

Lévi-Strauss was also much influenced by the work of Russian folklorist Vladimir Propp (1895–1970).[12] Propp had collected volumes of Russian folktales and had shown that they could be broken down into sets of constitutive elements (a hidden treasure, three sons, talking animals, etc.). These elements, he demonstrated, repeated themselves within the folktales and were recombined in various ways throughout the whole corpus. His pioneering work demonstrated that it was both possible and productive to read folktales and myths not as narratives, but as formal compositions of repeated semantic units.

---

tered were the ways a corpus of myths could be dismantled to reveal the repeated synchronic relations between contrastive meaning units, just as phonemes are to be understood as patterned relations of opposing sounds. Using a musical metaphor, we could say that Lévi-Strauss shifted the analysis of mythic texts from melody to harmony.

Of course, the elements that make up a sound have a physical basis in the sonic potentials of the human voice, whereas the elements that supposedly make up a semantic unit do not. They are decided upon by the analyst and therefore are subjective. Lévi-Strauss tried to escape solipsism by arguing that myths always confront fundamental quandaries within a particular social formation. The Oedipal myth that so inspired Freud, wherein Oedipus unknowingly married his mother and slew his father, was said by Lévi-Strauss to be about the irreconcilable paradox of human origins: born from the earth or born from woman.[13] This polarity is reworked again and again in the mythic cycle, not to reach a resolution, but to demonstrate through analogical paradoxes that both extremes are untenable. (See Figure 9.1.) So, whereas Durkheim had seen analogical pairings constructed on the basis of vague yet powerful emotional correspondences, Lévi-Strauss tried to offer a more intellectual cause: The repetition of paired oppositions were repeated attempts to resolve fundamental intellectual paradoxes of human life.

But Lévi-Strauss did agree with Durkheim that human thought is essentially analogical, and that the brain is driven to classify and categorize the universe in a binary fashion, and then to relate opposed elements to one another in systematic patterns. For Lévi-Strauss, then, totemic animals are classified together not because they are good to eat, but because they are good to think— that is, they offer semantic elements that are easily ramified into patterns of opposition. Human beings everywhere, he argued, apply the same binary constitutive logic to their surroundings; the only difference between "savage thought" and our own is that the savage combines sensory elements (odor, color, shape, texture) to make up symbolic systems, while civilized society uses abstract qualities (mass, energy, acceleration, time).[14]

Cadmos
seeks his sis-
ter Europa,
ravished by
Zeus

                                        Cadmos kills
                                        the dragon
                    The Spartoi
                    kill one an-
                    other

                                        Labdacos (Laios'
                                        father) = *lame (?)*

                    Oedipus kills   Laios (Oedipus'
                    his father,   father) = *left-sided
                    Laios   (?)*
                                Oedipus kills
                                the Sphinx

                                        Oedipus - *swollen-
                                        foot (?)*

Oedipus
marries his
mother,
Jocasta   Eteocles
                 kills his
                 brother,
                 Polynices
Antigone
buries her
brother,
Polynices,
despite
prohibition

FIGURE 9.1. Structural model of the Oedipal myth.
Source: Claude Lévi-Strauss, 1967, "The Structural Study of Myth," in C. Lévi-Strauss (ed.), Structural Anthropology, *Garden City, NY: Doubleday, p. 210.*

In America Lévi-Strauss's eclectic and philosophically informed work struck anthropologists with the force of a bolt of lightning. It reinvigorated the early anthropological mandate to develop a universal theory of the mind and inspired numerous attempts at the structural analysis of stories, films, and poems. But opponents of the new method deplored structuralism's apparent indifference to history and its restrictive model for consciousness. The validity Lévi-Strauss claimed for his analysis of myth was further undermined by the problem of subjectivity. His science of myth, some said, was actually a figment of Lévi-Strauss's fertile imagination and did not prove the existence of any underlying mental patterning. Nor was his picture of mental processes safe from dispute, since academic psychologists insisted there was no convincing evidence that cognition was actually as binary as Lévi-Strauss had claimed. As the psychologist Gustav Jahoda wrote, "one can admit the importance of binary oppositions in human thinking, but this may merely reflect the fact that they are also salient in our environment." For Jahoda and other critics, Lévi-Strauss's claim that his analysis of myth demonstrated universal cognitive patterns was nothing more than a leap of faith.[15]

Despite justified criticisms, it is clear that Lévi-Strauss's work—especially his emphasis on the importance of binary opposition in mental processes—does have a special affinity for recent research that takes as its model for the brain the workings of the computer, which are also based on binary oppositions. Furthermore, many of the intellectual influences that stood behind Lévi-Strauss's studies have strongly marked the development of American cognitive anthropology, a movement to which we now turn.

II. THE EVOLUTION OF COGNITIVE ANTHROPOLOGY

A Componential Analysis
   Culture as a cognitive system. The analysis of semantic domains, taxonomies, and cognitive maps.

B Universal Cultural Scripts
   The work of Anna Wierzbicka.

C Ethnoscience and the Classification of Nature
   Ethnoscience and the study of prototypes. Is there an objective model of the world encoded in the mind?

D The Body in the Mind: Experiential Linguistics
   George Lakoff and Mark Johnson's claim that the experience of the body is projected into the world.

E Ethnopsychology and the Interpretation of Culture
   Do others have psychologies radically different from our own? Theory and practice in ethnopsychology.

A. Componential Analysis

Beginning in the 1950s, a cadre of self-styled cognitive anthropologists, led by Yale linguist Floyd Lounsbury and ethnographer Ward Goodenough and inspired by the Yale tradition of empiricism, began to work toward achieving a cross-cultural study of the brain, moving warily away from the use of discredited psychological tests and toward the investigation of systems of meaning encoded in language—an area where anthropology was strong.[16] The goal of such an investigation, as cognitive anthropologists saw it, was to develop some way to make sense of cross-cultural data that could give objective insight into the way cognition operated across cultures. The aim, as one practitioner wrote, was to discover "what material phenomena are significant for the people of some culture; and how do they organize these phenomena."[17]

Culture itself was empirically defined by Goodenough "as whatever it is one has to know or believe in order to operate in a manner acceptable to its members."[18] Within this practical framework, symbolic and interpretive studies and all forms of psychological speculation were eschewed as impressionistic and unverifiable; what analysts sought instead were cognitive maps that could show how to negotiate the cultural system—from how to order a drink to how to arrange a marriage. Theoretically, these various maps could be analyzed and compared according to a method akin to formal logic or mathematics. This method was called componential analysis.

The basic assumption in componential analysis—as in Lévi-Strauss's structural analysis of myth—was that the linguistic method of categorization of phonemes could be extended to culture. It was thought that cultural knowledge could be divided into distinct meaning units, or semantic domains, such as kinship or disease or furniture or plants, that could be analyzed and compared. But the method for analysis was somewhat different from the method used by Lévi-Strauss, who had looked at the meaning units as elements within total symbolic systems. Instead, cognitive anthropologists imitated the methods of linguists and psychologists, breaking down the semantic units into their components and arranging them according to their significant features.

The exemplary arena for the application of this type of analysis was in the realm of kinship, where obvious distinctive features included sex, generation, and type of relationship (direct or collateral). For example, American terms for collateral relatives (uncle, aunt, cousin, niece, nephew) are derived from the contrastive features of generation $(+1, -1)$ and sex (M, F) of the relative. Uncle includes all $+1$, M; aunt, all $+1$, F; cousin, all 0 M and F; nephew, all -1, M; niece, all -1, F.[19] (See Figure 9.2.) In other cultures, this arrangement would not be so simple. For example, the Pukhtun with whom I worked discriminated collateral relatives not only by the generation and sex of the relative, but also by the sex of the person in the nuclear family with whom they are most closely related, so matrilateral relatives are discriminated from patrilateral relatives. Thus, ego calls his or her father's brothers by a term (tarbur) different from that used for the mother's brothers (mama).

Obviously, this type of analysis could also arrange terms in taxonomic hierarchies: Direct relatives include parents and children; children include sons and daughters; parents include father and mother. Similarly, the domain of furniture includes chairs, tables, beds; that of chairs includes easy chairs, kitchen chairs, and so on. This technique required careful elicitation procedures: Expert informants were asked to name all the members of a particular semantic class of entities. Then subclasses were categorized and contrasted internally according to informants' answers.

The semantic domains that were derived from this process were believed to be the cognitive guides by which individuals navigated their cultural system; once they had been collected and analyzed, it was fondly hoped that the researcher would have access to all the knowledge necessary to function correctly as a native in the culture. It was also hoped that these cognitive maps, once collected and broken into components, could be compared across cultures, thereby revealing the

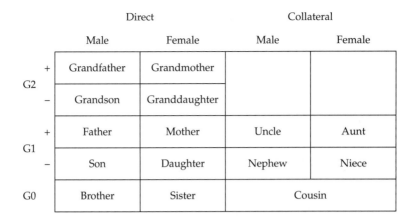

		Direct		Collateral	
		Male	Female	Male	Female
G2	+	Grandfather	Grandmother		
	−	Grandson	Granddaughter		
G1	+	Father	Mother	Uncle	Aunt
	−	Son	Daughter	Nephew	Niece
G0		Brother	Sister	Cousin	

FIGURE 9.2. Feature analysis of English kinship terms.
Source: Roy D'Andrade, 1995, The Development of Cognitive Anthropology, *Cambridge, England: Cambridge University Press, p. 29.*

Noam Chomsky's Universal Grammar

In 1957 the MIT linguist Noam Chomsky published his revolutionary book *Syntactic Structures.* In it he argued that the grammars of all languages are built up from a set of universal underlying rules that can account for different surface structures. The classic example is the passive and active voices (John was seen by Mary; Mary saw John), which have the same deep structure despite their different expressions. Like Lévi-Strauss, Chomsky went on to argue that his research demonstrated the existence of innate (and therefore probably genetic) mental capacities for the acquisition of language. In fact, he has argued that linguistic theory ought to be seen as a branch of cognitive psychology. Prior to Chomsky's work, linguists had been content to describe and analyze particular languages; afterward, the goal was to discover the basic grammatical limits of all languages. However, as in anthropology, there has of late been a swing away from universalistic theory and back toward more surface-oriented studies.[20]

manner in which the generic mind operated, much as the linguist Noam Chomsky had shown how a generic grammar lay beneath language usage everywhere.

Although componental analysis of native systems of classification led to some fascinating research,[21] and provided as well a new and interesting way to conduct an ethnographic interview,[22] its larger comparative project never really got off the ground. Partially, this was because of questions about its adequacy as a theory of mind. One problem was that all componental analysis seemed able to do was to generate ever proliferating domains, organized alike in neat taxonomies. But did this tell us how the brain worked, or were the models created out of thin air by creative informants trying their best to answer the ethnographer's arcane inquiries? Another problem was the highly linguistic nature of componential analysis. Many skeptical anthropologists wondered how much these complex and systematic domains of knowledge collected from local experts had to do with the real actions and mental processes of ordinary people in the world. The hierarchies of contrasting terms were, it was argued, too clearcut; in actual practice, terms could shift in meaning, and human cognition did not easily fit into such Procrustean beds. How was the variability that Anthony F. C. Wallace had discerned in culture to be accounted for? Did everyone carry around all of culture in their heads, or did people have access to cognitive maps only on an ad hoc basis, or did they perhaps make use of different or even contradictory maps according to their social status positions? (See Chapter 6 for more on Wallace.) Finally, what was one to do with anomalies in the classificatory systems themselves? Was a stool a chair? Was a stepfather a relative?[23]

B. Universal Cultural Scripts

Despite these many problems, which led to a general disenchantment with the field in the late 1970s, the componential analysis of culture produced some productive offshoots. One of the most ambitious has been the work on cultural scripts undertaken by the Australian linguist Anna Wierzbicka. Studying the basic vocabularies of many different societies, she has argued that fundamental cross-cultural norms and values can be expressed in terms of a few extremely simple lexical universals found in every language in the world. Cultural differences in notions of psychology and motivation can then be reduced to key words, and these can be translated into the universal lexicon to generate cultural scripts that may be stated in neutral terms.[24] For instance, she breaks the complicated Western notion of self-expression into the following universal script that could, in principle, be translated with no loss of meaning into any language in the world:

> "Everyone can say something like this: 'I think this, I don't think this.' "
> "It is good to say what I think."
> "When someone says something like this: 'I think this,' I don't have to say something like this: 'I think the same.' "[25]

According to Wierzbicka, this script expresses in a universally understandable manner the complicated reasoning lying beneath the notion of self-expression, that is, that everyone has her or his own thoughts, that those thoughts ought to be expressed, and that conformity is not necessary. Once this reduction has been accomplished, central terms of any language can be easily translated and cross-cultural comparisons undertaken to discover what is shared and what is not. This is what Wierzbicka and her colleagues have done in a number of cases, producing some striking results. For example, they argue that all cultures define persons in standard ways, and also always evaluate them as good or bad, that is, positively or negatively.

However, Wierzbicka's method strikes some observers as both too complex and too simplified: too complex in the sense that her reductions often are almost unintelligible to native speakers—as the example of self-expression graphically indicates, and must therefore be equally if not more difficult for people in an-other culture to understand when they are translated; too simple in the sense that the reductions do not do justice to linguistic and cultural variety. For ex-ample, where I did my fieldwork, people denied that they thought anything, be-cause the verb "to think" meant the same thing as "to worry"—and no one wanted to admit worrying. Similarly, limiting evaluation to simple "bad" and "good" obscures important distinctions: Do feelings of homesickness and feel-ings of terror carry the same evaluative charge? Is the badness of halitosis equiv-alent to the badness of incest?[26]

C. Ethnoscience and the Classification of Nature

A more influential form of linguistic analysis directly descended from compo-nential analysis was ethnoscience, which devoted itself to the comparative study of local classificatory systems that are relatively easily demarcated and complete, such as ethnobotany and ethnobiology.[27] These studies pursued the relatively modest goal of discovering the patterned taxonomies that organize data about the natural world across cultures. Yet their contribution to the anthropological study of the actual workings of the brain has been disproportionally great, since the ma-terial collected spoke to the old controversy in anthropology over whether the classification of natural objects is purely arbitrary, or whether it is somehow mo-tivated either by mental structures or by the nature of the world, or by both.

The usual social science position, shared by almost all parties, has always been that such semantic systems are wholly culturally generated and are there-fore arbitrary. Only some rebels, such as Charles Peirce and Victor Turner, sug-gested that symbols somehow resembled or reflected the world they referred to. In contrast, cognitive scientists have tended to follow a Cartesian objectivist view of knowledge: Categories are based on real properties, and symbols are in-ternal representations of an abstract external reality. Correct reason mirrors the logic that underlies the universe.

The contrasting models can be summed up as follows:

- *Cultural model.* Symbols are arbitrary; categories are mental constructs.
- *Objectivist model.* Symbols reflect the world; categories exist in reality.

The objectivist position was much strengthened and the anthropological as-sumption of arbitrariness was called into question when it was discovered that folk classifications of nature are, in fact, quite similar everywhere, though, as noted in Chapter 4, the simplest cultures may not contain the most inclusive taxon. Nor is organizational similarity the sole parallel; species, too, seem to be classed together in terms of morphological features in a way that is remarkably alike across cultures: Everybody, it seems, will class lions and tigers and bears as categorically different than, yet at the same taxonomic level as, monkeys and gibbons and chimpanzees. There are, of course, exceptions. For example, Lévi-Strauss records an indigenous American Indian categorization of charcoal ani-mals—bears, eagles, deer, and swans—that are classed together because they have dark extremities.[28] In spite of such anomalous instances, a number of the-orists have argued that cross-cultural similarities in classification systems

---

Human Attributes and Natural Kinds

The assumption of the integrity of natural kinds may help account for the difficulty people have in deciding what the limits of human existence might be. Many of us in the West believe that a person with no brain is still a human being, or that an egg at the moment of impregnation is human—which means termination of pregnancy is equivalent to murder. In the first instance, humanity is determined by appearance; in the second, by potential. Both attributions also rely on a religious notion of the sanctity of human life in any form—a notion that has become ever more prevalent as the West has become more individualistic.

It is worth noting that these concepts are not universal. Many cultures imagine that humanity ceases at the boundaries of their own tribe (a common self-designation of groups is human beings—while other groups are by implication nonhuman). And in many cultures children become human only incrementally, as they become capable of participation in social life. In such societies, abortion and infanticide are often not considered reprehensible.

---

demonstrates that people are somehow genetically programmed to respond to plants and animals differently than they respond to purely cultural artifacts. Plants and animals are perceived as natural kinds; thus a tiger without legs and stripes is still a tiger, with a presumed natural essence that is not defined by perceptual features. In contrast, a table without legs is not a table.[29]

Cognitive scientists—especially Eleanor Rosch—made a somewhat different argument, one that utilizes objectivist assumptions about the actual existence of external categories, but also moves toward a rapprochement with a more anthropological way of understanding these categories as culturally constructed. Rosch begins with a sensible utilitarian assumption: The brain seeks to get as much return with as little work as possible. The perceived world therefore is not apprehended as bits of random information that are somehow fit together, nor even as objects that incorporate a list of distinctive features. Both of these would tax the rather limited capacities of human memory. Rather, we organize the world to fit simple standardized configurations or prototypes. In other words, the mind perceives objects according to the categories it has manufactured. This works well in the natural world because objects there actually do conform to standardized forms: Birds do tend to be feathered, lay eggs, and have wings; an animal with fur is highly unlikely to fly, and an animal with wings is highly unlikely to have fur. This means that human beings can utilize idealized representations of objects that more or less correspond to their most commonly co-occurring sets of attributes, as they have been noticed by human observers.

Prototypes then are defined by Rosch as "the clearest cases of membership defined operationally by people's judgments of goodness of membership in the category" and as "those members of a category that most reflect the redundancy structure of the category as a whole."[30] For example, in American English, the most prototypical birds are robins and sparrows. They stand at the center of our commonsensical groupings of birds as the clearest cases; the boundaries of the cat-

TABLE 9.1. Prototypicality (Goodness of Example) Ratings for Birds

Member	Mean	Member	Mean	Member	Mean
Robin	1.02	Hummingbird	1.76	Owl	2.96
Sparrow	1.18	Seagull	1.77	Pelican	2.98
Bluejay	1.29	Woodpecker	1.78	Goose	3.03
Bluebird	1.31	Pigeon	1.81	Vulture	3.06
Canary	1.42	Thrush	1.89	Stork	3.10
Blackbird	1.43	Falcon	1.96	Buzzard	3.14
Dove	1.46	Crow	1.97	Swan	3.16
Lark	1.47	Hawk	1.99	Flamingo	3.17
Swallow	1.52	Raven	2.01	Duck	3.24
Parakeet	1.53	Goldfinch	2.06	Peacock	3.31
Oriole	1.61	Parrot	2.07	Egret	3.39
Mockingbird	1.62	Sandpiper	2.40	Chicken	4.02
Wren	1.64	Pheasant	2.69	Turkey	4.09
Redbird	1.64	Catbird	2.72	Ostrich	4.12
Finch	1.66	Crane	2.77	Titmouse	4.35
Starling	1.72	Albatross	2.80	Emu	4.38
Eagle	1.75	Condor	2.83	Penguin	4.53
Cardinal	1.75	Toucan	2.95		

Source: D'Andrade The Development of Cognitive Anthropology, *Cambridge, England: Cambridge University Press, p. 118.*

egory, however, are fuzzy: Are ostriches and penguins birds? We say yes. But is a bat also a bird? In some societies it is, in ours it is not, since we consider it a kind of anomalous mammal—a rodent with wings. However, in Jamaica, my friends called bats "rat-bat-birds," thus fusing the categories nicely. (See Table 9.1.)

Nonetheless, in general, there appears to be a fairly evident line, perceived by humans everywhere, that divides one natural category from another at a generic level; these natural categories, while not completely overlapping, do tend to be quite similar. What this appears to indicate is that human thought operates, at least in the formation of natural classes, by constructing prototypical structures out of strongly correlated attributes that exist in the real world. However, what is stressed in prototype theory is not the existence of the objective reality that is being mapped, but the capacity of the mind to construct models that permit rapid judgments and assumptions with a minimum of information.

D. The Body in the Mind: Experiential Linguistics

Beginning from prototype theory, the linguists George Lakoff and Mark Johnson have gone on to make the radical argument that many of our most important prototypical models of the world do not actually mirror objective physical differences existing "out there," but are metaphorical and metonymical reflections of our own embodied experiences of reality.[31] According to Lakoff and Johnson, the experiences we have through our bodies are central to our being and are projected into the world to serve as conventional mental models, shaping many sorts

Racial Categories

If it is true that the mind tends to construct prototypical natural categories out of associated physical elements, the question then arises as to whether the brain may sometimes produce categories and evaluations that are wholly inaccurate. For example, it has been postulated that one of the reasons for the intractablity of racism is that skin color is wrongly perceived as indicating a difference in natural kind with implicit significance for intelligence, physical ability, sexuality, and character.[32] If such concrete physical imagery is particularly central in our grasping of the world, then it becomes even more difficult to loosen the hold of prejudice based on visible physical distinctions. Ethnic bigotry may also take some of its strength from the same unfortunate human disposition to make moral judgments on perceived physical differences. However, adequate cross-cultural research on this topic remains to done.

of behavior and belief. For example, achieving success is said to be "moving up in the world," and bosses are "higher-ups." This image takes as its prototypical model a bodily experience of higher and lower that is then extended metonymically to status relationships. From Lakoff and Johnson's experientialist perspective, immediate physical experience provides the imagery (structural, orientational, and spatial) for our key categorizations of the world, focusing our attention on certain aspects of reality to the exclusion of others.[33] Note that this perspective returns to the Durkheimian (and structuralist) notion of thought as analogical, but whereas Durkheim placed the social first (we use up and down as categories because of the experienced reality of social hierarchy), Lakoff and Johnson turn his paradigm upside down, taking the physical immediacy of the body as the primary symbolic source for social categories.

The rise of experiential realism in linguistics has provided some confirmation of the theories of phenomenological anthropologists concerned with embodiment, as outlined in Chapter 7. But in moving away from objective external reality and turning radically toward the immediate phenomenal experiences of the body, experiential realism apparently removed culture from the picture altogether. All bodies, after all, are more or less the same everywhere, so our fundamental symbolic systems therefore also ought to be more or less the same.[34] But anthropologists have found comfort in the fact that physical states are usually vague and multidimensional; they require reworking and channeling through cultural mediation.[35] What anthropologists have taken from linguistic experientialism, then, is its opposition to objectivist Cartesian notions of the mind and its insistence on the central importance of (culturally mediated) metaphors and metonyms for thinking.

E. Ethnopsychology and the Interpretation of Culture

The vexing question of the degree to which indigenous categories actually form experience has been most vigorously taken up by ethnopsychology,[36] the branch of ethnoscience that has made the greatest effort to move beyond the study of natural kinds. Starting from the premise that we know little about the "questions people in other cultures ask about psychological matters, or the theories they draw on in formulating their answers,"[37] ethnopsychology has sought to fill that lacuna and discover the way people believe the mind operates. Like other forms of cognitive anthropology, ethnopsychology has relied on detailed linguistic analysis of native categories to gain insight into "the way they think they think." But whereas ethnobotanists and ethnobiologists, like other componential analysts, formally sorted responses to specific questions about categories into abstract taxonomies of plants and animals, proponents of ethnopsychology concentrated their attention on natural discourse and narrative, asking natives to give explanations of their beliefs and actions, decoding standard definitions of mental states, word usages, things left unsaid, common metaphors, similes, and metonyms.

By using more interpretive methods, ethnopsychologists largely dispensed with the scientific apparatus of formal componential analysis; in changing their methodology, they hoped to avoid the charges of unreality and oversimplification that plagued the earlier generation of cognitive anthropologists. They also accepted the fact that psychological reality is more complex than any simple cognitive models allow, that an act may have multiple purposes, that models may be inconsistent, that people may amend accounts of themselves and their actions in order to make themselves look better, and even that some knowledge may be held outside of awareness and perhaps repressed.

Despite giving concessions that seemed to demolish any possible claims for universal validity, ethnopsychologists still hoped that careful linguistic research using advanced techniques could facilitate a comparative study of indigenous psychologies. Such comparisons could be made because researchers assumed that ethnopsychologies were "an *organized* body of understandings."[38] If local psychological knowledge systems were in fact highly structured, it ought to be feasible to grasp their underlying axioms and make comparisons between them, discovering which postulates about the mind are universal, which are particular. Of course, the assumption of systematic organization had the peril, characteristic of all attempts to map semantic domains, of *petitio principii*, "taking for granted that which needs to be proved."

In truth, ethnopsychologists were not very interested in making a comparative taxonomy of the organized body of understandings people had about the mind. Inspired by Hallowell's earlier work on the cultural manufacture of self-awareness, they argued that indigenous models of psychology are not just abstract systems of expert knowledge, but are organizing principles that serve to stimulate, orient, and guide action in a particular cultural world. In other words, ethnopsychological models of reality were thought to have a directive force that makes them especially motivating.[39] The real ambition of ethnopsychology was to complete the work of Weber and his interpretivist descendants by using linguistic techniques to elicit and compare the belief systems presumed to lie beneath and motivate social action. More and more, then, the comparative objectives of ethnopsychology were set aside in favor of a quest for the content of indigenous directive knowledge systems.

Of special importance in this project was a blunt challenge to Western psychological models, which were regarded as no more accurate than any other culturally constructed theory of the mind. Psychoanalysis especially was subjected to ethnopsychological scrutiny in an effort to deconstruct its basic categories and reveal its underlying premises. Unsurprisingly, what was discovered were assumptions about the autonomy of the self, the private nature of emotions, the reality of inner experience, and the value of self-exploration. These egoistic aspects were then contrasted to non-Western ethnopsychologies that were said to be more social, public, and external in nature, and to organize and designate emotions in quite a different manner.[40] The challenge to the authority of psychoanalysis and its understanding of emotional order was probably ethnopsychology's most original and controversial contribution—one that will be discussed at more length in Chapter 10.

For the moment, however, I want to stress ethnopsychology's relationship to the rest of the ethnoscience enterprise. Although ethnopsychology did draw attention to the differences between indigenous psychologies, it lost considerable rigor because of its interpretative orientation. Unlike ethnobotany and ethnobiology, where the domains analyzed were clearly demarcated and clearly referred to natural kinds, ethnopsychology was studying worldviews—a far more ineffable and fuzzy area. As a result, like the more ambitious forms of componential analysis, it too was extremely vulnerable to criticisms that the coherent worldviews were created by informants in response to the questions the researchers were asking or, even worse, were constructed post hoc by anthropologists piecing together fragments that somehow must fit into a whole.

Small samples also sometimes made large conclusions appear rather suspect. For example, the contemporary cognitive anthropologist Roy D'Andrade undertook an impressive detailing of the American folk model of the mind that was based entirely on interviews with five college and high school students.[41] Furthermore, even if a coherent indigenous psychology could adequately be elicited, could it actually account for the full range of psychological reality? Perhaps, as some commentators have said, cultural conceptual systems do not express everything that individuals within the culture actually feel and may serve instead to mask certain emotions (see Chapter 10 for more on this argument).[42] By giving most credit to the local accounts of emotional-psychological structures and by denying psychoanalytic models any validity, ethnopsychology may in fact have closed the door to cross-cultural comparison.

At the same time, ethnopsychology also fell prey to its own assumptions that people are relatively conscious of and capable of discussing their own mental states—an assumption that is dubious at best.[43] Ethnopsychology also had the problem of relating the systems it claimed to have discovered to the rest of the society. Without an in-depth psychological theory of their own upon which to rest their premises, ethnopsychologists usually were left with only crude notions of hegemony and functionalism to explain the authority of any particular cultural theory of the self and the mind: People's ethnopsychologies became ratifications of predominant power relations.[44] A final problem is that ethnopsychology, like componential analysis, aimed primarily at constructing a coherent system; this means it tended to be ahistorical and insensitive to the nuances of context and conflict, reifying description of an abstract model over process, agency, and interest.[45] Despite these deficits, the new subdiscipline of ethnopsychology did begin to undertake research that is crucially important to the future of psychological anthropology: the study of indigenous beliefs about the nature of the mind.

III. COMPUTERS, CONSCIOUSNESS, AND CULTURAL MODELS

A Computer Science and Anthropology
>   The influence (and limitations) of the study of artificial intelligence for understanding human cognition.

B New Models of the Mind: Parallel and Serial
>   Connectionist and serial computer processing, and their relationship to habitual and analytic thought.

C Motivating Schemas and Cultural Models
>   Schema theory. How cognitive models can motivate behavior. Modularity: the mind as tidal pool.

D Critiques and Amplifications of Schema Theory
>   Problems of accounting for difference, contradiction, and the experience of psychic unity within the schema model.

A. Computer Science and Anthropology

The most recent and most productive efforts to expand the anthropological understanding of the relationship between the workings of the brain and the structure of society have been in alliance with a new and different universe of knowledge: computer science. The idea that the brain is a kind of thinking machine has had a long history, but until recently, real thinking machines were no more than science fiction fantasies. The advent of computers capable of the rapid analysis of billions of binary bits of information changed this. These artificial intelligences actually do appear to think, and to do it much better, in some ways, than human beings. The explosion in the study of artificial intelligence meant that it was now hard to avoid presuming that the brain is a kind of computer. And since we can understand the workings of a computer, we should be able to understand the brain as well. Cognitive scientists therefore began to hope that computer experts could develop programming that would replicate human thinking processes.

But here an impasse was reached. Traditionally, cognitive scientists had pictured the human brain as a kind of central processor, undertaking and completing cognitive tasks. Following Descartes's objectivist notions of the workings of the mind, many assumed that mathematics was the highest form of thought. If this were so, then computers were far superior to human beings: They could sort and analyze huge quantities of data and calculate accurate answers much faster and more accurately than any human being. They could even beat the greatest

Chess champion Garry Kasparov's match against Deep Blue, a computer that analyzes 200 million chess moves a second.

human chess players. However, it was also soon discovered that the superiority of computers over humans was quite limited. Even the most brilliant computer could not accomplish the simplest human actions: It could not recognize faces, negotiate a room, make sense of a poem, row a boat, or carry on a sensible conversation. The realization that computers, although able to solve complex equations almost immediately, could not do many of the things that are taken for granted by even the dimmest of human beings challenged some fundamental premises about what the brain really is. As the anthropologist Charles Frake writes:

> Ironically, it has been a machine that has made us aware of the mental richness of mundane human life. It has done so by demonstrating to us just how un-artificial our intelligence is. Cognitive scientists—some of them at least—are being forced to recognize that human cognition, whatever else it may be and whatever form or formula might best reveal it, is, unlike a computer, embodied, emotional, ecological, and social.[46]

B. New Models of the Mind: Parallel and Serial

Challenged by this insight, some computer scientists began to move away from programs based on a mathematical notion of knowledge.[47] In traditional serial processing, symbolic representations of the outside world (say, a chess game) are encoded within the computer in binary bits. The computer then achieves tasks (such as solving chess problems) by rapidly manipulating these representations in a sequential chain and methodically selecting the best possible answer according to rules of logic. This works well for some problems, but does not answer the ambiguities of daily life.

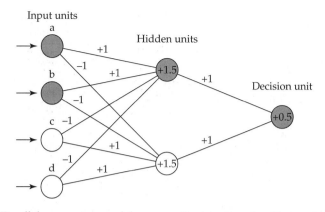

FIGURE 9.3. Parallel processing model—connectionist network with one decision unit. This unit is activated when input units a and b are active *or* when input units c and d are active, *but not both.*
Source: *Roy D'Andrade, 1995,* The Development of Cognitive Anthropology, *Cambridge, England: Cambridge University Press, p. 138.*

However, the serial processing model is not the only one possible for programming a computer. Another form, developed in the 1950s, is made up of a series of several inputs connected to outputs. When the activation of the inputs reaches a certain level, or "weight," the output they are connected to is triggered. This extremely rudimentary unit could be multiplied, and programmed to respond to a particular pattern by increasing the weight of input units activated by that pattern, while decreasing the weight of others.[48] (See Figure 9.3.) This type of processor had some negative features: It could not discriminate odd or even numbers, and it did not recognize which out of a particular set of inputs are active—factors that made it lose out to serial processing in the initial stages of computer research.

However, continued work on these networks led to improvements—especially the development of intermediate units between input and output that allowed for more sophisticated distinctions. These new devices—called neural nets, parallel distributing processing networks, or connectionist networks— soon proved to have some unusual properties relevant for our understanding of ourselves and our thoughts. For example, there are no strict rules in connectionist networks, only weights and combinations; they operate in terms of continua and associations, not in terms of encoded symbols, and quickly fill in missing data based on assumptions about the larger configuration. Neural nets can also blend different patterns into a coherent whole by searching for underlying structural similarities. This makes connectionist networks excellent for mapping relationships and for adapting to circumstances. Connectionist learning can be strongly influenced by physical impressions, and comprehends structure if structure is in the input; in other words, neural nets reflect the nature of objective reality.

In terms of learning, the development of strong connections by parallel distributing processing networks is incremental, and requires many repetitions of the same stimulus to be imprinted; but when something is learned, it is activated in a way that is automatic, rapid in execution, and hard to eradicate. This stands in contrast to the direct learning that occurs in traditional serial processing, which is quicker and easier, more abstracted from physical reality, and simpler to change, but not so immediate in execution, and far more likely to crash when input is altered.

As Roy D'Andrade writes, "there is little doubt that the brain, with its ten billion or so neurons, *is* a massively parallel connectionist network."[49] But it is also true that both types of processing go on in the mind: the pattern recognition and associational connections of a neural net and the symbolic coding and logical structuring of serial processing. In terms of human experience, the two kinds of models may well correspond to what we might call school learning— which is like serial processing—and habit—which is connectionist. School learning inculcates knowledge of abstract systems, formal theory, and analytical logic; in contrast, the ordinary skills of interaction, the taken-for-granted grasp of the world, the physical habits and skills, the capacity for recognition of faces and places, the regularities of language, are all learned not by study, but by repetition, pattern recognition, association, and gradual embedding.

The difference can be compared to the difference between learning the rules of the road by reading a driver's manual and learning to manipulate a stick shift by constant practice. Human beings, it is clear, utilize both types of learning. We have memories and habits deeply ingrained into our being; we also learn, think, and develop new theories. As Weber knew, some parts of our lives run more or less automatically and are almost impossible to change, while others are a matter of conscious awareness and choice. What is new is that the study of habit has now become possible.

Actors' and Observers' Models

The distinction between types of learning has interesting similarities to the distinction made by cognitive anthropologist Bradd Shore between observers' models and actors' models. Observers' models, Shore says, are formal. They are used to represent and coordinate abstract, general perspectives, and are organized more in terms of categories and mutual, not personal, orientation. Actors' models, in contrast, use symbols that are dynamic and graded; often tacit, they allow individuals to adapt to a changing environment. For instance, Shore writes that his informants in Samoa had a formal observers' model of their village layout that stressed the polar division between front and back; but they also had a more nuanced, personal, and implicit model of the village as concentric, divided between center and periphery. He was presented with the formal model, which his informants themselves saw as epitomizing the whole of culture. Only after long fieldwork was the more habitual, taken-for-granted actors' model made visible.[50]

The new notions of learning, in which routine takes a place alongside reason, occurred in conjunction with the development of computer models based on the actual way people adapt to new situations, that is, by scanning a new setting for basic resemblances to previous experiences and then enacting an appropriate script, or scenario. For example, once we have gone to a few restaurants, we have a good idea how to act in any place that fits the general prototype category of restaurant.[51] Computer science rediscovered what Goffman and G. H. Mead had known all along: Human beings are actors improvising in ongoing plays, learning through imitation, and continually adapting themselves to standardized patterns of action.

C. Motivating Schemas and Cultural Models

All this material was united in the notion of the schema, or cultural model, defined by cognitive anthropologist Roy D'Andrade as "a conceptual structure which makes possible the identification of objects and events."[52] These conceptual schemas, or cultural models, are larger, more vague, and more open than prototypes. They provide the organized framework of objects and relations waiting to be filled in by the specific sets of expectations contained in a particular prototype. Cultural models also are portrayed as similar to connectionist processing models: They are frequent, well organized, memorable, made from minimal cues, and resistant to change. Like parallel processing networks, they can arrive at an interpretation based on a small amount of information; they are relational, vague, incremental, multiple, and embodied, and are often matters of habit.[53] They also operate analogically, not digitally, and are activated by words that point to them as internal entities.

The next step taken was to try to link these pervasive but imprecise mental structures with action. The argument was that they may not simply be descriptive models, but could also be desired goals that people would struggle to achieve.[54] In other words, cultural models, or schemas, are the cognitive anthropologist's equivalent of worldviews. As emphasized by D'Andrade, not all schemas have directive force; only "a person's most general interpretations of what is going on will function as important goals for that person."[55] Beneath these general motivating interpretations are second-level schemas that require other goals to be initiated. At the lowest level are schemas that do not provoke action unless excited by higher-level goals. Some examples of general motivating interpretations are Freud's master schemas of love and work; middle-level schemas are said to include such things as marriage, job, and surfing; lower-level schemas are such things as how to write memos, what to do on birthdays, and what to use a water glass for.[56] Clearly, everything is included within these hierarchically nested schemas—even the kitchen sink. In fact, there seems no end to the variations, possibilities, and divisions of the schemas that are possible.

The most ambitious attempt to construct a comprehensive categorization of schemas was recently undertaken by Bradd Shore.[57] His basic contrast is between linguistic and nonlinguistic models. Linguistic models include scripts, propositional models (the Ten Commandments), sound symbolic models (onomatopoeia), lexical models (taxonomies, lists, dictionaries, etc.), grammatical models, verbal formulas (proverbs, sayings, etc.), and narratives. Nonlinguistic models include image schemas (such as the "higher-up" schema discussed by Lakoff and Johnson), emotion models, action sets (gestural models such as handshaking and clapping, as well as complex ritual performances), olfactory models, sound image models, visual image models (iconography, maps, etc.). And this is only a condensed list.

Nor is Shore's work yet complete: He divides these various models according to their functions. Any of them can be orientational, expressive-conceptual, or task. Orientational models give a framework for uniting people in their behavioral environment. They can be spatial, temporal, social, diagnostic, and so on. Expressive models are classificatory, playful, ritualized, dramatic, and theoretical. Task models are scripts, recipes, checklists, mnemonic devices, persuasive rhetoric.[58]

It remains as yet unproved whether this proliferation of categories will prove useful, or whether, like the epicycles used to try to save the principles of Ptolemaic astronomy, they simply reflect a fundamental incoherence at the core of the theory, that is, the failure to postulate any integrating element—a "me" that is in charge of the ramifying schemas.[59] This incoherence is a result of the way human beings are understood by D'Andrade, Shore, and other cognitivists as consisting of multiple modular computers busily communicating useful information to one another. As D'Andrade writes, from this perspective, individuals and culture are seen as sets of more or less interrelated modular subsystems operating to solve various problems "such as the problem of biological reproduction, or the problem of getting food out of the environment, or human cognitive limitations, or personality needs, or whatever."[60] The human mind is therefore not to be understood as a unified central consciousness; rather, it is pictured as consisting of independent cognitive modules, coexisting rather like the denizens of a tidal pool.

D. Critiques and Amplifications of Schema Theory

This functionalist modular perspective fragments human reality into an infinite set of never-ending riddles to be answered. Culture, as a multiple, all-purpose problem-solving device, has no more coherent content than the multiple computational subsystems who use it for "whatever."

There is much to be argued with here—not least of which is the contradiction between an instrumental image of human beings (or the modules that make up human beings) as problem solvers and the quasi-Weberian notion that cultural schemas themselves define what life's problems are. More to the point, the fragmentation of cultures and of persons into computational devices designed for answering multiple, unspecified problems tells us nothing about the impulses that propel human desire, nor does it explain why some schemas are far more likely to be master motives than others, or why some hierarchies of nested models are tightly organized and integrated while others are not, or why some cultural models are well articulated and others are tacit. Nor does it provide any explanation of the experiential reality of coherence, both in the self and in the environment. It seems to me that questions like these cannot be answered within the framework thus far provided by cognitivists—not without bringing in some concept of human motivation and psychic unity that stands outside—or alongside—cognition.

Another problem faced by cognitive anthropology is that most studies of schemas portray everyone in the culture learning and enacting cultural models without any strain or inner conflict—surely an overly rosy picture.[61] One solution has been to factor individual distinctions into the equation. This has been accomplished by returning to old notions of socialization and internalization: Not all schemas are accepted equally by everybody, as a result of variations in the learning environment, including the degree of emotional intensity surrounding the learning of a schema. Differences in personal libido may also enter in, though the emphasis in this theoretical model is very little on the push (where energy comes from) and very much on the pull (what energy is going toward). As D'Andrade puts it: "Human action is more directly understood by identifying the conceptual network of things toward which the creature strives than by identifying energy sources."[62] This viewpoint has its virtues, but it eliminates the very real possibility that we can be pushed in directions we do not wish to go, and that cultural goals can stand in direct contradiction to the desires that drive individuals.

At any rate, within the cognitivist theoretical framework, variations in the degree to which cultural schemas are internalized and shared (for whatever reason) account for differences between people. Some people find a particular schema very motivating, while others do not. For example, Claudia Strauss claims that blue-collar men are not motivated by the dominant American value of success, but are impelled by a more class-based value of being the breadwinner for the family. The first, she says, is recognizable as a passionless cliché because of the repetitive, standardized way it is discussed; the second, in contrast, is taken for granted as an unavoidable reality. In this case, the two schemas do not clash, but simply coexist at different levels of consciousness and salience.[63] This, of course, does not answer the more fundamental problem of why such collective differences should exist at all. Are class divisions or discrepancies in power always the most motivating of factors?

One valiant attempt to bring some needed tension into the schema framework has been attempted by Naomi Quinn, who uses interview material to show that American women's notions of marriage involve potentially antagonistic schemas of (1) equity, (2) obligation to the role, and (3) personal integrity. The first is based on underlying notions of fairness and equality. The second is based on acceptance of the wifely duties to her husband. The third is based on the notion that the individual has the obligation to maximize his or her own abilities.

These widely held schemas can be mutually exclusive. For example, some women want to fill the stereotypical role of ideal wife by putting their husband's career first, but this culturally favored goal is in tension with deeply held American notions of fairness, and with the equally potent ideal of trying to reach one's personal potential. Quinn concludes that incompatible cultural schemas about oneself and one's values may lead to moral conflicts and, sometimes, to resistance against the status quo.[64] Quinn's is one of the few studies to give credit to what Freud saw as central to the human experience: conflicting desires and existential ambivalence.

Another failing of cognitivist images of cultural models, conflicting or not, is the way models are seen to be directly available to consciousness, easily analyzed by articulate informants. This leaves out the obvious possibility of self-deception, bias, and concealment.[65] Cognitivist accounts tend as well to neglect or overlook the possibility of unconscious motivations that might conflict with conscious or standard models.[66]

Despite these weaknesses, schema theory claims to offer a better way to understand behavior. Discovering which schemas are motivating means we know why people do things. By defining what can and cannot be done, felt, or believed, schemas make our world for us, and we operate according to the dictates of that knowledge. The tremendous advances in artificial intelligence and contemporary linguistics have therefore led modern cognitive anthropology back to a very old conclusion: Our lives and our brains are constructed by our cultural understandings.

Summary

The study of the mind has always fascinated anthropologists, who have a mandate to discover not only the particular but also the universal, and to define what it is to be human. Perhaps the most daring early theory of the mind was proposed by Émile Durkheim, who argued that human beings are not primarily logical, causal thinkers but, instead, think by analogy, categorizing and cataloguing the world in ever expanding symbolic systems. His poetic vision was greatly extended by Claude Lévi-Strauss, who used linguistic theory to argue that myth can be broken down into contrastive elements linked analogically. On the basis of his analysis, Lévi-Strauss claimed to have uncovered the hidden structure of the mind itself, which he understood as a binary processor of symbols. However, his work, admittedly brilliant, was disparaged as reflecting more his own mind than the minds of others.

From another direction, but equally influenced by linguistics, American cognitive anthropologists also began exploring meaning systems, seeking a key to understanding thought. Componential analysis broke down semantic domains, such as kinship, into contrastive units, and generated cognitive maps and taxonomies derived from interviews. Though attempting to be rigorous, componential analysis, too, fell foul of accusations of subjectivity, and it also came to an intellectual dead end, producing only more and more taxonomies. Yet it spawned a number of exciting offspring: Anna Wierzbicka's theory of universal cultural scripts, which suffers from perhaps a too rigorous reduction of meanings; the comparative study of the botanical and zoological categorizations employed in other cultures, which turn out to be remarkably similar to our own; and Eleanor Rosch's theory of prototypes, defined as the best examples of a particular class of things or beings. The use of prototypes, Rosch has argued, allows the mind to make rapid and fairly accurate assessments with a minimum of information—particularly when dealing with natural kinds in the external world.

Developing from, but in contrast to, prototype theory, the linguists George Lakoff and Mark Johnson have claimed that prototypical linguistic categories—especially metaphors and metonyms—are internally generated by the actual physical and emotional experiences of individuals. It is from feelings and sensations, they say, that we draw our reality. In its extreme form, experiential realism would seem to deny culture its due place, replacing it with the body; but in a less radical incarnation, it offers an important qualification to the assumption that the human mind is purely rational and that the logic of the world imposes itself upon us.

Ethnopsychology makes a very different argument, concerning itself with the directive force of the psychological theories developed in different cultures. Here the external world has priority, as various ethnopsychologies are thought to motivate behavior and construct thought. In a real sense, ethnopsychology is another attempt to develop a Weberian *verstehen* approach to culture, offering a way to understand the way they think they think. But in assuming that people do indeed have coherent, organized, and motivating ethnopsychologies, the discipline may be making too great a leap of faith.

A different avenue to understanding the nature of the mind has been taken in the alliance between computer researchers and cognitive anthropologists. Advances in artificial intelligence would seem to offer a powerful new tool for understanding the principles of human thought, but, as it turns out, highly "intelligent" computers are actually woefully inadequate at negotiating ordinary human tasks. Perhaps this is because their programming is primarily serial—oriented toward the solution of mathematical problems—while the human mind operates in a more connectionist manner, through associations and analogies (though somewhat differently than Durkheim and Lévi-Strauss conjectured).

Computer programmers' research on neural nets was influenced by, and has greatly influenced, schema theory—a development from prototype theory. Schemas, or cultural models, are understood by cognitive anthropologists such as Roy D'Andrade as more complex and open than prototypes—much like a connectionist computer network. Multiple schemas are thought to provide us with the scripts for our daily lives; they are also hierarchically arranged, with higher-level schemas (Freud's love and work, for instance) motivating us to action.

Exciting though this new perspective is, there are serious problems with it, among them the difficulty of limiting the proliferation of schemas, the absence of any central organizing processor (and therefore the absence of any self), and the difficulty of dealing with contradiction or resistance. Nonetheless, the development of schema theory has given anthropologists a fresh way to think about thinking and a linkage between culture and the brain that was previously absent. On balance, then, cognitive anthropologists are right to be proud of their contributions. They have offered a provocative reworking of our knowledge of the relationship between the individual and society. Anthropologists have always tended to overemphasize socialization, ignoring mental processes. Cognitive scientists have been equally prone to the opposite error, forgetting culture and affirming the primacy of the mind alone. Cognitive anthropology has begun to bridge that intellectual gap, giving us a much clearer idea of the nature and patterning of the complex interrelationship between social life and the operations of the mind, and the emergence of consciousness within the context of culture.

Endnotes

1. For a more complete discussion, see Thomas Gladwin, 1970, *East Is a Big Bird*, Cambridge, MA: Harvard University Press; Edwin Hutchins, 1994, *Cognition in the Wild*, Cambridge, MA: MIT Press.
2. The task of social science, Weber wrote, was to supply "the interpretive understanding of social action and thereby . . . a causal explanation of its course and consequences." See Max Weber, 1978, *Economy and Society*, Berkeley: University of California Press, p. 4.
3. Ibid., pp. 21, 25, 24.

4. Chapter 11 will deal with Weber's concept of another type of nonrational action: charisma.

5. Durkheim and his colleague Marcel Mauss illustrated these patterns copiously in Durkheim and Mauss, 1963, *Primitive Classification,* Chicago: University of Chicago Press (original publication 1904). For an interesting critique, which claims that this type of polar categorization is actually an artifact of literacy, see Jack Goody, 1977, *The Domestication of the Savage Mind,* Cambridge, England: Cambridge University Press.

6. Émile Durkheim, 1965, *The Elementary Forms of the Religious Life,* New York: Free Press, pp. 169, 170 (original publication 1912).

7. Durkheim and Mauss, *Primitive Classification,* p. 86.

8. Quoted in Marc Augé, 1960, "Ten Questions Put to Claude Lévi-Strauss," *Current Anthropology* 31: 85–90, 86.

9. Robert Hertz, 1960, "The Pre-eminence of the Right Hand," in Robert Hertz, *Death and the Right Hand,* Glencoe, IL: Free Press (original publication 1909). For more recent essays on the topic of dualism, see Rodney Needham (ed.), 1973, *Right and Left: Essays on Dual Classification Systems,* Chicago: University of Chicago Press; David Maybury-Lewis and Uri Almagor (eds.), 1989, *The Attraction of Opposites: Thought and Society in the Dualistic Mode,* Ann Arbor: University of Michigan Press.

10. Claude Lévi-Stauss, 1969, *The Elementary Structures of Kinship,* Boston: Beacon Press, (Original French publication 1949).

11. See Roman Jakobson, 1956, *Fundamentals of Language,* The Hague, Netherlands: Mouton; Ferdinand de Saussure, 1959, *Course in General Linguistics,* New York: Philosophical Library (original publication 1916).

12. Vladimir Propp, 1958, *The Morphology of the Folktale,* Bloomington: Indiana University Press (original publication 1928).

13. Claude Lévi-Strauss, 1967, "The Structural Study of Myth," in C. Lévi-Strauss (ed.), *Structural Anthropology,* Garden City, NY: Doubleday.

14. Claude Lévi-Strauss, 1966, *The Savage Mind,* Chicago: University of Chicago Press.

15. Gustav Jahoda, 1982, *Psychology and Anthropology: A Psychological Perspective,* London: Academic Press, p. 219.

16. For seminal works, see Ward Goodenough, 1956, "Componential Analysis and the Study of Meaning," *Language* 32: 195–216; Floyd Lounsbury, 1956, "A Semantic Analysis of the Pawnee Kinship Usage," *Language* 32: 158–94.

17. Steven Tyler (ed.), 1969, *Cognitive Anthropology,* New York: Holt, Rinehart and Winston, p. 3.

18. Quoted in Roy D'Andrade, 1995, *The Development of Cognitive Anthropology,* Cambridge, England: Cambridge University Press, p. xiii. For another history of the discipline, see Ronald Casson, 1994, "Cognitive Anthropology," in Philip Bock (ed.), *Psychological Anthropology,* Westport, CT: Praeger.

19. See A. Kimball Romney and Roy D'Andrade, 1964, "Cognitive Aspects of English Kin Terms," *American Anthropologist* 66: 146–70; Ward Goodenough, 1965, "Yankee Kinship Terminology: A Problem in Componential Analysis," *American Anthropologist* 67: 259–87.

20. See Noam Chomsky, 1957, *Syntactic Structures,* The Hague, Netherlands: Mouton; for his later views, see 1988, *Language and Problems of Knowledge: The Managua Lectures,* Cambridge, MA: MIT Press. For an alternative, see Gerald Gazdar et al., 1985, *Generalized Phrase Structure Grammar,* Cambridge, MA: Harvard University Press.

21. For a survey, see Harold Conklin, 1972, *Folk Classification: A Bibliography,* New Haven, CT: Yale University, Department of Anthropology.

22. James Spradley, 1979, *The Ethnographic Interview,* New York: Holt, Rinehart and Winston.

23. For some cogent criticisms, see Roger Keesing, 1972, "Paradigms Lost: The New Ethnography and the New Linguistics," *Southwestern Journal of Anthropology* 28: 299–332; Charles Frake, 1977, "Playing Frames Can Be Dangerous: Some Reflections on Methodology in Cognitive Anthropology," *Quarterly Newsletter of the Institute for Comparative Human Development* 1: 1–7; Robert Randall, 1976, "How Tall Is a Taxonomic Tree? Some Evidence for Dwarfism," *American Ethnologist* 3: 543–53.

24. For an outline, see Anna Wierzbicka, 1993, "A Conceptual Basis for Cultural Psychology," *Ethos* 21: 205–31.

25. Anna Wierzbicka, 1996, "Japanese Cultural Scripts: Cultural Psychology and 'Cultural Grammar,' " *Ethos* 24: 527–55, 546.

26. For this critique, see D'Andrade, *The Development of Cognitive Anthropology,* Chap. 9.

27. For classic accounts, see Harold Conklin, 1954, "The Relation of Hanunoo Culture to the Plant World," Ph.D. dissertation, Department of Anthropology, Yale University, New Haven, CT; Brent Berlin, D. Breedlove, and P. Raven, 1973, "General Principles of Classification and Nomenclature in Folk Biology," *American Anthropologist* 75: 214–42.

28. Lévi-Strauss, *The Savage Mind,* p. 147.

29. See Scott Atran, 1990, *Cognitive Foundations of Natural History: Towards an Anthropology of Science,* Cambridge, England: Cambridge University Press.

30. Elinor Rosch, 1978, "Principles of Categorization," in E. Rosch and B. Lloyd (eds.), *Cognition and Categorization,* New York: Erlbaum, pp. 36, 37.

31. A metaphor derives from a perceived similarity between two entities (he is as fat as a pig) or experiences (love is blind), while a metonym is based on contiguity and association (I speak the English tongue). In a sense, these categories recapitulate Frazier's distinction between types of magic based on similarity and on contagion.

32. See Pascal Boyer, 1993, "Pseudo Natural Kinds," in P. Boyer (ed.), *Cognitive Aspects of Religious Symbolism,* Cambridge, England: Cambridge University Press; Lawrence Hirschfeld, 1997, "The Conceptual Politics of Race: Lessons from Our Children," *Ethos* 25: 63–92. See also the other articles in that issue.

33. See George Lakoff and Mark Johnson, 1980, *Metaphors We Live By,* Chicago: University of Chicago Press; George Lakoff, 1987, *Women, Fire and Dangerous Things: What Categories Reveal about the Mind,* Chicago: University of Chicago Press; Mark Johnson, 1987, *The Body in the Mind: The Bodily Basis of Meaning, Imagination, and Reason,* Chicago: University of Chicago Press.

34. Anthropologists have sometimes made this case as well, though always with caution. For instance, Rodney Needham has long called on anthropology to consider the perhaps archetypical ways in which the brain perceives and organizes color, noise, and texture (see, for example, Rodney Needham, 1978, *Primordial Characters,* Charlottesville: University of Virginia Press).

35. See, for instance, the discussion of Lakoff in Naomi Quinn and Dorothy Holland, 1987, "Culture and Cognition," in Dorothy Holland and Naomi Quinn (eds.), *Cultural Models in Language and Thought,* Cambridge, England: Cambridge University Press.

36. For an early usage of this term, see C. A. Valentine, 1963, "Men of Anger and Men of Shame: Lakalai Ethnopsychology and Its Implications for Sociopsychological Theory," *Ethnology* 2: 441–77. See also Raymond Fogelson, 1979, "Person, Self, and Identity: Some Anthropological Retrospects, Circumspects, and Prospects," in Benjamin Lee (ed.), *Psychosocial Theories of the Self,* New York: Plenum Press.

37. John Kirkpatrick and Geoffrey White, 1985, "Exploring Ethnopsychologies," in Geoffrey White and John Kirkpatrick (eds.), *Person, Self, and Experience: Exploring Pacific*

Ethnopsychologies, Berkeley: University of California Press, p. 7. For another important set of articles on ethnopsychology, written more from a psychological point of view, see Paul Heelas and Andrew Lock (eds.), 1981, *Indigenous Psychologies: The Anthropology of the Self,* London: Academic Press.

38. Kirkpatrick and White, "Exploring Ethnopsychologies," p. 22.
39. The question of directive force has also been important for understanding emotions. See Renato Rosaldo, 1983, "Grief and a Headhunter's Rage: On the Cultural Force of Emotions," in Edward Bruner (ed.), *Text, Play and Story: The Construction and Reconstruction of Self and Society,* Proceedings of the American Ethnological Society. See Chapter 10 for more on this topic. Washington, DC.
40. See, for example, Catherine Lutz, 1985, "Ethnopsychology Compared to What? Explaining Behavior and Consciousness among the Ifaluk," in Geoffrey M. White and John Kirkpatrick (eds.), *Person, Self, and Experience: Exploring Pacific Ethnopsychologies,* Berkeley: University of California Press.
41. Roy D'Andrade, 1987, "A Folk Model of the Mind," in Dorothy Holland and Naomi Quinn (eds.), *Cultural Models in Language and Thought,* Cambridge, England: Cambridge University Press.
42. This point has been made by Eleanor Ruth Gerber, 1985, "Rage and Obligation: Samoan Emotion in Conflict," in G. White and J. Kirkpatrick (eds.), *Person, Self and Experience,* Berkeley: University of California Press. See also Robert Levy, 1984, "Emotion, Knowing, and Culture," in Richard Shweder and Robert LeVine (eds.), *Culture Theory: Essays on Mind, Self and Emotion,* Cambridge, England: Cambridge University Press.
43. As the psychologist Lawrence Kirmayer notes, "there is little reason to assume that self-presentation and underlying cognitive schema are isomorphic and so an account of the person as a role-governed entity based on self-description is highly suspect." See Lawrence J. Kirmayer, 1989, "Cultural Variations in the Response to Psychiatric Disorders and Emotional Distress," *Social Sciences and Medicine* 29: 327–39, 335.
44. For this critique, see Charles W. Nuckolls, 1996, *The Cultural Dialectics of Knowledge and Desire,* Madison: University of Wisconsin Press, pp. 6–8.
45. Roger M. Keesing, 1987, "Models, 'Folk' and 'Cultural': Paradigms Regained?" in Dorothy Holland and Naomi Quinn (eds.), *Cultural Models in Language and Thought,* Cambridge, England: Cambridge University Press. The French cognitive anthropologist Dan Sperber has posited an alternative theory of consciousness that takes account of the incoherence and irrationality of human knowledge systems. He argues for an epidemiological model of knowledge in which information spreads rather like a disease, and is accepted or rejected according to elective affinities with the predispositions and interests of individual recipients. For a good statement of his perspective, see Dan Sperber, 1998, *Explaining Culture: A Naturalistic Approach,* Oxford: Basil Blackwell. For a complex and complete ethnographic account of the actual manner in which indigenous knowledge systems are generated and incorporated, see the groundbreaking work of Fredrik Barth, 1975, *Ritual and Knowledge among the Baktman of New Guinea,* New Haven, CT: Yale University Press; 1987, *Cosmologies in the Making: A Generative Approach to Culture Variation in Inner New Guinea,* Cambridge, England: Cambridge University Press.
46. Charles Frake, 1994, "Cognitive Anthropology: An Origin Story," in Marcelo Suarez-Orozco, George Spindler, and Louise Spindler (eds.), *The Making of Psychological Anthropology II,* Fort Worth, TX: Harcourt Brace, p. 248.
47. Much of the material in the next paragraphs is paraphrased from D'Andrade, *The Development of Cognitive Anthropology,* pp. 136–49.

48. Philip Quinlan, 1991, *Connectionism and Psychology,* Chicago: University of Chicago Press; Andy Clark, 1989, *Microcognition,* Cambridge, MA: MIT Press; David Rumelhart et al., 1986, "Schemata and Sequential Thought Processes in PDP Models," in J. McClelland and D. Rumelhart (eds.), *Parallel Distributed Processing,* Vol. II, Cambridge, MA: MIT Press.
49. D'Andrade, *The Development of Cognitive Anthropology,* p. 140.
50. Bradd Shore, 1996, *Culture in Mind: Cognition, Culture, and the Problem of Meaning,* New York: Oxford University Press. For a sophisticated and convincing ethnographic use of the techniques of cognitive anthropology, see Maurice Bloch, 1998, *How We Think They Think: Anthropological Approaches to Cognition, Memory and Literacy,* Boulder, CO: Westview Press.
51. R. Schank and R. Abelson, 1977, *Scripts, Plans, Goals and Understanding: An Inquiry into Human Knowledge Structures,* Hillsdale, NJ: Erlbaum.
52. Roy D'Andrade, 1992, "Schemas and Motivation," in Roy D'Andrade and Claudia Strauss (eds.), *Human Motives and Cultural Models,* Cambridge, England: Cambridge University Press, p. 28. The term "schema" was originated by Frederic Bartlett, 1932, *Remembering: A Study in Experimental and Social Psychology,* Cambridge, England: Cambridge University Press.
53. D'Andrade, "Schemas and Motivation," p. 29.
54. As Claudia Strauss argues, schemas "not only label and describe the world but also set forth goals (both conscious and unconscious) and elicit or include desires." See Claudia Strauss, 1992, "Models and Motives," in Roy D'Andrade and Claudia Strauss (eds.), *Human Motives and Cultural Models,* Cambridge, England: Cambridge University Press, p. 3.
55. D'Andrade, "Schemas and Motivation," p. 30.
56. Ibid.
57. Shore, *Culture in Mind.*
58. I presume that Shore's own model is a lexical one that aims to orient anthropologists in the quest for usable theory. Or, on second thought, perhaps his model is propositional, classificatory, and playful.
59. This same problem plagues the new rationalist models of the mind that rely on computer modeling and modularity. For a critique, see Jerry Fodor, 1998, "The Trouble with Psychological Darwinism," *London Review of Books,* January 22: 11–13.
60. D'Andrade, *The Development of Cognitive Anthropology,* p. 250.
61. Dorothy Holland, 1992, "The Woman Who Climbed Up the House: Some Limitations of Schema Theory," in Theodore Schwartz, Geoffrey White, and Catherine Lutz (eds.), *New Directions in Psychological Anthropology,* Cambridge, England: Cambridge University Press, p. 75.
62. D'Andrade, *The Development of Cognitive Anthropology,* p. 238.
63. Claudia Strauss, 1992, "What Makes Tony Run? Schemas as Motives Reconsidered," in Roy D'Andrade and Claudia Strauss (eds.), *Human Motives and Cultural Models,* Cambridge, England: Cambridge University Press.
64. Naomi Quinn, 1992, "The Motivational Force of Self-Understanding: Evidence from Wives' Inner Conflicts," in Roy D'Andrade and Claudia Strauss (eds.), *Human Motives and Cultural Models,* Cambridge, England: Cambridge University Press.
65. As Naomi Quinn and Dorothy Holland admit: "[Informants often] construct post hoc accounts of that behavior that are comprehensible, plausible, justifiable, and socially acceptable to themselves and other audiences, and that require a certain amount of smoothing, patching, and creative amendment to these ends." See Quinn and Holland, "Culture and Cognition," p. 7.
66. This point is made by Claudia Strauss, "Models and Motives," p. 15.

CHAPTER 10

Feeling and Being

In the United States, people tend to believe that emotions come from the center of their being; emotion is compelling, powerful, often overwhelming. People who do not feel strongly are dead and cold, lacking heart or soul; those who do feel strongly are lively and warm, full of passion and verve. Dissimulating one's feelings is a crime against the self and others; people who do so are fake and phony.

But among the Wolof speakers of Africa, only a certain group of individuals express strong emotions in public. These are the griot, the singers and poets of the society, who are thought to be passionately emotional by nature. Griot are experts in the display of emotion. Part of their profession is to communicate the feelings of the nobles whom they serve, inspiring the audience with their expressivity. The nobles, in contrast, are proud of their emotional restraint and sangfroid, which indicate their high status. While their lower-class griot servants sing their praises or express outrage on their behalf, the nobles stand silent and aloof, allowing the singers to exhibit the emotions a person of honor would never reveal.

A griot tells a story.

When considering these performances, how can we know what the griot or their noble masters really feel? Are the passionate griot faking the emotions they show so vividly; are the apathetic nobles repressing their true feelings? Or is the way emotions are understood and experienced by the Wolof actually very different from our own?[1]

These are the sorts of questions that have begun to intrigue psychological anthropologists, who have increasingly undertaken the study of emotional expression and experience in other cultures, offering their findings as a contrast to and test of Western assumptions about the nature and content of emotions. In so doing, they have added their voices, and data from their research, to a long-standing debate.

Chapter Outline

I Conceptualizing the Passions
   A Can Emotions Be Studied by Social Science?
   B Theories of Emotion
   C The Physiology of Feeling
   D The Search for the Basic Emotions

II Emotion as Embodied Thought
   A Does Culture Control Feeling?
   B The Social Construction of Emotional Control
   C Thinking-Feeling and Sociocentric Emotions

III The Dialectics of Emotion
   A Emotion and Culture
   B Hyper- and Hypocognized Emotions
   C Prototypes and Culturally Specific Emotions

I. CONCEPTUALIZING THE PASSIONS

A Can Emotions Be Studied by Social Science?
   Negative attitudes toward emotional experience.

B Theories of Emotion
   Plato, Aristotle, Aquinas, humoral-medical, Descartes. Capitalism and the taming of the passions. The romantic response.

C The Physiology of Feeling
   Physiological-adaptive theories of emotion versus cognitive evaluative theories. Modern theory: Emotions are organized and transformed by context.

D The Search for the Basic Emotions
   How many emotions are there? Which of them are fundamental? Contrasting arguments.

A. Can Emotions Be Studied by Social Science?

In the previous chapter, we considered in brief some anthropological evidence for the Cartesian hypothesis that human beings are fundamentally creatures of the mind—thinking animals who occupy themselves in constructing systems of meaning. But clearly there is more to human experience than reason alone. Romantics rebelled against the Enlightenment notion that the capacity for detached thought is the fundamental mark of humanity, arguing instead that it is emotion that makes us human; for them, authenticity was a matter of being in touch with one's feelings. Instead of human beings as thinking animals, this view portrays us as feeling machines—a vision recently popularized in science fiction, as mechanical robots struggle to experience emotion and thereby become more human.

Yet the study of emotion is a relatively recent topic in psychological anthropology. This is partly a reflection of the generally negative attitude of social sciences toward "matters of the heart." Hoping to be accepted as scientists, most anthropologists and sociologists have cautiously heeded Durkheim and Mauss's warning that emotions cannot be properly studied because they are fluid, mixed, not easily defined, and, consequently, impossible to analyze.[2] Similarly, Lévi-Strauss cautioned that "affectivity is the most obscure side of man [and]. . . what is refractory to explanation is ipso facto unsuitable for use in explanation."[3] In other words, emotions are too soft and too subjective to be appropriate topics for research by researchers seeking above all to be hard and empirical.

The obscurity of emotion is indicated in the ambiguity of the word itself: "Emotion" has its etymological origins in the Latin word *emovere,* "to move away," indicating both elusiveness and agitation. Like the notion of self, emotion is not easily translatable cross-culturally.[4] The French, for example, unite "feeling" and "emotion" in one word, *sentiment.* And even in English the use of the word "emotion" is relatively recent, dating only from the eighteenth century. Formerly, English spoke only of "the passions"—derived from the Latin *passus,* "suffered," "submitted," which suggests the overwhelming power of desire and the passivity of the individual, who is believed not to control feelings but to be enslaved by them.

Since strong emotion has been understood and experienced in the West as a force outside the range of conscious regulation, it has long served as the paradigm for irrationality: Those controlled by emotions are said to be wild, impulsive, impetuous, tempestuous, and incapable of reason. In the West, emotion has traditionally been the domain of women, who talk about their feelings twice as much as their male counterparts (though this may be rapidly changing).[5] In contrast, self-consciously rational men have, until recently, predominated in the sciences. For these men, a meaning-centered and cerebral Western model of social science naturally precluded the study of irrational and effeminate emotional states of being. From the masculine perspective, people controlled by vague yet powerful feelings cannot plan, cannot construct webs of significance, and are therefore outside the range of empirical investigation.

There is another disciplinary reason why emotion was not much studied by anthropologists or sociologists. Because emotion has been viewed in the West as a compulsive force arising in the inner core of the individual, it falls in the realm of the study of the individual personality, not within social science, the study of relationships. As a result, when emotion occasionally did become the object of scientific scrutiny, it was left entirely to professional psychologists who, naturally enough, measured, codified, and analyzed personal feelings within laboratory settings, leaving aside all cultural context.

B. Theories of Emotion

Despite the lack of social scientific interest in the emotions, the nature of the passions and their relationship to human well-being has been very much a matter of philosophical debate throughout Western history, a debate that forms current theorizing in often unexpected ways.[6] Plato was perhaps the first to talk systematically about emotion. In an argument that greatly influenced later utilitarian thinkers, he expressed his belief that all emotions could be put on a continuum between sensations of pleasure and those of pain. Painful feelings, Plato said, arose from intensity and discord; pleasure resulted from the restoration of balance. The best strategy, Plato thought, was to maintain neutrality and harmonize one's energies through the rational contemplation of the disembodied good.[7]

Aristotle (384–322 B.C.) and his followers, in contrast, were more interested in categorization and the ways emotions were connected to bodily experience and mental processes. They divided the passions into four fundamental classes: desire, fear, pleasure, pain; these were linked to pneuma, the vital spirits manifested in bodily heat or cold, and arose as a consequence of the rational appraisal of a situation.[8] This formula provided the basis for all later contextual theories of emotion.

The early Christian model, as expounded by St. Thomas Aquinas (1225–1274), combined Platonic idealism and situational-categorical aspects of the study of the feelings. For Aquinas, the body did not cause passions; rather, it was the restless movement of the soul that stimulated changes in the body: Anger is a result of the soul's appetite for vengeance, which leads to an inflamed heart and then to the felt experience of rage. All emotions, Aquinas said, were situational, aroused by various degrees of presence or absence of God's love in the human soul.

A combination of Aristotelian theory and popular medicine led to the notion of humors, which reached full flower in the medieval period. According to this doctrine, characteristic feelings were thought to predominate naturally in certain distinctive physical types. Some people were choleric (angry); others were splenetic (spiteful) or phlegmatic (dull) or melancholiac (depressed) as a consequence of their basic humors, which were shaped in turn by the relative predominance of one or the other of the elemental fluids in the body (blood, yellow bile, phlegm, black bile). This medical categorization was, in part, the origin of the later Jungian notion of archetypes.[9]

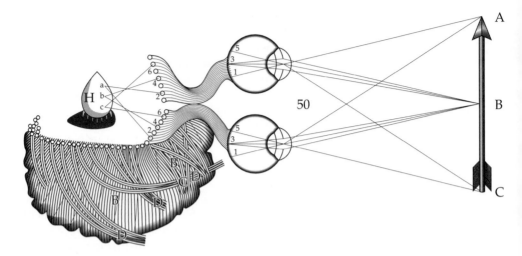

FIGURE 10.1. Sketch of the effect of visual perception on pineal gland by René Descartes.
Source: Charles Adam and Paul Tannery (eds.), 1897–1910, Oeuvres de Descartes, Vol. 11, "Les Passions de l'Ame". Paris: Leopold Cerf Publishers, (original publication 1649), no page number.

Centuries later, Descartes attempted to bring more scientific rigor to Aquinas's theory of emotion by arguing that the fundamental passions of love, hate, desire, joy, astonishment, and grief originate in an inner perception of an external disturbance that excites the movement of tangible spirits in the blood; this flux agitates the soul, which he thought was physically located in the pineal gland. (See Figure 10.1.) Ever the detached rationalist, Descartes believed emotions could be subdued and channeled by stifling any thoughts or perceptions that might arouse disturbing feelings.[10]

The early theories of emotion can be summarized as follows:

- *Plato.* Emotion is a continuum. Pleasure is neutrality and balance; pain is intensity and discord.
- *Aristotle.* Emotional states are distinct physical conditions caused by the appraisal of reality. They include desire, fear, pleasure, and pain.
- *Aquinas.* Emotion is caused by the presence or absence of God's love, which moves the soul, leading to distinctive changes in the body.
- *Humoral theory.* Emotion is a consequence of the predominance of elemental fluids in the body: Blood is associated with anger; yellow bile, with spite; phlegm, with dullness; black bile, with depression.
- *Descartes.* Emotional states are distinct physical conditions caused by external excitation of the pineal gland.

But most modern theorists of the emotions were not so optimistic as Descartes. In an argument that prefigures Freud, Nicolas Malebranche (1638–1715) stated that all vigorous and unfettered expressions of passion are highly pleasurable, whether aroused by good or evil inclinations; only frustration causes distress. As a result, the passions are very difficult to control; God's grace alone could strengthen the resolve needed to limit one's natural impulses. Similarly, Immanuel Kant believed that human feelings and appetite operate according to principles completely different from and contradictory to logic, and are not easily subdued.[11] And, as we have already seen, Hume claimed that emotion must always rule reason.

Accepting the intractable nature of sentiment, other authors argued that a better society could be built only through emphasizing certain primary emotions. As mentioned in Chapter 3, Hobbes accentuated the social importance of fear and the primal desire for self-preservation. He argued that fear and selfishness would press reasonable human beings to negotiate and enforce a pacifying social contract that would protect them all from their own worst instincts.

But the predominant theory of emotion in early modern times was put forward by utilitarian thinkers such as Jeremy Bentham who, like Plato, saw emotion primarily as a continuum between pleasure and pain. They argued that the pursuit of pleasure and avoidance of pain in a society governed by free economic exchange would naturally lead to peace and prosperity. In particular, they recommended the cultivation of the calm passion of greed, since the desire for profit would make men and women steadfast, single-minded, and methodical—and therefore resistant to the dangerous desires for glory or revenge that had caused so much violence in Europe. Greed, a deadly sin for earlier moralists, was therefore advocated by utilitarians as an impulse both morally good and socially useful, because it dominated and rationalized all other cravings.

However, as the economist and social theorist Albert O. Hirschman has remarked, there was a price to be paid for the victory of avarice over other more dangerous desires, since the new, calmer bourgeois world seemed to "lack nobility, grandeur, mystery, and, above all, passion."[12] In response to the spiritual desolation wrought by the pragmatic capitalistic fetish for methodical calculation and accumulation, a new romantic emphasis on the importance of feeling gradually developed throughout Western culture, inspiring Rousseau's assertion of his own authentic sensibility and rousing Nietzsche to praise the passionate excesses of "blond beasts." It led as well to Freud's alarming theory that a cauldron of powerful desires was seething beneath the surface of even the smoothest businessperson, erupting sometimes in symbolically disguised forms as neuroses and hysteria.

This capsule history of theories of emotion shows at minimum that concepts of feeling can affect feeling itself. The reevaluation of greed, for instance, made avarice a virtue, and many would-be capitalists subdued their more violent impulses in favor of calculated self-control. The pursuit of science also favors the cultivation of emotional detachment; nowadays the psychologist who cannot coolly dispose of a lab rat has little future in the field. Nor has all training been for restraint. When Johann Wolfgang Goethe (1749–1832) published his prototypical romantic novel, *The Sorrows of Werther,* in 1774, he inspired hundreds of young men throughout Europe to imitate his morbidly sensitive artist-hero and to commit suicide as the ultimate expression of their profound poetic sensibilities. And

---

Emotivism

The contemporary philosopher Alasdair MacIntyre has argued that the romantic and utilitarian strands have coalesced into what has been termed the modern creed of emotivism, that is, the doctrine that values and moral judgments are a matter of personal preference and can be justified simply on the grounds that they feel right for the individual.[13] The doctrine of emotivism coincided with the rise of what the educator Philip Rieff called the psychological man, for whom " 'I believe,' the cry of the ascetic, lost precedence to 'one feels,' the caveat of the therapeutic."[14] MacIntyre asserts that the modern tendency to validate judgment based on subjective taste reflects a social world in which traditional values have lost their hold, and where sacred pronouncements are no longer binding; it corresponds with an unrealistically high evaluation of individual autonomy and an unfortunate ignorance of the social consequences of action.

---

today, of course, novels (and movies) continue to provide us with larger-than-life models of how to love, how to grieve, and how to feel in every situation.

C. The Physiology of Feeling

Alongside philosophical ruminations on the ultimate nature of emotion, the scientific study of the physiology of the emotions continued apace. Advancing beyond Descartes's naive claims for the pineal gland as the physical seat of the soul, nineteenth-century French theory located emotion within the nervous system, while English-speaking theorists focused instead on processes of awareness and evaluation. Eventually, most scientific investigators followed Darwin's claim that emotions are adaptive mechanisms human beings share with their animal cousins: Fear and anger prepare the body for flight or fight, happiness is an expression of pleasure, grief of pain.[15] However, in the United States, the pragmatist philosopher John Dewey (1859–1952) suggested that emotions are a sign of conflict and interfere with adaptive activity—prefiguring the dismissive view of emotions as disorganized response that was to dominate American psychology in the middle part of the twentieth century.[16]

Thirty years later, Dewey's contemporary, the great psychologist and philosopher William James, returned to a Darwinian framework to propose that emotion is a by-product of the bodily responses caused by the stimulation of the senses. The various emotions, from this perspective, are unconscious, innate, and adaptive physiological reactions.[17] James's argument was later championed by a number of neurobiologists, who claimed that different emotions are associated with different autonomic processes and chemicals. Fear, for example, was correlated with the neurochemical epinephrine (E); anger, with norepinephrine (NE).[18]

In response to James's proposition, some psychologists argued that induced physical changes themselves do not necessarily arouse emotion, and that the same visceral changes may occur in states self-defined as emotional or as non-emotional.[19] This contextual theory was borne out by a famous (though ethically somewhat dubious) experiment conducted by the psychologists Stanley Schachter and Jerome Singer in which subjects were given injections of epinephrine, a drug that causes an accelerated heartbeat and a sense of excitement (the subjects were told it was a new drug called suproxin and that the experiment was to test the effect it had on their bodies). Some of the subjects were put into situations in which the "stooges" around them pretended to be irritated, while others were placed in situations where the stooges acted euphoric. As it turned out, the subjects interpreted the effects of their injections differently, according to context: Those surrounded by cranky people felt cranky themselves; those surrounded by happy people felt happy. Schachter and Singer concluded that the appraisal of the situation "determines whether the state of physiological arousal will be labeled as 'anger,' 'joy,' 'fear,' or whatever."[20]

To reiterate:

- *Darwin.* Emotion is physical and adaptive. As adaptive mechanisms, emotions can, for instance, prepare the body for fight or flight.
- *Dewey.* Emotion is physical and maladaptive. As a sign of conflict, emotions interfere with adaptive activity.
- *James.* Emotion is physical and adaptive. Different emotions result from different chemicals appearing in the body as responses to stimuli.
- *Schachter and Singer.* Emotion is cognitive and evaluative. The same chemical reaction can be appraised as different emotions according to circumstance.

For many, Schachter and Singer's finding appeared to invalidate any claims made for the physiological differences between emotional states, opening the door for a purely cultural and cognitive view of emotions. However, physiological explanations were soon resuscitated by more sophisticated neurobiological research on the brain, in which endorphins and other neurochemicals were discovered to have profound and quite specific effects on mood. Schachter and Singer's experimental procedures were also brought into question, both from an empirical point of view and, ironically enough, because of their failure to take into account the social relations among the subjects and the stooges.[21]

Because of these problems, a purely cognitive-evaluative theory of emotions failed to carry the day among most biologically and evolutionarily oriented psychologists, some of whom ended by arguing the equally extreme opposite case (the one already so strongly stated by Hume) that "cognitions have largely evolved in the service of emotions,"[22] or, more moderately, that emotions can exist in consciousness independent of cognition, aroused by unconscious drives or by other emotions.[23] Many psychologists, neurologists, and other researchers came to believe, as Durkheim and Freud had intuited, that choices we claim to have made for good, logical reasons may well be generated by unconscious emotional preferences encoded at a visceral level—much like the parallel processing type of learning discussed in the previous chapter.[24]

Perhaps the most balanced view was taken by Silvan Tomkins, who argued that emotion is best seen as a biological motivating system. "Without its amplification nothing else matters, and with its amplification anything else *can* matter."[25] His theory accepted the Freudian position that emotion (or affect) is the mechanism for directing the vague but potent drives arising in the unconscious. Affects rely on the innate libidinal drives for their power, and they also have certain panhuman characteristics—many of which were already known to Plato and Aristotle (sudden intense input, for instance, causes a startle reaction; increased stimulus leads to distress; lowered stimulus is pleasurable; some emotional reactions, such as disgust, are innate).

But alongside biological universals, Tomkins and other theorists admitted that the vast majority of emotional responses can be learned, blended, channeled, increased, reduced, and transformed almost infinitely, according to multiple cultural and personal inputs. It follows that cultural differences in the revelation and experience of feelings may be a result of divergent attitudes toward those particular feelings, not a consequence of differences in the innate character of the basic emotions themselves.[26] The appropriate scholarly task, then, would be to discover exactly what these fundamental emotions actually are, and how they are altered and channeled culturally.

D. The Search for the Basic Emotions

This search has proved to be a difficult enterprise indeed. As we have seen, unlike natural objects, emotions "do not form a natural class";[27] as Durkheim and Mauss warned, they are difficult even to describe, much less to name and arrange in any form of hierarchy. In consequence, despite considerable advances, the catalogue of basic emotions remains confused.

For example, the psychologist Carrol Izard has proposed eight primary emotions: interest, excitement, joy, surprise/startle, distress/anguish, disgust/contempt, anger/rage, shame/humiliation, fear/terror. Meanwhile, Paul Ekman, who, with his colleagues, has carried on Darwin's project of cross-cultural research on the emotions universally recognized on the human face, says he has discovered five essential categories—happiness, fear/surprise, sadness (or distress), anger, disgust—that can be blended in numberless ways. In con-

	Happiness	Disgust	Surprise	Sadness	Anger	Fear
United States (N = 99)	97%	92%	95%	84%	67%	85%
Brazil (N = 40)	95%	97%	87%	59%	90%	67%
Chile (N = 119)	95%	92%	93%	88%	94%	68%
Argentina (N = 168)	98%	92%	95%	78%	90%	54%
Japan (N = 29)	100%	90%	100%	62%	90%	66%

Ekman's photos of the primary emotions and the percentages of people in five cultures who correctly identified them.

trast, working from the standpoint of evolutionary adaption, Robert Plutchik has arranged a "color wheel" sequence of primary, but transient, emotions of joy, acceptance, fear, surprise, sadness, disgust, anger, and satisfaction. Mixtures of these primaries give rise to secondary, but more enduring, moods of love, submission, awe, disappointment, remorse, contempt, aggression, and optimism. (See Figure 10.2.) In contrast to this variety, the sociologist Theodore Kemper has argued for the existence of only four primary emotions—fear, anger, depression (sadness), and satisfaction (happiness)—that are culturally elaborated in an infinite variety of expressions.[28] The preceding theories are only the most well known of the many theories proposed.

It seems, then, that there is still no agreement among empirical researchers over the actual number and nature of the emotions. Nonetheless, there has been progress: Almost all categorizations of primary emotions include at least the four outlined by Kemper. According to some researchers, these emotions already can be discerned among infants only two months old, who express sadness, fear, anger, and happiness at appropriate occasions, crying to elicit care, and expressing fright at unexpected stimuli, anger when frustrated, and joy when engaged.[29] It is also recognized that emotions vary in intensity and duration; some are more gripping than others, more involving, more motivating, and more forceful: Nostalgia for the lilacs of yesteryear and overwhelming fear of a

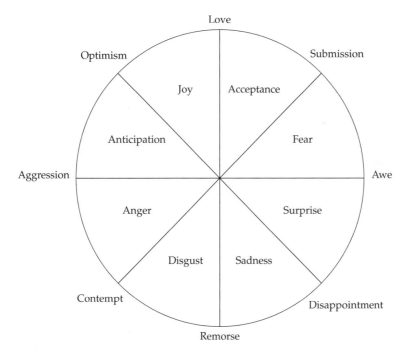

FIGURE 10.2. Robert Plutchik's "wheel" arrangement of primary (transient) and secondary (enduring) emotions.
Source: Robert Plutchik, 1982, "A Psychoevolutionary Theory of the Emotions," Social Science Information 21: 540.

Emotion and Force

The anthropologist Renato Rosaldo describes how the Ilongot headhunters he was studying always told him they killed their enemies to vent the rage caused by grief over the death of a loved one. He believed this simple answer must be wrong and, following his anthropological training, understood head-hunting instead as a form of exchange, and death as a kind of ritual event. But with the tragic accidental death of his wife Michelle (whose important work on emotion is discussed in this chapter), he realized from his own visceral experience how overwhelming rage can indeed arise from profound grief.

With his own ordeal in mind, Rosaldo has argued against anthropological work that tends to see emotion as the product of obligatory rituals; from this perspective, "wailing at the prescribed moment and in the prescribed manner creates within the wailer the proper sentiment."[31] Rather, Rosaldo says that compelling emotions can exist without ritual expression, while rituals can exist without emotional content, as mere platitudes. Eliminating the force and intensity of emotions such as anger, lust, and tenderness, Rosaldo asserts, is to dehumanize others, and to make it impossible to understand their deepest motivations.[32]

charging lion are obviously hugely different.[30] These powerful emotions need not be symbolically elaborated to be moving, and, in fact, the very simplicity of discourse about them may indicate their force. Perhaps most important for anthropologists, even evolutionary biologists agree that emotions are very definitely subject to cultural construction. The question is how.

II. EMOTION AS EMBODIED THOUGHT

A Does Culture Control Feeling?
    Claims and counterclaims.

B The Social Construction of Emotional Control
    Emotion as a resource, as a danger, and as an expression of identity.

C Thinking-Feeling and Sociocentric Emotions
    Can feeling be distinguished from thinking?

A. Does Culture Control Feeling?

For disciplinary reasons, the contributions of anthropologists to the debate about the nature of emotions have naturally emphasized the central importance of culture in the expression and experience of feeling.[33] As the anthropologist Hildred Geertz wrote in 1959, "culture presents not only a set of suggested answers on *how to behave* . . . but also clues on *how to feel* about his actions." It was nonetheless widely recognized that culturally constructed "ideas of what emotional states human beings ought to have"[34] did not necessarily accurately reflect or completely exhaust the emotional repertoires potentially available to individuals. In the light of the earlier arc of behavior model proposed by culture and personality theorists like Mead and Benedict (see Chapter 4), human emotional repertoires were assumed to be wider in range than any particular social configuration allowed—though it was never stated what the range actually was, nor what the basic emotions might be.

This vague but open-ended approach was set aside by some researchers who argued that it was not at all obvious that people in other cultures experienced the primary emotions of the West. For instance, Crow Indian men laughed about the deaths of their nearest and dearest; the Ik tribesmen of Africa seemed to have no compassion for others' suffering; men of the Iroquois bore the most hideous tortures while singing and joking; the Lepcha of Sikkim apparently had no sexual jealousy whatsoever; and the Mundurucu of South America showed no anger.[35] From this evidence it was possible to posit that emotions might be wholly culturally constituted; there was no autonomous realm of passion, no fundamental emotions felt by all humanity.

The most famous anthropologist making this argument was Clifford Geertz, who, as we saw in Chapter 7, claimed that the Balinese do not feel any emotions except for stage fright. According to Geertz, the Balinese lacked "individuality, spontaneity, perishability, emotionality, vulnerability";[36] they did not grieve at funerals, smiled regardless of stress, and devoted their entire energies to a public aesthetic performance of rituals. They were, in effect, all surface, with no depth whatsoever. Somewhat less radically, in her widely cited ethnography of the Alaskan Inuit, Jean Briggs declared that anger did not exist among her informants, who were motivated solely by feelings of nurturance and values of rationality.[37] And, in what was perhaps the most influential statement of a cultural theory of emotions, Michelle Rosaldo argued that the Ilongot tribesmen of the Philippines had the remarkable capacity to "throw away" anger at their fellows, since such anger would disrupt their egalitarian society.[38]

For some time, these strong assertions of the authority of public culture over private sentiment were allowed to stand without refutation. But in a reconsideration of her earlier findings, Briggs discovered that the Inuit child-raising techniques relied heavily on frightening questions, such as "Why don't you kill your new baby brother? Like this!" and "What a lovely new shirt. Why don't you die so I can have it?" As she writes, these proddings helped create "the awareness that one wants what one should not want, enjoys what one should fear, or fears what one should want."[39] Briggs asserted that by making children hyperaware of their antisocial temptations, Inuit socialization increased pressure on them to monitor and control their dangerous impulses, which were thought to never be far from the surface. Far from vanishing, Inuit anger was greatly feared and was held in continual check by vigilant socialization techniques.[40] Nonetheless, rage and cruelty did sometimes come to the fore, particularly in the treatment of animals, which children were encouraged not only to nurture, but also to mutilate and kill.

Geertz's portrait of the Balinese was also challenged on similar grounds by the anthropologist Unni Wikan. Undertaking fieldwork to reaffirm Geertz's research, she found instead that the outwardly calm and cheerful demeanor of Balinese

Above: Balinese men stab themselves while in possession trance.
Right: The stoic public face of a Pukhtun man.

society is deceptive. Beneath the smooth surface, the Balinese see their own and others' hearts as seething cauldrons of passions. These strong passions are extremely dangerous, so much so that the Balinese attribute one out of every four deaths to magical spells surreptitiously cast by angry hearts. Revealing their inner feelings, the Balinese believe, would expose them to spiritual attacks from one of their many secret enemies; as a result, they are careful to maintain an appearance of politeness and a smiling face.

Thus, according to Wikan, in Bali it is precisely the perpetually happy expression that indicates the turbulent depths beneath. Nonetheless, the rigorously controlled passions, urges, and drives of the Balinese do press toward the surface, exposing vulnerable elements of the self despite efforts at concealment. Those who are culturally knowledgeable can detect the quiver in the eyelid, the slight flush, that betray rigidly concealed feelings.[41] But for the uninitiated, these signs may go undetected, and the unruffled public face may be taken as inner reality. This is the mistake that Geertz made. If he had taken into account the emotionally charged content of Balinese rituals, the pervasive belief in witchcraft, and the propensity of the Balinese to spirit possession, perhaps he would not have been so easily misled.

B. The Social Construction of Emotional Control

The sort of radical emotional control found in Bali is in fact quite common in face-to-face societies where people cannot escape the long-term consequences of yielding to their immediate impulses in public. Sometimes in such cultures there is a class division of emotional labor, as among the Wolof people cited in the in-

troduction to this chapter, where the inferior griot are permitted and even required to enact the feelings more respectable persons ought not show.

More commonly, emotion is divided by gender, with men maintaining public stoicism, while women, as private creatures, are given emotional leeway. For
instance, among the Pukhtun whom I studied, an impassive demeanor was characteristic of men, while women were expected to express their feelings strongly.
At funerals men sat expressionless and silent, while women wailed and keened
hysterically in the background. The reasons for maintaining manly silence were
explained by the great Pukhtun warrior poet, Khushal Khan Khattack:

> If it is your hope never to be
> shamed before anyone
> it's best to keep within your heart
> even your least affair
>
> . . . .
>
> Let your heart bleed within itself,
> Khushal, if bleed it must,
> but keep your secrets well concealed
> from both stranger and friend.[42]

Nor is the control and manipulation of emotional expression found only in
primitive societies. As Norbert Elias (1897–1990) has shown, members of the
court society of France's Louis XIV (who reigned from 1654 to 1715) had to be
willing and able to enact emotional states that were pleasing to their superiors
and, of course, to keep their own immediate reactions strictly in check. Theirs
was a theatrical world of extreme sophistication and duplicity, as the courtier La
Bruyère attested in his memoirs:

> A man who knows the court is master of his gestures, of his eyes and his ex-
> pression; he is deep, impenetrable. He dissimulates the bad turns he does,
> smiles at his enemies, suppresses his ill-temper, disguises his passions, dis-
> avows his heart, acts against his feelings.[43]

Behind their well-controlled surface masks, the courtiers (like the Pukhtun)
had feelings much like our own, though their attitudes toward their feelings differed: We believe that to maintain mental health and personal authenticity,
we ought to express our emotions; they believed that for safety and self-
aggrandizement, they must disguise their strong feelings and (in the case of the
courtiers) express false emotions. The Pukhtun hid his feelings beneath a stoical
mask because of a well-founded fear that revealing them would give enemies
an advantage in a competitive and egalitarian environment. The courtier simulated false feelings to gain the confidence of the ruler in a never-ending game of
influence inside the closed hierarchical universe of the palace.

Obviously, the social structures of the two cultures are very different, but
there are underlying parallels that have significance for the way emotion is expressed in them. In both Pukhtun and court society, members are locked into
place in highly personalized, antagonistic, densely articulated social structures.
The Pukhtun social structure is based on the relationships between patrilineal
relatives, who continually struggle with one another for ephemeral positions of

Elias's Historical Psychology

Norbert Elias was a brilliant theorist and historian who wedded Weberian sociology with Freudian theory to construct what he called an historical psychology. He claimed that the civilizing process—that is, the evolution of more anonymous, interdependent, complex, and hierarchical societies—required the suppression of strong emotions, such as anger. In the absence of traditional social controls, these dangerous emotions had to be internally restrained, despite the psychic costs of increased frustration and anxiety.

Elias's theory of the civilizing process was illustrated through his history of manners. In the past, as Elias documented, behaviors that we find offensive were common. Our ancestors farted and belched freely, picked their teeth with table knives, wiped their hands on their clothes, slept together in a common bed, ate out of a common bowl, and blew their noses in their shirttails. The development of a cultivated etiquette coincided with larger processes of social mobility and alienation; it coincided as well with a heightened fantasy life, as revealed in greater artistic concern with acts of violence and sexuality.

Elias's work is powerful and convincing, particularly when he deals with the intertwined evolution of guilt and social controls in the West. But it suffers from unfounded assumptions that primitive societies are invariably bloodthirsty, vulgar, and generally more moved by unconstrained desire than more complex social formations.[44]

dominance. Similarly, the courtier seeks to advance his career at the expense of his rivals in a closed social system, though in this case the system is structured not by kinship, but by the absolute authority of the king. These sorts of constricted social systems favor a strong ethos of emotional constraint, both for purposes of protection and for purposes of manipulation.[45]

In contrast, consider the emotional life of another group: the Yanomamo, mobile swidden agriculturalists of the Northern Brazilian jungles, who are famous for their habitual public posture of rage. Whereas the Pukhtun wear a stoic mask defensively and manipulate their moods for advantage, the Yanomamo usually aim to intimidate with their appearance. But even though the Yanomamo pose is aggressive, it is often simulated, a bluff, and therefore resembles the masking behavior of the courtiers and Pukhtun.

There are, however, several differences in the three patterns of emotional masking that place the Yanomamo in an analytic category separate from those of the Pukhtun and the courtier. One difference is that the Yanomamo do not always portray themselves as enraged. They have a variety of other faces that they wear at appropriate times in public life. But their ethnography indicates that it is only rage that is consistently dissembled. This is unlike both the French, whose every emotion is carefully constructed, and the Pukhtun, who show almost no emotion in public.

In another sense, however, the Yanomamo fierce face is similar to the play-acting of the courtier, since imitating enraged behavior is a pretense aimed at de-

Segmentary Lineage Organizations

The Pukhtun have a social organization technically known by anthropologists as an acephalous segmentary lineage system. The classical form of this leaderless system was described by E. E. Evans-Pritchard (1902–1973) in his famous book on the Nuer cattle nomads of Africa.[46] According to Evans-Pritchard, in disputes the Nuer aligned themselves in relatively equal segments according to their genealogical distance from a common patrilineal ancestor. (See Figure 10.3.) The principle of alliance is put succinctly in a Middle Eastern proverb: I against my brothers; my brothers and I against my [patrilateral] cousins; my brothers and my [patrilateral] cousins against the world. The genealogical rela-

tionships between segments tend to be replicated on the ground, so that close patrilateral relatives live contiguously. Segments tend only to coalesce in contests with one another, and the principle of complementary opposition (the balancing out of equivalent units) theoretically prohibits any from ever gaining ascendance over the others.

Of course, the actual workings of political alliances may vary considerably from the ideal. Nonetheless, the principles of segmentary organization play a central ideological role in constraining and structuring all forms of conflict and alliances among groups such as the Pukhtun.[47]

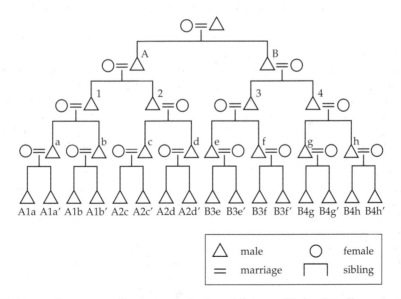

FIGURE 10.3. Segmentary lineage organization. All A are allied politically against all B, all A1 against all A2, all A1a against all A1b, and so on.
Source: Charles Lindholm, The Islamic Middle East: An Historical Anthropology; *Oxford: Basil Blackwell, p. 57.*

The fierce expression of a Yanomamo man.

luding and frightening an enemy, like the fearsome body paint or awe-inspiring costumes utilized in other warlike cultures, and like the courtier's dissembling of his true feelings to gain advantage. But this similarity is a superficial one. It is evident from the ethnographic record that the Yanomamo's elaborate system of feasts, duels, and sanctioned violence not only serves to give men the opportunity to display anger and therefore frighten enemies, just as the courtier's display aims to fool his rivals, but also, as the most famous ethnographer of the Yanomamo notes, has the purpose of goading the subject "into the appropriate state of rage for the business of killing enemies."[48]

In Swat and France, in contrast, the performance is primarily for the other, not for the self, and any merger between outward expression and internal feeling is unintended and undesirable. The Pukhtun wishes simply to hide his feelings beneath a shell of invulnerability; the courtier has the more complex task of both hiding his real feelings and displaying false ones. But neither wants to make the inner and the outer correspond—quite the contrary.

Why does this difference exist? Although the Yanomamo are like the Pukhtun in many respects, especially in their intense internal antagonisms, Yanomamo rivalry is not structured as is Pukhtun opposition. The Yanomamo do not, in fact, have anything resembling a comprehensive lineage structure, and their major allies are men who are unrelated to them. Furthermore, they are highly mobile, both as individuals and as groups, shifting from place to place and from group to group as circumstances demand. The flexibility and relative freedom of choice in the Yanomamo system is a far cry from the long-term and highly systematic genealogical (and geographical) linkages that locate and lock all the thousands of Pukhtun into one complex and well-articulated network within which each man knows his place, his duties, and his potential enemies and allies. Nor, more obviously, do the Yanomamo resemble the French court, united under the authority of the absolute monarch. It is the absence of structure in their exceptionally malleable world that helps explain the Yanomamo proclivity for merging inner feeling and outward display.

Within the pliable but hostile universe of the Yanomamo, the sanctioned expression of anger and the effort to incite anger through this expression may be seen as a way of invoking and experiencing the self in the absence of overarching and well-articulated structural or political constraints, constraints which provide, among other things, a mechanism for maintaining identity and gaining respect. The Yanomamo lack the organized structure so evident in France and Swat. They pretend fierceness not only to proclaim their identity to others, but also because they wish to live out a socially valorized emotional reality within themselves. In their performance, they become not only what they need to be in order to defend themselves but also what they ought to be in order to be proper men. In contrast, in Swat and France the structure gives a predetermined and highly constricted social status, one that is perhaps too solid for comfort, but that does offer an absolute grounding for the construction of personal identity.

In this theoretical perspective we expect to find other relatively loose societies such as the Yanomamo, which also imitate favored emotions in order to experience them. The content of the dominant emotion in each case will, of course, vary. Modesty, for instance, may be an equivalent pose in one society, while another society may habitually feign expressions of interest, or of dependency, or of joy, in hopes of actually feeling the emotions that are culturally favored. Thus the Balinese smile in the hope of actually becoming happy.

Social organization is therefore likely to have profound effects on the way individuals experience emotion. This truism operates as much within our own society as it does in others, as has been proved by the sociologist Arlie Hochschild. She has argued persuasively that changes in the economy have led to increasing concern among Americans about the authenticity of their own feelings and the feelings of others. This is because more people in the United States are now working in service industries, work that involves constant public interaction with customers and a high degree of emotional control. This pervasive "emotion work" can have pernicious effects. In her study of airline stewardesses (now called flight attendants), Hochschild found workers were required to be always smiling and friendly, regardless of their own moods. The obligatory maintenance of cheerfulness led many to experience deep feelings of self-estrangement and even a sense of emotional deadness. As Hochschild puts it: "When the product—the thing to be engineered, mass-produced, and subjected

An emotion worker: Airline stewardesses are required to look friendly while on the job.

to speed-up and slowdown—is a smile, a mood, a feeling, or a relationship, it comes to belong more to the organization and less to the self. And so in the country that most publicly celebrates the individual, more people privately wonder, without tracing the question to its deepest social root: What do I really feel?"[49] It is in reaction to the management of feeling that the value of authentic emotion, free of restraint or obligation, has risen greatly in the United States.

C. Thinking-Feeling and Sociocentric Emotions

Although the Pukhtun and the French courtiers work to control and even to manipulate their emotions, and the Yanomamo strive to become the angry men they wish to be, and Americans search for authenticity, and the Balinese try to be eternally happy, there is no suggestion that the fundamental feelings these groups are working on are essentially different—only that they are expressed in different manners.

However, a number of authors have indeed argued that in some other cultures, emotions are experienced in a way that is quite distinct. For example, Wikan says that the Balinese do not clearly distinguish thought and feeling— they think with their feelings and feel with their thoughts. There is also no unconscious in Balinese folk psychology: Emotions are not internal, but are believed to be socially generated by specific situations and quite controllable.

The Balinese ethnopsychology would seem, then, to portray an emotional life that is indeed quite at odds with anything experienced in the Western world. From Wikan's evidence, it is clear that the Balinese—like many other people— do not have the same notion of emotional authenticity as modern Westerners do; emotion is believed not to exist prior to thought, and the Balinese, like the Yanomamo, presume that by changing the exterior expression of emotion, one can, over time, change the internal feeling. As the Balinese say, "laughter *makes* happiness, it takes sadness out" and "if you only think good thoughts, it is impossible to feel sad."[50] In contrast, modern Westerners believe that despite ap-

---

Techniques of Acting

The contrast between the American and Balinese theories of emotion is somewhat similar to the contrast between the American and British styles of acting. American method actors believe that to play a part, one must deeply feel what the character is supposed to be feeling, and to do so, reach into one's own past to reexperience equivalent moments of pain, anger, disappointment, and the like that will then be expressed by the character played on stage. In contrast, British actors believe that attention to surface detail in the creation of a part is sufficient. One needn't feel sad in order to act sad; in fact, acting out the appearance of sadness with great dexterity will touch the audience more powerfully than the attempt to resurrect truly felt emotions, which can sweep away the actor's control. But the parallel between Balinese and Western theories of emotion and British and American acting techniques does not quite hold, since the British actor performing an emotion does not at all wish to feel the emotions portrayed, while the American actor is trying mightily to dredge emotion up from the inside that will make the performance "authentic."

---

pearances, felt emotions will continue to have their effect—as revealed in blushes and other inadvertent bodily signs. Even the courtiers did not think that smiling at one's enemy would eventually lead one to like him.

It is evident, then, that the Balinese ethnopsychology of emotion differs quite radically from our own. But does the difference in belief make for an equally deep difference in experience? In fact, the evidence for the actual unification of emotion and cognition among the Balinese is not convincing, since the Balinese themselves sometimes distinguish between the two and debate over which takes precedence. Also, dangerous feelings (those of anger and profound sadness) clearly have the power to overwhelm, despite the folk theory that a person ought to be able to control them and laugh them away. Nor are all feelings capable of being cognized or manipulated, as we see when Wikan asks a young woman why she is writing poetry for her dead beloved, and the woman "said she did not know, she just felt like that."[51] Furthermore, the strong tendency of the Balinese toward immersion in possession trance is not well explicated by the indigenous model of mental control over "feeling-thoughts." Obviously, those Balinese convulsed in a trance are hardly in conscious control of their emotions. A better causal explanation for this experience has been put forward by ethnographer Linda Connor, who sees violent Balinese trance behavior as a way to release pent-up feelings without having to take any direct personal responsibility for them.[52] This makes good sense in the psychologically threatening environment described by Wikan.

In stressing the unity of thought and feeling, and the absence of an unconscious, Wikan has followed the lead of a number of ethnopsychologists who have worked in the Pacific. Most notable among them is Catherine Lutz, who has championed a positive sociocentric concept of feeling-thoughts, in opposition to Western views of emotion as "a psychobiological structure and an aspect of the individual."[53] According to Lutz, the individualistic Western view of feeling can be traced to the rise of Cartesian positivism and a masculine Enlightenment rationality that split the body off from the mind, rendering the former inferior to the latter, and demeaning "feminine" emotionality.[54] She makes an alternative claim that emotion ought to be viewed as a positive moral force, relational and nurturant, drawing people together in communities of shared feeling.[55]

Since she conceives emotion primarily in terms of nurturance (she ignores emotions such as anger or contempt), it is appropriate that Lutz's major example of a feeling-thought is taken from her research on the small, peaceful, and non-competitive Pacific island of Ifaluk. The central feeling-thought there is *fago*, which translates as a combination of compassion, love, and sadness. Fago is said to be an automatic consequence of relationships of mutual exchange. As one woman says: "I fago you because you give me things . . . If I take care of you, give you things, and talk to you, I'll know you fago me." Yet fago turns out to be not quite as nurturant as it seems on the surface, since Lutz explains it as a functional technique for "sanctioning the display of resources and abilities in the act of helping others";[56] in other words, beneath nurturance is a hidden agenda—a quest for power in a small-scale social universe where overt power seeking is repudiated. Through fago, individuals can dominate one another by the supposedly selfless giving of succor.

A number of ethnopsychological studies have emulated Lutz in claiming that many cultures also see emotion not as a private inner experience, but as a consequence of typical public relationships: A person will always feel x when another person does y. Emotions in these cultures are described not in terms of personal stimuli and uncontrollable inner sensations as they are in the West (he acted so coldly that I just boiled over with rage) but in terms of formal obligations and public relationships (my cousin did not give the proper offerings at the ceremony, so I was angry). They also follow her in focusing on the way emotion is correlated with power and social hierarchy.[57] From this perspective, the claim is made that all emotion can properly be understood as a form of cognitive assessment that in some mysterious fashion arouses the body as well as the mind. This point of view is put most cogently by the anthropologist Michelle Rosaldo, whose work on the Ilongot has already been mentioned:

> What distinguishes thought and affect, differentiating a "cold" cognition from a "hot," is fundamentally a sense of the engagement of the actor's self. Emotions are thoughts somehow "felt" in flushes, pulses, "movements" of our livers, minds, hearts, stomachs, skin. They are *embodied* thoughts, thoughts steeped with the apprehension that "I am involved."[58]

As in the model put forward by Schachter and Singer, emotions are seen here as socially constituted and reflective of the conscious mental constructions that make up culture; they are the way the cultural habitus of power is embedded (or resisted) within the physical being of the relational self.

There is much to be said for this point of view, which is now dominant in the anthropological study of emotion. By emphasizing the way emotional rhetoric is deployed for political purposes, theorists of this school have opened up an important and fruitful avenue of research.[59] But the effort to bring the emotions within the range of cultural analysis through the route of cognition and ethnopsychology has ended by locating emotion in verbal definitions, which are then said to give the experience its content, so that thoughts and words alone determine the individual's reaction to the world.[60] From this perspective, emotions have no autonomy, no structure; there are no drives, no repression, no conflicts between internal desire and external constraint, no variations in emotional intensity and force. Feelings serve simply as the physical expression of authority (or resistance to authority). So, in principle, it would seem that anything can be felt, so long as it is expressed and defined in discourse.

III. THE DIALECTICS OF EMOTION

A Emotion and Culture
The case against cultural dominance over emotional experience, and for a dialectical relationship.

B Hyper- and Hypocognized Emotions
Cultural repression and elaboration of emotions.

C Prototypes and Culturally Specific Emotions
Universal emotions and emotions that are culturally unique. Ethnographic and linguistic cases.

A. Emotion and Culture

As we have seen, a convincing array of physiological and evolutionary evidence indicates that emotions are neither infinitely malleable, nor totally cognitive, nor completely relational; nor is the quest for power the only motivation of human beings. Primary affects are more varied than this, and the drives that impel them do have some autonomy, force, and structure, and press toward expression no matter how thoroughly they are denied. This more balanced case for a *dialectical* relationship between emotion and culture has increasingly been accepted by anthropologists.

For example, both Melford Spiro and Charles Nuckolls have disputed claims made by Lutz in her work in Ifaluk, and Michelle Rosaldo in her ethnography of the Ilongot of the Philippines, that individuals can be wholly public and situational in their emotional experiences. This assertion is undermined by Rosaldo's admission that the Ilongot themselves make the "despairing claim that 'one can never know the hidden reaches of another's heart.' " The same denial of cognitive awareness and assertion of privacy and inwardness was also made by people of Ifaluk, who told Lutz in response to her questions about their emotions that "we cannot see our insides" and so cannot be absolutely sure about what is going on there, and particularly so in the case of others' insides.[61]

Nor is it the case, Nuckolls and Spiro maintain, that the Ilongot and Ifaluk peoples can throw away anger. Spiro points out that the Ilongot were notorious headhunters, who say themselves that the act of murder is a powerful way of relieving feelings of grief. Such killing, Spiro argues, was also a way for the Ilongot to displace and express rage at their own fellows—an argument that makes good sense of the data. This reasoning does not hold for the Ifaluk, who are a nonviolent people. Yet all is not peaceful there either; as in Bali, the apparent surface harmony of their society is marred by an overwhelming sense of fear, in this case fear of ghosts and an unrealistic anxiety about the sharing of food. Nuckolls understands these frightening aspects of Ifaluk emotional life as transformations of the anger caused by a severe suppression of childhood sibling competition over the affection of the mother. The compassionate emotion of fago, from Nuckoll's perspective, is to be seen not as a way to assert power, but rather, as a demand for fusion and dependency denied in infancy. The strong value placed on charity and empathy coincides with an equally powerful, though repressed, threat of anger. Sociocentric societies, Nuckoll's plausibly argues, are always torn by ambivalence over egoism; the public affirmation of harmony always conceals inner resentment.

Other anthropological studies of exotic emotional systems have come to similar universalistic conclusions. We have already seen how Jean Briggs later repudiated her own picture of the Inuit as incapable of anger, and how Geertz's portrait of the eternally smiling Balinese was overturned by Wikan's in-depth study. Both of these cases indicate that a more universalistic and balanced view of emotional structure makes better sense of the data.

For example, it has long been known that Samoans, like the people of Ifaluk and other Pacific islands, do not speak of physical states when they talk of emotions, but of stereotyped situations and appropriate responses. Ethnopsychologists have sometimes taken this discourse as indicating that their actual feelings are equally detached and relational. But as the ethnographer Ruth Gerber has argued, when Samoans are engaged in an emotionally loaded situation, it is easy to see the physiological signs of strong affects (flushing, tears, clenched teeth), despite the fact that these signs are unmentioned. Like the Ilongot and Ifaluk, Samoans also vehemently deny the existence of certain feelings, especially any resentment toward one's parents, since such animosity is considered absolutely immoral. Nonetheless, Samoans sometimes do lose control of this pool of unexpressed anger, which floods into violence. This occurs especially during periodic drinking bouts, when a drunken man vents his rage against his peers, not against his elders; such violence is not owned by the perpetrator—he was under the influence of alcohol—and therefore it has no subversive meaning. (Alcohol has a similar function in the United States, allowing actions forbidden in daily life. See Chapter 11 for more on this subject.) By such unconscious balancing mechanisms, the equilibrium between social constraint and proscribed emotional impulse is maintained.[62]

B. Hyper- and Hypocognized Emotions

While the Ifaluk, Ilongot, and Samoans deny anger, Robert Levy has shown that the Tahitians do the opposite; among them anger is hypercognized; that is, there is a large vocabulary available for discussing it. Sadness, in contrast, is minimally elaborated; it is hypocognized. This means that in situations where we would talk about grief, the Tahitians talk about sensations of fatigue, aches and pains, and other forms of physical distress (I have been feeling tired since my mother died). Sadness is somatized as an objective perception of a bodily state, but not felt to be subjectively involving. (Levy calls the first state a feeling; the second, an emotion. His useful distinction makes emotion an internalized and subjective subsystem of the larger objective physical category of feeling.) Yet the lack of a vocabulary available to describe sadness does not mean that grief disappears. On the contrary, Levy demonstrates that the emotions denied in discourse are nonetheless subjectively manifested in powerful and uncanny ways, for example, as ego-alien sensations of being overcome by malevolent spirits or illness.

Anger and sadness are not the only emotions repressed and then revealed in disguised forms. As indicated in Chapter 7, among the rivalrous Pukhtun whom I studied, the advice of their poet made very good sense:

> The eye of the dove is lovely, my son,
> but the sky is made for the hawk.
> So cover your dovelike eyes
> and grow claws.[63]

Yet even in this antagonistic universe, hidden desires for love, mutuality, and nurturance were indirectly expressed in rituals of generosity and bonds of friendship. Deprived of attachment in reality, the Pukhtun sought it in ritual and idealized relationships.[64] I should think the same would occur in any society where fundamental emotions are forbidden or denied.

C. Prototypes and Culturally Specific Emotions

Levy's ethnographically based conclusion that "the central tendencies named by various emotional terms are probably universal but that the borders of the categories may differ"[65] has been seconded by the experientialist linguist George Lakoff, who was cited in the previous chapter. Lakoff has argued that when anger is metaphorically or metonymically conceptualized, it will always be seen as an increase in body heat, pressure, and agitation, building within the container of the body until there is an explosion. People are red-hot and ready to burst when they are inflamed with rage. This linguistic prototype corresponds remarkably well with the actual physiology of anger; thus "the physiology corresponding to each emotion has a great deal to do with how the emotion is conceptualized."[66] Cognitive anthropologists have made similar assertions for the continuity of emotional experience, as when an experiment demonstrated that there was a remarkable cross-cultural correlation in the colors people picked to represent various primary emotions.[67]

But what about emotional categories that do not exist across cultures? There are several possibilities. The first is that some culturally specific emotions are simply unique mixtures of basic feeling-states that, after all, do not have hard-

and-fast boundaries. Different cultures will therefor emphasize different blend-ings: as we have seen, the Ifaluk concept of fago mingles compassion, love, and sadness; the Inuit have a parallel category of nallik, implying nurturance, love, pity, and the suppression of all anger. Ekman found in his survey of facial ex-pressions that many preliterate societies merge fear and surprise. But even though some cultures may separate categories of emotion that others mix and elaborate experiences that other societies do not, this does not mean there is no common substrate. We have already cited the consensus among neurobiologists and psychologists that such a substrate exists. Though its exact contents are a matter of controversy, they must include at least the four basic emotions of fear, anger, depression, and satisfaction.

There also are culturally specific emotions that are barely emotions at all, since they do not move anyone; they are vague feeling-states like nostalgia for the lilies of the field—narrowly defined, shallow, and culturally specific, with little if any motivating affect behind them. According to Ruth Gerber, the Samoan concept of respect may be one such shallow feeling; while some Samoans say it is indeed a feeling inside, most say it is merely a form of ritual behavior. Nonetheless, such affectless affects probably are modeled after more highly charged feelings, in this case, a combination of love and fear.[68]

Another possibility is that the unique emotional category may be a cultur-ally specific transformation of a more fundamental impulse. One example is the Japanese emotion of *amae*, defined by the Japanese psychiatrist Takeo Doi as an asymmetric adult bond of helpless dependency modeled after early infantile attachment. In manifesting amae, Japanese subordinates commonly act in a childlike and dependent way toward superiors, expecting to elicit nurturance in return. This highly valued emotion—often called passive love—favors "a con-siderable blurring of the distinction between subject and object."[69]

Amae makes sense in the intensely group-oriented and hierarchical atmos-phere of Japan, where it obliges a kindly superior to offer protection and provides a safe way to indulge oneself by acting helpless in a needy manner. But it is an emotional constellation that is neither recognized nor valued in the United States, where personal independence is prized and where public expressions of helplessness and dependency among adults are strongly disapproved. Yet this does not mean that a need for nurturance and attachment is biologically unim-portant for Westerners, only that we have ways of expressing it that are cultur-ally specific. One way, as I shall argue in Chapter 12, is romantic love.[70]

As a result of these and other arguments, overbalanced anthropological claims for the power of culture over emotion have of late been very much muted. Even the cultural psychologist Richard Shweder, who has often vehe-mently argued for a relativist, interpretive view of culture, concedes that "it is ludicrous to imagine that the emotional functioning of people in different cul-tures is basically the same. It is just as ludicrous to imagine that each culture's emotional life is unique."[71] We can determine then that an adequate psycholog-ical anthropology ought not try to prove that every culture is emotionally unique (this is both obvious and fruitless), but that differences are culturally mo-tivated variations resting upon a common psychic ground. The real task is the double one of seeking to discover what that ground may be and of finding what factors determine the alternative paths taken in the repression, expression, and interpretation of desire.

Summary

Emotions are, as any number of theorists have noted, extremely difficult to study. Compelling, ambiguous, and subjective, they have served in the West as the epitome of the irrational. But they are also perhaps the most powerful motivating factors in our lives, and so have been the object of intellectual discourse for a very long time indeed. Many theories of emotion have been proposed, some of them concerned primarily with evaluation, others with typology. Emotions have also been the object of rational control, and have been apostrophized as the seat of true humanity. They have been seen as internally generated and as completely reflective of context.

Despite controversy, it is now recognized that emotions do have distinctive and universal physiological content, that they serve as a biological system of motivation. It is also recognized that some emotions are fundamental and powerful, while others are peripheral and less gripping. But exactly what these fundamental emotions are remains controversial, though there seems to be general agreement that fear, anger, sadness, and happiness ought to be included.

Some anthropologists have been slow to accept these findings and have tended instead to argue that emotions are completely culturally constructed. The Balinese, for example, have been said to have no feelings at all, while the Inuit feel no anger and the Ilongot can throw anger away. Yet restudies have discovered that these are overstatements that do not do justice to the complexity of the emotional experience of these peoples.

It is clear, though, that emotion is regulated differently in various cultures, with some strongly favoring masking or even simulating emotions for pragmatic purposes, while others alter their expression of feeling in the belief that this will change their inner reality. These differences are related to differences in social structure: Tight yet competitive structures where people have a known status and role are more likely to manipulate or mask feeling; looser and more ambiguous systems lead members to define themselves through the public expression of appropriate emotional states.

But if different societies have different concepts of emotion, does this mean that feelings themselves differ? Many anthropologists now argue that some cultures do not see emotion in Western fashion as internal, personal, and powerful. Instead, for them, emotion is public, relational, and controllable—an embodied form of thought. However, there are contradictions in this argument—not the least of which is the difficulty of accounting for the motivations of others in ways that do not simply reduce all interactions to quests for power. Also, conflating thought with emotion has the unintended consequence of reducing the autonomy of emotion. Feeling becomes another mode of discourse and thus all but disappears.

What is needed instead is a more dialectical view of emotion and culture as realms of being that are intertwined and mutually interrelated, but do not wholly overlap. Some emotions may be hypercognized, others may be hardly spoken of at all, yet the latter do not vanish and may appear in symbolic or somatic forms. Certainly, culturally specific emotional forms do indeed exist, as blends or as modifications of deeper drives. Nonetheless, for the anthropological study of emotion to go forward, it must be admitted that all human beings share a common heritage. To argue that fundamental emotional impulses exist and are engaged in a dialectic with cultural constraints does not undermine anthropological analysis. Instead, this premise provides a better basis for comparative work and, perhaps more importantly, gives a basis for the humane anthropological claim that others are not so different from ourselves. They too are driven by contradictory desires for attachment and for autonomy; they too are subject to fears, anxieties, and grief; they too are transported by love and communion.

Endnotes

1. For a discussion, see Judith Irvine, 1990, "Registering Affect: Heteroglossia in the Linguistic Expression of Emotion," in Catherine Lutz and Lila Abu-Lughod (eds.), *Language and the Politics of Emotion* Cambridge, England: Cambridge University Press; 1982, "Language and Affect: Some Cross Cultural Issues," in Heidi Byrnes (ed.), *Contemporary Perceptions of Language: Interdisciplinary Dimensions,* Washington DC: Georgetown University Press.
2. Émile Durkheim and Marcel Mauss, 1963, *Primitive Classification,* Chicago: University of Chicago Press, p. 87 (original publication 1904).
3. Claude Lévi-Strauss, 1963, *Totemism,* Boston: Beacon Press, p. 69.
4. This point is made by Anna Wierzbicka, 1993, "A Conceptual Basis for Cultural Psychology," *Ethos* 21: 205–31.
5. This argument has been made by Catherine Lutz, 1988, *Unnatural Emotions: Everyday Sentiments on a Micronesian Atoll and Their Challenge to Western Theory,* Chicago: University of Chicago Press. For a condensed version, see Catherine Lutz, 1990, "Engendered Emotion: Gender, Power, and the Rhetoric of Emotional Control in American Discourse," in Catherine Lutz and Lila Abu-Lughod (eds.), *Language and the Politics of Emotion,* Cambridge, England: Cambridge University Press.
6. For a good discussion, see H. M. Gardiner, Ruth Metcalf, and John Beebe-Center, 1937, *Feeling and Emotion: A History of Theories,* New York: American Book Company. The next few pages owe much to their work.
7. Plato, 1972, *Phaedrus,* Cambridge, England: Cambridge University Press.
8. See Aristotle, 1962, *Nicomanchean Ethics,* Tenth book, Indianapolis, IN: Bobbs-Merrill; 1991, *Rhetoric,* Second book, New York: Oxford University Press.
9. Discussed in Chapter 5.
10. See Descartes, 1897–1910, "Les Passions de l'Ame," In Charles Adam and Paul Tannery (eds.) *Oeuvres de Descartes,* Vol. 11. Paris: Leopold Cerf Publishers, (Original publication 1649).
11. See Immanuel Kant, 1931, *Critique of Judgement,* London: Macmillan (original publication 1781); 1977, *Anthropology from a Pragmatic Point of View,* Carbondale: Southern Illinois University Press (original publication 1798). In the latter work, Kant differentiates passions, long-lasting dispositions (*leidenschaften*), from short-term emotions of pleasure and pain (*affekle*). Both stand irreducibly opposed to moral reason.
12. Albert O. Hirschman, 1977, *The Passions and the Interests: Political Arguments for Capitalism before Its Triumph,* Princeton, NJ: Princeton University Press, p. 132.
13. Alasdair MacIntyre, 1981, *After Virtue: A Study in Moral Theory,* London: Duckworth.
14. Philip Rieff, 1987, *The Triumph of the Therapeutic: Uses of Faith after Freud,* Chicago: University of Chicago Press, p. 25.
15. See Charles Darwin, 1965, *The Expression of Emotions in Man and Animals,* Chicago: University of Chicago Press (original publication 1872).
16. John Dewey, 1894, "A Theory of Emotion," *Psychological Review* 1: 553–69.
17. C. Lange and W. James, 1922, *The Emotions,* New York: Macmillan, Hafner Press.
18. For a seminal article in this argument, see D. Funkenstein, 1955, "The Physiology of Fear and Anger," *Scientific American* 192: 74–80.
19. W. Cannon, 1927, "The James–Lange Theory of Emotion: A Critical Examination and an Alternative Theory," *American Journal of Psychology* 39: 106–24.

20. Stanley Schachter and Jerome Singer, 1962, "Cognitive, Social and Psychological Determinants of Emotional States," *Psychological Review* 69: 379–99, 380.
21. For a synopsis of this controversy, see Theodore Kemper, 1987, "How Many Emotions Are There? Wedding the Social and the Autonomic Components," *American Journal of Sociology* 93: 263–89.
22. Robert Plutchik, 1982, "A Psychoevolutionary Theory of the Emotions," *Social Science Information* 21: 529–53, 544.
23. For the best statements of this perspective, see Carrol Izard, 1971, *The Face of Emotion*, New York: Appleton-Century-Crofts; 1972, *Patterns of Emotions*, New York: Academic Press; 1977, *Human Emotions*, New York: Plenum.
24. See R. Zajonc, 1980, "Feeling and Thinking: Preferences Need No Inferences," *American Psychologist* 35: 151–75.
25. Silvan Tomkins, 1982, "Affect Theory," in P. Ekman (ed.), *Emotion in the Human Face*, Cambridge, England: Cambridge University Press, pp. 355–56. Similarly, anthropologist David Parkin writes: "Emotions are non-judgmental shapers of decisions. That is to say, emotions act autonomously, or at least appear to do so, in giving sense to an interpretation, not through comparison with other possible decisions, but by making *that* particular interpretation seem fitting." See David Parkin, 1985, "Reason, Emotion and the Embodiment of Power," in Joanna Overing (ed.), *Reason and Morality*, London: Tavistock, p. 142.
26. Carrol Izard, 1980, "Cross Cultural Perspectives on Emotion and Emotion Communication," in H. Triandis (ed.), *Handbook of Cross-Cultural Psychology*, Boston: Allyn and Bacon.
27. Amélie Rorty, 1980, "Explaining Emotions," in A. Rorty (ed.), *Explaining Emotions*, Berkeley: University of California Press, p. 104.
28. Izard, "Cross Cultural Perspectives on Emotion and Emotion Communication"; Paul Ekman, Wallace Friesen, and Pheobe Ellsworth, 1982, "What Emotion Categories or Dimensions Can Observers Judge from Facial Behavior?" and "What Are the Similarities and Differences in Facial Behavior across Cultures?" in P. Ekman (ed.), *Emotion in the Human Face*, Cambridge, England: Cambridge University Press; Plutchik, "A Psychoevolutionary Theory of the Emotions"; Kemper, "How Many Emotions Are There?" For his full account, see Theodore Kemper, 1978, *A Social Interactional Theory of Emotion*, New York: Wiley.
29. Colwyn Trevarthen, 1984, "Emotions in Infancy: Regulators of Contact and Relationships with Persons," in Klaus Scherer and Paul Ekman (eds.), *Approaches to Emotion*, Hillsdale, NJ: Erlbaum, p. 152.
30. Rorty, "Explaining Emotions."
31. Richard Huntington and Peter Metcalf, 1979, *Celebrations of Death: The Anthropology of Mortuary Ritual*, Cambridge, England: Cambridge University Press, p. 26.
32. Renato Rosaldo, 1983, "Grief and a Headhunter's Rage: On the Cultural Force of Emotions," in Edward Bruner (ed.), *Text, Play, and Story: The Construction and Reconstruction of Self and Society*, Proceedings of the American Ethnological Society, Washington, DC.
33. For reviews of the anthropological literature on emotion, see Catherine Lutz and Geoffrey White, 1986, "The Anthropology of Emotions," *Annual Review of Anthropology* 15: 405–36; Janis Jenkins, 1994, "The Psychocultural Study of Emotion and Mental Disorder," in P. Bock (ed.), *Psychological Anthropology*, Westport, CT: Praeger.
34. Hildred Geertz, 1959, "The Vocabulary of Emotions," *Psychiatry* 22: 225–37, 237, 233.
35. See Robert Lowie, 1935, *The Crow Indians*, New York: Farrar and Rinehart; Colin Turnbull, 1972, *The Mountain People*, New York: Simon and Schuster; Anthony F. C. Wallace, 1970, *The Death and Rebirth of the Seneca*, New York: Knopf; Geoffrey Gorer,

1938, *Himalayan Village: An Account of the Lepchas of Sikkim,* London: M. Joseph; Robert Murphy, 1960, *Headhunter's Heritage,* Berkeley: University of California Press.

36. Clifford Geertz, 1965, *Person, Time and Conduct in Bali: An Essay in Cultural Analysis,* New Haven, CT: Yale University, Southeast Asia Studies, p. 399.

37. Jean Briggs, 1970, *Never in Anger: Portrait of an Eskimo Family,* Cambridge, MA: Harvard University Press.

38. Michelle Rosaldo, 1980, *Knowledge and Passion: Ilongot Notions of Self and Social Life,* Cambridge, England: Cambridge University Press.

39. Jean Briggs, 1987, "In Search of Emotional Meaning," *Ethos* 15: 8–15, 13, 12. See also Jean Briggs, 1978, "The Origins of Nonviolence: Inuit Management of Aggression," in Ashley Montague (ed.), *Learning Non-Aggression: The Experience of Non-Literate Societies,* New York: Oxford University Press.

40. For another discussion of the expression of rage among a "peaceful people," see Robert Paul, 1978, "Instinctive Aggression in Man: The Semai Case," *Journal of Psychological Anthropology* 1: 65–79.

41. Unni Wikan, 1990, *Managing Turbulent Hearts: A Balinese Formula for Living,* Chicago: University of Chicago Press, pp. 229, 35, 116.

42. Khushal Khan Khattack, 1965, *Poems from the Diwan of Khushal Khan Khattack,* London: Allen and Unwin, p. 36. In private and among friends, Pukhtun men do show a range of emotions. The role of the joker is especially well-developed.

43. Quoted in Norbert Elias, 1982, *Power and Civility,* New York: Urizen, p. 272.

44. See Elias, *Power and Civility,* and Norbert Elias, 1978, *The Civilizing Process,* New York: Urizen. For an anthropological use of Elias's model, see Charles Lindholm, 1988, "The Social Structure of Emotional Constraint: The Court of Louis XIV and the Pukhtun of Northern Pakistan," *Ethos* 16: 227–46. A cross-cultural perspective is offered in Yi-Fu Tuan, 1982, *Segmented Worlds and Self: Group Life and Individual Consciousness,* Minneapolis: University of Minnesota Press.

45. For a more detailed comparative analysis of this point, see Lindholm, "The Social Structure of Emotional Constraint."

46. E. E. Evans-Pritchard, 1940, *The Nuer,* Oxford, England: Clarendon Press.

47. For a survey of the large and sometimes acrimonious body of literature on segmentary lineage systems, and a discussion of its operation among the Pukhtun, see Charles Lindholm, 1980, *Generosity and Jealousy: The Swat Pukhtun of Northern Pakistan,* New York: Columbia University Press. See also the relevant essays in Lindholm, 1996, *Frontier Perspectives: Essays in Comparative Anthropology,* Karachi, Pakistan: Oxford University Press.

48. Napoleon Chagnon, 1977, *Yanomamo: The Fierce People,* New York: Holt, Rinehart and Winston, p. 50.

49. Arlie Russell Hochschild, 1983, *The Managed Heart: Commercialization of Human Feeling,* Berkeley: University of California Press, p. 198.

50. Wikan, *Managing Turbulent Hearts,* pp. 123, 152.

51. Ibid., pp. 152, 149.

52. Linda Connor, 1982,"The Unbounded Self: Balinese Therapy in Theory and Practice," in Anthony Marsella, Geoffrey White, (eds.), *Cultural Conceptions of Mental Health and Therapy,* Dordrecht, Netherlands: D. Reidel.

53. Lutz, *Unnatural Emotions,* p. 4. See Chapter 9 for more on ethnopsychology, Chapter 8 for the controversy over sociocentricism.

54. For an influential claim that women are more nurturant and other-directed than men, see Carol Gilligan, 1982, *In a Different Voice: Psychological Theory and Women's Development,* Cambridge, MA: Harvard University Press.

55. Lutz, *Unnatural Emotions*, p. 80.

56. Ibid., pp. 139, 152. For a critique, see J. Russell, 1991, "Culture and the Categorization of Emotions," *Psychological Bulletin* 110: 426–50.

57. See, for example, Lila Abu-Lughod and Catherine Lutz, 1990, "Introduction: Emotion, Discourse and the Politics of Everyday Life," in Catherine Lutz and Lila Abu-Lughod (eds.), *Language and the Politics of Emotion*, Cambridge, England: Cambridge University Press.

58. Michelle Rosaldo, 1984, "Toward an Anthropology of Self and Feeling," in Richard Shweder and Robert LeVine (eds.), *Culture Theory: Essays on Mind, Self and Emotion*, Cambridge, England: Cambridge University Press, p. 143. For a fuller (and more convincing) account, see Michelle Rosaldo, *Knowledge and Passion*.

59. For an example, see Mary-Jo Good and Byron Good, 1988, "Ritual, the State, and the Transformation of Emotional Discourse in Iranian Society," *Culture, Medicine and Psychiatry* 12: 43–63.

60. For this critique, see Bruce Kapferer, 1995, "From the Edge of Death: Sorcery and the Motion of Consciousness," in Anthony P. Cohen and Nigel Rapport (eds.), *Questions of Consciousness*, London: Routledge.

61. Michelle Rosaldo, "Toward an Anthropology of Self and Feeling," p. 146; Lutz, *Unnatural Emotions*, p. 97.

62. Eleanor Ruth Gerber, 1985, "Rage and Obligation: Samoan Emotion in Conflict," in G. White and J. Kirkpatrick (eds.), *Person, Self and Experience*, Berkeley: University of California Press, p. 155.

63. Ghani Khan, 1958, *The Pathans: A Sketch*, Peshawar, Pakistan: University Books, p. 12.

64. Lindholm, *Generosity and Jealousy*.

65. Robert Levy, 1984, "Emotion, Knowing, and Culture," in Richard Shweder and Robert LeVine (eds.), *Culture Theory: Essays on Mind, Self and Emotion*, Cambridge, England: Cambridge University Press, p. 229.

66. George Lakoff and Zoltan Kovecses, 1987, "The Cognitive Model of Anger Inherent in American English," in Dorothy Holland and Naomi Quinn (eds.), *Cultural Models in Language and Thought*, Cambridge, England: Cambridge University Press, p. 221; George Lakoff, 1987, *Women, Fire and Dangerous Things: What Categories Reveal about the Mind*, Chicago: University of Chicago Press, p. 39. See also Paul Ekman, R. Levinson, and W. Friesen, 1983, "Autonomic Nervous System Activity Distinguishes between Emotions," *Science* 221: 1208–10. Of course, secondary sentiments such as nostalgia for the lilacs of yesteryear that have minimal specific physiological content would also not have universal application.

67. Roy D'Andrade and Michael Egan, 1974, "The Colors of Emotion," *American Ethnologist* 1: 49–63. The emotions cited were happiness, sadness, anger, and fear. Colors were also assigned to states such as good, bad, strong, and weak.

68. Gerber, "Rage and Obligation," p. 130.

69. John Bester, 1981, "Introduction," in Takeo Doi, 1981, *The Anatomy of Dependence*, Tokyo: Kodansha International, p. 8; see also Hisa Kumagai and Arno Kumagai, 1986, "The Hidden 'I' in Amae: 'Passive Love' and Japanese Social Perception," *Ethos* 14: 305–20.

70. See also James Averill, 1980, "Emotion and Anxiety: Sociocultural, Biological and Psychological Determinants," in A. Rorty (ed.), *Explaining Emotions*, Berkeley: University of California Press.

71. Richard Shweder, 1991, *Thinking through Cultures: Expeditions in Cultural Psychology*, Cambridge, MA: Harvard University Press, p. 252.

CHAPTER 11

Outsiders and Charismatics

Chapter 2 of this book begins with a description of St. Augustine's tortured search for some coherent meaning to his life. He wrote about how he felt himself torn asunder, alienated from his family and friends, unable to work or think, driven to the edge of madness, and how he was rescued from despair only when he heard the voice of God exhorting him to take up the Bible and read. As a result, he converted to Christianity and went on to become a central figure in church history. Today, we would probably diagnose his experience as a mental breakdown, describe the voice of God as an auditory hallucination, and recommend some form of therapy and drug treatment to alleviate his symptoms.

But in many societies, Augustine's encounter would be interpreted in quite a different manner. In these cultures individuals have experiences that we would also consider indicative of mental illness. They too may hear otherworldly voices, just as Augustine did, and may be tormented by frightening apparitions. For example, as a Tamang man of Nepal recounts: "I saw many evil spirits, some with long crooked fangs, others with no heads and with eyes in the middle of their chests, still others carrying decaying corpses. They attacked me and, before I knew it, they were all over me devouring my body."[1] For this man, as for Augustine, the terrifying visions were the prelude to spiritual transformation; but whereas Augustine went on to become a bishop and an interpreter of scripture, the Tamang became a shaman and healer, gaining supernatural power by embodying and controlling the very phantoms that had tortured him. Clearly, what we might define as delusions were understood very differently by the Tamang shaman, just as Augustine understood his own psychic disintegration and recovery very differently than we would.

Such accounts of dissociative states of consciousness and the metamorphosis of identity test the very limits of what we consider reality. How can these extraordinary experiences be understood? What role do they play in the construction of the self and in the organization of society? How much does culture define the boundaries between the normal and the deviant, the sane and the insane, the charismatic and the stigmatized? These are the central questions to be addressed in this chapter.

A Crow Indian shaman praying that the man on his right enter a trance and receive a healing vision.

Chapter Outline

I Understanding the Marginalized Individual
  A Configurationism and Heteroglossia
  B Labeling Theory
  C Rules for Breaking the Rules

II Culture and Insanity
  A The Biomedical Model of Mental Illness
  B The Cultural Expression of Mental Disorder
  C Culture-Bound Disorders in the United States

III The Social Structure of Stigma
  A Goffman's Theory of Stigma
  B The Powers of the Weak

IV Charisma
  A Turning Low into High
  B The Professional Abreactor
  C Complexity and Charisma

I. UNDERSTANDING THE MARGINALIZED INDIVIDUAL

A Configurationism and Heteroglossia
   Is deviance biological? Does it exist at all?

B Labeling Theory
   Society requires deviance for maintenance of moral order. Being labeled a deviant creates a deviant identity—to a degree.

C Rules for Breaking the Rules
   Social control of deviance. Some cultural constraints on accusations.

A. Configurationism and Heteroglossia

Despite the fact that our disciplinary mandate naturally emphasizes the authority of culture over nature, anthropologists have long had an interest in individuals who do not quite fit into the culture in which they were born. Partly, this is because anthropologists are often outsiders themselves, and so are sympathetic to the experiences of others like them; partly it is because the best informants are often the unconventional individuals who can offer a critical perspective on their own worlds; partly it is because fieldwork inevitably makes ethnographers sensitive to the fact that every society is made up of people with multiple perspectives and varied personal histories. As we saw earlier, this last point was made strongly by Edward Sapir and Anthony F. C. Wallace, who both underscored the diversity of personality types within any given culture.[2]

The same theme was taken up by the configurationist culture and personality theorists Margaret Mead and Ruth Benedict, who stressed the overwhelming power of culture to shape the psyche, but who also wrote sympathetically about individuals who simply could not fit into their milieu. Such persons, Mead and Benedict believed, were temperamentally unsuited to the world they were born into—they were, for example, the naturally timid in a society of warriors, or the naturally aggressive in a culture where tranquility was the norm. Social reactions to such persons varied: Some might be avoided or ridiculed; others might be punished as criminals or ostracized as insane; a few, such as Augustine, might be appointed leaders or, like the Tamang man described above, revered as shamans.[3]

In any case, configurationists assumed that deviance was a relative matter: What was regarded as aberrant, extraordinary, or deranged in one society might well be deemed normal, routine, and rational in another. It was also assumed that deviance was due to innate psychobiological factors, and that deviant individuals would appear everywhere, since no culture would permit complete expression of the entire great arc of human psychic potential. However, the configurationist-biological approach does imply that it is theoretically possible to construct a society in which there would be no deviants. A program in eugenics—or long-term in-marriage and a high degree of social control—might limit the range of psychobiological difference to the extent that everyone within a culture would share the same temperament, and no one would be strange, rebellious, or crazed.

More recent anthropological discourse has generally taken exactly the opposite position. The claim is that there are so many individual variations in any culture that the very notion of the exceptional or unusual is an error. While owing much to Sapir and Wallace, this position has also been inspired by the work of the twentieth-century Russian literary critic Mikhail Bakhtin (1895–1975), who explored the heteroglossia of literary production in exuberant writers such as François Rabelais (1494–1553) and Fyodor Dostoyevsky (1821–1881). Bakhtin showed that the texts written by these authors were fluid and decentered, made up of contesting alternative discourses. Bakhtin also stressed the carnivalesque aspect of literature: the overturning of rules in liberating eruptions of pure vitality and laughter.[4]

Some postmodernist anthropologists have appropriated Bakhtin's work in simplified form and have portrayed cultures as complex and multiple texts, made up of countless individual voices shouting and murmuring their separate messages to create a clamoring polyphony. This perspective does away with attributions of deviance: No voice can be seen to be out of tune with the totality, since there is no single tune being sung, no harmony sought.[5] This position can lead to a view of culture in which, as Renato Rosaldo writes, "nothing is thrust out, the good the bad and the ugly, nothing rejected, nothing abandoned."[6]

This is a creed admirable for its incorporative ambitions, but it is not very convincing. We might like to see everyone playfully united, without differentiation, prejudice, or antipathy. However, our discipline demands that we not imagine utopias and present them as realities, but portray the world as it actually works. We should also keep in mind that not to have standards is itself a kind of standard—one that makes intolerance a sin and excludes anyone who seeks to exclude. Finally, we must note that this perspective eliminates culture entirely, substituting an unjudgmental tolerance for the hard job of analysis, which requires an ability to make distinctions and generalizations.

B. Labeling Theory

Both the reduction of deviance to the expression of innate temperamental differences and the denial of moral judgment altogether in favor of an encompassing, egalitarian heteroglossia misconstrue the positive social function of exclusion. As Émile Durkheim knew, every society, no matter how homogenous and well controlled, *must* have deviants within it.[7] This is not due to biological differences in temperament; it is because society exists primarily as a moral entity that binds its members together through their shared beliefs and practices. And because normality *requires* abnormality for its definition, society manufactures and marks moral distinctions so that the rest can assure themselves that they are indeed good persons—however goodness is defined. Note that there is no notion here of any absolute ethics. As Hobbes remarked, an honest man is condemned in the company of pirates, while a monogamist is despised in a society of rapists. All that is necessary is *some* overarching moral order, whatever its rules, that will designate certain of the society's members negatively in order to reinforce the moral solidarity of the remainder. It is for this reason that Erving Goffman has written, "the normal and the stigmatized are not persons, but rather perspectives."[8]

According to this theory, the process of assigning people to the category of outsider depends not so much on their innate temperaments, as the configurationists thought, but on the way they are regarded by the society at large. Sociologists of deviance call this labeling theory. Relying on G. H. Mead's arguments about the importance of cultural input in manufacturing identity,[9] labeling theorists assume that people discover themselves in the eyes of the others surrounding them. Identified in some way as an outsider, the stigmatized individual will be socialized to act according to the definition of the deviant category, and will very likely identify with that definition and enact it in daily life: A boy designated by peers and adults as a bully is likely to take the role to heart, growing up to be a thug. For labeling theorists, society—not humankind's animal instincts—is the source of deviance.

Many anthropologists have found a modified version of the social labeling argument a more reasonable way to look at deviance than making assumptions about people's innate temperaments. For instance, Robert Levy has argued that the transvestite male prostitute mahu in Tahiti is not necessarily a man who is predisposed to homosexuality. Instead, every village selects and socializes only one mahu, whose obligatory effeminacy and sexual promiscuity affirms masculinity in a society where male-female differences are relatively slight. As a result, even though they are not strongly differentiated from women, Tahitian men can say to themselves, "I am a man, because I am not one of the mahu."[10] Notably, a mahu can decide he no longer wishes to fill the role; when this occurs, a new candidate must be selected and trained for the position. Similarly, Nancy Scheper-Hughes remarks on the tolerant attitude toward high levels of alcohol consumption in rural Ireland. There, drinkers compare themselves with the despised town drunk, who is in a stupor by noon. The majority can reassure themselves by saying, "I may drink heavily, but I am not an alcoholic. The alcoholic is already unconscious in the gutter."[11]

But while social labeling can explain a great deal, it is also evident that labels can be applied either to amplify or (more rarely) to mute the innate tendencies that do exist in a particular individual. For example, in any group of people, some are timid while others are risk takers, who prefer to bend or break the rules; more controversially, some persons may have a biologically based predilection to engage in certain behaviors, such as violence, homosexual acts, or overindulgence in alcohol, that can be culturally defined as deviant. And it is certain that some forms of serious mental illness—schizophrenia, bipolar disorder, and clinical depression—have important neurobiological aspects.

C. Rules for Breaking the Rules

Although we must accept the empirical reality of biological differences in character and in potential operating in tandem with the powerful influence of social labeling, we must also be careful to avoid turning tendencies and labels into destinies. While people everywhere are molded by their culture and impelled by their biological makeup, and while biology and culture can easily come into conflict (as Mead and Benedict realized), human beings are not wholly constituted by either factor; they are also independent agents capable of deciding exactly how they will respond to the conditions in which they find themselves.

An awareness of human freedom reminds us that norms not only provide guidelines about what is proper and what is aberrant, but also give opportunities for individual manipulation. As the anthropologist Robert Edgerton remarks in his book about deviance: "Durkheim was right in saying that rules themselves cause the possibility of deviance, but it is also true that men create rules that permit them to maneuver to their advantage and behave within one rule while violating another."[12] We should also recall Freud's dictum that laws are necessary only because of temptation, and that desire will always seek a channel for release. Every society therefore has rules about how to break rules, and rules about how to react when a rule has been broken.

For example, Unni Wikan has described how her female friends in the strictly Muslim Gulf state of Oman—all highly respectable and proper women in a society that greatly values female chastity—welcomed a well-known local prostitute into their circle. As long as their friend did not mention her illicit life and maintained public decorum, the other women were glad enough to enjoy her lavish hospitality. What might be seen here as hypocrisy was defined there as good manners: For the polite Omani, one's personal life is no one else's business, and only God can punish private sins.[13] In this way, the women maintained a smooth social surface and avoided the terrible consequences of a public accusation of sexual immorality—for in Omani society, an adulterous woman ought to be condemned to death.

The degree to which deviance from the moral norm is covertly permitted, concealed, or ignored can be a good baseline for making cross-cultural comparisons. For example, we could hypothesize that communally oriented face-to-face cultures, such as the Omani, might generally be more harsh than individualistic and impersonal societies such as ours in their punishment of deviance, since those who veer from the norm challenge the moral solidarity of the entire group. At the same time, as we have seen in Oman, such cultures might also be very reluctant to label anyone as abnormal, since that label would have such dire consequences both for the individual, who would be condemned severely, and for the group, which would be dishonored.

This indeed does seem to be the case in Japan, where group membership is so important for personal identity. Psychiatrists there are extremely loath to humiliate their patients and the patients' families; therefore even persons with serious mental illnesses such as paranoid schizophrenia may be ambiguously diagnosed as neurasthenic and allowed to continue their public careers, even to the point of disaster. As an example, a Japanese airline pilot with obvious delusions was not taken off duty and eventually crashed his plane, killing himself and his passengers. This is, of course, an extreme case, but not untypical. However, when the disorder becomes too obvious and publicly unmanageable, then

Omani women.

the deranged individual is likely to be permanently incarcerated somewhere far out of sight of the community and family.[14]

Similarly, clannish Irish-American families in Boston's culturally conservative South End put up with very irrational behavior from obviously schizophrenic relatives, excusing them as sensitive mystics or eccentric geniuses. The irrational behavior is excused because defining a family member as mentally disturbed means both shame for the family and the utter exile of the person from the tight-knit community.[15] Meanwhile, the disturbed individual generally cooperates in the charade by behaving circumspectly, dressing conservatively, and not voicing his or her delusions in public. So long as appearances are kept up, nothing is done, and the saving pretence of normality can be maintained.

II. CULTURE AND INSANITY

A The Biomedical Model of Mental Illness
   The biology of insanity and the limits of the medical model.

B The Cultural Expression of Mental Disorder
   Cultural influences on mental disease: somatization and depression, schizophrenia, the evaluation and treatment of culture-bound disorders.

C Culture-Bound Disorders in the United States
   American mental diseases: multiple personality disorder, posttraumatic stress disorder, and alcoholism

A. The Biomedical Model of Mental Illness

As the above examples indicate, insanity is in many senses the ultimate and most frightening form of deviance. Anyone, of any class or status, can be afflicted and rendered incapable of grasping the nature of reality and therefore incapable of making rational choices. Such people are said not to know what they are doing and cannot be held responsible for themselves. Simultaneously, the floridly delusional also appear outside culture, speaking and acting in ways that are apparently incomprehensible, without regard for social norms.[16] Everywhere in the world, madness is recognized as the triumph of disintegration, and it is probably the most stigmatized form of difference, despite (or perhaps because of) its prevalence. For example, in any given year nearly 2 million Americans have diagnoses of schizophrenia, while about 15 million suffer from clinical depression or bipolar disorder (manic depression). Because it challenges our very notions of reality and identity, insanity can serve us well as a test for the relationship between normative culture and the unconventional individual.

As mentioned earlier, we now know that the most virulent forms of mental illness have a major biological component. New diagnostic technologies, such as positron-emission tomography (PET), conclusively reveal alterations occurring in the electrical and chemical composition of the brains of individuals experiencing psychotic states. Genetic factors evidently are crucial in predispositions toward such states, though it is not clear exactly what those factors are. It also is accepted that many of the positive symptoms of major mental illnesses (hallucinations, delusions, incoherence, bizarre behavior, mood swings, rage) are associated with excessive or distorted neural activity and can therefore be allayed by sophisticated modern medications capable of regulating the level of neurotransmitters produced in the brain. Unfortunately, negative symptoms (passivity, flat affect, absence of drive and will, lack of pleasure) are less amenable to such treatments.[17]

Contemporary clinical psychologists, justifiably proud of the advanced chemical treatments now available, have naturally tended to focus on the neurobiological causation of major mental illnesses and have concluded that cultural differences are merely a veneer over a shared etiology. From this perspective, "the structure of delusions varies little, if any, across cultures, whereas the content may be influenced by culture." Therefore, cultural analysis must stay on the surface; it cannot illuminate the underlying nature of psychological disorders.[18]

But in making this formulation, clinicians have applied models evolved within a Western medical framework that privileges biology; mental diseases, like other diseases, are assumed to be the direct consequence of some form of injury or trauma, though in this instance the injury has been to the mind, not the body. The difficulty is that accurately diagnosing and treating a mental wound is not quite the same as diagnosing and treating a broken leg; the wound is invisible, its symptoms are neither clear-cut nor immutable, and sharp boundaries between cultural context and the experience of mental illness are very difficult, if not impossible, to maintain.[19]

B. *The Cultural Expression of Mental Disorder*

As mentioned above, and as all clinicians recognize, the surface content of mental delusions can be very different across cultures. Obviously, modern paranoids may have delusions that they are being directed by electronic messages from devices secretly planted in their tooth fillings, while people in less technologically advanced cultures—unfamiliar with electricity or fillings—fantasize instead about spirit possession or believe worms are eating their brains.

But culture is implicated in far more complex differences as well. Even within the United States, ethnic background has been shown to affect symptomology among schizophrenics. Irish Americans tend to be preoccupied with guilt and sexuality in their delusions and to display considerable disorganized thinking; at the same time, they generally are discreet about revealing their symptoms and maintain a respectable front. Italian Americans are more hypochondriacal and fixed in their delusional systems; they are also much more rebellious toward authority and more flagrant in their behaviors than the Irish-American group.[20]

Even what is defined as mental illness may vary considerably across cultures. As noted in the previous chapter, what Americans would call despondency or depression is generally presented as physical fatigue in Tahiti. This is hardly extraordinary since even in the United States, depression is closely associated with the actual experience of physical and social deprivation and discrimination.[21] Unsurprisingly, people who are poor, marginalized, badly treated, and hopeless are everywhere especially susceptible to feelings of worthlessness and enervation—which is probably the reason women in America are far more prone to depression than are men. The provision of better social circumstances and greater respect would without doubt be the most helpful therapy in such cases.[22]

Because of our own cultural preconceptions, in the United States we tend to ignore objective external conditions for despair and focus instead on the inner states of individuals. Diffuse reports of fatigue, listlessness, and chronic exhaustion are defined as depression and treated purely as a psychic disorder, to be alleviated by proper medication and therapy, not by social intervention. As the psychiatrist and anthropologist Arthur Kleinman has argued, this is a char-

Somatization

Unlike Americans, members of traditional cultures often stress bodily feeling more than emotion when discussing psychological distress or discomfort. Somatization, as this is called, has sometimes led psychologists to diagnose people from such cultures as suffering from alexithymia—a deficit in the capacity to express emotion. But in fact somatization usually occurs as an accompaniment to emotional distress, not as a substitute.[23] For example, among Iranians a high rate of anxiety about heart trouble is connected to a complex emotional-cultural constellation in which the heart is considered the seat of sadness and yearning.[24]

acteristic way in which the medical profession channels a variety of vague symptoms—an illness—into a preconceptualized medical category—a disease. This process necessarily neglects many of the subjective sensations of the patient for the sake of maintaining a biomedical model of distress.[25]

In particular, the common diagnosis of depression reflects the fact that Americans are extraordinary in their tendency to psychologize and internalize their sensations. For example, a friend of mine with a cold was quite certain his headache and cough were ultimately caused by conflicting feelings he had about his girlfriend. Excessive psychologizing has an elective affinity for a culture such as ours, with its values of personal autonomy, expressivity, and privacy, which incite people to attribute suffering to their inner moods and desires.[26] This characteristic overemphasis on inner emotional states can lead to a downplaying of the social world, thereby interfering with a proper appreciation of people's real-life physical ills, anxieties, and alienation.

Cultural attitudes and categorizations affect diagnosis and treatment in other ways as well.[27] For example, Americans—ever cheerful and optimistic—are quick to label someone depressed; the Chinese—who favor conventionality and a stiff upper lip—are much more inclined to tolerate depressive symptoms and to be far more concerned when people become extroverted, talkative, and pushy. Rates of hospitalization for depressive and manic disorders therefore differ noticeably in the two countries.[28] Even more remarkable, what may be seen as serious mental illness in one cultural context can be understood quite positively in another. People who in America might well be regarded as paranoid masochists are revered in the Mediterranean area as visible saints whose public suffering has ennobled them. As Obeyesekere has shown, in Sri Lanka the symptoms of withdrawal and sadness we associate with depression are treated by some religious groups as the onset of wisdom, while severe self-laceration can be seen as evidence of divine inspiration. Similarly, experiences of depersonalization that would be seen in the West as symptomatic of severe psychosis may be interpreted by Indian Yogis as indicators of enlightenment.[29]

More damning to a purely biological view of mental illness is the finding that different cultural inputs are associated with a different course and outcome in schizophrenia, which is recognized as both the most severe and the most physiologically based mental disorder. It was discovered in these studies that schizophrenic patients in the developing third world had a more acute onset of symptoms than individuals in modern societies, but that they also recovered more quickly and completely.[30] Most psychologists believe that social factors are responsible for this distinction, including the steady support of extended family members, integrative healing rituals, an absence of stigma, and the relative simplicity of the environment. Also, a guilty sense of responsibility for the illness can be alleviated by notions of causation emphasizing external influences. Finally, societies that accept notions of spiritual possession offer a culturally valid explanation and cure for what the individual is suffering. Often, as we shall see at more length below, the notion of possession may permit distressed individuals to weave themselves back into the cultural fabric by taking on new and valued social roles as shamans and spiritual healers.

These facts challenge the accepted biomedical notion that schizophrenia is a psychobiological disorder that has the same symptoms and the same rate of occurrence everywhere. This challenge is made more persuasive when we consider ethnographic reports noting that permanent states of psychosis were extremely rare among peoples not subjected to Western influence. More common were occasional manic outbursts, often caused by some unexpected setback or obstacle.[31] Such periodic hysterical fugues and frenzies are clearly not equivalent to the withdrawal, flat affect, and highly abstract and generally incomprehensible thought forms that are characteristic of chronic schizophrenia in the West. This is so much the case that the psychologist Louis Sass (following the pioneering work of the psychological anthropologist Georges Devereux) has recently argued that schizoid disorders are primarily a modern Western phenomena, a mental illness that afflicts human beings isolated and turned inward upon themselves in an ever more complex and fragmented environment. In contrast, small-scale, communal, and coherent societies favor mental disorders consisting of hysterical outbursts, which are interpreted as spirit possession and which serve to gain the attention and care of the collective.[32]

Claims for a universal medical paradigm for mental illness are also challenged by the existence of a great variety of culturally specific diseases that would be defined in the West as psychologically caused. These range from koro (the panic fear among some East Asian men that the penis will withdraw into the body)[33] to latah (a compulsion to imitate, common in Malaysia)[34] to windigo psychosis (an Ojibwa syndrome in which individuals are possessed by a cannibalistic demon).[35] None of these, it should be remarked, are indigenously regarded as mental problems. Locally, they are treated by various physical remedies or by intervention from shamans, who seek to exorcise the possessed victims of their demons. It should also be noted that these treatments, more often than not, are quite successful.

C. Culture-Bound Disorders in the United States

History also shows us that the identification of mental disorders has not remained stable, even in the West, but has shifted over time. New disorders, such as anorexia and bulimia, certainly reflect changing cultural values, as does the appearance of narcissistic personality disorders and borderline personality disorders.[36] But here I wish to consider another new mental illness: multiple personality disorder (MPD). MPD was frequently reported a hundred years ago, then lost favor as Freudian notions came to dominate. Of late, as psychoanalysis has become less fashionable, MPD has again come to the fore in America (though it is apparently unknown elsewhere), but in a form quite different from its earlier incarnation, when consciousness was only double or at most triple. Now 25 distinct personalities are the mean, with some patients developing literally hundreds of alters—all supposedly caused as dissociative defenses against the traumatic experience of child abuse.[37] Unlike schizophrenics who hear multiple voices in their heads, the alters in MPD are not insane, though they vary greatly in character: Some are infantile, others promiscuous, others aggressive; some alters have alters of their own, in seemingly endless proliferation. Multiples can appear and disappear with bewildering rapidity, much like channels flicking by on the television.[38]

The anthropologists Paul Antze and Michael Lambeck contend that the sudden clinical appearance of MPD directly responds to present-day social fragmentation and to the erosion of family ties. In compensation, lonely people now create a "family within the individual."[39] MPD also mirrors the contemporary disintegration of political systems and the multiple demands of each ethnic group for its own state. Like these groups, every mood and interest within the individual can now make parallel claims for full autonomy: Every alter has its own right to independence. The shattering of the self coincides as well with the contemporary modular theory of the mind as a set of computational devices, each serving a different purpose, but without any central "me" in control.[40] Finally, the belief that MPD is a response to forgotten incidents of child abuse offers the afflicted individual someone to blame for present misery and provides a coherent explanation for an incoherent life—but at the cost of portraying the sufferer as a permanent victim. This too reflects modernity, as people very often quite understandably feel themselves out of control of their fragmented lives, victimized by uncontrollable circumstances, and afflicted by an inner sense of emptiness.[41]

A related disorder, even more widespread, is post-traumatic stress disorder (PTSD). This diagnosis began as an explanation of the varied symptoms and dysfunctions of hospitalized Vietnam veterans. Like MPD, PTSD is said to be caused by a trauma—originally, by the terrifying events of battle. PTSD is the descendant of diagnoses of shell shock and battle fatigue among soldiers in World Wars I and II,[42] and of nineteenth-century theories that physical injuries could cause psychological disorder. According to medical anthropologist Allan Young, the diagnosis of PTSD has served several social purposes: It helped veterans expiate their guilt while also offering them a convincing explanation for the alienation they suffer—an explanation that cannot be refuted, since, like the explanation of MPD, it depends on the repressed memory of a psychic injury.[43]

The diagnosis of PTSD has since been extended to cover many other indeterminate forms of mental distress among nonsoldiers, distress now thought to be caused by the childhood equivalent of shell shock: sexual abuse (also said to be the root cause of MPD). This paradigm effectively eliminates the Freudian premises of conflicting drives and the problem of ambivalence. The only aspect of psychoanalysis retained is the notion of repression, which is invoked to explain the fact that the purported original trauma is not remembered. Culture also more or less vanished from these diagnoses, since mental illness is assumed to be a universal reaction to abuse.

In the 1980s, the idea that generalized unhappiness and anxiety were probably caused by forgotten incidents of incest became prevalent among many therapists seeking some way to explain and cure the large numbers of female patients suffering from a mixture of vague symptoms, such as malaise, difficulty in relating, sexual coldness or promiscuity, and nameless fears. Appropriating the diagnosis of PTSD, these therapists assumed that sexual abuse of children must necessarily be extremely common in American families, and made every

Battle fatigue during the Korean War.

effort to get their patients to "remember" more and more traumatic hidden memories. For many, recollection had a therapeutic effect.

However, egged on by demands for remembrances, some women recounted incredible tales of parents who were members of covens of devil worshipers, who repeatedly gang-raped their children and cannibalized the babies that resulted. Under hypnosis and with prompting, parents too searched their unconscious and remembered that they were guilty of the hideous crimes that their daughters had accused them of committing.[44] Elsewhere, children in day care centers, inspired by the same sorts of relentless questioning and the lead-

---

Trauma and Psychoanalysis

In Freud's early theory, he stated that sexual abuse probably was the source of subsequent neurosis, but he later abandoned this view. This does not mean that he denied the existence of sexual abuse or the destructive effect of traumas. In fact, it was the success of psychoanalysis in treating shell-shocked World War I veterans that led to the wider acceptance of the psychoanalytic method of the talking cure.

However, for Freud, what was important in terms of furthering psychoanalytic theory was not the trauma itself. Rather, it was the response of the individual to sexual assault (whether imagined or real) that mattered. Children, Freud said, feel attracted as well as repelled by adult sexuality and can have a strong sense of guilt about those illicit feelings. It is guilt over repressed desires that leads to later neurosis, not the simple act of seduction, which could be repudiated if the child did not feel complicit.

Similarly, shell shock and battle fatigue were not simply responses to awful violence, but reflected deeper anxieties that could be alleviated by psychoanalysis. One of the most influential proponents of this method was the pioneering psychological anthropologist W. H. R. Rivers (discussed in Chapter 4), who discovered that the aviators most prone to shell shock were not the fighter pilots, who had a horrifyingly high death rate, but those who manned observation balloons, whose rates of death were comparatively low. He reasoned that the high incidence of shell shock among balloonists resulted from their having almost no control over their fates, while the pilots could at least maneuver their planes and fight the enemy. Discussing these issues often aided healing.[45]

---

ing suggestions of well-meaning therapists, described fantastic sexual and physical abuse at the hands of their teachers. These charges sometimes resulted in long prison sentences, but courts have since found most of the testimony of abuse unreliable, and many of the accused have been released.[46]

It is now recognized that many of these lurid memories served to project disavowed impulses onto a convenient target. The repeated charges of sexual molestation and satanism also reflected both the religious beliefs of Americans and their deep cultural anxieties about the family, which is supposed to be held together solely by love, and yet is actually often full of underlying tension. Confession had the complementary psychological function of allowing the accused to express and expiate their existential guilt. The recovered memory movement operated within the framework of the current and culturally bound biomedical model that inevitably explains existential despair and ennui as a result of a previous psychological trauma.

This is not to say that trauma does not cause serious psychic damage. The devastating effects of sexual abuse or wartime violence are only too obvious.[47] And it is not to deny that the cures offered did sometimes offer relief. It *is* to claim that the sudden flood of extreme and wholly implausible accusations of abuse tells us more about the hidden fears and fantasies of Americans and about the workings of the unconscious than it does about real events.

Another likely culture-bound malady is alcoholism, considered the inability to control one's drinking behavior. Alcoholism is treated in America as an addiction, defined as a compulsive mental disorder with a biomedical basis. But, as the anthropologist Gerald Erchak (among others) has argued, the assumption that human beings are out of control can occur only within a culture where self-control is normative, and where being out of control is both very appealing and very dangerous.[48] Alcohol, culturally designated as an agent that inevitably erodes control, permits the beleaguered individual to abdicate responsibility—an abdication justified by the biomedical model of addiction as irresistible compulsion. Alcoholic personalities are then assumed to be people who have little or no capacity to restrain their drinking, and who must therefore be treated medically to prevent them from ever using alcohol again.

The American model assumes that there is a unitary cause for alcoholism and that alcoholics are victims of an underlying mental-biological disease. But there is little proof for these assumptions.[49] Rather, alcohol use varies greatly between alcoholic individuals, and even more greatly across cultures, as does behavior when inebriated.[50] In most premodern societies where alcohol is drunk, it is a central aspect of ritual and community, and is highly valued as a social lubricant. It is only with the intrusion of modernity, the collapse of community, the rise of individualism, and the anxieties and frustrations that follow, that compulsive heavy drinking appears in traditional societies. Therefore, even if we do accept that certain people are addictive personalities, it is quite clear that addiction in general, and alcoholism in particular, has an elective affinity for certain kinds of societies, and must be understood, at least in great part, in cultural terms.

To reiterate: As the biomedical model claims, the most crippling forms of psychological disorder are certainly connected to neurobiological factors. However, the manifestation, causation, treatment, and outcome are equally powerfully affected by interpretation and context. Culture makes a difference, even in the most extreme pathologies of self-disintegration.

III. THE SOCIAL STRUCTURE OF STIGMA

A Goffman's Theory of Stigma
    Discredited and discreditable roles. Options for the stigmatized. Why are the stigmatized also hated? Internalization of negative identity.

B The Powers of the Weak
    Ambivalence, pollution, the projection of repressed desire, the psychology of the witch-hunt.

A. Goffman's Theory of Stigma

As mentioned, the mentally ill are at the most extreme end of a continuum of the excluded and socially tainted. For an adequate theory of what it means to be ostracized, we must move away from a focus on the supposed cause of exclusion, and recognize, as did Durkheim, that exclusion can best be understood structurally and culturally as the attribution of a negative stigmatized identity to an individual or a group. The master of this type of analysis of stigma is Erving Goffman, whose work on life as theater was synopsized in Chapter 6.[51]

As we saw there, in his early writing, Goffman argued that social life, and indeed personal identity itself, is a consequence of role playing. But he soon realized that some roles—those that are repudiated by the mainstream—are not freely chosen, but rather are forced upon individuals and groups. As a result, he developed a theory of stigma and identity that divided the stigmatized into two categories:

1. Those who have identities that are discredited.
2. Those who have identities that are discreditable.

In the first category are those whose differences from the norm are evident. Typical markers are skin color, weight, height, scars or other disfigurements, physical handicaps, and behavioral abnormalities such as tics. Again, sociologically speaking, there is no intrinsic significance to any of these distinctions; they are important only insofar as they are taken to represent disapproved characteristics. For example, to be obese in our culture is devalued; in many other cultures it is considered beautiful and is prized.

The ideal female body of the seventeenth century: Peter Paul Rubens's *The Three Graces.*

In the second category are those who can pass for normal (whatever that may be), but who have an aspect of the self that they believe they must keep hidden, such as criminal record, sexual preference, mental disorder, or ethnic or religious background. The first type of stigma is usually associated with negative views about certain aspects of the body; the second usually has to do with the suspect moral character of the individual or with the supposed bad character of a group.

Goffman devoted much of his work to considering how stigmatized people deal with the social exclusion they must endure and the effect stigma has on their self-images. A number of strategies can logically be employed. For example, those with obviously discredited identities may acquiesce to the mainstream attitude toward them and try to be more normal. They may even feel a sense of obligation to be cheerful and optimistic to make their mainstream companions feel more comfortable around them. Or they may adopt the opposite tactic, asserting that they are the normal ones and the mainstream is deviant. Or they may simply repudiate mainstream values entirely and drop out.

Those with discreditable identities have somewhat different options. They are interested primarily in maintaining appearances and controlling the information they reveal, which requires constant vigilance. However, the stress of concealment can lead to a search for groups of individuals with similar stigma, where secrets need not be kept; these groups can sometimes accept their stigma, become public, and demand equal recognition by the mainstream. However, this strategy can lead the now discredited person to become wholly invested in the aspect of the self that had formerly been a source of shame—a maneuver that can lead to an impoverishment of the alternatives available for the individual.

In summary:

- *Discredited identity.* Differences are visible; strategy involves accommodation to or rejection of mainstream.
- *Discreditable identity.* Differences are hidden; strategy involves concealment or revelation.

Goffman notes that the problems of the stigmatized are, in a real sense, universal. For example, few, if any, of us can actually live up to the central ideals of American society and be admired as what he calls the "young, married, white, urban, northern, heterosexual Protestant father of college education, fully employed, of good complexion, weight and height and a recent record in sports."[52] Even the exemplary American white male Protestant is likely to be tormented by doubts and anxieties. As Goffman says, he too must "suppress his immediate heartfelt feelings" and continually wear the masks appropriate to his role. This common dilemma corresponds with a crucial discrepancy between our all-too-human selves and our socialized selves.[53] In truth, none of us can actually be what we ought to be. We are all, Goffman says, bound together by the guilty secret of the discrepancy between "is" and "ought," and cooperate to avoid embarrassing one another with our failures. Moreover, we also are likely to diminish our own defects by showing conspicuous contempt for those who stand outside the norm too obviously.

Unfortunately, as labeling theory has informed us, constant denigration is very likely to penetrate the psyches of those who are discredited, ostracized, and

---

Tearoom Trade

The relationship between deviance and intolerance was tested in controversial sociological research undertaken in the 1950s by Laud Humphreys,[54] who observed illicit homosexual encounters in public toilets (euphemistically called tearooms). Humphreys took note of the car license numbers of the participants and then secretly traced them to their suburban homes. He had them sent versions of a national test of attitudes, including tests of attitudes toward nonconformity and sexual deviance. Perhaps unsurprisingly, these men (many of whom were married) generally tested out as rigid moralists, extremely uncharitable toward unconventional behavior.

---

demeaned, and they may believe themselves guilty of the sins of which they have been accused (else why should they be universally condemned?). As a result, they may then be prone to high rates of violence, insanity, suicide, and disease.[55] As we saw in Chapter 8, Frantz Fanon documented the psychic injuries of racism and colonialism, where the values of the oppressor were internalized by the oppressed, who then judged themselves as inferior. And, as noted above, depression and other disorders that are diagnosed as mental diseases are often a consequence of actual experiences of the stresses resulting from impoverishment, exclusion, and degradation.

B. The Powers of the Weak

Yet the public attitude toward the deviant is not quite so negative as it may seem at first glance. There is also considerable attraction to deviance, as can be seen during periodic celebrations, such as Mardi Gras in New Orleans or Brazil's carnival, when behaviors that are usually punished are rewarded instead. Like the festive moments described by Bakhtin, these rituals of reversal can serve as safety valves, allowing people to overturn ordinary constraints and hierarchies for a well-demarcated instant, secure in the knowledge that the moral order is not threatened and will be reasserted after the celebration is over.[56] Or, in a more positive sense, such rituals offer needed moments of communitas, when all the opposing elements of society are drawn harmoniously together.[57]

As Victor Turner argued, in complex societies some people are believed to be permanently in touch with the dark and forbidden side of experience. These are the liminal outsiders who marshal the powers of the weak—magic, ecstasy, creativity—that are not under the authority of the dominant structure. Such persons can stimulate exciting fantasies among the populace at large, who are hungry for an escape from boredom and order, yet afraid of the consequences; they can admire the outsiders' creativity, while also eagerly awaiting their eventual punishment and destruction, and the ultimate ratification of the status quo.[58]

An example of this phenomenon can be found in a characteristic popular American attitude toward musicians, actors, and painters. If successful, these creative people are thought to have mysterious powers; they are applauded for their revelations in the sacred spaces of concert hall, theater, and museum. As outsiders, artists are expected by the public to live in odd and rebellious ways and have license to turn bourgeois morality upside down. Through the media, the public obsessively observes and takes pleasure in the artists' excesses. But there is a price for entering into the role of rule breaker, and it is paid in high rates of divorce, drug addiction, alcoholism, mental illness, and suicide. The scandal-loving public can then enjoy the downfall of those people whom it had previously adulated.

Public ambivalence toward the outsider and rule breaker has been somewhat differently understood by the structural anthropologist Mary Douglas, in her famous discussion of matter out of place.[59] Objects, animals, and people that stand outside or athwart the ordinary order of things are polluting; they represent the forces of chaos, always threatening to spill across boundaries and taint our tidily scheduled lives. At the same time, it is only through breaking out of structure and routine that creativity is ever released. Rigid order is clean and safe, but dead; the breakdown of order is dirty and dangerous, but vitalizing.[60] Because the excluded and transgressive are by definition outside the mainstream, they symbolize the erosion of order and are often thought to possess the special spiritual and psychic powers attributed to matter out of place. Artists in our society gain their ambiguous and exciting power because they cross symbolic boundaries, and they may suffer the disintegrative consequences as well.

For an ethnographic example, consider the subjugated Bushmen of the Kalahari Desert in Africa, who are despised by the dominant Bantu-speakers for the "primitivity" of their culture. Yet the same Bushmen are sought as spiritual healers by their overlords, and it is the Bushmen who are feared for their capacity to bewitch.[61] Similarly, the warrior Nayars of India employ subordinate castes as exorcists. In a state of possession trance, these low-caste shamans have the power to expunge evil spirits from their superiors. At the same time, the exorcists are suspected of secretly sending their spiritual familiars to attack their rulers. As the anthropologist I. M. Lewis has noted, these are just two instances of a very common association "between low caste status, spirit possession, exorcism, and witchcraft." The logic is this: Excluded people stand outside the constraints of the society and therefore have access to the dangerous magical power of pollution and transgression. They can use this power to cure diseases that are caused by the breakdown of the natural order; however, these same marginal and magical individuals may also use their uncanny powers to harm those who have ostracized them.[62]

These structural-symbolic explanations for the ambivalence and fear of the excluded and liminal are commensurate with a psychoanalytic perspective. From this point of view, forbidden impulses and unacceptable desires are often projected outward and located in a detested other, who can then be repudiated and punished; this pattern of projection and punishment also allows normally prohibited aggressive urges to be enacted without threat to the social fabric. Hurting someone who is evil wins accolades, not condemnation. This mechanism helps explain the pogroms and witch-hunts that periodically erupted in European history. As the medieval historian Norman Cohn writes, witches and devils represented "desires which individual Christians have, but which they dare not acknowledge as belonging to themselves."[63] Jews, strangers, and lonely old women were presumed to indulge in precisely the crimes most repressed in the imaginations of their accusers—cannibalism, perverse eroticism, and other inversions of the moral order—and were tortured and killed in retribution.[64]

1555: German engraving of the burning of a suspected witch.

Witchcraft and Spirit Possession

Witchcraft has often been explained by anthropologists as a force for social control in small-scale, interdependent societies. Tensions in these tightly knit communities cannot be resolved by any higher judicial authority and lead instead to accusations of spiritual predation. For example, in matrilineal societies where a man's property is inherited by his sister's son, witchcraft accusations often are directed at the inheriting nephew, who is thought to cast spells to gain access to his uncle's wealth more quickly.[65] (Note that these forms of witchcraft are far removed from their mild contemporary manifestations, which are conceived as attempts to revive a pre-Christian pagan religion.[66])

I. M. Lewis has argued persuasively that witchcraft accusations generally occur between equals, while possession by malevolent spirits is found primarily among those who are outcasts. The reason for the difference is simple. While both serve to make the afflicted person the center of attention, witchcraft accusations blame others for afflictions; in contrast, possession is caused by inhuman forces. There is no blame and therefore no threat to those higher up—at least not unless the possessed absorb the spirit's magical power and actively seek to overturn the old order.[67]

As we know to our dismay, witch-hunts are not a thing of the past. Of late, those condemned have been feared minorities, as in the ethnic cleansing in Bosnia and in the dirty war against leftists in Argentina, the genocide of the Jews and Gypsies in Nazi Germany, and the persistent prejudice against African Americans in the United States. In these modern witch-hunts and pogroms, scapegoated groups are demeaned and exterminated in expiation for the repressed desires of their persecutors.

IV. CHARISMA

A Turning Low into High
    Those stigmatized at the center can be charismatic leaders on the periphery.

B The Professional Abreactor
    Shamanism as the prototype for charisma. Parallels to mental illness. Healing through trance. The physical conditions for dissociation. Benefits.

C Complexity and Charisma
    Difficulties of experiencing trance in modern society. Exclusion of charismatic groups and the consequences. The continued need for charisma.

A. Turning Low into High

There is yet another side to the dialectic of peripheralization. Although attributing dangerous powers of the weak to the outsider serves mainly to justify the cruelty of the strong, those powers are not completely illusory. The excluded may actually believe in their own spiritual strength, and under certain circumstances, the low do sometimes seek to overthrow the high and to install a new order in the land. As I. M. Lewis has shown, these redressive movements are very often led by persons whom the mainstream designates as monsters or, in more modern parlance, as lunatics. Yet those most negated by the center are sometimes those most elevated on the periphery; what is insanity or impurity according to the privileged may be charismatic inspiration for the downtrodden.[68]

The polarized dialectic of charismatic deification and demonization, worship and stigma, revelation and lunacy, regularly occurs when communities are subjected to conditions of oppression. For instance, some Kalahari Bushmen (whom I described above) have become paid professional shamans with their own traveling troops of musicians, going from place to place, dancing and engaging in healing trance. They are few in number, wealthy, and prestigious, and they are idolized by Bushmen boys and young men, who imitate their idiosyncrasies and their songs; at the same time, they are greatly feared as powerful witches by the dominant Bantu. According to the ethnographer of the region, in the event of a rebellion by the Bushmen against Bantu rule, one of these charismatic performers would certainly be the instigator.[69]

The Concept of Charisma

The term "charisma" is taken from Christian theology, where it referred to the disciples' recognition of Jesus's divinity. It was introduced into sociology as a value-free term by Max Weber, who contrasted the emotional power of charismatic authority to the traditional power of the patriarch and the rational rule of law. Weber distinguished two distinct forms of charisma, one—institutional charisma—arising out of the other—pure charisma. The secondary form, institutional charisma, can be inherited or passed along with accession to an office. This is the charisma that gives an aura of sacred power to whoever has the right to wear the bishop's robe, or sit in the king's throne, regardless of that person's actual personal characteristics.[70]

Institutional charisma arises from the primary form, an original experience of pure charisma, which is by its very nature irrational and emotional. Instead of following laws or custom, followers yield to the commands of their prophet, who is obeyed solely because he or she emanates a mysterious power to command. Whatever the leader says or demands is right, even if it is self-contradictory. It is right *because the leader has said it*. In its primal expression, charisma obeys no fixed lines of authority; those involved aim at the overthrow of all structure, the disintegration of all the chains of custom.[71]

Many charismatic movements of precisely this type have been recorded worldwide, particularly in colonial contexts, where local tradition has been undermined by the authority of the invaders and new values are required to make sense of a world turned upside down. In these tumultuous environments, magnetic individuals who believe themselves to have a special transformative mission may become the vehicles for what Anthony F. C. Wallace termed "revitalization movements" of the colonized and culturally disenfranchised. According to Wallace, profound crisis provides an opening for the inspired prophet to offer followers a "mazeway resynthesis" of their old values into a new form.[72]

Although according to Weber, charisma overturns everything traditional, in fact, the content of the existing symbolic system has a profound effect on the direction a charismatic movement can take, and on the character of the leader, who must fit within a preexistent image of spiritual power. For example, Gandhi's chastity and general abstinence resonated with an Indian paradigm of the conservation of spiritual power, but would not have appealed to Indonesians, who were thrilled instead by Sukarno's much publicized sexual vitality; Ayatollah Khomeini's austerity, esoteric knowledge, and unyielding demeanor tapped into traditional Iranian models of spiritual authority; Hitler's aggressive speeches, polarized anti-Semitic worldview, and theatrical rages played into the fantasies of Germans.[73] But in all instances, true believers were emotionally attached to their leader as a person of special power, capable of transforming the world, whom they would follow even to death. Opponents, in contrast, saw these leaders as criminals, lunatics, or charlatans. It is only history that decides which is the case.

B. *The Professional Abreactor*

According to Max Weber, modern charismatic leaders are only the most recent incarnations of figures who once were central to culture. These were the shamans,[74] who, like the Bushmen healers mentioned above, were capable of entering into altered and intensified states of consciousness, arousing others to experience similarly heightened states. The powerful feelings stimulated during the collective trance were then attributed to the shaman's supernatural capacity, and he or she became an object of worship—a god on earth. For Durkheim, as for Weber, this ur-experience of communal ecstasy was "the very type of sacred thing," existent prior to any message conveyed.[75] And, in fact, according to some historians of religion, shamanistic trance was found throughout the pre-literate world, though it was interpreted and evaluated differently according to context.[76]

As a religion based on trance, shamanism relies on an extraordinary capacity of the human mind that is judged very differently across cultures. A person who experiences auditory and visual hallucinations and who enters into states of dissociation is regarded in Western society as severely mentally ill. Yet the anthropologist Erika Bourguignon estimates that nearly 90 percent of all societies have understood trance and dissociation as an avenue to higher spiritual consciousness.[77] In these societies, trance is institutionalized, and those capable of being possessed and entranced cross the line between the worlds of human and divine, as they embody the gods within themselves.

When called to their vocation, these extraordinary individuals often have felt themselves torn apart and overwhelmed by malevolent forces, as the account from Nepal cited in the introduction to this chapter indicates. Western psychiatrists would regard these experiences as evidence of mental breakdown, perhaps paranoid schizophrenia; in simpler societies, they are an expected part of the shaman's initiation. Beginning shamans also typically manifest other behaviors and mental states, such as withdrawal, extreme depression, hallucinations, hysterical seizures, and depersonalization, that coincide with Western notions of mental breakdown. These too are believed to indicate the shaman's divine calling.[78]

Yet, although many cultures accept the shaman's psychological disintegration as the beginning of the journey to the spirit world, they also clearly distinguish between the authentic shaman's mental state and that of the truly insane. This distinction is made even though the mental states and behaviors of both are similar, and in spite of the fact that insanity (often culturally defined as spirit possession) is the precursor of the shamanic gift in an initiate. But the shaman is a person who, as an Alaskan practitioner says, "goes out of his mind, but not crazy."[79] Though initially torn asunder, the shaman "alleviated the psychic sufferings of the others by alleviating his own, and conversely, alleviated his own by curing the others."[80]

This reciprocal healing process is accomplished through the healing seance, as the shaman dramatically reenacts the psychic crisis and rebirth of the original calling. As Claude Lévi-Strauss has remarked, this entranced performance is a form of abreaction—a psychoanalytic term for the "decisive moment in the treatment when the patient intensively relives the initial situation from which his disturbance stems, before he ultimately overcomes it."[81] But whereas the modern psychoanalytic patient is the one who relives a psychic trauma under the uninvolved eye of the analyst, in shamanism, healers cure by reexperiencing their original journeys through madness, drawing the onlookers and the patient alike into a communal, revitalizing drama of disintegration, absorption into the spirit world, and redemption.

In shamanistic societies the insane are defined as those individuals who, for whatever reason, cannot achieve this resolution; they are buffeted and broken by the spirits they feel possessing them. But cultures where possession and shamanism are part of the belief system do offer psychologically fragile persons the possibility of filling a valued role if they can learn to rein in their demons.[82] As we have seen, such societies have a far better rate of recovery from psychotic episodes than occurs in the West. I noted above some of the reasons why this might be so, citing family support, nonjudgmental notions of causation, collective healing, and so on. We can add that control over dissociative states can also be encouraged by socialization. Children in societies where trance regularly occurs learn how possessed individuals act, play at being possessed themselves, and are prepared to have the actual experience when they become adults. Others who have already become shamans also train the neophytes in proper techniques of ecstasy and help them make sense of their experiences.

As a result, in some societies a large proportion of the population may eventually become capable of entering dissociative states to some degree. Among the !Kung San Bushmen of the Kalahari, for example, fully half the men and 10 percent of the women enter ecstatic states,[83] while in Ojibwa society virtually every person has some shamanistic ability.[84] However, there are always differences in degree, and in these cultures, only a few individuals are revered as true virtuosos.

Even in our own complex society, evidence shows that almost everyone can be drawn into a some form of trance under the right circumstances. This can be accomplished through physical inputs, such as drumming, dancing, chanting, hyperventilation, physical fatigue, hunger, thirst, disease, torture, and the use of psychotropic drugs, often taken in conjunction with a group ritual performance. Trance can be achieved as well by understimulation (solitude, darkness, immobility) and by extreme mental concentration.[85] These inputs appear to act mechanically to break down the ordinarily ordered structures of consciousness that pattern our perceptions. As Weber asserted, we usually live by rote, unaware of the world around us. But the techniques and conditions cited above, as well as many others, disrupt the normal funneling of attention and excite powerful physiological reactions in the brain.[86] Biologically speaking, such disruptions can lead to a state wherein people are gripped by sensations of psychic disintegration that can be felt as either horrifying or transcendent, according to expectations and context.

If the setting is favorable, then a number of benefits may accrue. According to some observers, long-term experience of positively valued trance states correlates with a consistent personality change in which emotions become more

A !Kung bushman in trance healing a Herero woman.

powerful, while the intellect remains intact.[87] The psychically charged performance of ritualized ecstatic trance also permits a therapeutic reliving of traumatic
events and the enactment of repressed fantasies and alternative lives, providing
cathartic purging within a safe atmosphere of collective support, as well as an
avenue for the expression of creativity.[88] Furthermore, the exposure of a whole

---

Group Psychology

Anthropology has had little to say about the importance of group psychology, and has tended to assume that individuals are rationally seeking to maximize the benefits that are culturally valued. But this assumption ignores the profound effects of the emotional tenor of a collective, which can blur the boundaries between self and other, and incite mental states that are far from rational. Durkheim recognized this in his portrait of collective effervescence, which he saw as the positive source of the sacred; Freud painted a far more negative picture of crowd excitement kindling the basest impulses of its members. Certainly, the modern history of movements such as the Nazis shows us that collectives can behave in ways that are hard to place within a rational framework. The development of a theory of such states remains a challenge for social science in general and anthropology in particular.[89]

---

group to common driving stimuli may synchronize their mental, emotional, and physical states, inspiring in them a strong sense of group identity and fellow-feeling.[90] In other words, just as Durkheim thought, the communal experience of trance does have the power to bind a society together, while also providing a powerful therapeutic experience for psychologically distressed individuals. It is not hard to see, then, that the devaluation of collective trance in our society would correlate with a high rate of alienation and depression.[91] But it is also evident that the pursuit of dissociated states in unfavorable environments can easily lead to ostracism and, in the worst cases, to severe forms of mental distress and fragmentation, as we shall see in the next section.

C. Complexity and Charisma

As stated earlier, psychobiological and cross-cultural evidence demonstrates conclusively that the capacity for trance is rooted in the human brain. Social circumstances will shape the manner in which such dissociated forms of consciousness are interpreted, experienced, and allocated. For example, in the simplest societies, where shamans hold considerable political authority, men dominate in the role. But as society becomes more complex and ecstatic experience is marginalized, more and more women (as well as peripheralized and therefore effeminate men) become shamans.[92]

In present-day society, the form of consciousness known as charisma is not favored. As Weber noted, the devaluation of charisma is partly a result of the disenchantment of the world brought about by the complexity and increased bureaucratic rationality demanded by a modern capitalist system. No longer believing in the power of spirits, we find such experiences of inspiration to be a threat to our intricate social organization and to our rationality. For most of us, dissociative states are now temporarily achieved only through secular celebrations such as parties or sporting events, where people gather in an atmosphere of emotional intensification, heightened by music and alcohol. More permanently and perilously, a few of us experience dissociation in schizoid breakdowns.

Some, however, do still participate in charismatic movements, but when these arise, they are usually marginalized into cults. Speaking only to themselves and reliant for direction solely on the visionary trances of the leader, the charismatic group may believe (with some justice) that the larger society is bent on their destruction. In response, the threatened cult may store up weapons for defense, encouraging the very aggression from the mainstream they had feared. Or a charismatic movement may elect to attack first, hoping to destroy the world and bring the millennium. It is also possible that the members may decide to kill themselves, rejecting the world that has rejected them, and search for their true divine destinies in death.

For melancholy instances of this trajectory, we can recall the mass suicides of the sect surrounding Jim Jones, the apocalyptic destruction of the fortified compound of the Branch Davidians in Waco, the suicides of the Heaven's Gate group, the sarin attack waged in the Tokyo subways by the Om Shin Rikyo cult, and a host of other frightening events. All these were set off by the inevitable collision between small groups worshiping their own charismatic gods on earth and the larger rationalized modern society, which is frightened and appalled by these apparently incomprehensible and fanatical alternative worlds.

However, members in these groups are not necessarily psychologically disturbed, though participation in a closed sect, where there is no testing against the taken-for-granted reality of the mainstream, can lead to the development of some quite extraordinary belief systems. Most converts join charismatic groups because their friends have joined them, or they join out of loneliness or in a sincere quest for enlightenment. And these communities do offer something notably lacking in daily life: an immediate and powerful connection to transcendent forces through participation in the faith of the believers—in other words, the experience of collective ecstacy. For this reason, it is not surprising that the fastest-growing religious movement in the United States (and perhaps in the world) is Pentecostalism, which offers immediate communion with God as its central tenet. The millions who have had this empowering experience are hardly mentally imbalanced; instead, they are reacting against the mechanization of the dominant culture and the bureaucratization of religion. It is also noteworthy that Pentecostalism is a movement that lacks a central leader, which makes it far less threatening to the mainstream.

Before judging the sanity of cult members, we should remember that Christianity itself began as a peripheral charismatic movement and that many charismatic groups ever since have succeeded in rationalizing themselves and integrating into the mainstream. The Quakers and the Anabaptists, along with old-world Mennonites and Amish, were all regarded in their early days as subversive extremists; we can recall as well that Mormons were once persecuted and killed for their beliefs and for their devotion to their charismatic leader, and were forced to flee into the desert, where they found their promised land. But the Mormons are now full-fledged citizens, whose charismatic past is largely forgotten. And in the present day the Unification Church has struggled mightily to outgrow its status as a cult, while still continuing to worship its charismatic founder, Sun Myung Moon.

As I have implied here and argued more extensively elsewhere,[93] immersion in a charismatic relationship is a universal human potential. It reflects an existential need to escape from the boundaries of the self and the constraints of rational structure. In charismatic relations, this need can be met by emotional devotion to the authority of a divine leader and by ecstatic participation in a collective wherein the boundaries of the self are dissolved. As both Durkheim and Weber argued, this experience lies at the heart of community, since it generates commitment to the sacred group; but under the right circumstances it also can be the source of innovation and revolution.

In simpler societies, charisma was a part of ordinary life; the shaman was the spiritual leader, reliant on visions to heal and command, incarnating the gods occasionally and otherwise living a relatively normal life. But in more complex and rationalized society, such experiences become exceptionally dangerous, since they threaten to break apart the central order of things and the rationality of the individual. As a result, charismatic groups are likely to be shunted to the periphery, which generates in their membership a sense of estrangement. In what Bateson would have described as schizmogenesis, the peripheralization and denigration of these movements often lead them to become more extreme, more oppositional, more encompassing, and more threatening to the mainstream, and therefore more likely to be persecuted and more likely to engage in radical and even violent behaviors. Nonetheless, such movements sometimes do succeed in reintegrating themselves into the larger culture, rationalizing their message of revitalization.

The human demand for self-loss and a release from structure does not cease in modern society. Rather, it may be intensified, as people feel themselves more isolated and alienated within an increasingly impersonal, fluid, and competitive social world. The yearning for a charismatic relation may be especially powerful in the United States, where mobility, individualism, and competitiveness are at their maximum, and where there is also a long history of a spiritual thirst for community and a deep appreciation of inner spirituality as the source of ultimate meaning. For these reasons, America has always been home to many charismatic movements and will continue to be in the future. But modern American society has also developed alternative forms of transcendent experience, as we will see in the next chapter.

Summary

This chapter deals with the complex topic of exclusion and marginalization, and with the paired processes of stigmatization and charisma. Every society, it was argued, always must categorize certain individuals and groups as outsiders, since it is through such attributions that the moral solidarity of the society as a whole is affirmed. Those labeled outsiders often take on the identity they have been assigned and live out lives that divide them from the mainstream. However, although every culture has deviants within it, the manner in which deviance is dealt with varies considerably. Some societies may be more likely to make accusations of deviance, others may favor a policy of silence; some may punish disfavored behavior severely, others may be more tolerant. These differences may be correlated with the degree of communal solidarity in the particular culture.

The claim for the importance of labeling is not to deny that there may be biological and characterological components at play in the assumption of a deviant identity. This is certainly the case with the most frightening and disturbing form of nonconformity to social norms: mental illness. Nonetheless, it is also clear that cultural attitudes do profoundly alter the symptomology and trajectory of even the most serious mental diseases, such as schizophrenia. It is also evident that behavior considered insane in one society can be highly valued in another, and that many mental disorders are culture-bound. This is so even in the United States where new mental illnesses such as multiple personality disorder and post-traumatic stress disorder reflect prevailing societal values and tensions. Even alcoholism has a strong cultural component.

Mental illness, then, is simply one among many human conditions that is stigmatized and treated with hostility. As Erving Goffman has argued, stigma is a structural relation in which certain identities are held to be discredited or discreditable by the larger society. Everyone, Goffman says, is subject to this process, since none of us is wholly what we ought to be; we all are subject to the all-too-human errors in our public presentation of self. The universal discrepancy between "is" and "ought" binds us as co-conspirators, acting together to maintain the smooth running of the social machine. But it also leads us to ostracize those who are too far outside the range of the acceptable—they remind us of our own failures.

Similarly, psychoanalytic theory argues that marginalized individuals serve as the foci for the projection outward of unacceptable aspects of the personality. They can then be repudiated with impunity, as a symbolic act of purification of the self. Yet the very act of projection attributes dark powers of the unconscious to the stigmatized person. A structural anthropological analysis makes an equivalent case. Outsiders are despised as polluting because they subvert the order of the central social organization. However, exclusion also puts outsiders in touch with the creative forces that are stifled by the rigidity of structure, and they become sources of dangerous energy. It is for these reasons that stigmatized people are feared as well as hated, and some are violently persecuted as witches and devils.

But the devils for members of the mainstream may well be the saviors for the peripheralized and disenchanted, who can be moved by the charismatic appeal of radical individuals who seek to overturn the authority of the existing system. Charisma is an emotional relation of unreasoning attraction—the reverse of the unreasoning repulsion of stigma. It is a universal human potential that becomes activated when the social order no longer has authority or legitimacy, allowing radical iconoclasts the space to spread their subversive messages to a receptive audience.

The expression of charisma varies historically, and charismatics appear in different guises in different cultural contexts. According to Max Weber, its origins are in the mind-shattering experiences of possession, psychic fragmentation, and eventual reintegration of shamanism. When this experience was reenacted in public, the audience participated in the emotional force of the performance, were revitalized by it, and attributed godlike powers to the performer. Trance, interpreted as possession by the gods, is the central experience of shamanism. Although designated as indicative of mental illness in our society, trance can be found in most of the world's preliterate cultures. Even in our own society, trancelike states can be induced through various techniques that disrupt the ordinary flow of information into the brain and precipitate a sense of dissociation, which can be interpreted as spirit possession.

But under modern conditions the interpretation is usually far more negative. Those who participate in charismatic relationships are often considered mentally deranged, and the groups they belong to are designated cults. Because collective experiences of dissociation can threaten the social order, charismatics and their groups are relegated to the periphery. Such estrangement often leads to an escalating dialectic of aggression and demonization that ends in destruction, as the tragic fates of several contemporary charismatic cults indicate. But participation in charismatic relationships also is an effort to touch the divine. As such, it is an ineradicable part of the human experience.

Endnotes

1. Quoted in Larry Peters, 1982, "Trance, Initiation and Psychotherapy in Tamang Shamanism," *American Ethnologist* 9: 21–46, 23.
2. See Chapters 4 and 6, respectively.
3. See Chapter 4.
4. See the essays in Mikhail Bakhtin, 1981, *The Dialogic Imagination,* Austin: University of Texas Press (original publication 1975).
5. Ibid. Note that Bakhtin was a far more dialectical thinker than many of his modern followers, and was well aware of issues of power and the difficulties of change. Bakhtin also knew that not every novel is equally multiplex in voicing, nor is every voice equally important.
6. Gloria Anzaldúa quoted in Renato Rosaldo, 1989, *Culture and Truth: The Remaking of Social Analysis,* Boston: Beacon Press, p. 216. See also Philip Rieff, 1986, *The Triumph of the Therapeutic: Uses of Faith after Freud,* Chicago: University of Chicago Press, for a meditation on the nature of constraint and the quandaries of a therapeutic model of society in which acceptance replaces morality. Also, see Chapter 8 for a longer discussion of some of the problems of a postmodern approach to anthropological research.
7. Émile Durkheim, 1984, *The Division of Labor in Society,* New York: Free Press (original publication 1893).
8. Erving Goffman, 1963, *Stigma: Notes on the Management of a Spoiled Identity,* New York: Simon and Schuster, p. 138.
9. As discussed in Chapter 6.
10. For a different interpretation, see Niko Besnier, 1996, "Polynesian Gender Liminality through Time and Space," in Gilbert Herdt (ed.), *Third Sex, Third Gender: Beyond Sexual Dimorphism in Culture and History,* New York: Zone Books.
11. Nancy Scheper-Hughes, 1979, *Saints, Scholars and Schizophrenics: Mental Illness in Rural Ireland,* Berkeley: University of California Press.
12. Robert Edgerton, 1976, *Deviance: A Cross-Cultural Perspective,* Menlo Park, NJ: Cummings, p. 110.
13. Unni Wikan, 1991, *Behind the Veil in Arabia: Women in Oman,* Chicago: University of Chicago Press. A similar relationship is reported by Janice Boddy, 1989, *Wombs and Alien Spirits: Women, Men and the Zar Cult in Northern Sudan,* Madison: University of Wisconsin Press.
14. For this material, see Tsunetsugu Munakata, 1989, "The Socio-Cultural Significance of the Diagnostic Label 'Neurasthenia' in Japan's Mental Health Care System," *Culture, Medicine and Psychiatry* 13: 203–13.
15. N. Scheper-Hughes, 1987, " 'Mental' in 'Southie': Individual, Family, and Community Responses to Psychosis in South Boston," *Culture, Medicine and Psychiatry* 11: 53–78. The attitude of the community is epitomized in a sign carried in protest

against the building of a psychiatric clinic in the neighborhood: Keep Mental Health Out of Southie!

16. Though with patience, interpretation of the delusions is possible. For an example, see Atwood Gaines, 1988, "Delusions: Culture, Psychosis and the Problem of Meaning," in Thomas Oltmanns and Brendan Maher (eds.), *Delusional Beliefs*, New York: Wiley.

17. For discussions, see Nancy Andreasen, 1984, *The Broken Brain: The Biological Revolution in Psychiatry*, New York: Harper and Row. The standard reference is American Psychiatric Association Committee on Nomenclature and Statistics, 1994, *Diagnostic and Statistical Manual of Mental Disorders* (4th ed.), Washington, DC: American Psychiatric Association.

18. Joseph Westermeyer, 1988, "Some Cross-Cultural Aspects of Delusions," in Thomas Oltmanns and Brendan Maher (eds.), *Delusional Beliefs*, New York: Wiley, p. 218. See also H. W. Dunham, 1976, "Society, Culture and Mental Disorder," *Archives of General Psychiatry* 33: 147–56.

19. The best discussion of the limitations and premises of Western psychiatry is found in Arthur Kleinman, 1988, *Rethinking Psychiatry: From Cultural Category to Personal Experience*, New York: Free Press. See also Horacio Fabrega, Jr., 1988, "An Ethnomedical Perspective on Anglo-American Psychiatry," *Journal of Psychiatry* 146: 588–96; Horacio Fabrega, Jr., 1987, "Psychiatric Diagnosis: A Cultural Perspective," *Journal of Nervous and Mental Disease* 175: 383–94.

20. Jerome Singer and Morris Opler, 1956, "Contrasting Patterns of Fantasy and Motility in Irish and Italian Schizophrenics," *Journal of Abnormal and Social Psychology* 53: 42–47; Morris Opler, 1959, "Cultural Differences in Mental Disorders," in M. Opler (ed.), *Culture and Mental Health*, New York: Macmillan. See also Scheper-Hughes, " 'Mental' in 'Southie.' " For a discussion of racial differences, see Horacio Fabrega, Jr., Juan Mezzich, and Richard Ulrich, 1988, "Black-White Differences in Psychopathology in an Urban Psychiatric Population," *Comprehensive Psychiatry* 29: 285–97.

21. For evidence, see Michael Blakey, 1994, "Psychophysiological Stress and the Disorders of Industrial Society: A Critical Theoretical Formulation for Biocultural Research," in Shepard Forman (ed.), *Diagnosing America: Anthropology and Public Engagement*, Ann Arbor: University of Michigan Press.

22. See Arthur Kleinman, 1986, *Social Origins of Distress and Disease*, New Haven, CT: Yale University Press; Arthur Kleinman and Byron Good (eds.), 1985, *Culture and Depression: Studies in the Anthropology and Cross-Cultural Psychiatry of Affect and Disorder*, Berkeley: University of California Press; G. Brown and T. Harris, 1978, *Social Origins of Depression: A Study of Psychiatric Disorder in Women*, New York: Free Press. Note, though, that clinical depression is a major mental illness that involves considerable brain disorder. It should be distinguished from feelings of melancholy and affliction.

23. Horacio Fabrega, Jr., 1990, "The Concept of Somatization as a Cultural and Historical Product of Western Medicine," *Psychosomatic Medicine* 52: 653–72.

24. Byron Good, 1977, "The Heart of What's the Matter: The Semantics of Illness in Iran," *Culture, Medicine and Psychiatry* 1: 25–58.

25. Kleinman, *Social Origins of Distress and Disease*.

26. See Lawrence Kirmayer, 1989, "Cultural Variations in the Response to Psychiatric Disorders and Emotional Distress," *Social Sciences and Medicine*, 29: 327–39; Atwood Gaines, 1982, "Cultural Definitions, Behavior and the Person in American Psychiatry," in A. Marsella and G. White (eds.), *Cultural Conceptions of Mental Health and Therapy*, Dordrecht, Netherlands: D. Reidel.

27. For an early statement, see Nancy Waxler, 1974, "Culture and Mental Illness: A Social Labeling Perspective," *Journal of Nervous and Mental Disease* 159: 379–95.

28. Cited in Kirmayer, "Cultural Variations."
29. Atwood Gaines and Paul Farmer, 1986, "Visible Saints: Social Cynosures and Dysphoria in the Mediterranean Tradition," *Culture, Medicine and Psychiatry* 10: 295–330; Gananath Obeyesekere, 1985, "Depression, Buddhism and the Work of Culture in Sri Lanka," in Arthur Kleinman and Byron Good (eds.), 1985, *Culture and Depression: Studies in the Anthropology and Cross-Cultural Psychiatry of Affect and Disorder,* Berkeley: University of California Press; Richard Castillo, 1991, "Divided Consciousness and Enlightenment in Hindu Yogis," *Anthropology of Consciousness* 2: 1–6. See Chapter 7 for more on Obeyesekere's argument.
30. K. M. Lin and A. Kleinman, 1988, "Psychopathology and the Clinical Course of Schizophrenia," *Schizophrenia Bulletin* 14: 555–67.
31. For a review, see R. Warner, 1985, *Recovery from Schizophrenia,* London: Routledge and Kegan Paul.
32. Louis Sass, 1992, *Madness and Modernism: Insanity in the Light of Modern Art, Literature and Thought,* Cambridge, MA: Harvard University Press. See also Georges Devereux, 1980, *Basic Problems in Ethnopsychiatry,* Chicago: University of Chicago Press.
33. G. Leng, 1985, "Koro—A Cultural Disease," in R. Simons and C. Hughes (eds.), *The Culture-Bound Symptoms,* Dordrecht, Netherlands: D. Reidel.
34. Michael Kenny, 1978, "Latah: The Symbolism of a Putative Mental Disorder," *Culture, Medicine and Psychiatry* 2: 209–31.
35. L. Marano, 1985, "Windigo Psychosis: The Anatomy of an Emic-Etic Confusion," In R. Simons and C. Hughes (eds.), *The Culture-Bound Symptoms,* Dordrecht, Netherlands: D. Reidel.
36. For a discussion, see Christopher Lasch, 1978, *The Culture of Narcissism: American Life in an Age of Diminishing Expectations,* New York: Norton.
37. For a recent multibiography of MPD, see Joan F. Casey, 1991, *The Flock,* New York: Knopf.
38. As Ian Hacking remarks, it may be significant that the TV remote control became widely used at the time that MPD began to flourish. For more, see Ian Hacking, 1995, *Rewriting the Soul: Multiple Personality and the Sciences of Memory,* Princeton, NJ: Princeton University Press.
39. Michael Lambeck and Paul Antze, 1996, "Introduction: Forecasting Memory," in Paul Antze and Michael Lambeck (eds.), *Tense Past: Cultural Essays in Trauma and Memory,* New York: Routledge, pp. xxiii–iv.
40. For a defense of MPD as a model of the mind appropriate for comparative anthropology, see Richard Castillo, 1994, "Spirit Possession in South Asia: Dissociation or Hysteria," *Culture, Medicine and Psychiatry* 18: 1–21, 141–62. For a discussion of the modular theory of mind, see Chapter 8.
41. See Janice Haaken, 1994, "Sexual Abuse, Recovered Memory, and Therapeutic Practice," *Social Text* 40: 115–45.
42. Some of the best of these studies, interestingly enough, were undertaken during World War I by W. H. R. Rivers (whose pioneering studies of the primitive mind were mentioned in Chapter 4) and in World War II by Abram Kardiner (whose attempted synthesis between Freud and anthropology was described in Chapter 5).
43. Allan Young, 1995, *The Harmony of Illusions: Inventing Post-Traumatic Stress Disorder,* Princeton, NJ: Princeton University Press.
44. For an example, see Lawrence Wright, 1994, *Remembering Satan,* New York: Knopf.
45. For a moving novelistic account of Rivers's wartime work, see Pat Barker, 1991, *Regeneration,* Harmondsworth, England: Penguin Books.

46. For a discussion of the excesses of the recovered memory movement, see Richard Ofshe and Ethan Watters, 1994, *Making Monsters: False Memories, Psychotherapy and Sexual Hysteria,* New York: Scribners.

47. For an example, see Nancy Venable Raine, 1998, *After Silence: Rape and My Journey Back,* New York: Crown.

48. See Gerald Erchak, 1992, *The Anthropology of Self and Behavior,* New Brunswick, NJ: Rutgers University Press, pp. 149–59.

49. Herbert Fingarette, 1988, *Heavy Drinking: The Myth of Alcoholism as a Disease,* Berkeley: University of California Press.

50. For an example, see Mac Marshall, 1979, *Weekend Warriors: Alcohol in a Micronesian Culture,* Palo Alto, CA: Mayfield.

51. For an anthropological appreciation of Goffman, see Philip Bock, 1988, *Rethinking Psychological Anthropology,* New York: Freeman.

52. Erving Goffman, 1963, *Stigma: Notes on the Management of a Spoiled Identity,* New York: Simon and Schuster, p. 128.

53. Erving Goffman, 1959, *The Presentation of Self in Everyday Life,* New York: Doubleday, p. 9.

54. Laud Humphreys, 1970, *Tearoom Trade: Impersonal Sex in Public Places,* Chicago: Aldine.

55. See also Émile Durkheim, 1966, *Suicide: A Study in Sociology,* New York: Free Press (original publication 1897), which relates rates of crime, insanity, and suicide to a sense of alienation (a sense of meaninglessness) or anomie (a frightening feeling of an absence of boundaries) associated with social fragmentation.

56. For the classic statement of the "safety valve" theory of ritual, see Max Gluckman, 1954, *Rituals of Rebellion in Southeast Africa,* Manchester, England: Manchester University Press.

57. This is the perspective taken by Victor Turner, 1977, *The Ritual Process: Structure and Anti-Structure,* Chicago: Aldine, and developed in Roger Abrahams and Richard Bauman, 1978, "Ranges of Festival Behavior," in Barbara Babcock (ed.), *The Reversible World: Symbolic Inversion in Art and Society,* Ithaca, NY: Cornell University Press.

58. See Turner, *The Ritual Process,* for examples. See also Victor Turner, 1974, "Passages, Margins, and Poverty: Religious Symbols of Communitas," in V. Turner (ed.), *Dramas, Fields, and Metaphors: Symbolic Action in Human Society,* Ithaca, NY: Cornell University Press. In this article, Turner breaks the liminal into three categories. The liminar, who is moving between structural categories; the outsider, who is permanently excluded from structure; and the marginal, who is moving between categories, but may not succeed in making the transition. In this section, I am dealing primarily with the outsider, though liminars and marginals also partake of some of the same supernatural power. See Chapter 7 for more on Turner.

59. Mary Douglas, 1966, *Purity and Danger: An Analysis of Concepts of Pollution and Taboo,* London: Routledge.

60. See Edmund Leach, 1976, *Culture and Communication: The Logic by Which Symbols Are Connected,* Cambridge, England: Cambridge University Press.

61. Mathias Guenther, 1975, "The Trance Dance as an Agent of Social Change among the Farm Bushmen of the Ghanzi District," *Botswana Notes and Records* 7: 161–66.

62. I. M. Lewis, 1971, *Ecstatic Religion: An Anthropological Study of Spirit Possession and Shamanism,* Harmondsworth, England: Penguin Books, pp. 121.

63. Norman Cohn, 1975, *Europe's Inner Demons,* New York: Basic Books, p. 73.

64. Alan MacFarlane, 1970, *Witchcraft in Tudor and Stuart England: A Regional and Comparative Study,* New York: Harper and Row; Keith Thomas, 1971, *Religion and the Decline of Magic,* New York: Scribners.

65. Max Marwick, 1965, *Sorcery in Its Social Setting*, Manchester, England: Manchester University Press.
66. Tanya Luhrmann, 1989, *Persuasions of the Witch's Craft: Ritual Magic and Witchcraft in Present-day England*, Cambridge, MA: Harvard University Press.
67. For the paradigmatic statement, see I. M. Lewis, 1970, "A Structural Approach to Witchcraft and Spirit Possession," in Mary Douglas (ed.), *Witchcraft Confessions and Accusations*, London: Tavistock.
68. I. M. Lewis, 1986, *Religion in Context: Cults and Charisma*, Cambridge, England: Cambridge University Press.
69. Guenther, "The Trance Dance," p. 165.
70. See Edward Shils, 1965, "Charisma, Order, Status," *American Sociological Review* 30: 199–213; Clifford Geertz, 1977, "Centers, Kings and Charisma," in Joseph Ben-David and T. N. Clark (eds.), *Culture and Its Creators*, Chicago: University of Chicago Press.
71. Max Weber, 1946, "The Sociology of Charismatic Authority," in Hans Gerth and C. Wright Mills (eds.), *From Max Weber: Essays in Sociology*, New York: Oxford University Press; 1968, "The Nature of Charismatic Authority," in S. N. Eisenstadt (ed.), *Max Weber on Charisma and Institution Building*, Chicago: University of Chicago Press.
72. Anthony F. C. Wallace, 1956, "Revitalization Movements," *American Anthropologist* 58: 264–81.
73. See Ann Ruth Willner, 1984, *The Spellbinders: Charismatic Political Leadership*, New Haven, CT: Yale University Press. The study of leadership in general offers a fertile field for psychological anthropology, since leaders must express and channel the values, hopes, and desires of their followers. A psychosocial study of the complex intersection between cultural form, individual character, and the assertion of power was pioneered by Erik Erikson (1958, *Young Man Luther: A Study in Psychoanalysis and History*, New York: Norton; 1969, *Gandhi's Truth on the Origins of Militant Nonviolence*, New York: Norton) but has been little explored since by anthropologists, who have left the field to political scientists. For an exception, see Waud Kracke, 1978, *Force and Persuasion: Leadership in an Amazonian Society*, Chicago: University of Chicago Press.
74. The term "shaman" is an anthropological neologism taken from the Siberian Tungus. For them, it designates one who is excited, moved, raised. As a verb, it means "to perceive in an ecstatic manner." For the classical account, see S. Shirokogoroff, 1935, *The Psychomental Complex of the Tungus*, London: Kegan Paul, Trench, Trubner.
75. Émile Durkheim, 1965, *The Elementary Forms of the Religious Life*, New York: Free Press, p. 140 (original publication 1912).
76. Mircea Eliade, 1964, *Shamanism: Archaic Techniques of Ecstasy*, Princeton, NJ: Princeton University Press, p. 504.
77. Erika Bourguignon, 1972, "Dreams and Altered States of Consciousness in Anthropological Research," in F. Hsu (ed.), *Psychological Anthropology*, Chicago: Dorsey Press.
78. The question of the shaman's sanity has long been a topic of debate among anthropologists. The traditional opinion was that the shaman is psychologically unbalanced. See Waldemar Borgoras, 1904, *The Chukchee: Memoirs of the Jesup North Pacific Expedition*, Vol. 11, New York: American Museum of Natural History, pp. 426–28; V. Jochelson, 1926, *The Yukaghir and the Yukaghirized Tungus: Memoirs of the Jesup North Pacific Expedition*, Vol. 14, New York: American Museum of Natural History, p. 187; Alfred Kroeber, 1952, "Psychosis or Social Sanction," in A. Kroeber (ed.), *The Nature of Culture*, Chicago: University of Chicago Press; Eliade, *Shamanism*, p. 306; Georges Devereux, 1961, "Shamans as Neurotics," *American Anthropologist* 63: 1088–90. On the other hand, Boyer claims that Apache shamans are actually saner than others in the

group, with more ability to "use regression in the service of the ego." See L. Bruce Boyer et al., 1964, "Comparison of Shamans and Pseudoshamans of the Apaches of the Mescalero Indian Reservation: A Rorschach Study," *Journal of Projective Techniques* 28: 173–80, 173. See also Richard Shweder, 1972, "Aspects of Cognition in Zinacanteco Shamans, Experimental Results," in Alexander Lessa and Evon Vogt (eds.), *Reader in Comparative Religion*, New York: Harper and Row; Don Handelman, 1968, "Shamanizing on an Empty Stomach," *American Anthropologist* 70: 353–58.

79. Quoted in J. Murphy, 1964, "Psychotherapeutic Aspects of Shamanism on St. Lawrence Island, Alaska," in A. Kiev (ed.), *Magic, Faith and Healing*, London: Free Press, p. 58. For a psychologically astute model of shamanic initiation, see I. M. Lewis, 1971, *Ecstatic Religion: An Anthropological Study of Spirit Possession and Shamanism*, Harmondsworth, England: Penguin Books.

80. Lawrence Krader, 1978, "Shamanism: Theory and History in Buryat Society," in V. Dioszegi and M. Hoppal (eds.), *Shamanism in Siberia*, Budapest, Hungary: Adademiai Kiado, p. 185.

81. Claude Lévi-Strauss, 1967, "The Sorcerer and His Magic," In Claude Lévi-Strauss (ed.), *Structural Anthropology*, New York: Basic Books, p. 175.

82. See the section on Obeyesekere in Chapter 7 for examples.

83. Richard Katz, 1982, *Boiling Energy: Community Healing among the Kalahari Kung*, Cambridge, MA: Harvard University Press.

84. John Grim, 1983, *The Shaman: Patterns of Siberian and Ojibway Healing*, Norman: University of Oklahoma Press.

85. Richard Castillo (1995, "Culture, Trance and the Mind-Brain," *Anthropology of Consciousness* 6: 17–32) suggests that intense focusing of attention is the key psychological mechanism for all forms of trance induction.

86. Ernst Gellhorn and William Kiely, 1972, "Mystical States of Consciousness: Neurophysiological and Clinical Aspects," *Journal of Nervous and Mental Disease* 154: 399–405; Raymond Prince, 1982, "The Endorphins: A Review for Psychological Anthropologists," *Ethos* 10: 303–16; 1982, "Shamans and Endorphins: Hypothesis for a Synthesis," *Ethos* 10: 409–23.

87. Michael Winkelman, 1986, "Trance States: A Theoretical Model and Cross-Cultural Analysis," *Ethos* 14: 174–203, 174, 185. See also Arnold Mandell, 1980, "Toward a Psychobiology of Transcendence: God in the Brain," in Julian Davidson and Richard Davidson (eds.), *The Psychobiology of Consciousness*, New York: Plenum.

88. For a good discussion, see T. J. Scheff, 1979, *Catharsis in Healing, Ritual and Drama*, Berkeley: University of California Press.

89. For my own attempt to do so, see Charles Lindholm, 1990, *Charisma*, Oxford, England: Basil Blackwell.

90. Scheff, *Catharsis in Healing, Ritual and Drama*.

91. Charles Lindholm, 1992, "Charisma, Crowd Psychology and Altered States of Consciousness," *Culture, Medicine and Psychiatry* 16: 287–310.

92. For examples, see Lewis, *Ecstatic Religion*; Emiko Ohnuki-Tierney, 1980, "Shamans and *Imu* among Two Ainu Groups," *Ethos* 8: 204–18.

93. See Lindholm, *Charisma*; Lindholm, "Charisma, Crowd Psychology and Altered States of Consciousness."

PART FIVE

Applications

CHAPTER 12

Love and Culture

For most of his life, Max Weber, the great sociologist who wrote so insightfully about the emotional power of charisma, felt himself to be ugly and cold-blooded, without the capacity for passion: "I am . . . like a tree stump, which is able to put out *buds,* again and again—without playing the part of being a whole tree." Cut off from his emotions, sexually frustrated in his marriage, he sought salvation in the austere pleasures of the intellect. But when he met and fell in love with the aristocratic and sensual Else Von Richthofen, she became his pathway to a different kind of existence. As he wrote in a love letter to her, "I can live toward only one person in truth, and that I can and must do that is the last and decisive necessity in my life, loftier and stronger than any god." Erotic love, he now felt, is the "royal road . . . away from enslavement to the lifeless routines of everyday existence and from the pretentiousness of unrealities handed down from on high."[1] Through rapture, Weber proclaimed, one could escape from the modern chains of specialization and rationality.

But although Weber praised the immanent power of love to reveal the truest aspects of the self, most social scientists have ignored it, or if they have mentioned love, they have claimed that it does not exist at all, except as an illusion promulgated in Hollywood movies. This position was best stated in 1931 by the American anthropologist Robert Lowie (1833–1957), who wrote that everywhere in the world "passion, of course is taken for granted; affection, which many travellers vouch for, might be conceded; but Love? Well, the romantic sentiment occurs in simpler conditions, as with us–in fiction."[2]

The romantic ideal: Clark Gable and Vivien Leigh in *Gone with the Wind.*

Is love indeed an illusion—or is it the transformative experience that Weber said it was? Anthropologists, historians, and others have only recently begun to address this question.[3] In this chapter we will utilize some of their work to discuss the psychological anthropology of love in its multiple dimensions. And while we certainly will not be able to unravel its inner mystery, we can at least begin to answer the question of "what we talk about when we talk about love."[4]

Chapter Outline

I Paths to Selflessness
 A Charisma and Its Alternatives
 B The Love Schema
 C Love and Charisma

II Love in History
 A Love before Capitalism
 B Marriage, Modernity, and the Function of Love
 C Transcendence and Pragmatism

III Looking for Love
 A Does Romantic Love Exist Only in the West?
 B Do Other Cultures Experience Romantic Love?
 C Love, Sex, and Reproduction

IV The Nature of Love
 A Chaste Love
 B Case Studies: Love and Social Structure
 C The Future of Love

I. PATHS TO SELFLESSNESS

A Charisma and Its Alternatives
 The location of various charisma-like experiences in modern society.

B The Love Schema
 Love is the major modern alternative to charisma. The Western love schema is defined.

C Love and Charisma
 Charisma and romantic love are compared and contrasted.

A. Charisma and Its Alternatives

One way to talk about love is to do so indirectly, through comparison with experiences that resemble it. Charisma is just such an experience. As we learned in the previous chapter, it is defined as the attraction of a group toward its idolized leader, who is thought to be a kind of god. Charisma provides salvation from

Secular Religion

The notion of secular religion goes back to Durkheim, who insisted that religion could not be defined as a belief in God, but as a division of the world into opposed sacred and profane domains. For him, the essence of the sacred is communion in the group, as the ecstatic experience of collective effervescence transforms the participants and merges them into a moral unit. Durkheim believed that the contemporary state, with its ceremonies and pomp, its calendrical celebrations of itself, and the awe and self-sacrifice it inspires, is equivalent to a secular religion, with the flag as its unifying symbol. Those who do not find this convincing might recall the passions aroused when protestors have burned the American flag in public.

isolation and alienation by drawing people out of themselves and into a communal relationship that is subjectively felt to be a connection with the divine. However, charismatic relations are also perilous—they threaten the complex social structure and can lead to ostracism and various forms of pathology.

Instead of participating in pure charismatic relations, most people today seek safer, less intense, more rationalized routes to escape from loneliness and to gain some of the benefits offered by charisma. These alternatives include participation in mainstream religions, which supply the sacred in diluted, institutionalized forms. The state too provides its own secularized religion that gives citizens feelings of belonging and empowerment.

Of course, there is also the more profane and trivial, but also more personal and exciting, community provided by sports, with its exemplary heroes, expressive performances, and local attachments. For more aesthetic souls, the cult of the arts serves a similar purpose, furnishing the faithful with superhuman figures to worship and with temples for contemplation of the holy objects. Yet all these moneymaking forms of charisma are much weakened by the professionalism of the performers, the variety of "products" available, the fickleness of the consuming public, and the consequent lack of commitment to any particular charismatic individual or group.

More intimate and more satisfying communion is achieved in smaller-scale gatherings. Psychotherapy and its New Age cousins, the numerous 12-step programs, give troubled individuals the opportunity to participate in emotionally empathetic groups, while the therapist provides someone with whom patients are expected to "fall in love" through the mechanism of transference. But therapists who try to prolong and intensify the emotional ties with their patients are likely candidates for disciplinary action, since the whole point of therapy is to work through the transference and eventually terminate the relationship, leaving the patient cured and capable of solitary self-actualization.

A similar process also undermines the intimate institution that therapy is meant to heal: the family. Ideally speaking, the middle-class American family provides the major alternative to the competitive world of business and trade. As the anthropologist David Schneider has shown, Americans have strong faith that the family is a place of "diffuse, enduring solidarity" held together solely by shared love and affection.[5] In Christopher Lasch's famous words, for Americans, home is the "haven in a heartless world."[6] As the prototypical location for intimacy and caring, the family provides the model for the loving community that is sought in charismatic groups. It is no accident that the members of such communities habitually call one another Brother and Sister, and that the leader is regularly referred to as Father or Mother.

Yet the reality of the family is often very different from its idealized form, as unconditional love and participation are undercut by the practical need to raise children who are capable of independence and detachment, and who are trained in the necessary skills of negotiation and entrepreneurship. As Erik Erikson has written, instead of a comfortable love nest, what exists in the American home is a miniature marketplace, with each individual bargaining "to accrue claims for future privileges justifiable on the basis of one's past concessions."[7] Cultural values favoring protection of privacy, freedom of choice, and individual control over personal resources also erode middle-class family solidarity, as the children have their own inviolate, private spaces and are taught to express their preferences, to work for themselves, and to accrue their own personal property. These values coincide with the fact that the average American family—like the therapy group—exists to disintegrate, since children are expected to leave home and embark on their independent careers.

Friends provide the secondary alternative to family life, and the usual trajectory for American children in early adolescence is to attach themselves to peer groups, leaving the family behind. Like the family, friends too are supposed to be loving, giving, and caring; they provide the community lacking in the marketplace; they are the people to whom one can reveal one's true self, the people who can be wholly trusted and with whom one can feel at home. Yet the reality of social mobility, which requires rapid changes in both status and location, means that trusted old friends must often be left behind and forgotten. New ones must be found at work or school, where intimacy is challenged by rivalry, or in clubs, sports leagues, action groups, and so on, where intimacy is limited by the narrow range of the shared interest. As a result, friendships often are adaptive and fleeting, with little depth or intensity. The smiley-face icon and the generalized niceness of Americans reflect this reality.

B. The Love Schema

Most Americans would agree with Weber that today the most effective and moving way to seek redemption from emotional aridity is through romantic love. This truth is testified to by the popular movies, television shows, songs, and literature of our culture, which are preoccupied with love and its vicissitudes. So, if love is an illusion, as many social scientists have said, it is an extremely pervasive and persuasive one.[8] The relationship between constructed image and felt experience is, of course, neither simple nor direct; but from the perspective of psychological-cognitive anthropology, we can see that the conventional media stereotypes of romance convey an emotionally motivating master schema that is widely held and followed in modern American society—and perhaps in other societies as well.[9] This master schema both shapes and is shaped by the actual experiences of individuals. It helps constitute our hopes and dreams, our goals, our emotional lives in a powerful way precisely because it answers the most profound quandary of our existence: our desire to transcend our separateness and finitude.

What are the prototypical attributes of the romantic love schema? Above all, love is conceptualized as a mysterious, overwhelming, compulsive attraction directed toward a particular unique other. For the true lover, life is not worth living alone, while simply being close to the beloved is of ultimate value in itself. This kind of love is conceived as occurring spontaneously, to just happen, and the intrusion of planning is almost as great a sin against love as selfishness. Romantic love is risky, since it may not be returned, but it must have at least the potential for mutuality, and so cannot be for a thing, or a cause, but only for a person. Unlike the often chaste romances of the medieval courtier, which always emphasized the inferiority of the male lover to his lady, falling in love in the modern world is equalizing and sexual, and cannot include the love of a mother for a child or the love of God. Also, love is blind; the reciprocal attraction of the lovers is believed to pay no attention to boundaries of age, class, and race. Many of the dramas of love have plotlines constructed around the conflicting claims of love and status (though in fact most love relationships are with people much like oneself). Love also thrives on obstacles, and interference is likely to increase, not lessen, romantic attachment.[10]

As the modern philosopher Robert Unger writes, the ennobling sentiments and capacity for transcendence felt by those inside the dyadic love world constitute "the most influential mode of moral vision in our culture."[11] Love, it is said, makes the world go around, just as love's euphoria makes the heads of lovers spin. As an emotional state, it is unique in its capacity to create a shared world of mutual adoration. As an ideal, it is aspired to by most Americans, though it may be felt in all its aspects by only a few.[12] As a point in a life course, the emotional rush of falling in love (the risky romantic moment) is believed to lead to the calmer and more rational state of being in love, which is the basis of a lasting companionate marriage.

C. Love and Charisma

Obviously, the parallels between the experience of falling in love and the experience of charisma are multiple. For instance, in Western ideology, love, like charisma, is thought to completely enthrall the parties involved. Like charisma, romantic involvement is felt to be timeless, intense, and compelling. Unlike other social ties that are either obligatory, like kinship, or chosen, like friendship, love, like charisma, is conceived to be a spontaneous, overwhelming emotional attraction. Love cannot be organized or predetermined, it cannot be assigned or controlled; it is involuntary and compulsive. And, as in charismatic relations, the great sins against love are planning and egoism.

The parallel between charisma and romantic love is most evident in the apotheosis of the leader/beloved. In both cases there is an idealization and sense of fusion with the other that endows the master/lover with a unique status and authority.[13] By identification, the follower shares in the leader's power, just as the lover finds self-fulfillment in pleasing the beloved. Both recognize the beloved other as vivid, extraordinary, preternaturally attractive, full of intense emotion—the embodiment of all that is good and desirable. Because of these imputed qualities, lovers, like followers, want to obey the ones they adore, and try to intuit and immediately satisfy their desires. Devotion to the beloved one in both charisma and romance is felt as ennobling and ecstatic; self-sacrifice becomes a gain, not a loss. Because of these extensive parallels, falling in love has been described as "the simplest form of a collective movement" replicating in small scale the ecstatic sensations and transformative power of great revolutions.[14]

There are, however, vast differences between the experiences. In contrast to the hostility that usually occurs between present-day charismatic groups and the mainstream, all the world loves a lover. Despite the lovers' subjective sense of rebellion and spontaneity, romantic love exists within and supports the modern social system, and is the expected precursor to the central institution of marriage. For the society at large, it is the opposite of radical. Love has another valuable social function as well. It gives an accepted image of rapture and communion, an escape, potentially available to all, from the world of competitive individualism—anyone can fall in love; anyone can be loved. All the world loves the lover because the lovers' regard for one another reaffirms the possibility of transcendence over human hostility and alienation. The tremendous quantity of love songs, stories, movies, and poems testifies to the function of love imagery in soothing and pacifying the public and in reducing the tension of existence in the modern world.

Love, because it is so powerful and so involving, so spontaneous and inspiring, and yet so socially useful, is the best and most efficient channel for the

Realizing the ideal: A bride and groom exit the church.

intense emotions that might otherwise be directed into dangerous charismatic social movements. Instead of being turned to critique or outright rejection of the mainstream, in romance the transcendent impulse and the desire for selfless fusion are confined to the mutuality of the intimate couple.

Because each demands a complete identification of self and other in the relationship, love and charisma are always antagonistic to one another: A person cannot be part of a charismatic group and still be in a separate love relationship. Charismatic communities everywhere devalue and break any intense bonds between couples and focus sexual desires upon the leader. The intolerance of charismatic groups for couples may be seen quite clearly in many examples, such as the strict sanctions against special love (love between couples) in John Humphrey Noyes's Oneida community. The Shakers solved the problem by obliging all members to take a vow of chastity, while the ecstatic Russian sect of the Skopzi endorsed castration as an indication of commitment. The same extreme strategy was followed by the ill-fated Heaven's Gate commune. Other cults, such as the one led by Jim Jones, have required all members to have sex with the leader, who also assigned sexual partners to one another. The opposite pattern also holds true; as Freud noted, "lovers are sufficient to themselves" and are hostile to the demands made by the group.[15] Ex–cult members regularly attest that their decision to leave the group was a direct consequence of establishing or managing to retain a romantic dyad in spite of group pressure.

II. LOVE IN HISTORY

A Love before Capitalism
   Sex and love in the classical world. Courtly love in medieval Europe.

B Marriage, Modernity, and the Function of Love
   Capitalism and the rise of love marriage. The rating and dating complex.

C Transcendence and Pragmatism
   Love and the quest for authenticity. The tension between irrational romance and institutionalized matrimony.

A. Love before Capitalism

Like religion, romantic love can best be known by its effects. It is crucial in maintaining social stability in contemporary society. It induces people to marry and have children; it also draws them away from potentially dangerous charismatic involvements. It provides the experience of ecstasy and communion to ordinary individuals, and so alleviates alienation and promotes social cohesion and mental health. It is probably the most intense emotional experience available in our culture and is the major avenue of escape from the pressures of competitive individualism. Love is clearly not an illusion, since its consequences are so tangible and profound.

But even though Weber was right about the subjective importance of love, and even though lovers may feel their love is both timeless and natural, in reality, romantic love as we know it is a modern phenomenon, created by the intersection of human needs and historical-cultural context. Among the ancient Greeks and Romans, love was understood not as idealization, but as an irre-

The Dangers of Eros

The separation of eroticism from marriage through the expansion of the institutions of prostitution and concubinage has often led to problems. For example, in the Roman Empire, sexual pleasure (at least for patrician men) was to be found mainly in the arms of slaves in brothels. Unfortunately, as a result, the birthrate of legitimate children among the nobility became dangerously low; also, the clients sometimes became enamored of their concubines.[16] In a reversal of the actual relationship, the prostitute might then be called Domina—the ruler of her lover. One embittered lover named his faithless beloved Nemesis—the sister of tenderness and deceit.[17] Patrician women too could be destroyed by the attacks of Eros and compulsive attraction to the wrong man, as Virgil's story of Dido and Aeneas attests. In this epic tale, Dido is the powerful ruler of her own kingdom. But she is brought low by Cupid's arrow, and is forced to fall in love with the wandering hero Aeneas. When he eventually leaves her to follow his destiny, the distraught Dido burns herself alive in a gigantic funeral pyre.

Aeneas tells the story of his travels to an enraptured Dido.

sistible erotic desire. Sexual craving was worshiped as a fecund force emanating from the gods, but also feared because it could draw young people into inappropriate and dangerous liaisons, dissolve arranged marriages, and cause untold conflict and misery. To protect against these threats, mechanisms such as child betrothal, chaperonage, and institutionalized prostitution were developed to maintain corporate group control over reproduction, either by suppressing wayward erotic desire or by channeling it to a sphere entirely separate from marriage.[18] Many of these forms of control are still found in contemporary societies where family and lineage retain their importance.

Early Christians, with their millenaristic and moralistic attitude toward life, looked askance at Roman licentiousness. Instead of relegating erotic desire to the brothel, they tried to banish it entirely by valuing chastity as the conquest of the body by the spirit. For them, Eros was inferior to the higher asexual love of agape, understood as a reflection of God's infinite and unstinting love of humankind. Agape was portrayed as altruistic; it created value in its object, regardless of the beloved other's objective beauty or virtue; it was imagined to be an overflowing and selfless love, the opposite of possessive and appraising Eros. As one commentator put it: "Eros *recognizes value* in its object, and loves it—Agape loves, and *creates value in its* object."[19]

The reader will recognize that our modern concept of romantic love mixes both paradigms. For us, romantic love is always sexual, yet cannot be reduced to erotic desire, nor can a lover calculate the value of the beloved; rather, love has become idealizing and mystical. This transformation has been chronicled by the philosopher and intellectual historian Irving Singer, who has argued that for medieval Christianity, God is love; for the Romantic ideology, love is God.[20] And if love is God, then the beloved takes on qualities of a divinity.

Eros and Bestowal

According to Irving Singer, there are two traditions in Western philosophy about love. The first is the Eros tradition, which portrays romantic idealization as a disguise for sexual attraction, reproduction of the species, or some other ulterior motive. The most subtle version of this paradigm was proposed by Plato, who believed that attraction to human beauty was a lesser form of the desire for pure knowledge. Accordingly, he counseled sexual promiscuity as a path to recognizing the eternal truth that lies beneath varied sensual experience.

The second way of looking at love is the bestowal tradition. From this alternative perspective, love is not motivated by the desire to reproduce, or by lust, or by the ideal of beauty; rather, the beloved others are adulated in themselves as the fountainheads of all that is beautiful, good, and desirable. This adulation is offered in spite of the beloved's actual characteristics; the beloved can even be loved for his or her very faults. From within this framework, any overt or covert calculated appraisal of the other as a good provider, as a useful ally, or even as an avenue to God is considered to be a sin against the very nature of love.

According to historians of personal life in the West, intense erotic attraction to physical beauty was transformed into quasi-mystical idealization of the beloved only when traditional feudal society began to disintegrate in the late medieval era. As outlined in Chapters 2 and 3, this accelerating process eroded the solid hierarchical social base that had previously supplied people with stability. Instead, newly autonomous free agents were forced to compete for places within an ever-growing and constantly shifting multiplicity of roles. As the traditional institutions crumbled, the old feudal statuses based on noble lineage began to be replaced by more individualistic routes to social rank. This was especially the case for the dispossessed younger sons of lesser nobility, who were obliged to forage about for their livelihoods and find alternative routes to acclaim. Since there were no great wars where enterprising young men could gain recognition by heroism, they sought to prove themselves instead by their ability to express deep feelings in love poetry and music. By artistically revealing a profound capacity for selfless passion, the troubadour could claim to be a better man than the rich or powerful who patronized him.

It was in this context that romantic lyrics were first composed in Europe in the twelfth century. Influenced in part by ancient Middle Eastern notions of romantic love brought back by European knights from the Crusades, the first European romances also made use of religious imagery from the already existent cult of the worship of Mary, mother of Jesus. Weaving these threads together, itinerant minstrels showed themselves to be men of spiritual depth, aesthetic delicacy, and intense passion through the ballads they dedicated to the ladies they adored. Ideally speaking, such romances were chaste affairs, though the ideal was certainly not met in every case. But in any instance, the relations of courtly lovers were by definition between a superior woman and an inferior

An illustration from a thirteenth-century manuscript shows a minstrel kneeling before Queen Mary of France.

man (a reversal of the relationship between the sexes in daily life) and were always outside marriage, which was regarded as a functional and prosaic relationship, not at all conducive to passion.[21]

B. Marriage, Modernity, and the Function of Love

It was only very gradually that marriage based on idealized romantic attraction replaced marriage based on pragmatic or familial requirements. This shift is usually associated with capitalism's final triumphant destruction of ties of the past and the integration of atomized individuals into the burgeoning industrial system.[22] The argument is that alienated workers sought refuge and solace from the competitive and often hostile economic world in the close emotional warmth of the nuclear family. It was only at home that one could find nurturance and love. As one historian writes:

> Intimate relationships, as we understand them today, emerged during the early decades of the nineteenth century . . . with the self conscious bourgeois individual whose life is torn between the separated worlds of work and home. Individualism and intimacy are the Siamese twins of modernization.[23]

But how could separate individuals ever achieve a nurturant family in a fluid and anonymous society where marriage was no longer arranged and where people no longer had any way of making objective decisions about who would be appropriate mates?

The anthropologist and cultural historian Alan MacFarlane has answered this question by arguing that in a free marketplace of potential marriage partners "some external force of desire is needed to help the individual to make a choice. Hence passionate 'love' overwhelms and justifies and provides compulsive authority."[24] Many sociologists agree that romantic love is a necessity in a society where strong kin groups and arranged marriages are largely absent.[25] From this point of view, falling in love is a functional response to a preexistent and overriding social need for cohesion in a fragmented world—an ideology somehow transmuted into an emotional compulsion that substitutes for the marriage arrangements formerly made by the extended family in a stable social environment.

For these theorists, romantic love thrives in the contemporary world because it provides a mechanism for the manufacture of the nuclear family, and because it is congruent with modern core values of individualism, autonomy, and free choice. It is also compatible with the Christian ideal of personal salvation through mystical union—achieved now not with God, but in the arms of the beloved other. And romantic love, despite its selfless quality, also fits well with the capitalist ideal of possession, since lovers demand each other's total commitment and loyalty, and so are withdrawn from the sexual marketplace.

This functional view of romantic love correlates with a view of romantic idealism as a disguise for the real utilitarian quest for power and status among maximizing entrepreneurs competing with one another for scarce goods—in this case, attractive sexual partners. From this free-market perspective, the

---

Love and Capitalism

Some anthropologists and historians[26] have claimed that the family patterns, property relations, and courtship customs of Northern Europe favored a romantic base for marriage among ordinary people from at least the thirteenth century. This was especially so in England, where spatial mobility and individual choice in marriage have a very long history. According to these theorists, this setting helped provide the grounding for the capitalist revolution. As Alan MacFarlane concludes: "If love can exist without capitalism, it is more questionable as to whether capitalism could have existed, or could continue to exist, without love."[27]

---

idealizations reported by lovers are self-deceptions, and the purpose of research is to show the more calculating reality that lies beneath. In this vein, the sociologist Willard Waller undertook his famous "rating and dating" survey of female American college students in the 1930s, showing how coeds coolly ranked their suitors according to social status, looks, and potential income.[28]

More recent anthropological studies have shown that considerable calculation still goes into dating, and that there are asymmetric expectations of intimate relationships according to gender. For instance, the cognitive anthropologists Dorothy Holland and Debra Skinner interviewed a number of college students, coded the answers, and discovered that for their respondents, dating is constructed through "a negotiation in which she and he work out whether his prestige or attractiveness is higher than, equal to, or lower than hers."[29] Women with lower status are expected to be more sexually available, men with lower status must compensate by being especially attentive —and romantic love is simply a way in which maximizing sexual computation is dressed up in socially acceptable clothing.

C. Transcendence and Pragmatism

However, portraying love as nothing more than a practical reckoning of costs and benefits stands at odds to the prototypical American belief that romance completely sweeps away any self-conscious calculation of pluses and minuses. It would not be socially acceptable for someone who claims to be in love to rate the beloved on a scale of prestige or income, and a sexual relationship entered into for personal profit certainly cannot be defined as love—quite the contrary, it verges on prostitution. It seems likely then that Waller and Holland and Skinner have described a model for relationships that is reflective of the overriding influence of a marketplace mentality in American culture. This pragmatic and opportunistic paradigm may be the one people utilize when they plan their casual sexual encounters, but it stands in stark contrast to romantic love—which is what most Americans say they hope to find, even though they may be obliged by circumstances to seek sex and social status in less satisfactory encounters. Nonetheless, the hope for love has a strong limiting effect on the pursuit of sexuality—as we can see when 66 percent of the respondents to a national survey said they would not have sex with someone unless they were in love with that person.[30]

It is true then that romantic love does have a history and does serve a number of functions in modern society, but functional usefulness cannot explain the subjective emotional power of love—only the reasons love occupies a central place within our culture. A more psychological analysis is required to conceptualize love's force, one that appreciates romantic love as the fulfillment of a deep desire for transcendence through the passionate attachment to an idealized beloved. According to many theorists, this desire is likely to grow more intense under the dehumanizing pressures of an increasingly confusing and alienating modern world. As the sociologist Hugo Beigel has put it:

> What love does . . . is to satisfy man's most urgent psychological needs, those produced by social isolation, by lack of any conceptual hold on the world in which he lives, and by lack of work satisfaction . . . Reduced through technological progress to a negligible nut in an incomprehensible machine, confused by tumbling and contradictory social values, he can regain the feeling of self-importance only in love.[31]

From within this framework (one that Weber would have favored), romantic love offers the ordinary person an idealizing fusion with a beloved other and a repudiation of the fragmentation, rationalization, and vacuity of the everyday world. True identity, the lover believes, is gained through passionate devotion to the beloved.

Although falling in love is subjectively felt to overturn all social constraints, as we noted above, it is in actual fact the prelude to the rationalized relationship of marriage and the production of a family. The ambiguous combination of transcendence and practicality in American love relations has been analyzed by another cognitive anthropologist, Naomi Quinn,[32] who used linguistic data to show that the American model of marriage emphasizes calculation of reciprocal benefits and the labor-intensive aspects of being in love and building a relationship, all of which stand in direct contradiction to the precipitate, irrational, compulsive, and risky experience of falling in love.[33]

This tension reflects the larger problem of transforming the compelling, ecstatic experience of romance into a lasting but prosaic marriage. In American society, romantic love is understood as the emotional foundation upon which a nurturant, rationalized, and sustainable familial unit can be built. But this new unit requires the conversion of sexual love between the parents into nonsexual love for children.[34] The cultural symbol of this difficult transition is the honeymoon—typically, a period of socially sanctioned sexual indulgence on a tropical fantasy island—followed by a return to the community and the hard work of maintaining a companionate marriage.

But this transition is rarely complete, and the desire to reexperience romantic fulfillment remains powerful even in stable families, which helps account for many domestic dramas of infidelity and the high frequency of divorce in America, as people seek to recapture their original romantic thrill. In other words, a high divorce rate does not indicate that Americans do not believe in romantic love. Quite the reverse, as is demonstrated by the extremely high rate of remarriage and serial monogamy in our society. The romantic ideal also helps account for the high rates of sexually transmitted diseases in our culture, since use of a condom is a calculated act of self-protection and is thus thought to indicate an absence of spontaneity, trust, and romantic attachment between partners.[35]

III. LOOKING FOR LOVE

A Does Romantic Love Exist Only in the West?
   Anthropological and psychological arguments contending that romance is uniquely Western and cannot exist elsewhere.

B Do Other Cultures Experience Romantic Love?
   Data show that a type of romantic love does exist—at least in non-Western state societies.

C Love, Sex, and Reproduction
   Sociobiological explanations of romantic attraction.

A. Does Romantic Love Exist Only in the West?

Most social historians assume that romantic love is a uniquely Western construction. In a trivial sense, this must be true, simply because every aspect of human culture always has a specific historical trajectory and a distinctive flavor. But psychological anthropology cannot be content with this, since our mandate is to seek comparative understanding of the relationship between culture and the self. The notion of romantic love offers special opportunities for making this exploration. As the linguist Harvey Pitkin writes: "The notion of love is freighted with meanings, diverse in various cultures, susceptible to metaphorical extension, and a window into the complex symbolism of a people."[36] Just as we have investigated the capacity of people in other cultures to perceive colors or optical illusions, or the way emotions are conceptualized, we can ask how love is understood and experienced elsewhere, and what this may tell us about human experience in general.

In the standard historical argument I outlined above, romantic love is understood as characteristic of modern societies that emphasize autonomy, where individuals are mobile and flexible in their relationships, where personal choice is exercised in mating and marrying, where intimacy is highly valued, and where Who am I? is a central question.[37] From this social structural perspective, it follows that in precapitalist societies where the extended family is intact and highly valued, people do not experience romantic love. The psychological anthropologist Francis Hsu has argued this point very convincingly, claiming that in traditional China the dominant model for all social interaction was the hier-

archical and respectful relation of father and son, not the Western-style romantic, erotic bond of husband and wife. In fact, according to Hsu, the sexual passions of Chinese men were reserved for courtesans, not wives (how wives felt
about this was not discussed by Hsu, reflecting female subordination within
Chinese society). The predominance of the father-son relationship indicates the
crucial importance of corporate clans and a patrilineal social structure in China,
whereas in the fluid social world of the West, all that ties people together is the
fragile bond of male-female love. By implication, other lineage-based societies
should have a similar antipathy toward romantic attachment—an argument
made plausible by the example from classical Rome that was cited above, where
eroticism was also separated from marriage and directed toward prostitutes.[38]

Similar assertions have been made by authors with much less ethnographic
authority. For example, one writes that among the Japanese and Chinese, "the individual was not sharply distinguished from the collectivity, and hence there was
no basis for romantic idealization."[39] In the same vein, a popular history of romantic attachment claims that primitives do not perceive any great difference between individuals; consequently, they are not concerned with establishing unique
relationships. According to this author, such deindividuated people can easily detach themselves from love objects, since they gain all the affection they require
from their extended families.[40] Taking a different perspective, the historian
Lawrence Stone claims that prior to the Industrial Revolution the "intensity of the
struggle to satisfy the basic need for food and shelter leaves little room for humane
emotions and affective relationships."[41] Only with relative affluence could people
afford the luxury of romantic attraction.

The argument that the wealthy, individualist, modern West is really the
only home of romantic love has recently been given a psychological basis by
Robert Endelman, a psychoanalyst with a strong interest in anthropological
research. Endelman says that romantic love is characteristic of the West because of the intense bonding between mother and child that takes place within
the nuclear household. He believes falling in love is an attempt to recapitulate
that bond, as is indicated by the delusory idealization of the beloved, and the
sensation of fusion, which is like the early merger of mother and child. Endelman then goes on to claim that such idealization cannot exist in primitive societies because in extended family systems, the requisite dyadic bonding between mother and child does not occur, since other caretakers intervene. What
we usually find instead, he says, is predatory lust, and he cites several ethnographies to make his case.[42] We thus have a variety of psychoanalytic, historical, and cultural arguments purporting to show that Western family structure,
wealth, individualism, and social organization are so unique that romantic
love cannot exist anywhere else.

B. Do Other Cultures Experience Romantic Love?

In contrast, a number of other authors have contended that some form of romantic love does indeed exist elsewhere than the modern West, and have used
ethnography and historical accounts as proof. One such case has been made by

the anthropologist Yehudi Cohen, who has argued that "the strength of affective ties between spouses tends to be in inverse proportion to the strength of bonds in the wider kin group." His premise is the familiar functionalist one: Love compensates for the erosion of tribe and clan. But Cohen gives functionalism a political aspect when he argues that many precapitalist state systems actively promoted romantic love and free choice in marriage as a way to undermine potentially powerful lineages and other solidary groups that arrange marriages in order to maintain their unity. Cohen concludes that "the romanticization of the husband-wife relationship in a statement such as 'after all, we have each other,' and romantic love in general, is an adaption to pressures of life in a state society."[43]

Even a cursory look at world literature shows that Cohen was certainly right about the presence of something very much like romantic love in non-Western state systems. For instance, the popular love plays in the Tokugawa period all concerned impossible love affairs that could end only in death, while in medieval Japan, Lady Murasaki's great *Tale of Genji* portrayed the transforming power of extramarital love in the Japanese court of the tenth century. In India, the myths of Krishna as a lover, the ancient legend of Pururavas and Urvasi, the stories of the Mahabharata (especially of Ruru and Pramadvara), and the erotic poetry of Bhartrihari and Bilhana, all showed aspects of the compulsive, idealizing, and transcendent power of erotic love, as did the romantic poetry of the Middle East, which so much influenced the troubadours. Clearly, many of the aspects of romantic love that we recognize were present in these texts, and others.

The great lover Krishna surrounded by admirers.

But Cohen's case for exact parallels founders when we note that at least among the elite, romantic love in Japan, or India, or the Middle East, was (like courtly love in feudal Europe) outside marriage, which functioned solely for the public end of achieving social mobility and prestige. Far from providing a nurturant and loving haven from the state, in these societies marriage was one of the most political acts in a highly politicized world. As we saw in the Roman case cited above, the only actual erotic attachments possible for elite men in these societies were prostitutes (female and male), married women, or women of a much lower social standing. When these illicit relationships became too intense, they led to catastrophe, which is why love and suicide are often so closely linked in the literature of these premodern states.

We can conclude then that at least some people in premodern state systems did experience powerful romantic attractions to one another, but that love and marriage did not go together as they do in our society. Instead, parents and other corporate groups attempted to control and channel passionate desire among young people; when romantic love appeared, it did so in spite of the restrictions, and against the conventional morality, not with it, as in our culture.[44]

Of course, the situation may have been very different for poor people who, lacking lineage obligations or property, were free to choose their spouses and, in theory, could have married for love.[45] Equally, these men and women may have been attracted to their mates less because of idealized love and more for pragmatic reasons: strength, childbearing ability, intelligence, or cooking skill. As men of the Lepcha tribe of Sikkim simply state, they love their wives because their wives feed them.[46]

At any rate, since the poor in other cultures, and (until recently) our own, were illiterate and anonymous, we will never know why they married or if they fell in love in a way similar to modern Americans. All we do know are the experiences of elites who were motivated by their particular requirements of power, and who in general did not marry for love, though they apparently did sometimes fall in love with people whom they could not marry. In sum, the historical research demonstrates a potential for idealized romantic love among the elite in complex premodern state systems—though the relationship between love and marriage was very different than it is for us.

C. Love, Sex, and Reproduction

Other researchers have taken a different tack to argue for the ubiquity of romantic love, finding it not only in state systems but even in the simplest societies. Influenced by sociobiology, they are the new avatars of the Eros tradition of Greece and Rome, and assume that romantic love and erotic desire are more or less the same thing. They assume as well that since erotic desire must be universal, the potential for romantic love must also be universal, though it can be channeled by cultural factors. The argument, in a nutshell, is that romantic love is a genetically innate mechanism serving to offset the male's natural tendency to maximize his gene pool through promiscuity. According to this reasoning, romantic idealization ties the wandering male to a particular female and the enhanced pair bonding that results serves the evolutionary purpose of increasing

TABLE 12.1. Culture Area and Romantic Love

	Romantic Love	
	Found (% of all groups in area)	Not found (% of all groups in area)
Circum-Mediterranean	22 (95.7)	1 (4.3)
Sub-Saharan Africa	20 (76.9)	6 (23.1)
East Eurasia	32 (94.1)	1 (5.9)
Insular Pacific	27 (93.1)	2 (6.9)
North America	24 (82.8)	5 (17.2)
South and Central America	22 (84.6)	4 (15.4)

Source: William Jankowiak and Edward Fischer, 1992, "A Cross-Cultural Perspective on Romantic Love,"
Ethnology 31: 152.

the overall rate of survival for human children. This case is well argued in a comprehensive ethnographic survey undertaken by William Jankowiak and Edward Fischer, who discovered evidence of a strong erotic attraction they consider equivalent to romantic love in almost every culture, even where there are sanctions against it.[47] (See Table 12.1.)

Though convincing as a demonstration of the universal existence of sexual passion, this argument has some serious flaws as an account of romantic love.[48] For instance, even though it is a fact that in almost every known culture, married couples produce and raise the vast majority of children, it is also a fact that the correlation between passionate attraction and marriage is rare indeed. Instead, as we have seen, it is far more usual, cross-culturally, for love to be reserved for those whom one does not and cannot marry, while marriage itself is generally a mundane affair based on contracts between lineages and other corporate groups. Moreover, if idealization of one's mate is assumed to correlate with reproductive success, one would expect that the West, which has the world's most elaborated ideology of romance, would also have one of the highest birthrates. In fact, the converse is the case. Cultures where marriages are arranged by parents between unloving strangers for political and economic benefit have generally had far higher birthrates than the West.

We can say, then, that if romantic love is the means used by nature to assure human reproduction, nature has been made a fool of by culture, since an absence of romance correlates positively with population growth. Therefore, there is no necessary connection between sexual lust and marriage, or even reproduction. And it remains questionable whether people in every culture experience the idealizing passions of love.

IV. THE NATURE OF LOVE

A Chaste Love

Are love and sex equivalents? Arguments and examples. Romantic love as an experience of transcendence.

B   Case Studies: Love and Social Structure
    Asymmetric and desexualized romantic love between those who can
    never marry versus mutual, sexualized romance leading to marriage.

C   The Future of Love
    Is love vanishing today? What could replace it?

A. Chaste Love

Sociobiologically inspired theorists assume that romantic love and passionate,
heterosexual, erotic attraction are equivalent. But psychologically speaking, the
two may be in contradiction, since recent research has shown that callous and
violent impersonal sexual fantasies of rape, bondage, and interchangeable partners cause far more sexual arousal than do the tender emotions of romance.[49] I
have already noted above that even in the West, our particular linkage of idealization and carnality in romance is a culturally specific intertwining of two
strands of thought that were historically quite separate: erotic attraction to physical beauty and a mystical love for God. The medieval courtier, who first
brought these elements together in the West, followed a Middle Eastern poetic
tradition that gave primacy to mystical adoration of the beloved, who was never
a sexual object. Nor was this tradition simply a literary production of unworldly
aesthetes. According to Ibn al-Jawzi (d. 1200), who was the most prolific medieval Muslim writer on romantic love, the convention of chastity derived from
the early Bedouin, who "loved passionately but spurned physical union, believing that it destroys love. As for the pleasure resulting from union, it is the
affair of animals, not of man." His portrait was validated by the Arabian philol-
ogist al-Asmai (d. 828), who did research among the remote tribes. He wrote:

> I said to a Bedouin woman: "What do you consider love to be among you?"
> "Hugging, embracing, winks, and conversation," she replied. Then she asked:
> "How is it among you, city-dweller?" "He sits amidst her four limbs and
> presses her to the limit," I answered. "Nephew," she cried, "this is no lover, but
> a man after a child!"[50]

The high evaluation of chaste love documented by these ancient writers has
been traced by the Orientalist scholar Louis Massignon (1883–1962) to the seventh-
century Bedouin Yemeni tribe of the Banu Udhra, who believed that "to die of love
is a sweet and noble death." This form of chaste love was linked to a deep notion
of the "election to a religious and sacrificial life by the unexpected appearance of a
'kindred soul.'"[51] The transcendent other who inspired this elevated state was believed to be a spirit embodied in a human being, and the relationship with that divine spirit was not to be sullied by physical contact. Instead, the beloved was regarded as pure and internalized through avid contemplation, so that eventually
the two became one. The mystical ideal of sexless merging was later transformed
into an esoteric practice among some Sufis, who sought spiritual bliss by gazing at
beautiful boys.

The separation of sex from romance is quite common cross-culturally. I have
already noted the chaste ideal of the troubadour. A similar disentangling of the

---

Homosexual Romantic Love

The Western notion that romantic love must be heterosexual is not necessarily the case elsewhere. For example, some of the great classics of Middle Eastern romantic literature concern romantic love between men—the most famous being the love of King Mahmud of Ghazna for his Turkish slave Ayaz, with the king becoming a slave of his slave through love. Homosexual romance is characteristic of societies where there is a patrilineal ideology that is highly ambivalent about female sexuality. For example, in the Middle Eastern popular tradition, it is believed that a girl who has been sexually initiated has much greater passion than any man and therefore must be contained in purdah to protect herself and her family from dishonor. The pornography of the culture also stresses female insatiability and the humiliation of men. Under these circumstances, homosexual idealization (for both men and women) is not hard to understand.

---

erotic from the romantic is to be found in many other societies, such as the Marri Baluch of Pakistan, where secret lovers meet, exchange tokens of affection, gaze longingly into one another's eyes, recite poetry, and talk without the restraint and asymmetry characteristic of ordinary male-female relations in this strictly patrilineal society. Sexuality between lovers is thought to be a violation of the equality and affection of this much-desired romantic relationship.[52]

The separation between sexual desire and romantic love may be especially common in patriarchal societies such as the Marri, where sexual penetration is regarded as an act of violence and domination, or in cultures where sexuality is fraught with pollution and spiritual danger. An example of the latter is found in Manus, described by Margaret Mead, where sex is regarded as a perilous and disgusting act, and marriage itself is a distasteful and shameful business. As among the Marri, Manus men and women are drawn into extramarital liaisons, but, as Mead writes: "Illicit love affairs, affairs of choice, are, significantly enough, described as situations in which people need not have sex relations if they do not wish to, but can simply sit and talk and laugh together . . . The wonderful thing about lovers is that you don't have to sleep with them."[53]

A negative attitude toward sexuality is very much at odds with modern American opinion, which generally agrees with Woody Allen's comment that sex is the only thing on earth that's good even when it's bad. But this is hardly the case across cultures; nor was it even the case in our own history. Proper public, Victorian, middle-class morality portrayed sexual desire as a degrading intrusion on reason, to be resisted and controlled by men, denied completely by women. Nor is this attitude unusual. In South Asia, men fear debility from semen loss, while Chinese are terrified of being afflicted by koro (the withdrawal of the penis into the body) as the result of excessive sexual activity. Fear of sexuality often correlates with a social configuration where chastity is inordinately valued, as among the Dugum Dani of New Guinea, who practice almost complete abstinence.[54]

In the light of this material, it makes anthropological and psychological sense to stop seeing romantic attraction as a mask for disguising and focusing erotic desire, or reducing romantic love to a secondary effect of the capitalist marketplace or to a mode for negotiating prestige and power. Instead, romantic love might be better comprehended as a kind of religious experience, one that is expressed in worship of and spiritual fusion with the beloved other. Any number of enamored poets have versified about this enraptured state, but let me quote someone rarely regarded as a great romantic: Sigmund Freud. He writes that "at the height of being in love the boundary between ego and object threatens to melt away. Against all evidence of his senses, a man who is in love declares that 'I' and 'you' are one, and is prepared to behave as if it were a fact."[55] For Freud, this union was the only revelation adults could have of selfless bliss, and it served as the model for religious ecstasy.

Historical, social, and psychological evidence therefore leads us to conclude that romance is a culturally specific experience, one that reverses the individualistic and competitive milieu of our contemporary world, and offers instead an irrational and overwhelming sensation of self-loss in merger with the beloved, who takes the place of the deity. If we look at romance in this way, we have a more sensitive understanding of the sacred aura that differentiates love from sex in our culture, a differentiation that gives romance its distinctive character wherever it appears. We have as well a deeper awareness of the way romantic love serves to supply an identity that can carry human beings beyond their ordinary isolation, since idealization of and fusion with the beloved erases the boundaries of the self. Such selfless merger can easily be experienced in sexual intercourse, as it is in our culture, but it may also be detached from sexuality altogether.

B. Case Studies: Love and Social Structure

Can romantic idealization be correlated with specific kinds of social and familial structure? This is difficult to do since little real research has been done about the prevalence of romantic love cross-culturally, perhaps because of the reluctance of earlier anthropologists to take the matter seriously. Particularly in Africa, which was studied primarily by British functionalists, intimate relationships were rarely registered. As a result, investigators have to make do with fragmentary and inconclusive suggestions, and their findings reflect this lack of conclusive data. For instance, Jankowiak and Fischer[56] discovered romantic attraction in 147 of 166 cultures, using the standard cross-cultural sample, while Rosenblatt[57] found it in 37 of 75 societies in his sample. My assistants and I were able to find good indications of a romantic love complex in only 20 of the 248 prestate cultures reviewed, while 20 more societies had very weak evidence of romantic idealization.[58] This large discrepancy shows the dangers of cross-cultural surveys, and also indicates that the researchers were actually looking for different things. My survey stressed items such as love suicide and other indicators of a culturally elaborated notion of romantic idealization, whereas Jankowiak and Fischer were looking for powerful erotic attraction, and Rosenblatt correlated companionate marriage choice with romantic love.

Despite the confusion and lack of evidence, we can still make some plausible claims about the sorts of social structures that favor romantic love of some sort. For instance, we have already seen that the social conditions of complex, hierarchical, precapitalist state systems do apparently stimulate a taste among the elite for romantic love outside marriage. These societies are sites of intense internal rivalry, where marriage relationships function solely for the public end of achieving social mobility and prestige. The court society of Louis XIV (discussed in Chapter 10) is a case in point. There, cynical noblemen struggled against one another for favor from the king and married women who could help them in their battles for prestige. Family relations were distant, and the aristocratic child was often actually raised by a series of wet nurses and servants; religion was merely formulaic. For an adult man, emotional engagement was in relationships with courtesans and married women, around whom a desexualized romantic cult of gallantry and service was elaborated. The lover was portrayed as friend and confidant with whom a nobleman could interact freely and without constraint, and whom he could idolize, but whom he could never marry.[59]

The Marri Baluch, whose ideal of chaste love was discussed above, are another such group. Highly individualistic, self-interested, and competitive, the Marri live in closed patrilineal, patrilocal campsites. However, this minimal group is not one of cooperation and friendship. Despite their kinship ties, men work separately, have their own tents and property, and cooperate as little as possible; they expect opportunism and manipulation from all social transactions. Their personal lives are dominated by fear, mistrust, and hostility; secrecy and social masking are at a premium, while collective action and cooperation are minimal. If they could, they would separate, but the need for defense and a varied labor pool keeps the camps together, a need validated by the formal rights and duties of shared descent.

Reflecting this hostile yet highly constrained context, Marri marriage is never for love. It is, in fact, shameful even to show affection for one's spouse. Rather, marriage is a matter of political alliances between small patrilineal kin groups, jockeying for position in a never-ending quest to gain points over one's nearest, and most disliked, lineage mates and rivals.[60] Women are treated as chattel, to be controlled and dominated for the honor and benefit of the patriarch. As one woman says: "You know what rights a woman has among us Marris. She has the right to eat crap—that's all."[61]

In this harsh setting, romantic involvement, with all its risk, is the only human relationship in the whole of Marri culture felt to be of value in and for itself, and not simply as a means to the instrumental ends of personal power and prestige. It is understood by the Marri Baluch to be opposed to marriage in every way. Marriage is a public and sanctioned relationship between superior men and inferior women, often within the camp and the lineage, and always among allies; it is preeminently politically motivated, and it is expected to be cold and hostile at best. Romance, on the contrary, is secretive and private, and is conducted with strangers who are actually potential enemies. Its only possible political consequences are disastrous enmity and feud. Romantic love has the potential for dividing groups while it unites the lovers, whereas marriage

Northern Pakistan: A young bride is unveiled in her husband's house, surrounded by her new in-laws.

aims to solidify groups while permitting no attraction within the asymmetrical couple. In marriage, the woman is inferior and despised; in romance, she is honored and revered. And, as we have seen, in romance, sexuality is denied, while in marriage, reproduction is the only way a woman can gain respect.

The differences can be summed up as follows:

Marriage	*Romance*
Asymmetrical (male is superior)	Equal
Ingroup; unifying	Outgroup; divisive
Political alliance	Personal bond
Public	Private and secret
Hostile	Tender
Sexual	Chaste
Mundane	Idealized

For the Marri, then, romance is with a distant other, and it is consciously perceived as negating the rivalries of power, the inferiority of women, and the constraints of the marriage tie. It is chaste and highly idealistic. This romantic complex occurs within a relatively rigidly structured, but characteristically competitive, social formation that is parallel in striking ways to that of the court society: closed, rivalrous, relatively highly organized.[62] Far from providing the basis for reproducing the dominant social configuration, romance in these cases opposes it in every way.

Societies like the court society and the Marri Baluch, where romantic relations are in opposition to the central social institutions, tend to evolve notions of the complementarity of love relations that equalize or even reverse the actual sexual asymmetry of sexes in the public world. As we have seen, this complementarity could sometimes coincide with an exaggerated idealization and desexualization of beloved women, as in medieval romances and among the French courtiers and Baluch lovers. Male worship of a chaste beloved is probably related to the aloof relationships between parent and child, the competitive struggles between equals, the persistence of arranged marriages, and the inequality of the sexes—all of which might promote fantasizing about an ideal love world where these aspects of life are reversed or negated.

If asymmetric and desexualized romantic love between those who can never marry is common in complex hierarchical and cosmopolitan state societies, a mutual, sexualized pattern of love leading to marriage is to be found in some simple and relatively egalitarian societies.[63] These social groups resemble our own in specific ways: They generally are based on independent nuclear families, are individualistic and atomized, and place a strong emphasis on personal autonomy, initiative, and flexibility. Love is especially likely in societies where mutual aid (often found in hunting and gathering groups) has been eroded by extremely harsh conditions, forcing a struggle for survival that, like capitalism, puts human beings into conditions of stress and competition. We arrive, then, at an ironic congruence between our extremely complex society and some of the most simple forms of social organization—both being not only highly individualistic and fluid but also extremely contentious and risky, with little communal life.

An example of one such society can be found in ethnographic accounts of the tribe of Ojibwa Indians who inhabit the Northern Great Lakes region of the United States and Canada. As portrayed by A. I. Hallowell (discussed in Chapter 6) and by Ruth Landes, the Ojibwa had a concept of romantic love quite comparable with that of contemporary America.[64] Love was described by the Ojibwa as an overwhelming attraction to be pursued at the cost of great risk and self-sacrifice; it was focused on one idealized and beloved other who was sought as a lifelong mate.

Along with their belief in love, the Ojibwa were like modern Americans in other crucial ways. Their society was exceptional in its extremes of competitive individualism; this was coupled with a highly developed concept of personal property, which was held even within the nuclear family. As in the United States, there were few, if any, primordial groups or ties among the Ojibwa to provide them with a wider sense of solidarity and identity. There were no ascribed positions of authority, few communal rituals, no stable structures of hierarchy, no important extended kinship units. Even the social roles of men and women were not highly articulated, and each could do the work of the other. Easy divorce made the family insecure, residence was fluid, and people had a deep fear of being betrayed by their friends, relatives, and neighbors. Life was extremely risky, with starvation a constant menace.

In this society, as in ours, people sought safety, meaning, and communion in the mutuality of romance, which—unlike romance in more structured societies—was sexual and symmetrical, and was expected to coincide with a life-long marriage. Here the couple, united by love, became the ultimate refuge against the hostile world, and the emotional and reproductive nucleus of an atomized and perilous social organization, where constant dissimulation was a necessity for mere survival.[65]

We can hypothesize then that romantic love does have an elective affinity, as Weber said, with certain kinds of social formations that are especially risky, competitive, and individualistic—though the type of love varies with the type of social structure: Closed, highly structured sex-segregated societies tend to have desexualized love between people who cannot marry; egalitarian societies have sexualized love that turns into companionate marriage.

The links between type of social structure and type of love relationship can be summarized as follows:

- *Type 1.* Society is closed, competitive, individualistic, and highly structured. Marriage is arranged and involves marked gender asymmetry. Romance is extramarital, chaste, courtly, and gallant; it reverses the male-female relation.
- *Type 2.* Society is open, competitive, individualistic, and fluid. Marriage is chosen and involves relative gender equality. Romance is sexual and leads to companionate marriage.

Under both conditions, romantic love is not a mask for erotic desire; it arises as an expression of the existential human impulse to escape—however temporarily—from the twin restrictions of the self and the social system.

Finally, there appears to be a third kind of social formation that also favors romantic love, but this type is not so well defined as the first two, and I can discuss it only in abbreviated form here. These societies are group-oriented, non-individualistic cultures that strictly control marriage but also permit the youth institutionalized, premarital sexual freedom in their age-segregated clubhouses. This freedom may lead to powerful romantic attachments that can never end in marriage, and that stand in radical contrast to the cool relations expected between husband and wife. Stories are common of young lovers committing suicide out of despair at the inevitable separation that is entailed by marriage. Such doomed relationships are regarded as of the highest possible cultural and aesthetic value, and are celebrated in song and story. Examples of this kind of romantic involvement are found in tribal India, Southeast Asia, and Oceania, particularly in disharmonic societies where the residence and inheritance do not correlate, that is, societies that are matrilocal and patrilineal, or vice versa. This disjuncture between residence and inheritance means that members of a village are not lineage mates. Romance, confined to unmarried members of the group in the clubhouse, may provide an emotional glue in these fragile social formations, binding people to the memory of the sexual paradise of their youth.[66]

C. The Future of Love

As the French anthropologist and philosopher Georges Bataille has written: "Only the beloved can in this world bring about what our human limitations deny, a total blending of two beings, a continuity between two discontinuous creatures."[67] We can ask then what will happen if the ideal of romantic love is devalued in the West and replaced by the pursuit of personal authenticity. Many social thinkers believe this is precisely what is occurring today, partly as a result of the decreasing importance of the family, which is declining in inverse proportion to the increasing importance of work outside the home for both parents, and the subsequent appearance of more rational alternatives to the nuclear family, such as day care, play groups, and camps. As the family becomes less necessary, the social usefulness of the romantic couple as the precursor to the institution of the family may be also be reduced. People may be less willing to give up pleasures and preferences for the sake of unwanted and unnecessary chains of obligation to a partner. This shift is favored by the dominant institutions, since it frees the workforce from private loyalties and dissolves the one remaining bulwark against full integration into a bleak but rationalized world.

Perhaps, then, as the sociologist Anthony Giddens argues, in the future, idealized romantic fantasy will be replaced by freely and frankly negotiated relationships based on the utilitarian exchange of "reciprocal sexual pleasure." These relationships will be easily terminated when the relationship ceases to offer sufficient erotic satisfaction to either partner.[68] Giddens welcomes this possibility, maintaining that the removal of romantic illusion will permit more choice, more pleasure, and, surprisingly, more democracy, since people will become accustomed to negotiating for their erotic desires in personal life, and will extend their negotiating skills into politics as well.

Others have been much less sanguine about the replacement of romantic idealization with pure erotic attraction. Weber feared that a modern eroticization of human relationships would lead us to view others brutally, as the means to pleasure, not as ends in themselves,[69] while Robert Bellah and his colleagues have worried that the expansion of contractual relationships from the "boardroom to bedroom and back again is what threatens to obsure the ideals of personal virtue and public good."[70] However, from the perspective of psychological anthropology outlined here, the supposed erosion of romantic love (which may or may not occur), can be viewed in a less utopian or alarmist manner. If romantic love is best seen as a kind of religious quest for an escape from the limits of the self and the constraints of social order, and if human beings are always impelled to seek such forms of communion, then should romantic love lose its force, transcendence will be sought elsewhere.

In small-scale, well-integrated, precapitalist societies, transformative experiences psychically equivalent to love may well have been a part of daily life, provided by participation in the seances of the shaman and by the close and continuing emotional ties within the group itself. But in the complex, mobile, rationalized, and individualistic world of today, these possibilities have been lost. The alternatives that are available within the mainstream of contemporary social life have already been outlined, and we can expect that expressive public arenas of religion, art, sport, and entertainment will be more and more important in people's lives if the potential for romantic love fades. And we can expect greater fusion between individual and the personalized nation as well. New emphasis on friendship and family might also ensue, though inevitably the intensity of familial relations would be severely injured by the disappearance of the love ideal upon which they are now based.

Somewhat more likely is an upsurge of involvement in the workplace, which may increasingly provide a substitute for the family, a location for sexual adventure, a group to belong to, and a charismatic leader to adulate. However, the merger of work and love has its own perils, not least being the difficulty of reconciling group loyalty with the harsh necessities of bureaucratic efficiency and the maximization of profit.

But none of these alternatives offers the convulsive physical fusion that romantic love provides, and so it is probable that the future of love is quite secure, despite pressures. In fact, those pressures may make romantic love more, rather than less, compelling. Individuals struggling simply to stay afloat in an impersonal, bureaucratized, and meaningless flood of paper are likely to seek refuge from their dehumanizing conditions in the private world of romantic idealization.

This may be especially the case as women enter the marketplace in greater numbers. Contrary to popular belief, women have always tended to be the less romantic sex. Because their social status traditionally derived from marriage, they had to try to balance irrational romantic attraction with hardheaded pragmaticism. Thus the standard romantic woman's novel was one in which an attractive but inappropriate admirer (a handsome but destitute poet, for instance) turns out to be slumming from his wealthy and socially prominent family. Men, in contrast, had their statuses located in work and looked to women for intimacy and romantic excitement, regardless of their practical contributions to the relationship. But now that both men and women share the work world, female pragmatism may be on the wane, and women may be freed (or impelled) to pursue idealized love without regard to consequences.

Whatever the future may bring, we can predict that the deep human longing to go beyond individual limits and societal regulations will not vanish, even though the locations available for achieving such transcendence have been diminished by the universalizing and disenchanting processes of capitalism. The human quest for moments of selflessness and communion is, for better or worse, part of our existential condition. As Bataille has put it: "We are discontinuous beings, individuals who perish in isolation in the midst of an incomprehensible adventure, but we yearn for our lost continuity."[71]

Summary

In this chapter we have seen that romantic attraction has much in common with other types of idealizing relationships. Such necessary illusions are essential to the human condition since they obliterate the limitations of self and the boredom of banal existence through a relationship felt to be greater and more valuable; they are at the heart of religion and its secular equivalent, nationalism. They also underlie our adulation of artists and athletes, as well as the transference experienced with therapists. The feeling of love binds us to family and friends. Most spectacularly, the idealizing love of a deified leader unites charismatic groups.

Romantic love shares much with charisma, in that it too is idealizing and compelling, overwhelming the lover. In neither love nor charisma is there choice or calculation, nor can either relationship be assigned by any authority or left at will. Each is also liable to rationalization—in the one case, into marriage; in the other, into a church. Romantic love is the individual's major alternative to charismatic involvement, since the two offer very much the same sensations of merger and an ecstatic blurring of the boundaries of the self. For this reason, charisma and romance are antagonists. One cannot be involved in a charismatic group and in a romantic relationship at the same time. They are also opposed because in our highly organized social order, charisma is dangerous, while romance is safe. It is through romance that families are founded, and it is the experience of romance that provides a living example of transcendence within a competitive and often alienating world.

But even though romantic love is a powerful, positive force in modern Western life, it has not always been experienced in the same way. The ancient Greeks and Romans imagined attraction as an uncontrollable sexual urge that could disrupt social life. Idealization had no part in this animalistic compulsion. Christian clerics, in contrast, removed sexual desire from this world, denigrating Eros and praising disinterested and selfless agape. In Hegelian fashion, these two antagonistic perspectives were synthesized in courtly love, where the courtier chastely worshiped his beloved lady. The connection between love and marriage, many historians claim, arose later, with the rise of capitalism, as arranged marriages and solidary communities were undermined by individual social and spatial mobility.

From this functional sociological perspective, romance was a requisite for modernity. It correlated with novel notions of individualism and free choice, while reflecting—in secular form—the old Christian value of mystical merger; it also fit in with capitalist ambitions for possession and control over others. But most importantly, the new ideology of love served to validate marriage choices among egalitarian individualists, and thus provided an external basis for the continuation of the family. And because love is supposed to lead to marriage, many theorists have argued that it is really nothing more than an ideological veneer masking the practical calculation of the suitability of others as sexual partners and potential mates.

A prosaic weighing of the pluses and minuses of entering into an affair does accurately reflect the realities of a highly competitive sexual marketplace. But it is not part of the model for romantic love that is recited and believed by so many Americans. According to this model, in true love individuals will be adored just as themselves, regardless of their objective weaknesses or failings. This disjuncture shows us that however much romantic love supports the social structure, it still must be understood on its own terms—as a subjective experience of ecstasy and adulation. This means that falling in love—the transcendent moment of merger—stands in contrast to its usual consequence—the mundane establishment of a family. The difficulty of resolving this contradiction leads to much of the unhappiness of modern American family life.

We can assert then that romantic love, as we know it, suits a modern mobile social world where choice and autonomy are favored, where private intimacy is valued as a counter to public bureaucratization, where personal choice is exercised in mating and marrying, and where identity is conditional and problematic. In this universe, love answers the question Who am I? very immediately. I am the one who is lost in love, filled with a passionate desire to be held close to the beloved.[72]

Anthropologically speaking, the question then arises as to whether the idealization characteristic of romantic love exists in other societies, and, if so, what form it takes. Many theorists have argued that the imaginative bestowal of perfection on the beloved that is central to romance does not and cannot exist elsewhere, because of differences in social organization and family structure. But convincing data indicate that at least in premodern states, romantic love did occur, and was actually fairly typical, among elites. Taking heart from this finding, some authors, influenced by evolutionary biology, have gone on to argue that romantic love must actually exist everywhere, since it bonds naturally polygamous males to innately monogamous females in order to provide support for their helpless offspring. This argument loses much of its force when it is recalled that romantic love in other cultures and times rarely led to marriage or to children, and that Western society, which places the highest value on love marriage, has a relatively low birthrate.

Instead of conflating romantic love and sexuality, it makes more anthropological and psychological sense to recognize that the two are conceptually quite distinct. Some societies, such as our own, tie them together, but others do not and actually see sex as destructive to love. Chastity, fantasies about purity, and reversals of gender hierarchy are more likely to be found in societies where sexuality is considered degrading or polluting, and where romantic love is outside marriage. This configuration is likely to correlate with social worlds that are relatively closed, highly structured, and internally rivalrous. A converse pattern—romantic love as sexual, equalizing, and oriented toward marriage—is more likely in equally competitive but more fluid social formations, such as our own, where identity is open to question. Furthermore, many societies probably do not know romantic love at all.

If love is a historical-cultural creation, then it could disappear as the society changes. This is what many commentators think is happening as the ideology of individualism becomes more prevalent, and it becomes difficult to justify the self-sacrifice of romantic involvement. Some greet this possibility with applause; others approach it with fear. But from the perspective of the synthetic psychological anthropology outlined here, the underlying impulse for transcendence and merger that has found expression in romantic love cannot vanish as long as human beings yearn to be more than they are.

Endnotes

1. Quoted in Martin Green, 1974, *The Von Richthofen Sisters: The Triumphant and the Tragic Modes of Love*, New York: Basic Books, pp. 114, 164, 170. Weber was later rejected by Else, but his relationship with her changed his view of the importance of erotic love.
2. Robert Lowie, 1931, "Sex and Marriage," in John McDermott (ed.), *The Sex Problem in Modern Society*, New York: Modern Library, p. 146.
3. Some of these writings can be found in recent edited collections by William Jankowiak (1995, *Romantic Love: A Universal Experience?* New York: Columbia University Press); Victor de Munck (1998, *Romantic Love and Sexual Behavior: Perspectives from the Social Sciences*, Westport, CT: Praeger); and Mike Featherstone (1999, *Love and Eroticism*, London: Sage). Other anthropological research includes an early series of articles and counterarticles that attempted, with ambiguous results, to make cross-cultural statistical correlations between love marriage and residence patterns: R. Coppinger and P. Rosenblatt, 1968, "Romantic Love and Subsistence Dependence of Spouses," *Southwestern Journal of Anthropology* 24: 310–18; Carol Mukhopadhyay, 1979, "The Function of Romantic Love: A Re-appraisal of the Coppinger and Rosenblatt Study," *Behavior Science Research* 14: 57–63; Paul Rosenblatt, 1966, "A Cross-Cultural Study of Child Rearing and Romantic Love," *Journal of Personality and Social Psychology* 4: 336–38; Paul Rosenblatt, 1967, "Marital Residence and the Functions of

Romantic Love," *Ethnology* 6: 471–80. R. Berndt and Lila Abu-Lughod have written about the love poetry of their respective field sites: R. Berndt, 1976, *Love Songs of Arnhem Land*, Chicago: University of Chicago Press; Lila Abu-Lughod, 1990, "Shifting Politics in Bedouin Love Poetry," in Catherine Lutz and Lila Abu-Lughod (eds.), *Language and the Politics of Emotion*, Cambridge, England: Cambridge University Press. My own work on the subject has been drawn on for much of the remainder of the chapter. For more detail, see Charles Lindholm, 1981, "Leatherworkers and Love Potions," *American Ethnologist* 9: 512–25; 1988, "Lovers and Leaders: A Comparison of Social and Psychological Models of Romance and Charisma," *Social Science Information* 27: 3–24; 1995, "Love as an Experience of Transcendence," in William Jankowiak (ed.), *Romantic Love: A Universal Experience?* New York: Columbia University Press; 1998, "The Future of Love," in V. de Munck (ed.) *Romantic Love and Sexual Behavior: Perspectives from the Social Sciences*, Westport, CT: Greenwood; 1999, "Love and Structure," in Mike Featherstone (ed.), *Love and Eroticism*, London: Sage.

4. This is the title of Raymond Carver's (1981, New York: Knopf) fine book of short stories.
5. For this model, see David Schneider, 1968, *American Kinship: A Cultural Account*, Chicago: University of Chicago Press. Of course, there are class, ethnic, and racial variations: For example, poor black families often have extended family structures, in which kinship—both real and fictive—is used to knit together a loose alliance of mutual aid (on this, see Carol Stack, 1975, *All Our Kin: Strategies for Survival in a Black Community*, New York: Harper and Row).
6. Christopher Lasch, 1977, *Haven in a Heartless World*, New York: Basic Books. See also Erik Erikson, 1950, *Childhood and Society*, New York: Norton. On love as the central metaphor of American culture, see Hervé Varenne, 1977, *Americans Together: Structured Diversity in an American Town*, New York: Teachers College Press. Chapter 13 will treat this topic in more detail.
7. Erikson, *Childhood and Society*, p. 317.
8. A number of attitudinal tests by social psychologists show that Americans by and large continue to believe in and live out the stereotypes of romantic involvement. For typical examples, see T. Huston and R. Burgess, 1979, "Social Exchange in Developing Relationships," in R. Burgess and T. Huston (eds.), *Social Exchange in Developing Relationships*, New York: Academic Press; Zick Rubin, 1973, *Liking and Loving*, New York: Holt; G. Levinger, 1977, "The Embrace of Lives: Changing and Unchanging," in G. Levinger and H. Raush (eds.), *Close Relationships: Perspectives on the Meaning of Intimacy*, Amherst: University of Massachusetts Press.
9. See Chapter 9 for more on cultural models. For an analysis of love lyrics, see James Carey, 1969, "Changing Courtship Patterns in the Popular Song," *American Journal of Sociology* 74: 720–31.
10. For an objective test of this, see D. Driscoll, K. Davis, and M. Lipetz, 1972, "Parental Interference and Romantic Love: The Romeo and Juliet Effect," *Journal of Personality and Social Psychology* 24: 1–10.
11. Roberto Unger, 1984, *Passion: An Essay on Personality*, New York: Free Press, p. 29.
12. See James Averill, 1985, "The Social Construction of Emotion: With Special Reference to Love," in Kenneth Gergen and Keith Davis (eds.), *The Social Construction of the Person*, New York: Springer-Verlag, on love as a conglomerate of disparate experiences unified through a cultural paradigm. Michael Moffatt's ethnography of college students (1989, *Coming of Age in New Jersey: College and American Culture*, New Brunswick, NJ: Rutgers University Press) showed that while some were cynical about love, the vast majority believed in its existence. My own research with students in Boston bears this out.

13. James Miller, 1980, "Romantic Couples and Group Process," in Kenneth Pope (ed.), *On Love and Loving*, San Francisco: Jossey-Bass.

14. Francesco Alberoni, 1983, *Falling in Love*, New York: Random House.

15. Sigmund Freud, 1962, *Civilization and Its Discontents*, New York: Norton, p. 55 (original publication 1930).

16. Pierre Grimal, 1986, *Love in Ancient Rome*, Norman: University of Oklahoma Press; Norbert Elias, 1987, "The Changing Balance of Power between the Sexes—A Process-Sociological Study: The Example of the Ancient Roman State," *Theory, Culture and Society* 4: 287–316.

17. Quoted in Grimal, *Love in Ancient Rome*, p. 164.

18. For a cross-cultural analysis of these mechanisms, see William Goode, 1959, "The Theoretical Importance of Love," *American Sociological Review* 24: 38–47.

19. Anders Nygren, 1958, *Agape and Eros*, Philadelphia: Westminster Press, p. 210. St. Augustine was one of the foremost proponents of sexual asceticism, and his moral repugnance has resonated in Christian theology ever since.

20. Irving Singer, 1984, *The Nature of Love: Plato to Luther*, Vol. 1, Chicago: University of Chicago Press.

21. For an outline, see Roger Boase, 1977, *The Origin and Meaning of Courtly Love*, Manchester, England: Manchester University Press.

22. For standard accounts, see Lawrence Stone, 1988, "Passionate Attachments in the West in Historical Perspective," in W. Gaylin and E. Person (eds.), *Passionate Attachments: Thinking about Love*, New York: Free Press; Edward Shorter, 1977, *The Making of the Modern Family*, New York: Basic Books.

23. Howard Gadlin, 1977, "Private Lives and Public Order: A Critical View of the History of Intimate Relations in the United States," in George Levinger and Harold Raush (eds.), *Close Relationships: Perspectives on the Meaning of Intimacy*, Amherst: University of Massachusetts Press, p. 34.

24. Alan MacFarlane, 1987, *The Culture of Capitalism*, Oxford, England: Basil Blackwell, p. 142.

25. See, for example, Gideon Sjoberg, 1960, *The Preindustrial City, Past and Present*, Glencoe, IL: Free Press, pp. 139–40.

26. Alan MacFarlane, 1986, *Marriage and Love in England: 1300–1840*, Oxford, England: Basil Blackwell; MacFarlane, *The Culture of Capitalism*; Peter Laslett, 1977, *Family Life and Illicit Love in Earlier Generations: Essays in Historical Sociology*, Cambridge, England: Cambridge University Press; Jack Goody, 1983, *The Development of the Family and Marriage in Europe*, Cambridge, England: Cambridge University Press.

27. MacFarlane, *The Culture of Capitalism*, p. 143.

28. Willard Waller, 1937, "The Rating and Dating Complex," *American Sociological Review* 2: 727–34.

29. Dorothy Holland and Debra Skinner, 1987, "Prestige and Intimacy: The Cultural Models behind American's Talk about Gender Types," in Dorothy Holland and Naomi Quinn (eds.), *Cultural Models in Language and Thought*, Cambridge, England: Cambridge University Press, p. 93.

30. For this statistic, see Edward O. Laumann, John H. Gagnon, Robert T. Michael, and Stuart Michaels, 1994, *The Social Organization of Sexuality: Sexual Practices in the United States*, Chicago: University of Chicago Press, p. 514. For an anthropological study of the way love and sex are morally and cognitively united in the United States, and of the problems caused by transgression, see Joyce Canaan, 1986, "Why a 'Slut' Is a 'Slut': Cautionary Tales of Middle-Class Teenage Girls' Morality," in Hervé Verenne (ed.), *Symbolizing America*, Lincoln: University of Nebraska Press. Michael Moffatt

(*Coming of Age in New Jersey*) indicates that even those undergraduates who separate romance and sex still generally believe that marriage should be to someone with whom one is in love.

31. H. Beigel, 1951, "Romantic Love," *American Sociological Review* 16: 326–34, 333.
32. Naomi Quinn, 1987, "Convergent Evidence for a Cultural Model of American Marriage," in Dorothy Holland and Naomi Quinn (eds.), *Cultural Models in Language and Thought*, Cambridge, England: Cambridge University Press.
33. For a critique of Quinn, see Janet Keller, 1992, "Schemes for Schemata," in Theodore Schwartz, Geoffrey White, and Catherine Lutz (eds.), *New Directions in Psychological Anthropology*, Cambridge, England: Cambridge University Press. For the response, see Naomi Quinn, 1996, "Culture and Contradiction: The Case of Americans' Reasoning about Marriage," *Ethos* 24: 391–425. In this article, Quinn agrees with Keller that in the United States, the schema for the security and stability of a lasting marriage is in conflict with an equally powerful schema for personal fulfillment.
34. Schneider, *American Kinship*. For classic accounts, see Ralph Linton, 1949, "The Natural History of the Family," and Talcott Parsons, 1949, "The Social Structure of the Family," in Ruth N. Anshen (ed.), *The Family: Its Function and Destiny*, New York: Harper.
35. Ellen Sobo, 1993, "Inner-city Women and AIDS: The Psycho-Social Benefits of Unsafe Sex," *Culture, Medicine, and Psychiatry* 17: 455–85.
36. Harvey Pitkin, 1985, "A Wintu Etymology: 'Love,' " *International Journal of American Linguistics* 51: 536–38.
37. For the best statement of this perspective, see Robert Solomon, 1981, *Love, Emotion, Myth and Metaphor*, Garden City, NY: Anchor Books.
38. Francis Hsu, 1983, "Eros, Affect and Pao," in F. Hsu (ed.), *Rugged Individualism Reconsidered*, Knoxville: University of Tennessee Press. For rather different perspectives on romantic love in China, see William Jankowiak, 1992, *Sex, Death and Hierarchy in a Chinese City: An Anthropological Account*, New York: Columbia University Press; R. Moore, 1998, "Love and Limerence with Chinese Characteristics: Student Romance in the PRC," in V. de Munck (ed.), *Romantic Love and Sexual Behavior: Perspectives from the Social Sciences*, Westport, CT: Praeger.
39. Quoted in James Averill, 1985, "The Social Construction of Emotion: With Special Reference to Love," in Kenneth Gergen and Keith Davis (eds.), *The Social Construction of the Person*, New York: Springer-Verlag, p. 101.
40. Morton Hunt, 1959, *The Natural History of Love*, New York: Knopf.
41. Lawrence Stone, cited in MacFarlane, *The Culture of Capitalism*, p. 130.
42. Robert Endelman, 1989, *Love and Sex in Twelve Cultures*, New York: Psyche Press.
43. Yehudi Cohen, 1969, "Ends and Means in Political Control: State Organization and the Punishment of Adultery, Incest, and Violation of Celibacy," *American Anthropologist* 71: 658–87, 665, 666.
44. William Goode, "The Theoretical Importance of Love."
45. See MacFarlane, *The Culture of Capitalism* and *Marriage and Love in England*.
46. Geoffrey Gorer, 1938, *Himalayan Village: An Account of the Lepchas of Sikkim*, London: M. Joseph.
47. William Jankowiak and Edward Fischer, 1992, "A Cross-Cultural Perspective on Romantic Love," *Ethnology* 31: 149–55. See also Dorothy Tennov, 1979, *Love and Limerence: The Experience of Being in Love*, Chelsea, MI: Scarborough House.
48. See Lindholm, "Love as an Experience of Transcendence."
49. See Duncan Cramer and Dennis Howitt, 1998, "Romantic Love and the Psychology of Sexual Behaviour: Open and Closed Secrets," in Victor de Munck (ed.), *Romantic Love and Sexual Behavior: Perspectives from the Social Sciences*, Westport, CT: Praeger.

50. Quoted in Joseph Bell, 1979, *Love Theory in Later Hanbalite Islam*, Albany: State University of New York Press, pp. 33–34, 134.
51. Louis Massignon, 1982, *The Passion of al-Hallaj: Mystic and Martyr of Islam, Vol. I, The Life of al-Hallaj*, Princeton, NJ: Princeton University Press, pp. 348, 349.
52. See Robert Pehrson, 1966, *The Social Organization of the Marri Baluch*, Chicago: Aldine.
53. Margaret Mead, 1956, *New Lives for Old: Cultural Transformation—Manus, 1928–1953*, New York: Morrow, pp. 361, 405.
54. See Karl Heider, 1970, *The Dugum Dani: A Papuan Culture in the Highlands of West New Guinea*, Chicago: Aldine.
55. Freud, *Civilization and Its Discontents*, p. 13.
56. Jankowiak and Fischer, "A Cross-Cultural Perspective."
57. Rosenblatt, "Marital Residence and the Functions of Romantic Love."
58. See Lindholm, "Love and Structure," for the actual data.
59. Norbert Elias, 1983, *Court Society*, New York: Pantheon Books.
60. The potential for minimal social movement is of crucial importance, not the degree of movement possible. An absolutely rigid structure would not evolve the love complex noted here because social pressure, risk, and competition would be absent.
61. Pehrson, *The Social Organization*, p. 59.
62. For a similar analysis of the types of emotional responses characteristic of such societies, see Chapter 10.
63. See Lindholm, "Love and Structure."
64. Ruth Landes, 1937, *Ojibwa Sociology*, New York: Columbia University Press.
65. See Andrew Buckser, 1986, *Love in a Cold Climate: Romantic Love and Social Structure among the Canadian Ojibwa*, Undergraduate honors thesis, Department of Anthropology, Harvard University, Cambridge, MA.
66. For more, see Charles Lindholm, "Love and Structure."
67. Georges Bataille, 1962, *Eroticism*, London: Calder, p. 20.
68. Anthony Giddens, 1992, *The Transformation of Intimacy: Sexuality, Love and Intimacy in Modern Societies*, Stanford: University of California Press, p. 62.
69. For a discussion of Weber's views, see Margareta Bertilsson, 1986, "Love's Labour Lost? A Sociological View," *Theory, Culture and Society* 3: 19–35.
70. Robert Bellah et al., 1985, *Habits of the Heart: Individualism and Commitment in American Life*, New York: Harper and Row, p. 127.
71. Bataille, *Eroticism*, p. 15.
72. See Solomon, *Love, Emotion, Myth and Metaphor.*

CHAPTER 13

Being an American

I recently taught a course on the anthropology of the United States. When I began by talking about our shared cultural values, one of the students objected. "Americans don't really have a culture," she said. "We are all different!" I asked the students how many agreed with this statement. All of them enthusiastically raised their hands.

Of course, if everyone agrees that everyone is different, then everyone is, in a certain sense, the same. This point about American culture[1] has been made in another context by the anthropologist Michael Moffatt, who spent considerable time doing ethnographic research in an environment usually considered too dangerous and alien to explore: a college dorm. One of the major problems faced by the students was a racial divide: The dorm was half white and half black. Whites often perceived the black contingent as unfriendly, while the blacks sometimes saw the whites as pushy and insensitive. Neither appreciated the others' musical tastes. Each felt misunderstood by the other. But when Moffatt talked to a resident Jamaican undergraduate about the diff___ __s between the two groups, the response was incomprehension: "T___ ___ ___ericans to me."[2]

How can the Ame___ ___nd individual and group differences be recon___ ___ess of all concerned—a shared identity quick___ ___y Americans themselves? How can we not hav___ ___t? More to the point, what effect does the pa___ ___isjuncture between the individual and the c___ ___ons and experiences of ourselves and others ___ psychological anthropology can help provide s___ ___g the way history, structure, culture, and psyche intersect to co___ ___ a distinctive American worldview.

Ideally, such an inquiry would provide person-centered perspectives on American cultural values from individuals occupying different status positions. But that is too large a project for this chapter.[3] Instead, the effort here is to provide a shared framework of values within which person-centered research could take place. The chapter then focuses on one of the central tensions endemic to our culture—the difficulty Americans have conceptualizing distinctions in the economic and political realms—to show how the contradictions inherent in our shared worldview help shape our lives and relationships.

Americans: All different or all the same?

Chapter Outline

I. DISTINCTIONS

A   Anthropology and Self-Reflection
   Anthropology and the Western quest for authenticity.

B   Regional Differences in the United States
   Regional identity. The example of the South. The process of
   homogenization.

C   Ethnic Identity in the United States
   Ethnic identity, Americanization, and the illusion of variety.

D   Race as Destiny: The Fates of African Americans
   Evidence of racism in the United States. Its effect on psyche and
   worldview.

A. Anthropology and Self-Reflection

As we saw in the first section of this book, the self-certainty of Europeans was challenged not only by the critical spirit of the Enlightenment, but also by the discovery, during the age of exploration, of cultures holding values and beliefs very different from those held in the West. These cultures offered an opportunity for testing the validity of accepted Western paradigms and self-concepts. Anthropology arose out of this confrontation between "the West and the rest." The anthropological quest to decipher the thoughts, feelings, perceptions, and worldviews of others was thus never solely for the sake of accumulating abstract knowledge. There has always been a moral aspect to the search, the hope that through comparison with the other we can discover our own deepest and truest selves.

Throughout this book, I have accentuated this reflexive dimension of the anthropological inquiry, drawing attention whenever possible to the cultural uniqueness of what is thought to be natural and normal in America. As an example, our belief that children need both privacy and praise is highly unusual across cultures. Far more common is the constant participation of children in groups of adults who rarely praise them, on the grounds that compliments would lead to unhealthy self-regard. Americans also playfully interact with and speak baby talk to infants, and believe that this is the natural way to behave. Elsewhere, such play is seen as stimulating unnecessary excitement, while talking to infants is considered ridiculous. Many of our attitudes toward and relationships with small children are therefore not natural at all, but reflect pervasive cultural values of autonomous individualism, a concomitant emphasis on self-esteem and self-expression, and a deep faith in the importance of inculcating knowledge through talk. These traits and attitudes are adaptive in a modern social world where people are increasingly responsible for and reliant upon themselves, and where formal education is crucial for success.[4]

At the same time, I have pointed to the sometimes unsuspected ways others share our sense of being in the world, despite surface dissimilarities: The Japanese, who appear so interdependent that they are often portrayed as the polar opposites of the independent West, actually are quite concerned with protecting their egos and pursuing their personal goals, while Americans are in truth extremely worried about fitting in with the group and gaining the respect of others. Sociocentric and egocentric cultures are, it turns out, less at odds than they seem.[5]

In sum, anthropology has always had the mission of making the strange familiar and the familiar strange, shaking the complacency of those ignorant or arrogant enough to imagine their world is the only one that exists. But anthropology cannot be satisfied with exciting a sense of wonder; its ultimate duty is to use the knowledge gained elsewhere to analyze ourselves and our own culture.

B. Regional Differences in the United States

The anthropological study of American identity[6] is difficult simply because the notion of a shared culture is so actively resisted here, while assumptions of ineluctable individual and group differences are so deeply ingrained. Research on the United States has tended to reflect these values and has focused very much on local, ethnic, and racial distinctiveness, at the expense of developing a coherent portrait of the values and premises of American culture as a whole.[7]

And it is true that considerable variation does exist within the United States. For instance, regional differences are evident, especially in the South, which is the largest geographical region in the country, spreading all the way from the Atlantic to Texas. Southern Baptism is culturally unique, as is the characteristic Southern accent, while Nashville is the center of a distinctive Southern musical tradition (country and western). Beneath these surface differences are more important cultural contrasts: The South retains strong beliefs in manly honor, gentility, and military valor; gender differences are greater in the South, as is the level of acceptable violence; murder rates are higher, and capital punishment is more common.[8]

Yet, although Southerners do sometimes feel like (and are sometimes treated like) foreigners in their own country, in fact, their differences from the rest are very minor compared with differences between, for example, northern and southern Italians, who cannot even understand each other's dialects. And even the differences that do exist are disappearing, largely as a result of the relocation of the textile industry to the South after World War II and the diversification of the Southern economy. These factors have integrated the South into the American mainstream. This blending has been furthered by increased media penetration into the region and by massive population shifts, as people from other areas of the country move to the South and vice versa. And finally, there is the nationalizing process that was begun by Lincoln, who introduced the holiday of Thanksgiving as a way to unite the nation after the Civil War. Other commemorative celebrations followed. Nowadays, nearly everyone in the United States—North, South, East, and West—not only observes the same holidays, but also watches the same TV programs, goes to the same movies, buys the same products, votes in the same national elections, participates in the same sports, works for the same companies, and shares the same essential ethical principles. Local distinctions do remain, but they are relatively superficial.[9]

C. Ethnic Identity in the United States

Also subjectively important for identity are the ethnic identities that Americans cling to. When asked their nationality, most people in this country will give the place of origin of their ancestors, and it is this history of immigration that people often refer to when justifying their claim that all Americans are different. The premise is: We cannot have a shared culture when almost all of us (or our ancestors) came from so many countries. The easy answer, of course, is that it is precisely the experience of immigration that unites the country. Everyone here (except the American Indians) is descended from immigrants, so it is difficult for members of any group to make convincing claims of an aristocratic heritage or innate superiority over other citizens, as is the case in more homogeneous and ancient nations. We are all equivalent in our liberation from historical chains and in our shared faith that we can remake ourselves and become all we can be.

The heady appeal of this emancipating aspect of American life is evident in a letter sent by a French migrant to California during the Gold Rush:

> In the midst of this world of adventurers, who change their occupation as often as they do their shirt, egad, I did as the others. As mining did not turn out remunerative enough, I left it for the town, where in succession I became a typographer, a slater, plumber, etc. In consequence of thus finding out that I am fit for any sort of work, I feel less of a mollusk and more of a man.[10]

For such adventurous souls, America indeed offered—and continues to offer— an opportunity for shedding an old identity so as to take on a new one, for making "a man out of a mollusk." Though it must immediately be noted that not everyone cashes in on the promise and new immigrants continue to be discriminated against in America, the American dream of shedding old identities and constraints for new freedoms and opportunities is a powerful one that still motivates—a master schema, in the terms of cognitive anthropology.

Nonetheless, ethnic backgrounds, though often many generations distant, do sometimes make a difference in the personal lives of Americans. For example, people who consider themselves of Irish background may march in the St. Patrick's Day parade, wear green a lot, give money to Irish causes, and enjoy drinking beer, eating corned beef, and reading Irish literature. Or they may not. Unlike in Europe, the display of ethnic affiliation in America is voluntary, not obligatory.[11] Although the content of one's ethnic display may vary, the pattern does not: The Irish American's celebrations of ethnicity are structurally equivalent to those of her or his Chinese or Bulgarian or French or Pakistani neighbor, who also can march in ethnic parades, occasionally wear indigenous costumes, eat ancestral foods, feel proud of the literature and music from the home country, and wax nostalgic about tradition. To paraphrase Lévi-Strauss, the differences between American ethnic groups tend to resemble one another and are invoked when group members wish to validate their uniqueness against the overwhelming anonymity of American mass society: We are (name the group) and so have our own primordial community and authentic identity.

Some of the most striking ethnic differences are not really related to tradition at all. For instance, ethnographers report that Mexican Americans tend to

The celebration of ethnicity: Chinese New Year in Philadelphia.

live in large, extended families, unlike mainstream Americans, who are raised mainly in nuclear settings; Japanese Americans are much more concerned with filial piety than are their white neighbors.[12] However, these and other seemingly traditional practices are best seen as functional adaptions to the American setting, affirming a useful solidarity in the face of poverty or discrimination. These social forms are not equivalent to practices in the home country in any direct or recognizable way. Meanwhile, these same groups emulate what their members believe to be the practices of ordinary Americans, celebrating the national holidays, cheering for the local teams, attending school, learning English, and—above all—trying to realize the American dream of success.[13]

In fact, ethnic groups are integrated into the majority American culture far more than the members themselves may like to think. As anthropologists George and Louise Spindler have remarked, the extraordinary assimilative power of America is reflected in national tests of attitudes where "responses from ethnic minorities are indistinguishable from those produced by the mainstream—except that minority respondents tend to be more traditional, more 'American' in their value orientations."[14] In other words, in many instances the minorities are themselves the best examples of the ordinary Americans they believe themselves to be emulating.

Hispanics in the USA

Americans unduly worried about the coherence of their society have recently been perturbed by the increasing numbers of Hispanics in the United States, where they now make up the third-largest ethnic group. A major fear is that English is being challenged by Spanish in some areas, raising the specter of a language-based separationist movement. It is evident, however, that most Spanish speakers would like to learn English if they could, and that the major factor holding them back is the absence of affordable schooling. Furthermore, it is also clear that Hispanics are by no means a unified community: Cubans, Puerto Ricans, Spaniards, and Mexicans rarely identify with one another.

A more positive view of Latino immigration might focus on the fact that people from these cultures—especially from Mexico—could serve as examples of cultural and racial hybridity, because of their own mixed backgrounds. Mestizo, or "mixed race," people now make up 85 percent or more of the population of Mexico, though it is hard to tell, since race has not been a category in the Mexican census since 1921.[15]

Independence coerced?

D. Race as Destiny: The Fates of African Americans

Of course, the greatest rebuke to American ideals of assimilation are the African Americans, who are among the earliest immigrants to the United States, though their immigration was often coerced. They remain disproportionately impoverished, ghettoized, and politically underrepresented. Although they constitute 12 percent of the population, they hold only 1.4 percent of political offices. Blacks also constitute half the murder victims and half of those convicted for murder; as a group, their educational achievement is depressingly low, as is their income. Despite these disheartening statistics, it is also clear that racial prejudice in the United States is losing force. In 1940 only 10 percent of black men could claim middle-class status; the proportion now is 40 percent. Interracial friendships and marriages have also increased considerably.

In spite of their successes, African Americans often do not feel they are accepted in white society. And for good reason, since psychological tests show that white Americans are still very reluctant to treat people with dark skin with the same respect they treat people with light skin. As various studies reveal, whites who see a videotape of a shove often interpret it as violence from a black actor, but as play from a white one. Whites tend to sit farther away from blacks than they do from other whites, make nervous speech errors in talking to blacks, have less eye contact, conduct shorter interviews, and evaluate their work as inferior.[16] Prejudice is also seen in a 1990 survey that asked a cross section of whites to rank racial and ethnic groups in order of intelligence, industriousness, and willingness to be self-supporting. Blacks were ranked lowest on every measure.[17] Negative white attitudes toward blacks are so ingrained that the anthropologist John Ogbu has argued that despite proclamations of equality, the

United States is actually a caste society consisting of two mutually exclusive, hierarchcially ranked groups: white and black.[18]

There are many complex reasons for this situation. One is the biologizing of difference that permits whites to see blacks as naturally inferior. The same categorizing technique can justify any kind of oppression: In the Second World War anyone with one-sixteenth Japanese blood was automatically interred; women too have often been denied their rights on the grounds of biological inferiority.[19] On top of the use of color as a natural marker for difference is added the African-American heritage of slavery, which is an historical taint difficult to erase or compensate for in American culture where autonomy is so highly valued.[20] A third factor is the symbolic necessity for a free people to posit an unfree other, against whom they can favorably compare themselves. Blacks, because of their racial distinctiveness and history of slavery, easily fall into this slot.[21]

This layering of negative images is compounded by the actuality of continued poverty and the high incidence of crime and drug addiction among ghettoized urban African Americans. The much publicized violent lifestyles of black gangs help reinforce disapproving attitudes of whites toward African Americans while also solidifying the group's own sense of exclusion and indignity—which is felt even more deeply by middle-class blacks than by those who are impoverished.[22] The continued existence of disgraceful urban conditions for poor African Americans is partially a result of the structural shift in the American economy toward service industries, which has eliminated traditional male jobs and left urban black men with no work. This same process has coincided with liberalized social policies that have drawn middle-class blacks away to the suburbs. The combination has left black urban areas bereft of both resources and positive role models, and thus has promoted alienation and isolation.[23]

A more encouraging reading is that African Americans are best seen not as eternal victims of discrimination, but as transitional internal migrants who have left the stagnant plantation and small-farmer economy of the South for wage labor in the North only fairly recently—mostly after World War II. As such, they can be compared with other immigrant populations, such as the Irish, who overcame terrible prejudice and social marginalization to enter the middle-class after two or three generations. It is also worth remembering that the Irish and other non-Anglo-Saxon immigrants were commonly thought to belong to completely different and inferior races, as distinct from the mainstream as African Americans are now thought to be.[24] According to this model, black Americans are gradually moving away from their status as unskilled immigrants; their slow entrance into the middle class, which is well documented, will lead eventually to an end to prejudice. Of course, this reading does not account for the ever-increasing cultural and moral distance between the suburban black middle class and the slum dwellers who continue to inhabit decaying city centers.

Do the burning problems of prejudice and inequity mean that African Americans have values that are distinctly different from those of other Americans? Certainly, this is true to a degree—particularly because of their shared history of discrimination and the memory of slavery, and the psychological and ethical repercussions those experiences entail. But these differences are objectively relatively minor, though subjectively, they may be felt to be major. In fact, survey data show that black Americans have much the same values, beliefs, hopes, and dreams as their white neighbors. With few exceptions, they too affirm equality of opportunity, self-reliance, and the right to pursue the American dream of success. And of course African Americans have made many distinctive and irreplaceable contributions to mainstream American culture. In particular, their strong faith that they can and should struggle against discrimination and for justice and equity shows the depth of their Americanness.[25]

II. AMERICAN VALUES

A Sources and Paradoxes of Egalitarian Individualism
>   Historical, cultural, and structural origins of egalitarian individualism. Capitalism, conformity, and consumerism.

B Righteousness, Moderation, and Moral Minimalism
>   Sacred values of Americans: social trust, tolerance, nonjudgmental moral minimalism, and generalized niceness.

C Love and the Construction of Community
>   Love in the family and the community.

D The Price of Association: Bigotry and Paranoia
>   Naturalizing of inferiority. Paranoia and conspiracy theories.

A. Sources and Paradoxes of Egalitarian Individualism

We can say, then, that American regions are more alike than different, and that ethnic and racial divisions within the society do not correlate with very great distinctions in worldview. We can also note in passing that the United States is far from unique in the variety of peoples who live within it. Canada and Australia, which are also immigrant societies, have equally complex ethnic mixes, as do some Latin American countries. Much of what we Americans see as unique diversity is neither as diverse nor as unique as we like to believe.

What *is* singular about the United States is the way that individual difference and autonomy are glorified, and the paradoxical manner our faith in personal distinctiveness and freedom unites the whole society. As the social theorist Robert Bellah and his colleagues have noted, "the idea we have of ourselves as individuals on our own, who earn everything we get, accept no handouts or gifts, and free ourselves from our families of origin turns out, ironically enough, to be one of the things that holds us together."[26] In other words, my student's proud assertion that everyone in the United States is irreducibly different and unique (a belief shared by all her classmates) marks her (and her fellows) as quintessentially American.

The value placed on personal uniqueness has deep historical, cultural, and structural roots. It grows out of the origins of the United States as a culture built by mobile and entrepreneurial pioneers who were heavily influenced by the moral premises of Protestantism. For these settlers, questing for religious freedom and personal salvation, their new society was never seen as preexisting or commanding. Rather, it was envisioned as a covenanted community, knit together by voluntary agreements between free and equal individuals, each responsible for his or her own acts and each seeking personal salvation within the group. Even though one had to belong to a sacred association, the individual's conscience always had priority; as a result, the church congregation was bound together only by the loyalties of kindred spirits. In practice, within the mobile environment of the United States, this meant that the authority of any church could be opposed, and members of the congregation could find new preachers, organize new churches. The history of American Protestantism is one of continual schism and the rise of new faiths and sects as dissatisfied parishioners sought new, greener, spiritual pastures.[27]

Esteem for personal independence was furthered even more by the revolutionary history of the United States, which imbued Americans with a deep distrust for any form of central authority. This individualistic value system coincided with the ease of social and spatial movement in the New World, where entrenched class hierarchies and status limitations did not exist. As a result, American towns, like American churches, were founded with enthusiasm by boosters who made hopeful claims to community and solidarity, but who then left whenever something better was offered. The United States remains the most mobile nation on earth, with families commonly scattered across the whole continent. The mind-set that has resulted from the confluence of Protestant ideology, material reality, and historical circumstances assumes the value of the individual is paramount, regardless of position, place, or power.

In practice, this has meant that from colonial times onward, material inequalities in the United States have always been balanced by a democratic demand for personal respect. As David Fischer, an historian of early America, remarks, on the colonial frontier, rich and poor "wore similar clothing and addressed each other by first names. They worked, ate, laughed, played and fought together on a footing of equality."[28] A distaste for snobbery and the related demand for respect for individuals regardless of actual hierarchical distinctions are also evident in the horrified report from the British consul in Boston in 1840 that servant girls "are, when walking the streets, scarcely to be distinguished from their employers."[29]

Today, in spite of huge and ever-increasing distinctions in wealth and power, most Americans remain just as careful to disguise authority relations behind the trappings of equality. On the job, subordinates are team members whose consent and cooperation are requested by their supervisors.[30] As Margaret Mead's English disciple Geoffrey Gorer wrote, in America we find bosses who are "glad-handed, extrovert, mindful of first names, seeing their subordinates in their shirt sleeves and with their feet on the desk, democratically obscene in their language, with private interests, if any, simple and within the reach of all."[31] The shared egalitarian ideal means that Americans can have servants and send their children to elite schools, but the servants can't be dressed in livery nor can the children speak in a genteel accent.

Homogeneous Speech in America

The unity of American culture is indicated in part by the amazing homogeneity of speech throughout the country. While this standardization has been greatly enhanced by the spread of mass media, it was already remarkable before the American Revolution; European visitors were astonished at the uniformity of pronunciation across regions and classes. The reasons, according to the historian Daniel Boorstin, have to do with widespread literacy, the ubiquity of the spelling bee, the absence of an aristocratic dialect or a cultural center, and the American passion for self-improvement through education.[32] Shared speech, Americans continue to believe, is one of the few things holding the country together—hence the widespread fear of ebonics and the dislike of schools' teaching children in Spanish.

The casual American outfit of blue jeans and work shirt can be worn by everyone, to demonstrate that even the richest are workers at heart, while in restaurants, waiters cheerily introduce themselves by name to their customers. In short, in the United States it is perfectly fine to be rich and powerful just as long as one does not make claims to be different and better. Such public denials of rank and affirmations of equality would be ludicrous in class-bound European cultures, but they are standard in America, where people confront one another as individuals, not as members of hierarchical status groups. For Americans, even the beggar on the street demands and deserves recognition.[33]

Studies by cognitive anthropologists have verified this characteristic American stance toward life and relationships. Roy D'Andrade concluded from tests given to a sampling of American students that they greatly disliked any semblance of control by others or being treated as inferiors. Instead, they strongly preferred mutual caring and mutual sharing among equals. D'Andrade concludes that American cognitive schemas of the world are exceptionally "anti-authoritarian and pro-egalitarian."[34]

Yet the American ethic of caring and sharing among co-equals coexists with an intense competition for status, as each individual seeks to gain resources in a never-ending game of entrepreneurship. The seemingly paradoxical combination of equality and self-assertion was explained by Alexis de Tocqueville (1805–1859), the French aristocrat who visited the United States in 1831 and wrote *Democracy in America*, the greatest of all ethnographies of our country.[35] In this book, he made a social structural argument demonstrating that a democratic society based on a free-market economy is bound to be torn by continuous competition. The logic is as follows: Lacking the security and stability granted by inherited positions found in more traditional and hierarchical cultures, and immersed in a capitalist system with no safeguards, people in a capitalist democracy must struggle continually to defeat their nearest rivals and establish positions of safety for themselves. In short, democratic, egalitarian individualism within a market economy fosters rivalry rather than cooperation.

Consumerism and Democratic Identity

Capitalism relies on consumption, and in America consumption has been democratized in department stores and malls. Until the nineteenth century, luxury goods were to be found only in intimate shops catering to the elite, but with the inauguration of huge, open urban emporiums, the entire public could now become part of a consumption community drawn together by the sumptuous display of merchandise.[36]

It is hard to overestimate the symbolic importance of consumption in the construction of American identity, especially now that the suburban mall has become ubiquitous. In these artificial, hygienic, and homogeneous environments, people can explore various possibilities for manufacturing themselves; they can parade their status positions while also demonstrating their individuality by purchasing lifestyle goods. Regardless of all race, class, and ethnic divisions, shoppers move in unison through a controlled environment where the common fantasy of achieving and displaying wealth is publicly played out in an atmosphere of collective enthusiasm. In the overflowing abundance of the public marketplace, it is made quite clear that the system offers Americans every dream that money can buy.[37]

Tocqueville also believed that egalitarianism would inevitably place psychological tensions upon Americans that would impel them toward a high degree of conformity, despite their proud claims to independence. He puts his argument as follows:

> The more alike men are, the weaker each feels in the face of all. Finding nothing that raises him above their level and distinguishes him, he loses his self-confidence when he comes into collision with them. Not only does he mistrust his own strength, but even comes to doubt his own judgement, and he is brought very near to recognizing that he must be wrong when the majority hold the opposite view. There is no need for the majority to compel him; it convinces him.[38]

Fearful of being in the wrong and of being ostracized by the majority, Americans must carefully monitor their behavior, "keeping up with the Joneses" while still not "rocking the boat." Conformity also coincides psychologically with acute status anxiety, which is far greater than would be found in a traditional society where groups and their appropriate manners are well demarcated, and where people automatically know their place. As Tocqueville says, in the egalitarian democracy of the United States, "each man wants to appear as something he is not."[39] This anxiety helps account for the compulsive consumerism of Americans, as each seeks to prove his or her worth by accumulation of measurable possessions.

B. Righteousness, Moderation, and Moral Minimalism

The complex combination of egalitarianism, individualism, competition, status seeking, conformity, and consumerism coincides with another characteristic aspect of the self-identity of Americans: a strong sense of their own morality and righteousness, and of the morality and righteousness of the nation as a whole. As the English author G. K. Chesterton (1874–1936) observed, the United States is "a nation with the soul of a church,"[40] meaning that, unlike citizens in other societies, citizens of the United States see themselves participating in a universal sacred mission and attribute a holy aura to the nation and its symbols.[41] Largely because America began in a spiritual quest, the ideal of the nation as God's country has deep and lasting roots. The mythic charter of the country describes the United States as the city on the hill, the land of the free and the home of the brave, with a mission to save the world from tyranny and evil. Citizens are sanctified by their shared participation in this exalted task and have a deep faith that their fellows will act instinctively in righteous and ethical American ways. As one man said in a recent survey:

> People are inherently good and they will make the right decisions based on what's right and what's wrong, not necessarily because that's what their religion taught them. If you don't have religion, there's still right and wrong.[42]

From this perspective, Americans naturally know for themselves what is right to do in their own particular circumstances and naturally want to be moral and just. What the society at large must do is allow each individual to follow his or her innate sense of morality: All will then be well. Differences in preference are not to be argued with, but confirmed. A faith in the essential goodness of fellow Americans coincides with a belief that "good people will always make the right kinds of choices."[43] Davey Crockett's famous maxim—Be sure you're right, then go ahead—still has resonance among American egalitarian individualists, certain that their fellow citizens share their faith in the moral superiority of their nation and of the American people.

Vaguely counting on the general decency of others, whom they consider good people very much like themselves, Americans also tend to be suspicious of strong opinions and of any sort of zealotry. For example, a 1987 Gallup poll reported that 44 percent of Americans would not like to live next door to a religious fanatic; in comparison, 11 percent would not like to live next door to an Afro-American. Racial prejudice, while it definitely exists, takes a backseat to an intolerance for religious extremism. This attitude is ideologically justified since zealots make claims to moral authority—the cardinal sin in an egalitarian ethos where a superior attitude leads to accusations of being a snob or a know-it-all, which are some of the worst insults that can be directed at an American. This determinedly moderate attitude has recently been encapsulated by the sociologist Alan Wolfe: "[Americans] believe in the importance of leading a virtuous life but are reluctant to impose values they understand as virtuous for themselves on others; strong believers in morality, they do not want to be considered moralists."[44]

The value of moderation is expressed in a characteristic American stance of moral minimalism, that is, avoiding any conflictual interactions and refraining from trying to control the actions of another person.[45] It may seem odd that one of the ordinary American's strongest moral values is a reluctance to impose moral values, but this is simply an expression of the premise that all individuals ought to have equal freedom to make their own fates without restraint from their neighbors; concomitantly, they too should not meddle with anyone else. In other words, no one has any right to tell anyone else what to do. Because Americans do not want to confront their neighbors, anonymous calls to the police are the primary means of resolving minor nuisances (the majority of suburban police calls are to silence a neighbor's barking dog).[46]

Exceptions to the rule, such as violent pro-life extremists or racist hate groups and paranoid militias, would seem to overturn this premise—but these groups, though they gain a great deal of publicity, are not numerous, and are viewed with distaste by the vast majority of Americans, who find their exclusionary principles and unwillingness to compromise repellent. Those who keep on shouting out moralistic calls to action tend to be castigated as troublemakers and demagogues, and even as un-American, since nothing is more American than moderation and tolerance. Those enthusiastic or enraged enough to embrace confrontational tactics may unify a core of true believers, but they will inevitably be marginalized outside the vast, homogenizing mainstream of American culture.

In the past, the pervasive spirit of avoidance suited the openness and rough-and-ready equality of a frontier society; today it correlates with the world of the middle-class suburb, where there is usually no need for neighbors to confront one another, where it is even possible for members of the family household to have separate rooms, separate schedules, and separate meals, and almost never come in contact with one another. The same ethic prevails as well in America's automated factories and construction sites, where the motto is "Do your own work and don't mess with anybody's shit."[47] Cultivating indifference, Americans can interact smoothly with others as long as those others make no demands on one's time and autonomy or interfere in the efficient completion of one's task.

Working-Class Worldviews

There has not been enough ethnographic literature on the differences between the worldviews of the working class and those of the middle class in America. In general, we can say that working-class relationships in America tend to be more volatile and confrontational—a consequence both of differing attitudes toward life and of more constrictive social settings. For example, according to one recent ethnographic study of the complex relationship between class and concepts of self in America, working-class children are trained to see themselves in an adversarial light and to harden themselves for the struggle against a hostile world. In contrast, upper-middle-class children are socialized to imagine themselves flowering in a nurturant environment and are encouraged to seek cooperative relations with others.[48] However, these class-based differences pale in comparison with the stark distinctions between working class and middle class that prevail in England, for instance.[49]

Labor Day barbecue in the suburbs.

The social trust and nonjudgmental tolerance of Americans are also a legacy of the original Protestant covenanted church, now transferred to the larger, secularized social world, where the primary goals are no longer sanctity and salvation, but simply being well liked while pursuing success. This attitude corresponds with the cordial informality and compulsive niceness of Americans that is so often commented on with amusement or condescension by foreign visitors, who are far more formal in their public expression of emotion. As the American historian Daniel Boorstin has noted, easy amiability is appropriate for a "new realm of uncertain boundaries . . . an affable, communal world which, strictly speaking, was neither public nor private: a world of first names, open doors, front porches, and front lawns."[50] In this changeable and open public universe, an easygoing, friendly expression allows strangers to negotiate a social minefield where there are no clear status markers and where authority is decentralized and relatively weak. This unstable and potentially threatening universe is made livable by the expectation that one's own friendliness and helpfulness will usually be returned by one's equally nice fellow citizens.[51]

C. Love and the Construction of Community

The family both expresses and inculcates the American ethos of niceness and toleration. As noted in the previous chapter, Americans believe that the family is held together not through rules and regulations or through coercion and charisma, but by means of mutual consensus and loving affection.[52] In the prototypical middle-class American family setting, equality and negotiation are the watchwords. The father is not a commanding patriarchal authority figure; like other family members, he too must bargain to get his way. The relative absence of paternal power in suburban middle-class America correlates with the very real independence of children, who work for themselves; often have their own private rooms, property, and incomes; and have almost no long-term interests to bring them together with their parents. In keeping with the overriding ethic of autonomy, American children generally expect to be paid for their labor around the home, and can even be fired if their work is not up to par.

In this businesslike atmosphere, the only thing holding the family together is love. As sociologist M. P. Baumgartner writes in her study of an American suburb, parents "are aware that unless they can bind their children to them with ties of affection, no material compulsion will keep those children deferential to them—or even in touch with them—in later years."[53] This fragile emotional bond, however, is supposed to be enough: Love is believed to have the power to dissolve hierarchy and to bind independent individuals together in an egalitarian community of unselfish mutuality.[54] The familial anti-authoritarian expression of positive emotion has great resonance and extension in American culture. As Gorer wrote, for Americans, "unsmiling subservience produces discomfort; unsmiling arrogance, fear and hostility. The emotional egalitarianism of America demands that all relationships shall bear some resemblance to those of love and friendship."[55]

The expansion of familial affection into the public sphere is centrally important since it appears to resolve the tension between personal freedom and participation in the community. This is a tension that Americans feel especially strongly. In most other cultures the community precedes the individual, who finds a place within it. In contrast, as we have seen, for Americans, society is thought to be constituted only by the voluntary agreement of its members. As the astute French ethnographer of America, Hervé Varenne, puts it, Americans believe that "individualism is natural, community problematical. *Society has to be built.*"[56]

Because community—whether sacred or secular—is both highly valued and yet felt to be extremely fragile, Americans tend to place great emphasis on the emotional solidarity of groups, just as they place great emphasis on love between couples. The belief in the power of ties of love—or, minimally, of liking—allows competitive, egalitarian individualists to conceptualize and experience participation in the civic sphere. Within this cultural model, community members, like marriage partners, recognize each other as independent individuals united primarily by personal affection rather than by rules, laws, interests, or authority. Affection can cool and membership can shift, as in marriage, but the anti-authoritarian, individualistic notion of a voluntaristic community united by caring remains the same.[57] In love or in community, Americans reserve for themselves the right to continue to search for personal happiness through relations with others; for them, divorce is not an act of despair, but the prelude to a better and more fulfilling relationship. Towns, organizations, clubs, and every other form of voluntary group are joined and left in the same adventurous and romantic spirit.

Of course, there are variations along a continuum here. Condominium associations, for example, are convened for practical matters, and considerable painful conflict may occur among members; in contrast, participants in therapeutic self-help groups are expected to give unconditional support to one another. But, ideally at least, disagreement within all forms of voluntary communal associations is kept to a minimum. "It doesn't matter whether the members of a community are objectively alike," Varenne writes, speaking of his research in a small American town, "as long as they agree not to insist on expressing whatever differences may indeed exist." He found this to be so much the case that "some of my informants could literally be brought to tears if someone they considered close to them appeared to seriously disagree with them."[58] Community, for Americans, is a moral good, but it can never be dictated and can be arrived at only through repressing differences and the cooperation of co-equals.

D. The Price of Association: Bigotry and Paranoia

There is a dark side to American egalitarianism and communalism. We have already seen how Americans tend to naturalize inferiority for certain categories of person—especially African Americans, but also other ethnic and racial minorities, as well as women. Biologizing inferiority allows maintenance of the faith in human equality in the face of blatant bigotry and oppression through the simple expedient of denying some people full human status.[59] At the same time, the fundamental credo of equality means that any such assertions of rank are always contested. Denigrated groups can and do resist being consigned to inferior categories, and call on the egalitarian values of the mainstream for support. This was the strategy followed by Martin Luther King, Jr., and it has made overt expressions of bigotry less and less socially acceptable in American culture.

Another dark side of the American stress on the emotional source of community and faith in the niceness of its members is a pervasive ambiguity about those who are not participants. Americans typically tend to refer to their own group as "everybody" and believe they act as everybody should act, that is, with love and generosity. But the attribution of virtue to one's own group implies, as Freud said, the demonization of others. Thus Americans tend to be extremely suspicious of the motives of strangers and outsiders who, they think, may be hiding nefarious plots beneath smiling faces. For this reason, American college students see their own group as an egalitarian bunch of nice guys, while they disparage other groups as cliques of snobs.

Pervasive suspicion of collectives other than one's own fuels the characteristic American anxiety about conspiracies. If one's own friends and colleagues are prototypically good and righteous Americans, then some evil countergroups must be working in hidden ways to keep "us" from power. This paranoia is exacerbated by the actual decentralization of the political system, which means, as we shall see, that many important decisions are, in fact, made by cabals outside public surveillance. A propensity to blame conspiracies for failures of the American dream has sometimes led to witch-hunts, such as the anti-Communist phobias stirred up by Joseph McCarthy in the 1950s. In compensation, generalized suspicion of groups makes it hard for any organization to present itself as the savior of the American way, and helps provide the basis for a social order founded on a trust of Americans as individuals, coupled with anxious suspicion of them in groups.

In sum, the shared American understanding of the nature of the individual has powerful effects on the experience of the self and the construction of relationships in America. It correlates directly with pervasive cultural patterns of competitiveness, conformity, moral minimalism, social trust, participation in community, and notions of love, along with the biologizing of inferiority, a tendency toward self-righteousness, and an inclination to paranoia.

III. WEALTH AND EGALITARIANISM

A Pretending Class Doesn't Exist
    Explaining the absence of class warfare in the United States.

B The Pursuit of the American Dream
    Competition, capitalism, individualism, and the cultural acceptance of income inequity.

A. Pretending Class Doesn't Exist

As we have seen, the creed of equality and individualism, like the notion of caste discussed in Chapter 8, has its own logic and its own implicit contradictions and tensions that trouble the minds and hearts of Americans, whoever they are. The rest of this chapter will explicate some of the ramifications of one aspect of the ambiguous social, psychological, and cultural underpinnings of American life outlined above. The question to be addressed is, How can an egalitarian society justify the reality of inequality among categorical equals? In other words, how do Americans manage to cope with the manifest superiority of the rich and powerful?[60]

It has long been remarked that one of the most striking features of class in America is the fact that most people do not believe it exists.[61] Of course, there are many structural and historical reasons for this remarkable fact, not least of them being the extraordinary productivity of the American economy, which has elevated many skilled workers into the expansive ranks of the middle class—the class group that the vast majority of Americans identify as their own. This positive effect was coupled with the brutal suppression of the socialist labor movement around the turn of the century, effectively eliminating any class-based challenge to the status quo in the United States.[62]

In this section, however, I want to concentrate primarily on some cultural and psychological reasons for the relative lack of class antagonism in America. In part, this absence stems from the fact that most Americans divide the world in two, with the public marketplace viewed as the proper arena for continuous contests between rivalrous co-equals. In this, the market is contrasted to the private world of friends, family, and community where love and reciprocity are supposed to prevail. Although rivalry is expected in business, this does not solve the problem of justifying the enormous differences that result when one entrepreneur wins and the other loses: If all Americans are essentially equivalent, how is it that one has a mansion while another lives in a slum?

The evident difficulty of reconciling the American faith in human equality with the existence of extreme wealth and poverty has long been a source of great alarm among members of the propertied classes, such as the English lord who wrote to an American correspondent in the mid-eighteenth century: "Your government will never be able to restrain a distressed and discontented majority. For with you, the majority is the government, and has the rich, who are always a minority, absolutely at its mercy."[63] Yet, despite the fears of the Right (and the hopes of the Left), American radicals have often tended to be romantic anarchists demanding a recognition of autonomy within a community of love, rather than socialist revolutionaries seeking to overturn the class hierarchy.[64] Young, white radicals of the 1960s, for example, almost universally demanded not an end to riches, nor even more equitable income redistribution; instead, they wanted a more nurturant society, where there would be no unjust wars and where people would be allowed the freedom to grow and find themselves. In other words, social critique was not directed primarily against an unjust division of wealth, but against the Vietnam War and the inability of the political realm to provide an environment of trust.

This pattern followed a tradition in American politics, where resistance to war and dislike for government interference in people's personal lives have always been intermingled,[65] but where—with the exception of the New Deal— there has rarely been popular support for even such minimal redistributive mechanisms as a ceiling on income or wage and price controls. Instead, the vast majority continue to believe in the American dream of self-reliance and prosperity. This is true even of the most disadvantaged. Two-thirds of the poor in America believe they can improve their standard of living by working harder— three times the number in Europe. It seems then that, as the great American historian Charles Beard (1874–1948) wrote, "modern egalitarian democracy . . . does not destroy economic classes or economic inequalities. It ignores them. Herein lies the paradox, the most astounding political contradiction that the world has ever witnessed."[66]

B. The Pursuit of the American Dream

This paradox is difficult to understand if we accept the utilitarian premise that individuals are indeed maximizing free agents seeking personal wealth. The poor, as the English lord feared, should then rationally want a redistribution of income that would raise their standards, and ought to disrupt society in order to gain this reasonable goal. But this has not happened. Is this because the less privileged hope instead to move up the ladder of success and do not want to destroy their chances? If so, it is mostly a false hope, since strong wealth differentiation, rather than upward mobility, has generally been the rule rather than the exception in America,[67] and since differences between haves and have-nots have noticeably accelerated in recent decades.[68]

If American acceptance of vast differentials in wealth is not based primarily on rational reasons, what then is it based on? Research indicates that consent is due to the way values of egalitarian individualism are applied to the economic realm. We have already noted the polar conceptual opposition between the private ideal of selfless mutuality among beloved intimates and the public domain of the marketplace characterized by competitive rivalry. In this cutthroat arena, equality of opportunity is emphasized. Inequality of result is justified by the abilities of the individual: Capitalist success is thereby reconciled with American egalitarian ideals, since prosperity is believed to be a goal all can (and should) pursue, but only the best can actually gain.

The polarized spheres of American culture can be summarized as follows:

- *Public marketplace.* Competition, egoism, equality of opportunity, differential success or failure as a consequence of ability.
- *Private relationships.* Cooperation, interdependence, mutuality and reciprocity, equality in a shared community of love.

Although the marketplace stands against the private virtues of caring and sharing, it has its own ethical standards. For instance, because of the Protestant faith that work is a value in itself, wealth must be earned, not inherited, to be respected. Earned wealth is thought to demonstrate a person's capacity to do work that deserves high compensation. Thus the value of the individual—his or her perfectibility, to borrow a Protestant term—can be measured in monetary terms. In a secularized transvaluation of the Protestant ethic, money then becomes a sign of an individual's admirable qualities: assertiveness, initiative, courage, efficiency, individual effort, and personal ability.[69] As a result of this faith, even the poorest accept the morality of differentiation in wealth. It is simply an accepted reality "not unlike the law of gravity."[70] Even more astonishingly, survey data show that Americans of every status and occupation are remarkably uniform in their agreement on the proper disparity of wealth for occupational groups, with businesspeople unquestioningly accepted as deserving top salaries while unskilled labor are believed to be entitled to the lowest pay—though it is true that most people on the low end of the scale have no idea how vast is the actual disparity between their incomes and the incomes of the elite.[71]

But the main difference between the attitudes of the haves and the have-nots toward wealth is that the poor believe they have not had the opportunity to show their diligence and good character, and hope for the chance to escape from the lowly world of unskilled labor into the lucrative realm of business; the rich, in contrast, generally believe the poor simply have not worked hard enough. For both, the ideal is not to flatten the income curve, but to reach, or remain atop, the peak. Katherine Newman, who has done pioneering anthropological work on class and status in America, notes that even those who fail in the race for wealth continue to accept the existence of a meritocracy, and "prosecute themselves on its behalf, turning criticisms against themselves and against one another: victims blaming victims."[72] Newman has documented the human misery of administrators fired from their jobs, who have lost not only their income but also their sense of self-respect. The same mechanism of self-blame occurs among the impoverished as well. For instance, in 1985, 60 percent of the poor people surveyed thought women would have babies simply to get child welfare benefits, while only 45 percent of the nonpoor thought this was the case.[73]

Despite the undeniable fact that wealth and power in the United States are actually concentrated in a relatively small portion of the population, who have access to family fiduciary trusts, who are guaranteed admission into elite universities and membership in exclusive clubs, and who control the most powerful institutions,[74] Americans still retain the individualistic belief that the accumulation of riches is a result of personal struggle by ordinary people who have succeeded through their own unaided efforts at the same game everyone plays, or should be able to play. Nor is wealth considered permanent; instead, it is thought the wealthy will lose their riches over time, and new entrepreneurs will take their places.[75] These beliefs, though largely false, are understandable within the context of the American value system of egalitarian individualism.

Political arguments about the justice of economic inequality do not challenge these basic assumptions about the legitimacy of wealth. From the Right, the argument is that the race is indeed fair; the poor have failed to take advantage of the opportunities offered to them and to everyone else and so deserve their poverty. The argument from the Left is the reverse: The playing field is not level; therefore, those players who fail are not at fault and should be helped to achieve parity. Both sides accept without debate a cultural belief, inherited from Protestantism, that only those who are trying seriously to escape poverty and succeed in the competition should be given aid; there is no warrant to help those who are lazy and little value placed on the spiritual value of charity for its own sake.

To summarize, in the public sphere of the marketplace, all participants are thought to be free agents struggling for the desirable but temporary benefits of success. The actual predominance of elites and the existence of class is ignored, masked by assumptions of essential human equality. As a result, those who do succeed are believed to be individuals who have the sorts of character traits Americans see as both morally good and typical of themselves: independence, efficiency, innovation, courage, hard work, ambition, personal drive. While there may be resentment at the fat cats, it is believed that they will eventually fall from grace. Anyway, their wealth is deserved and reflects their virtues. In sum, most Americans do not see anything wrong with great gulfs of income. Rather, whether black or white, poor or middle-class, they want to be on the right side of that gulf.[76] For these cultural and psychological reasons (along with others that are more structural and political-historical), Americans have shown little interest as yet in undertaking even a minimal restructuring of the economy.

IV. POLITICS AND COMMUNITY

A Sacred Power
   Politics as the locus of the sacred community of co-equals.

B Central Paradoxes of American Politics
   Cynicism and idealism. The ambiguities of special interest politics, presidential authority, and group influence.

A. Sacred Power

A second arena in which Americans must wrestle with the problem of distinction is far more problematic; this is the realm of politics and the state, which, as Durkheim noted, opposes the pragmatism of the marketplace by relying upon sacred values for its legitimation. This is especially the case in the United States, where there is no spiritual myth of ethnic origin. As a nation of immigrants, Americans must look instead to the documents and symbols of the past for their sacred charter. The Declaration of Independence, the Bill of Rights, and the Constitution are our sacred texts, housed in the civil pilgrimage center of Washington; the revolutionary flag is our totem; the history of the nation and its heroes are celebrated on the holy days of July Fourth, Thanksgiving, Memorial Day, and on other holidays; we recite our allegiance to our faith at the beginning of every sporting event; we are ready to die for it in the event of war. Lacking a national religion, we have made a religion of the nation.[77]

The political community in this vision of America takes on a powerful ethical life as an actively constructed metaphysical entity. As the anthropologist Elvin Hatch writes in his ethnography of a small American town: "It was assumed not only that a community *does* exhibit cooperation, cohesion, and collective action, but that it *should* do so . . . regions that lack a community life altogether—and therefore are not communities—lack merit."[78] This view coincides with the revolutionary and Protestant American premise, noted above, that society is not a preexistent institution with its own rules and orders, but is a moral corporation that must be continuously knit together by voluntary agreements between independent co-equals who each bear personal responsibility for their own acts. In

---

Trust and Government

Robert Bellah and his colleagues[79] have made a convincing case that Americans idealize government at the level of local representation, which is generally seen through rose-colored glasses as a homey New England town meeting of neighborly equals (the reality, of course, is quite different, as any small-town New Englander knows). They also idealize presidential authority as the symbolic unifying force for the whole nation.

However, the vast range of political action between these two extremes is viewed with distaste. In particular, the House of Representatives—both national and local—is disdained, because the House is where the most pressing political battles are fought, compromises are reached, and special interests are mollified. In other words, it is where real politics is practiced, and therefore it is symbolically tainted. Those who doubt this analysis should note that no matter how unpopular a president, the House has always been more unpopular. For example, when Richard Nixon's approval rating fell to 30 percent, the House was approved by only 21 percent of the public.

July Fourth in Washington, D.C.

this context, it becomes the job of every individual American citizen, working together with his or her neighbors, to manufacture a new nation, one "conceived in liberty" where "all men are created equal"—a replication, in other words, of the American family, where authority is democratically exercised only through consensus and affection, as we elect leaders whose power is not their own, but who are supposed to represent the sacred unity of the community.[80]

Within this idealized framework, proper political action is understood as the voluntary participation of independent individuals cooperating to build and maintain the town, the state, and the nation. Like the private world of the family, the ideal community is thought to be bound together by the unselfish love and caring of its members. The American sacred vision of citizenship is symbolically enacted in a number of ways. For instance, each individual casts a vote in the privacy and isolation of the voting booth, giving up personal political responsibility via a personal contract with the elected official, who then must act for all the individual voters in the aptly named Congress. Criminals are punished by being permanently stripped of the fundamental right to vote; they are thereby excluded from the sacred covenant of co-equal citizens.

Because American government represents the sacred community, holders of political power are imagined to be exemplary figures who represent the whole electorate and express the harmony of the group. Political leaders in America must therefore always demonstrate that they are not egoists, but rather agents of consensus and selfless servants of the popular will. This is most evident in local, face-to-face political relationships where, as Hatch documents, a leader "tried to avoid any appearance that it was he who determined the goals sought."[81] Even national leaders must show that they can build consensus and serve their constituents; all must fervently deny that they favor any special interests; all must return to their home districts to display their common touch by shaking the hands and kissing the babies of their local constituency.[82] Since American politics is the public manifestation of sacred values, it is no coincidence that political upheaval in America is always accompanied by religious revivalism and by a passionate rediscovery of the moral, egalitarian, and individualistic community of the Founding Fathers.[83]

B. Central Paradoxes of American Politics

Readers may be amazed at this characterization of political life in America as sacred, since Americans are quite proud of their contempt for politicians and their hatred of the insiders in Washington. It is axiomatic that no one in American politics can campaign as a believer in central power; presidential candidates especially need to affirm their rebellious status as outsiders who aim to reform a system that is automatically assumed to be corrupt. This scorn has historical roots in American anti-authoritarianism derived from our history of revolution against the English crown.

But cynicism is the refuge of the disillusioned romantic, and the general American contempt for politics paradoxically indicates the high ideals Americans hold for political life, as well as the unfortunate fact that these ideals must inevitably be disappointed. The American dream of politics without special interests could be realized only in a Rousseauean small-scale, face-to-face community with little conflict, little mobility, and a subsistence economy of farms and local enterprises—in other words, in the conflict-free communal-familial world Americans wistfully imagine they once lived in. But because of the realities of the individualistic American culture, which presses for the decentralization of political power and undermines party control, politicians are necessarily forced to represent the interests of their local financial supporters. Politicians therefore do not act simply for themselves—as economic entrepreneurs are expected to do in the profane realm of the marketplace—but neither can they act wholly for the sacred community as ideal politicians ought to do. Instead, by representing hated special interests, they fall between the realms of sacred community and profane market, and are roundly excoriated as desecrators of the American ideal.

The characteristic American dislike of interests in politics also helps explain the fact that powerful businesspeople and insiders can exercise inordinate influence on the political process, while not exciting the outrage of the electorate.[84] The wealthy and powerful have close, personal connections to the politicians they bankroll; they can use their leverage in private conversations at the club and in quiet deals that are not noticed by the public at large.[85] In contrast, relatively impotent groups, such as blacks or feminists, must engage in confrontations at the statehouse to reach governmental officials. Because these weak groups make loud public demands for influence, they are seen by the general populace as threats to social unity and harmony, and their influence is usually lessened rather than increased, unless they can alert the electorate to a danger to the whole American social contract, as occurred in the civil rights movement and the protests against the Vietnam War.

Popular response to the contradictions of politics is also to be discovered in the extraordinary attitude of Americans toward their presidents, who portray themselves and are portrayed in the cultural imagination as expansive and encompassing figures appointed by the sacred community to lead God's own country. Their task is to reach beyond interest groups and despised party politics in order to achieve the good of the nation by representing all the people. The emotional expressiveness and assertion of personal character that are increasingly demanded of presidential figures are indicators of this symbolic function, since the revelation and sharing of emotion demonstrates the president's common humanity, which policies cannot do either directly or convincingly. Voters who can sympathize with a president's tragedies and family trials will feel a comforting communion with him—he is a good man who suffers just as I do; his nobility and compassion are like my own. Similar revelations of weakness and tragedy are not demanded of entrepreneurs; all that is needed to identify with them is a shared desire for wealth.

Psychologically speaking, on the other side of idealization and identification is an incessant desire to unmask and sully. Americans eagerly denigrate their politicians, especially their presidents, by revealing their sexual and moral faults. The increased scrutiny of public figures and the widely reported mass detestation of them reflect the deep tensions within the political realm as sacred ideals of selfless community service are increasingly seen to clash with realities of difference and interest, and as politicians are shown up as heroes with feet of clay. This cannot happen to entrepreneurs, who are expected to be knee-deep in the mud—albeit rich mud.

As noted above, a major reason for public mistrust of politicians is the politician's necessary reliance on political action groups representing special interests. Yet, inside political action groups themselves, the stated ideal remains that of the public at large: equivalence for all participants in the democratic process. Labor leaders, businesspeople, bankers, consumers, farmers, feminists, media people, blacks, students—all agree that every American should share equally in political power. But because of the general atmosphere of paranoia about groups other than one's own, coupled with the difficulty of discerning where power really lies in the decentralized and diffuse American political process and the widespread distrust of the institutions of government, all disagree about who *actually* does have influence, and each group sees itself as the victim in an unfair system that plays favorites.[86] Distrusting others, leery of the system, every group believes it should dominate, since it alone expresses the true will of the people. This circle of mistrust and self-delusion among influence groups validates public qualms about the corruption and degeneration in the political realm, fuels further paranoia, and leads to a retreat into the private world of family and friends, where one can ignore ambiguity and hope for unselfish love and caring. Of course, there are problems there too, as mentioned in the previous chapter.

Voter Apathy

Political activists in America are usually appalled at low voter turnout, forgetting that voter turnout hardly guarantees an enlightened society. High voter participation in Weimar Germany brought Hitler into power. Also, it should be recalled that the United States has more elections annually than any other nation except Switzerland (where turnout is equally low). Exceptionally concerned with maintaining popular control over government, we vote on judges and on amendments to law; we can even vote to change the Constitution. Such high demands on the electorate lead to voter fatigue.

Culturally speaking, there is another reason for voter indifference. As we have seen, politics is viewed with considerable ambivalence by most Americans, and they prefer to leave it to politicians, who are specialists in the dirty business of compromise. But we should also note that Americans do become politically active when their interests are directly at stake, as is evident in the rapid appearance and disappearance of single-issue pressure groups, both nationally and locally. Despite fears, America is in no danger of losing its civil society.

In conclusion, as Gregory Bateson long ago pointed out, deep-seated ambivalences, derived from contradictions within and between fundamental cultural values, are part of any living society and serve to give it its dynamism. This is clearly so in the United States, as values of egalitarian individualism inevitably clash with necessary distinctions of rank and corporate authority. What is distinctive is that Americans believe no such tension between "is" and "ought" should exist. This belief derives from the American cultural premise that society is knit together only through bonds of affection between autonomous individuals. Americans are therefore especially likely to feel that stability is precarious and to fear that any tension is likely to lead to destruction.

Yet in truth we are inevitably entangled in contradiction—and not only in the areas I have already outlined. The leading theorist of American studies, Seymour Martin Lipset has recently provided a list of problems implicit in the American worldview:

> The lack of respect for authority, anti-elitism, and populism contribute to higher crime rates, school indiscipline, and low electoral turnouts. The emphasis on achievement, on meritocracy, is also tied to higher levels of deviant behavior and less support for the underprivileged . . . Concern for the legal rights of accused persons and civil liberties in general is tied to opposition to gun control and difficulty in applying crime-control measures.[87]

Any number of other problematic implications of American values can be added to this list: Suburban youth's emulation of the styles of ghetto gangs expresses a characteristic American romance with rebellion and risk; excessive use of drugs and alcohol is a perpetual temptation for individualists who are socialized to seek salvation through personal sensation; the persistence of oddball therapies and excessive cults is a modern expression of the old American quest for frontiers to conquer; and so on.

The truth is that despite their faith in themselves as self-manufactured free agents, Americans are nonetheless part of a hierarchical and complex social world. All too often the freedom that is desired is a negative "freedom from," without any content, and coincides with loneliness and a sense of deprivation; choice is often not between moral alternatives, but between types of toothpaste; the material success Americans dream of is ever more difficult to realize and spiritually unsatisfactory even when it is achieved. But most important, from the perspective taken in this book, is that the American faith in autonomy ignores the collective, historical, and cultural aspects of existence, and places extraordinary psychological burdens on the individual.

If the approach I have outlined here has any concrete value, it is that it can help illuminate some of the social and psychological constraints that limit our lives and channel our energies. Paradoxically, knowledge of limits can have a liberating effect, since a greater awareness of the influences acting upon us alleviates the oppressive psychic weight of absolute self-responsibility demanded by our culture.

In conclusion, in seeking to give an objectively accurate portrait of the multiple ways we construct and are constructed by our lived-in reality, psychological anthropology aims to provide the critical knowledge that is a precondition for any significant social or spiritual transformation. As Franz Boas said, only by understanding our world and our places within it can we bring about meaningful changes in our communities—and in ourselves.

Summary

These few pages have sketched out some of the implications of the egalitarian, individualistic values that help construct notions of the person and community in the United States, including competitiveness, conformity, status anxiety, moral minimalism, social trust, a pervasive quest for love, and a tendency toward racism and paranoia. I have considered in some detail two spheres of action in America—the economic and the political—where the ideology of equality makes a difference in the social perception of and expression of distinction. In contrast to the quandaries of the hierarchical system of caste discussed in Chapter 8, the problem in the United States is how to validate the reality of difference when everyone, according to the cultural ideal, is supposed to be equal.

I have argued that in the marketplace, distinction is validated by the ideology of equality of opportunity and a notion that individual pursuit of economic success is a natural and moral act. The cultural assumption is that the successful deserve their rewards since they have won at a game everyone plays or wants to play, and have acted as every rational person would act if given the opportunity. Within this conceptual framework, rank in the economic sphere is not especially problematic; it is a result of what is perceived as pragmatic, natural, personal striving. It is easily measured and easily enjoyed and displayed by individuals. Those who fail in competition hope to succeed by trying again or else attempt to increase their chances by changing the level of the field, but few seem to doubt the basic premises. As yet, there is no great resentment against the achievements of the winners, nor is there any imputation of special qualities to the rich. They are imagined to be ordinary people whom other ordinary people want to emulate.

In contrast, the political world is conceived of as a sacred realm that is highly egalitarian in terms of result. This realm is imagined to be constructed by participatory power sharing among autonomous, co-equal individuals bound together in a community united solely by ties of shared love and mutual caring. Within this context, political leadership takes on a sanctified and familial quality that morally opposes the pragmatic role of the entrepreneur. Political rank is justified by conceptualizing politicians as self-sacrificing servants of the people who are supposed to be motivated by the higher ethical goals of the communities they serve.

Idealism coincides with highly negative attitudes toward the politicians, who are believed to be constantly betraying the public trust and selling out to special interests. Groups are also suspected as undermining the sacred unity of the community, and there is a strong tendency toward conspiracy theories of power. A widespread contempt for politicians is a consequence of disappointment in their inability to live up to the elevated moral position they are thought to hold—a moral position that stands in opposition to the real workings of political authority in a complex and hierarchical society that is nevertheless deeply imbued with the notion of human equality. This is a central contradiction of America politics.

Endnotes

1. I recognize, of course, that the United States is not all of America, but the usage is standard and the neologism "Unitedstatesian" is atrocious. Another adjectival possibility would be "gringo," but that has unfortunate connotations.

2. Michael Moffatt, 1989, *Coming of Age in New Jersey: College and American Culture,* New Brunswick, NJ: Rutgers University Press, p. 155. However, after two months, this student was less willing to make such comments.

3. For the classic (and still unsurpassed) ethnography of an American town that takes multiple perspectives, see W. Lloyd Warner, J. O. Low, Paul S. Lunt, and Leo Srole, 1963, *Yankee City,* New Haven, CT: Yale University Press.

4. See Chapter 8. For more, see Robert LeVine et al., 1994, *Child Care and Culture: Lessons from Africa,* Cambridge, England: Cambridge University Press.

5. Again, see Chapter 8.

6. Much of the following draws on the analysis presented in John A. Hall and Charles Lindholm, 1999, *Is America Breaking Apart?* Princeton, NJ: Princeton University Press.

7. For exceptions, see H. Varenne, 1986, "Introduction," and J. Caughey, "Epilogue: On the Anthropology of America," in H. Varenne (ed.), *Symbolizing America,* Lincoln: University of Nebraska Press; James Peacock, 1994, "American Cultural Values: Disorders and Challenges," and Roy Rappaport, 1994, "Disorders of Our Own," in S. Foreman (ed.), *Diagnosing America: Anthropology and Public Engagement,* Ann Arbor: University of Michigan Press.

8. For a clear discussion of American regionalism, see R. Gastril, 1992, "Cultural Regions of America," in Luther S. Luedtke (ed.), *Making America: The Society and Culture of the United States,* Chapel Hill: University of North Carolina Press.

9. For a discussion of the historical origin of American regionalism, see David H. Fischer, 1989, *Albion's Seed: Four British Folkways in North America,* Oxford, England: Oxford University Press.

10. Quoted in C. Degler, 1959, *Out of Our Past: The Forces That Shaped Modern America,* New York: Harpers, p. 129.

11. For more on ethnicity in the United States, see Chapter 8.

12. For these cases, see C. Velez-Ibanez, 1994, "Plural Strategies of Survival and Cultural Formation in US-Mexican Households in a Region of Dynamic Transformation: The US-Mexico Borderlands," in Shepard Forman (ed.), *Diagnosing America: Anthropology and Public Engagement,* Ann Arbor, University of Michigan Press; Sylvia Yanagisako, 1985, *Transforming the Past: Tradition and Kinship among Japanese Americans,* Stanford, CA: Stanford University Press.

13. Yanagisako, *Transforming the Past;* Karen Blu, 1980, *The Lumbee Problem: The Making of an American Indian People,* Cambridge, England: Cambridge University Press.

14. George and Louise Spindler, 1986, "Foreword," in H. Varenne (ed.) *Symbolizing America,* Lincoln: University of Nebraska Press, p. x.

15. Carlos Fernandez, 1992, "La Raza and the Melting Pot: A Comparative Look at Multiethnicity," in Maria Root (ed.), *Racially Mixed People in America,* Newbury Park, CA: Sage.

16. For this information, see Jennifer Hochschild, 1995, *Facing Up to the American Dream: Race, Class, and the Soul of the Nation,* Princeton, NJ: Princeton University Press, Chap. 5. For a more positive account of race relations, see S. Thernstrom and A. Thernstrom, 1997, *America in Black and White,* New York: Simon and Schuster.

17. D. Shipler, 1997, *A Country of Strangers: Blacks and Whites in America,* New York: Knopf. For what are still the best illustrations of American prejudice against blacks,

see W. Lloyd Warner, 1952, *The Structure of American Life*, Edinburgh, Scotland: University of Edinburgh Press.

18. John Ogbu, 1978, *Minority Education and Caste: The American System in Cross-Cultural Perspective*, New York: Academic Press.

19. See Chapter 9 on race as a natural kind, Chapter 8 on the biologizing of race.

20. The pernicious effect of the combination of race and a history of slavery was noted by Alexis de Tocqueville, 1969, *Democracy in America*, Garden City, NY: Doubleday, p. 341 (original publication 1835).

21. See Orlando Patterson, 1991, *Freedom*, New York: Basic Books.

22. Reasons for this are discussed by Hochschild, *Facing Up to the American Dream*; Hall and Lindholm, *Is America Breaking Apart?*

23. See William J. Wilson, 1996, *When Work Disappears: The World of the Urban Poor*, New York: Knopf. For an ethnographic account, see Philippe Bourgeois, 1995, *In Search of Respect: Selling Crack in El Barrio*, Cambridge, England: Cambridge University Press.

24. For this argument, see Richard E. Williams, 1990, *Hierarchical Structures and Social Value: The Creation of Black and Irish Identities in the United States*, Cambridge, England: Cambridge University Press. See Chapter 8 for more on American notions of race and miscegenation.

25. For data, see Hochschild, *Facing Up to the American Dream*. For interviews with black suburbanites, see Alan Wolfe, 1998, *One Nation, After All*, New York: Viking.

26. Robert Bellah et al., 1985, *Habits of the Heart: Individualism and Commitment in American Life*, New York: Harper and Row, p. 62.

27. For the best discussion of this subject, see Max Weber, 1985, " 'Churches' and 'Sects' in North America," *Sociological Theory* 3: 7–11. For an analysis of Weber's ideas, see Steven Kalberg, 1997, "Tocqueville and Weber on the Sociological Origins of Citizenship: The Political Culture of American Democracy," *Citizenship Studies* 1: 199–222.

28. Fischer, *Albion's Seed*, p. 754. This was the case throughout colonial America, except in Virginia, where aristocratic values, exaggerated by the institution of slavery, prevailed.

29. Quoted in Daniel Boorstin, 1995, "A Democracy of Clothing," in Ruth Boorstin (ed.), *The Daniel J. Boorstin Reader*, New York: Modern Library, p. 231.

30. For these, and more, examples, see David Potter, 1964, "Individuality and Conformity," in M. McGiffert (ed.), *The Character of Americans*, Chicago: Dorsey Press.

31. Geoffrey Gorer, 1948, *The American People: A Study in National Character*, New York: Norton, p. 40.

32. Daniel J. Boorstin, 1995, "Culture by the Book: The Spelling Fetish," in Ruth Boorstin (ed.), *The Daniel J. Boorstin Reader*, New York: Modern Library.

33. Adam Seligman, 1992, *The Idea of Civil Society*, New York: Free Press, p. 155.

34. Roy D'Andrade, 1995, *The Development of Cognitive Anthropology*, Cambridge, England: Cambridge University Press, p. 88.

35. Tocqueville, *Democracy in America*.

36. See Daniel Boorstin, 1995, "Consumer Palaces," in Ruth Boorstin (ed.), *The Daniel J. Boorstin Reader*, New York: Modern Library.

37. For an ethnography of the suburban mall, see Jerry Jacobs, 1984, *The Mall: An Attempted Escape from Everyday Life*, Prospect Heights, NJ: Waveland Press.

38. Tocqueville, *Democracy in America*, p. 643.

39. Ibid., p. 467. Many theorists since have commented on American conformity, especially Seymour M. Lipset (1963, *The First New Nation: The United States in Historical and Comparative Perspective*, New York: Basic Books) and David Riesman, with

Nathan Glazer and Reuel Denney (1961, *The Lonely Crowd,* 2d ed., New Haven, CT: Yale University Press). Riesman's famous other-directed man, who was supposed to have been a product of modernity, was already outlined in his most fundamental particulars by Tocqueville in 1835 and understood as a result of the American ethic of egalitarianism. See Chapter 5 for more on Riesman and other American national character studies.

40. G. K. Chesterton, 1923, *What I Saw in America,* New York: Dodd, Mead, pp. 11–12.

41. The most important discussion of America's civil religion is Robert Bellah, 1992, *The Broken Covenant: American Civil Religion in a Time of Trial,* 2nd ed., Chicago: University of Chicago Press. For more anthropological views, see Warner et al., *Yankee City;* Milton Singer, 1986, "The Melting Pot: Symbolic Ritual or Total Social Fact?" in Hervé Varenne (ed.), *Symbolizing America,* Lincoln: University of Nebraska Press. S. Bercovitch, 1992, *Rites of Assent: Transformations in the Symbolic Construction of America,* London: Routledge, offers a literary perspective.

42. Wolfe, *One Nation, After All,* p. 87.

43. Ibid., p. 85.

44. Ibid., p. 278.

45. For the best discussion of this subject, see M. P. Baumgartner, 1988, *The Moral Order of a Suburb,* Oxford, England: Oxford University Press. Following Riesman's analysis in *The Lonely Crowd,* Baumgartner believes the American ethic of avoidance is a result of social fragmentation associated with modernity. But she also notes that moral minimalism is, in fact, a dominant form of conflict resolution in many small-scale societies.

46. For an analysis of disputes in suburban America, see Constance Perin, 1988, *Belonging in America: Reading between the Lines,* Madison: University of Wisconsin Press.

47. G. Genier et al., 1992, "On Machines and Bureaucracy: Controlling Ethnic Interaction in Miami's Apparel and Construction Industries," in Louise Lamphere (ed.), *Structuring Diversity: Ethnographic Perspectives on the New Immigration,* Chicago: University of Chicago Press, p. 86.

48. Adrie Kusserow, 1999, "De-Homogenizing American Individualism: Socializing 'Hard' and 'Soft' Individualism in Manhattan and Queens," *Ethos* 27: 210–34.

49. See Paul Willis, 1977, *Learning to Labor: How Working Class Kids Get Working Class Jobs,* Farnborough, England: Saxon House.

50. Daniel Boorstin, 1995, "Palaces of the Public," in Ruth Boorstin (ed.), *The Daniel J. Boorstin Reader,* New York: Modern Library, p. 131.

51. For the American requirement to be friendly, see Hervé Varenne, 1986, "Creating America," in Hervé Varenne (ed.), *Symbolizing America,* Lincoln: University of Nebraska Press; Steven Kalberg, n.d., "The Sociology of Friendliness," unpublished manuscript; Nancy Rosenblum, 1998, *Membership and Morals: The Personal Uses of Pluralism in America,* Princeton, NJ: Princeton University Press. See also Chapter 8.

52. See David Schneider, 1968, *American Kinship: A Cultural Account,* Chicago: University of Chicago Press. Of course, there are class, ethnic, and racial variations: For example, poor black families often have extended family structures in which kinship— both real and fictive—is used to knit together a loose alliance of mutual aid (on this, see Carol Stack's 1975 classic, *All Our Kin: Strategies for Survival in a Black Community,* New York: Harper and Row).

53. Baumgartner, *The Moral Order of a Suburb,* p. 66.

54. For some characteristic statements about the American family, see Christopher Lasch, 1977, *Haven in a Heartless World,* New York: Basic Books; and (in a very different mood) Erik Erikson, 1950, *Childhood and Society,* New York: Norton. On love as the central metaphor of American culture, see Hervé Varenne, 1977, *Americans Together: Structured Diversity in an American Town,* New York: Teachers College Press.

55. Gorer, *The American People,* p. 133.

56. Varenne, *Americans Together,* p. 70 (emphasis in original). Compare Bernard Bailyn, 1967, *The Ideological Origins of the American Revolution,* Cambridge, MA: Harvard University Press; and J. R. Pole, 1978, *The Pursuit of Equality in American History,* Berkeley: University of California Press.

57. For a superb anthropological account of the ambiguities of neighborliness in America, see Perin, *Belonging in America.*

58. Varenne, *Americans Together,* pp. 205, 92.

59. For the general argument, see Louis Dumont, 1980, *Homo Hierarchicus: An Essay on the Caste System,* Chicago: University of Chicago Press. See Chapters 8 and 9 for more on the naturalizing of race.

60. In asking this question, we also essay an implicit comparison with the more hierarchical societies of the world, especially India, where the problem is exactly the opposite: the assertion of human equality. See Chapter 8 for more on this subject.

61. A point made most clearly by Edward Pessen, 1992, "Status and Class in America," in Luther S. Luedtke (ed.), *Making America: The Society and Culture of the United States,* Chapel Hill: University of North Carolina Press.

62. For a more complete analysis and a bibliography, see Hall and Lindholm, *Is America Breaking Apart?*

63. Quoted in Jennifer Hochschild, 1981, *What's Fair? American Beliefs about Distributive Justice,* Cambridge, MA: Harvard University Press, p. 9.

64. There were radical and violent exceptions, such as the International Workers of the World, but they were offset by the accommodative ethos of the Knights of Labor and later by Samuel Gompers's business unionism.

65. For an anthropologically informed history of antiwar movements in the United States, see Sol Tax, 1968, "War and the Draft," in Morton Fried, Marvin Harris, and Robert Murphy (eds.), *War,* Garden City, NY: Doubleday.

66. Quoted in Sidney Verba and Gary Orren, 1985, *Equality in America: The View from the Top,* Cambridge, MA: Harvard University Press, pp. 8–9.

67. In 1670 an estimated one-third of all wealth was held by 5 percent of the population; a century later, 3 percent owned one-quarter of the wealth; when Tocqueville visited America, 1 percent of the population owned more than a third of all wealth. For these figures, see Pessen, "Status and Class in America."

68. For a synopsis of theoretical arguments in favor of demands for redistribution, as well as a review of some of the reasons such seemingly sensible demands have not been part of the American political discourse, see Katherine S. Newman, 1988, *Falling from Grace: The Experience of Downward Mobility in the American Middle Class,* New York: Free Press; John Laslett and Seymour M. Lipset, 1974, *Failure of a Dream?* New York: Doubleday Anchor; Hochschild, *What's Fair?* Of course, in the present positive economic climate, the poor have gained advantages that help validate their faith in the system.

69. David Potter, 1964, "Individuality and Conformity," in Michael McGiffert (ed.), *The Character of Americans,* Chicago: Dorsey Press.

70. Newman, *Falling from Grace,* p. 77.

71. Verba and Orren, *Equality in America.*

72. Newman, *Falling from Grace,* p. 75. She also argues that membership in a shared community can offset this pattern of self-doubt and blame.

73. Cited in Hochschild, *Facing Up to the American Dream.*

74. The psychological anthropology of elites in America is an understudied subject, largely because of their inaccessability, since they naturally wish to maintain their secrecy and privacy in an egalitarian universe. See George Marcus (ed.), 1983,

Elites: Ethnographic Issues, Albuquerque: University of New Mexico Press; for a discussion of the social and cultural mechanisms by which American elites retain power, see Michael Lind, 1995, *The Next American Nation: The New Nationalism and the Fourth American Revolution*, New York: Free Press; for a sociological study of the elites, see G. William Domhoff, 1975, *The Bohemian Grove and Other Retreats: A Study in Ruling Class Cohesiveness*, New York: Harper and Row. Marcus has also written a provocative study of the depersonalizing effects of wealth on the psyche. See Marcus, 1995, "On Eccentricity," in Deborah Battaglia (ed.), *Rhetorics of Self-Making*, Berkeley: University of California.

75. There are structural reasons for this, since wealth and power in the United States are not centralized but are distributed regionally. Because there is no national elite, it is more difficult to recognize the extent and stability of class differentiation.

76. There is, of course, some ambiguity about the inequalities that result from this laissez-faire attitude. Hochschild found that many of her respondents, when questioned, say "other people would not permit equality to work, even though they themselves might welcome it" (Hochschild, *What's Fair?* p. 171).

77. Bellah, *The Broken Covenant*; Singer, "The Melting Pot."

78. Elwin Hatch, 1979, *The Biography of a Small Town*, New York: Columbia University Press. In a classic work, Page Smith (1966, *As a City upon a Hill: The Town in American History*, New York: Knopf) argues this is an attempt by cumulative frontier communities typical of Middle and Western America to recapture the unity of the covenanted communities of the Puritan Northeast. But one need not invoke nostalgia; the tensions implicit in contradictory values of equality and community press toward symbolic expressions of unity as a means of denying actual processes of fission and fragmentation.

79. The argument in the next few pages follows Bellah and his colleagues' *Habits of the Heart*.

80. Ibid.

81. Hatch, *The Biography of a Small Town*, p. 235.

82. This concept of political equality, in which all citizens are united in a moral community and leaders are merely representatives of the whole, finds its first and greatest theorist in Jean Jacques Rousseau, 1967, *The Social Contract and Discourse on the Origins of Inequality*, New York: Washington Square Press (original publication 1762 and 1755). See Chapter 3 for more.

83. Samuel Huntington, 1981, *American Politics: The Promise of Disharmony*, Cambridge, MA: Harvard University Press; Seymour Lipset, 1968, *Revolution and Counterrevolution*, New York: Basic Books; William G. McLaughlin, 1978, *Revivals, Awakenings, and Reforms*, Chicago: University of Chicago Press.

84. This analysis follows Samuel Huntington's persuasive dissection of the antipower ethic in his 1981 classic *American Politics: The Promise of Disharmony*. Huntington has been rightly castigated by anthropologists for his unnecessarily conflictual view of the relationship between "the West and the rest," but the anthropological failings of some of his work do not vitiate the remainder.

85. As mentioned earlier, vague public awareness of the hidden and personalized structure of power lies behind the conspiracy theories pervading popular culture.

86. Verba and Orren, *Equality in America*, p. 189.

87. S. M. Lipset, 1996, *American Exceptionalism: A Double-Edged Sword*, New York: Norton, p. 290.

Bibliography

ABRAHAMS, ROGER, and RICHARD BAUMAN. 1978. "Ranges of Festival Behavior." In Barbara Babcock (ed.). *The Reversible World: Symbolic Inversion in Art and Society.* Ithaca, NY: Cornell University Press.

ABU-LUGHOD, LILA. 1990. "Shifting Politics in Bedouin Love Poetry." In Catherine Lutz and Lila Abu-Lughod (eds.). *Language and the Politics of Emotion.* Cambridge, England: Cambridge University Press.

———. 1993. *Writing Women's Worlds: Bedouin Stories.* Berkeley: University of California Press.

ABU-LUGHOD, LILA, and CATHERINE LUTZ. 1990."Introduction: Emotion, Discourse and the Politics of Everyday Life." In Catherine Lutz and Lila Abu-Lughod (eds.). *Language and the Politics of Emotion.* Cambridge, England: Cambridge University Press.

ADORNO, THEODOR, ELSE FRENKEL-BRUNSWIK, DANIEL J. LEVINSON, and R. NEVITT SANFORD. 1950. *The Authoritarian Personality.* New York: Harper.

ALBERONI, FRANCESCO. 1983. *Falling in Love.* New York: Random House.

AMERICAN PSYCHIATRIC ASSOCIATION COMMITTEE ON NOMENCLATURE AND STATISTICS. 1994. *Diagnostic and Statistical Manual of Mental Disorders* (4th ed.). Washington, DC: American Psychiatric Association.

ANDERSON, BENEDICT. 1991. *Imagined Communities: Reflections on the Origin and Spread of Nationalism* (rev. ed.). London: Verso.

ANDREASEN, NANCY. 1984. *The Broken Brain: The Biological Revolution in Psychiatry.* New York: Harper and Row.

AOKI, MASAHIKO. 1988. *Information, Incentives and Bargaining in the Japanese Economy.* Cambridge, England: Cambridge University Press.

ARISTOTLE. 1962. *Nicomanchean Ethics,* Tenth book. Indianapolis, IN: Bobbs-Merrill.

———. 1991. *Rhetoric,* Second book. New York: Oxford University Press.

ATRAN, SCOTT. 1990. *Cognitive Foundations of Natural History: Towards an Anthropology of Science.* Cambridge, England: Cambridge University Press.

AUGÉ, MARC. 1960. "Ten Questions Put to Claude Lévi-Strauss." *Current Anthropology* 31: 85–90.

AUGUSTINUS, ST. AURELIUS. 1961. *Confessions.* Baltimore: Penguin Books. (Written 397–401.)

AVERILL, JAMES. 1980. "Emotion and Anxiety: Sociocultural, Biological and Psychological Determinants." In A. Rorty (ed.). *Explaining Emotions.* Berkeley: University of California Press.

———. 1985. "The Social Construction of Emotion: With Special Reference to Love." In Kenneth Gergen and Keith Davis (eds.). *The Social Construction of the Person.* New York: Springer-Verlag.

AVRUCH, KEVIN. 1990. "Melford Spiro and the Scientific Study of Culture." In David K. Jordan and Marc J. Swartz (eds.). *Personality and the Cultural Construction of Society: Papers in Honor of Melford E. Spiro.* Tuscaloosa: University of Alabama Press.

BAILEY, FREDERICK. 1957. *Caste and the Economic Frontier: A Village in Highland Orissa.* Manchester, England: Manchester University Press.

BAILYN, BERNARD. 1967. *The Ideological Origins of the American Revolution.* Cambridge, MA: Harvard University Press.

BAKHTIN, MIKHAIL. 1981. *The Dialogic Imagination.* Austin: University of Texas Press. (Original publication 1975.)

BARKER, PAT. 1991. *Regeneration.* Harmondsworth, England: Penguin Books.

BARNOUW, VICTOR. 1985. *Culture and Personality* (4th ed.). Chicago: Dorsey Press.

BARTH, FREDRIK. 1975. *Ritual and Knowledge among the Baktman of New Guinea.* New Haven, CT: Yale University Press.

———. 1987. *Cosmologies in the Making: A Generative Approach to Culture Variation in Inner New Guinea.* Cambridge England: Cambridge University Press.

———. 1997. "How Is the Self Conceptualized? Variations between Cultures." In Ulric Niesser (ed.). *The Conceptual Self in Context: Culture, Experience, Self-Understanding.* Cambridge, England: Cambridge University Press.

BARTLETT, FREDERIC. 1932. *Remembering: A Study in Experimental and Social Psychology.* Cambridge, England: Cambridge University Press.

BATAILLE, GEORGES. 1962. *Eroticism.* London: Calder.

BATESON, GREGORY. 1936. *Naven: A Survey of the Problems Suggested by a Composite Picture of the Culture of a New Guinea Tribe Drawn from Three Points of View.* Cambridge, England: Cambridge University Press.

———. 1972. *Steps to an Ecology of Mind.* San Francisco: Chandler.

BATTAGLIA, DEBORAH (ed.). 1995. *Rhetorics of Self-Making.* Berkeley: University of California Press.

BAUMGARTNER, M. P. 1988. *The Moral Order of a Suburb.* Oxford, England: Oxford University Press.

BEIGEL, H. 1951. "Romantic Love." *American Sociological Review* 16: 326–34.

BELL, JOSEPH. 1979. *Love Theory in Later Hanbalite Islam.* Albany: State University of New York Press.

BELLAH, ROBERT. 1992. *The Broken Covenant: American Civil Religion in a Time of Trial* (2d ed.). Chicago: University of Chicago Press.

BELLAH, ROBERT, RICHARD MADSEN, WILLIAM SULLIVAN, ANN SWIDLER, and STEVEN TIPTON. 1985. *Habits of the Heart: Individualism and Commitment in American Life.* New York: Harper and Row.

BENEDICT, RUTH. 1934. "Anthropology and the Abnormal." *Journal of General Psychology* 10: 59–80.

———. 1946. *The Chrysanthemum and the Sword: Patterns of Japanese Culture.* Boston: Houghton Mifflin.

———. 1989. *Patterns of Culture.* Boston: Houghton Mifflin. (Original publication 1934.)

BERCOVITCH, S. 1992. *Rites of Assent: Transformations in the Symbolic Construction of America.* London: Routledge.

BERLIN, BRENT. 1978. "Ethnobiological Classification." In E. Rosch and B. Lloyd (eds.). *Cognition and Categorization.* New York: Erlbaum.

BERLIN, BRENT, D. BREEDLOVE, and P. RAVEN. 1973. "General Principles of Classification and Nomenclature in Folk Biology." *American Anthropologist* 75: 214–42.

BERLIN, BRENT, and PAUL KAY. 1969. *Basic Color Terms: Their Universality and Evolution.* Berkeley: University of California Press.

BERNDT, R. 1976. *Love Songs of Arnhem Land.* Chicago: University of Chicago Press.

BERTILSSON, MARGARETA. 1986. "Love's Labour Lost? A Sociological View." *Theory, Culture and Society* 3: 19–35.

BESNIER, NIKO. 1994. "Polynesian Gender Liminality through Time and Space." In Gilbert Herdt (ed.). *Third Sex, Third Gender: Beyond Sexual Dimorphism in Culture and History.* New York: Zone Books.

BESTER, JOHN. 1981. "Foreword." In Takeo Doi. *The Anatomy of Dependence.* Tokyo: Kadansha International.

BETTELHEIM, BRUNO. 1954. *Symbolic Wounds: Puberty Rites and the Envious Male.* Glencoe, IL: Free Press.

———. 1983. *Freud and Man's Soul.* New York: Knopf.

BHABHA, HOMI. 1994. *The Location of Culture.* London: Routledge.

BLAKE, WILLIAM MILTON. "Preface." In Michael Mason (ed.). *William Blake: Poems, Selections.* Oxford, England: Oxford University Press.

BLAKEY, MICHAEL. 1994. "Psychophysiological Stress and the Disorders of Industrial Society: A Critical Theoretical Formulation for Biocultural Research." In Shepard Forman (ed.). *Diagnosing America: Anthropology and Public Engagement.* Ann Arbor: University of Michigan Press.

BLOCH, MAURICE. 1998. *How We Think They Think: Anthropological Approaches to Cognition, Memory and Literacy.* Boulder, CO: Westview Press.

BLOCK, JACK. 1981. "Some Enduring and Consequential Structures of Personality." In A. Rabin (ed.). *Further Explorations in Personality.* New York: Wiley.

BLU, KAREN. 1980. *The Lumbee Problem: The Making of an American Indian People.* Cambridge, England: Cambridge University Press.

BOAS, FRANZ. 1910. "Psychological Problems in Anthropology." *American Journal of Psychology* 21: 371–84.

———. 1938. "An Anthropologist's Credo." *The Nation,* August 27: 201–2.

BOASE, ROGER. 1977. *The Origin and Meaning of Courtly Love.* Manchester, England: Manchester University Press.

BOCK, PHILIP. 1988. *Rethinking Psychological Anthropology.* New York: Freeman.

BODDY, JANICE. 1989. *Wombs and Alien Spirits: Women, Men and the Zar Cult in Northern Sudan.* Madison: University of Wisconsin Press.

BOORSTIN, DANIEL. 1995. "A Democracy of Clothing"; "Culture by the Book: The Spelling Fetish"; "Consumer Palaces"; "Palaces of the Public." In Ruth Boorstin (ed.). *The Daniel J. Boorstin Reader.* New York: Modern Library.

BORGORAS, WALDEMAR. 1904. *The Chukchee: Memoirs of the Jesup North Pacific Expedition,* Vol. II. New York: American Museum of Natural History.

BOURDIEU, PIERRE. 1977. *Outline of a Theory of Practice.* Cambridge, England: Cambridge University Press.

BOURGEOIS, PHILIPPE. 1995. *In Search of Respect: Selling Crack in El Barrio.* Cambridge, England: Cambridge University Press.

BOURGUIGNON, ERIKA. 1968. "World Distribution and Patterns of Possession States." In Raymond Prince (ed.). *Trance and Possession States.* Montreal: Burke Memorial Society.

———. 1972. "Dreams and Altered States of Consciousness in Anthropological Research." In F. Hsu (ed.). *Psychological Anthropology.* Chicago: Dorsey Press.

——. 1979. *Psychological Anthropology: An Introduction to Human Nature and Cultural Difference.* New York: Holt.

BOYER, L. BRYCE, BRUNO KLOPFER, FLORENCE BRAWER, and HAYAO KAWAI. 1964. "Comparison of Shamans and Pseudoshamans of the Apaches of the Mescalero Indian Reservation: A Rorschach Study." *Journal of Projective Techniques* 28: 173–80.

BOYER, PASCAL. 1993. "Pseudo Natural Kinds." In P. Boyer (ed.). *Cognitive Aspects of Religious Symbolism.* Cambridge, England: Cambridge University Press.

BRIGGS, JEAN. 1970. *Never in Anger: Portrait of an Eskimo Family.* Cambridge, MA: Harvard University Press.

——. 1978. "The Origins of Nonviolence: Inuit Management of Aggression." In Ashley Montague (ed.). *Learning Non-Aggression: The Experience of Non-Literate Societies.* New York: Oxford University Press.

——. 1987. "In Search of Emotional Meaning." *Ethos* 15: 8–15.

BROWN, G., and T. HARRIS. 1978. *Social Origins of Depression: A Study of Psychiatric Disorder in Women.* New York: Free Press.

BUCKSER, ANDREW. 1986. *Love in a Cold Climate: Romantic Love and Social Structure among the Canadian Ojibwa.* Undergraduate honors thesis. Department of Anthropology, Harvard University, Cambridge, MA.

BURKHARDT, JACOB. 1960. *Civilization of the Renaissance in Italy.* New York: Mentor Books.

CAMPBELL, JOSEPH. 1949. *The Hero with a Thousand Faces.* New York: Pantheon.

CANAAN, JOYCE. 1986. "Why a 'Slut' Is a 'Slut': Cautionary Tales of Middle-Class Teenage Girls' Morality." In Hervé Verenne (ed.). *Symbolizing America.* Lincoln: University of Nebraska Press.

CANNON, W. 1927. "The James–Lange Theory of Emotion: A Critical Examination and an Alternative Theory." *American Journal of Psychology* 39: 106–24.

CAREY, JAMES. 1969. "Changing Courtship Patterns in the Popular Song." *American Journal of Sociology* 74: 720–31.

CARRITHERS, MICHAEL. 1997. "Culture." In Thomas Barfield (ed.). *The Dictionary of Anthropology.* Oxford, England: Basil Blackwell.

CARVER, RAYMOND. 1981. *What We Talk About When We Talk About Love.* New York: Knopf.

CASEY, JOAN F. 1991. *The Flock.* New York: Knopf.

CASSON, RONALD. 1994. "Cognitive Anthropology." In Philip Bock (ed.). *Psychological Anthropology.* Westport, CT: Praeger.

CASTILLO, RICHARD. 1991. "Divided Consciousness and Enlightenment in Hindu Yogis." *Anthropology of Consciousness* 2: 1–6.

——. 1994. "Spirit Possession in South Asia: Dissociation or Hysteria." *Culture, Medicine and Psychiatry* 18: 1–21, 141–62.

——. 1995. "Culture, Trance and the Mind-Brain." *Anthropology of Consciousness* 6: 17–32.

CAUGHEY, JAMES. 1986. "Epilogue: On the Anthropology of America." In Hervé Varenne (ed.). *Symbolizing America.* Lincoln: University of Nebraska Press.

CELLINI, BENVENUTO. 1927. *Autobiography.* Garden City, NY: Garden City Publishing. (Original publication 1728.)

CHAGNON, NAPOLEON. 1977. *Yanomamo: The Fierce People.* New York: Holt, Rinehart and Winston.

CHAO, RUTH. 1995. "Chinese and European American Cultural Models of the Self Reflected in Mothers' Childrearing Beliefs." *Ethos* 23: 328–54.

CHESTERTON, G. K. 1923. *What I Saw in America.* New York: Dodd, Mead.

CHODOROW, NANCY. 1999. *The Power of Feelings: Personal Meaning in Psychoanalysis.* New Haven, CT: Yale University Press.

CHOMSKY, NOAM. 1957. *Syntactic Structures.* The Hague, Netherlands: Mouton.

———. 1988. *Language and Problems of Knowledge: The Managua Lectures.* Cambridge, MA: MIT Press.

CHRISTIE, RICHARD, and MARIE JAHODA (eds.). 1954. *Studies in the Scope and Method of "The Authoritarian Personality."* Glencoe, IL: Free Press.

CLARK, ANDY. 1989. *Microcognition.* Cambridge, MA: MIT Press.

COHEN, YEHUDI (ed.). 1961. *Social Structure and Personality.* New York: Holt, Rhinehart and Winston.

———. 1969. "Ends and Means in Political Control: State Organization and the Punishment of Adultery, Incest, and Violation of Celibacy." *American Anthropologist* 71: 658–87.

COHLER, BERTRAM. 1992. "Intent and Meaning in Psychoanalysis and Cultural Study." In Theodore Schwartz, Geoffrey White, and Catherine Lutz (eds.). *New Directions in Psychological Anthropology.* Cambridge, England: Cambridge University Press.

COHN, NORMAN. 1975. *Europe's Inner Demons.* New York: Basic Books.

COLE, M., J. GAY, J. GLICK, and D. W. SHARP. 1971. *The Cultural Context of Learning and Thinking.* New York: Basic Books.

COLE, M., and S. SCRIBNER. 1974. *Culture and Thought.* New York: Wiley.

COLE, MICHAEL. 1996. *Cultural Psychology: A Once and Future Discipline.* Cambridge, MA: Harvard University Press.

CONKLIN, BETH A., and LYNN M. MORGAN. 1996. "Babies, Bodies, and the Production of Personhood in North America and a Native Amazonian Society." *Ethos* 24: 657–94.

CONKLIN, HAROLD. 1954. "Hanunoo Color Categories." *Southwestern Journal of Anthropology* 11: 339–44.

———. 1954. "The Relation of Hanunoo Culture to the Plant World." Ph.D. dissertation. Department of Anthropology, Yale University, New Haven, CT.

———. 1972. *Folk Classification: A Bibliography.* New Haven, CT: Yale University, Department of Anthropology.

CONNOR, LINDA. 1982. "The Unbounded Self: Balinese Therapy in Theory and Practice." In A. Marsella and G. White (eds.). *Cultural Conceptions of Mental Health and Therapy.* Dordrecht, Netherlands: D. Reidel.

COPPINGER, R., and P. ROSENBLATT. 1968. "Romantic Love and Subsistence Dependence of Spouses." *Southwestern Journal of Anthropology* 24: 310–18.

CRAMER, DUNCAN, and DENNIS HOWITT. 1998. "Romantic Love and the Psychology of Sexual Behavior: Open and Closed Secrets." In Victor de Munck (ed.). *Romantic Love and Sexual Behavior: Perspectives from the Social Sciences.* Westport, CT: Praeger.

CRAPANZANO, VINCENT. 1973. *The Hamadsha: A Study in Moroccan Ethnopsychiatry.* Berkeley: University of California Press.

———. 1980. *Tuhami: Portrait of a Moroccan.* Chicago: University of Chicago Press.

———. 1990. "On Self-Characterization." In James Stigler, Richard Shweder, and Gilbert Herdt (eds.). *Cultural Psychology: Essays on Comparative Human Development.* Cambridge, England: Cambridge University Press.

———. 1992. "Some Thoughts on Hermeneutics and Psychoanalytic Anthropology." In Theodore Schwartz, Geoffrey White, and Catherine Lutz (eds.). *New Directions in Psychological Anthropology.* Cambridge, England: Cambridge University Press.

———. 1994. "Rethinking Psychological Anthropology: A Critical View." In Marcelo Suarez-Orozco, George Spindler, and Louise Spindler (eds.). *The Making of Psychological Anthropology II.* Fort Worth, TX: Harcourt Brace.

CSORDAS, THOMAS. 1994. *The Sacred Self: A Cultural Phenomenology of Charismatic Healing.* Berkeley: University of California Press.

D'ANDRADE, ROY. 1987. "A Folk Model of the Mind." In Dorothy Holland and Naomi Quinn (eds.). *Cultural Models in Language and Thought.* Cambridge, England: Cambridge University Press.

———. 1989. "Culturally Based Reasoning." In A. Gellatly, D. Rogers, and J. Sloboda (eds.). *Cognition and Social Worlds.* Cambridge, England: Cambridge University Press.

———. 1992. "Schemas and Motivation." In Roy D'Andrade and Claudia Strauss (eds.). *Human Motives and Cultural Models.* Cambridge, England: Cambridge University Press.

———. 1995. *The Development of Cognitive Anthropology.* Cambridge, England: Cambridge University Press.

D'ANDRADE, ROY, and MICHAEL EGAN. 1974. "The Colors of Emotion." *American Ethnologist* 1:49–63.

DANIEL, E. VALENTINE. 1984. *Fluid Signs: Being a Person the Tamil Way.* Berkeley: University of California Press.

DARNELL, REGNA. 1986. "The Fate of the Sapirian Alternative." In George Stocking (ed.). *Malinowski, Rivers, Benedict and Others: Essays on Culture and Personality.* Madison: University of Wisconsin Press.

DARWIN, CHARLES. 1965. *The Expression of Emotions in Man and Animals.* Chicago: University of Chicago Press. (Original publication 1872.)

DAVIS, ALLISON, and JOHN DOLLARD. 1964. *Children of Bondage.* New York: Harper and Row. (Original publication 1940.)

DE GÉRANDO, JOSEPH-MARIE. 1969. *The Observation of Savage Peoples.* Berkeley: University of California Press. (Original publication 1800.)

DEGLER, C. 1959. *Out of Our Past: The Forces That Shaped Modern America.* New York: Harper.

DEMOS, VIRGINIA. 1988. "Affect and the Development of the Self." In Arnold Goldberg (ed.). *Frontiers in Self Psychology,* Vol. 3. Hillsdale, NJ: Analytic Press.

DE MUNCK, VICTOR (ed.). 1998. *Romantic Love and Sexual Behavior: Perspectives from the Social Sciences.* Westport, CT: Praeger.

DESCARTES, RENÉ. 1897–1910. "La Dioptrique" (original publication 1637); "Les Passions de l'Ame" (original publication 1649). In Charles Adam and Paul Tannery (eds.) *Oeuvres de Descartes.* Paris: Leopold Cerf Publishers.

———. 1972. *Discourse on Method and Meditations on First Philosophy.* Harmondsworth, England: Penguin. (Original publication of *Meditations on First Philosophy* 1641.)

DEVEREUX, GEORGES. 1961. "Shamans as Neurotics." *American Anthropologist* 63: 1088–90.

———. 1969. *Reality and Dream: Psychotherapy of a Plains Indian.* New York: New York University Press.

———. 1980. *Basic Problems in Ethnopsychiatry.* Chicago: University of Chicago Press.

DEVOS, GEORGE. 1973. *Socialization for Achievement: Essays on the Cultural Psychology of the Japanese.* Berkeley: University of California Press.

DEWEY, JOHN. 1894. "A Theory of Emotion." *Psychological Review* 1: 553–69.

DIRKS, NICHOLAS. 1987. *The Hollow Crown: Ethnohistory of an Indian Kingdom.* Cambridge, England: Cambridge University Press.

DOI, TAKEO. 1981. *The Anatomy of Dependence.* Tokyo: Kodansha International.

DOMHOFF, G. WILLIAM. 1975. *The Bohemian Grove and Other Retreats: A Study in Ruling Class Cohesiveness.* New York: Harper and Row.

DOUGHERTY, J. W. 1978. "Salience and Relativity in Classification." *American Ethnologist* 5: 66–80.

DOUGLAS, MARY. 1966. *Purity and Danger: An Analysis of Concepts of Pollution and Taboo.* London: Routledge.

DRISCOLL, D., K. DAVIS, and M. LIPETZ. 1972. "Parental Interference and Romantic Love: The Romeo and Juliet Effect." *Journal of Personality and Social Psychology* 24: 1–10.

DU BOIS, CORA. 1960. *The People of Alor.* Vol. I. New York: Harper and Row. (Original publication 1944.)

DUMONT, LOUIS. 1980. *Homo Hierarchicus: An Essay on the Caste System.* Chicago: University of Chicago Press.

DUNHAM, H. W. 1976. "Society, Culture and Mental Disorder." *Archives of General Psychiatry* 33: 147–56.

DURKHEIM, ÉMILE. 1965. *The Elementary Forms of the Religious Life.* New York: Free Press. (Original publication 1912.)

———. 1966. *Suicide: A Study in Sociology.* New York: Free Press. (Original publication 1897).

———. 1984. *The Division of Labor in Society.* New York: Free Press. (Original publication 1893).

DURKHEIM, ÉMILE, and MARCEL MAUSS. 1963. *Primitive Classification.* Chicago: University of Chicago Press. (Original publication 1904.)

EAGLETON, TERRY. 1996. *The Illusions of Postmodernism.* Oxford, England: Basil Blackwell.

EDGERTON, ROBERT. 1976. *Deviance: A Cross-Cultural Perspective.* Menlo Park, NJ: Cummings.

EKMAN, PAUL, WALLACE FRIESEN, and PHEOBE ELLSWORTH. 1982. "What Emotion Categories or Dimensions Can Observers Judge from Facial Behavior?" "What Are the Similarities and Differences in Facial Behavior across Cultures?" In P. Ekman (ed.). *Emotion in the Human Face.* Cambridge, England: Cambridge University Press.

EKMAN, PAUL, R. LEVINSON, and W. FRIESEN. 1983. "Autonomic Nervous System Activity Distinguishes between Emotions." *Science* 221: 1208–10.

ELIADE, MIRCEA. 1964. *Shamanism: Archaic Techniques of Ecstasy.* Princeton, NJ: Princeton University Press.

ELIAS, NORBERT. 1978. *The Civilizing Process: The Development of Manners.* New York: Urizen. (Original publication 1939.)

———. 1982. *Power and Civility.* New York: Urizen.

———. 1983. *Court Society.* New York: Pantheon Books.

———. 1987. "The Changing Balance of Power between the Sexes—A Process-Sociological Study: The Example of the Ancient Roman State." *Theory, Culture and Society* 4: 287–316.

ENDELMAN, ROBERT. 1989. *Love and Sex in Twelve Cultures.* New York: Psyche Press.

ENGELS, FRIEDRICH. 1902. *The Origin of the Family, Private Property, and the State.* Chicago: Kerr. (Original publication 1884.)

ERCHAK, GERALD. 1992. *The Anthropology of Self and Behavior.* New Brunswick, NJ: Rutgers University Press.

ERIKSON, ERIK. 1950. *Childhood and Society.* New York: Norton.

———. 1958. *Young Man Luther: A Study in Psychoanalysis and History.* New York: Norton.

———. 1969. *Gandhi's Truth on the Origins of Militant Nonviolence.* New York: Norton.

EVANS-PRITCHARD, E. E. 1940. *The Nuer.* Oxford, England: Clarendon Press.

EWING, KATHERINE. 1990. "The Illusion of Wholeness: Culture, Self and the Experience of Inconsistency." *Ethos* 18: 251–73.

———. 1992. "Is Psychoanalysis Relevant for Anthropology?" In Theodore Schwartz, Geoffrey White, and Catherine Lutz (eds.). *New Directions in Psychological Anthropology.* Cambridge, England: Cambridge University Press.

———. 1997. *Arguing Sainthood: Modernity, Psychoanalysis and Islam.* Durham, NC: Duke University Press.

FABREGA, HORACIO, JR. 1987. "Psychiatric Diagnosis: A Cultural Perspective." *Journal of Nervous and Mental Disease* 175: 383–94.

———. 1988. "An Ethnomedical Perspective on Anglo-American Psychiatry." *Journal of Psychiatry* 146: 588–96.

———. 1990. "The Concept of Somatization as a Cultural and Historical Product of Western Medicine." *Psychosomatic Medicine* 52: 653–72.

FABREGA, HORACIO, JR., JUAN MEZZICH, and RICHARD ULRICH. 1988. "Black-White Differences in Psychopathology in an Urban Psychiatric Population." *Comprehensive Psychiatry* 29: 285–97.

FAIRBAIRN, W. R. 1954. *The Object-Relations Theory of the Personality.* New York: Basic Books.

FANON, FRANTZ. 1965. *The Wretched of the Earth.* London: Macgibbon and Kee. (Original publication 1961.)

———. 1968. *Black Skin, White Masks.* London: Macgibbon and Kee. (Original publication 1952.)

FEATHERSTONE, MIKE (ed.). 1999. *Love and Eroticism.* London: Sage.

FERNANDEZ, CARLOS. 1992. "La Raza and the Melting Pot: A Comparative Look at Multiethnicity." In Maria Root (ed.). *Racially Mixed People in America.* Newbury Park, CA: Sage.

FERNANDEZ, JAMES W. 1982. "The Dark at the Bottom of the Stairs: The Inchoate in Symbolic Inquiry and Some Strategies for Coping with It." In Jacques Maquet (ed.). *On Symbols in Anthropology: Essays in Honor of Harry Hoijer.* Malibu, CA: Uneda.

FINGARETTE, HERBERT. 1988. *Heavy Drinking: The Myth of Alcoholism as a Disease.* Berkeley: University of California Press.

FISCHER, DAVID H. 1989. *Albion's Seed: Four British Folkways in North America.* Oxford, England: Oxford University Press.

FODOR, JERRY. 1998. "The Trouble with Psychological Darwinism." *London Review of Books,* January 22: 11–13.

FOGELSON, RAYMOND. 1979. "Person, Self, and Identity: Some Anthropological Retrospects, Circumspects, and Prospects." In Benjamin Lee (ed.). *Psychosocial Theories of the Self.* New York: Plenum Press.

FOUCAULT, MICHEL. 1980. *Herculine Barbin: Being the Recently Discovered Memoirs of a Nineteenth Century French Hemaphrodite.* New York: Pantheon.

FRAKE, CHARLES. 1977. "Playing Frames Can Be Dangerous: Some Reflections on Methodology in Cognitive Anthropology." *Quarterly Newsletter of the Institute for Comparative Human Development* 1: 1–7.

———. 1994. "Cognitive Anthropology: An Origin Story." In Marcelo Suarez-Orozco, George Spindler, and Louise Spindler (eds.). *The Making of Psychological Anthropology II.* Fort Worth, TX: Harcourt Brace.

FRASER, S. (ed.). 1995. *The Bell Curve Wars.* New York: Basic Books.

FRAZER, JAMES. 1890. *The Golden Bough.* 2 vols. London: Macmillan.

FREEMAN, DEREK. 1983. *Samoa: The Making of an Anthropological Myth.* Cambridge, MA: Harvard University Press.

FREUD, ANNA. 1936. *Ego and the Mechanisms of Defense.* New York: International Universities Press.

FREUD, SIGMUND. 1950. *Totem and Taboo: Resemblances between the Psychic Lives of Savages and Neurotics.* New York: Norton. (Original publication 1918.)

———. 1959. *Group Psychology and the Analysis of the Ego.* New York: Norton. (Original publication 1921.)

―――. 1960. *The Ego and the Id.* New York: Norton. (Original publication 1923.)

―――. 1960. *Jokes and Their Relation to the Unconscious.* New York: Norton. (Original publication 1905.)

―――. 1961. *Civilization and Its Discontents.* New York: Norton. (Original publication 1930.)

―――. 1965. *New Introductory Lectures in Psychoanalysis.* New York: Norton. (Original publication 1931.)

―――. 1989. *The Psychopathology of Everyday Life.* New York: Norton. (Original publication 1904.)

FRIEDMAN, JONATHAN. 1997. "Global Crises, the Struggle for Cultural Identity and Intellectual Porkbarrelling: Cosmopolitans versus Locals, Ethnics and Nationals in an Era of De-Hegemonisation." In Pnina Werbner and Tariq Modood (eds.). *Debating Cultural Hybridity: Multi-Cultural Identities and the Politics of Anti-Racism.* London: Zed Books.

FROMM, ERICH. 1941. *Escape from Freedom.* New York: Holt, Rinehart and Winston.

FUNKENSTEIN, D. 1955. "The Physiology of Fear and Anger." *Scientific American* 192: 74–80.

GADLIN, HOWARD. 1977. "Private Lives and Public Order: A Critical View of the History of Intimate Relations in the United States." In George Levinger and Harold Raush (eds.). *Close Relationships: Perspectives on the Meaning of Intimacy.* Amherst: University of Massachusetts Press.

GAINES, ATWOOD. 1982. "Cultural Definitions, Behavior and the Person in American Psychiatry." In A. Marsella and G. White (eds.). *Cultural Conceptions of Mental Health and Therapy.* Dordrecht, Netherlands: D. Reidel.

―――. 1988. "Delusions: Culture, Psychosis and the Problem of Meaning." In Thomas Oltmanns and Brendan Maher (eds.). *Delusional Beliefs.* New York: Wiley.

GAINES, ATWOOD, and PAUL FARMER. 1986. "Visible Saints: Social Cynosures and Dysphoria in the Mediterranean Tradition." *Culture, Medicine and Psychiatry* 10: 295–330.

GARDINER, H. M., RUTH METCALF, and JOHN BEEBE-CENTER. 1937. *Feeling and Emotion: A History of Theories.* New York: American Book Company.

GASTRIL, R. 1992. "Cultural Regions of America." In Luther S. Luedtke (ed.). *Making America: The Society and Culture of the United States.* Chapel Hill: University of North Carolina Press.

GAY, J., and M. COLE. 1967. *The New Mathematics and an Old Culture.* New York: Holt, Rinehart and Winston.

GAZDAR, GERALD, EWAN KLEIN, GEOFFREY and PULLUM, IVAN SAG. 1985. *Generalized Phrase Structure Grammar.* Cambridge, MA: Harvard University Press.

GEERTZ, CLIFFORD. 1965. *Person, Time and Conduct in Bali: An Essay in Cultural Analysis.* New Haven, CT: Yale University, Southeast Asia Studies.

―――. 1975. "From the Native's Point of View: On the Nature of Anthropological Understanding." *American Scientist* 63: 47–53.

―――. 1977. "Centers, Kings and Charisma." In Joseph Ben-David and T. N. Clark (eds.). *Culture and Its Creators.* Chicago: University of Chicago Press.

―――. 1979. "Suq: The Bazaar Economy in Sefrou." In C. Geertz, H. Geertz, and L. Rosen (eds.). *Meaning and Order in Moroccan Society.* Cambridge, England: Cambridge University Press.

GEERTZ, HILDRED. 1959. "The Vocabulary of Emotions." *Psychiatry* 22: 225–37.

GELLHORN, ERNST, and WILLIAM KIELY. 1972. "Mystical States of Consciousness: Neurophysiological and Clinical Aspects." *Journal of Nervous and Mental Disease* 154: 399–405.

GELLNER, ERNEST. 1981. "Flux and Reflux in the Faith of Men." In E. Gellner (ed.). *Muslim Society.* Cambridge, England: Cambridge University Press.

―――. 1983. *Nations and Nationalism.* Oxford, England: Basil Blackwell.

GENIER, G., A. STEPICK, D. DRAZIN, A. LABORWIT, and S. MORRIS. 1992. "On Machines and Bureaucracy: Controlling Ethnic Interaction in Miami's Apparel and Construction Industries." In Louise Lamphere (ed.). *Structuring Diversity: Ethnographic Perspectives on the New Immigration.* Chicago: University of Chicago Press.

GENNEP, ARNOLD VAN. 1960. *The Rites of Passage.* Chicago: University of Chicago Press. (Original publication 1909.)

GERBER, ELEANOR RUTH. 1985. "Rage and Obligation: Samoan Emotion in Conflict." In G. White and J. Kirkpatrick (eds.). *Person, Self and Experience.* Berkeley: University of California Press.

GERGEN, KENNETH. 1988. "If Persons Are Texts." In Stanley Messer, Louis Sass, and Robert Woolfolk (eds.). *Hermeneutics and Psychological Theory: Interpretive Perspectives on Personality, Psychotherapy, and Psychopathology.* New Brunswick, NJ: Rutgers University Press.

GIDDENS, ANTHONY. 1992. *The Transformation of Intimacy: Sexuality, Love and Intimacy in Modern Societies.* Stanford, CA: Stanford University Press.

GILLIGAN, CAROL. 1982. *In a Different Voice: Psychological Theory and Women's Development.* Cambridge, MA: Harvard University Press.

GILROY, PAUL. 1993. *The Black Atlantic: Modernity and Double Consciousness.* Cambridge, MA: Harvard University Press.

GINZBURG, CARLO. 1980. *The Cheese and the Worms: The Cosmos of a Sixteenth Century Miller.* Baltimore: Johns Hopkins University Press.

————. 1983. *The Night Battles: Witchcraft and Agrarian Cults in the Sixteenth and Seventeenth Centuries.* Baltimore: Johns Hopkins University Press.

GLADWIN, T., and S. SARASON. 1953. *Truk: Man in Paradise.* New York: Wenner-Gren.

GLADWIN, THOMAS. 1970. *East Is a Big Bird.* Cambridge, MA: Harvard University Press.

GLUCKMAN, MAX. 1954. *Rituals of Rebellion in Southeast Africa.* Manchester, England: Manchester University Press.

GOFFMAN, ERVING. 1959. *The Presentation of Self in Everyday Life.* New York: Doubleday.

————. 1961. *Asylums: Essays on the Social Situation of Mental Patients and Other Inmates.* Garden City, NY: Doubleday.

————. 1963. *Stigma: Notes on the Management of a Spoiled Identity.* New York: Simon and Schuster.

GOOD, BYRON. 1977. "The Heart of What's the Matter: The Semantics of Illness in Iran." *Culture, Medicine and Psychiatry* 1: 25–58.

GOOD, MARY-JO (ed.). 1992. *Pain as Human Experience: An Anthropological Perspective.* Berkeley: University of California Press.

GOOD, MARY-JO, and BYRON GOOD. 1988. "Ritual, the State, and the Transformation of Emotional Discourse in Iranian Society." *Culture, Medicine and Psychiatry* 12: 43–63.

GOODE, WILLIAM. 1959. "The Theoretical Importance of Love." *American Sociological Review* 24: 38–47.

GOODENOUGH, WARD. 1956. "Componential Analysis and the Study of Meaning." *Language* 32: 195–216.

————. 1965. "Yankee Kinship Terminology: A Problem in Componential Analysis." *American Anthropologist* 67: 259–87.

GOODY, JACK. 1977. *The Domestication of the Savage Mind.* Cambridge, England: Cambridge University Press.

————. 1983. *The Development of the Family and Marriage in Europe.* Cambridge, England: Cambridge University Press.

————. 1996. *The East in the West.* Cambridge, England: Cambridge University Press.

GORER, GEOFFREY. 1938. *Himalayan Village: An Account of the Lepchas of Sikkim.* London: M. Joseph.

———. 1948. *The American People: A Study in National Character.* New York: Norton.

GORER, GEOFFREY, and JOHN RICKMAN. 1950. *The People of Great Russia: A Psychological Study.* New York: Chanticleer Press.

GRAMSCI, ANTONIO. 1971. "The Study of Philosophy." In Quintin Hoane and Geoffrey N. Smith (eds.). *Selections from the Prison Notebooks of Antonio Gramsci.* New York: International Publishers.

GREEN, MARTIN. 1974. *The Von Richthofen Sisters: The Triumphant and the Tragic Modes of Love.* New York: Basic Books.

GREENFELD, LIAH. 1992. *Nationalism: Five Roads to Modernity.* Cambridge, MA: Harvard University Press.

GRIM, JOHN. 1983. *The Shaman: Patterns of Siberian and Ojibway Healing.* Norman: University of Oklahoma Press.

GRIMAL, PIERRE. 1986. *Love in Ancient Rome.* Norman: University of Oklahoma Press.

GUENTHER, MATHIAS. 1975. "The Trance Dance as an Agent of Social Change among the Farm Bushmen of the Ghanzi District." *Botswana Notes and Records* 7: 161–66.

GUHA, RANAJIT (ed.). 1982–83. *Subaltern Studies,* Vols. I and II. New Dehli: Oxford University Press.

HAAKEN, JANICE. 1994. "Sexual Abuse, Recovered Memory, and Therapeutic Practice." *Social Text* 40: 115–45.

HACKING, IAN. 1995. *Rewriting the Soul: Multiple Personality and the Sciences of Memory.* Princeton, NJ: Princeton University Press.

HADDON, ALFRED. 1901–35. *The Cambridge Anthropological Expedition to Torres Straits* (6 vols). Cambridge, England: Cambridge University Press.

HALL, JOHN A. 1987. *Liberalism.* Chapel Hill: University of North Carolina Press.

HALL, JOHN A., and CHARLES LINDHOLM. 1999. *Is America Breaking Apart?* Princeton, NJ: Princeton University Press.

HALLOWELL, A. I. 1976. "Psychology and Anthropology" (original publication 1954); "Ojibwa Ontology, Behavior, and World View" (original publication 1960); "Ojibwa World View and Disease" (original publication 1963); "Personality, Culture and Society in Behavioral Evolution" (original publication 1963). Reprinted in A. I. Hallowell. *Contributions to Anthropology: Selected Papers of A. Irving Hallowell.* Chicago: University of Chicago Press.

HAMACHER, WERNER. 1986. " 'Disgregation of the Will': Nietzsche on the Individual and Individuality." In Thomas C. Heller, Morton Sosna, and David E. Willbery (eds.). *Reconstructing Individualism: Autonomy, Individuality, and the Self in Western Thought.* Stanford, CA: Stanford University Press.

HANDELMAN, DON. 1968. "Shamanizing on an Empty Stomach." *American Anthropologist* 70: 353–58.

HANDLER, RICHARD. 1986. "Vigorous Male and Aspiring Female: Poetry, Personality and Culture in Edward Sapir and Ruth Benedict." In George Stocking (ed.). *Malinowski, Rivers, Benedict and Others: Essays on Culture and Personality.* Madison: University of Wisconsin Press.

HARKNESS, SARA. 1992. "Human Development in Psychological Anthropology." In Theodore Schwartz, Geoffrey White, and Catherine Lutz (eds.). *New Directions in Psychological Anthropology.* Cambridge, England: Cambridge University Press.

HARKNESS, SARA, CHARLES M. SUPER, and CONSTANCE H. KEEFER. 1992. "Learning to Be an American Parent: How Cultural Models Gain Directive Force." In Roy D'Andrade and Claudia Strauss (eds.). *Human Motives and Cultural Models.* Cambridge, England: Cambridge University Press.

HARRIS, GRACE. 1989. "Concepts of Individual, Self and Person in Description and Analysis." *American Anthropologist* 91: 599–612.

HARRIS, MARVIN. 1985. *Good to Eat: Riddles of Food and Culture*. New York: Simon and Schuster.

HARTMANN, HEINZ. 1958. *Ego Psychology and the Problem of Adaption*. New York: International Universities Press. (Original publication 1939.)

HATCH, ELWIN. 1979. *The Biography of a Small Town*. New York: Columbia University Press.

HEATH, SHIRLEY BRICE. 1983. *Ways with Words: Language, Life and Work in Communities and Classrooms*. Cambridge, England: Cambridge University Press.

———. 1986. "What No Bedtime Story Means: Narrative Skills at Home and School." In B. Schieffelin and E. Ochs (eds.). *Language Socialization across Cultures*. Cambridge, England: Cambridge University Press.

HEBDIGE, DICK. 1979. *Subculture: The Meaning of Style*. London: Methuen.

HEELAS, PAUL, and ANDREW LOCK (eds.). 1981. *Indigenous Psychologies: The Anthropology of the Self*. London: Academic Press.

HEGEL, G. W. F. 1967. *The Phenomenology of Mind*. New York: Harper and Row. (Original publication 1808.)

HEIDER, ELEANOR. 1972. "The Structure of Color Space in Naming and Memory for Two Languages." *Cognitive Psychology* 7: 532–47.

HEIDER, KARL. 1970. *The Dugum Dani: A Papuan Culture in the Highlands of West New Guinea*. Chicago: Aldine.

HENRY, JULES. 1963. *Culture against Man*. New York: Random House.

HERDT, GILBERT. 1994. "Mistaken Sex: Culture, Biology and the Third Sex in New Guinea." In Gilbert Herdt (ed.). *Third Sex, Third Gender: Beyond Sexual Dimorphism in Culture and History*. New York: Zone Books.

HERNSTEIN, RICHARD, and CHARLES MURRAY. 1994. *The Bell Curve*. New York: Free Press.

HERTZ, ROBERT. 1960. "The Pre-eminence of the Right Hand." In Robert Hertz. *Death and the Right Hand*. Glencoe, IL: Free Press. (Original publication 1909).

HIRSCHFELD, LAWRENCE. 1997. "The Conceptual Politics of Race: Lessons from Our Children." *Ethos* 25:63–92.

HIRSCHMAN, ALBERT O. 1977. *The Passions and the Interests: Political Arguments for Capitalism before Its Triumph*. Princeton, NJ: Princeton University Press.

HOBBES, THOMAS. 1980. *Leviathan*. Indianapolis, IN: Bobbs-Merrill. (Original publication 1651.)

HOCHSCHILD, ARLIE RUSSELL. 1983. *The Managed Heart: Commercialization of Human Feeling*. Berkeley: University of California Press.

HOCHSCHILD, JENNIFER. 1981. *What's Fair? American Beliefs about Distributive Justice*. Cambridge, MA: Harvard University Press.

———. 1995. *Facing Up to the American Dream: Race, Class, and the Soul of the Nation*. Princeton, NJ: Princeton University Press.

HOLLAN, DAVID. 1992. "Cross-Cultural Differences in the Self." *Journal of Anthropological Research* 48: 283–300.

HOLLAND, DOROTHY. 1992. "The Woman Who Climbed Up the House: Some Limitations of Schema Theory." In Theodore Schwartz, Geoffrey White, and Catherine Lutz (eds.). *New Directions in Psychological Anthropology*. Cambridge, England: Cambridge University Press.

HOLLAND, DOROTHY, and DEBRA SKINNER. 1987. "Prestige and Intimacy: The Cultural Models behind American's Talk about Gender Types." In Dorothy Holland and Naomi Quinn (eds.). *Cultural Models in Language and Thought*. Cambridge, England: Cambridge University Press.

HOLMBERG, ALLAN. 1969. *Nomads of the Long Bow: The Siriono of Eastern Bolivia*. Garden City, NY: Natural History Press. (Original publication 1950.)

HOLMES, LOWELL. 1987. *Quest for the Real Samoa: The Mead/Freeman Controversy and Beyond.* South Hadley, MA: Bergin and Garvey.

HONIGMANN, JOHN. 1954. *The Kaska Indians: An Ethnographic Reconstruction.* New Haven, CT: Yale University Publications in Anthropology, 51.

———. 1967. *Personality in Culture.* New York: Harper and Row.

HORNEY, KAREN. 1939. *New Ways in Psychoanalysis.* New York: Norton.

HOWARD, ALAN. 1985. "Ethnopsychology and the Prospects for a Cultural Psychology." In G. White and J. Kirkpatrick (eds.). *Person, Self and Experience.* Berkeley: University of California Press.

HSU, FRANCIS. 1963. *Clan, Caste and Club: A Comparison of Chinese, Hindu and American Ways of Life.* Princeton, NJ: Van Nostrand.

———. 1983. "Eros, Affect and Pao." In F. Hsu (ed.). *Rugged Individualism Reconsidered.* Knoxville: University of Tennessee Press.

———. (ed.). 1961. *Psychological Anthropology: Approaches to Culture and Personality.* Chicago: Dorsey.

HUME, DAVID. 1956. *The Natural History of Religion.* Stanford, CA: Stanford University Press. (Original publication 1757.)

———. 1978. *A Treatise of Human Nature.* London, England: Oxford University Press. (Original publication 1739.)

HUMPHREYS, LAUD. 1970. *Tearoom Trade: Impersonal Sex in Public Places.* Chicago: Aldine.

HUNT, MORTON. 1959. *The Natural History of Love.* New York: Knopf.

HUNTINGTON, RICHARD, and PETER METCALF. 1979. *Celebrations of Death: The Anthropology of Mortuary Ritual.* Cambridge, England: Cambridge University Press.

HUNTINGTON, SAMUEL. 1981. *American Politics: The Promise of Disharmony.* Cambridge, MA: Harvard University Press.

HUSTON, T., and R. BURGESS. 1979. "Social Exchange in Developing Relationships." In R. Burgess and T. Huston (eds.). *Social Exchange in Developing Relationships.* New York: Academic Press.

HUTCHINS, EDWIN. 1994. *Cognition in the Wild.* Cambridge, MA: MIT Press.

INGHAM, JOHN. 1996. "Oedipality in Pragmatic Discourse: The Trobriands and Hindu India." *Ethos* 24: 559–87.

———. 1996. *Psychological Anthropology Reconsidered.* Cambridge, England: Cambridge University Press.

IRVINE, JUDITH. 1982. "Language and Affect: Some Cross Cultural Issues." In Heidi Byrnes (ed.). *Contemporary Perceptions of Language: Interdisciplinary Dimensions.* Washington DC: Georgetown University Press.

———. 1990. "Registering Affect: Heteroglossia in the Linguistic Expression of Emotion." In Catherine Lutz and Lila Abu-Lughod (eds.). *Language and the Politics of Emotion.* Cambridge, England: Cambridge University Press.

IZARD, CARROL. 1971. *The Face of Emotion.* New York: Appleton-Century-Crofts.

———. 1972. *Patterns of Emotions.* New York: Academic Press.

———. 1977. *Human Emotions.* New York: Plenum.

———. 1980. "Cross Cultural Perspectives on Emotion and Emotion Communication." In H. Triandis (ed.). *Handbook of Cross-Cultural Psychology.* Boston: Allyn and Bacon.

JACKSON, MICHAEL. 1989. *Paths toward a Clearing: Radical Empiricism and Ethnographic Inquiry.* Bloomington: Indiana University Press.

JACOBS, JERRY. 1984. *The Mall: An Attempted Escape from Everyday Life.* Prospect Heights, IL: Waveland Press.

JAHODA, GUSTAV. 1954. "A Note on Ashanti Day Names in Relation to Personality." *British Journal of Psychology* 45: 192–95.

———. 1982. *Psychology and Anthropology: A Psychological Perspective.* London: Academic Press.

JAKOBSON, ROMAN. 1956. *Fundamentals of Language.* The Hague, Netherlands: Mouton.

JANKOWIAK, WILLIAM. 1992. *Sex, Death and Hierarchy in a Chinese City: An Anthropological Account.* New York: Columbia University Press.

———. (ed.). 1995. *Romantic Love: A Universal Experience?* New York: Columbia University Press.

JANKOWIAK, WILLIAM, and EDWARD FISCHER. 1992. "A Cross-Cultural Perspective on Romantic Love." *Ethnology* 31: 149–55.

JENKINS, JANIS. 1994. "The Psychocultural Study of Emotion and Mental Disorder." In P. Bock (ed.). *Psychological Anthropology.* Westport, CT: Praeger.

JOCHELSON, V. 1926. *The Yukaghir and the Yukaghirized Tungus: Memoirs of the Jesup North Pacific Expedition,* Vol. 14. New York: American Museum of Natural History.

JOHNSON, FRANK. 1985. "The Western Concept of Self." In Anthony Marsella, George de Vos, and Francis Hsu (eds.). *Culture and the Self: Asian and Western Perspectives.* London: Tavistock.

JOHNSON, MARK. 1987. *The Body in the Mind: The Bodily Basis of Meaning, Imagination, and Reason.* Chicago: University of Chicago Press.

JUNG, CARL, M. L. VON FRANZ, JOSEPH HENDERSON, JOLANDE JACOBI, and ANIELA JAFFE. 1964. *Man and His Symbols.* London: Aldus.

JUNOD, HENRI. 1927. *The Life of a South African Tribe.* London: Macmillan.

KALBERG, STEVEN. 1997. "Tocqueville and Weber on the Sociological Origins of Citizenship: The Political Culture of American Democracy." *Citizenship Studies* 1: 199–222.

———. n.d. "The Sociology of Friendliness." Unpublished manuscript.

KANT, IMMANUEL. 1931. *Critique of Judgement.* London: Macmillan. (Original publication 1781.)

———. 1977. *Anthropology from a Pragmatic Point of View.* Carbondale: Southern Illinois University Press. (Original publication 1798.)

KAPFERER, BRUCE. 1995. "From the Edge of Death: Sorcery and the Motion of Consciousness." In Anthony P. Cohen and Nigel Rapport (eds.). *Questions of Consciousness.* London: Routledge.

KARDINER, ABRAM. 1939. *The Individual and His Society: The Psychodynamics of Primitive Social Organization.* New York: Columbia University Press.

———. 1945. *The Psychological Frontiers of Society.* New York: Columbia University Press.

KATZ, RICHARD. 1982. *Boiling Energy: Community Healing among the Kalahari Kung.* Cambridge, MA: Harvard University Press.

KEESING, ROGER. 1972. "Paradigms Lost: The New Ethnography and the New Linguistics." *Southwestern Journal of Anthropology* 28: 299–332.

———. 1987. "Models, 'Folk' and 'Cultural': Paradigms Regained?" In Dorothy Holland and Naomi Quinn (eds.). *Cultural Models in Language and Thought.* Cambridge, England: Cambridge University Press.

KELLER, JANET. 1992. "Schemes for Schemata." In Theodore Schwartz, Geoffrey White, and Catherine Lutz (eds.). *New Directions in Psychological Anthropology.* Cambridge, England: Cambridge University Press.

KEMPER, THEODORE. 1978. *A Social Interactional Theory of Emotion.* New York: Wiley.

———. 1987. "How Many Emotions Are There? Wedding the Social and the Autonomic Components." *American Journal of Sociology* 93: 263–89.

KENNY, MICHAEL. 1978. "Latah: The Symbolism of a Putative Mental Disorder." *Culture, Medicine and Psychiatry* 2: 209–31.

KHAN, GHANI. 1958. *The Pathans: A Sketch.* Peshawar, Pakistan: University Books.

KHATTACK, KHUSHAL KHAN. 1965. *Poems from the Diwan of Khushal Khan Khattack.* London: Allen and Unwin.

KIRKPATRICK, JOHN, and GEOFFREY WHITE. 1985. "Exploring Ethnopsychologies." In Geoffrey White and John Kirkpatrick (eds.). *Person, Self, and Experience: Exploring Pacific Ethnopsychologies.* Berkeley: University of California Press.

KIRMAYER, LAWRENCE J. 1989. "Cultural Variations in the Response to Psychiatric Disorders and Emotional Distress." *Social Sciences and Medicine* 29: 327–39.

KIRSCHNER, SUZANNE. 1996. *The Religious and Romantic Origins of Psychoanalysis: Individuation and Integration in Post-Freudian Theory.* Cambridge, England: Cambridge University Press.

KLEIN, MELANIE. 1975. *Envy and Gratitude and Other Works.* New York: Dell.

KLEINMAN, ARTHUR. 1986. *Social Origins of Distress and Disease.* New Haven, CT: Yale University Press.

———. 1988. *Rethinking Psychiatry: From Cultural Category to Personal Experience.* New York: Free Press.

KLEINMAN, ARTHUR, and BYRON GOOD (eds.). 1985. *Culture and Depression: Studies in the Anthropology and Cross-Cultural Psychiatry of Affect and Disorder.* Berkeley: University of California Press.

KOHUT, HEINZ. 1977. *The Restoration of the Self.* New York: International Universities Press.

———. 1985. *Self Psychology and the Humanities.* New York: Norton.

KONDO, DORINNE. 1990. *Crafting Selves: Power, Gender and Discourse of Identity in a Japanese Workplace.* Chicago: University of Chicago Press.

KRACKE, WAUD. 1978. *Force and Persuasion: Leadership in an Amazonian Society.* Chicago: University of Chicago Press.

———. 1994. "Reflections on the Savage Self: Introspection, Empathy, and Anthropology." In Marcelo Suarez-Orozco, George Spindler, and Louise Spindler (eds.). *The Making of Psychological Anthropology II.* Fort Worth, TX: Harcourt Brace.

KRADER, LAWRENCE. 1978. "Shamanism: Theory and History in Buryat Society." In V. Dioszegi and M. Hoppal (eds.). *Shamanism in Siberia.* Budapest: Adademiai Kiado.

KROEBER, ALFRED. 1920. "Totem and Taboo: An Ethnologic Psychoanalysis." *American Anthropologist* 22: 48–55.

———. 1939. "Totem and Taboo in Retrospect." *American Journal of Sociology* 45: 446–57.

———. 1952. "Psychosis or Social Sanction." In A. Kroeber (ed.). *The Nature of Culture.* Chicago: University of Chicago Press.

KUMAGAI, HISA, and ARNO KUMAGAI. 1986. "The Hidden 'I' in Amae: 'Passive Love' and Japanese Social Perception." *Ethos* 14: 305–20.

KUPER, ADAM. 1994. "Culture, Identity and the Project of a Cosmopolitan Anthropology." *Man* N.S. 29: 537–54.

KURTZ, STANLEY. 1991. "Polysexualization: A New Approach to Oedipus in the Trobriands." *Ethos* 19: 68–101.

———. 1992. *All the Mothers Are One: Hindu India and the Cultural Reshaping of Psychoanalysis.* New York: Columbia University Press.

KUSSEROW, ADRIE. "De-Homogenizing American Individualism: Socializing 'Hard' and 'Soft' Individualism in Manhattan and Queens." *Ethos* 27: 210–34.

LA BARRE, WESTON. 1958. "The Influence of Freud on Anthropology." *American Imago* 15: 275–328.

———. 1972. *The Ghost Dance.* New York: Delta Press.

LAKOFF, GEORGE. 1987. *Women, Fire and Dangerous Things: What Categories Reveal about the Mind.* Chicago: University of Chicago Press.

LAKOFF, GEORGE, and MARK JOHNSON. 1980. *Metaphors We Live By.* Chicago: University of Chicago Press.

LAKOFF, GEORGE, and ZOLTAN KOVECSES. 1987. "The Cognitive Model of Anger Inherent in American English." In Dorothy Holland and Naomi Quinn (eds.). *Cultural Models in Language and Thought.* Cambridge, England: Cambridge University Press.

LAMBECK, MICHAEL, and PAUL ANTZE. 1996. "Introduction: Forecasting Memory." In Paul Antze and Michael Lambeck (eds.). *Tense Past: Cultural Essays in Trauma and Memory.* New York: Routledge.

LANDES, RUTH. 1937. *Ojibwa Sociology.* New York: Columbia University Press.

LANGE, C., and W. JAMES. 1922. *The Emotions.* New York: Macmillan, Hafner Press.

LAQUEUR, THOMAS. 1990. *Making Sex: Body and Gender from the Greeks to Freud.* Cambridge, MA: Harvard University Press.

LASCH, CHRISTOPHER. 1977. *Haven in a Heartless World.* New York: Basic Books.

———. 1978. *The Culture of Narcissism: American Life in an Age of Diminishing Expectations.* New York: Norton.

LASLETT, JOHN, and SEYMOUR M. LIPSET. 1974. *Failure of a Dream?* New York: Doubleday Anchor.

LASLETT, PETER. 1977. *Family Life and Illicit Love in Earlier Generations: Essays in Historical Sociology.* Cambridge, England: Cambridge University Press.

LAUMANN, EDWARD O., JOHN H. GAGNON, ROBERT T. MICHAEL, and STUART MICHAELS. 1994. *The Social Organization of Sexuality: Sexual Practices in the United States.* Chicago: University of Chicago Press.

LEACH, EDMUND. 1976. *Culture and Communication: The Logic by Which Symbols Are Connected.* Cambridge, England: Cambridge University Press.

LEE, DOROTHY. 1959. *Freedom and Culture.* Englewood Cliffs, NJ: Prentice-Hall.

LENG, G. 1985. "Koro—A Cultural Disease." In R. Simons and C. Hughes (eds.). *The Culture-Bound Symptoms.* Dordrecht, Netherlands: D. Reidel.

LEVINE, ROBERT. 1973. *Culture, Behavior and Personality: An Introduction to the Comparative Study of Psychosocial Adaption.* Chicago: Aldine.

———. 1979. "The Self and Its Development in an African Society: A Preliminary Analysis." In Benjamin Lee (ed.). *Psychosocial Theories of the Self.* New York: Plenum Press.

———. 1981. "Psychoanalytic Theory and the Comparative Study of Human Development." In R. H. Munroe, R. L. Munroe, and B. Whiting (eds). *Handbook of Cross-Cultural Human Development.* New York: Garland Press.

———. 1990. "Infant Environments in Psychoanalysis: A Cross-Cultural View." In James Stigler, Richard Shweder, and Gilbert Herdt (eds.). *Cultural Psychology: Essays on Comparative Human Development.* Cambridge, England: Cambridge University Press.

LEVINE, ROBERT, SUZANNE DIXON, SARAH LEVINE, AMY RICHMAN, P. HERBERT LEIDERMAN, CONSTANCE H. KEEFER, and T. BERRY BRAZELTON. 1994. *Child Care and Culture: Lessons from Africa.* Cambridge, England: Cambridge University Press.

LEVINE, SARAH. 1979. *Mothers and Wives: Gusii Women of East Africa.* Chicago: University of Chicago Press.

LEVINGER, G. 1977. "The Embrace of Lives: Changing and Unchanging." In G. Levinger and H. Raush (eds.). *Close Relationships: Perspectives on the Meaning of Intimacy.* Amherst: University of Massachusetts Press.

LÈVI-STRAUSS, CLAUDE. 1963. *Totemism.* Boston: Beacon Press.

———. 1966. *The Savage Mind.* Chicago: University of Chicago Press.

———. 1967. "The Sorcerer and His Magic." "The Structural Study of Myth." In C. Lévi-Strauss (ed.). *Structural Anthropology.* Garden City, NY: Doubleday.

———. 1969. *The Elementary Structures of Kinship.* Boston: Beacon Press. (Original French publication 1949.)

———. 1985. "Race and Culture." In Claude Lévi-Strauss (ed.). *The View from Afar.* Oxford, England: Basil Blackwell.

LEVY, ROBERT L. 1973. *Tahitians: Mind and Experience in the Society Islands.* Chicago: University of Chicago Press.

———. 1984. "Emotion, Knowing, and Culture." In Richard Shweder and Robert LeVine (eds.). *Culture Theory: Essays on Mind, Self and Emotion.* Cambridge, England: Cambridge University Press.

LEVY-BRUHL, LUCIEN. 1926. *How Natives Think.* London: Allen & Unwin. (Original publication 1912.)

LEWIS, I. M. 1970. "A Structural Approach to Witchcraft and Spirit Possession." In Mary Douglas (ed.). *Witchcraft Confessions and Accusations.* London: Tavistock.

———. 1971. *Ecstatic Religion: An Anthropological Study of Spirit Possession and Shamanism.* Harmondsworth, England: Penguin Books.

———. 1986. *Religion in Context: Cults and Charisma.* Cambridge, England: Cambridge University Press.

LIFTON, ROBERT JAY. 1970. *Boundaries: Psychological Man in Revolution.* New York: Vintage.

LIN, K. M., and A. KLEINMAN. 1988. "Psychopathology and the Clinical Course of Schizophrenia." *Schizophrenia Bulletin* 14: 555–67.

LIND, MICHAEL. 1995. *The Next American Nation: The New Nationalism and the Fourth American Revolution.* New York: Free Press.

LINDHOLM, CHARLES. 1980. *Generosity and Jealousy: The Swat Pukhtun of Northern Pakistan.* New York: Columbia University Press.

———. 1981. "Leatherworkers and Love Potions." *American Ethnologist* 9: 512–25.

———. 1988. "Lovers and Leaders: A Comparison of Social and Psychological Models of Romance and Charisma." *Social Science Information* 27: 3–24.

———. 1988. "The Social Structure of Emotional Constraint: The Court of Louis XIV and the Pukhtun of Northern Pakistan." *Ethos* 16: 227–46.

———. 1990. *Charisma.* Oxford, England: Basil Blackwell.

———. 1992. "Charisma, Crowd Psychology and Altered States of Consciousness." *Culture, Medicine and Psychiatry* 16: 287–310.

———. 1995. "Love as an Experience of Transcendence." In William Jankowiak (ed.). *Romantic Love: A Universal Experience?* New York: Columbia University Press.

———. 1996. *Frontier Perspectives: Essays in Comparative Anthropology.* Karachi: Oxford University Press.

———. 1996. *The Islamic Middle East: An Historical Anthropology.* Oxford, England: Basil Blackwell.

———. 1997. "Does the Sociocentric Self Exist? Reflections on Markus and Kitayama's 'Culture and the Self.' " *Journal of Anthropological Research* 53: 405–22.

———. 1997. "Logical and Moral Problems of Postmodernism." *Journal of the Royal Anthropological Institute* 3: 745–60.

———. 1998. "The Future of Love." In V. de Munck (ed.). *Romantic Love and Sexual Behavior: Perspectives from the Social Sciences.* Westport, CT: Greenwood.

———. 1999. "Love and Structure." In Mike Featherstone (ed.). *Love and Eroticism.* London: Sage.

LINTON, RALPH. 1949. "The Natural History of the Family." In Ruth N. Anshen (ed.). *The Family: Its Function and Destiny.* New York: Harper.

LIPSET, SEYMOUR M. 1963. *The First New Nation: The United States in Historical and Comparative Perspective.* New York: Basic Books.

————. 1968. *Revolution and Counterrevolution.* New York: Basic Books.

————. 1996. *American Exceptionalism: A Double-Edged Sword.* New York: Norton.

LOCK, MARGARENT, and NANCY SCHEPER-HUGHES. 1987. "The Mindful Body." *Medical Anthropology Quarterly* 1: 6–41.

LOCKE, JOHN. 1959. *Essay Concerning Human Understanding.* New York: Dover. (Original publication 1690.)

LOUNSBURY, FLOYD. 1956. "A Semantic Analysis of the Pawnee Kinship Usage." *Language* 32: 158–94.

LOWIE, ROBERT. 1931. "Sex and Marriage." In John McDermott (ed.). *The Sex Problem in Modern Society.* New York: Modern Library.

————. 1935. *The Crow Indians.* New York: Farrar and Rinehart.

LUHRMANN, TANYA. 1989. *Persuasions of the Witch's Craft: Ritual Magic and Witchcraft in Present-day England.* Cambridge, MA: Harvard University Press.

————. 1994. "Psychological Anthropology as the Naturalist's Art." In Marcelo Suarez-Orozco, George Spindler, and Louise Spindler (eds.). *The Making of Psychological Anthropology II.* Fort Worth, TX: Harcourt Brace.

————. 2000. *Of Two Minds: The Growing Disorder in American Psychiatry.* New York: Knopf.

LURIA, A. R. 1976. *Cognitive Development: Its Cultural and Social Foundations.* Cambridge, MA: Harvard University Press. (First published in Moscow 1974.)

LUTZ, CATHERINE. 1985. "Ethnopsychology Compared to What? Explaining Behavior and Consciousness among the Ifaluk." In Geoffrey M. White and John Kirkpatrick (eds.). *Person, Self, and Experience: Exploring Pacific Ethnopsychologies.* Berkeley: University of California Press.

————. 1988. *Unnatural Emotions: Everyday Sentiments on a Micronesian Atoll and Their Challenge to Western Theory.* Chicago: University of Chicago Press.

————. 1990. "Engendered Emotion: Gender, Power, and the Rhetoric of Emotional Control in American Discourse." In Catherine Lutz and Lila Abu-Lughod (eds.). *Language and the Politics of Emotion.* Cambridge, England: Cambridge University Press.

LUTZ, CATHERINE, and GEOFFREY WHITE. 1986. "The Anthropology of Emotions." *Annual Review of Anthropology* 15: 405–36.

MACFARLANE, ALAN. 1970. *Witchcraft in Tudor and Stuart England: A Regional and Comparative Study.* New York: Harper and Row.

————. 1986. *Marriage and Love in England: 1300–1840.* Oxford, England: Basil Blackwell.

————. 1987. *The Culture of Capitalism.* Oxford, England: Basil Blackwell.

MACINTYRE, ALASDAIR. 1981. *After Virtue: A Study in Moral Theory.* London: Duckworth.

MACPHERSON, CHARLES B. 1962. *The Political Theory of Possessive Individualism: Hobbes to Locke.* Oxford, England: Oxford University Press.

MAGEO, JEANNETTE-MARIE. 1996. "Samoa, on the Wilde Side: Male Transvestism, Oscar Wilde, and Liminality in Making Gender." *Ethos* 24: 588–627.

MAKDISI, GEORGE. 1981. *The Rise of Colleges: Institutions of Learning in Islam and the West.* Edinburgh: Edinburgh University Press.

MALINOWSKI, BRONISLAW. 1927. *Sex and Repression in Savage Society.* New York: Harcourt Brace.

————. 1948. *Magic, Science and Religion.* Boston: Beacon Press.

————. 1967. *A Diary in the Strict Sense of the Term.* New York: Harcourt, Brace and World.

MANDELL, ARNOLD. 1980. "Toward a Psychobiology of Transcendence: God in the Brain." In Julian Davidson and Richard Davidson (eds.). *The Psychobiology of Consciousness.* New York: Plenum.

MANSON, WILLIAM. 1986. "Kardiner and Neo-Freudian Alternative." In George Stocking (ed.). *Malinowski, Rivers, Benedict and Others: Essays on Culture and Personality.* Madison: University of Wisconsin Press.

———. 1988. *The Psychodynamics of Culture: Abram Kardiner and Neo-Freudian Anthropology.* Westport, CT: Greenwood Press.

MARANO, L. 1985. "Windigo Psychosis: The Anatomy of an Emic-Etic Confusion." In R. Simons and C. Hughes (eds.). *The Culture-Bound Symptoms.* Dordrecht, Netherlands: D. Reidel.

MARCUS, GEORGE (ed.). 1983. *Elites: Ethnographic Issues.* Albuquerque: University of New Mexico Press.

———. 1995. "On Eccentricity." In Deborah Battaglia (ed.). *Rhetorics of Self-Making.* Berkeley: University of California Press.

MARCUSE, HERBERT. 1968. *Eros and Civilization.* Boston: Beacon Press.

MARKUS, HAZEL, and SHINOBU KITAYAMA. 1991. "Culture and the Self: Implications for Cognition, Emotion and Motivation." *Psychological Review* 98: 224–53.

MARRIOTT, MCKIM. (ed.). 1990. *India through Hindu Categories.* New Dehli: Sage.

MARRIOTT, MCKIM, and RONALD INDEN. 1974. "Caste Systems." *Encyclopaedia Britannica,* Vol. 3, pp. 982–91.

MARSHALL, MAC. 1979. *Weekend Warriors: Alcohol in a Micronesian Culture.* Palo Alto, CA: Mayfield.

MARTIN, EMILY. 1987. *The Woman in the Body: A Cultural Analysis of Reproduction.* Boston: Beacon Press.

MARWICK, MAX. 1965. *Sorcery in Its Social Setting.* Manchester, England: Manchester University Press.

MASSIGNON, LOUIS. 1982. *The Passion of al-Hallaj: Mystic and Martyr of Islam, Vol I., The Life of al-Hallaj.* Princeton, NJ: Princeton University Press.

MATHEWS, GORDON. 1996. "The Stuff of Dreams, Fading: Ikigai and 'the Japanese Self.' " *Ethos* 24: 718–47.

MAUSS, MARCEL. 1979. "A Category of the Human Mind: The Notion of Person, the Notion of 'Self' " (original publication 1938); "Body Techniques" (original publication 1935). In Marcel Mauss (ed.). *Sociology and Psychology: Essays.* London: Routledge and Kegan Paul.

MAYBURY-LEWIS, DAVID, and URI ALMAGOR (eds.). 1989. *The Attraction of Opposites: Thought and Society in the Dualistic Mode.* Ann Arbor: University of Michigan Press.

MCLAUGHLIN, WILLIAM G. 1978. *Revivals, Awakenings, and Reforms.* Chicago: University of Chicago Press.

MEAD, GEORGE HERBERT. 1934. *Mind, Self and Society.* Chicago: University of Chicago Press.

MEAD, MARGARET. 1928. *Coming of Age in Samoa: A Psychological Study of Primitive Youth for Western Civilization.* New York: Morrow.

———. 1942. *And Keep Your Powder Dry.* New York: Morrow.

———. 1956. *New Lives for Old: Cultural Transformation—Manus, 1928–1953.* New York: Morrow.

———. 1962. "Retrospect and Prospect." In T. Gladwin and W. Sturtevant (eds.). *Anthropology and Human Behavior.* Washington, DC: Anthropological Society of Washington.

———. 1963. *Sex and Temperament in Three Primitive Societies.* New York: Morrow. (Original publication 1935.)

MILLER, JAMES. 1980. "Romantic Couples and Group Process." In Kenneth Pope (ed.). *On Love and Loving.* San Francisco: Jossey-Bass.

————. 1984. *Rousseau: Dreamer of Democracy.* New Haven, CT: Yale University Press.

MILLER, PEGGY J., HEIDI FUNG, and JUDITH MINTZ. 1996. "Self-Construction through Narrative Practices: A Chinese and American Comparison of Early Socialization." *Ethos* 24: 237–80.

MOFFATT, MICHAEL. 1979. *An Untouchable Community in South India.* Princeton, NJ: Princeton University Press.

————. 1989. *Coming of Age in New Jersey: College and American Culture.* New Brunswick, NJ: Rutgers University Press.

MONTAIGNE, MICHEL DE. 1958. "Apology for Raymond Sebond" (original publication 1580). In *The Complete Essays of Montaigne.* Stanford, CA: Stanford University Press.

MOORE, R. 1998. "Love and Limerence with Chinese Characteristics: Student Romance in the PRC." In V. de Munck (ed.). *Romantic Love and Sexual Behavior: Perspectives from the Social Sciences.* Westport, CT: Praeger.

MORGAN, L. H. 1963. *Ancient Society.* Cleveland: World Publishing. (Original publication 1877.)

MUKHOPADHYAY, CAROL. 1979. "The Function of Romantic Love: A Re-appraisal of the Coppinger and Rosenblatt Study." *Behavior Science Research* 14: 57–63.

MUNAKATA, TSUNETSUGU. 1986. "Japanese Attitudes toward Mental Illness and Mental Health Care." In T. Lebra and W. Lebra (eds.). *Japanese Culture and Behavior.* Honolulu: University of Hawaii Press.

————. 1989. "The Socio-Cultural Significance of the Diagnostic Label 'Neurasthenia' in Japan's Mental Health Care System." *Culture, Medicine and Psychiatry* 13: 203–13.

MUNROE, ROBERT, and RUTH MUNROE. 1994. *Cross Cultural Human Development* (2d ed.). Prospect Heights, IL: Waveland Press.

MURPHY, J. 1964. "Psychotherapeutic Aspects of Shamanism on St. Lawrence Island, Alaska." In A. Kiev (ed.). *Magic, Faith and Healing.* London: Free Press.

MURPHY, ROBERT. 1960. *Headhunter's Heritage.* Berkeley: University of California Press.

NEEDHAM, RODNEY. 1985. "Skepticism and Forms of Life." In Rodney Needham. *Exemplars.* Berkeley: University of California Press.

————. 1973. *Right and Left: Essays on Dual Classification Systems.* Chicago: University of Chicago Press.

————. 1978. *Primordial Characters.* Charlottesville: University of Virginia Press.

NEWMAN, KATHERINE S. 1988. *Falling from Grace: The Experience of Downward Mobility in the American Middle Class.* New York: Free Press.

NIESSER, ULRIC. 1988. "Five Kinds of Self-Knowledge." *Philosophical Psychology* 1: 35–59.

NIETZSCHE, FRIEDRICH. 1967. *Birth of Tragedy and the Case of Wagner.* New York: Vintage. (Original publication 1872.)

————. 1969. *On the Genealogy of Morals and Ecce Homo.* New York: Vintage. (Original publication *On the Genealogy of Morals* 1887.)

————. 1977. *The Twilight of the Idols and the Anti-Christ.* Harmondsworth, England: Penguin. (Original publication *The Twilight of the Idols* 1889.)

————. 1996. *Human, All Too Human: A Book for Free Spirits.* Lincoln: University of Nebraska Press. (Original publication 1878–79.)

————. 1990. "Schopenhaver as Educator" (original publication 1874) In Friedrich Nietzsche (ed.). *Unmodern Observations.* New Haven, CT: Yale University Press.

NISBETT, R., and L. ROSS. 1980. *Human Inference: Strategies and Shortcomings of Social Judgment.* Englewood Cliffs, NJ: Prentice-Hall.

NUCKOLLS, CHARLES W. 1996. *The Cultural Dialectics of Knowledge and Desire.* Madison: University of Wisconsin Press.

NYGREN, ANDERS. 1958. *Agape and Eros.* Philadelphia: Westminster Press.

OBEYESEKERE, GANANATH. 1981. *Medusa's Hair: An Essay on Personal Symbols and Religious Experience.* Chicago: University of Chicago Press.

———. 1985. "Depression, Buddhism and the Work of Culture in Sri Lanka." In Arthur Kleinman and Byron Good (eds.). *Culture and Depression: Studies in the Anthropology and Cross-Cultural Psychiatry of Affect and Disorder.* Berkeley: University of California Press.

———. 1990. *The Work of Culture: Symbolic Transformation in Psychoanalysis and Anthropology.* Chicago: University of Chicago Press.

OCHS, ELINOR, and BAMBI SCHIEFFELIN. 1984. "Language Acquisition and Socialization: Three Developmental Stories and Their Implications." In Richard Shweder and Robert LeVine (eds.). *Culture Theory: Essays on Mind, Self and Emotion.* Cambridge, England: Cambridge University Press.

OFSHE, RICHARD, and ETHAN WATTERS. 1994. *Making Monsters: False Memories, Psychotherapy and Sexual Hysteria.* New York: Scribners.

OGBU, JOHN. 1978. *Minority Education and Caste: The American System in Cross-Cultural Perspective.* New York: Academic Press.

O'HANLON, R. 1988. "Recovering the Subject: Subaltern Studies and Histories of Resistance in South Asia." *Modern Asian Studies* 22: 189–224.

OHNUKI-TIERNEY, EMIKO. 1980. "Shamans and *Imu* among Two Ainu Groups." *Ethos* 8: 204–18.

OPLER, MORRIS. 1959. "Cultural Differences in Mental Disorders." In M. Opler (ed.). *Culture and Mental Health.* New York: Macmillan.

ORANS, MARTIN. 1996. *Not Even Wrong: Margaret Mead, Derek Freeman, and the Samoans.* Novato, CA: Chandler and Sharp.

PADEL, RUTH. 1981. "Madness in Fifth-century (BC) Athenian Tragedy." In Paul Heelas and Andrew Lock (eds.). *Indigenous Psychologies: The Anthropology of the Self.* London: Academic Press.

———. 1992. *In and Out of the Mind: Greek Images of the Tragic Self.* Princeton, NJ: Princeton University Press.

PARISH, STEVEN M. 1994. *Moral Knowing in a Hindu Sacred City: An Exploration of Mind, Emotion and Self.* New York: Columbia University Press.

———. 1996. *Hierarchy and Its Discontents: Culture and the Politics of Consciousness in Caste Society.* Philadelphia: University of Pennsylvania Press.

PARKIN, DAVID. 1985. "Reason, Emotion and the Embodiment of Power." In Joanna Overing (ed.). *Reason and Morality.* London: Tavistock.

PARRY, JONATHAN. 1982. "Sacrificial Death and the Necrophagous Ascetic." In M. Bloch and J. Parry (eds.). *Death and the Regeneration of Life.* Cambridge, England: Cambridge University Press.

PARSONS, ANNE. 1964. "Is the Oedipus Complex Universal? The Jones–Malinowski Debate Revisited and a South Italian 'Nuclear Complex.' " In W. Muensterberger and S. Axelrad (eds.). *The Psychoanalytic Study of Society,* Vol. III. New York: International Universities Press.

PARSONS, TALCOTT. 1949. "The Social Structure of the Family." In Ruth N. Anshen (ed.). *The Family: Its Function and Destiny.* New York: Harper.

PATTERSON, ORLANDO. 1991. *Freedom.* New York: Basic Books.

PAUL, ROBERT. 1978. "Instinctive Aggression in Man: The Semai Case." *Journal of Psychological Anthropology* 1: 65–79.

PEACOCK, JAMES. 1994. "American Cultural Values: Disorders and Challenges." In S. Foreman (ed.). *Diagnosing America: Anthropology and Public Engagement.* Ann Arbor: University of Michigan Press.

PEHRSON, ROBERT. 1966. *The Social Organization of the Marri Baluch.* Chicago: Aldine.

PEIRCE, CHARLES. 1940. *Philosophical Writings of Peirce.* New York: Dover.

PERIN, CONSTANCE. 1988. *Belonging in America: Reading between the Lines.* Madison: University of Wisconsin Press.

PESSEN, EDWARD. 1992. "Status and Class in America." In Luther S. Luedtke (ed.). *Making America: The Society and Culture of the United States.* Chapel Hill: University of North Carolina Press.

PETERS, LARRY. 1982. "Trance, Initiation and Psychotherapy in Tamang Shamanism." *American Ethnologist* 9:21–46.

PITKIN, HARVEY. 1985. "A Wintu Etymology: 'Love.' " *International Journal of American Linguistics* 51: 536–38.

PLATO. 1972. *Phaedrus.* Cambridge, England: Cambridge University Press.

PLUTCHIK, ROBERT. 1982. "A Psychoevolutionary Theory of the Emotions." *Social Science Information* 21: 529–53.

POLE, J. R. 1978. *The Pursuit of Equality in American History.* Berkeley: University of California Press.

PORTEUS, S. D. 1931. *The Psychology of a Primitive People.* London: Edward Arnold.

———. 1965. *Porteus Maze Test.* Palo Alto: Pacific Books.

POTTER, DAVID. 1964. "Individuality and Conformity." In M. McGiffert (ed.). *The Character of Americans.* Chicago: Dorsey Press.

PRICE-WILLIAMS, D. R. 1969. "A Study concerning Concepts of Conservation of Quantities among Primitive Children." In D. R. Price-Williams (ed.). *Cross-Cultural Studies.* Harmondsworth, England: Penguin.

PRINCE, RAYMOND. 1982. "The Endorphins: A Review for Psychological Anthropologists." *Ethos* 10: 303–16.

———. 1982. "Shamans and Endorphins: Hypothesis for a Synthesis." *Ethos* 10: 409–23.

PROPP, VLADIMIR. 1958. *The Morphology of the Folktale.* Bloomington: Indiana University Press. (Original publication 1928.)

PROSKAUER, STEPHEN. 1980. "Oedipal Equivalents in a Clan Culture: Reflections on Navaho Ways." *Psychiatry* 43: 43–50.

QUINLAN, PHILIP. 1991. *Connectionism and Psychology.* Chicago: University of Chicago Press.

QUINN, NAOMI. 1987. "Convergent Evidence for a Cultural Model of American Marriage." In Dorothy Holland and Naomi Quinn (eds.). *Cultural Models in Language and Thought.* Cambridge, England: Cambridge University Press.

———. 1992. "The Motivational Force of Self-Understanding: Evidence from Wives' Inner Conflicts." In Roy D'Andrade and Claudia Strauss (eds.). *Human Motives and Cultural Models.* Cambridge, England: Cambridge University Press.

———. 1996. "Culture and Contradiction: The Case of Americans' Reasoning about Marriage." *Ethos* 24: 391–425.

QUINN, NAOMI, and DOROTHY HOLLAND. 1987. "Culture and Cognition." In Dorothy Holland and Naomi Quinn (eds.). *Cultural Models in Language and Thought.* Cambridge, England: Cambridge University Press.

RADIN, PAUL. 1920. *The Autobiography of a Winnebago Indian.* Berkeley: University of California Press.

———. 1926 .*Crashing Thunder: The Autobiography of an American Indian.* New York: Appleton.

———. 1927. *Primitive Man as Philosopher.* New York: Appleton.

RAINE, NANCY VENABLE. 1998. *After Silence: Rape and My Journey Back.* New York: Crown.

RANDALL, ROBERT. 1976. "How Tall Is a Taxonomic Tree? Some Evidence for Dwarfism." *American Ethnologist* 3: 543–53.

RAPPAPORT, ROY. 1994. "Disorders of Our Own." In S. Foreman (ed.). *Diagnosing America: Anthropology and Public Engagement.* Ann Arbor: University of Michigan Press.

REICH, WILHELM. 1970. *The Mass Psychology of Fascism.* New York: Farrar, Straus and Giroux.

———. 1972. *Sex-Pol: Essays 1929–1934.* New York: Random House.

REYNA, STEVE. 1994. "Literary Anthropology and the Case against Science." *Man* N. S. 29: 555–82.

RIEFF, PHILIP. 1987. *The Triumph of the Therapeutic: Uses of Faith after Freud.* Chicago: University of Chicago Press.

RIESMAN, DAVID, with NATHAN GLAZER and REUEL DENNEY. 1961. *The Lonely Crowd* (2d ed.). New Haven, CT: Yale University Press. (Original publication 1950.)

RIESMAN, PAUL. 1986. "Person and the Life Cycle in African Social Thought and Life." *African Studies Review* 29: 71–138.

ROHEIM, GEZA. 1968. *The Origin and Function of Culture.* New York: Johnson Reprint Corporation. (Original publication 1943.)

ROHRER, JOHN, and MUNRO EDMUNSON. 1960. *The Eighth Generation Grows Up.* New York: Harper and Row.

ROLAND, ALAN. 1988. *In Search of Self in India and Japan: Toward a Cross-Cultural Psychology.* Princeton, NJ: Princeton University Press.

ROMNEY, A. KIMBALL, and ROY D'ANDRADE. 1964. "Cognitive Aspects of English Kin Terms." *American Anthropologist* 66: 146–70.

ROOT, MARIA. 1992. "Within, Between, and Beyond Race." In Maria Root (ed.). *Racially Mixed People in America.* Newbury Park, CA: Sage.

RORTY, AMÉLIE. 1980. "Explaining Emotions." In A. Rorty (ed.). *Explaining Emotions.* Berkeley: University of California Press.

———. 1988. *Mind in Action: Essays in the Philosophy of Mind.* Boston: Beacon Press.

ROSALDO, MICHELLE. 1980. *Knowledge and Passion: Ilongot Notions of Self and Social Life.* Cambridge, England: Cambridge University Press.

———. 1984. "Toward an Anthropology of Self and Feeling." In Richard Shweder and Robert LeVine (eds.). *Culture Theory: Essays on Mind, Self and Emotion.* Cambridge, England: Cambridge University Press.

ROSALDO, RENATO. 1983. "Grief and a Headhunter's Rage: On the Cultural Force of Emotions." In Edward Bruner (ed.). *Text, Play and Story: The Construction and Reconstruction of Self and Society.* Proceedings of the American Ethnological Society, Washington, DC.

———. 1989. *Culture and Truth: The Remaking of Social Analysis.* Boston: Beacon Press.

ROSCH, ELINOR. 1978. "Principles of Categorization." In E. Rosch and B. Lloyd (eds.). *Cognition and Categorization.* New York: Erlbaum.

ROSEMAN, MARINA. 1990. "Head, Heart, Odor, and Shadow: The Structure of the Self, the Emotional World, and Ritual Performance among Senoi Temiar." *Ethos* 18: 227–50.

ROSEN, LAWRENCE (ed.). 1995. *Other Intentions: Cultural Contexts and the Attribution of Inner States.* Santa Fe, NM: School of American Research Press.

ROSENBERGER, NANCY (ed.). 1992. *The Japanese Sense of Self.* Cambridge, England: Cambridge University Press.

ROSENBLATT, PAUL. 1966. "A Cross-Cultural Study of Child Rearing and Romantic Love." *Journal of Personality and Social Psychology* 4: 336–38.

———. 1967. "Marital Residence and the Functions of Romantic Love." *Ethnology* 6: 471–80.

ROSENBLUM, NANCY. 1998. *Membership and Morals: The Personal Uses of Pluralism in America.* Princeton, NJ: Princeton University Press.

ROUSSEAU, JEAN JACQUES. 1953. *The Confessions of Jean Jacques Rousseau.* Harmondsworth, England: Penguin. (Original publication 1781.)

———. 1967. *The Social Contract and Discourse on the Origins of Inequality.* New York: Washington Square Press. (Original publication 1762 and 1755).

———. 1979. *Reveries of the Solitary Walker.* London: Penguin. (Original publication 1782.)

ROZIN, PAUL, and CAROL NEMEROFF. 1990. "The Laws of Sympathetic Magic: A Psychological Analysis of Similarity and Contagion." In James Stigler, Richard Shweder, and Gilbert Herdt (eds.). *Cultural Psychology: Essays on Comparative Human Development.* Cambridge, England: Cambridge University Press.

RUBIN, ZICK. 1973. *Liking and Loving.* New York: Holt.

RUMELHART, D., P. SMOLENSKI, E. HINTON, and J. L. MCCLELLAND. 1986. "Schemata and Sequential Thought Processes in PDP Models." In J. McClelland and D. Rumelhart (eds.). *Parallel Distributed Processing,* Vol. II. Cambridge, MA: MIT Press.

RUSSELL, J. 1991. "Culture and the Categorization of Emotions." *Psychological Bulletin* 110: 426–50.

SAPIR, EDWARD E. 1923. "The Two Kinds of Human Beings." *Freeman* 8: 211–12.

———. 1929. "The Status of Linguistics as a Science." *Language* 5: 207–14.

———. 1933. "Personality." *Encyclopedia of the Social Sciences.* Vol. XII, pp. 85–87.

———. 1949. "Culture, Genuine and Spurious." In David Mandelbaum (ed.). *Selected Writings of Edward Sapir on Language, Culture and Personality.* Berkeley: University of California Press. (Original publication 1924.)

SASS, LOUIS. 1988. "The Self in Contemporary Psychoanalysis: Commentary on Charles Taylor." In Stanley Messer, Louis Sass, and Robert Woolfolk (eds.). *Hermeneutics and Psychological Theory: Interpretive Perspectives on Personality, Psychotherapy, and Psychopathology.* New Brunswick, NJ: Rutgers University Press.

———. 1992. *Madness and Modernism: Insanity in the Light of Modern Art, Literature and Thought.* Cambridge, MA: Harvard University Press.

SAUSSURE, FERDINAND DE. 1959. *Course in General Linguistics.* New York: Philosophical Library. (Original publication 1916.)

SCHACHTER, STANLEY, and JEROME SINGER. 1962. "Cognitive, Social and Psychological Determinants of Emotional States." *Psychological Review* 69: 379–99.

SCHAFER, ROY. 1978. *Language and Insight.* New Haven, CT: Yale University Press.

SCHANK, R., and R. ABELSON. 1977. *Scripts, Plans, Goals and Understanding: An Inquiry into Human Knowledge Structures.* Hillsdale, NJ: Erlbaum.

SCHEFF, T. J. 1979. *Catharsis in Healing, Ritual and Drama.* Berkeley: University of California Press.

SCHEPER-HUGHES, NANCY. 1979. *Saints, Scholars and Schizophrenics: Mental Illness in Rural Ireland.* Berkeley: University of California Press.

———. 1987. " 'Mental' in 'Southie': Individual, Family, and Community Responses to Psychosis in South Boston." *Culture, Medicine and Psychiatry* 11: 53–78.

———. 1990. "Mother Love and Child Death in Northeast Brazil." In James Stigler, Richard Shweder, and Gilbert Herdt (eds.). *Cultural Psychology: Essays on Comparative Human Development.* Cambridge, England: Cambridge University Press.

———. 1992. *Death without Weeping: The Violence of Everyday Life in Brazil.* Berkeley: University of California Press.

———. 1994. "The Violence of Everyday Life: In Search of a Critical and Politically Engaged Psychological Anthropology." In Marcelo Suarez-Orozco, George Spindler, and Louise Spindler (eds.). *The Making of Psychological Anthropology II.* Fort Worth, TX: Harcourt Brace.

SCHNEIDER, DAVID. 1968. *American Kinship: A Cultural Account.* Chicago: University of Chicago Press.

SCHWARTZ, THEODORE. 1992. "Anthropology and Psychology: An Unrequited Relationship." In Theodore Schwartz, Geoffrey White, and Catherine Lutz (eds.). *New Directions in Psychological Anthropology.* Cambridge, England: Cambridge University Press.

SEGAL, MARSHALL, DAVID CAMPBELL, and MELVILLE HERSKOVITZ. 1966. *The Influence of Culture on Visual Perception.* Indianapolis, IN: Bobbs-Merrill.

SELIGMAN, ADAM. 1992. *The Idea of Civil Society.* New York: Free Press.

SHAH, IDRIES. 1972. *The Exploits of the Incomparable Mulla Nasrudin.* New York: Dutton.

SHILS, EDWARD. 1965. "Charisma, Order, Status." *American Sociological Review* 30: 199–213.

SHIPLER, D. 1997. *A Country of Strangers: Blacks and Whites in America.* New York: Knopf.

SHIROKOGOROFF, S. 1935. *The Psychomental Complex of the Tungus.* London: Kegan Paul, Trench, Trubner.

SHKLAR, JUDITH. 1969. *Men and Citizens: A Study of Rousseau's Social Theory.* Cambridge, MA: Harvard University Press.

SHORE, BRADD. 1996. *Culture in Mind: Cognition, Culture, and the Problem of Meaning.* New York: Oxford University Press.

SHORTER, EDWARD. 1977. *The Making of the Modern Family.* New York: Basic Books.

SHWEDER, RICHARD. 1972. "Aspects of Cognition in Zinacanteco Shamans, Experimental Results." In Alexander Lessa and Evon Vogt (eds.). *Reader in Comparative Religion.* New York: Harper and Row.

———. 1977. "Likeness and Likelihood in Everyday Thought: Magical Thinking in Judgements of Personality." *Current Anthropology* 18: 637–58.

———. 1979–80. "Rethinking Culture and Personality Theory." *Ethos* 7: 255–311; 8: 60–94.

———. 1984. "Anthropology's Romantic Rebellion, or There's More to Thinking than Reason and Evidence." In Richard Shweder and Robert LeVine (eds.). *Culture Theory: Essays on Mind, Self and Emotion.* Cambridge, England: Cambridge University Press.

———. 1986. "Storytelling among the Anthropologists." *New York Times Book Review,* September 21: 1, 38–39.

———. 1991. *Thinking through Cultures: Expeditions in Cultural Psychology.* Cambridge, MA: Harvard University Press.

SHWEDER, RICHARD, and EDMUND BOURNE. 1984. "Does the Concept of the Person Vary Cross-Culturally?" In Richard Shweder and Robert LeVine (eds.). *Culture Theory: Essays on Mind, Self and Emotion.* Cambridge, England: Cambridge University Press.

SHWEDER, RICHARD, and JOAN G. MILLER. 1991. "The Social Construction of the Person: How Is It Possible?" In Richard Shweder. *Thinking Through Cultures: Expeditions in Cultural Psychology.* Cambridge, MA: Harvard University Press.

SINGER, IRVING. 1984. *The Nature of Love: Plato to Luther,* Vol. 1. Chicago: University of Chicago Press.

SINGER, JEROME, and MORRIS OPLER. 1956. "Contrasting Patterns of Fantasy and Motility in Irish and Italian Schizophrenics." *Journal of Abnormal and Social Psychology* 53: 42–47.

SINGER, MILTON. 1984. *Man's Glassy Essence: Explorations in Semiotic Anthropology.* Bloomington: Indiana University Press.

———. 1986. "The Melting Pot: Symbolic Ritual or Total Social Fact?" In Hervé Varenne (ed.). *Symbolizing America.* Lincoln: University of Nebraska Press.

SJOBERG, GIDEON. 1960. *The Preindustrial City, Past and Present.* Glencoe, IL: Free Press.

SKINNER, B. F. 1953. *Science and Human Behavior.* New York: Macmillan.

SLATER, PHILIP. 1971. *The Glory of Hera.* Boston: Beacon Press.

————. 1976. *The Pursuit of Loneliness: American Culture at the Breaking Point.* Boston: Beacon Press.

SMITH, PAGE. 1966. *As a City upon a Hill: The Town in American History.* New York: Knopf.

SOBO, ELLEN. 1993. "Inner-city Women and AIDS: The Psycho-Social Benefits of Unsafe Sex." *Culture, Medicine, and Psychiatry* 17: 455–85.

SOLOMON, ROBERT. 1981. *Love, Emotion, Myth and Metaphor.* Garden City, NY: Anchor Books.

SPERBER, DAN. 1998. *Explaining Culture: A Naturalistic Approach.* Oxford, England: Basil Blackwell.

SPINDLER, GEORGE. 1955. *Sociocultural and Psychological Processes in Menomini Acculturation.* Berkeley: University of California Publications in Culture and Society, Vol. 5.

————. (ed.). 1978. *The Making of Psychological Anthropology.* Berkeley: University of California Press.

SPINDLER, GEORGE, and LOUISE SPINDLER. 1971. *Dreamers without Power: The Menomini Indians.* New York: Holt, Rinehart and Winston.

————. 1986. "Foreword" In Hervé Varenne (ed.). *Symbolizing America.* Lincoln: University of Nebraska Press.

SPIRO, MELFORD. 1951. "Culture and Personality: The Natural History of a False Dichotomy." *Psychiatry* 14: 19–47.

————. 1965. "Religious Systems as Culturally Constituted Defense Mechanisms." In M. Spiro (ed.). *Context and Meaning in Cultural Anthropology.* New York: Free Press.

————. 1982. "Collective Representations and Mental Representation in Religious Symbol Systems." In Jacques Maquet (ed.). *On Symbols in Anthropology: Essays in Honor of Harry Hoijer.* Malibu, CA: Uneda.

————. 1982. *Oedipus in the Trobriands.* Chicago: University of Chicago Press.

————. 1984. "Some Reflections on Cultural Determinism and Relativism with Special Reference to Emotion and Reason." In Richard Shweder and Robert LeVine (eds.). *Culture Theory: Essays on Mind, Self and Emotion.* Cambridge, England: Cambridge University Press.

————. 1992. "Oedipus Redux." *Ethos* 20: 358–76.

————. 1993. "Is the Western Conception of the Self 'Peculiar' within the Context of the World Cultures?" *Ethos* 21: 107–53.

SPIVAK, GAYATRI C. 1993. "Can the Subaltern Speak?" In P. Williams and L. Chrisman (eds.). *Colonial Discourse and Post-Colonial Theory: A Reader.* Hemel Hempstead, England: Harvester Wheatsheaf.

SPRADLEY, JAMES. 1979. *The Ethnographic Interview.* New York: Holt, Rinehart and Winston.

SRINIVAS, M. N. 1962. *Caste in India and Other Essays.* London: Asia Publishing House.

STACK, CAROL. 1975. *All Our Kin: Strategies for Survival in a Black Community.* New York: Harper and Row.

STOCKING, GEORGE. 1974 (ed.). *The Shaping of American Anthropology, 1883–1911: A Franz Boas Reader.* New York: Basic Books.

————. 1986. "Malinowski's Encounter with Freudian Psychoanalysis." In G. Stocking (ed.). *Malinowski, Rivers, Benedict and Others: Essays on Culture and Personality.* Madison: University of Wisconsin Press.

————. 1992. "Polarity and Plurality: Franz Boas as Psychological Anthropologist." In Theodore Schwartz, Geoffrey White, and Catherine Lutz (eds.). *New Directions in Psychological Anthropology.* Cambridge, England: Cambridge University Press.

STOLLER, ANN. 1995. *Race and the Education of Desire: Foucault's History of Sexuality and the Colonial Order of Things.* Durham, NC: Duke University Press.

STOLLER, PAUL. 1997. *Sensuous Scholarship.* Philadelphia: University of Pennsylvania Press.

STONE, LAWRENCE. 1988. "Passionate Attachments in the West in Historical Perspective." In W. Gaylin and E. Person (eds.). *Passionate Attachments: Thinking about Love.* New York: Free Press.

STRATHERN, ANDREW. 1996. *Body Thoughts.* Ann Arbor: University of Michigan Press.

STRAUSS, CLAUDIA. 1992. "Models and Motives." In Roy D'Andrade and Claudia Strauss (eds.). *Human Motives and Cultural Models.* Cambridge, England: Cambridge University Press.

———. 1992. "What Makes Tony Run? Schemas as Motives Reconsidered." In Roy D'Andrade and Claudia Strauss (eds.). *Human Motives and Cultural Models.* Cambridge, England: Cambridge University Press.

SUAREZ-OROZCO, MARCELO. 1994. "Remaking Psychological Anthropology." In Marcelo Suarez-Orozco, George Spindler, and Louise Spindler (eds.). *The Making of Psychological Anthropology II.* Fort Worth, TX: Harcourt Brace.

SUAREZ-OROZCO, MARCELO, GEORGE SPINDLER, and LOUISE SPINDLER (eds.). 1994. *The Making of Psychological Anthropology II.* Fort Worth, TX: Harcourt Brace.

TAUSSIG, MICHAEL. 1980. *The Devil and Commodity Fetishism in South America.* Chapel Hill: University of North Carolina Press.

———. 1992. *The Nervous System.* New York: Routledge.

———. 1993. *Mimesis and Alterity: A Particular History of the Senses.* New York: Routledge.

TAX, SOL. 1968. "War and the Draft." In Morton Fried, Marvin Harris, and Robert Murphy (eds.). *War.* Garden City, NY: Doubleday.

TAYLOR, CHARLES. 1989. *Sources of the Self: The Making of the Modern Identity.* Cambridge, MA: Harvard University Press.

TENNOV, DOROTHY. 1979. *Love and Limerence: The Experience of Being in Love.* Chelsea, MI: Scarborough House.

THERNSTROM, S., and A. THERNSTROM. 1997. *America in Black and White.* New York: Simon and Schuster.

THOMAS, KEITH. 1971. *Religion and the Decline of Magic.* New York: Scribners.

TOBIN, JOSEPH J., DAVID Y. H. WU, and DANA H. DAVIDSON. 1989. *Preschool in Three Cultures: Japan, China, and the United States.* New Haven, CT: Yale University Press.

TOCQUEVILLE, ALEXIS DE. 1969. *Democracy in America.* Garden City, NY: Doubleday. (Original publication 1835.)

TOMKINS, SILVAN. 1982. "Affect Theory." In P. Ekman (ed.). *Emotion in the Human Face.* Cambridge, England: Cambridge University Press.

TREVARTHEN, COLWYN. 1984. "Emotions in Infancy: Regulators of Contact and Relationships with Persons." In Klaus Scherer and Paul Ekman (eds.). *Approaches to Emotion.* Hillsdale, NJ: Erlbaum.

TRUMBACH, RANDOLPH. 1994. "London's Sapphists: From Three Sexes to Four Genders in the Making of Modern Culture." In Gilbert Herdt (ed.). *Third Sex, Third Gender: Beyond Sexual Dimorphism in Culture and History.* New York: Zone Books.

TUAN, YI-FU. 1982. *Segmented Worlds and Self: Group Life and Individual Consciousness.* Minneapolis: University of Minnesota Press.

TURNBULL, COLIN. 1972. *The Mountain People.* New York: Simon and Schuster.

TURNER, BRYAN. 1991. "Recent Developments in the Theory of the Body." In Mike Featherstone, Mike Hepworth, and Bryan Turner (eds.). *The Body: Social Process and Cultural Theory.* San Francisco: Sage.

TURNER, VICTOR. 1957. *Schism and Continuity in an African Society: A Study of Ndembu Village Life.* Manchester, England: Manchester University Press.

———. 1967. *The Forest of Symbols: Aspects of Ndembu Ritual.* Ithaca, NY: Cornell University Press.

————. 1969. "Forms of Symbolic Action." In R. Spencer (ed.). *Forms of Symbolic Action.* Seattle: University of Washington Press.

————. 1974. "Passages, Margins, and Poverty: Religious Symbols of Communitas." In V. Turner (ed.). *Dramas, Fields, and Metaphors: Symbolic Action in Human Society.* Ithaca, NY: Cornell University Press.

————. 1977. *The Ritual Process: Structure and Anti-Structure.* Chicago: Aldine.

————. 1985. "The Anthropology of Performance." In Edith L. B. Turner (ed.). *On the Edge of the Bush: Anthropology as Experience.* Tucson: University of Arizona Press.

TYLER, STEVEN (ed.). 1969. *Cognitive Anthropology.* New York: Holt, Rinehart and Winston.

TYLOR, E. B. 1865. *Researches into the Early History of Mankind.* London: Murray.

————. 1871. *Primitive Culture: Researches into the Development of Mythology, Philosophy, Religion, Art and Custom* (2 vols.). London: Murray.

UNGER, ROBERTO. 1984. *Passion: An Essay on Personality.* New York: Free Press.

VALENTINE, C. A. 1963. "Men of Anger and Men of Shame: Lakalai Ethnopsychology and Its Implications for Sociopsychological Theory." *Ethnology* 2: 441–77.

VAN DER MEER, THEO. 1994. "Sodomy and the Pursuit of a Third Sex in the Early Modern Period." In Gilbert Herdt (ed.). *Third Sex, Third Gender: Beyond Sexual Dimorphism in Culture and History.* New York: Zone Books.

VARENNE, HERVÉ. 1977. *Americans Together: Structured Diversity in an American Town.* New York: Teachers College Press.

————. 1986. "Creating America." In Hervé Varenne (ed.). *Symbolizing America.* Lincoln: University of Nebraska Press.

VELEZ-IBANEZ, C. 1994. "Plural Strategies of Survival and Cultural Formation in US-Mexican Households in a Region of Dynamic Transformation: The US-Mexico Borderlands." In Shepard Forman (ed.). *Diagnosing America: Anthropology and Public Engagement.* Ann Arbor: University of Michigan Press.

VERBA, SIDNEY, and GARY ORREN. 1985. *Equality in America: The View from the Top.* Cambridge, MA: Harvard University Press.

VERNANT, JEAN-PIERRE, and PIERRE VIDAL-NAQUET. 1981. *Tragedy and Myth in Ancient Greece.* Sussex, England: Harvester Press.

VONNEGUT, KURT. 1976. *Wampeters, Foma and Granfalloons.* New York: Dell.

WALLACE, ANTHONY F. C. 1950. "A Possible Technique for Recognizing Psychological Characteristics of the Ancient Maya from an Analysis of Their Art." *American Imago* 7: 239–58.

————. 1952. *The Modal Personality Structure of the Tuscarora Indians.* Bureau of American Ethnology Bulletin 150. Washington, DC: Smithsonian Institution.

————. 1956. "Revitalization Movements." *American Anthropologist* 58: 264–81.

————. 1961. *Culture and Personality.* New York: Random House.

————. 1970. *The Death and Rebirth of the Seneca.* New York: Knopf.

WALLACE, EDWIN. 1983. *Freud and Anthropology: A History and Reappraisal.* New York: International Universities Press.

WALLER, WILLARD. 1937. "The Rating and Dating Complex." *American Sociological Review* 2: 727–34.

WARNER, R. 1985. *Recovery from Schizophrenia.* London: Routledge and Kegan Paul.

WARNER, W. LLOYD. 1952. *The Structure of American Life.* Edinburgh: University of Edinburgh Press.

WARNER, W. LLOYD, J. O. LOW, PAUL S. LUNT, and LEO SROLE. 1963. *Yankee City.* New Haven, CT: Yale University Press.

WATERS, MARY. 1990. *Ethnic Options: Choosing Identities in America.* Berkeley: University of California Press.

WATSON, JOHN B. 1930. *Behaviorism.* New York: Norton.

WAXLER, NANCY. 1974. "Culture and Mental Illness: A Social Labeling Perspective." *Journal of Nervous and Mental Disease* 159: 379–95.

WEBEL, CHARLES. 1983. "Self: An Overview." In B. Wolman (ed.). *International Encyclopedia of Psychiatry, Psychoanalysis, Psychology and Neurology.* New York: Asclepias.

———. 1996. "From Self-Knowledge to Self-Obsessed Self-Interest." *New Ideas in Psychology* 14: 189–95.

WEBER, MAX. 1930. *The Protestant Ethic and the Spirit of Capitalism.* New York: Scribner. (Original publication 1920.)

———. 1946. "Politics as a Vocation" (original publication 1919); "The Sociology of Charismatic Authority" (original publication 1921); "Social Psychology of the World Religions" (original publication 1922–23); "Religious Rejections of the World and Their Directions" (original publication 1915). In Hans Gerth and C. Wright Mills (eds.). *From Max Weber: Essays in Sociology.* New York: Oxford University Press.

———. 1968. "The Nature of Charismatic Authority." In S. N. Eisenstadt (ed.). *Max Weber on Charisma and Institution Building.* Chicago: University of Chicago Press.

———. 1978. *Economy and Society.* Berkeley: University of California Press.

———. 1985. " 'Churches' and 'Sects' in North America." *Sociological Theory* 3: 7–11.

WEIL, SIMONE. 1986. "The Poem of Force." In Sian Miles (ed.). *Simone Weil: An Anthology.* New York: Weidenfeld and Nicholson.

WEINTRAUB, KARL JOACHIM. 1978. *The Value of the Individual: Self and Circumstance in Autobiography.* Chicago: University of Chicago Press.

WELLENKAMP, J. 1988. "Notions of Grief and Catharsis among the Toraja." *American Ethnologist* 15: 486–500.

WERBNER, PNINA. 1997. "Essentialising Essentialism, Essentialising Silence: Ambivalence and Multiplicity in the Constructions of Racism and Ethnicity." In Pnina Werbner and Tariq Modood (eds.). *Debating Cultural Hybridity: Multi-Cultural Identities and the Politics of Anti-Racism.* London: Zed Books.

WESTERMEYER, JOSEPH. 1988. "Some Cross-Cultural Aspects of Delusions." In Thomas Oltmanns and Brendan Maher (eds.). *Delusional Beliefs.* New York: Wiley.

WHITE, MERRY. 1993. *The Material Child: Coming of Age in Japan and America.* New York: Basic Books.

WHITING, BEATRICE, and JOHN WHITING. 1975. *Children of Six Cultures: A Psycho-Cultural Analysis.* Cambridge, MA: Harvard University Press.

WHITING, J., R. KLUCKHOHN, and A. ANTHONY. 1958. "The Function of Male Initiation Ceremonies at Puberty." In E. Maccoby, T. Newcomb, and E. Hartley (eds.). *Readings in Social Psychology.* New York: Holt.

WHITING, JOHN. 1990. "Adolescent Rituals and Identity Conflicts." In James Stigler, Richard Shweder, and Gilbert Herdt (eds.). *Cultural Psychology: Essays on Comparative Human Development.* Cambridge, England: Cambridge University Press.

WHITING, JOHN, IRVIN CHILD, WILLIAM LAMBERT, et al. 1966. *Field Guide for a Study of Socialization.* New York: John Wiley.

WHORF, BENJAMIN. 1956. "Science and Linguistics" (original publication 1940). In J. Carroll (ed.). *Language, Thought and Reality: Selected Writings of Benjamin Lee Whorf.* Cambridge, MA: MIT Press.

WIERZBICKA, ANNA. 1993. "A Conceptual Basis for Cross-Cultural Psychology." *Ethos* 21: 205–31.

———. 1996. "Japanese Cultural Scripts: Cultural Psychology and 'Cultural Grammar.' " *Ethos* 24: 527–55.

WIKAN, UNNI. 1990. *Managing Turbulent Hearts: A Balinese Formula for Living.* Chicago: University of Chicago Press.

————. 1991. *Behind the Veil in Arabia: Women in Oman.* Chicago: University of Chicago Press.

————. 1995. "The Self in a World of Urgency and Necessity." *Ethos* 23: 259–85.

WILLIAMS, RICHARD E. 1990. *Hierarchical Structures and Social Value: The Creation of Black and Irish Identities in the United States.* Cambridge, England: Cambridge University Press.

WILLIS, PAUL. 1977. *Learning to Labor: How Working Class Kids Get Working Class Jobs.* Farnborough, England: Saxon House.

WILLNER, ANN RUTH. 1984. *The Spellbinders: Charismatic Political Leadership.* New Haven, CT: Yale University Press.

WILSON, WILLIAM J. 1996. *When Work Disappears: The World of the Urban Poor.* New York: Knopf.

WINKELMAN, MICHAEL. 1986. "Trance States: A Theoretical Model and Cross-Cultural Analysis." *Ethos* 14: 174–203.

WINNICOTT, D. W. 1965. *The Maturational Process and the Facilitating Environment.* London: Hogarth.

WOLFE, ALAN. 1998. *One Nation, After All.* New York: Viking.

WORDSWORTH, WILLIAM. 1888. "The World Is Too Much with Us." In *The Complete Poetical Works of William Wordsworth.* New York: Crowell. (Original publication 1807.)

WRIGHT, LAWRENCE. 1994. *Remembering Satan.* New York: Knopf.

YANAGISAKO, SYLVIA. 1985. *Transforming the Past: Tradition and Kinship among Japanese Americans.* Stanford, CA: Stanford University Press.

YANS-MCLAUGHLIN, VIRGINIA. 1986. "Mobilizing Culture and Personality for World War II." In George Stocking (ed.). *Malinowski, Rivers, Benedict and Others: Essays on Culture and Personality.* Madison, University of Wisconsin Press.

YOUNG, ALLAN. 1995. *The Harmony of Illusions: Inventing Post-Traumatic Stress Disorder.* Princeton, NJ: Princeton University Press.

YOUNG, FRANK. 1965. *Initiation Ceremonies.* Indianapolis, IN: Bobbs-Merrill.

ZAJONC, R. 1980. "Feeling and Thinking: Preferences Need No Inferences." *American Psychologist* 35: 151–75.

Index

NOTE: Page numbers in italics refer to figures and tables.

Photo Credits